ARTHUR SULLIVAN

A VICTORIAN MUSICIAN

Second edition

For Betty

ARTHUR SULLIVAN
A Victorian Musician

Second edition

ARTHUR JACOBS

Scolar Press

First edition published by Oxford University Press in 1984 and in paperback in 1986

Second edition published by
SCOLAR PRESS
Gower House
Croft Road
Aldershot
Hants GUII 3HR
England

ML
410
.S95
J28
1992b

British Library cataloguing-in-publication data is available.

ISBN 0 85967 905 5

Typeset in 10/12 Plantin by Photoprint, Torquay, Devon
and printed in Great Britain by Billing & Sons Limited, Worcester.

Arthur Sullivan: anonymous cartoon from
The Roundabout, 2 December 1882

'We may be a musical nation, but our taste
would seem to require some refinement.'
DISRAELI, 'Lothair' (1870), chapter 30

Contents

Preface		xi
Acknowledgements		xiii
List of illustrations		xiv
Sources and references		xv
Coinage and currency		xv
1	Beginnings	1
2	Mentors	10
3	Leipzig and London	20
4	In Demand	30
5	In search of Schubert	41
6	Love and Operetta	49
7	From Tennyson to Gilbert	58
8	A Partnership and a Patron	67
9	Broadening	77
10	Fanny	88
11	A College and an Aquarium	97
12	Collaborators	108
13	'Pinafore' and Piracy	117
14	Transatlantic	130
15	'We select an Englishman'	139
16	The Martyr and the Dairymaid	146

17 Diarist and Traveller   159

18 Loss   174

19 With Electric Light   183

20 Conflict   194

21 At the Centre   207

22 To California   218

23 Triple Assignment   231

24 In Others' Eyes   249

25 'I am not Strong'   264

26 The Furthest Point   279

27 'Monarchs of all they Savoy'   293

28 Transitions, translations   307

29 On the Carpet   316

30 'English Grand Opera'   325

31 Return to the Savoy   339

32 Satire   348

33 The End of the Partnership   361

34 Jubilee   374

35 Valedictions   389

36 Legacy   404

37 1842–1992   413

    Notes on the text   428

Appendices

1   Arthur Sullivan's Family Tree   451
2   The supposed Jewish connection   454
3   List of Sullivan's works   456
4   Bibliography   467

    Index   479

Preface

ARTHUR SULLIVAN was the best-known figure of Victorian music, in both his countrymen's and foreigners' eyes. As a young man he sat at the feet of Rossini; in his prime he greeted Liszt in London; late in life he encouraged the young Elgar. He worked in creative partnership with Jenny Lind and Henry Irving, with Tennyson and Kipling. He knew Dickens, Browning, Hardy, Millais, Burne-Jones, and five Prime Ministers (Gladstone, Disraeli, Salisbury, Rosebery, Balfour). With several members of the royal family he probably mixed more intimately than anyone else who did not hold a court position. The interest of his personal and professional life goes far beyond the collaboration with W. S. Gilbert for which posterity has cherished him.

A word may be said about the terminology of his stage works with Gilbert. As a matter of musical classification they are best called 'operetta': curiously enough, that is the heading Gilbert gave to his first version (in the pages of *Fun*) of *Trial by Jury*. But for the stage productions the dignity of the word 'opera' was preferred, generally with a qualifying adjective ('an aesthetic opera' for *Patience*, 'a Japanese opera' for *The Mikado*). In this book it has been found convenient to make use of both terms, 'opera' and 'operetta', according to context. It may be noted that 'Savoy opera' was not, in its day, a term exclusive to Gilbert and Sullivan but was applied by Richard D'Oyly Carte to similar works presented by him with the participation of other, now virtually forgotten, librettists and composers.

It is now well over half a century since the appearance of what may be called the official biography of Sullivan, the joint work (1927) of Sir Newman Flower and the composer's nephew, Herbert Sullivan. A second edition appeared in 1950. Among the prime tasks of a new biography is the correction of the mistakes and omissions of that book, with its ignorant and careless transcriptions from the composer's letters and diaries. The authors' musical competence is sufficiently shown in their transcriptions of Norma, Adalgisa, and Oroveso (principal characters from Bellini's *Norma*) as Norman, Adalliri, and Ovovess, not to mention their *cachnalia* for Sullivan's own *cachucha*. Labouring to produce an acceptably 'clean' image of their subject, they suppressed references not only to sex but even to gambling.

At the time, those letters and diaries were in private possession. Subsequent writers have been heavily dependent (and, at times, needlessly baffled) by the transcriptions offered. But the new accessibility of this material (see the note on page xv on 'Sources and References') makes possible a new wholeness of portraiture. It may be hoped that, as has already occurred with recent studies of Victorian writers and painters, frankness may lead to a truer understanding of an artist's life.

ARTHUR JACOBS

London · New York · Huddersfield
1980–3

Note to the New Edition

The new, expanded edition provides the opportunity to bring the book abreast of the new developments in performance and research, as also to correct some factual errors and misprints. For help and suggestions in both these respects I am indebted to colleagues and fellow-enthusiasts in Sullivan's cause, particularly Stephen Turnbull (the energetic secretary of the Sir Arthur Sullivan Society), David Eden, John Gardner, Roger Harris, Dr David Russell Hulme, Christopher Knowles, Peter Joslin, Andrew Lamb, Dr Terence Rees, Philip Scowcroft, Martin Thacker, the Rev Selwyn Tillett, Fredric Woodbridge Wilson, and John Wilson. Other (1983) acknowledgements are on pp. xiii–xiv; the decease of a number of these original helpers does not diminish my appreciation of their kindnesses.

A new set of illustrations has been kindly supplied by Peter Joslin.

A. J.
Wolfson College, Oxford,
November 1991

Acknowledgements (1983)

FOR permission to reproduce extracts from the letters and diaries of Arthur Sullivan, and other manuscript material, I am grateful to the trustees of the Pierpont Morgan Library, New York and to the Beinecke Rare Book and Manuscript Library, Yale University. The guidance provided by Reginald Allen, the curator of the Gilbert and Sullivan collection at the former institution, and by his assistant Gale d'Luhy was of the utmost value. That assistance has been continued by Mr Allen's successor, Fredric Woodbridge Wilson. The Leverhulme Trust, by its award of a year's research fellowship, financially enabled me to extend my research in American and other libraries, after which a visiting fellowship at Wolfson College, Oxford, facilitated the actual writing of the first part of the book. A grant was also made by the Central Research Fund, University of London. The library and other facilities at Merton College, Oxford, where I was once an undergraduate, were also placed at my disposal.

I feel a special debt to those colleagues in the field who unstintingly placed information in my hands: Jane W. Stedman (Chicago), George S. Emmerson (London, Ontario), Andrew Lamb, Peter Joslin and Terence Rees. Peter Joslin read the typescript, to my great benefit, and also researched and prepared the illustrations, most of which have never previously appeared in book form. Leslie Weaver of Liverpool and Thomas O. Jones of Rockville, Maryland, placed at my disposal a prodigious number of items of documentary information relating to Sullivan's career and his antecedents. At a late stage Dame Bridget D'Oyly Carte gave access to her invaluable stock of press-cutting books and typed transcripts of a number of letters to and from Sullivan (the originals having perished), and to the autograph full score of *Iolanthe*. She also directed me to the archives held by the Savoy Hotel, London.

The BBC provided quotations from remarks by Princess Alice (Queen Victoria's granddaughter) in the television programme *Victorian Memory*, 1978. I was able to avail myself of material at the Royal Military School of Music; the Bodleian Library, Oxford; the British Library, Reference Division; the New York Public Library; the Library of Congress, Washington, D.C.; the Newberry Library, Chicago; the Lilly Library, Indiana University (Bloomington, Indiana); the libraries of the University of California at Los Angeles and at Berkeley; the Sterling Memorial Library, Yale University; the State Library (West Berlin) and the Vienna City Libraries; the public central libraries of Manchester, Leeds, Bradford, and Liverpool; the libraries of the Royal College of Music, the Royal Liverpool Philharmonic Society, and the Museum of London. I received useful information also from the Royal Archives, Windsor Castle; from the Head Archivist, Director-General's Department, Greater London Council; and in Ottawa from the National Library of Canada. The Swiss National Tourist Office in London helped me to become acquainted with some of the principal places in Switzerland which Sullivan visited.

Adrian Williams was my zealous professional researcher and my thanks go also to the following for information and assistance: George Barr, Marianne Barton, Harry Benford, Chalmers Burns, Kathryn Copisarow, A. R. Davis, John Earl, David Eden, Brian Harrison, George Hauger, Roger Highfield, Ernst Hilmar, Nicholas Holding, H. Montgomery Hyde, George Jellinek, Patricia Kelvin, John Lehmann, David Lisle, Frederic Lloyd, Beryl Normand, the late Sir Cecil Parrott, Henry Pleasants, Colin Prestige, Harold Rosenthal, Lord Rothschild, Simon Schama, Paul D. Seeley, Richard Telfer, Constance Thompson, Christine Vann, Alan Walker, John Warrack, Leslie Wilson, R. J. Witts, Sir Hugh Wontner, Percy M. Young.

Julia Nash nursed the typescript of the greater part of this book with the utmost conscientiousness and Joanna Harris and Susan Welton valuably supplemented that work.

The contributions of my wife Betty and sons Julian and Michael, on all levels from historical and stylistic to clerical and domestic, have been indispensable.

A. J.

List of Illustrations

*Between pages **248** and **249***

1 The Lost Chord – poster for a film, 1933

2 Teachers and interpreters

3 An anthem by the young Sullivan

4 *The Mikado* in German guise

5 Mary Frances Ronalds

6 'Cox and Box' with Fred Sullivan (left)

7 Places of fame: *top* Leeds Town Hall; *bottom* Savoy Theatre, London

8 W.S. Gilbert

Sources and references

NOTES, including the identification of quoted sources, will be found at the back of this book, p. 428. A catch-phrase from the main text introduces the references in the notes, so that readers desirous of further information can easily find their place in the notes.

Letters to or from Sullivan are – unless otherwise noted – reproduced from the originals in the Pierpont Morgan Library, New York. The initials BDC identify transcripts kindly provided by the late Dame Bridget D'Oyly Carte. Entries from Sullivan's diary are similarly reproduced from the original manuscript volume in the Pierpont Morgan Library (for 1879–80) and from the originals in the Beinecke Rare Book and Manuscript Library of Yale University (for all other years).

Spelling of quoted sources has been modernized ('quartet' for 'quartette', 'clarinet' for 'clarionet', etc.) and punctuation of manuscript sources has been revised where a hasty or ill-formed style of writing would have needlessly raised difficulties for today's reader. Omissions [. . .] and conjectures [in square brackets] are, however, always noted as such.

Coinage and currency

THE internal and external value of British currency, being based on a gold standard, was more or less stable during Sullivan's lifetime. The pound sterling (£) was represented by a gold coin, the sovereign; the pound divided into 20 shillings (s.) and the shilling into twelve pence (d.). The half-sovereign, crown and half-crown (10s., 5s., 2s.6d.) were coins as well as values but the guinea (£1.1s.), common in quotation of professional fees and in various other contexts, had ceased to be coined since 1813 and was a notional sum only. The half-penny (usually spelt ha'penny and pronounced 'hay-penny') and farthing (¼d.) were the coins of smallest value.

Sums are expressed in this book in the style then current, e.g. £8.15s.6d. Where helpful, an approximate 'translation' in modern decimal coinage (£8.77) is given. British equivalents for sums in foreign currencies are given at appropriate points in the text: in 1880 the US and Canadian dollar was worth 4s.2d. (about 21p), the French and Swiss franc 9½d. (nearly 4p), the German mark 1s. (5p), and the Austro-Hungarian florin 1s.11d. (nearly 10p). The franc divided into 100 centimes, the mark into 100 pfennigs.

1 Beginnings

Two hundred men bearing shoulder-high posters – and wearing top-hats, a necessary badge of respectable occupation – marched about the streets of London to proclaim the birth of the *Illustrated London News*.[1] The first issue of the new weekly publication offered an unprecedented 32 illustrations in 16 pages, and was priced at sixpence, or 2½p in modern currency. On the Friday of that week, 13 May 1842, Arthur Sullivan was born in Lambeth, South London.

The new journalism was one of the features of dramatic social change between the beginning and end of the reign of Queen Victoria (1837–1901), within which fell the whole of Arthur Sullivan's life (1842–1900). The circulation of the *Illustrated London News*, initially 26,000, had doubled by the end of the year, and by 1863 exceeded 300,000. The illustrations, hand-drawn and produced from wood-engravings, depicted incidents or personalities in the news. Increasingly, the newspaper artist copied from photographs, which could not be reproduced directly until after 1860. By means of such illustrations the Crimean War of 1854–6 was to acquire a more vivid public image than any previous event of suffering and conflict. In like manner the illustrated press made familiar not only the characters and scenes from Gilbert and Sullivan's theatrical works but also the lineaments of the creators themselves. The bluff, burly Gilbert and the suave, smaller Sullivan lived in faithful image and fantastic caricature.

In the pages of the *Illustrated London News* in 1850 Joseph Paxton published his plans for a gigantic glass-walled exhibition building – this in order to appeal directly to public enthusiasm, over the heads of a procrastinating official committee. It was in *Punch* that Douglas Jerrold gave the building its inspired name: the Crystal Palace. The first Crystal Palace, in Hyde Park, housed the Great Exhibition of the Works of Industry of All Nations (invariably known just as 'the Great Exhibition') in 1851; the greatly enlarged second Crystal Palace, making use of materials from the first, was erected in London's south-east outskirts at Sydenham. Finished in 1854, it would shortly house Britain's first long-lasting series of popular-priced orchestral concerts, where Arthur Sullivan – long before his collaboration with Gilbert – would romantically find fame overnight.

Improved technical processes in manufacturing and engineering, so proudly on display at the Great Exhibition, benefited music directly. Factory-made brass instruments made possible the working-class brass bands as well as the newly precise symphony orchestra. The annual output of pianos rose from about 23,000 in 1850 to 25,000 in 1870 and about 50,000 in 1890.[2] In 1871, in a book called *Music and Morals*, the Rev. H. R. Haweis guessed that there were about 400,000 pianos in the British Isles and about one million pianists. The spreading railway network (1,331 miles of track in 1840, rising to 17,935 miles by 1880) enabled leading performers to leave London for a rehearsal and concert the same day in a provincial city.[3]

In 1841, the year before Arthur Sullivan's birth, the first census of the United Kingdom revealed a population which was under 27 million and mainly agricultural. By 1901 the population was over 41 million and mainly industrial. It was, especially after Forster's Education Act of 1870 took effect, a better educated population and also one with an increased purchasing-power for things of leisure: real wages increased during the second half of the century by more than 80 per cent. For the most depressed of all, the poor of the urban slums, things grew no better: though cholera had been conquered, Charles Booth's famous surveys revealed that in 1889 over 30 per cent of London's population,[4] about 1,800,000 people, lived in the direst and filthiest poverty. But at least from the 1870s the class of tradesmen, shop-assistants and clerks was able to take some share of civilized entertainment from the museum to the music-hall. The 'steady-and-stolid-y, jolly-Bank-Holiday, everyday young man' from *Patience* was in a literal sense the creation of the Bank Holiday Act, 1871; and, as Saturday afternoons as well as Sundays became free of labour, *la semaine anglaise* brought itself to the notice of Continental visitors.

It was indeed into an expanding world of entertainment that Arthur Sullivan grew up. Through its purchasing-power and its strongly defined patterns of leisure, the middle class took the lead, and the nation joined in. The jaunty tunes of *HMS Pinafore* and *Iolanthe* captured a public which also responded to the sentimental appeal of *The Lost Chord*, said to have sold an average of 20,000 copies annually for 25 years.[5] From such ballads and facile piano pieces to the grandest occasions of opera and concert, the Victorian press catered strongly for its readers' musical interests. Chorley of the *Athenaeum*, Davison of *The Times*, Joseph Bennett of the new, more popularly slanted *Daily Telegraph* – all these were music critics of strong opinion and considerable influence. With each of them, and later with Hermann Klein of the *Sunday Times*, Arthur Sullivan was to develop a personal relationship.

In its infancy during that summer of 1842, the *Illustrated London News* grasped its opportunities. Its fourth weekly number apologized for its inattention hitherto to 'music and theatricals' and began to make immediate amends. A German opera company had just given London its first hearing of Meyerbeer's *Les Huguenots*. At a concert to raise funds for sufferers from a fire which had devastated Hamburg, the visiting Mendelssohn played a piano duet with Ignaz Moscheles – who, carrying from Beethoven's Vienna a reputation as pianist, composer, and conductor, was now a prominent and resident figure in London's musical life. In the issue of 11 June, the longest of the paper's articles on any topic, musical or other, was a report on 'the singing-classes at Exeter Hall',[6] at which the admiring spectators included the Queen Dowager (Queen Adelaide, widow of William IV) and other members of 'the Court and *haut ton*'.

These classes, directed by John Hullah, pursued the ideal proposed in the phrase *Singing for the Million* – the title of a textbook by another popularizer, Joseph Mainzer. Hullah demonstrated to school-teachers, who would pass it on to their pupils, his method of learning to sing at sight, with physical actions as an aid to memory. The counting of beats by a repeated 'crotch, crotch, crotch, crotch' reminded the *Illustrated London News* reporter of the noises of a duck-pond, but the demonstrations were a much-approved public wonder in an age when self-help and education were so highly esteemed. In July 1842 there were said to be 50,000 Hullah pupils, and singing in schools began to be recognized as 'an important means of forming an industrious, bright, loyal and religious people'. The phrase is that of Dr James Kay (later Sir James Kay-Shuttleworth), secretary of the Privy Council's committee on education.

British social stability is encapsulated in Kay's words. The throngs of Parisian labourers in their *bleu de travail* whom Mainzer had assembled for his singing-classes alarmed the French authorities: for fear of insurrection the enterprise was banned in 1839. The British ruling class, however, was strong enough to contain and repress the radical Chartist movement (1839–48), and revolutionary impulse was weakened by social reform and rising prosperity. National cohesion was encouraged by the moral, disciplinary verses favoured in British school songs as in many larger choral works. Within that morality, W. S. Gilbert and Arthur Sullivan were to gain recognition as licensed jesters.

During Sullivan's lifetime the provision of concerts increased dramatically. Whereas London's population between 1848 and 1898 increased only twofold (to a total exceeding four million), newspaper advertisements suggest a fivefold rise in the provision of orchestral and choral-orchestral concerts. Add the miscellaneous concerts (including 'ballad concerts' at which publishers profitably pushed their wares through the medium of celebrated singers) and the increase is even more remarkable. By 1886, when *The Mikado* was enjoying its record-breaking run, the magazine *Truth* implied that the London musical scene was not merely full, but congested:

Arrangements are being made for 14 Popular, 20 Crystal Palace, 16 Henschel, 13 Richter, 14 Ballad, 6 Sacred Harmonic, 6 Novello's Choir, 6 Albert Hall, 6 Sarasate, 7 Ambrose Austin, 6 Philharmonic, 3 Strolling Players, 2 Bach Choir, 2 London Musical Society, and a large number of other concerts.[7]

Moreover, the new halls were bigger. St James's Hall, with a capacity of 2,127, had opened in 1858; the Albert Hall (about 7,000) in 1871; Queen's Hall (2,500) in 1893. In Sullivan's early years the Philharmonic Society – the most prestigious of London promoters, though confining its concerts to about eight each year – was performing in the Hanover Square Rooms, seating only about 850; it moved to St James's Hall in 1869 and to Queen's Hall in 1894.

Good music became not only more plentiful, but cheaper. From the 1840s, promenade concerts – at which, in those days, the audience *did* promenade –

attracted large audiences, the programmes often mingling popular dance-arrangements and solo items with overtures and symphonic works, and often employing a military band as well as an orchestra. The great exponent was the French conductor Jullien – a showman who would seize a violin or piccolo at the climax of a dance-arrangement of military or naval airs, but would don a pair of white kid gloves to conduct a Beethoven symphony. At the end of his career, the *Musical World* in July 1859 recalled that it was he who 'taught the crowd that they can hear, for a shilling or half-a-crown [5p., 12½p.], several times during the winter season, performances quite as good as those for which the Philharmonic directors charge one guinea [£1.05]'.

Jullien's main appearances, however, were in summer, the 'monster concerts' at the Surrey Gardens being among his special attractions. Even at such a place of popular, suburban entertainment he could mount a 'classical' programme with financial success. An all-Mozart concert in June 1857 included the Piano Concerto in C minor (Arabella Goddard as soloist) and the 'Jupiter' symphony. The symphony 'was executed without curtailment', noted *The Times* – whose critic, James W. Davison, happened to be Arabella Goddard's husband. The review went on:

Who, after this, can venture to question the artistic taste of Southwark, Camberwell, Kennington, Lambeth, and Walworth, where the influence of M. Jullien seems to be quite as good as that which he has exercised for so many years in the cis-pontine regions? And who will dare assert that a metropolis is not *musical*, when Handel, Mozart, Beethoven and Mendelssohn are so much and so continually in request?

The terms *cis-pontine* and *trans-pontine*, indicating the 'near' and 'far' side of the bridges across the Thames, were often invoked to differentiate the taste of the fashionable and wealthy from that of meaner folk. (Thirty years later, Gilbert and Sullivan's *Ruddigore* would be disparaged as redolent of 'transpontine melo-drama'.) The raising of musical taste was a process characterized in Davison's posthumous memoirs as 'the democratization of good concerts'. The implication of political homogeneity should not be missed.

The vortex of London's expanding musical life attracted the musical celebrities of Europe. During Sullivan's boyhood not only Mendelssohn and Moscheles came, but also Chopin, Verdi, Wagner, Berlioz, Meyerbeer, Liszt. No home-grown talent could compare with that; nor could any native conductor rival, for sheer capability, the Neapolitan who achieved British naturalization and knighthood as Sir Michael Costa (1808–84). Into Costa's hands fell not only the Royal Italian Opera at Covent Garden but the Philharmonic Society (he was its first 'permanent' conductor, from 1846 to 1854), the Birmingham Festival, the Leeds Festival, and the Sacred Harmonic Society, London's leading amateur choir, staunch proponents of Handel. Were British composers and conductors never to draw abreast? What was called the 'native talent question' – the phrase is yet again from Davison's memoirs – was constantly under discussion, with no case more prominent than Sullivan's.

Lambeth, his birthplace, was a populous London borough on the south (Surrey) side of the Thames, with more than 100,000 inhabitants.[8] Since the Reform Act of 1832 it had sent two members to Parliament. It would maintain a strong local identity even when absorbed in 1888 into the new administrative County of London. A short walk from the Sullivans' house stood Lambeth Palace, the residence of the Archbishop of Canterbury – one of about 50 'places which a stranger in London must see', according to Peter Pellingham's two-volume *Handbook for London* of 1849. Lambeth Bridge being as yet unbuilt, the Archbishop's palace was connected with the other side of the river by a horse-ferry. (The present Horseferry Road recalls it.) On the north bank, where the Tate Gallery is now located, stood the menacing six-pentagon structure of the Millbank Penitentiary.

The house was in Bolwell Street, numbered as 8 Bolwell Terrace (no longer standing). Civil registration of births having come into force six years previously, the son of Thomas and Mary Clementina Sullivan was registered on 24 June 1842 with the one forename, Arthur. At his baptism on 31 July in the nearby parish church of St Mary – the building was pulled down in 1851 and replaced – a second forename, Seymour, was added. It was the middle name also of one of his mother's cousins. At the age of 31, apparently irritated by jokes at the sequence of his three initials, Arthur Seymour Sullivan was to drop the middle name from both his correspondence and the title-pages of his compositions.

He was fortunate in his mother. Mary Clementina (born at Marlow, Bucks, on 2 November 1811) combined energy and forethought with a charm that was to win the affection of both the eminent and the humble in her son's future circle. She was to guide and encourage him, to be secretary, companion, and confidante, to 'air his linen, dry his tears', as the line was to go in *The Sorcerer*. From the beginning, she preserved his letters – and more than his letters. The tiny garment labelled as 'Arthur Sullivan's first shirt', with a note in his mother's hand bearing the date of his birth, rests in the Gilbert and Sullivan collection of the Pierpont Morgan Library, New York. If she ever did the same for her elder son Frederic (born 25 December 1837), the results have not come down to us. There were no other children.

Mary Clementina (her nickname was variously spelt Clemma or Clema)[9] herself compiled a family tree – of her own side only, not her husband's. The information in it is incorporated into what follows and also into the family tree on pp. 452–3 of this book. Her maiden name was Coghlan, her father James Coghlan being Irish. (It seems unlikely, since there is no mention of it in family correspondence, that they were related to the Irish actor Charles Coghlan, active in the London theatre at this period.) Her mother, born Mary Louisa Margaret Righy, was a daughter of Joseph Righy – born in Nice, which under the Italian name of Nizza was then part of the Kingdom of Sardinia. Joseph Righy, having settled in England, died in 1824 at Camberley in Surrey.

'Righy' was apparently a French or English re-spelling of the Italian name 'Righi': Arthur Sullivan described his mother as descending from 'an old Italian family'. Another daughter of Joseph's, Maria Victoria Righy (Arthur Sullivan's great-aunt), married Edward Philipps, who died in Barbados. The composer was to establish a warm contact with cousins of that surname. It is from his mother's side that Sullivan was supposed – by writers in his lifetime, and afterwards – to draw a partly Jewish descent. There is no evidence for that supposition and indeed a strong presumption against it. But the matter throws such a curious light on Victorian attitudes to Jewishness in music that it deserves to be dealt with in some detail (Appendix 2, pp. 452–3).

On 2 November 1836, her 25th birthday, Mary Clementina Coghlan married Thomas Sullivan, who was born on 4 June in 1805 or 1806 (his wife could not be sure but the former is apparently correct).[10] She had evidently known him almost all her life, as Arthur Sullivan was to note (see p. 44) at the time of his father's death. Thomas's father (also named Thomas Sullivan) was a soldier: born in County Cork, Ireland (near Tralee, in a hamlet called Caherweeshen, disguised in army documentation as 'Kerryshane'), he enlisted in the 58th Regiment of Foot in mid-1806 and was discharged as a private from the 66th Regiment of Foot on 11 October 1821. The statement that he rose to the rank of sergeant is incorrect, and various other family traditions as reproduced in the biography of Arthur Sullivan by Herbert Sullivan and Newman Flower are fanciful.[11] Military records confirm, however, that Thomas Sullivan senior served in the Peninsular War, in Upper Canada and in the detachment sent to guard Napoleon at St Helena. He died in London as a pensioner of the Royal Hospital, Chelsea, on 6 February 1838, when his age was given as 60.

Thomas junior, the composer's father, attended 'the Duke of York's School'[12] (the familiar name for the Royal Military Asylum for the children of soldiers of the regular army) adjoining the Royal Hospital in Chelsea. It was designed to accommodate as many as 700 boys and 300 girls. Training for the boys was on military lines, with their own band. It is not surprising that, since a talent for music was discovered, Thomas Sullivan was sent at the age of 15 as a bandsman to the Royal Military College at Sandhurst, joining in September 1820 and remaining until 31 December 1834.

The Royal Military College had moved to Sandhurst from Marlow in 1812. Since Mary Clementina Coghlan as a baby made the same move, it may be presumed that her father, James Coghlan, had business with the College. Later she is said to have assisted in running a girls' school at the nearby village of Blackwater. So Thomas junior met his future wife. A letter of 1831 from Mary Clementina's younger brother, Fred Coghlan, to 'Dear Tom' testifies to the intimacy between the families and to the nature of Thomas Sullivan's employment at the age of about 25. Though the syntax and some of the references may be obscure ('Hunt's Matchless' was a proprietary boot-polish), the musical indication is clear.

I am sure I think you have been highly honoured if the papers speak true, and I am sure if the Worthy Band of the R. M. College in the full Regimentals was on this immense boot which I was told was of the highest polish, there could have been no necessity for Hunt's Matchless. I am confident your *Royal Patrons* were highly pleased . . .

Thomas Sullivan's move from the Sandhurst area to Lambeth, some time after his marriage, indicates a resolve to explore the greater musical opportunities of London. The salary he earned as clarinettist in the Surrey Theatre, only a guinea [£1.05] a week, was supplemented by music-teaching and music-copying.[13] It must have been a sadly pinched existence, for on 28 April 1845 (the year when Arthur was nearly three) his father returned to the Royal Military College as sergeant bandmaster.[14] His name was not mentioned, but the band was, when a pamphlet in defence of the College was issued in 1849 in reply to criticism in the *Quarterly Review*. The anonymous author ('An Experienced Officer') praised the educational facilities provided at Sandhurst for the young officers and cadets. He commended the discipline and comradeship instituted without the bullying, fagging and flogging prevalent in educational establishments elsewhere. Moreover,

there is a very good military band, consisting of a master, 12 boys and youths, who are usually the sons of old soldiers; and as the commencement and termination of all studies, parades, meals, etc, etc. are made known by bugle-calls, they are all trained to act in the capacity of buglers as well as musicians.

So the young Arthur Sullivan came to live at Sandhurst. The house in Albany Place lay in the area designated by the military authorities as York Town (named after the Duke of York, late Commander in Chief). While living here he attended the Yorktown National (i.e. Church of England) School; and through his father's occupation, to quote his own words, he 'learned to play every wind instrument, with which I formed not merely a passing acquaintance, but a real, life-long intimate friendship'.[15] The bandsmen, numbering only 12, are likely to have 'doubled' on different instruments.

The post of sergeant bandmaster was paid at a rate of 3 shillings per day, plus his keep. Thomas Sullivan may have taken private pupils too, and was able to afford a piano at home: his son later recollected making musical 'discoveries' on the instrument at the age of about five, and forming then the intention of making music his career.

Clementina Sullivan may have raised additional income by going out to teach again, making use of the opportunities offered in a garrison town. Without such an addition, it is difficult to see how funds could have been available to place Arthur Sullivan at about nine or ten years of age as a boarder in a London school.[16] It was an establishment maintained and taught by one William Gordon Plees, at 20 Albert Terrace in Bayswater.

According to his own later recollection,[17] Arthur Sullivan was only eight (that is, he had not yet arrived at Plees's school) when he composed an anthem, *By the Waters of Babylon*. Attendance at Sandhurst parish church had evidently been a formative experience.[18] Whether he received musical training at the school, or only encouragement, is not known. He seems to have taken the initiative himself in seeking a place in the Chapel Royal, the ancient foundation which provided residence and maintenance as well as education for its choristers. His imagination may well have been struck by seeing the choristers, in their dress uniform of scarlet and gold, marching through the streets to Sunday services in St James's Palace, or on less elevated occasions wearing their uniforms of navy blue with red cord stripes on the trousers, and crown buttons.[19] Mrs Sullivan had written her approval of her son's ambitions, so Plees and his young aspirant called on 8 April 1854 without appointment on the patriarchal Sir George Smart, for 32 years joint organist and composer to the Chapel Royal. He had known Haydn and Beethoven and had himself been a boy chorister at the Chapel some 60 years before.

Smart did not concern himself with the selection and training of the choristers and directed his callers to their 'master', the Rev. Thomas Helmore. Presumably through inadvertence, Smart gave them the address which Helmore and his young wife had recently left, in Onslow Square, South Kensington. When they found it empty and were at a loss for the new address, it was Sullivan himself (according to his own later recollection) who said: 'He must have had meat – let us ask at the nearest butcher's'. The address being thus found, the pair set out on foot again and at 7 p.m. arrived at 6 Cheyne Walk, Chelsea. It was a house large enough to accommodate not only Helmore and his family but the ten 'Children of the Chapel Royal' (that is, the boy choristers) to whom he acted as moral guide and general schoolmaster, as well as musical instructor. Plees's report to the boy's mother next day (9 April 1854) told of the promising interview:

Mr Helmore stated that . . . he had a great many candidates so that, had Arthur not seen him, there would have been no chance of success. As it is, there seems great reason to succeed. Mr Helmore was pleased with your son's voice, more so too that he had been properly exercised, in fact everything that he could wish but in two points: (1) his age (2) the distance of his home from the scene of his duties.

The first was a disadvantage as his voice would be breaking too soon. In this respect after five years' service with a good certificate, the pupils get as a reward from the Government the sum of £30, and £10 from the Bishop. Besides these, Mr Helmore is in expectation of obtaining ulterior advantages for them. But Arthur's voice will probably not last the five years.

The distance of his home was against him thus. There is no remission of Sunday duty although there are four or five weeks' vacation at midsummer and Christmas, besides a few days at Easter and Michaelmas. Therefore to Mr Helmore it was an inconvenience to have boys who could not go home during the vacation and yet do their Sunday duty. I however begged him not to let that stand in the way, as he could always find a home with me during the vacations.

Next day Helmore himself wrote to Sullivan's father, confirming that only the boy's age raised some doubt as to his suitability ('as there happens to be a vacancy'). The matter was referred to the Bishop of London, the Bishop evidently gave the necessary authorization, and with Arthur Sullivan's enrolment in the Chapel Royal on 12 April 1854 his musical career began.[20] A three-month probationary period was soon passed. What the boy and his parents could not know is that he had been placed, at exactly the right moment, in the care of the one man best capable of firing his imagination. Thomas Helmore (1811–90) embodied the strength of musical revival in the Church of England.

2 Mentors

THE Chapel Royal had known better and grander days. Historically, the title referred to an institution rather than a place: its members, serving the Sovereign's musical needs on ecclesiastical and sometimes other occasions, had included Byrd, Tallis and Morley in the reign of Elizabeth I, Purcell in the reign of Charles II. But with the growth of secular music and the changed function of royal patronage, it had lapsed in the eighteenth and nineteenth centuries into an almost domestic unimportance. Its musical standards had sunk with those of most cathedrals. In November 1842 a letter in the *Musical World* from Dr E. F. Rimbault deplored the musical laxity of the Chapel Royal services in St James's Palace as well as those of St Paul's Cathedral.

The boy choristers at the chapel, left to regulate themselves when off duty (with inevitable bullying) were roughly treated by Helmore's predecessor. 'Mistakes in the rendering of the services were generally corrected by the Master, William Hawes, aided by a charming little riding-whip, which he applied to their backs with benevolent impartiality.' Such was the recollection of one former chorister, W. H. Cummings, who later became principal of the Guildhall School of Music.[1] Helmore replaced that by a disciplined but kindly regime. He did so, moreover, as part of a remarkable career. Serving the Church of England when the Church was itself in ferment, he was a leader of the movement to strengthen its musical dignity and to reclaim for its use the traditions of plainsong and sixteenth-century polyphonic music typified by the names of Tallis and Byrd.

Musical reform in the Victorian church followed architectural and liturgical reform. Under the inspiration of Augustus Pugin (1812–52), the pointed style of architecture was identified, because of its association with the medieval Age of Faith, as the proper expression of Christian devotion. Solidified into Victorian Gothic, it was to dominate the construction (and, alas, the restoration) of churches in nineteenth-century England, and to overflow into other monumental buildings such as the Houses of Parliament, begun in 1840 by Sir Charles Barry. A certain Romantic feeling – a yearning to recapture, through symbols, the essence of an earlier and purer age than one's own – suggests itself both in that architectural movement and in the theological effort to restore to the Church of England her 'Catholic' inheritance. An emphasis on the values of the sacraments, on the liturgy rather than the sermon, on ritual and robing – this was characteristic of the 'high church' movement known as Tractarianism (from its series of *Tracts for the Times*). Under its spell, Helmore forsook his Congregationalist background, accepted Anglican baptism, and set himself to fulfil the musical demands which sprang from the reformers' ideals.

It had become common practice in churches for a mixed male-and-female choir to be placed, with supporting instrumentalists, in the west gallery. The Tractarians' ideal was a robed choir of trained boys and men seated face-to-face in the chancel and accompanied by the organ where appropriate. The officiant should not merely recite the prayers but intone them, the people responding in like manner. Similarly, the psalms were not to be read as speech but chanted, either in Anglican chant (the harmonized form used in cathedrals) or, better, in single-line Gregorian chant (plainsong), reclaimed from Roman Catholic usage and fitted with English words. If possible, the service itself should be sung by the choir and not just said.

The cradle of the whole movement, and the place where practicability of its methods was demonstrated, was the Church of England's first national training college for (male) teachers – St Mark's, Chelsea. As its vice-principal and precentor (musical director), Helmore set up daily choral worship, open to the public. A robed choir of men and boys sang unaccompanied; prayers were intoned, and the psalms chanted to Anglican or Gregorian chants. 'Services' and anthems were sung to settings by such composers as Tallis, Byrd, Gibbons, Palestrina and Lassus. Helmore's own edition of the Psalms set to plainsong (*The Psalter Noted*, 1849, later amplified as *A Manual of Plainsong*) was a milestone of the reform movement. To a modern musical historian such as Nicholas Temperley the musical changes in Anglican worship during Victorian times are part of a wider social change: 'an expression of secular middle-class values and tasks, a part of the . . . growth in appreciation of professional musical performance which marked the age.'[2] Even 'low' churchmanship approved of the fuller use of music: 'Nobody was now against organs, choirs, anthems and counterpoint, as the Puritans had been in the sixteenth century. Both chanting and hymn-singing were practised by high and low churchmen alike.'

The 'ritualistic' services as St Mark's were the occasional object of hostile public demonstration. Among those who approved and occasionally worshipped there, however, was Dr C. A. Blomfield, Bishop of London. On his nomination, Helmore became in 1846 the first priest since the Reformation to be Master of the Children of the Chapel Royal. He retained his musical duties at St Mark's, though ceasing to be vice-principal, and occasionally brought his Chapel Royal boys to sing with the resident choir there.

To Sullivan and his fellow-choristers, Helmore was the complete tutor. An amateur player of the flute and cello, he nourished their musical tastes and personally instructed them in English, Latin, history, geography, Euclid (geometry), scripture, and church history – subjects which he had previously taught at St Mark's College. In Arthur Sullivan's letters home, there is the record of a hard-working but highly enjoyable apprenticeship under a kindly supervision. The manuscript of a madrigal 'O lady dear',[3] written in this period, bore the surely humorous inscription: 'Written while lying outside the bed one night, undressed, and in deadly fear lest Mr Helmore should come in'.

The chief duty of the boys was to sing at morning and evening services on Sundays at St James's Palace. Christmas also claimed them: 'I shall miss your little happy face and black eyes at my dinner table', his mother wrote to Sullivan on 23 December 1855.[4] Helmore also accepted engagements for the boys to sing at oratorio and other performances, both public and private. (The promoters of such events paid Helmore a fee which no doubt would contribute to the boys' welfare but was not passed on to them directly.) Hardly had Sullivan entered the Chapel when he found himself participating on 11 May 1854 at the 'Sons of the Clergy' Festival in St Paul's Cathedral. Next year (10 June 1855) he and his fellow-choristers were among the vocal force of 1,500 who delivered Handel's 'Hallelujah Chorus' when Queen Victoria attended the reopening of the Crystal Palace at its new Sydenham site.[5] In May 1855, at the Chapel Royal in St James's Palace itself, an anthem by the 12-year-old Sullivan (*Sing unto the Lord and bless His name*) was given under Sir George Smart's own direction.[6]

An undated letter of Sullivan's inscribed 'Tuesday evening' (1856?) refers to a concert series, almost certainly that of the Madrigal Society. Not only cultivating old English and Italian madrigals but encouraging the composition of new ones, its members were gentlemen amateurs who met under the guidance of a professional director (at that time Cipriani Potter, principal of the Royal Academy of Music) and evidently relied on Chapel Royal voices to supply the treble lines.

My dear Father,

   I saw Fred [his brother] today at the concert. I gave him a ticket to admit him. I understand you want one of the big bills to stick up in your room. Well, I will try to get you one. I gave Fred a book of the words to send home to you. I will send you one each concert. I am getting introduced to the public nicely, ain't I? Everything went off very well today – there was a pretty *good house*. I can't write much more tonight as I am tired and I ought to be at Latin. Goodbye, God bless you,

Arthur

P.S. When are you going to sing my psalm?

'My psalm' was a setting of Psalm 103, 'Bless the Lord, O my soul, and all that is within me bless his holy name'. The question 'When are you going to sing it?' suggests that his father's musical duties at the Royal Military College embraced Sunday church services – doubtless at Sandhurst parish church, since the college had no chapel at this time. This psalm-setting was never published; a madrigal accepted by the Madrigal Society, but likewise never published, was presumably the 'O lady dear' already referred to: both survive in manuscript in a private collection. But by this time a work of Sullivan's had already seen print. 'O Israel', a 'sacred song', was published by Novello in 1855. Helmore himself had apparently arranged for this publication, leaving unaltered some musical crudities so that the song could claim to be the composer's unaided work. Helmore also enlisted the youthful prodigy's assistance to provide harmonizations for another of his own publications, the second part of *The Hymnal Noted*.

By 1856 Arthur Sullivan's voice and reliable musicianship had made him a chosen favourite when individual solos were required. On 6 October he wrote home that he had become 'first boy'.[7] (Alfred Cellier, a future colleague in D'Oyly Carte days, was 'second boy'.) Because at least twice in that year he was kept at home by illness, letters survive from Helmore to 'my dear Arthur' which indicate an affectionate tutorial relationship.

You do not forget Mr Townsend's . . . party on Thursday, I suppose. Madame Goldschmidt dines with them and will probably stay . . . Pray do not come if you are at all unwell, but if you feel refreshed by your trip to Blackwater, we shall all be glad to see you again.

'Madame Goldschmidt' was Jenny Lind (1820–87); in the midst of a dazzling career in opera she had abandoned it for the more earnest field of oratorio and solo performance. This value-judgement, common in Victorian times, was not usually so drastically demonstrated. As the wife of Otto Goldschmidt (1829–1907), the German-born conductor of London's Bach Choir, she continued to radiate charm and benevolence. No one was to gain a more secure place in the affections of the boy whom she may have first met on this occasion. Certainly it was about this time that Sullivan first heard her sing, as he was to recall in a heartfelt letter to Goldschmidt on the occasion of her death 31 years later.

In 1848 Jenny Lind had given her services in a London concert to help endow a scholarship in memory of Mendelssohn. Not until July 1856 did the organizing committee proceed as far as selecting the first recipient, who would initially receive one year's free training at the Royal Academy of Music. Out of 17 competitors the oldest and the youngest tied for first place. Joseph Barnby (later a well-known choral conductor, and the composer of the popular *Sweet and Low*) was barely a month off his 18th birthday; Arthur Sullivan was 14. A deciding round was held, at which it was announced that the winner would be informed by letter next day. More than 40 years later Sullivan recounted the suspense:

I spent the day in a fever of excitement. Every time I heard a knock at the door, my heart was in my mouth. The day wore on, but still no letter. Two o'clock came – three – four, I was beginning to lose hope. At last, rat-tat! The postman's knock! It was unmistakable. I crept into the hall. The maidservant passed by me, and went to the letter box. 'A letter for you, Master Sullivan', she said. I took it from her, tore it open and then – I had won it. I don't think I ever felt such joy in my life.

The letter was dated 4 July 1856. Framed, it would occupy a place on the wall of his study at 1 Queen's Mansions, his London home from 1882 until his death. Sullivan's success, in so far as it was not in his own native gifts, must largely be ascribed to Helmore's training. His father, who received the news in a letter from Helmore, replied: 'It would indeed be difficult to describe what I felt at that moment. Should the Almighty spare him, I think he will at no distant day achieve much greater things.'[8] The wish that he should be spared was no routine piety, for the boy's health continued to be delicate, as Helmore's daughter was to recall:

'On Sundays between services[9] he always had to lie down in the afternoon in order to recover from the fatigue of the morning service and the walk to and from the Chapel Royal in his heavy gold-adorned coat.'

So, as Mendelssohn Scholar from 21 September 1856, Arthur Sullivan began study at the Royal Academy of Music. (Earlier that month, in a letter to a 'Mr Russell' written from the family home at York Town, he already signed himself 'A.S. Sullivan, R.A.M.!)[10] The Academy was not then, as it is now, a place of higher education inviting entrants at the age of 17 or 18 as an alternative to university. Nor was it a full conservatory, designed for the concluding as well as the intermediate stage of a musical education. Complaints were frequently made that Britain lacked any equivalent to the conservatories of Paris and Leipzig: indeed, such complaints led to the advocacy of a *new* training institution for London (see p. 103). Occupying premises in Tenterden Street near Hanover Square, the Academy had begun operations in 1823, admitting male and female pupils aged between 10 and 15. Most were boarders; only in 1853 was the basis changed to one of day students only.

With a new freedom the 14-year-old boy must have walked about London's streets, where pillar-boxes had recently begun to appear, and in the parks where the end of the Crimean War had been celebrated with firework displays in the previous spring. There were sights to see, including the new South Kensington Museum (1856), dubbed by the *Builder* magazine the 'Brompton Boilers'. There were sights a young boy was supposed not to see: women and little girls (the legal age of consent was only 12) offering their favours in the West End with the query 'Are you good-natured, dear?', the standard fee being five shillings (25p). A sensational cartoon of 1857 by John Leech in *Punch*[11] depicts two prostitutes meeting, 'not a hundred miles from the Haymarket'. Says Bella: 'Ah! Fanny! How long have you been gay?' (i.e., 'on the game'). On the wall behind is a theatrical poster: 'Great success – *La traviata*': Verdi's opera about the world of the Parisian courtesan had reached London in the previous year.

Verdi was not, however, a composer likely to have been commended to the young Sullivan at the Royal Academy. His piano teacher was William Sterndale Bennett (1816–75), a noted composer whose allegiance was to English vocal music and the Austro-German symphony. His instructor in harmony was John Goss (1800–80)[12] through whom may be traced an interesting though tenuous line of musical descent: Goss had been the pupil of Thomas Attwood (1765–1838), who had in turn been the pupil of Mozart in Vienna. In fact a fair copy in Sullivan's hand (dated 1858) of a three-part fugue, 'after Mozart', was formerly supposed to be Sullivan's own composition, but is actually a student exercise by Attwood. Sullivan's instruction at the Academy also included violin lessons – it is not known with what teacher.

His voice having not yet broken when he entered the Academy, he remained a Chapel Royal chorister living at Helmore's house in Cheyne Walk. On 29 September 1856 (the feast of St Michael and All Angels) he was taken to sing at the dedication service for St Michael's College, Tenbury, Herefordshire, endowed by Sir Frederick Gore Ouseley, who was a baronet and a cleric and a respected composer as well. The 'true musicianly pathos' of Arthur Sullivan's treble voice in Goss's anthem, *Praise the Lord*, and the 'prodigious sensation' caused by it among the regular St Michael's choirboys were remembered almost half a century later by one of them. As Bishop Charles J. Corfe[13] he was to write from Korea to the *Musical Times* after Sullivan's death:

There was, I think on the following day, an incident which amazed us still more. To entertain his numerous musical friends, Sir Frederick asked them to his house in the evening. We boys had, of course, to go in order to provide the soprano parts of the concerted music with which he entertained them. . . . We knew, of course, that Sullivan was Mendelssohn Scholar, and that he could play the piano. But I do not think anyone in the room was prepared for what then happened. Suddenly Ouseley, in his joyous and impulsive way, said, 'Sullivan, I challenge you to play an extempore duet with me.' This savoured of the impossible, considering one was a chorister and the other the Professor of music at Oxford. But Sullivan said, very modestly and quietly, 'Very good, Sir Frederick.' The room was pretty still by this time, and every one looked on, prepared to listen with attention, and, I doubt not, an amused curiosity. 'You take the treble, Sullivan, because it will be easier, and I will take the bass.' Forthwith they sat down at the piano, agreed upon the key and the rhythm, and fell to.

Here my story must end abruptly. I remember nothing about the music, and, of course, could not pronounce upon its merits. I stood near Sullivan – behind him – and watched keenly his fingers, and noticed that there was no hesitation. I do not suppose that *as music* it was very remarkable, but they played on without stopping until the piece came to a natural end; and I thought then, as I have thought ever since that, as a *tour de force*, it was very wonderful.

Shortly after that Tenbury event he and a fellow-chorister, Christopher Bridgeman, were chosen by Helmore to go with him to St Neots, Cambridge-shire, to take part in another special church service – not on a Sunday, for the Chapel Royal services in St James's Palace had absolute claim on that day. Sullivan being again at home, unwell, Helmore wrote on 8 December 1856 to 'my dear Arthur':

The next train after the 5 p.m. (by which Bridgeman and I are to go to St Neots) starts from the King's Cross Station at 8 p.m. and gets in at 10.21. You will on arriving at St Neots get into an omnibus, and direct them to put you down at the house of the Rev Mr Vaughan, the vicar (fare to St Neots, 7s, so you will need a few shillings more than I gave you). This will give you ample time for Dr Bennett's lesson [at the Royal Academy of Music], *and a meal after it* – but be very careful not to miss the train. . . .

Helmore's own report[14] was given in a letter to Arthur's mother:

Arthur sang a very elaborate solo in church today, with a good many divisions [florid passages] in it, requiring flexibility of voice, very nicely, and his expression was beautiful. It brought the tears very near my eyes (although the music itself was rubbish), but as I was immediately to enter the pulpit, I was obliged to restrain myself. . . . He had a headache yesterday which he attributes to riding in omnibuses – but I think it is more likely to proceed from irregularity in eating. I am sure he (and most children) require, as we do ourselves, the regular meals not much altered in time or quantity. They got themselves a nice dinner of chops here [St Neots' Vicarage] and this set Arthur up for the time, but he was fagged at rehearsal so I got him to bed as soon as possible and today he is 'all right'.

On Sullivan's death his fellow-chorister Bridgeman was to write in the *Musical Times* a memorial of those days. It is embellished with a highly circumstantial anecdote of a solo sung by Sullivan at the christening of Prince Leopold, Duke of Albany – and a comment made at rehearsal by Sir Michael Costa, who was conducting. The account, reproduced by various biographers, is unfortunately fictitious: Leopold was christened in June 1853, a year before Sullivan's entry into the Chapel Royal, and on no other occasion at this period did Costa participate in such an event. But another letter of Sullivan himself (to his father – undated, but probably of 1857) gives an authentic glimpse of life at Cheyne Walk seen through boyish eyes:

I went to Novello's on Saturday and found that the price of *Judas Maccabaeus* is four shillings, professional three shillings [i.e. less a discount], which I can get it for. We went to the Bishop's party on Thursday and had such a jolly dinner. After that we went and had a game at cricket with the Bishop's two sons, two very nice gentlemen. Then we went into tea. After that we sung [*sic*] in the evening. I sang *With verdure clad*, with which the Bishop was very much pleased and patted me on the head. He then gave us 2s. 6d. each. So I bought *Samson* when we went to Novello's, as one of the boys owed me sixpence. Shan't we be well stocked with oratorios? I went to King's [his brother's lodging] on Saturday to see Fred but he was at his office so I stopped there till he came home. He came with me and got his parcel. I am very much obliged for all the nice things you sent me, particularly the *marmalade*. It was beautiful. The same night my new cloak came home. It is such a beauty. . . . This is my last sheet of paper and very near the last envelope. The edition of Novellos of the oratorios is scarlet cloth and gold. Fred came the other night and was saying about 'the Horgin [*organ*] Days!' when Mr Helmore comes down. He told me I shouldn't bring my friends down into the schoolroom while lessons where [*sic*] about. Goodbye, God bless you, love to dear Mother and Helen.
    Your affectionate and dutiful son,

                                                                                  Arthur Sullivan

'Helen' was perhaps a cousin staying with the family. If it now seems odd that Sullivan's letters appear to have been exclusively addressed to his father (despite the exceptional closeness to his mother as evidenced later), the explanation must surely be that his father was the financial provider to whom an account had to be rendered.

On one occasion at least he went to the opera and heard Giulia Grisi and the tenor Giovanni Mario, both of great celebrity.[15] But oratorio and church music remained the dominant influence in Arthur Sullivan's musical upbringing. (Bernard Shaw was to find Sullivan's operettas 'most unexpectedly churchy after Offenbach'.) It might be supposed that an equally important and contrasting influence would arise from the idiom of the military band – his father's vocation. But there was no distinctive, original band style during Sullivan's boyhood. Popular band fare drew mainly on operatic and other adaptations among which marches were included. Vigorous, swinging tunes such as Donizetti's 'Per te d'immenso giubilo' (the wedding march from *Lucia di Lammermoor*, 1835) inspired the typical band style, not the other way round; and when Shaw came to write *Major Barbara* in 1905, he used that very march for the evangelizing strains of the Salvation Army band.

The life of Sullivan's father now underwent an important change. The military abuses exposed during the Crimean War spurred a wave of army reforms. British bands had shown themselves inferior to those of France, where a central army school of music had been in existence since 1836. At a massed parade in Scutari, the British bands had distinguished themselves by playing *God Save the Queen* in different keys simultaneously.[16] In a drive to raise the standards of army bands and institute reasonable uniformity between them, the Royal Military School of Music was brought into being at Kneller Hall, Twickenham – where it still stands. It opened in 1857 under a civilian director of music, Henry (originally Heinrich) Schallehn (1815–93), late bandmaster of the 17th Lancers, whose quarterly salary at Kneller Hall was £87.10s. A staff of three other instructors was provided.

Of these, Thomas Sullivan shortly became one. His post at Kneller Hall[17] was that of 'chief professor of the clarinet', according to the entry on Arthur Sullivan written by George Grove in the first (1879) edition of Grove's *Dictionary of Music and Musicians*. There is every reason for preferring this authority to a tradition at Kneller Hall which attaches Thomas's name exclusively to 'lower brass'. The clarinet had, after all, been his wage-earning instrument in the theatre. Probably, however, the instrumental versatility which had been a necessity at Sandhurst found scope in the newer post.

According to a later copy of the original register of Kneller Hall, his first salary was paid in the quarter ending 30 June 1857 and amounted to £19.3s.4d. – evidently a two-month salary, two-thirds of a full quarter's salary of £28.15s. which he received subsequently. He must therefore have joined at the beginning of May 1857. But it was not a direct transfer from his previous post. The records of the Royal Military College at Sandhurst show him as receiving his army discharge on the last day of December 1856. Perhaps he had simply determined to try his fortunes in London again, and was lucky to find the Kneller Hall job available. From 22 June 1857 Arthur Sullivan ceased to be a member of the Chapel Royal (his voice having broken) and would need a London address in order to continue at the Royal Academy.

At £115 per annum, Thomas Sullivan's salary was sufficient to rank him in the middle class (just!), though below the level at which income tax fell due. A skilled industrial labourer in the 1860s might earn £60 or £70 per annum,[18] an agricultural or unskilled labourer between £20 and £40. On Thomas Sullivan's social level, a maid-of-all-work could be engaged by a family for about £10 per annum plus her keep. By the autumn the family was established at 3 Ponsonby Street in the Pimlico district (on the north bank of the Thames, opposite Lambeth), to which Thomas Sullivan returned nightly after his work at Kneller Hall. A few pence would have taken him to Twickenham daily by an early morning workmen's train – not necessarily the 'parliamentary train' (required by statute to run daily at a maximum third-class fare of a penny a mile), which, in the mouth of Gilbert's Mikado, was to baffle twentieth-century listeners.

Pimlico was a respectable middle-class district, adjoining fashionable Belgravia.[19] It was conspicuous in ecclesiastical circles for St Barnabas's Church, with its ritualistic practices – alleged by opponents to lead to Popery, if not worse:

> The Reverend Pimlico Poole was a saint
> Who averted from sinners their doom,
> By confessing the ladies until they felt faint
> All alone in a little dark room.

More to the point for the Sullivan brothers, the district had a flourishing amateur dramatic society[20] which soon enlisted the participation of Fred. For one of its productions, Arthur arranged the participation of a 26-strong orchestra mainly consisting of fellow-students from the Royal Academy of Music. Like them, the young conductor appeared in the Academy's uniform, wearing a blue jacket with gilt buttons, and thus made what was probably his first contact with theatrical entertainment.

Sullivan's studies at the Academy bore fruit. An overture (apparently untitled) was performed on 13 July 1858 and four days later was praised in the *Musical World*: it showed 'an independent way of thinking, which, in one so young as the Mendelssohn scholar, looks well'. A year before, on 14 July 1857, an Academy concert had included a setting for duet and chorus of 'It was a lover and his lass' – an early showing of that attraction to Shakespeare which lasted throughout his musical life.

Arthur Sullivan's prowess in his first academic year (1856–7) was sufficient to induce the extension of his Mendelssohn Scholarship for a second year. His teachers furthered his acquaintance with professional concert life. In 1856 Sterndale Bennett himself had become conductor of the Philharmonic Society. Lacking Costa's decisiveness with the baton, he represented a lapse into the Society's too-comfortable traditions. His relationships with his fellow-musicians on the Society's committee of management were not of the happiest, as a letter from Sullivan to his father (24 March 1857) makes clear:

Mr Goss particularly wishes me to subscribe to the Philharmonic this season. He tried first to see if Dr Bennett could get me in for nothing. Dr B could have done it but he won't ask a *favour* of the *present committee*. I suppose you have read the correspondence about the shameful behaviour of the committee in the *Musical World* – if not, I will send you one or two numbers. Well, the *professional* subscription is two guineas for the six concerts. May I subscribe? I daresay I shall be able to make it up to you again. . . . Today is a concert at the Academy. H.R.H. Prince Albert is going to honour us with a visit. So we must all go *very swell*.

In a further and extraordinary gesture of confidence, the Mendelssohn Scholarship Committee now decided to extend Arthur Sullivan's scholarship for a third year (beginning 21 September 1858) in order that the 16-year-old prodigy could proceed to the Leipzig Conservatory for more advanced study than London could offer. The chairman of the committee was Sir George Smart, who had maintained a warm and helpful interest in the former Chapel Royal soloist; its secretary was the German-born Carl Klingemann, who had been an intimate friend of Mendelssohn. Klingemann's wife volunteered to give the boy free lessons in German. The composer Julius Benedict – Weber's former pupil, who had settled in London 20 years before – was evidently also consulted by Smart. Supporting the recommendation that Sullivan should be sent to Leipzig, Benedict suggested[21] entrusting him there to the guidance of Moritz Hauptmann, 'who is very much opposed to the music of the future' (i.e. to Liszt and Wagner, the latter's pamphlet on *The Art-Work of the Future* having appeared in 1849). Evidently there were dangerous sparks in the Leipzig air.

Henry Broadwood, of the celebrated piano firm of that name, added his own private donation to the scholarship money, in order to make adequate provision for a boy with no financial resources of his own. Sullivan could not have been more generously treated – and it was a generosity stirred not only by his musical worth but by a charm of manner which persisted through life, making him as welcome to ladies in the drawing room as to clubmen and colonels, bankers and brother artists. 'He is so great a favourite of all of us', wrote Lady Smart (speaking no doubt on behalf of her young daughter and niece too) to Mrs Sullivan, acknowledging a portrait of Arthur which the proud mother had sent.

3 Leipzig and London

WHEN the taste of the most cultivated British musicians was so dominated by Austrian and German music from Haydn to Mendelssohn, the attraction of Leipzig needed no advertising. It was the city where Sterndale Bennett, Sullivan's teacher, had played his own Third Piano Concerto in 1836 and had won the friendship of Mendelssohn and Schumann. The Conservatory was a beacon of musical excellence: Mendelssohn had been its first director (1843) and Schumann had taught there. It was in the best sense an international finishing-school for the most talented of young musicians. Grieg was a fellow-student of Sullivan's, but one year younger; Sullivan's letters make no mention of him, nor of Dudley Buck (1839–1909), an American who was to win some attention as a composer, and to make a musical setting of Longfellow's *The Golden Legend* before Sullivan did.

The principal professor of the piano was Moscheles, now 62 years old, who had left London in 1846. Smart wrote to him a commendation of Sullivan which survives in a copy made by Sullivan's mother.

I take a lively interest in Mr Sullivan and recommend him to your notice with confidence, as his talent will ensure your favourable attention, and his modesty as to his pretensions is not among the least of his qualifications. Composition is what he shines most in. An overture of his was performed with considerable success at the last concert of the season at the Royal Academy of Music . . .

Smart's letter was apparently forwarded to Moscheles by Klingemann, to whom Moscheles replied from Leipzig. Klingemann translated it for Smart, using 'Leipsic' as the customary English form. Mention was made not only of Wagner's 'music of the future' (those dangerous sparks again!) but of Bach as Leipzig's greatest son.

Sullivan's excellent talent and the manifold instruction he got from his former masters gives him a rank among the young musicians which claims the highest interest, and cannot but be flattering to our Conservatorio which he is to enter.[1] I owe to my oldest friend Sir George Smart and to the house of Broadwood fatherly to provide for their protégé. The Conservatorio founded by Mendelssohn is still administered after his intention. Pianoforte and violin players have to learn the truly beautiful in the classics. You know who are the teachers: Hauptmann for counterpoint, Richter for organ, Rietz for instrumentation and composition. Although Leipsic only *tolerates* the 'music of the future' ('Zukunftmusik'), the taste here is not for being so rigid as *only* to like the music of Sebastian Bach's deep learning and antiquated manner. We like our young composers to find a *juste milieu* and develop elements fit for every school of art. . . The course of lessons will be arranged entirely according to the ability and speciality of the pupil. Therefore I cannot yet say anything regarding it for Mr Sullivan, and only promise to take a lively interest in him and to recommend him to the other teachers. As you tell me Sullivan has a peculiar talent for composition, it stands to reason that his chief time will be devoted to this branch. . . .

Having arrived in Leipzig in September 1858, Sullivan became thoroughly caught up in his new academic and social life, and waited four months before sending to Smart the account which must have been expected much earlier.

I have one lesson a week from Professor Moscheles and two from Mr Plaidy on the pianoforte; in counterpoint, weekly one from Mr Hauptmann and one from Mr Richter; one composition lesson from Kapellmeister Rietz; on the violin one a week from Concertmeister Dreyschock (brother to the celebrated pianoforte player) and two from Herr Röntgen. Then there are the Gewandhaus concerts every Thursday night and an Abend-Unterhaltung (evening entertainment) in the Conservatory every Friday . . .

I cannot tell you how [kind] Mr and Mrs Moscheles are to me. From the first day I came here they have treated me more as a son than a stranger. I am sure I shall always love and respect them. I have nothing to do with money matters. Mr Moscheles pays everything for me and whenever I want some money I go to him.

Of these teachers the oldest and most eminent, apart from Moscheles himself, was Moritz Hauptmann (1792–1868), whose pupils in composition included Joachim and von Bülow, and who held Bach's former position as cantor (musical director) of St Thomas's School. Ernst Friedrich Richter (1808–79), who was to succeed Hauptmann in that post, was the author of an internationally noted textbook of harmony. As well as working with Julius Rietz (1812–77), Raimund Dreyschock (1824–69), Louis Plaidy (1810–74), and the Dutch violinist Engelbert Röntgen (1829–97), Sullivan probably studied conducting with Ferdinand David (1810–73), who had been an intimate of Mendelssohn's and who taught both violin and conducting at the Conservatory.

David was also leader ('Concertmeister', as it was then spelt) of the orchestra in the celebrated series of concerts in the Gewandhaus (Cloth Hall). Its standards could startle musical visitors from London, where rehearsal-time was skimped. Sullivan's own reactions may have been similar to those of his friend Frederic Clay (see p. 34), who went later to Leipzig for a brief period of study and reported back to Sullivan in 1863 in terms of the utmost enthusiasm:

I can say without hesitation that all the orchestral playing I have ever heard in my life is amateurs' work beside these men.[2] A good proof of this is that, at the first concert, they played Beethoven's C minor Symphony, and turned my head with surprise and delight. Tonight they repeated it and I went fully (and not unnaturally) expecting that they would not reach the immense standard which my remembrance of their first performance now required. My boy, they played it better tonight than before. . .

In his first month at Leipzig, however, Sullivan wrote home that he would not be attending the first two Gewandhaus concerts 'as they are on a Sunday'[3] – a youthful sabbatarianism which contrasts with his later advocacy of Sunday concerts in London as a socially beneficial recreation. His references to his

London family circle now include Charlotte Louisa Lacy, to whom his brother Fred had become engaged.

His finances permitted him a summer trip by rail to Dresden and then by boat up the Elbe as far as Schandau. In the company of Plaidy and of an English fellow-student, Walter Bache (1842–88), he also went by rail to Halle where a bicentenary ceremony in honour of Handel, the town's most illustrious citizen, provoked the 17-year-old visitor to trenchant criticism in a further letter to Smart (14 August 1859).

We, that is to say, a large party of English, and some German admirers of Handel, went by an early train and arrived in Halle about half past 8. The uncovering of the statue took place at 9. The Bürgermeister and another man made each a short speech, to hear which I was too far off. The cloth was then taken off the statue, the people cheered a little, and a brass band in a balcony played 'See the conquering hero' a great deal too quickly, and an old Chorale of some one else's composition, the suitability of which I could not quite recognize. There was then a general adjournment into the church to listen to a performance of *Samson*, and a more wretched performance it was never my good fortune to hear. All the tempi were taken wrong, many of the best things left out, and altogether is quite unworthy of the occasion. The fact is that they do not understand Handel in Germany and have not the traditional reading of it like we have. Johanna Wagner sung [*sic*], Mr David played first violin and Robert Franz the celebrated composer conducted. That finished the ceremony of the day. I think without pride I may venture to assert it would have been otherwise in England. The statue itself is a very fine one of bronze.[4]

Another letter to Smart was dated 'Maundy Thursday' (i.e. 21 April) 1859, and referred to the Austrian invasion of Piedmont to oppose the Italian nationalist uprising, supported by Napoleon III.

I have played once in the Abend-Unterhaltung . . . intended to give the players confidence and am going to play again next Friday, a sonata of Mendelssohn's in E.

Telegraphic dispatches have just brought news war has broken out in the south. The general opinion is that it will not come near here, at least not this summer. Leipzig is a capital place for a battle. It lies on an immense plain . . .

Among the students, Sullivan formed a close friendship with his fellow-Londoner John Francis Barnett (1837–1916), and with the latter's cousins Domenico, Clara, and Rosamond Barnett, who were also students there under the eye of their mother while their father, the composer John Barnett (1802–90), remained in England.[5] To Clara Barnett (recalling it long afterwards), Sullivan was a 'smiling youth with an oval, olive-tinted face, dark eyes, a large generous mouth, and a thick crop of dark curly hair which overhung his low forehead . . . the sight of him excited in me a strange emotion never before experienced!' Alas, Sullivan was inclined to flirt with her sister, dedicating to Rosamond and not to Clara a German song, *Ich möchte hinaus es jauchzen*, to words by the Swiss poet, Wilhelm August Corrodi (1826–85). At this time he also composed another German song to words by Eichendorff (a poet much favoured by Schumann) beginning *Lied mit Thränen halb-geschrieben*.

On one occasion he sent back to the family a photograph of some students, and received from 'Jack' (his nickname for his brother Fred) a drawing based on the photograph and a request for identifications. He replied by sending a drawing of his own. His reference to Charlotte is ironic in his usual vein: she had (one presumes) written *no* letter.

I have just received Jack's letter, which cheered me up and amused me very much. The picture is as follows. (I can draw better than he can.)

1. Emil Krause, from Hamburg, pianist and composer
2. John F. Barnett, pianist and composer
3. Carl N. Rose, from Hamburg, violinist
4. Arthur S. Sullivan, highly distinguished pianist, tenor [viola] player and composer
5. Robert Lienau, from Lübeck, pianist
6. Frederick Hegar, from Basel, in Switzerland, violinist and composer
7. Eugene Albrecht, from St Petersburg, violinist

What a capital hand Charlotte is at corresponding! I have been so charmed with the numerous letters I have received from her. When you write again send me a full account of how you are getting on at Broadwood's, what sort of music you play, and if they are all tolerably decent players, or if you have to teach them all from the beginning, etc, etc. I enclose you a translation of a criticism of the Miss Barnetts' playing which appeared in one of the daily papers here.

What I want Fred to do is this. You know how very kind Mr and Mrs Barnett have been to me. Well, I think if they saw any notice taken of their children in an English paper, it would please them immensely, and I should like to be the means of it, as a small return for their kindness, etc. Now let him (Jack) take the enclosed to Mr Davison [J. W. Davison, the music critic], give him my best remembrances, explain the matter to him, making him understand that Barnetts have nothing whatever to do with it and that it is solely my own doing to beg him to put something about it in the *Musical World*. Appeal to his national feelings, tell him that his countrymen are distinguishing themselves abroad while we are paying an enormous price in England for foreign talent which is very often not half so good.

Those words of Fred's are very neat, I must confess. They inspired me with brilliant ideas directly – all good words do: something of the following classical style came into my head. Don't you admire it?

!!

!!

Tell Jack that if he wishes me to set any words to music they must be proper ones, not such rubbish as that, where sense, rhythm, etc are all wrong and confused.

'Carl N. Rose', listed among the photographed figures, was to be better known as Carl Rosa (1842–89), founder of the English opera company bearing that name. Sullivan's self-description as a viola player suggests that he may have been required to study the instrument in order to make up numbers in the Conservatory orchestra. (On at least one occasion in orchestral rehearsal he played the double-bass part on the piano, evidently 'filling-in' in the absence of the proper players.[6]) The letter also reveals the renewed generosity of Broadwood. Not only had he again added his own contribution when the

Mendelssohn Scholarship Committee extended Sullivan's stay in Leipzig for a second year; he also engaged Sullivan's father to superintend a band of his factory employees – with a result to be noted in the next chapter.

Gradually, as Sullivan's studies progressed, the piano took second place to composition and conducting. 'I come in for all the conducting now,' he wrote to his father, describing how in March 1860 he conducted a farewell concert of Julius Rietz's own works when Rietz took a post at Dresden.[7] The following month, in the examinations marking the end of his second academic year, Sullivan conducted an overture of his own under the German title of *Der Rosenfest*. This was 'The Feast of Roses' as described in Thomas Moore's narrative Oriental poem *Lalla Rookh*:

> . . . The merry laughter, echoing
> From gardens where the silken swing
> Wafts some delighted girl above
> The top leaves of the orange grove;
> Or, from these infant groups at play
> Among the tents that line the way
> Flinging, un-awed by slave or mother,
> Handfuls of roses at each other!

The poetry of Thomas Moore (1779–1852) was in fashion, and not only in England – *Lalla Rookh* itself had been translated into many languages, and Schumann's cantata *Paradise and the Peri* was one of the better-known musical works based on it.

On a less formal occasion Sullivan, playing a tambourine, was among the contingent of Anglo-American students who put on a 'grand nigger performance'[8] in emulation of the blacked-up troupes who were already popular in London.

There was no chance of extending the Mendelssohn Scholarship beyond a second year, but Sullivan was pressed by his teachers to stay. Remarkably, it seems to have been Thomas Sullivan who raised enough money – aided by £5 from Smart – for his son's further period of study. (Whether Arthur Sullivan himself found additional income from work during the two summer vacations is not known.) By a benevolent gesture of the Conservatory, Sullivan was exempted from tuition fees during this last year: that is, a 'scholarship' was granted by the Conservatory itself. His informal activities were to reinforce his professional skills. Unanimously elected president of the student music committee, he wrote in December 1859 that he was to conduct an operetta by Carl Reinecke, Rietz's successor as the regular conductor of the Gewandhaus concerts.[9]

Attendance at the Gewandhaus concerts doubtless sharpened his own musical taste. The programmes were conservative, but not so conservative as at the Philharmonic concerts in London. The season was more substantial – 20 concerts over eight months, as compared with London's eight in four months – and more varied.[10] Extracts from Wagner's latest opera, *Lohengrin*, had been given just before Sullivan's arrival in the autumn of 1858. During the first two years of his studies, the programmes included not only the standard works of Beethoven,

Mendelssohn, and Schumann but the duet 'Wie aus der ferne' from Wagner's *Flying Dutchman*. The youthful Brahms came and played his first piano concerto (27 January 1859) to a largely indifferent, uncomprehending audience. Of Schubert, who was to be one of Sullivan's favourites, the 'Great C major' symphony was given, and the Grand Duo in Joachim's orchestral arrangement – but not yet the 'Unfinished' Symphony, still awaiting its discovery.

Joseph Joachim (1831–1907), with whom Sullivan was to develop a warm friendship, was among the violinists appearing at this period, and Pauline Viardot-Garcia among the singers.[11] At a party given by Ferdinand David, Sullivan was introduced to Liszt. A letter home gives evidence that he met Spohr (whose Violin Concerto no. 9, Symphony no. 3 and other works were given at Leipzig in this period), and won his approval of a string quartet – which, however, was judged not sufficiently good for an official Conservatory concert.

Opera and church music must also have attracted the students. In 1859 and 1860 Leipzig's operatic fare included Rossini's *The Barber of Seville*, Meyerbeer's *Les Huguenots*, Nicolai's *The Merry Wives of Windsor*, and Wagner's *Lohengrin* – all these, be it noted, works by living composers! – as well as Mozart's *Don Giovanni* and *The Impresario*. In the spring of 1861 a visiting Italian company brought Verdi's *Il trovatore* and *La traviata*. Among Leipzig's churches Sullivan can hardly have failed to attend one service or more at St Thomas's, with its inheritance from Bach. We know that out of curiosity he visited the Leipzig synagogue[12] and heard in its service a striking musical progression that he was deliberately to employ 30 years later in characterizing the Jewess Rebecca in *Ivanhoe* (see p. 333).

Two Leipzig press reviewers found Mendelssohn's influence strong in *The Feast of Roses*. His next work, which marked a decisive step in his career, relied on Mendelssohn's example not so much in matters of style as in formal conception. On the analogy of the music to *A Midsummer Night's Dream*, Sullivan set himself the task of writing incidental music to *The Tempest*. A selection of six items from it (out of an eventual 12) was given at the Conservatory's end-of-year examination concert on 6 April 1861 – as usual, a public event at the Gewandhaus. Four days later his official diploma was granted by the Conservatory.

The concert was opened by an English fellow-student, Walter Bache,[13] playing the first movement of Bennett's third piano concerto (the one which the composer himself had played in Leipzig 25 years before). Carl Rose played the most celebrated of Spohr's violin concertos (no. 8, 'in the form of a song scena'), and there were six other items. With acknowledged competence Arthur Sullivan conducted his own work – given under the German title, *Der Sturm*, and with Ariel's song, 'Where the bee sucks' (also in German translation) sung by a fellow-student, Minna Giesinger. He was thrice called upon to take a bow, and the critics of the two Leipzig musical papers gave his score their cordial approval.[14] Sullivan must already have felt that to be a composer was his vocation. But it was not, at the age of 20, a living. As for his ability with the baton, Sullivan may have found more than a jest in a letter from his brother Fred: 'You say you have been told by your masters that you were born to be a conductor. In that case you will have no chance in London, should you aspire to a position, for the market's overstocked with omnibuses!'[15]

The horse-drawn double-decker omnibus, of which the conductor stood on a board at the back and held on by a strap, was indeed a feature of the streets of London. Here Sullivan rejoined his family, who had moved from no. 3 Ponsonby Street to no. 6 in the same street. A professional notice in the *Musical World*, May 1861, advertised his return from Germany: 'All communications respecting pupils, etc., etc., are to be addressed to his residence, 6 Ponsonby Street, Pimlico.'

The 'etc.' which his advertisement sought was not much more than a hopeful fiction, and the 'pupils' (that is, piano pupils) could not be depended on. Helmore helped Sullivan by engaging him for some teaching (not of music, but of reading, writing, and arithmetic![16]) to the Chapel Royal boys. The one steady salaried position that was normally open to such a young musician was that of church organist. Jenny Lind's husband, Otto Goldschmidt, evidently anxious to assist the former Mendelssohn Scholarship winner, pointed out the availability of such a post at a Lutheran church. Sullivan declined the offer, ostensibly on the ground of his own Anglican convictions, and was lucky to find a Church of England position within two miles of his home – at St Michael's, Chester Square, where constables from the local police station assisted in the choir.[17] Having never trained as an organist, he was now prudent enough to take a few lessons. If the statement in Percy M. Young's biography that his salary was £80 is correct then he was exceptionally fortunate, since about this time young Joseph Barnby was receiving £30 per annum from a London church.

In Leipzig he had become friendly with Ignaz Moscheles's son Felix, who now paid a visit to London and for a time left his dog with Sullivan and his family. A letter 'from' the dog to Moscheles starting '(*mf*) Bowwowwowwow – (*pp*) Gr-r-r-r-r-r (*f*) wow' carries a 'translation of the foregoing by A. S. Sullivan'.

I was very low-spirited the whole day after leaving you, and appeared to feel the parting very much, but it soon wore off under the influence of biscuit, bones and kindness . . . I have several little idiosyncrasies and failings of which my master (*pro tem*) is trying to correct me, but finds it rather hard work for I am not easily brought out of them. I have a will of my own, but Sully says: Train up a dog in the way it should go, and he will not depart from it, etc., etc. and Sully is right.

For some reason this friendship did not persist, though Felix Moscheles (1833–97) became a fashionable London portrait-painter and a crony of George du Maurier, whose circle overlapped with Sullivan's. But another friendship made at this time was among the most enduring of his life. George Grove (1820–1900), known to posterity as founder-editor of the *Dictionary of Music and Musicians* which still bears his name, was by training a civil engineer but music, literature and biblical scholarship were his enthusiasms. Having 'rubbed up my Hebrew',[18] and having twice visited Palestine, he became a chief contributor to the vast *Dictionary of the Bible* which appeared in 1862. From 1866 to 1883 he was to be the editor of *Macmillan's Magazine*, and had already been appointed to the post which gave him such an influential sway in music – that of secretary (administrator) of the Crystal Palace in its new location at Sydenham.

Admission to the Crystal Palace and its grounds, where the gardens and fountains were said to outstrip those of Versailles, cost 2s 6d on a Saturday but only 1s on other days.[19] Inside the 1,600-foot long building itself were botanical displays, an art museum on historical principles, an industrial and technological museum, and a gallery where pictures were sold as well as exhibited. Inside the structure too was the enormous area for performers (as many as 4,000 could be, and were, accommodated on special occasions) and their audience. The gardens were not only ornamental but afforded facilities for cricket, archery, and rifle shooting. Here Blondin was to walk a tight-rope slung between two water towers, pausing midway to cook himself an omelette.

Concerts of light music were daily fare. Only on Saturday afternoons, however, was the Crystal Palace orchestra expanded to symphonic size, with programmes that sought the highest musical level, with good representation of living composers British and foreign. The importance of this series not only from the public's point of view but from that of two generations of British composers is incalculable. The series lasted until 1901, conducted throughout by one extraordinary musician, the German-born August Manns (1825–1907), who shared with Grove the choice of programmes. The critic Hermann Klein[20] was to observe him

in the prime of life, a man of 46, with a leonine head of grey hair; tall, straight, alert, with a fierce-looking moustache, suggesting something of the aspect of a drum-major as he wielded his baton with a wide, noble rhythmic sweep. . . . His full Saturday orchestra only gathered for rehearsal on the morning of the concert.

Grove's meeting with Sullivan took place not at the Crystal Palace but at a concert in St James's Hall in the West End. Twenty-two years Sullivan's senior, he became the younger man's champion and friend, making him his frequent guest at his family home – in Sydenham, near the Crystal Palace itself. In correspondence with one another, George Grove and Arthur Sullivan later expressed mutual affection in terms which are not in the least inconsistent with Victorian manly sentiment, and in which a subsequent age would be quite wrong to suspect homosexuality. Grove was a family man with (later) a long extra-marital relationship with a much younger woman; Sullivan's own strong heterosexual drive will be sufficiently shown in later chapters of this book.

It was perhaps through Grove that Sullivan also began a friendship with Nina Lehmann. Daughter of the Edinburgh publisher Robert Chambers, she was the wife of Frederick Lehmann, a prosperous metal merchant.[21] He and his brother, the painter Rudolf Lehmann, both German-born, had settled in England. Some eleven years older than Sullivan, she became his cherished confidante. In his letters, 'My dear Mrs Lehmann' changed to 'Dear Nina' and 'Dear Ni'. Sullivan spent his 21st birthday (May 1863) with the Lehmanns and, 31 years later, was to recall to Nina that 'with every gaiety of London open to us, we chose the delirious dullness of Madame Tussaud's'.

But before he was 21, he was famous. Grove, who chose the programmes jointly with Manns, decided to put on *The Tempest* at the Crystal Palace. The complete score (not just a selection, as in Leipzig) was to be given. In a letter to Grove of 12 February he spoke of still having to 'work' at it, probably indicating that some of the twelve numbers were still being composed (or at least retouched or re-orchestrated) for the Crystal Palace.

A narration was specially written by Henry F. Chorley – such a narration being necessary because, envisaging the possibility of a theatrical performance, Sullivan had made use of *melodrama* in the technical sense of that word, i.e. music accompanying speech. Some spoken substitute for the lines of the missing actors had therefore to be provided. Chorley (1808–72), not content with his influence as music critic of the weekly *Athenaeum*, fancied his independent literary powers. His dreadful translation of Gounod's *Faust* ('Even bravest heart may swell', etc.) remained long in use. He, too, sensed the young composer's talent and shortly afterwards would begin writing an opera libretto for him.

At the concert on 5 April 1862 Sullivan's music to *The Tempest*, with Arthur Matthison as narrator, took up much the greater part of the programme. The masque in the fourth act of the play had been particularly seized on by the composer. An overture to that act, written in conventional sonata-form, was the longest single item, and one of its brisk tunes was slowly recalled (against speech) in the epilogue to the whole. The well-known 'Miss Banks' (May Banks)[22] was joined in the one duet ('Honour, riches, marriage-blessing') by Robertina Henderson, 'the best and most promising singer the Royal Academy of Music has recently sent forth', according to *The Times*.

The work was an immediate success, five items being encored. Two days later *The Times* (probably in Davison's pen)[23] decisively praised Sullivan's achievement.

He, and those who first discerned the germs of talent in him, may well be proud . . . As we understand that the work is to be performed again (and indeed after such a success it will be strange if it were otherwise), we shall not pay Mr Sullivan the ill compliment of judging him critically by a single hearing. Enough at present to say that his music to *The Tempest*, while betraying a strong partiality for Mendelssohn's fascinating style, exhibits remarkable merits, and among the rest a decided vein of melody, a strong feeling of dramatic expression, and a happy fancy in the treatment of the orchestra . . . At the conclusion there was a loud call for 'the composer' who, being led forward by Herr Manns, was greeted with the heartiest applause on all sides.

The weekly *Athenaeum* (Chorley was its reviewer) was even more categorical.

It was one of those events which mark an epoch in a man's life; and, what is of more universal consequence, it may mark an epoch in English music, or we shall be greatly disappointed. Years on years have elapsed since we have heard a work by so young an artist so full of promise, so full of fancy, showing so much conscientiousness, so much skill, and so few references to any model elect.[24]

Four days after the triumphant performance of *The Tempest* at the Crystal Palace, Sullivan sent to Helmore a letter showing both the punctiliousness and the charm that won so many older people to his support:

If any little success attends me in my professional career, surely *you* ought not to be overlooked amongst those to whom the chief credit is due. For to you I owe more than anyone else perhaps . . . The care and attention bestowed upon every branch of my education, and the constant and kindly interest taken in my progress, have been in no small manner influential in making me what I am, viz, an earnest labourer in the cause of true Art . . .[25]

Jenny Lind and her husband, Otto Goldschmidt, in whose circle Sullivan now moved, joined in the acclamation – Jenny Lind 'repeatedly singing the pretty song and duet' at home, according to a letter from her husband inviting Sullivan for Christmas, 1862. A vocal score of the work was published, with accompaniment for piano duet, though the full score was not to appear in print until 30 years later. At the Lind-Goldschmidts' home, Argyle Lodge, the illustrious Viennese music critic Eduard Hanslick met Sullivan briefly in 1862 (as he was to recall in a publication of almost 30 years later).[26] Thus, with influential friends and a favourable press, with a musical style as secure as England's and Germany's best training could provide, with personal determination and no domestic cares, Sullivan was triumphantly launched.

4   In Demand

Of those who gave their patronage to Shakespearean music in the concert-hall, some at least would not have followed the composer into a theatre. Royalty and 'Society' might cultivate the opera, but an influential middle-class opinion suspected the theatre of sinfulness – in the plots of the plays, in the supposed overlap between the career of actress and that of prostitute,[1] even in the opportunities given to theatregoers for illicit rendezvous. The old Puritan denunciation of 'the playhouse' re-emerged in the moralizing of influential Victorian clerics.

One of the fiercest diatribes against the dramatic art was lately [1862] delivered by Mr Spurgeon . . . As Mr Spurgeon is an eloquent preacher, but borrows several of his best effects from theatrical action, it has been asked whether a little professional jealousy has not been mixed up with his attacks.

The ironic comment on the message and method of the revivalist preacher C. H. Spurgeon, whose 'tabernacle' accommodated 4,000 of the faithful, was made by Henri-François Alphonse Esquiros, a French observer of the English scene in the 1850s and 1860s.[2] By the 1880s such denunciations from the pulpit would be old-fashioned, precisely because the theatre *had* become respectable, with Henry Irving the dignified head of his profession. But that time was not yet. The composer whose name was to be synonymous with a theatre as yet unbuilt, the Savoy, entered a musical world dominated on the one hand by the choral and orchestral concert and on the other by the undemanding fare of the drawing-room.

On that Saturday when Arthur Sullivan first took his bow at the Crystal Palace with *The Tempest*, the Sacred Harmonic Society advertised as forthcoming its 'usual Passion Week performance' of Handel's *Messiah*. The Philharmonic Society under Sterndale Bennett still gave its eight regular concerts a year at the Hanover Square Rooms – but had reduced its seat-price to 15s., perhaps stung by the rivalry of the upstart 'New Philharmonic Concerts' (on the same night!) conducted by Henry C. Wylde at the newer St James's Hall. The 'old' Philharmonic itself tried out the newer and more commodious hall for an extra concert on 14 July 1862.

The programmes offered at such concerts, considerably longer than those of today, relied heavily on solo instrumental items and operatic extracts. The repertory was rooted in the period from Haydn to Mendelssohn: Schumann's place was still debatable, and even more so Liszt's and Wagner's. The rival programmes for 7 April were typical:

Philharmonic	New Philharmonic
Haydn, Symphony [no 91] in E flat	Beethoven, Overture, 'Egmont'
	Beethoven, 'Choral Fantasia'
Beethoven, Symphony no 7 in A	Mozart, Piano Concerto [K.466] in D minor
Mendelssohn, Overture, 'Ruy Blas'	(Arabella Goddard)
Auber, Overture, 'Masaniello'	Mendelssohn, Symphony no 3 in A minor
Molique, Violin Concerto in D minor (Joseph Joachim)	Rossini, Meyerbeer, operatic excerpts
Mozart, Spohr, Meyerbeer, operatic excerpts (Louisa Pyne, Charles Santley)	(Therese Titiens)

Here were distinguished performers indeed. Therese Tietjens (to give the spelling more often used later) was an operatic soprano of German origin who had made her home in England: in girth she typified the nineteenth-century image of the prima donna, and in vocal command and dramatic power she was irresistible. Joachim, playing a concerto by another violinist-composer, Bernhard Molique (1802–69), was a regular and much admired visitor to London, where his brother Henry lived. Arabella Goddard was a performer of distinction, one of the few pianists bold enough at this time to perform late Beethoven sonatas in public. Charles Santley, to be knighted almost half a century later (1905), was the most distinguished of English baritones. At Covent Garden, where the management profited from the recent lifting of the Lord Chamberlain's ban on theatrical performances in Lent, he appeared in April 1862 as the Count of Luna in *Il trovatore* – a rare native participant among imported stars.

A week after its first performance the Crystal Palace gave a repetition of *The Tempest* ('which was received with so much enthusiasm at the concert last Saturday'). In that day's advertisements, the Sacred Harmonic Society added to its announcement the information that its 'orchestra' for *Messiah* would number 'nearly 700 performers' ('orchestra' meaning band and choir together),[3] this being 'the largest available in Exeter Hall'. Likewise advertised was a 'Grand Concert' in St James's Hall on 9 May 'in which the military band of Messrs John Broadwood and Sons' Manufactory will perform, under the direction of the bandmaster, Mr Thomas Sullivan. Eminent artists will appear.' The 'eminent artists' certainly justified that description: they included Hallé as pianist, Ernest Vieuxtemps as cellist (brother of the celebrated violinist), Santley among the singers, and Arthur Sullivan himself as song-accompanist and as one of the performers in a quartet by Walter Macfarren for two pianos, four players.

Broadwoods must have spent a good deal of money that night for their workmen's sake, and Arthur Sullivan's.

St James's Hall, located on the site of the present Piccadilly Hotel, had been open only since 1858. It was there that the publishing firm of Chappell established the 'Monday Popular Concerts' – which soon dropped the 'popular' repertory (ballads, instrumental solos, and the like) and were re-started in 1864 as programmes devoted to 'classical' works, principally chamber music. *These* 'Monday pops', to be satirically immortalized by Gilbert's Mikado, passed their thousandth concert on 4 April 1887. Joachim and the cellist Alfredo Piatti (1822–1901) were pillars of its programmes. Browning (who wrote a poem about the concerts) was one of the regular attenders, Tennyson and Swinburne were also seen there, and so were such painters as Leighton, Alma-Tadema and Dante Gabriel Rossetti. An important feature of the programmes differentiated them from those of today: chamber music by itself, e.g. a programme entirely of string quartets, was never heard. The programmes were mixed, with solos and songs. Another important feature was the price:

Where else could the humble music-lover have heard – for a shilling [5p] in the gallery and three shillings in the balcony – the *chefs-d'œuvre* of the great composers, interpreted by the greatest artists of the nineteenth century?

Such was the tribute later paid by another of Sullivan's critic-friends, Hermann Klein.

The spread of good music took other forms. The music-hall, where the audiences both drank and listened, had not weakened its claim to its literal title. Operatic excerpts were favourite fare. At the Islington Philharmonic Hall (a variety house, despite the name) the management advertised not only 'comic talent the most original and racy' but the 'triumphant success' of a nightly selection from Weber's *Oberon*, with soloists, 'chorus and band'. Well established also were the black-faced American 'minstrel' shows. In April 1862 two companies claiming to be the 'original' Christy Minstrels competed in advertisements in *The Times*. Such shows were to retain popularity long enough for Sullivan to make a fiercely humorous allusion three decades later in the score of *Utopia Limited*.

Spoken recitals of various kinds were also in favour. 'Mrs Macready' – presumably the second wife of the great actor, who had himself retired from the stage – offered a recitation of *A Midsummer Night's Dream* in which she would 'by change of voice and manner, personate each character in the play'. Charles Dickens was to be heard on 3 April 1862,[4] and again a week later, reading from *David Copperfield* and *The Boots at the Holly-Tree Inn* at St James's Hall. For such an occasion 'sofa seats' were available at four shillings, other seats being cheaper. The result brought to the author the exceptionally high revenue of £190 a night. He was just 50 and at the height of his fame, having recently published *A Tale of Two Cities* and *Great Expectations*. In 1846, when he had been installed as the first editor of the *Daily News*, he had appointed his father-in-law, George Hogarth, as music critic. Dickens remained in his post for three weeks, Hogarth for 20 years. From 1850 until 1864 (when he was past 80) Hogarth was also secretary of the Philharmonic Society. Dickens had other musical friends, including Chorley and the Lehmanns, and it was in Chorley's company that he attended the second Crystal Palace performance of the music to *The Tempest*.[5] Afterwards, according to Sullivan: 'He seized my hand with his iron grip and said: "I don't pretend to know much about music, but I do know that I have been listening to a very great work".'[6]

The triumph of Sullivan's *Tempest* at the Crystal Palace was repeated in Manchester, where an adventurous taste guided Charles Hallé in organizing and conducting his own series of concerts at the newly rebuilt Free Trade Hall. (Those of the Gentlemen's Concert Society, of which he was the paid conductor, were more conservative.) An enthusiast for Berlioz, whom he knew personally, Hallé was a distinguished pianist and, as a conductor, was the exponent of an assured and modern technique – in the class of Manns, decisively above that of Bennett. He gave the *Tempest* music twice, on 2 and 22 January 1863; May Banks was the principal soloist. On the second occasion Hallé made the composer his house-guest. Still aglow with success, Sullivan wrote next day from Hallé's home to 'Dear Mrs Lehmann':

Shall I tell you all about last night's proceedings, but in few words, for I have not ten minutes? First, however, on Wednesday I was received by Miss Hallé most graciously, who entertained me until the return of her parents to dinner. We went to the 'Gentlemen's Concert' in the evening: very classical and, *ergo*, very slow – Hallé [as pianist], Molique, Piatti, Reeves, &c. Then I was taken to a ball and shown about like a stuffed gorilla! . . . I stood about the room in easy and graceful postures, conscious of being gazed upon; walked languidly through the Lancers, and then talked a good deal to Mrs Gaskell the authoress, and at half-past 2 was in bed. The next day we went down to the rehearsal, where I met with a most enthusiastic reception by the band on being introduced by Mr Hallé. They played through the whole thing with good-will and took no end of pains about it. Then I went and got shaved (!), had an Eccles cake, a glass of sherry, and a cigar – looked at a few things of Hecht with him; home to dinner, and then to the concert.

I sat with the Hallés in the two front rows (I on only one, of course). A splendid hall and well filled – nearly 3,000, I am told:

Overture, 'Egmont'	BEETHOVEN
Song	MISS BANKS
Music to 'The Tempest'	A.S.S.!

Well, I felt calm and collected, and smiled blandly at the few people that I knew. The 'Storm' begins, ends, and is warmly applauded. Things go on. The 3rd act prelude, also warmly applauded, at which your correspondent looks gratified, and wishes that a certain lady friend of his could hear the way in which certain points were taken up and certain passages got through without bungle.

However, the audience warms up and applauds everything, especially the 4th act overture, which your correspondent thought as near perfection as anything he had ever heard. The band was superb – so bright! Well, it is all over, and loud applause follows. The band applaud at me. Hallé leans over and applauds at me. The audience see that something is up, and continue. At last Hallé beckons to me to come up. I wink, I nod, I interrogate with my eyebrows, and at last rush madly from my seat and up the platform.

When I show myself my breath is literally taken away by the noise. It is gratifying, though. I bow six times, twice to the orchestra (who throughout have been so kind and friendly), and shake hands with Hallé; then down again, and all is over. I stay behind during the 15 minutes interval, and am overwhelmed with – not reproaches – from critics, artists, rich merchants with hooked noses, &c. One gentleman sitting near Mrs Hallé, seeing me rush away, said, 'What! is *that* Sullivan, that boy!' (Oh that I had a dagger!) 'I thought he was a relation of yours.' Others thought I was a contemporary of Beethoven, or at least his immediate successor.

Hallé won't let me go back today. He is teaching all the morning, and says he has much to say to me, and stay I must. Mrs Hallé waits now in the carriage to take me to a sewing-school, forsooth! My love to the children. Is my little angel-wife better?[7]

The reference to 'merchants with hooked noses' alludes to the prominent support given to music in Manchester by the German business community, much of it Jewish. (Back in 1848, when he first came to Manchester, Hallé himself had noted the role taken by 'the German colony' in welcoming him.)[8] Sullivan perhaps met Piatti and Sims Reeves (1818–1900) here for the first time. The finest of English tenors, as Santley was of baritones, Reeves would be among the foremost performers of Sullivan's music, and it was to Piatti that he would dedicate his cello concerto.

The 'little angel-wife' in Sullivan's letter is the Lehmanns' infant daughter – also named Nina (or, in Sullivan's later affectionate correspondence, 'Little Ni'). Their son Rudolph, who was to become known as the writer R. C. Lehmann, was seven in January of that year. As 'my dear Rudie' he received a mock-moral greeting sent from the Sullivans' modest home in Ponsonby Street – or rather from 'Ponsonby Castle, sketched from life and from the street by a distinguished artist', to which Sullivan appended his own scrawled picture of himself.

I write to wish you many happy returns of the day – in other words to tell you how I hope you may live to be a fine old man, honest, upright, and good, always doing what is right, and especially being kind and affectionate to your parents, for think what they do for you.

Now the sermon is over, we will proceed to lighter matters. In the first place I shall be delighted to avail myself of your kind invitation for tomorrow which you did me the honour to send. The prospect of tea and buns which you hold out is far too tempting to resist, particularly as buns are the one great comfort of my life – in fact the sole object, almost, for which I live. If you could throw in a few biscuits and a pickled onion in red-currant jelly my happiness would, indeed, be more than I could well bear. No more of this, however, until we meet.

Goodbye, my dear boy, ever your affectionate friend.

Arthur S. Sullivan
his X mark[9]

Another friend – and indeed he was to remain the closest friend Sullivan ever made among his fellow-composers – was Frederic Clay (1838–89), a Bohemian by temperament who held a Civil Service post at the Treasury but later gave it up for music. Writing variously for stage and concert-room, Clay was to win his chief fame with the still-remembered song 'I'll sing thee songs of Araby'. Rapidly as Sullivan's circle grew, he did not neglect his old benefactor, Sir George Smart, now in his mid-80s and perceptibly frailer. 'We shall be most happy to see you on

Saturday,' wrote Lady Smart from Blackheath, where they were temporarily staying:

and as country air will do you good, come down here as early as you like, to breakfast if you please; there are plenty of steamboats from Pimlico Pier or Cadogan Pier to Hungerford or London Bridge Piers – where steamers go every 20 minutes to Greenwich . . . *Do come.* The air of Blackheath is the most invigorating in England, it will do you good in every way. We have nothing to offer but a sincere and hearty welcome, and a very fair pianoforte direct from Broadwoods, together with perfect quiet. If you can stay all day so much the better; but if you must return to your opera, you can go back at any quarter of an hour you like by railway, or by boat every 20 minutes . . . Our usual dinner hour here is 5 – but we would make it suit you . . .

'Your opera' was *The Sapphire Necklace*, with Chorley as librettist, on which Sullivan was evidently working as early as the time of this letter (August 1862). Only an overture and two vocal numbers emerged for performance, but later references suggest that the complete work was written and retitled *The False Heiress*.[10] On 20–24 September Sullivan stayed as Grove's guest at Sydenham, inviting Helmore to dinner there; on Saturday 22 November three orchestral items from *The Tempest* were repeated at the Crystal Palace, after the composer had made certain revisions.[11] He and Chorley had evidently been invited by the Lehmanns, who were already in Paris, to join them there. Sullivan wrote to Nina Lehmann on 23 November:

Joachim is very low-spirited at [the prospect of] our being all together, in perfect enjoyment, without his being able to join us. He asked most affectionately after you and Miss Dickens. Is he smitten? I see a great deal of him. They did a little *Tempest* at the Crystal Palace concert yesterday, and he, Clay, and myself dined at Grove's afterwards, and spent the pleasantest of evenings playing Bach's sonatas for violin and piano, *Salon Stücke* of Spohr's (very slow), talking no end of pleasant nonsensical small-talk (your superior mind is smiling contemptuously – I see it already), and finally all coming home together smoking gorgeous cigars, running down Meyerbeer and praising Auber.

At a time when the crisp *opéra-comique* style of Auber (in such works as *Fra Diavolo*) could be pitted against the grandiose ostentation of *Les Huguenots*, this musical preference identifies Sullivan himself.

Joining the Lehmanns in Paris, Sullivan heard Pauline Viardot-Garcia in her celebrated interpretation of the title-role of Gluck's *Orpheus* (in the edition prepared for her by Berlioz). Thirty years later he described the occasion to his biographer, Arthur Lawrence, as 'one of the greatest things I have ever seen on the stage'. Sullivan also called personally on Viardot-Garcia, who gave him an introduction to Rossini. Having composed *William Tell* for the Paris stage 33 years before, Rossini had lived in the city since 1855, composing only intermittently and not for the theatre. Rossini was born on 29 February in Leap Year (1792): it is tempting to suppose that Sullivan later dropped a hint of this chronological oddity to the librettist of *The Pirates of Penzance*. The young composer made a note of his visit, accompanied by a singer he refers to simply as 'Courtenay'.[12] The reference to 'Delle Sedie' identifies Enrico Delle Sedie, a baritone beginning to be well known in London.

Went with Courtenay to see Rossini at 3½. He was out. Went back in half an hour and were admitted to his bedroom, *à la française*. The old gentleman was very kind and affable; asked me if l sang . . . Invited me to his reception the same evening. I found Carl Rose there playing a new violin sonata by a young German. Rossini introduced us: 'M. Sullivan – M. Rose.' We looked at each other and burst out laughing. The idea of being introduced to each other by Rossini was too droll. I went again in the evening with Courtenay, saw a lot of blue and red ribbons – Delle Sedie, Lacource, and his wife, etc. – accompanied Courtenay in Fred Clay's [song] *Point du Jour* and slipped away unseen. Thursday at 9½ a.m. I was at Rossini's house and found him alone, composing a little pianoforte piece for his dog! He played us a new minuet, very pretty and quaint.

Sullivan also apparently induced Rossini to join him at the piano in playing part of his *Tempest* music – no doubt pressing on the elderly composer his published vocal score with piano duet accompaniment. The next day Rossini reciprocated with a photograph inscribed 'à mon jeune collègue Arthur S. Sullivan'. In later recollection of this Paris visit, Sullivan was to stress the lively companionship of Dickens: it is curious that Dickens himself seemingly left no record of having been in Sullivan's company either on this or any other occasion.[13]

It must have been through Grove – who had received royal visitors at the Crystal Palace – that Sullivan obtained, so early in his career, an opportunity to compose for a royal occasion. The marriage of the Prince of Wales to Princess Alexandra of Denmark on 10 March 1863 signalled a national rejoicing, breaking the sombre tone maintained at court since the death of the Prince Consort two years before.[14] 'The roaring rather than the shouting of an excited multitude' was noted by the *Illustrated London News* as the Princess, having taken ship to Gravesend, arrived by train at Bricklayers' Arms Station in the Old Kent Road (the line from Gravesend had not yet acquired a terminus in central London). The report made no mention of Sullivan's own contribution – a march to be played, as he said, by 'all the military bands'.[15] But there was an inevitable ode from Tennyson as Poet Laureate:

> Sea-Kings' daughter from over the sea,
> > Alexandra!
> Saxon and Norman and Dane are we
> But all of us Danes in our welcome of thee,
> > Alexandra!

Sullivan's work, under the title of *The Princess of Wales's March*, was published as a piano solo with a dedication 'by special permission' to the Prince of Wales. The same dedication headed Sullivan's song *Bride from the North*, with words by the indefatigable Chorley, and also his *Royal Wedding March*, performed orchestrally at the Crystal Palace on 10 March 1863 and published in an arrangement for piano solo. There is no indication that this was actually played at the magnificent but ill-rehearsed ceremony held in St George's Chapel of Windsor Castle.[16] The lasting effect of the Prince's marriage was to make him socially powerful, independent of the Queen. His London residence, Marlborough House, became identified with a fast set where wit and wealth were as good credentials as any titles of nobility. Here members of the Anglo-Jewish banking families, Rothschilds and Sassoons, became socially acceptable; here an Arthur Sullivan or a John Millais was received in free-and-easy opulence. A little later (13 March 1869) Sullivan was formally presented to the Queen at Buckingham Palace.[17]

How much Sullivan earned by his 'royal' works is not known. From the publishing firm of Metzler he received a mere five guineas each for his six *Shakespeare Songs* (1863–4) including 'Orpheus with his Lute' – sold outright. By contrast 'Will He Come?', published in 1865 by Boosey and 'composed expressly' for the popular contralto Madame Sainton-Dolby, was paid on a royalty basis – so much per copy sold. The difference in marketing reflects the musical contrast between the two songs. 'Orpheus with his Lute' would not earn much but represents Sullivan's most refined 'German' taste, recalling (with its little recurring independent theme in the piano accompaniment) Schubert's own Shakespearean setting, 'Who is Sylvia?'. 'Will He Come?' is of the more obvious and sale-worthy English ballad type. The verse by Adelaide A. Procter describes a woman waiting for a horseman and dying when he fails to arrive; the music is in a supposedly solemn style, melodramatically heightened in the third verse by a galloping motive to represent what the watcher *thinks* she hears. The 'effectiveness' that made it a money-spinner is the very quality that now torpedoes it.

If the writing of such a song was a challenge only to Sullivan's facility, the writing of a symphony was a challenge of a different kind: at 21 the enterprise was bold in the extreme. British audiences had embraced no later symphony than Mendelssohn's: Schubert's were hardly known, Schumann's considered too eccentric. Exceptionally among English composers, Cipriani Potter (1792–1871) had written nine, with a brief flash of glory when Wagner conducted one of them (in G minor) at the Philharmonic Society in 1855. Benedict, with the impeccable 'pedigree' of having studied with Weber, did not turn to the symphonic form until the 1870s. But now, almost at the same time as his teacher Bennett brought forth *his* first and only work in that genre (1864), Sullivan conceived his symphony while on holiday in northern Ireland. 'Already', he wrote to his mother:

I feel my ideas assuming a newer and *fresher* colour, and I shall be able to work like a horse on my return. Why, the other night as I was jolting home from Holestone (15 miles from here) through wind and rain on an open jaunting-car, the whole first movement of a symphony came into my head with a real Irish flavour about it – besides scraps of the other movements. I shall get it ready for the Musical Society next season . . .

The Musical Society was a concert-promoting body run by a spirited conductor, Alfred Mellon, from 1858 until his death in 1867. The symphony, a four-movement work in E, would later be known as 'the Irish Symphony' (and was so published after his death) but Sullivan's original thought had been to avoid the implied comparison with Mendelssohn's no. 3 ('the Scotch'). Whether he actually completed it in 1863, as is generally assumed, may be doubted, since its first performance did not take place 'next season' but three years later – not at the concerts of the Musical Society, but at the Crystal Palace.

That same summer in Ireland – he had stayed at Richmond Lodge, Holywood, Belfast – provided an experience of a different kind. Sullivan's personal charm awoke the passionate feelings of a young girl whose letters later that year bore the signature 'Aramis' (the notepaper also bears that name as an embossed heading). A *very* young girl, perhaps: she reprimands him for having referred to her as 'a comic child'. She addresses Sullivan as 'dear brother' and signs as 'your sister', recalling his visit or visits to her family.

Do you know, it strikes me that when you become a great man and an eminent musician, *my* letters may be published if your biography is written (which it is sure to be), and the idea is not a pleasant one. This is itself reason enough for destroying them, is it not, dear brother?

Arthur Sullivan did not generally keep letters but evidently could not bring himself to destroy those of 'Aramis', who was apparently Annie Tennent, later Mrs de la Cherris. But there is no indication that her outpourings were in any way encouraged – much less reciprocated – by the composer himself. A letter of October 1866 to Sullivan's friend A. J. Hipkins (of Broadwood's, the piano firm) recommends him, on his forthcoming visit to Ireland, to the Tennents – a clear sign that Sullivan's intimacy with the family was not broken.[18]

Back in London (the family had moved to 47 Claverton Street, still in the Pimlico area, by April 1863), Sullivan broadened his musical life by an association with the Royal Italian Opera, the enterprise which functioned at Covent Garden theatre during the 'season' (April–July), all works being sung in Italian. The assumption that Italian was the best language for singing, and the only one that could be demanded of an international cast, was by no means confined to that theatre: at Drury Lane Wagner's *Flying Dutchman* made its first London appearance in 1870 as *L'Olandese dannato* ('The Damned Dutchman'). Even Sullivan later referred to Mozart's *Il flauto magico* rather than *Die Zauberflöte*.

As musical director at Covent Garden, Sir Michael Costa was unwilling to admit Sullivan on a casual basis to rehearsals, and instead offered him an engagement as the company's organist. It gave him freedom of access to the theatre without a constant tie. Opera scores involving an organ were (and are) few. But:

One night whilst I was playing the organ solo in the church scene in *Faust*, the wire that connected the pedal under Costa's foot with the metronome stick at the organ, broke. This meant disaster in the concerted music as I relied entirely upon the stick, not being able to hear anything but the organ. Quick as thought, I called a stage hand and said: 'Tell Mr Costa the wire is broken – tell him he must keep his ears open and follow me.' The scene went well but at the end of the act I approached Costa nervously, for I thought he would certainly resent my arrogant message, for which I began to apologize. But he stopped me and shook my hand and said: 'No, no, no, good boy. You kept your head and did quite right.'[19]

Sullivan 'thinks *Faust* the best possible subject for an opera, and wishes it had fallen to his lot to set it', so the poet William Allingham (1824–89) wrote in his diary on visiting the composer in 1863.[20] Browning, having presumably got to know Sullivan through Grove, had recommended Allingham to Sullivan as a possible word-provider. 'A.S. is short and tight, with dark complexion and thick curly hair parted in the middle. Perhaps partly Jew?' (See p. 6 and Appendix 2.) Sullivan invited Allingham to hear Covent Garden's *Faust* but they did not proceed to a collaboration.

Within the Royal Italian Opera season, ballet was performed as a 'filler' when a short opera did not make up the long evening expected – especially an opera which did not incorporate its own ballet scene. So it was with a ballet and not with an opera or operetta that Arthur Sullivan made his first professional appearance as a composer for the stage. *L'Ile enchantée* (French was the conventional usage of ballet), with choreography by Desplaces, was performed on 16 May 1864, as an after-piece to Bellini's opera *La sonnambula*.[21] The star was the celebrated ballerina Salvioni. The work did not remain long in the repertory, but the score was to be quarried again in later output – including the incidental music to *The Merry Wives of Windsor* and the ballet *Victoria and Merrie England*. The Covent Garden assignment at least gave Sullivan an enjoyable test of adaptability:

A *variation* (solo-dance) was required, at the last moment, for the second *danseuse* who had just arrived. 'What on earth am I to do?' I said to the stage manager, 'I haven't seen her dance yet, and know nothing of her style.' 'I'll see,' he replied, and took the young lady aside. In five minutes he returned. 'I've arranged it all,' he said. 'This is exactly what she wants (giving it to me rhythmically), *Tiddle-iddle-um, tiddle-iddle-um, rum-tirum-tirum*, sixteen bars of that; then *rum-tum rum-tum*, heavy you know, sixteen bars, and then finish up with the overture to *William Tell*, last movement, 16 bars and *coda*.' In ten minutes' time I had composed it and written out a *répétiteur's* part [for piano], and it was at once rehearsed.

Costa was also the conductor of the Birmingham Festival, an important triennial event. Nominally a festival committee ordered the programmes, but the conductor's recommendation was generally decisive, and it is not surprising that Sullivan wrote directly to Costa asking for his favour.[22] The result was a commission for a cantata: *Kenilworth*, with words written inevitably by Chorley. Punctiliously, Sullivan wrote again to thank Costa and ask whether he might send his work for the conductor's critical opinion when completed.

Kenilworth (with reference to an episode in Scott's novel of that name) took the form of a supposed welcome to Queen Elizabeth I and was styled 'A Masque'. It was a longer, more elaborate but not necessarily better example of its kind than the *May Day* cantata which the composer George Macfarren (1813–87) had produced in 1857, where the 'Elizabethan' touches included a lively pipe-and-tabor dance. In a *Slow Dance* Sullivan for the first time evoked the 'old English' manner which was to serve him in the operettas, and here linked it to an unusual five-bar phrasing.[23] Perhaps the best thing in Sullivan's score was the inter-polated setting (for soprano and tenor) of 'How sweet the moonlight sleeps upon this bank' – in which, however, Chorley had the temerity to change Shakespeare's 'Such harmony is in immortal souls' to '. . . immortal sounds'. At the Birmingham première which Costa conducted on 8 September 1864 the duet was sung by Sims Reeves and a leading British soprano of her time, Helen Lemmens-Sherrington.

The music to *The Tempest* having originated in concert form, it has been implied by previous writers on Sullivan that it received no theatrical showing. Not so: on 15 October 1864, Charles Calvert chose the play to open his much-remarked series of productions at the Prince's Theatre, Manchester, and incorporated some or all of Sullivan's music, 'which was most favourably received last season at Mr Hallé's concerts'.[24] The *Manchester Guardian* reviewer, here quoted, considered that the 'very fitness' of Sullivan's contribution made it unobtrusive, and it was therefore not greeted with any unusual acclaim. The production made use of other composers' music too.

Next month (12 November 1864) *Kenilworth* made its appearance at the Crystal Palace, whose programmes were to remain hospitable to him throughout his life. Commissions for two orchestral works marked an important stage in his ability to command work as a composer: an overture, *Marmion* (another Scott subject), was to be written for the Philharmonic Society of London, and another overture as yet untitled for the Norwich Festival.

Perhaps through Costa's influence Sullivan became a Freemason. On 11 April 1865, described as 'a professor of music', he was initiated into the 'Lodge of Harmony' which met at the Greyhound Hotel, Richmond, Surrey.[25] (The 'harmony' of the title had no musical significance.) He was to be designated Grand Organist of England in 1887. Though neither the records of that Lodge nor the private documents of his life show an active role in Freemasonry, membership of the order may have strengthened his social advancement at a time when the Royal Princes and other notables lent their names to it.

5 In search of Schubert

NOTHING more important could happen in a young composer's life than to have such links forged with the country's major festivals. Most of these festivals depended on that new type of public building, the large concert hall, as distinctive in the Victorian city landscape as the railway station. Usually but not always a town hall with civic functions, it was required to accommodate chorus and orchestra and to have an organ at which an eminent local musician would often (in newspaper language) 'preside'. Though Birmingham's festival had older roots, it was the new Town Hall (1834) that reinvigorated it: here Mendelssohn came to conduct his *St Paul* in 1837 and his new *Elijah* nine years later. Norwich, where Sullivan's new overture was commissioned, had one of the older, cathedral-type festivals – providing an East Anglian counterpart to the celebrated Three Choirs Festival, rotating annually between Worcester, Hereford and Gloucester.

The basis of the festival performances was a large amateur chorus, specially raised. Orchestral players were generally brought from London, though sometimes the Hallé Orchestra was engaged. An essential was the engagement of eminent solo singers – perhaps to launch a new work, certainly to illuminate favourite fare by Handel and Mendelssohn. No public subsidy was required: on the contrary, festivals were designed to be profitable – not for private ends but to benefit hospitals or similar local charities. Bernard Shaw, writing as a music critic in 1893, would take a radical stance in protesting that 'as music has earned the money it should go to her own support, and that a good orchestra is every whit as important to a town as a good hospital'.[1]

To the Victorian composer – and indeed to later composers right up to the era of Vaughan Williams and Walton – festivals afforded the principal way to present a substantial new choral work, 'sacred' or other. With the vocal score probably printed by Novello (a firm which had largely cornered that market through its pioneering of cheap music-printing), a work successfully launched at a major festival and fully reported in the national and musical press was assured of further performances by local societies all over the country as well as in London. New orchestral works also had their place. At Norwich the conductor was (and had been since 1845) Sir Julius Benedict, Jenny Lind's former accompanist. He had perhaps exerted direct influence in the festival's commissioning an overture from Jenny Lind's favourite young composer, and had conducted a selection from Sullivan's *Tempest* music at the 1863 festival.

Meanwhile Sullivan, sufficiently supported by older friends and colleagues, was able to make the gesture – unprecedented for one of his years – of mounting a 'grand orchestral concert' almost entirely of his own music, conducted by himself, at St James's Hall. His symphony had already received its première, under Manns, at the Crystal Palace, on 10 March 1866, and had been given at St James's Hall in Mellon's 'Musical Society' series on 11 April. Now on 11 July it was to have this third performance, supplemented by the 'Brisk Dance' from *Kenilworth*, the duet 'In such a night as this' from the same work (sung by Edith Wynne and W. H. Cummings), and his overture to *The Sapphire Necklace*. In the same programme Jenny Lind-Goldschmidt sang his settings of 'Sweet Day, so Cool' and 'Orpheus with his Lute' and Santley sang 'O Mistress Mine' (both, of course, without fee), helping to guarantee a large and fashionable audience. It must have greatly gratified Sullivan that his old Leipzig mentor Ignaz Moscheles was in London and could be present. The programme accordingly included Moscheles's *Recollections of Ireland* for piano and orchestra, composed long before Sullivan was born, the soloist being Anna Mehlig, a 20-year-old pupil of Liszt. The choice of Bennett's overture *The Naiads* to open the programme was a suitable tribute to another of his principal mentors.

Each movement of the symphony was heartily applauded. Not until Elgar's no. 1 in 1908 would a British symphony be launched with such *élan* and such acclaim. *The Times*, in an anonymous notice which can be confidently ascribed to Davison, praised it warmly:

The symphony . . . is not only by far the most noticeable composition that has proceeded from Mr Sullivan's pen, but the best musical work, if judged only by the largeness of its form and the number of beautiful thoughts it contains, for a long time produced by any English composer . . . Mr Sullivan should abjure Mendelssohn, even Beethoven, and above all, Schumann, for a year and a day – like the vanquished knight errant, who, when conquered, foreswore arms for a like period. Not that Mr Sullivan has been conquered, but that he must conquer; and the best way to do this is to study the most legitimate and natural models, in the works of Haydn and Mozart, trusting to himself for the rest . . .

Meanwhile, Mr Sullivan, who, though young, is already shrewd enough to have steered clear of that dangerous quicksand, Spohr, the most mannered of all mannerists, has composed a first symphony, which, or we are greatly mistaken, will, for some time hence, engage the attention of the musical world, and lead to a second that may possibly fix it for at least a generation.

'It was a great triumph', wrote his old Royal Academy teacher John Goss to Sullivan five days later,

and that Mme Goldschmidt should have given her help crowned it to perfection! Her you can never repay except in the way that the greatest of artists, as herself, desire. I mean by going on—on—on—on until (as I hope) you may prove a worthy compeer of the greatest of the symphonists.

Such a concert also helped to establish Sullivan as a conductor. Even before this, in 1865, the Liverpool Philharmonic Society had considered him for the vacancy of conductor of their orchestral concerts – and he was only 23.[2] He was not appointed, but when the successful candidate, Alfred Mellon, died two years later, Sullivan's name was again put forward. The much senior Julius Benedict was preferred. Conducting was to remain one of Sullivan's principal occupations, though in the last 15 years of his life the arrival of a more vigorous, more positively interpretative school of conductors was to make his style old-fashioned.

Meanwhile it was August Manns, not Sullivan, who conducted (at the Crystal Palace on 24 November 1866), Sullivan's next full-length orchestral work – a three-movement cello concerto composed for, and played by, Piatti. It was cordially received, and Piatti repeated it in Edinburgh on 17 December 1866. But the work never appeared in print (even in cello-and-piano form); the autograph score is lost – though a reconstruction has proved possible (see p. 417). While the 'disappearance' of juvenile works is more or less understandable, the fate of the cello concerto remains odd – even allowing for the destruction of a copy in the fire at Chappell's, the publishers, on 6 May 1964. Why, in view of the high reputations of both Sullivan and Piatti, was this work simply 'dropped'? After a performance at an 'all-Sullivan' promenade concert at Covent Garden on 18 October 1873, with Walter Pettitt as soloist, an amateur performance at Westminster Town Hall on 16 February 1887 seems to have been the sole revival in the composer's lifetime. In a letter of 8 April 1867 Sullivan himself said the concerto was in the press and that the slow movement was being arranged as an organ voluntary. The proposal for such a transcription had been made by the *Musical Examiner*, praising this 'gem of loveliness' in its review of the première.

By apparent coincidence, Sullivan's two other works for cello date from approximately this period. *An Idyll* for cello and piano (a mere 71 bars) was 'composed for and dedicated to his friend Col P. Paget (Farnham)'[3] and is dated on the manuscript 31 July 1865. In the previous week Col Patrick Paget had been his host at Farnham, a town not far from the Sandhurst garrison area: Sullivan cherished, then and later, an affection for his boyhood location. In 1868 a more formally titled *Duo Concertante* for cello and piano was published with a dedication to the Welsh composer and pianist Henry Brinley Richards (1817–85), who had recently written *God Bless the Prince of Wales*.

Between 1862 and 1868 Sullivan also published nine pieces for solo piano – two *Thoughts*, six *Day Dreams*, and *Twilight*. They came at a time when the taste of amateurs was broadening from merely flashy or sentimental pieces to embrace Mendelssohn, Chopin and Schumann – or at any rate the more obviously 'songful' strains of those composers. The limitations of amateur playing technique were observed in these pieces of Sullivan's, mostly in the Mendelssohnian vein. (Sullivan himself had been preparing for the publisher Cramer an edition of the *Songs without words*.) Exceptionally, *Twilight* (1868) suggests a homage to one of the smooth, arpeggio-accompanied Nocturnes of Chopin – or those of Chopin's predecessor in this style, the Irish composer John

Field. Presumably because its technique is more challenging and its harmony marked by fierce discords, an *Allegro risoluto* in the unusual key of B flat minor (1868) remained unpublished at the time. Its toccata-like energy is resolved, not too happily, in a mawkish final cadence.

The hospitality of the Crystal Palace was extended on 13 April 1867 to Sullivan's overture, *The Sapphire Necklace*, and to the two songs made available from that opera: a recitative and prayer beginning 'They come not yet', and a song 'Over the roof'. Manns again conducted, and Edith Wynne was the soprano soloist. (The second song was encored.)[4] The Philharmonic was less receptive to new works and it was a sign of favour that the *Marmion* overture was the only native work to receive a first performance in the 1867 season (3 June). But the Philharmonic seems to have withheld its commissioning fee on the ground that, presumably in breach of some agreement, Sullivan let the Crystal Palace have the overture, somewhat revised, on 7 December of the same year.

Arthur Sullivan's brother Fred had married Charlotte Lacy in 1862 and moved to Fulham – at that time a village detached by fields from London itself. The composer was still living with his parents (they moved, still within Pimlico, to 47 Lupus Street) but was often to be found at Grove's house at Sydenham and at one time seems to have taken rooms over a shop nearby. In Sydenham he became intimate also with the family of John Scott Russell, FRS (1808–82), the celebrated Scottish engineer and naval architect, who had been Grove's predecessor as secretary of the Royal Society of Arts. From the Russells' house Sullivan wrote to his father in September 1866 alluding to the unsatisfactory progress he was making on the overture for Norwich: 'Although I meant it to be bright, it has turned out of the most gloomy and dismal character. It is needless to say that it won't do.'

His happy family life now received its first blow. On the night of 22–23 September he was staying at Sydenham (possibly at Grove's) when his brother Fred arrived in haste at 4 a.m. Their father was dead.

My dear, dear father, whom I loved so passionately and who returned my love a hundredfold, if that were possible! Oh, it is so hard – it is so terribly hard – to think that I shall never see his dear face again, or hear his cheery voice saying, 'God bless you, my boy' . . . I am able to be strong all day for my poor mother's sake who is nearly broken-hearted (they have been married 30 years and have known each other intimately nearly 50!); but at night, when I am alone, then the wound bursts out, and I think of him and his tender love and care for me, and his pride in all I did – and now he is gone for ever. Perhaps he can look upon me and see all I do; and please God I will try and never do anything that will make him turn away his head and regret that he left me alone here.

So he wrote in a letter to his young friend 'Rudie' Lehmann. He transfused the loss in the re-worked version of his new overture. It was now given the sub-title *In Memoriam* – which in general usage (including the composer's own) became the main title. It was duly unveiled by Benedict at the Norwich Festival on 30

October 1866 – the start of a considerable popularity which, with the change of taste, has slumped to nothing. In the slow, hymn-like opening tune it is the repetition of the single note which traps Sullivan into banality – as later, and even more obviously, in *The Lost Chord*.

On 7 February 1867, in a letter to the Liverpool Philharmonic Society, he declined an invitation to compose a piano quintet since 'at the present moment I have so much on my hands'.[5] Still holding his post as church organist, Sullivan now added the conductorship of an amateur choir, the Civil Service Musical Society. Presumably with leave of absence from these two commitments, Sullivan embarked on a voyage of musical discovery which arose from the enthusiasm for Schubert which he shared with Grove. Though it had been a decade since the 'Great C major' was first presented at the Crystal Palace, the listing of Schubert's works in Kreissle von Hellborn's biography published in Vienna in 1865 (which appeared in English the following year)[6] made it clear that there were still tasks of rescue to be done. Manuscript copies obtained from Vienna enabled two entr'actes from *Rosamunde* to be performed at the Crystal Palace on 10 November 1866. But only an investigation on the spot could determine what else from Schubert's pen might lie hidden.

As Manns could not leave his Crystal Palace post, the person 'better able, perhaps than anyone else to advise and assist me in my search' (as Grove put it) was Sullivan. He was not only fluent in German but could – with some difficulty – read German handwriting in the old script. In any case the joys of friendship supplied enough reason for the voyage on which the travellers set out on 26 September 1867. Fred Sullivan was with them, at least for the first part of the journey.[7] 'What shall I say of Grove?', Arthur wrote to his mother:

It would be painting the lily to try and describe his goodness and charm, so I refrain. We take great care of each other, are very economical, haggle over centimes and get on famously. I shall read this part to him, so have made it strong!

The travellers had crossed the Channel and brightened an inclement sea-crossing by sharing the company of 'Strauss' on board. The reference in Sullivan's letter home is probably not to Johann the younger (who had not yet appeared in England) but to Sullivan's professional acquaintance, the viola-player Ludwig Straus, whose surname was prone to mis-spelling (see p. 48). In Paris, Sullivan had been engaged to supervise the British musical contribution to the international exhibition of that year. He had paid a previous visit to Paris in July on this account, and now directed a group of English male singers at a ceremonial dinner. Their performance of *Non nobis domine* as a grace (presumably in the traditional setting ascribed to Byrd) excited enthusiastic applause and cries of '*Bis! bis!*' But Sullivan, to the surprise of the guests, withheld a repetition. No doubt his boyhood training with Helmore had persuaded him that an appeal to the Deity is not to be subjected to an encore.

After Paris and Baden-Baden (where they called not only on Clara Schumann but also on Pauline Viardot-Garcia) they proceeded to Munich and Salzburg, and paid the obligatory visit to the Mozarteum containing letters and other relics of the composer. Sullivan found that his fame was beginning to spread: 'When we wrote our names in the Visitors' Book, the librarian asked me if I was the composer of whom he had often read in the *Signale* and other musical papers. I modestly owned that I did now and then write a little music.'[8]

Once in Vienna itself (they arrived on Saturday 5 October, and stayed at the Hotel Kaiserin Elisabeth), their expectations were more than fulfilled. Through Carl Anton Spina (1827–1906), proprietor of the publishing firm which had handled Schubert's music, they were introduced to a nephew of Schubert himself, Eduard Schneider. They met an old clerk in the publishing firm who had actually known Schubert and claimed to have been at his christening.[9] From Schneider they unearthed the overture to the opera *Die Freunde von Salamanca* and two symphonies, the so-called 'Tragic' in C minor (no. 4, D. 417) and another in C major (no. 6, D.589). They made arrangements to have copies made from which performances were duly given at the Crystal Palace.

'But I had failed', wrote Grove, in prose so vivid that it would be an impertinence to paraphrase it,

in one chief object of my journey. The *Rosamunde* music was almost dearer to me than the symphonies. Besides the Entr'actes in B minor and B flat, the Ballo No. 2 and the Ballet Air No. 9 which we had already acquired [by previous inquiry from London], we had found at Mr Spina's an entr'acte after the second act, and a *Hirten-melodie* [Shepherd Melody] for clarinets, bassoons, and horns; but we still required the accompaniments to the romance and the two Choruses, as well as the total number of pieces and their sequence in the drama. To quit Vienna without these would have been too cruel, and yet neither from Dr Schneider nor Mr Spina, nor in the library of the Musik-Verein – where the admirable librarian Mr C. F. Pohl was entirely at our service – had we succeeded in finding a trace of them.

It was Thursday afternoon, and we proposed to leave on Saturday for Prague. We made a final call on Dr Schneider, to take leave and repeat our thanks, and also, as I now firmly believe, guided by a special instinct. The doctor was civility itself; he again had recourse to the cupboard, and showed us some treasures which had escaped us before. I again turned the conversation to the *Rosamunde* music – he believed that he had at one time possessed a copy or sketch of it all. Might I go into the cupboard and look for myself? Certainly, if I had no objection to being smothered with dust. In I went, and after some search, during which my companion kept the doctor engaged in conversation, I found, at the bottom of the cupboard and in its farthest corner, a bundle of music books two feet high, carefully tied round, and black with the undisturbed dust of nearly half a century.

When we had dragged out the bundle into the light, [we] found that it was actually neither more nor less than what we were in search of . . . There were the part-books of the whole of the music in *Rosamunde*, tied up after the second performance, in December 1823, and probably never disturbed since . . . It was now late in the day, but we summoned our kind and faithful friend Pohl to our aid, and by dint of dividing our work into three, and writing our hardest, we contrived before two in the morning to get all the missing accompaniments copied, as well as every note and stage direction that could throw light on the connection between the drama and the music.[10]

Sullivan and Grove concluded their labours with a game of leap-frog, and it was only a few weeks later (10 November 1867) that the complete *Rosamunde* was given – for the first time anywhere – under Manns at the Crystal Palace.

After leaving Vienna, Sullivan made his way to Prague (12–13 October) and then to Leipzig. There he would not merely renew old acquaintance. Using as intermediaries both Ignaz Moscheles and Carl Reinecke, he had sought to have the *In Memoriam* overture included in the Gewandhaus orchestra's regular series.[11] Sullivan himself conducted it there on 17 October 1867 with 'great success . . . I think it has laid a firm foundation to a good reputation in Germany'.[12] So he reported to his mother, with the news also of an orchestral run-through of the symphony: it was not actually given in the Gewandhaus concert series. A trip to Dresden enabled him to see Wagner's early opera, *Rienzi*.[13] Acquainted as he was with Wagner's later works, it is not surprising that he found it 'a great disappointment – a mixture of Weber, Verdi and a touch of Meyerbeer. The whole very commonplace, vulgar and uninteresting.' On his return he wrote to Davison, with an intimacy which had not been his a few years before:

My poor old boy, I am grieved to hear you have been in such a wretched state so long . . . Grove and I have just come back from Vienna and have had great sport in the Schubert preserves. Two symphonies (both in C, but neither so fine as *the* C major), two overtures (both in D), all the music to *Rosamunda* [sic], a string quartet, a lovely trio for violin, viola and cello, never performed or printed and several little songs – perfect gems. When will you come here and have a quiet chop with Grove and talk matters over? The sooner the better. I expect everything (from the Vienna copyist) next week.

Then I went to Leipzig and had a great success with *In Memoriam* in the Gewandhaus and I am to send them *Marmion* or a new symphony. Also I commenced transactions with publishers there. But no pleasure was equal to the delight of travelling with G.G., whose looks, manners and conversation won all hearts there even as they have won yours and mine.

A letter to an unidentified friend begins: 'Reverend and dear Sir' – the 'Reverend' perhaps as jocular as the rest of the letter:

A young and rising composer, one Schubert, has written a very meritorious quartet in B flat which I wish to make known to some of my English friends as it has never been performed in this country. For this purpose I have effected an arrangement with Mr Arthur Chappell, who will bring his celebrated performing troupe, the Bowing Brothers of Bond Street (consisting of Le Petit Piatti, the Toneless Blagrove, Striding Strauss, and the inimitable serio-comic player Ries) next Saturday at half past eight, to try it through. I rely also upon you to see that all cigars are kept alight, and that any man who refuses to drink his brandy and soda shall be instantly ejected. So don't fail to come.

The allusion was to Chappell's publishing house (in Bond Street) as well as to its promotion of the 'Monday Pops' at St James's Hall. In string quartets of that series of performances, Louis Ries (1830–1913) as second violinist was no less well known than Piatti as cellist. Other musicians to whom Sullivan makes his Brandy & Soda shall be instantly ejected — So don't fail to come.

I come by night. I come by day. I neurah! never can

stay a—way.

yr. ever

A. S. S.

6 Love and Operetta

THE first rapturous outburst of enthusiasm for Sullivan as an orchestral composer did not last. Avid reader of the press that he was,[1] he must have been aware of such coolly critical voices as that of Henry C. Lunn, editor of the *Musical Times* from 1863.

> Of his overture to *The Sapphire Necklace* we may say that there is very much to admire and that, without contrasting it with mature works, it contains sufficient to show that Mr Sullivan has power to advance to a high place provided that power be rightly directed in time . . .[2]

In the slow movement of the symphony 'all who love mere tune' could be gratified, but

> although we consider this symphony remarkable as a bold experiment by a young composer, we are by no means inclined to believe that it is a step in the right direction. Mr Sullivan's unquestionable talent should make him doubly careful not to mistake popular applause for artistic appreciation. . . . If Mr Sullivan be not already spoiled by unique laudation, there is every hope for his future . . .

Of *In Memoriam*, Lunn declared that

> Mr Sullivan has thoughts which so dazzle by their brilliancy that he is too little prone to reflect where they lead him. . . . His present overture is one more instance that continuity of design cannot be compensated for by facility of invention. . . . The power to grasp these ideas and mould them into a perfect work is wanting.

The *Manchester Guardian* took a similar line with the symphony when Charles Hallé gave it in Manchester on 5 December 1866. Its movements were 'fragmentary and disjointed':

> Although the sound may be pleasant to hear, and the ingenuity of the constructive artist may be freely acknowledged, there is no substitute for the true, spirited inspiration that they should reveal, but do not.

Even with more favourable winds it was not possible for a British composer to make a living from orchestral music. Commissions were too scarce, repetitions were too rarely programmed, and orchestras were too few. London had no such thing as a self-governing or in today's sense a 'permanent' symphony orchestra; orchestral players were mustered *ad hoc*, for one or a few performances, by promoters and concert societies. Not orchestral pieces, not festival cantatas but ballads offered rich reward – ballads which were pushed by famous vocalists and sung by amateurs in thousands of drawing-rooms. The currently favoured type of English opera had ballads 'built in', readily transferable to domestic use in separate song-copies. During Sullivan's boyhood, 'I dreamt I dwelt in marble halls' from Balfe's *The Bohemian Girl* (1843) and 'Scenes that are brightest' from Wallace's *Maritana* (1845) became two of the most popular songs of the Victorian era, precisely by that route.

Despite the domination of Italian opera in London, it was possible for an English opera to be famous. In the dozen years following its birth at Drury Lane, *The Bohemian Girl* went to at least 15 Continental opera houses as well as to New York and Sydney. Moreover, from 1858 the performance of opera in English (both original works and translations from French, German and Italian) had been re-established in London under the auspices of the Pyne-Harrison company, which took a regular lease of the Covent Garden theatre outside the Royal Italian Opera season.[3] In 1862 ears were charmed there by Benedict's new opera *The Lily of Killarney*, based on Dion Boucicault's very successful Irish play, *The Colleen Bawn*. (This was 'the pathos of Paddy, as rendered by Boucicault', which Gilbert was to recall in *Patience*.) *The Lily of Killarney* managed to marry the operatic inheritance of Weber (Benedict's teacher) with characteristic English style and the necessary Irish flavouring. The score launched several solo songs into popularity as well as the duet, 'The moon hath raised her lamp above'.

Unfortunately for an aspirant composer's hopes, the Pyne-Harrison enterprise – under the name of the Royal English Opera – failed in 1864; a company newly formed to succeed it ('The Royal English Opera Company Ltd') likewise failed early in 1866. Sullivan's thoughts had soared high. In 1864 or 1865, learning that Verdi had been interested in,[4] but had finally rejected, an operatic scenario drafted in English and based on Shakespeare's *Cymbeline*, he inquired whether he himself might have access to it. (Shakespeare never ceased to stimulate him musically.) But now no reasonable prospect could be envisaged for staging a 'grand' opera of this nature. It is not surprising that he was willing to consider the more modest facilities offered at the institution run by Mr and Mrs German Reed – the Royal Gallery of Illustration, located in Regent Street.

Its very name avoided any suggestion of impropriety which might linger around the word 'theatre'. There was no space for a normal theatre orchestra, and musical accompaniment was necessarily restricted to a string quartet, or a piano and harmonium, or the like. Its presentations, however, were genuinely theatrical. In a series entitled 'Opera di Camera' (chamber opera), using only piano accompaniment, the German Reeds presented in 1863 a brief two-act work called *Jessy Lea* by George Macfarren. By this time blind but still active, the 50-year-old Macfarren was not new to operatic work: he had won some success with a full-scale opera, *Robin Hood*, presented three years before at Covent Garden under the Pyne-Harrison regime. The plot of the new piece, with words by John Oxenford, was unashamedly reminiscent of Donizetti's *L'elisir d'amore*, so popular at this time. A bottle of supposed magic power so reinforces a bashful suitor's confidence that he wins the girl – and finds himself incidentally rich too.

Macfarren's four characters are absolutely from stock – the village belle who teases her suitor, the shy suitor himself, the baleful gypsy girl, and the jolly Jack

Tar (soprano, tenor, mezzo-soprano, and baritone). Such characters indeed might have come almost straight from Arne's *Thomas and Sally* or *Love in a Village* in the old English comic opera style of a century before. What is so assured and so significant in Macfarren is the brisk dramatic pace and the light-hearted operetta style, harnessed to the use of learned musical techniques (including a canon for three voices). Contrasting musical sections often run straight into each other, without intervening speech. *Jessy Lea* may be considered one of the two starting-points from which Sullivan's own operetta style took off.

The other starting-point was Offenbach, whose operettas had for ten years enlivened the London stage in both French and English versions. *Orpheus in the Underworld*, given in English at Her Majesty's Theatre on Boxing Day in 1865, was to stay unrivalled in popularity. Two years later *The Grand Duchess of Gerolstein* arrived, only six months after its Paris première. An operetta of Offenbach's in more intimate style was *Les deux aveugles* ('The Two Blind Men') – given in London by Offenbach's own troupe, the Bouffes Parisiens, as far back as 1857 but not yet translated.[5] It had only two singing characters, tenor and baritone, and one tiny walk-on part. Each of the supposedly blind beggars comically discovers the other's imposture.

In Offenbach's *Les deux aveugles* itself are two musical devices worth pointing out, one of them paralleled in *Cox and Box*, the other to be exploited elsewhere by Sullivan. The first is the comic imitation (vocal, acted, or both) of musical instruments – in a tradition going back to Piccini (*La buona figliola*, 1760), and probably before. The other is the device of presenting one tune for one character, another tune for another character, and then unexpectedly combining them in counterpoint. Not that Sullivan would have lacked examples elsewhere; he certainly knew Berlioz's *The Damnation of Faust*, where the soldiers' and students' choruses are so brilliantly combined. He had himself already effected a similar contrapuntal combination of themes in his overture to *The Sapphire Necklace*.

It was *Les deux aveugles*, sung at a private amateur gathering, that directly prompted Sullivan's first operetta. The 'Moray Minstrels' were a convivial all-male group who met on Saturday evenings at Moray Lodge in Kensington, the home of Arthur Lewis. A partner in the drapery firm of Lewis and Allenby in Regent Street, he had a passion for music and theatricals and was to marry Kate Terry, an actress like her famous sister Ellen. His was a circle that embraced both Sullivan and Francis C. Burnand (1836–1917), an experienced writer for the theatre and a contributor to *Punch*, of which he was to become editor in 1880. George du Maurier (1834–96), the celebrated *Punch* artist and future author of *Trilby*, was in the same circle. To provide a companion-piece for the Moray Minstrels' performance of the Offenbach operetta, Burnand and Sullivan wrote *Cox and Box*. The text was an adaptation of the already successful one-act farce by J. Maddison Morton (1811–91), *Box and Cox*.

Morton's play had been first given in 1847 and, even after its operatic transformation, was often to be revived (and to be translated into Dutch, German and Russian). Two bachelor lodgers, unknown to each other, have rented the same room – one absent at work by night, one by day – in the house of a Mrs Bouncer. With the all-male Moray Minstrels in mind, Burnand replaced the landlady by Sergeant Bouncer, a landlord given to interminable military reminiscences. In other respects Morton's plot was kept intact, with its masterly final stroke of comedy:

Box. The more I gaze on your features, the more I'm convinced that you're my long-lost brother.
Cox. The very observation I was going to make to you!
Box. Ah – tell me – in mercy tell me – have you such a thing as a strawberry mark on your left arm?
Cox. No!
Box. Then it is he. (*They rush into each other's arms.*)

So *Cox and Box, or The Long-lost Brothers* was given by the Moray Minstrels in Lewis's house on 26 May 1866, with George du Maurier (an enthusiastic amateur singer) as Box, Harold Power as Cox, and John Forster as Bouncer.[6] Almost a year later, the death of the *Punch* artist Charles Bennett prompted its first public performance on 11 May 1867[7] at the Adelphi Theatre, London, as part of a 'benefit' to aid the widow and eight children ('The number of the latter will shortly be increased', read the announcement.) George du Maurier retained his role, with a 'Mr Quintin' (actually Quintin Twiss) as Cox and Arthur Blunt as Bouncer.[8] It was announced in the programme that 'the lodging, including the little second-floor back room, has been furnished with original music by Mr Arthur Sullivan'. The composer conducted, and *Les deux aveugles* was among the other items on the bill.

Du Maurier had been nervous about this performance – his first public stage appearance. He drank and smoked furiously beforehand and nearly missed his entrance. But in his own diary he recorded the confidence that came to him with the applause earned by the mock-lullaby 'Hush'd is the bacon':

All the theatre was of course in a mist as I did not wear my glasses. . . . Then Twiss sang his song very well – then I flung his chop out of the window and we managed the duet 'Who are you, Sir?' very well – recovered all my self-possession. The second duet got an encore. The grand scena went off all right and so did 'Sixes'; I was watching Arthur Sullivan for my cues – triumphant finish. Blunt was splendid in 'Rataplan', Twiss a regular old stager.[9]

Only on 23 July in Paris,[10] however, did Sullivan complete an overture,[11] first used in a further 'benefit' performance in aid of Bennett's dependants, given at the Theatre Royal, Manchester on 29 July, after being rehearsed in London at Arthur Lewis's house. At this performance Du Maurier, Twiss and Blunt repeated their roles. Thus was launched the first work of the modern Sullivan theatrical canon.

Cox and Box was styled 'a triumviretta in one act' – suggesting to a classically educated audience the absurd comparison of these three operetta characters with the *triumviri* or board of three rulers in Ancient Rome. Puns were irresistible to Burnand, of whom Gilbert was to say that he would have made *The Pirates of Penzance* into *The Pirates of Pun-zance*. On the title-page of the vocal score, published in 1869, Burnand's name was larger than Morton's but not as large as Sullivan's – and the dedication was 'to his [Sullivan's] friend J. W. Davison'. Ten musical numbers, including the overture, are present – the last two of which were suppressed in modern printings of the score in order to conform with D'Oyly Carte cuts in production.

These two last numbers both incorporate a *reprise* of previous music – a typically operatic device, and one which Offenbach himself had borrowed for operetta. Offenbach also provided Sullivan's model in humorous incongruity. It might be a dramatic incongruity, when both composer and librettist simulated a heroic or tender mood in a trivial context – a lullaby addressed not to a baby in the cradle but to a piece of bacon resting in a frying pan. Or it might be a purely musical incongruity – elements of the high-flown 'grand opera' style, especially recitative and cadenzas, deliberately mismatched with commonplace words. Here were two essentials of what audiences were to relish as the 'Gilbert and Sullivan' manner.

Neither device is technically parody, but very near to parody is the incessant *rat-a-plan* as uttered by Sergeant Bouncer, the other two characters being almost hypnotically compelled to join in the imitation of the drum. Its use mocks the *rat-a-plan* which evokes military glory in *La Fille du régiment* – another Donizetti favourite. To a future generation it would recall the similar *rat-a-plan* in Verdi's *La forza del destino* – a work which at that time was still to receive its first performance.

The German Reeds did not immediately take the successful piece into a regular repertory. Instead, a new and longer (two-act) piece was commissioned from the successful author and composer. It was to be produced at the German Reeds' larger premises, St George's Hall, Langham Place (near the present Broadcasting House). 'Burnand was here all Saturday and Sunday and we settled a capital little opera for German Reed, which I am sure will be a success,' wrote Sullivan to his mother while staying at John Scott Russell's house. *The Contra-bandista, or The Law of the Ladrones* opened on 18 December 1867, being Sullivan's first stage work in more than one act. Here, as later, he followed the Italian comic-opera pattern in writing the finale of the first act as an unbroken chain of numbers with solos, ensembles, and choruses. Here too (no. 12, the trio of Act 2) is the contrapuntal harnessing of two tunes representing different characters. In the second act also, a *bolero* and a *cachucha* (the former already brought into opera by Weber and Auber) served in lively dance to indicate the Spanish location – effectively as music, but with a clumsy interruption to the action, which Sullivan would avoid when reintroducing such dances in *The Gondoliers*.

The Contrabandista, however, was of no strong merits as a whole. (In 1894 Sullivan and Burnand would revise it as *The Chieftain*.) Not much comic value is extracted from Mr Grigg, a camera-carrying English tourist in Spain, who is chosen against his will as the leader of a robber band. Some of Burnand's extravagances of rhyme barely made their point on paper, let alone in sound. ('If by shock awry, Knock'd like crockery . . .') Sullivan also showed a clumsy hand in dealing with Mr Grigg's song of longing to be back home with 'my spouse, my cows, and my sows, ha, ha!' It is a happy jingle of a tune, but its recurrence in the first-act finale, *with the robbers joining in*, is quite undramatic. The composer never made that mistake again.

The Contrabandista had been staged at St George's Hall with a full orchestra and chorus. At their smaller theatre, the Royal Gallery of Illustration, the German Reeds now brought *Cox and Box* into the repertory on 29 March 1869. The artistic loss caused to *Cox and Box* by the absence of an orchestra was noted by both *The Times* and *The Athenaeum* – the composer having perhaps dropped a hint in the friendly ears of Davison and Chorley. Sullivan had already developed a commercial sense and was determined to get full market value for the work. He had sanctioned the separate reissue of the lullaby to the bacon as a sentimental ballad with new words by Lionel Lewin ('Birds in the Night'), and resisted the librettist's readiness to think only of the short term. Addressing him as 'my dear Frank', he wrote to Burnand:

I don't consent to let Reed have C & B for 50 nights for £50, and have written him to say so. It's ridiculous in every respect, and entirely cuts away the ground from under our feet in the country for the future. I can't conceive what you can be thinking of.

Seeing we can make £100 in a week if we like to set about it, it is absurd to accept £25 for 50 performances spread over an indefinite period – and moreover I am not arranging for it to go down in the country in the form of a drawing-room entertainment.

We must wait our time. Opportunity and orchestra will turn up some day. In the meantime we shall not starve for the want of £25.

I will give no *exclusive* rights for the country and Reed must pay for *every* performance.

You are not a bit astonished that Boosey has published different words to the Lullaby, because I told you of it over and over again and you said, 'Quite right'. Moreover, the new words are excellent – done in my own house and every line carefully considered with regard to the requirements of the music.

P.S. £25 may pay you, because you have absolutely nothing to do since you wrote the libretto, but it does *not* pay me (hardly for the musical labour of copying all the music for the performance) who have had to teach the singers, attend all the rehearsals, and a hundred other things *besides* the composition.

While he was composing *Cox and Box*, Sullivan's fires of ambition were being stoked by his first serious love-affair. His passionate involvement with Rachel Scott Russell (1845–82) had been growing since 1865. Known to her family as Chenny, Rachel was the second of John Scott Russell's three daughters.[12] The parties which united the Groves, the Russells and other friends after the Saturday concerts at the Crystal Palace brought Sullivan constantly into the Russells' company. Theirs was a lively and not purely musical circle which included Burnand and the painter John Millais (1829–96), the latter remaining one of Sullivan's close friends.

Sullivan respectfully dedicated a song, 'If doughty deeds my lady please', to Mrs Russell and was made freely welcome at the family home – from which address come a number of his letters at this period. As Sullivan wooed Rachel, Frederic Clay (likewise introduced into the circle by Grove) courted the youngest daughter, Alice. Consent for Clay's marriage with Alice had been given, and preparations made, when the couple terminated their understanding. Sullivan's case was very different: he was barred from his suit by the young woman's parents. Learning how deeply Rachel had given her affections, her mother wrote to Sullivan on 29 July 1867:

It has come upon me with a shock to learn that you could not be content on merely the terms of intimate friendship in this family . . . It grieves me to tell you that under *no* circumstances could I ever consent to a different relationship. And therefore I ask you, if you *cannot* bring yourself to be satisfied with that which hitherto subsisted, to abstain from coming here till you can do so, and to cease all correspondence. . . . I grieve that I reposed in you a confidence to which you were not equal. I did it in absolute good faith . . .

After this it was by secret meetings (Grove's office, apparently, serving as one rendezvous) that the lovers continued to see each other.

What reason made Clay acceptable as a suitor, and Sullivan not? The reason of money. Clay, the son of an M.P., was wealthy and would give up his Treasury post on the death of his father. Sullivan depended on his profession and could make no promise of 'prospects'. Rachel did not want to start marriage without financial security: 'Do you not see', she wrote to Sullivan, 'that, even if everything befell so that I could say tomorrow "Take me", you would have to answer, "I cannot, you must wait"?'

Sullivan had dedicated to her his published song-setting of Jean Ingelow's words 'O fair dove, O fond dove', and Rachel's letters are sometimes signed 'Fond Dove' (or 'F.D.'), at other times 'Passion Flower'. She was constantly urging him to the creation of great music. As a subject for an opera she proposed *Francesca da Rimini*, to be based on Byron's translation from Dante; when he preferred the subject of Guinevere (taken from Tennyson's *Idylls of the King*) she spurred him on in her rather naive way.

Do it with your whole soul and your strength – working at it intensely and religiously as the old masters worked, like dear old Bach – and it *must* be a great work, for you have the power in you.

He did indeed get his friend Lionel Lewin to write a libretto on *Guinevere* for him, but it remained uncomposed.

Having an amateur's skill in music, she is stated by George S. Emmerson, the biographer of John Scott Russell, to have helped Sullivan with the 'scoring' of *Cox and Box*. It is more likely that she helped with the hasty copying of the orchestral parts for the Adelphi performance. After their enforced separation, the lovers were permitted a reunion in Zurich (Rachel was there with her father) in September 1868. Asking her suitor to bring from London a jacket of his which she liked, she slipped as she often did into Victorian baby-talk:

You looked so sweet in it . . . I like that better than anything else and so oo does it to please oo's bird – please do darling . . . I always liked that coat – so oo gives up oo's will to oo's bird . . . your little Passion Flower.

During his courtship of Rachel it is clear that the good-looking, dark-haired young musician had also stirred the affections of a third Russell sister – Louise, the eldest (1841–78). Letters to 'My dearest Arthur' from 'your truly loving' or 'your own devoted Little Woman' pass beyond the role of sisterly go-between; how far beyond is a matter of inference. In Louise's 'you have taken as your right the only thing I have to give', the obvious interpretation may be the correct one. The same physical intimacy is suggested by Rachel's 'Ah me! when I think of those days when cooing and purring was enough for us, till we tried the utmost – and that is why I fancy *marriage* spoils love. When you can drink *brandy*, water tastes sickly afterwards.'

Rachel continued to send ardent letters. But from the letter sent (over the signature 'F.D.') on the composer's 27th birthday it would appear that Arthur Sullivan's feelings had cooled. He was evidently working already on *The Prodigal Son*, commissioned for the Three Choirs Festival at Worcester later in 1869.

This is the first 13th of May since 1863 that I have not wished you 'many happy returns' – with my hand held out to welcome you. It is so bright and sunny and the birds are singing – and God grant this may be a happy day to you – and with all my heart I pray that there may be many in store for you yet.

I send you some of our flowers – they will bring back everything to you so vividly, as picking and choosing them has done to me. For a long time I have been trying to think what I could give you. I knew you would not care merely for a bought thing – and so I decided to do what has no intrinsic merit of its own beyond being as much as the work of my own hands as it is possible for anything to be. Doctor Pole has arranged – as you know – your symphony – *my* symphony – for me and I thought it would please you if I made a copy of it for you. But I could only get one part in time and I have had to work without ceasing two days to get it done. You shall have the others later and then put them all together and keep them. I am sure it is full of mistakes, but you know you always scolded me for not copying accurately and I am not improved.[13]

I am too sad to write much as it seems to me so curious that you could resist my letters – but if it saves you pain, God knows I would not ask you to do it. I am so utterly sad that I long to go away where the daily pain may be a little less . . . I paid a visit to Lady Victoria the other day and afterwards to the Byngs. I like them so much and I hope they are coming down to us on Saturday.

I am doing a translation of that letter of Hiller's on Wagner and I will send it to you when it is done. But it is *so* difficult that I almost despair at times. Will you not write to me now?

If I can help you in any way in copying or anything with your *Prodigal Son* do give it me to do. Did G. [Grove] ask you to put in a quartet unaccompanied for me? I think that with *your* harmonies it would be too beautiful.

Oh, Arthur, I pray God with my whole soul to bless you and to make you happy. The tears drop down over the poor little face you used to love as I write. You know all I would say and cannot. God have mercy on us both.

They met yet again, on Christmas Day 1869, when he gave her a camellia. He knew that she was to leave next month for a prolonged visit to St Petersburg, where her brother Norman was working for an English engineering firm. 'Spread your wings, my beautiful eagle,' she wrote in parting, 'and show how you can soar!' He would indeed soar, his music winning riches and respectability enough even to satisfy the most circumspect of parents; but the direction his music took was not the one which Rachel had urged.

Early in 1872 Rachel Scott Russell was married to William Holmes. It would be long after that before Arthur Sullivan unexpectedly met 'Chenny' again.

7 From Tennyson to Gilbert

A YOUNG man moving in Grove's orbit in the middle and late 1860s might have met such luminaries as Browning, Tennyson, George Eliot, Christina Rossetti, Edward Lear, T. H. Huxley, the architect Sir Gilbert Scott, the millionaire philanthropist Baroness Burdett-Coutts, and the liberal theologian Dean Stanley of Westminster.[1] If he did not meet them, he could hardly have avoided hearing their work and personalities discussed from intimate acquaintance. Some were friends of Grove, some were contributors to *Macmillan's Magazine* under his editorship, and some were both.

The striking thing about Sullivan is how little he was affected by the intellectual stirrings and social activities represented by those names. His many letters, and likewise the diary entries chronicling his later life, show an acute and humorous observation, a ready sympathy, and no trace of snobbish disdain for the class from which he was beginning to rise. But there are only the rarest references to public affairs. What came his way in music and the theatre was, of course, his professional concern and the subject of decisive judgement. But he was barely touched by general questions in the arts and literature, in science or philosophy. He stood aside from politics too. The successive widening of the parliamentary suffrage in 1867 and 1884, the partisanship attaching to the rivalry of Disraeli and Gladstone, the turmoil of Irish rebellion and the violence of the 'Fenian outrages' in London – to Sullivan, such things were news of the day, no doubt discussed, but not arousing action or commitment.

Financially, though he might not have achieved the 'prospects' desired by an ambitious fiancée, he was steadily progressing. In June 1867 he exchanged his organist's appointment for one at a newly built and more fashionable church (St Peter's, Cranley Gardens, in Kensington) – presumably at higher pay. In September 1867 he sold three songs to Metzler for 35 guineas (£36.75) – more than double the rate of the previous year.[2] In April 1868 he switched publishers, signing an agreement with Boosey[3] for a three-year 'retainer' (as it would now be called) at £400 per annum. This sum simply gave Boosey the right to publish his works – but not in lieu of royalties, which were to be paid as well. Earlier that year he was apparently too busy with other work to accept Hallé's proposal that he should conduct a choral festival at Leeds – a forerunner of the regular Leeds Festivals (see p. 144).

It was a mark of standing that in March 1869 he was elected to the Garrick Club, that favourite of artists and writers: he was to develop a taste for the dining, card-playing and all-male *bonhomie* of Victorian club life. Gambling, whether at card games or abroad on the roulette-wheel, became an obsession. Travel also became his pleasure as well as a matter of business, and he would soon accustom himself to the pleasures of the 'Season' – fashionable London's height of the social year, from April to July, with its balls and its race-meetings (Epsom, Ascot, Newmarket, Goodwood).

Meanwhile, thanks to Grove's initiative, Sullivan made a literary contact in a more exalted sphere than that of ballad-versifiers and commercial playwrights. Alfred Tennyson, though not raised to the peerage until 1884, was a commanding figure almost from the beginning to the Queen's reign: a state pension of £200 yearly was conferred on him in 1845 and he was made poet laureate (succeeding Wordsworth) in 1851. Many of his works, including the long narrative poem, *The Princess* (1847) had already inspired music by various composers. Among the Victorians' own favourites were Barnby's setting of 'Sweet and Low' and Balfe's of 'Come into the Garden, Maud' (from Tennyson's longer *Maud*, 1855). Tennyson himself, unlike Browning, had no knowledge of music but was fully aware of the 'musical' content of his own poetry. There could be no more suitable writer to collaborate with a composer in a deliberately planned set of songs.

The concept of such a set sequence hanging on narrative, like Schubert's *Die schöne Müllerin*, was as yet unfamiliar in English. In correspondence, Grove and Tennyson referred to the prospect not as a song-cycle but as a *liederkreis*. To stimulate the poet, Grove sent him some of Heine's verses – presumably those which had furnished one of Schumann's two Heine cycles. The projected collaboration between ageing poet and young composer was to be supplemented in print with an illustration to each song. John Millais was, apart from being an intimate of Sullivan's, an obvious choice of artist.[4] The days were past when, as a pre-Raphaelite rebel, he had shocked with the 'realism' of *Christ in the House of his Parents* (1850); Dickens in *Household Words* had called it 'mean, odious, revolting and repulsive'. Now the romantic and anecdotal had taken over his art, and he was both respectable and popular.

Tennyson reacted enthusiastically to the proposal for a song-cycle. He received Sullivan at his home in the Isle of Wight and visited him (in the flowing garb which he affected as a poet) in Pimlico. But, having written the verses, the poet grew cool to the project and delayed in giving permission to publish. According to Sir Newman Flower's biography of Sullivan, written in collaboration with the composer's nephew, Tennyson even offered Sullivan the very large sum of £500 as an inducement *not* to publish (which the composer refused). Because of Tennyson's procrastination, Millais allowed his series of drawings to be dispersed; one, depicting a girl at a window, was published as *A Reverie* in *Cassell's Family Magazine*, 1875. When the song-cycle was eventually published as *The Window, or The Songs of the Wrens* in 1871, the poet insisted on a prefatory note which Sullivan could not help but resent:

Four years ago Mr Sullivan requested me to write a little song-cycle, German fashion, for him to exercise his art upon. He has been very successful in setting such old songs as 'Orpheus with his Lute', and I drest up for him, partly in the old style, a puppet, whose almost only merit is, perhaps, that it can dance to Mr Sullivan's instrument. I am sorry that my four-year-old puppet should have to dance at all in the dark shadow of these days [i.e. of the Franco-Prussian War]; but the music is now completed, and I am bound by my promise.

Moreover, Tennyson's standing apparently made it imperative that the words be printed separately in the music-copy as well as underlying the music itself – and Tennyson himself had re-written one of the poems *after* its musical setting. The composer thus had the embarrassment of seeing the new, 'correct' version of the poem printed as though in contradiction to his setting of the earlier version. The poet's conduct seems in retrospect churlish – but if he was worried that the poems would be criticized as banal, he was surely right:

> The frost is here
> And fuel is dear
> And woods are sear
> And fires burn clear
> And frost is here
> And has bitten the heel of the going year.

In these twelve poems (Sullivan set only eleven) the utterance is supposedly that of a shy but successful wooer. The window in the beloved's home forms an object of anxious scrutiny – an echo, it would seem, of Schubert's *Die schöne Müllerin* rather than of the Schumann/Heine collaborations. But the reference to 'wrens' is misleading and not fully worked out: why the beloved should be called 'Queen of the Wrens' remains an obscure point, certainly less clear than why Maud should have been 'queen rose of the rosebud garden of girls'.

Sullivan's own inspiration flagged also. The first song has a rich promise not only in atmosphere but in possibilities of thematic development through the whole cycle. But the later songs settle for static, obvious expression. The hoped-for transplanting of the German seed into English soil did not happen.

By this time, in more conventional fulfilment of an English composer's role, Sullivan had successfully launched his first oratorio at Worcester. (The word may be taken in its strict sense – not merely a vaguely religious cantata, but a narrative work based directly on the Scriptures.) He wrote swiftly, taking only three weeks to compose *The Prodigal Son*, having selected his own biblical text. But a composer proposing to conduct his own new work was likely to run into difficulties – notably over rehearsal, as Goldschmidt forewarned in the most courteous terms:

In the case of Hereford two years ago, the chorus – numbering, I think, about 160 – came from Hereford, Worcester, Gloucester, Bristol, Bradford [and] London. They had not met together until the general rehearsal [for both choir and orchestra] in the Cathedral on the Monday. Your choruses may be so well written and easy that this single hasty rehearsal is sufficient. As a rule I should say it was not. Certainly it did not prove so in my case. I had again and again asked for one joint rehearsal, but the answer was that it was impossible. . . . Experience, however, has shown me that though the chorus may not be able to meet collectively before the Monday noon, they *can* meet after, viz. in the evening of that day. . . . You will know how to profit by this friendly hint . . .

It may be presumed that Sullivan *did* profit, and the impact of *The Prodigal Son* (with Sims Reeves in the title-part, Santley as the father and Tietjens as the soprano soloist) was such that it was repeated at the Hereford meeting of the festival in the following year. Vigorous musical strokes illustrate the sudden changes of the Prodigal's fate, and the composer's Chapel Royal training emerges in the solidly wrought choruses. That the slow, moralizing soprano aria, 'O that thou hadst harkened' should bring a lapse into sub-*Elijah* is not surprising.

Naturally the work was taken up by Sullivan's champions at the Crystal Palace. But there (11 December 1869) ill-fortune struck the composer both musically and financially. Sims Reeves absented himself on the usual plea of illness, other good tenors were unobtainable,

. . . and finally I am thrown back upon Perren! The choruses went well, Santley as usual was magnificent, giving me the idea that he was working all the harder to make up for my disappointment . . . [But] as far as the Prodigal's part, thank God not a note of it was heard except the accompaniment – it left no impression at all upon the audience. In fact it was *Hamlet* with the part of Hamlet omitted. I must say that the public were very good-natured and . . . enthusiastic to me personally . . . *In Memoriam* went superbly.[5]

The absence of Reeves and also of Tietjens (a 'Mlle Vanzini' sang the part) moreover, cut down the composer's fee, which was perhaps originally fixed at 100 guineas. 'My dear Sullivan', wrote Grove from the Crystal Palace in his official capacity on 18 December 1869:

Enclosed I hand you this company's cheque for 75 guineas with form of receipt, which be kind enough to sign and return.

You are aware that the offer of the Board was made on the understanding that Mme Titiens [so spelt] and Mr Sims Reeves were to be among the principals; and as neither of these eminent artists took part in the performance the Board do not feel that they will be justified in adhering fully to that offer – satisfactory as it would have been to pay you the whole sum . . .

Reeves was, it seems, notoriously unreliable: when *The Prodigal Son* was given by Hallé in Manchester, 'the farce of announcing Mr Sims Reeves, and of publishing the usual telegram from him stating his inability to attend, was once more enacted on this occasion' (*Musical Standard*, 22 January 1870). In Edinburgh, where Sullivan himself conducted *The Prodigal Son* on 14 November 1870, Sims Reeves participated but failed to sing the two Handel items on the programme – leading to a legal action about how much of his 90-guinea fee should be deducted.[6] In return for singing songs currently on a publisher's list, leading singers customarily received a royalty on each song-copy sold, but Reeves had a soft spot for his young composer friend and helped to turn the royalty system to the composer's advantage for once: 'Littleton [managing director of Novello's] will give you £100 down provided I sing it and *I will do so*. Am I not as good as a father to you? I hope you have not parted with it.' The letter was signed

'Tenorino'. The song for which Sullivan presumably got this very high fee is unidentified.

At this time, in addition to songs, anthems and hymns, he wrote a number of part-songs for male or mixed voices without accompaniment. In this specialized sense the part-song – unlike the madrigal, which the Victorian composer cultivated as a prized antique form, and the glee, which had become obsolete – was a harmonized composition with the melody on the top line and with the music either repeated in successive stanzas or varied to suit a poetic narrative. Both Mendelssohn and Schumann had written admirable examples and Sullivan's 'The Long Day Closes' (1868) to words by Chorley, may be not unworthily ranked with them.

John Goss, Sullivan's old teacher from Academy days, was cordial but critical about *The Prodigal Son*.

All you have done is most masterly – your orchestration superb, and your effects many of them original and first-rate . . . Some day you will, I hope, try another oratorio, putting out all your strength, but not the strength of a few weeks or months, whatever your immediate friends may say. . . . Only don't do anything so pretentious as an oratorio or even a symphony without *all your power*, which seldom comes in one fit.[7]

The phrase 'or even a symphony' (as though that were a lesser feat than an oratorio) may have an odd Victorian ring, but the advice was perceptive. Sullivan *did* have facility; the ability to work fast would serve him well in composing operetta with a première approaching and a cast already engaged in rehearsal. To symphony and concerto he never returned. It is as if he were conscious of a lack of sustaining-power, or more specifically of the power of thematic development in the German tradition. In fact, only three times thereafter did he essay a substantial composition for orchestra without voices. Far ahead lay the *Macbeth* overture (1888) and the *Imperial March* (1893) but on 31 August 1870, at the Birmingham Festival, he showed himself as both composer and conductor in a new concert-overture which was to remain freshly attractive into our own day.

This was the work generally known (and eventually printed) as the *Overture di Ballo*. The odd mixture of English and Italian was not Sullivan's – but his was perhaps the fault. On the Birmingham programme and in the composer's letters the work was entitled *Overtura di Ballo*. Knowing *ouverture* as a French word, Sullivan rashly and wrongly presumed the existence of an Italian form, *overtura*.[8] A pity that Sullivan did not feel bold enough to call it simply *A Dance Overture* as a later English composer would have done! He himself later referred to it on occasion as his '*Ballo* overture'.

Notably, this work does not depend on thematic development but on thematic metamorphosis – the notes of a tune altered in rhythm and in harmonic implication to make another tune. The procedure is most familiar in Liszt, but nothing else in the work is Lisztian. In a ten-minute span the *Ballo* overture links Sullivan's inheritance of Mendelssohn's orchestral grace with his own purely individual gift of melody. The syncopation in 6/8 prophesies the quintet from *Patience*, the cross-rhythms point to the more distant *Iolanthe*, and the whole work stands without parallel in Victorian music. That severe critic, Henry Lunn, was much impressed, declaring in the *Musical Times* that

Mr Sullivan's themes are so melodious and instinct with refined feeling, his instrumentation so graceful and ingenious, and his treatment of the subjects so thoroughly musician-like, that his composition appeals as much to the educated as to the uneducated ear.

For the amateur choral society which was conducted by his friend Barnby and supported by the firm of Novello's (to which Barnby was adviser), he produced 'additional accompaniments' to Handel's *Jephtha* in 1869 – the type of treatment, with added wind parts, which was accepted almost without question at this period, to balance choral forces which were so much more numerous than Handel's own. (Sullivan's own later preference for 'authentic' Bach orchestration makes a striking contrast.) A longer-lasting task was his work on Boosey's 'Royal Edition' of operatic vocal scores by composers ranging from Mozart to Wagner (*Lohengrin*). In 25 of these editions Sullivan's name as editor is coupled with that of Josiah Pittman; in seven scores Sullivan worked unaided.[9] Presumably the piano reductions are the editor's. Along with the rival series of vocal scores published by Novello, these were vital tools of Britain's operatic life. The actual phrases of the English translations provided – 'Home to our mountains' from *Il trovatore*, 'Not a lady, not a beauty' from *Faust* – became widely, almost proverbially, known.

On his own behalf, Sullivan rightly looked abroad – to Paris first of all. For eight years the conductor Jules Pasdeloup (1819–87) had run his own concerts with a wide-ranging repertory. As a visitor in 1869 Sullivan admired the responsiveness of Pasdeloup's audience, more than 4,000 strong: 'If people like the things, they applaud vigorously; if they don't, they hiss with equal energy'.[10] He persuaded the conductor to give *In Memoriam* at least a run-through at rehearsal, but apparently no performance eventuated until 1879 (see p. 125). In July 1870 he was back in Paris staying at the 'New Club', the English haunt on the Avenue Matignon – much cheaper than a hotel, he noted when writing to his mother. A concert at which 'we' [British] had a great artistic success but which was mismanaged made him depressed with 'this beastly hole'.

But such an expression represented, for him, a more momentary mood. In general Paris held for him – as for other Englishmen of means – the fascination of art, of social gaiety, of risqué theatre, and, not least, of sexual freedom. Though the number of registered brothels was falling (240 in 1840, 145 in 1870, 125 in 1881) the number of clandestine, unregistered brothels was growing: in 1888 the latter were estimated to house some 15,000 prostitutes in Paris alone.[11] The diaries which Arthur Sullivan kept later have strong indications of his patronizing such establishments, and in younger days he would be at least as likely to do so.

Correspondence with his mother indicates that Sullivan was already on terms of friendship with the wealthy woman – living partly in Nice, partly in Paris – to whom he always refers as 'Madame Conneau'.[12] Her husband was physician to the emperor Napoleon III and a senator; she (Juliette Conneau) was a close companion of Napoleon's consort, the Empress Eugénie. She was a keen amateur singer, of a standard that enabled her to participate in public performance. In her company, Sullivan met Ambroise Thomas (1811–96), whose *Mignon* had been lately produced in London (at Drury Lane, 7 July 1870). The prodigious success won in Paris by this opera had elevated Thomas to a position in French opera second only to that of Charles Gounod (1818–93). While in Paris, Sullivan may well have met Gounod too: at any rate, when the latter came to London a few months later, Sullivan paid a call on him and received a charming reply from a composer so much his senior.

[translated]

I was extremely sorry to miss your kind visit yesterday [14 December 1870], and I regret it more keenly because I had already been prevented from meeting you at the house of a friend of yours, the charming Miss Romanes,[13] who came to invite me with such warm entreaties.

Would you like to do me a kindness? Then ask me to dinner next Wednesday, the 21st, at 6.30. You will give me the pleasure of talking with you about our beloved art, of which I know you as a fervent apostle, a brilliant hope, and already a celebrity.[14]

It was not a casual visit to London on Gounod's part. He came as a refugee from war-torn Paris: Napoleon's empire had fallen to the power of Prussia, in a war which Bismarck had deliberately provoked. On 4 September 1870 the Third Republic was proclaimed – and the war against Germany continued with Napoleon III in exile. (The broad boulevards of Haussmann, the plays of the younger Dumas and the operettas of Offenbach would remain as the monuments of Napoleon's Paris.) In his self-imposed five-year exile Gounod exploited English taste, acquiring a new status as a composer of oratorios and a choral conductor. His appointment as conductor of the choral society established at the newly opened Royal Albert Hall provoked patriotic disapproval and must have reinforced Sullivan's own mortification at the way England treated her own musicians when posts of distinction were allotted. But Sullivan had no direct cause for jealousy. Unlike his friend Barnby, he was not a specialist choral conductor.

Nor was he yet stamped as a man of the theatre and a composer of operetta. *Cox and Box* had been a success; *The Contrabandista* had not. There was no forewarning that an invitation to collaborate with Gilbert would begin a transformation of his life and his fame. The likelihood is that Gilbert and Sullivan must have been at least casually acquainted by the time of the opening of the Gaiety Theatre in 1868 (to be referred to in the next chapter). But a tradition started by Gilbert places their meeting later in that year at a rehearsal of *Ages Ago*, a short dramatic piece written by Gilbert for the German Reeds, with music by Sullivan's friend Clay.[15] After Clay had introduced Sullivan, Gilbert addressed him in the following manner:

My friend Fred Clay and I have been discussing a technical point upon which you may be able to throw some light. My contention is that if a musician who is a master of all instruments has a musical theme to express, he can express it as readily upon the simple tetrachord of Mercury, in which, as we all know, there are no diatonic intervals whatever as upon the more elaborate disdiapason with the three tetrachords and the redundant note which, as I need not remind a composer of your distinction, embraces in its perfect consonance all the single, double and inverted chords.

Gilbert's account continues (without disclosing that this brilliant nonsense comes from his own play, *The Palace of Truth*):

Sullivan reflected for a moment, and asked me to oblige him by repeating my question. I did so, and he replied that it was a very nice point, and he would like to think it over before giving a definite reply. That took place about 20 years ago, and I believe he is still engaged in hammering it out.

William Schwenck Gilbert's character and work will necessarily be a subject of constant reference in the following pages. Born before Sullivan – on 18 November 1836, in London – he was to survive him by 11 years. His middle name was that of his godmother, and a letter from the classical scholar Gilbert Murray (1866–1957) to Leslie Baily[16] makes it clear that his family called him by this middle name: 'W. S. Gilbert was my mother's first cousin. We all knew the Gilbert family quite intimately: Schwenck himself, his sisters, and his very interesting and handsome old father, after whom I was called.' William Gilbert senior (1804–90) was himself a novelist and man of letters. He and his more famous son liked to suppose, without any known authority, that the Elizabethan explorer Sir Humphrey Gilbert (1539–83) was an ancestor of the family.

Gilbert had been a Civil Service clerk and then an unsuccessful barrister before making letters his profession. His legal experience was, at any rate, to stimulate the production of a whole set of stage lawyers from *Trial by Jury* to *The Grand Duke*. One occurrence of his childhood also reads like a slice out of one of the operas – if, indeed, we believe his story that at the age of two he was kidnapped near Naples by bandits, who released him on the payment of a ransom of £25. As well as verse, he wrote some short stories and drama criticism. When he turned to the theatre, it was at first in the genre known as burlesque or extravaganza. *Dulcamara, or The Little Duck and the Great Quack* (St James's Theatre, 29 December 1864) was based on the plot of Donizetti's *L'elisir d'amore*: the double title with the punning relation between the 'duck' (nice girl) and 'quack' (doctor), is characteristic. Indeed, puns in H. J. Byron's most reckless manner bespatter the text of *Dulcamara* at every few lines. Songs and choruses are interpolated, the words being written to scan exactly to such popular melodies as *Johnny Comes Marching Home* or operatic extracts, two of them from *L'elisir d'amore* itself. Here Gilbert was writing for pre–existent music, which denotes a skill not given to every versifier. His own later self-depreciation – 'I only know two tunes: one is *God Save the Queen* and one isn't' – was ironically defensive.

No Cards (29 March 1869, in the same bill as *Cox and Box*) was Gilbert's first play for the German Reed management, followed on 22 November 1869 by *Ages Ago*. Then came *Our Island Home* (20 June 1870), with a prophetic confusion between 'pilot' and 'pirate', and *A Sensation Novel* (30 January 1871). Of these, *Ages Ago* was easily the most successful: it ran for more than 350 performances, a figure much in excess of what was to be achieved by the first three Gilbert-and-Sullivan works. Clay's score, with piano and harmonium serving as 'orchestra' (as usual at the Royal Gallery of Illustration), was published with a dedication to Sullivan. A serious play, *Pygmalion and Galatea* (Haymarket Theatre, 1871, with the celebrated Madge Kendal as Galatea) is said to have netted Gilbert £40,000 from its original production and various revivals.[17]

From 1861, anonymously and then under his nursery nickname of Bab, he was a frequent contributor of light verse to the magazine *Fun*, which had been deliberately founded as a rival to *Punch*, at that time under the editorship of that celebrated Victorian punster H. J. Byron (1834–84). Moreover, both in *Fun* and when his work appeared in book form as *The Bab Ballads* (1869, with a second volume following), Gilbert was his own illustrator, mainly with ludicrous caricature but with an occasional sensual image of a young girl. His imagination was extraordinarily visual for a versifier; the sense of movement and spacing in his early drawings points towards his later success as a stage director.

It may be argued that a repressed sexuality lurks behind the impossibly 'proper' plots which Gilbert provided for the Savoy operas. Hesketh Pearson, among students of Gilbert's life and work, surmised that an unpleasant childhood with a father given to irrational temper was responsible for

the absence of human feeling in most of his plays, the false exaggeration of the sentiment whenever it occurs, his inability to portray real people, his constant resort to the fancies of fairyland, his frequent pictures of a topsy-turvy universe.

His upbringing may also have nurtured the brusque, irascible manner which made Gilbert such a difficult partner in creative and business matters.

Successful as he was with the combination of Gilbert and Clay, German Reed had evidently not given up Sullivan on account of the failure of *The Contrabandista*. He approached him in 1870 with a new idea:

Gilbert is doing a comic one-act entertainment for me – soprano, contralto, tenor, baritone and bass. Would you like to compose the music? If so – on what terms? Reply at once, as I want to get the piece going without loss of time.[18]

Nothing came of this. Sullivan's orchestral and choral commissions doubtless pre-empted his time. Thus vanished the historical possibility that the long-term partnership might have been 'Gilbert, Sullivan, and German Reed' rather than 'Gilbert, Sullivan, and D'Oyly Carte'. To another management, that of John Hollingshead at the Gaiety Theatre, belongs the actual credit of first jointly commissioning the composer and librettist, as will be seen. It none the less remains true that the partnership of Gilbert and Sullivan was 'cradled among the Reeds', as a wit of the time put it. The Bible-quoting Britons of former days would not miss the allusion.

8 A Partnership and a Patron

NAMED after the Prince Consort, who had died ten years before, the Royal Albert Hall was declared open, or rather not declared open, by Queen Victoria on 29 March 1871. Beforehand, quantities of Rimmel's scent were wafted upwards via the ventilation system at 20-minute intervals. The National Anthem was played on the not-quite-completed Willis organ, the Prince of Wales as president of the hall read a welcoming address, the Bishop of London pronounced a prayer. The Queen's declaration was to follow. But, under an emotion apparently associated with memories of her late husband, she did not trust her voice and called the Prince to her side. It was he who announced, in front of a crowd of about 10,000, 'The Queen declares this hall now open'. Among other royal personages attending was the Queen's music-loving second son, Alfred, Duke of Edinburgh.

Henry Cole (1808–82), that energetic public servant who had been the prime mover in the planning of the Great Exhibition 20 years before, was prime mover also in the construction of the new hall. The 1851 Exhibition had yielded a public profit of over £200,000. From that, with a government grant added, the commissioners for the exhibition had bought the Kensington Gore Estate and had erected the South Kensington Museum (today the Victoria and Albert Museum) there. Cole's ambition had been to open a great permanent hall, suitable for musical and other purposes, in time for another major exhibition planned for 1861. But that exhibition – deferred till 1862 – had to be held without it, in its own temporary building (where the Natural History Museum now stands). Included in that exhibition was a large collection of Japanese prints, fans and other objects and a display of painted furniture and rich embroideries from William Morris's firm of Morris, Marshall and Faulkner. From here the line is direct to the Aesthetic Movement of the 1870s and 1880s – and to *Patience* and *The Mikado*.

In 1871 the Royal Albert Hall was at last in being, though with seating for only 6,000 instead of 30,000 as at one time envisaged. Arthur Sullivan was chosen to represent his country at the hall's first major musical occasion – on 1 May 1871, to mark the opening of yet another international exhibition in the adjacent area. (The plan had been for exhibitions at ten-yearly intervals after 1851.) Gounod, as a refugee from France, composed and conducted his cantata *Gallia*; Ferdinand Hiller (1811–85), a German composer much admired at the time, contributed a *Triumphal March*; Sullivan's composition was a cantata called *On Shore and Sea* (with words by the dramatist and future editor of *Punch*, Tom Taylor). The cantata had been commissioned by Cole, who had evidently been impressed with the young musician.

On Shore and Sea is styled a dramatic cantata – that is, it allots solos to specific characters. A sailor and his bride (curiously given the Italian appellations of Il Marinaio and La Sposina) are separated when he goes to fight for the Cross against the Crescent, and then are reunited. Rocking 'nautical' themes and a Moorish strain for the enemy both suggest the influence of Weber's *Oberon*. The sentiment of bellicose Christianity is hastily switched for a final invocation to international peace and domestic prosperity:

> Bless the land whose Prince is wise
> Peaceful progress to devise.

It was a serviceable piece for an inaugural occasion (Sullivan himself was the conductor) and was published with a dedication to Grove. Cole retained his regard for Sullivan. He consulted him when the Society of Arts considered the advisability of Britain's adopting the French low standard pitch instead of the higher one which was prevalent in British use.[1] Sullivan seems to have given it support in principle but it was Barnby in his oratorio concerts from 1869 – at St James's Hall, with the organ newly built to French pitch – who decisively promoted it.

A warm friendship grew between Cole's son Alan and the composer. A note to 'Dear Alan', inscribed 'Saturday night' and possibly sent by messenger, evidently dates from the time when Sullivan was engaged in *On Shore and Sea*. It shows that Sullivan had by now adopted the habit of late-night composition which he was to retain throughout his life.

I never go out night or day. Can you come and smoke a bacca any time tonight before 1? I am writing as usual and if you come after eleven, that is to say after the lamp is out, ring the bell *twice* loud and distinct. That's my signal, arranged with the concierge. Tom Taylor couldn't send you his words, because we have been altering them a good deal.

Sullivan and his mother had by now moved to 8, Albert Mansions, Victoria Street – a wide thoroughfare which had swept away nauseous slums and had been opened in 1851. At one end of the street was Westminster Abbey; at the other was Victoria Station (1862), from which the rapid regular transit by rail and steamer to France had such attraction for the composer.

To Paris, nearly four years after his previous visit, Sullivan returned in the aftermath of war, siege and revolution. On 26 January 1871 the government of the new French republic under Adolphe Thiers had capitulated to the Germans. That government's legislative assembly, now based in Versailles, had abandoned the administration of the capital. On 11 March a popular elected council, calling itself the Paris Commune, took control. The Versailles army retook Paris and did not shrink from ruthlessness against fellow-Frenchmen. After the Commune carried out its last official act on 21 May, seven days of hand-to-hand fighting ensued – the 'Bloody Week' in which 25,000 people died.[2]

A feeling for the France he loved led Sullivan to join the Relief Committee set up in London to assist 'the re-stocking of Paris' – work for which he subsequently received an official French medal.[3] With Grove and another friend from London he visited the stricken city. Sullivan's previous biographers have drawn a picture of their hero surrounded by violent upheaval. But in his letter home (5 June 1871) the reference to shells and cannon must have been ironic: they had ceased well before, though individual shots were no doubt fired as arrests by the new authorities continued. The opening phrase 'After a series of thrilling adventures, not unaccompanied by danger' was evidently something of a family joke: it recurs in a letter of 1874 (about an equally non-dangerous situation, this time in Cologne).

Ma chère Maman,
    After a series of thrilling adventures, not unaccompanied by danger, I just find time amidst the rattling of the shells and the thunder of the cannon to write and say that hitherto I am safe and unwounded. I found Grove [and] Willie Glehn just dressing and their surprise was only equalled by their delight. We had a small open carriage and drove all through the city to see the ruins – it is something too shocking to see the result of the uncontrolled devilish spite of these ruffians of the Commune. The people all wear a sad miserable look and this added to the wet [*illegible*] day and the absence, for the greater part, of the population makes a very dismal effect.
    Tomorrow we drive out to the western part – the Bois de Boulogne, Neuilly, Passy, Meudon, etc., and return to London by the night mail. We shall arrive on Wednesday morning and I should like breakfast at 8 o'clock. Tell Stockman to have *two* baths ready in my bedroom, to take before breakfast. Bacon, kidney, omelette, toast, tea and coffee . . .
God bless you, your –
A.S.S.

The signature A.S.S. was not to be retained for long: from October 1873 the composer retained only the 'Arthur', dropping the 'Seymour' or 'S.' from correspondence and publications. It was apparently Mrs Helmore, the wife of his late teacher, who had first pronounced a decisive preference for 'Arthur' alone.[4]

In May 1870, probably at Cole's instigation, Sullivan had given some lectures on vocal music at the South Kensington Museum. A draft (which Sullivan, considering himself a poor speaker, may well have read out word-for-word) survives at the Pierpont Morgan Library in New York. It shows Sullivan drawing on his wide range of experience and acquaintance.

. . . thus we see that each [female] voice has an average compass of about two octaves. We cannot accept this of course as arbitrary [= binding], as voices are so varying in their compass and quality. Some sopranos can go up to the F above the treble stave and some contraltos down to the C below it, but I am bound to declare honestly that I had rather they did it when I am not in the room.
    The great song of the Queen of Night in the *Flauto Magico*, 'Gli auguri dell'inferno' ['Der Hölle Rache'] was written for a singer with an exceptional voice (it goes up to F) and is now generally transposed a whole note [down] even by a singer like Mademoiselle [Christine] Nilsson.[5] Mademoiselle Ilma de Murska has sung it hitherto in the original key, and it is of course a question of individual taste whether the effect is pleasant or not. But she told me on Friday night that as the pitch is so high in England, she means in future to sing it a note lower.

Even if singers possess these high notes they should use them very sparingly as the effect they are intended to produce is soon weakened by frequent employment, and palls upon the ear. Besides it is not artistic, it is too *tricky*. If a painter has a great gift of representing a mist, or a brilliant sunset, it would be ridiculous to introduce it into every picture he painted. And yet that is not more absurd than what many of our friends both artists and amateurs do: some singers are never happy unless they can introduce a high note into every piece of music they sing, whatever may be its character, and if they find a high note already placed there by the composer, how they revel in it! . . . They don't care how they murder the composition, or utterly destroy the intention of the poor composer – always the last person thought of in such cases.

Among other plans cherished by Cole for the South Kensington area was one for a new school of music – a project which would soon make more pressing demands on Sullivan's time. Meanwhile in March 1871 he was moved to draft a memorandum on 'continuing the culture of music in schools'. By 'the culture of music' Sullivan meant only sight-singing which, it was feared, would not be eligible for financial support under Forster's Education Act of 1870, because it might be considered not amenable to standardization and inspection. The act itself was perhaps the century's most important legislation on the subject, instituting local government expenditure on education for the first time, via 'School Boards'. It is somewhat curious that such a matter should occupy Sullivan when, at 28, he was so evidently concerned with his own advancement and not with issues of public policy. Although the document survives, and was presumably intended for print, no publication is known, and the concern seems to have been ill-grounded.

Theatrical, but not operatic, work beckoned from Manchester. Evidently remembering his production of *The Tempest* with Sullivan's pre-existent music in 1864, Charles Calvert enlisted him expressly for *The Merchant of Venice*. In that production (19 September 1871) Calvert reshuffled the scenes of the play, making 'Venice the scene of the whole of the first, second and fourth acts, and Belmont the locality of the third and fifth'.

The masque at the end of Act I, which diverts attention from Jessica's escape out of her father's house, was 'enlivened by some very sparkling and characteristic music by Mr Sullivan, who was warmly received on his appearance in the orchestra'.

The report is from a Manchester correspondent for *The Orchestra*, 22 September 1871. The music comprised seven instrumental numbers and one vocal (a 'serenata' with Italian words, 'Nel ciel seren') which were duly brought to the Crystal Palace in the following month (28 October), with Mme Conneau as vocal soloist.

The dedication of the published score was to a Manchester friend of the composer's, J. H. Agnew, with whom the composer then headed to Scotland to experience the pleasures of the grouse season – pleasures duly reported to 'Dearest Mum':

Fancy me getting up at *six* this morning, going into the stables and getting a game-keeper to pour buckets of water over me (there are no baths in this little inn) then breakfast, cigarette, etc., and starting at eight for the moors in a wagonette to begin to shoot at a quarter to nine! That's what happened today and I've got to do two days more. We have been shooting eight hours, or rather walking up and down these awful endless hills they call moors, and never a bird of any sort could we get near. The rain and wind kept them off.

I was drenched through without by the rain, and soaked inwardly by whisky. I never thought I could have drunk so much raw spirit and it had about as much effect as cold water. In the meantime, here I am, after a warm water tub and a complete change, sitting before the fire within ten minutes of post time.

The shooting here belongs to a friend of Agnew's, Roger Green by name, and as there is no house, we live in this little inn and are very comfortable. The party consists of Green, Agnew, another and myself, and all my expenses including railway are paid! So I am fortunate. My love to Jack [Fred] and Charlotte. God bless you.

Before the end of the year (1871) occurred the first theatrical production of the Gilbert and Sullivan partnership. It was to be the most celebrated partnership in the British theatre, lasting 25 years until *The Grand Duke* took the stage in 1896. By that time, 'Gilbert and Sullivan Opera' had long been recognized not merely as a series but as a type. Gilbert himself was later to stress the freshness, distinction, and propriety of the type:

Sullivan and I . . . resolved that our plots, however ridiculous, should be coherent; that our dialogue should be void of offence; that, on artistic principles, no man should play a woman's part and no woman a man's. Finally, we agreed that no lady of the company should be required to wear a dress that she could not wear with absolute propriety at a private fancy-dress ball.

Gilbert's recollection (he was looking back on the occasion of his 70th birthday celebrations in 1906) was reasonably accurate as a description of the highly 'proper', not to say prudish, form of operetta established in the D'Oyly Carte years. But it was not at all true of the partners' first collaboration – written for the Gaiety Theatre, a home of broadly humorous entertainment where the *ad lib* gag was as prominent as the female leg.[6] John Hollingshead, who spoke of keeping alight 'the sacred lamp of burlesque', had been its manager since it opened in 1868. Females in juvenile male roles (the 'principal boy' tradition later surviving in English pantomime) were favoured, and Nelly Farren was as much a celebrity in such 'breeches parts' as was J. L. Toole in the 'low comedian' roles. Toole was a great 'draw': at a time when a theatrical chorus-singer could expect only a pound or two in weekly salary, Hollingshead paid him £100 a week in 1873.[7]

The Gaiety was a large and very well equipped theatre, seating upwards of 2,000 (the Savoy was to seat fewer than 1,300) with a restaurant attached. The opening bill had included 'a new operatic extravaganza' by Gilbert (the terms 'burlesque' and 'extravaganza' were practically synonymous). Based on the plot of Meyerbeer's *Robert le Diable*, it was entitled *Robert the Devil, or The Nun, the Dun and the Son of a Gun*. In the first-night audience was Sullivan. Probably through a Garrick Club connection, he was on terms of warm friendship with Hollingshead and at Christmas 1870 presented him with an autographed copy of his Tennyson song-cycle *The Window*.

On 26 December 1871, preceded by H.J. Byron's three-act play, *Dearer than Life*, Gilbert and Sullivan's Christmastide entertainment opened at the Gaiety as *Thespis, or The Gods Grown Old*.[8] With an opening 'Chorus of Stars' and with lines of dialogue like 'Why, who's this? Jupiter, by Jove!', *Thespis* must have reminded audiences then, as it would now, of Offenbach's *Orpheus in the Underworld*. Indeed the press more than once referred to it as an 'English *opéra bouffe*'. It was in two acts, with an overture and (apparently) 15 musical numbers including a stretch of recitative to 'mysterious music', plus a ballet – for which Sullivan may have raided his *L'Ile enchantée*. The action of the play supposed the functions of the Olympian gods to be temporarily carried out by members of a theatrical troupe, with unlooked-for results, of course. Characters with such pseudo-Greek names as 'Nicemis' and 'Stupidas' bore witness to the current love of punning: 'Sparkeion' was a 'sparky one', a spritely and flirtatious young man. There was a topical slant in the replacement of Bacchus by an ex-drunkard, who wore a large medal round his neck to signify his conversion to fanatical teetotalism.

To Nelly Farren ('Miss Ellen Farren', as she was formally named on the programme) was given the *travesti* role of Mercury; Toole's role was that of Thespis, 'manager of a travelling theatrical company'. Sparkeion, another *travesti* role, went to a 'Mademoiselle Clary', who had arrived in London with a Belgian company a few months before. The small part of Apollo was played by Fred Sullivan, and Arthur Sullivan himself conducted, with Gilbert as 'stage manager' (the equivalent term, in those days, for what is now called 'director' in theatrical usage). A short ballet formed part of the entertainment.

The score of *Thespis* is lost. It is therefore tempting to pass quickly over a work which was hissed on its opening night, never published in musical form, and never revived. Yet it was never disowned by its creators. In the last year of his life, Gilbert judged it worth including in a volume of his *Original Plays* (unfortunately with mistakes from the 1871 theatrical libretto uncorrected). In the printing of vocal scores of later operettas, from *The Mikado* onwards, the title *Thespis* is included in the list of Gilbert and Sullivan's previous collaborations. In its original run it survived until 8 March 1872 and was then brought back as a 'benefit' performance (matinée of 27 April) for Mademoiselle Clary. As Terence Rees points out, it cannot have been ranked a failure if it was chosen (by the beneficiary, as always) for a performance expressly designed to raise money.

The first-night audience's hostile reception may have been provoked by hasty preparation and poor performance. If Gilbert's memory of 1902 can be relied on, *Thespis* 'was invented, written, composed, rehearsed and produced within five weeks'. But one might wish to hear the song with which Toole, in the traditional phrase, 'brought down the house', supported by 'a screaming, whistling and shouting chorus', as the *Era* (the theatrical newspaper of the period) reported.

> I once knew a chap who discharged a function
> On the North South East West Diddlesex junction,
> He was conspicu*ous* exceeding,

For his affable ways and his easy breeding.
Although a Chairman of Directors,
He was hand in glove with the ticket inspectors.
He tipped the guards with brand-new fivers,
And sang little songs to the engine drivers.

Moreover, as the *Pall Mall Gazette* told its readers, 'the orchestration is very novel, including, as it does, the employment of a railway bell, a railway whistle, and some new instrument of music imitating the agreeable sound of a train in motion' – a piece of sandpaper rubbed on wood, perhaps.

During the second act a quartet of simultaneous perplexity looked forward in words, and perhaps in music, to the matrimonial tangles of 'Here is a case unprecedented' in *The Gondoliers*. Its models were perhaps the ensembles of a similar nature in Auber's *Fra Diavolo* (1831) or Flotow's *Martha* (1847).

By this golden wedding ring,
I'm his $\left.\right\}$ wife and $\left\{\right.$ you're $\left.\right\}$ a 'thing'.
She's my $\left.\right\}$ I'm $\left.\right\}$
Please will someone kindly tell us
Who are our respective kin?

All of $\left\{\begin{array}{l} \text{us} \\ \text{them} \end{array}\right\}$ are very jealous

Neither of $\left\{\begin{array}{l} \text{us} \\ \text{them} \end{array}\right\}$ will give in.

Detective work in 1990 (see p. 418) was to trace the ballet music of *Thespis*, but only two vocal numbers transparently survive. The ingeniously inventive chorus 'Climbing over rocky mountain' was transferred to *The Pirates of Penzance* (see p. 136). It incorporates the characteristic device already discussed – the simultaneous combination of two tunes previously presented as if quite independent. The other survival is Sparkeion's song 'Little Maid of Arcadee', published afterwards as a self-contained ballad with altered words. As music it is as trivial as Sullivan ever wrote, but the changes enforced on the words point the contrast between the Gaiety Theatre's suggestiveness and the prudery expected in the drawing-room. In the theatre the little maid had 'sat on cousin Robin's knee', but in the ballad she sat *by* his knee; and before jilting her, Robin did not 'weary of his lover's play' but now became 'fickle as the month of May'.

But why was *Thespis* never revived when its creators had become successful under D'Oyly Carte's management? Carte did show some interest in a revival in 1875 (immediately after *Trial by Jury*) but grew cool, provoking Gilbert's comment: 'It's astonishing how quickly these capitalists dry up under the magic influence of the words "cash down".'

Carte's coolness, however, was commonsense. *Thespis* was Gaiety entertainment, and slightly *risqué* at that. Carte would attract his audience by following the 'respectable' path of the German Reeds, not that of Hollingshead with his brazen girls in tights and short skirts. Hollingshead later described Gilbert and Sullivan's subsequent entertainments as 'burlesque in long clothes'.

The year of Sullivan's first collaboration with Gilbert was also that of his most famous hymn. His was not the first setting of *Onward, Christian Soldiers*:[9] the Rev Sabine Baring-Gould's words had appeared in 1868, in an appendix to *Hymns Ancient and Modern* to a tune adapted by J. B. Dykes from the slow movement of Haydn's Symphony no. 53. In the same section of the appendix, devoted to 'processional' hymns, appeared *Brightly gleams our banner* by Henry Smart (1813–79), Sir George Smart's nephew. It is this hymn that may be taken as the model for Sullivan's *Onward, Christian Soldiers*: it even has (at the start of the refrain) the identical four-note repetition with which Sullivan's hymn begins. When he comes to the refrain, Sullivan takes the four-note repetition down from its original pitch (the dominant) to the lower keynote, so that the tune can rise dramatically to the upper keynote just before the end. Moreover, at the half-way point Sullivan provides the sudden exhilaration of an *oom-pah* or 'marching' bass (of an instrumental rather than a hymn type).

Such differences precisely demonstrate Sullivan's superiority as a melodist – and as something more. Written as a contribution to *The Hymnary* (a new collection brought out by Novello's under Barnby's editorship), Sullivan's hymn first appeared as an appetizer for that collection in the *Musical Times* of December 1871. Its success was immediate and lasting. That the tune should remain popular, even into a secular age which equipped it with the nonsense-text of 'Lloyd George knew my father', should cause no surprise. The taste which it served may be deprecated (see p. 426), but within that taste it is a subtle and truly original composition.

In an age which made a best-seller out of *Hymns Ancient and Modern* (it first appeared in 1861 and was to sell a million copies a year for over a century), the writing of hymn-tunes was not unprofitable. A composer retained his copyright and would charge a fee for reprinting in each successive collection. The hymns of Henry John Gauntlett (1805–76), composer of *Once in Royal David's city*, are said to run into thousands. Sullivan's interest in hymn-composition had been stirred a few years previously by his friendship with an enthusiast, the Rev Robert Brown, who changed his surname to Brown-Borthwick on his marriage in 1868.[10] (Sullivan was his groomsman at Westminster Abbey, promising to appear in 'a blue coat of superior texture, which together with an unaccompanied anthem in four parts will contribute, I hope, to the festivity of the occasion'.) Himself an amateur composer, Brown-Borthwick was the compiler of *A Supplemental Hymn and Tune Book* (1868).

For this collection Sullivan wrote *The Son of God goes forth to War* and also the remarkable setting of *The Strain Upraise*, combining metrical singing with chant and repeated alleluias. During the 1870s he wrote at least 45 hymns (none of them approaching *Onward, Christian Soldiers* in popularity)[11] and even acted as musical editor for a collection of *Church Hymns with Tunes* published in 1874 by the Society for the Promotion of Christian Knowledge. His comment to Brown-Borthwick on this task was: 'Had I known the wearisome labours of it, I would not have undertaken it for a *thousand pounds*.' And to his mother: 'I hope that the hymn-book will be a blessing to the Church. It's a curse to me.' Later fame made such drudgery unnecessary.

To the tune of *Onward, Christian Soldiers* Sullivan gave the name 'St Gertrude', Gertrude being the wife of his friend Ernest Clay Ker Seymer, with whom he often stayed.[12] Like Brown-Borthwick, Ernest (elder brother of the composer Frederic Clay) had added his wife's surname to his own on marriage. As hers was already 'double-barrelled', his became Clay Ker Seymer. Sullivan often stayed at Ernest and Gertrude's home, a mansion called Hanford, near Blandford in Dorset. Another friend was the Hon. Seymour ('Sym') Egerton (1839–98), a keen amateur musician who was shortly to succeed to the title of Earl of Wilton and the ownership of about 9,000 acres. When a trial of the Albert Hall's musical qualities was needed, shortly before its opening, the amateur society which Egerton conducted supplied the programme, while the workmen and their relatives supplied part of the audience. The Society's name was *The Wandering Minstrels* – a pleasing pre-*Mikado* fancy.

The young Sullivan's social graces eased him into ready friendship with the rich and titled, particularly those who were keen, practising musical amateurs. Most remarkably, he won the patronage of Alfred, Duke of Edinburgh. In the Royal Albert Hall Orchestral Society (later renamed the Royal Amateur Orchestral Society) Sullivan was conductor and the Duke the violinist-leader as well as president. The Duke showed his admiration by going to see *Thespis* as well as many works of Sullivan's later celebrity. By career a naval officer, rising to be Commander-in-Chief in the Mediterranean, the Duke (known in royal circles as Affie) had the ill-luck to be a 'spare' member of Victoria's brood on whom dynastic and diplomatic pressure could be exerted.

Born in 1844, he was elected King of Greece in 1862 but had been compelled (not by Victoria's personal wish, but by the British government) to decline: twelve years later, to strengthen that linkage of European royalty of which Queen Victoria was the apex, he was married in St Petersburg to the Grand Duchess Marie Alexandrovna – daughter of Britain's late enemy in the Crimean War, Tsar Alexander II. Finally, on the death of an uncle and in fulfilment of a treaty drawn up more than 30 years before, Alfred succeeded in 1893 to the German dukedom of Saxe-Coburg-Gotha, subject to the all-powerful German Empire – and in so doing lost his English title, home, and succession. His death occurred a few months before Sullivan's own.

Brusque in his public manner, the Duke was no extrovert and popular figure as the Prince of Wales was: 'London society counts on all princes as being charming: this appreciation is part of its religion. The type of perfect charmer is the Prince of Wales. The Duke of Edinburgh is far from approaching that.' As for the Duchess, she was under suspicion merely for being Russian. Moreover 'her face rarely lights up with a smile. She is not, and never will be, a popular personage.' So an anonymous French account of London society (*La société de Londres par un diplomate étranger*) declared. But in Sullivan the Duke evidently found a congenial spirit, often receiving him at Clarence House in London and making him a house-guest in his newly built residence at Eastwell Park, near Ashford, Kent. On such occasions Sullivan travelled with his own manservant. 'Dearest Mum' received a letter dated 27 November 1874:

I am very glad I came by the 4.45 instead of the 4.50, as, when I arrived, one of the royal footmen was on the platform to meet me. A large waggonette drove me, my suite, and luggage over here in about 20 minutes – awfully cold but a bright fine night. I was shown into the library by the Duke and Duchess, Lady Emma Osborne, and Clerk but I was very cold, so the Duke immediately plied me with a sherry and bitters. Then he brought me up to my room, which is exceedingly comfortable, and has just left me. Now I scribble these few lines whilst Jack puts out my things for me. The dressing-bell has already sounded so I must conclude or else I shall be late. God bless you,

A.

'My suite' as a humorous expression for a single attendant is a joke which Sullivan was to repeat in another letter a month later – and which Gilbert was to repeat in *The Gondoliers*. On such visits, the Duchess would play piano duets with Sullivan. The Duke's own pleasure was to have Sullivan as pianist to his violin, for which purpose he would call informally at Sullivan's London home. Such exceptional royal favour to a musician was known to the public and fed the gossip columns. But what remains unknown is how the very first steps towards friendship were taken – between a formal introduction in 1863 and the intimacy of the 1870s. Sullivan himself was both too discreet, and too loyal, to tell, and the eventual publication of a biography (1984) of this curious royal figure failed to fill the gap.[13]

9 Broadening

To neither Sullivan nor Gilbert did *Thespis* bring the revelation of a change of destiny. Neither perceived that the partnership was to revolutionize their artistic lives – and their incomes. It was to be over three years before they rejoined forces, not on their own initiative but on that of Richard D'Oyly Carte. Gilbert meanwhile commonly brought out three or four plays a year – including, at the Criterion Theatre in 1874, a one-acter (with a few interpolated songs) called *Topsyturvydom*, set in an imaginary kingdom and exhibiting the ideas of paradox and role-reversal which were later so familiar.

Quop. Tomorrow our monarch attains his majority. Born at the age of 80, he is now 59, and the event is to be celebrated with the usual tokens of rejoicing. Is all prepared to do honour to this auspicious occasion?
Crambo. Everything – the streets are to be draped in black – medicines are to be distributed gratuitously to the poor – tenpence in the pound will be put upon the income tax, and all the operating theatres of the hospitals will be thrown open to the public.

Arthur Sullivan had 'an appalling amount of work'. The phrase is his, in a letter to Kate Helmore, the daughter of his former teacher, in September 1872. The name of 'Mr Arthur S. Sullivan' appears as teacher of 'pianoforte and ballad-singing' in the 'Ladies' Division' of the School of Art, Science and Literature organized at the Crystal Palace[1] – but by the end of October 1873 no more pupils were to be accepted, 'on account of Mr Sullivan's professional engagements'.

Making the most of his royal connections, he obtained Queen Victoria's permission to include Prince Albert's only two hymn-settings in his own *Church Hymns with Tunes* and dedicated his next oratorio, *The Light of the World*, to the Duke of Edinburgh's Russian bride. He composed a gigantic *Te Deum* for the day designated (1 May 1872) as a national occasion of thanksgiving for the recovery of the Prince of Wales from typhoid, and was allowed to dedicate the work to Victoria herself. 'I am to say,' wrote Sir Thomas Biddulph from Windsor on her behalf, 'that H.M. rarely accords this privilege to anyone, and is only induced to do so on the occasion in question, in consequence of the particular circumstance of the case, and the performance taking place under the immediate patronage of the Royal Family.'

The first performance, not at the thanksgiving service in St Paul's but at the Crystal Palace, employed more than 2,000 performers and (as was reported in the journal *The Orchestra*,[2] at that time weekly) drew an audience of 26,000 people. The composer and his publishers made sure that this *Festival Te Deum* might later serve for non-royal occasions: the printed score carefully gives, as an alternative to 'O Lord Save the Queen', a repetition of some words from the *Te Deum* proper. The grandiose use of a military band in addition to full orchestra and organ indicates a debt to Jullien's 'monster' concerts in Sullivan's youth – and not, as might be supposed, to Berlioz's *Grande Messe des Morts* or Verdi's *Requiem*, with their extra brass remote from the main body of performers. Berlioz's work did not reach Britain until 1883 and Verdi's was as yet unwritten.

At the Crystal Palace Sullivan was 'uproariously cheered' when taking his bow after Manns had conducted the *Festival Te Deum*. Tietjens sang the soprano solo (and also led the singing of *God Bless the Prince of Wales* at the end of the concert). Sullivan's skilful counterpoint pleased the reviewer in the *Orchestra*, who noted the introduction not only of the hymn-tune *St Anne* but of a Gregorian psalm-tone (when the chorus sings of 'the glorious company of the Apostles'). The reviewer, probably Davison, also approved of the structural recurrence of the opening music, in the final number. Curiously, however, he did not pick out what would most strike any modern listener: the jaunty and even humorous effect when the band strikes up its quick march – with irregular phrase-lengths – across which the words and music of the familiar hymn-tune are then thrown, almost in Sullivan's operetta manner.

A work which seemed further to point Sullivan along the road of oratorio was *The Light of the World*, produced under the composer's baton on 27 August 1873 at the Birmingham Festival (which was still under Costa's direction). Its words, directly from the Bible without additions, were selected by the composer himself. The Duke of Edinburgh travelled to hear the performance; the principal soloists – Tietjens, Trebelli, Sims Reeves, Santley – added to the brilliance of the occasion. It was widely heard in British cities in the ensuing years.

In February 1872 Sullivan had been a principal mourner at the funeral of Henry Chorley, the critic who had given such encouragement to him in youth and had become – like Davison – an elder friend. Henceforth the critic who watched over Sullivan's mature career was Joseph Bennett (1831–1911).[3] He was friend, counsellor, and supplier of verses for musical setting, as Chorley had been. From 1876 Bennett plied his trade on the *Daily Telegraph*, London's first 'popular' daily paper; its circulation of 24,000, the largest in the world, far outstripped that of *The Times*. In reviewing Sullivan's compositions Bennett still paraded a professional detachment, and Sullivan was careful that any priming on his part should not overstep propriety. *The Merry Wives of Windsor* was about to be presented at John Hollingshead's Gaiety Theatre with the veteran Shakespearean actor Samuel Phelps as Falstaff – a rare revival of the play, for which the friendly Hollingshead had commissioned music from Sullivan. Two days before the opening, the composer wrote on 17 December 1874 to 'My dear Jo', with a jocular confusion between his own music and that of a more eminent composer.

I was rather dismayed when I first got the commission to do *The Merry Wives* for I could see no opportunity for music. However in the last act I have been able to do a little, and it will I hope be bright. . . . I wouldn't write an overture, because I did not care about competing with the very pretty one of Nicolai.

Your masterly judgement, my dear Joseph, will at once enable you to see that as the fairies are not *real* fairies (if such exist) but only flesh and blood imitations, I have endeavoured to indicate this, and have not written music of the same character as I wrote for *The Midsummer Night's Dream*, or that Mendelssohn wrote for the third act of *The Tempest*. I have only had three weeks to do the whole thing in . . . All the music is new, but (and this is not necessarily for publication) if you remember a ballet called *L'Ile enchantée* which I wrote for the Italian Opera, Covent Garden, many years ago, you will recognize two of the themes . . .

The song-setting of the last act is not Shakespearean. Hollingshead had secured from Swinburne's pen a lyric for Anne Page, beginning 'Love laid his sleepless head'. Sullivan was obliged, as he told Bennett, to make it 'very simple and easy' for the actress playing the part, and feared it might turn out commonplace. Published separately, it survives as the only setting by Sullivan of Algernon Charles Swinburne (1837–1909), whose 'aesthetic' art is supposed to have been one of the inspirations for *Patience*. There is no actual record of a meeting between Sullivan and the poet, though a letter from Swinburne to his sister announces his intention of being present at the opening of that production of *The Merry Wives*.[4]

All of his widening acquaintance, not excluding the Duke of Edinburgh, were thrown into his mother's informal company when they called. Many cordial messages to her were included in letters to Sullivan from his friends. Mary Clementina (she passed her 60th birthday in 1871) was never abashed by rank or authority, nor ever backward in giving advice. She was gently mocked in a letter from Sullivan's friend Frederic Clay – who had not yet left his post in the Treasury and wrote a letter to her on official notepaper, marked 'confidential'. Noting that he had secured a messenger's job for some youth of her acquaintance, he went on:

I am desired to add that vacancies may shortly be expected in the episcopal and the judicial branches and it is the hope of the Prime Minister that you will have no hesitation in making known to him your views with regard to the promotion of any particular person or persons to the rank of judge or bishop.

On one occasion when she was away from home, her son wrote that he had just come back

from Wimbledon – the Goldschmidts' ball. . . . You seem to be having *larx* up at Hendon.[5] Be very careful with the ice. I know how reckless you are and am in a constant state of fidget. Don't come home tomorrow as I have a succession of lady visitors all the afternoon beginning with Miss Romanes and must go down to Byng's at 6. We have a midnight service and choral Communion tomorrow and a supper to the choir previously.

The jocular misspelling for *larks* in the manner of Edward Lear shows Sullivan's fondness for word-play – an unusual facility for a musician, of obvious relevance to his aptitude in setting comic verse. 'To Byng's' indicated a visit to the perpetual curate of St Peter's, Cranley Gardens: he was the Hon. and Rev. Francis Byng, later to become Lord Strafford. Sullivan maintained his organist's post at the church until 1872. 'Miss Romanes' (see also p. 64) may have been a sister of the eminent scientist and philosopher, George John Romanes (1848–94).

More often, however, it was Sullivan who was away from home, fulfilling an ever-wider list of engagements and cultivating more and more aristocratic acquaintances. Twice in 1872 – for a house party and then when he conducted the *Festival Te Deum* at the Norwich Festival in September – he stayed with Lord and Lady Stafford at the magnificent Cossey (or Costessey) Hall, near Norwich. Lord Stafford (not to be confused with Lord Strafford) was 'president' of the festival – a post which, in those days, carried the sole right to command encores. He came from an old Roman Catholic family. On the second of these occasions Sullivan reported to his mother the altar-light burning in the chapel and the party scene which had greeted him: 'They were dancing when I arrived and a priest was playing a choice selection of waltzes.'

She seems to have relished the multiple demands imposed on her as housekeeper, hostess, and secretary to her unmarried son. About to return home with a guest, he wrote on 5 April 1874:

We shan't want dinner on Tuesday, only supper, as we leave Stafford at 5- something and get into Town about half-past-eight, I think. I will send Jack [manservant] by an earlier train. You will of course smarten yourself up for the occasion. The rats and mice must be looked to, for they keep me awake at nights and annoy me dreadfully.

On another occasion she was instructed to 'send into Strand for two or three bottles of *dry champagne* – good'. On 12 August 1874 Sullivan sounded almost a scolding note: 'Try and answer every letter you can *finally*, so I shan't have to waste days in writing when I return. I always dread that heap whenever I come home.'

In April 1874 he was one of a house-party at Ingestre, near Stafford, the country seat of the Earl of Shrewsbury, president of the Birmingham Festival. There were donkey races, at which Sullivan's servant Jack distinguished himself, and

tonight [14 April] there is a great servants' ball. Every servant invites a friend, and some of the tradespeople and others also come, and as we of the house-party are twenty-four in number (without our servants of course) there will be a great gathering. We stay till about twelve or so, then retire, and the servants keep it up until it is time for the housemaids to go and change their dresses for the morning!

From Ingestre, Sullivan had written home asking his mother to send him some of his store of music paper – 'Eighteen staves or any more but not less . . . barred if there is any – please send it *by return* as I must do the *Notturno* for the Brit. Orch. Soc.'[6] The piece so identified may be the *Prelude – Moonlight* from *The Merry Wives of Windsor*, needing for concert performance a fuller orchestra than it had in the theatre; otherwise it must be an independent piece commissioned but never completed. The British Orchestral Society was nearing the end of its life (1862–74): under the conductorship of George Mount, it engaged only British orchestral musicians and only British soloists, though its programmes were cosmopolitan.

A house-party in January 1873 had found him the palatial home of Baron Meyer Rothschild in Buckinghamshire.[7] Mentmore was 'Solomon's temple adapted to the nineteenth century,'[8] as Sullivan wittily described it to his mother, 'all blazing with gold, and beautiful tapestries, porcelain and other magnificent things . . . Miss Hannah, Lord Rosebery and I are just going for a walk.'

A fairly large footnote to British history may be said to be encapsulated in that comment. Meyer Rothschild (1818–74) was a younger brother of Lionel Rothschild (1808–79), whose election to Parliament in 1847 had been chiefly responsible for the removal of Jewish disabilities in England. Meyer's home was renowned for its hospitality as well as for its collection of works of art; his daughter Hannah was to marry Lord Rosebery, the future prime minister, in 1878. Jewish acquisition of landed wealth and a position in society was new and in some influential quarters resented: Mr Wharton in Trollope's *The Prime Minister* (1876) observed with particular distaste that 'peers' daughters were bestowing themselves on Jews and shopkeepers'. The Prince of Wales frequented the society of the Rothschilds, who were suspected of paying his debts. Sullivan himself was soon to develop a friendship with Lionel's sons, Alfred and Leopold Rothschild.

Meanwhile, he struck up a happy intimacy with a Scottish baronet, Sir Coutts Lindsay, and his wife, Lady (Caroline Blanche Elizabeth) Lindsay,[9] repeatedly enjoying their hospitality at Balcarres, Colinsburgh, Fife – despite the time taken to get there by changes of train. Exceptionally on one occasion, he complained that it had taken 7½ hours for the sixty miles from Glasgow, with an hour's wait at each of four junctions and a seven-mile cab drive through the rain at the end. Lady Lindsay, whose mother was born a Rothschild, was a little younger than Sullivan. Her husband, considerably older (1824–1913), had been a Grenadier Guards officer when a young man, but later devoted his energies to the arts. In 1877 he was to become the founder-proprietor of the Grosvenor Gallery in New Bond Street, with its stone façade in Italian renaissance style. The declared aim of the gallery was 'to afford to pictures and sculptures the advantage they receive in private homes for the background of harmoniously patterned walls and appropriate furniture'. It was there that Rossetti and other pre-Raphaelites exhibited, providing the butt of Gilbert's 'Grosvenor Gallery, greenery-yallery' joke in *Patience*.

Between 21 July and 23 August 1874 Sullivan travelled, partly as the Lindsays' guest, on the first of those prolonged continental journeys which were to become a regular pleasure, savoured every year or two (and, later, even more frequently). They were different from his quick business trips to Paris and often included a period of treatment at a spa (usually in Germany) for the kidney trouble which began to affect him in 1872.[10] Such journeys might encompass a professional object, but their essential motive was a delight in the Continental scene at a time when the well-to-do British traveller commanded the most respectful attention. Hotels greeted him in English, the pound was master, the London newspapers arrived by fast train to be read the following day.

Switzerland and Italy beckoned: in 1871 the opening of the Mont Cenis rail tunnel through the Alps brought Turin within 33 hours' journey from London. The French Riviera was being virtually created by the British as a winter resort. This time Sullivan's destination was the German duchy of Coburg, and then Dresden where the Lindsays awaited him.

As befitting a gentleman of his position, Sullivan took his manservant with him when he caught the paddle-steamer from Dover to Calais and then started the continental rail journey. At Brussels a change to another train was necessary. Here Jack 'ran off for a minute' (the account is in Sullivan's letter to his mother) 'and . . . judge my feelings when I felt the train move off without him!' Furious at first, Sullivan descended at the next station, Schaerebeek, but could not take his three big luggage trunks off the train with him, as they were registered to Cologne.

I found a very pleasant and obliging telegraph clerk, and I immediately telegraphed back to the station-master to keep Jack until I returned. He sent word back 'Il vous attend' and after kicking my heels about that beastly little station (like Herne Hill [a South London suburban station]) for two mortal hours, I returned to Brussels and found Jack, the station-master and an interpreter! They seemed to have got on capitally together. Jack had filled up the time by having a very good meal and I have no doubt treated his foreign friends. I couldn't be angry, for the scene was so ludicrous.

At Coburg, as he reminded his mother in another letter, Prince Albert had been born and Queen Victoria had stayed. The reigning Duke Ernst II (no doubt on the initiative of the Duke of Edinburgh, his nephew and heir-presumptive), received and honoured him.

This morning, breakfast at 9, lunch at 1. Grand Court reception (full dress) at 3 and dinner at 6 will fill out the rest of the day. Between you and me I expect I shall be bored to death – but fortunately I have got a lot of words here and shall write some songs.

Just over a week later he received (sent via a privy councillor) the grand-ducal order of knighthood, 'so I swagger about with a ribbon and star'.

Also at Coburg, and also honoured by a grand-ducal award, was the Swedish operatic soprano Christine Nilsson, well known to Sullivan from London. Two years before at Westminster Abbey, she had married Auguste Rouzeaud of Paris. The pair now took Sullivan as their companion on an excursion over the border to Franzensbad in Bohemia, within the Austrian Empire (now Frantiskovy Lazne, Czechoslovakia). There the Rouzeauds were awaited by an American friend, Mrs Grant. She was living in or near Paris (her husband having remained in New York, apparently) and was 'a perfect specimen of a high-bred, charming American lady – a style of woman I thoroughly enjoy and appreciate'. Mrs David Beach Grant was to become one of Sullivan's closest friends, always on terms of propriety.

In a letter home dated 8 August, Sullivan declared the spa town of Franzens-bad to be

quiet, pretty, and unexciting – everyone living more or less out of doors, taking their meals and listening to the music under the shade of the trees, which are all over the place. It is rather a relief, after the life we have been leading, to be free and unfettered and not have to dress in different costumes three or four times a day . . . There is a church just opposite here, and a priest's house next door – it is a handsome villa and looks beautifully furnished. The priest is a venerable-looking old man and I suppose he has private means of his own, or else he couldn't afford such a luxurious home. *I* believe he is a gay old dog. But that's between ourselves.

At length he arrived, with the Rouzeauds and Mrs Grant in tow, at Dresden where he was to be the guest of the Lindsays – who 'are really kind beyond belief. We got on splendidly, having the same tastes and habits.' There were former teachers of his to be revisited in Dresden – and in Leipzig, to which he went for a day-trip, rising to catch a 5.45 a.m. train in order to make the two-hour journey. There were regretful farewells to the Rouzeauds and Mrs Grant, who were going together to Paris. The Lindsays decided to extend their stay in Dresden, and that of Sullivan as their guest, and it was not until 20 August that he wrote announcing his intention to be back in London three days later. 'Jack' was instructed to wash Orpheus, Arthur Sullivan's dog, in time for his master's return.

Would the Coburg knighthood be followed by a similar recognition in his own country? Already, nine years before he *did* receive it, the rumour was raised. 'Dearest Mum', he wrote on 25 February 1874 from Manchester, where he was to conduct *The Light of the World* next day,

if you are bothered again by newspaper reporters, just say that so far as I am concerned, I know nothing about the proposed knighthood beyond what I have seen in the newspapers. I don't see why I should be 'interviewed' on everything that may be said about me. There is of course no foundation for such a thing and [it] only grows out of the good-natured fancy of the *Hornet*.

'Interview' as a verb was in quotation marks as a foreign, i.e. American, usage. Once back from Germany, he was soon on his way to the Lindsays at Balcarres. So was Mrs Grant. She had been in London and he at Liverpool, where *The Light of the World* was due to be performed on 29 September – unhappily shortened, as the *Orchestra* would declare.[11] After a rehearsal there, he made a railway rendezvous:

joined the Limited Mail [train from London] at Wigan . . . Neither Mrs Grant nor I could sleep so we talked all the way to Edinburgh, where we got some breakfast at an hotel, and then started again on our perilous journey. On arrival at Kilconquhar Station we found Sir Coutts and my Lady and the Rouzeauds waiting for us, and we at once felt ourselves at Dresden again. . . . The place is beautiful and we can see the sea spread out before us. We walk and potter about, the usual country house life, but I am hard at work in my room today as I only lark about after lunch and work every morning . . . The post doesn't come in today until one o'clock as it is ungodly in Scotland to read letters before you have been to church.

(At least, today's reader may reflect, there *was* in that church-going age a Sunday delivery as well as collection of mail.)

A letter *from* his mother about a troublesome (and probably young) friend drew a characteristic reply: 'If Agnes gives you so much trouble, why don't you give her a painless death – slow poison or a couple of hours of my music? The latter perhaps would carry her off soonest . . .'; and later, 'Give my love to Fred and Charlotte, also to Agnes if she has survived the slow poison'. This is presumably the girl to whom he referred in a delicious parody of Victorian moralizing: 'Give my love to Agnes King. I hope she is a good girl and always bears in mind the solemn warning that every moment may be her next!'

Another, briefer continental trip took him to Paris, this time with the professional purpose of finding a librettist. (The example of Balfe, who had written operas in French and Italian, might serve to remind Sullivan that there was no need to confine himself to a British collaborator if 'grand' opera was his aim.) He reported a pleasant visit to 'Albert Millaud, the author' – the librettist or joint-librettist of several Offenbach operettas – but nothing came of it. There was, however, Offenbach's newer, expanded version of *Orpheus in the Underworld* to be seen ('which I did not like so well as the old') and also his *La Périchole* and *Madame l'Archiduc*.

Moreover Mrs Grant was to be visited in Paris

– and her children, all delighted to see me . . . There were some charming Americans – the Parsons, who have invited me to dine with them next Thursday [5 November 1874] to meet Mrs Grant and other nice people . . .

His visits to Balcarres must have been particularly congenial because the Lindsays provided not only country-house sociability but an artistic atmosphere – as was only to be expected of the proprietors of the Grosvenor Gallery. The word 'aesthetic' was appropriately used in a poem of thanks written by a fellow-guest from a railway junction on his route home. The writer was a man of eminence: G. J. Goschen (1831–1907), M.P., lately a member of Gladstone's cabinet.

> Dear Lady Lindsay, just one line to say
> How much my wife and I enjoyed our stay,
> And of our grateful thoughts how great a share is
> Due to our charming hostess at Balcarres.
> The noises in this God-forsaken station
> Are 'base accompaniment' to inspiration,
> But, fresh from you, my mind is so aesthetic,
> That, even here, I'm forced to be poetic.
> Melons and models, melodies and mirth
> Still float before us on our way to Perth,
> Yet scarce I dare to sing in doggerel rhyme
> The bright impressions of that 'handsome time'.
> Fitly to sing its glories, I'd require
> To drink of Sullivan's melodious fire.
> Duly to paint its warm and sunny flush,
> I'd need the colours of fair Jopling's brush.

How shall I tell the zest with which we fell on
The luscious lumps of the 'nine-pounder' melon?

Goschen finally pictured himself 'looking back' – the phrase, in quotation marks, referring to one of Sullivan's most successful songs, 'Looking Back' (1870). The 'fair Jopling' is the artist Louise Jopling (1843–1933), and the 'nine-pounder' allusion is to naval cannon-balls, as in *HMS Pinafore*.

Visiting Oxford, Sullivan heard one of the great orators of the age. John Ruskin (1819–1900) had been long celebrated for his political as well as artistic writings when he was appointed the first Slade Professor of Fine Art in 1869. So well attended were his lectures that they generally had to be given in the Sheldonian Theatre (the university's largest auditorium) and sometimes repeated to a second audience. In 1873 Sullivan was visiting his young friend Lionel Lewin, who had become an undergraduate at Pembroke College at the late age of 25 and who was to die in the following year.[12] Sullivan not only heard Ruskin, but called on the famous Greek scholar, Dean Liddell of Christ Church, whose eldest daughter Lorna Charlotte 'sang *Orpheus* charmingly'.[13] (Sullivan's own song, 'Orpheus with his Lute', is meant.) Nothing is known of any possible meeting with Lorna's sister Alice (then 21), who had been immortalized by Lewis Carroll as 'Alice in Wonderland'.

All this activity testifies to a comfortable standard of living, but in January 1872 an acute financial embarrassment obliged him to write to his friend Frederick Lehmann (Nina's husband):

You could do me a very great kindness but I scarcely like to ask you, as it is rather a strain upon your good nature. I have had a final letter from Boosey (my publishers) tonight which has left me in a fix – upsetting my calculations and reducing me to a state of great anxiety. The result is that I am in great need of £300 for a short time. Can you and will you lend me this till the end of June, when I can pay you without difficulty? I will not bother you with a long letter entering into details but if you would care to know why I am obliged to ask for money, or what my means of repaying it are, I would gladly come and tell you *viva voce* if you would give me ten minutes' talk.

Even if you don't see your way to lending me the money, I think it would be rather a comfort to me to come to talk the matter over with you. You will probably give me counsel which would be valuable . . .

The answer was wisely brief. 'I must say no to your request, and I have not the heart to add another word to so disagreeable a communication.'

Happily, his good relations with the Lehmanns seem not to have been interrupted by the incident. The financial embarrassment – very likely, in view of later references in Sullivan's diary, to have been caused by gambling debts – did not last. Sullivan's income was growing. Besides royalties from the sale of his songs and other profitable works, there were fees to be derived from the performance of his larger works and fees for conducting them. The former were not easily controlled by the composer in those days – before the establishment of the modern Performing Right Society. Sympathizing with the complaint of a fellow-composer, Edouard Silas (1827–1909), about performances unpaid-for,

Sullivan wrote (30 October 1873) urging the formation of just such a fee-collecting body, 'like the Paris one'.

On one occasion at least there was an unsolicited tribute.[13] An old English silver goblet and a purse containing £200 were presented to him after he had conducted the Manchester performance of *The Light of the World* in 1874. Manchester was also the scene of a revival of Sullivan's two Burnand operettas, with his brother Fred in the company. The composer conducted some, at least, of the performances. After he had returned home, he sent to his influential Manchester friend E. J. Broadfield a letter which indicates quite a few 'second thoughts'. The original billing had evidently begun with *Cox and Box* but then a change was made:

> We began with *The Contrabandista* last night, as I found that *Cox and Box* killed it nearly, and the consequence was that we had a capital performance and the people seemed to enjoy it thoroughly. Go and see it again as soon as you can. I hope Fred will do well, as a little money will be of great use to him now. If he has a 'benefit', I think I shall run down again to help.
>
> You are quite right about the contralto air [Inez: 'Let others seek the peaceful plain']. It was stuffed in later, as the singers all grumbled dreadfully at having no song at all, but it doesn't come in well. We want a song with chorus in the finale to the first act, a good, lively, bold rhythm.

His developing skill as a conductor was recognized. In September 1871 his name, along with that of Sims Reeves, had been featured in advertisements for a so-called Royal National Opera, giving performances in English at the Lyceum Theatre, but he was never placed under contract. It was an ill-organized enterprise which performed lamely for a few weeks and then disintegrated. But he had other ambitions, among them a plan for an independent series of concerts under his own direction. A proposal for what was to be called 'The Concert Society'[15] survives in a document in his hand (apparently from 1873, before October) with a letter addressed to 'My dear B'. A season of ten concerts was envisaged, on Wednesdays from 3 to 5 p.m., i.e. presupposing an entirely leisured audience. Orchestral concerts on a week-day afternoon would have been a novelty, though recitals by eminent soloists would not. 'The concerts will be short and the programmes eclectic – a beautiful waltz is as much worth playing delicately and well as a symphony of Beethoven's: it is good in itself.'

The financial calculations were based on an orchestra of 60, of whom 40 would require a fee of two guineas (total £84) and the rest three guineas (£63). The hire of a concert room, no doubt for only a single rehearsal in addition to the concert, was estimated at £21. It was proposed to offer 500 subscriptions at five guineas each. The resultant £2,625 would show a substantial profit over the estimated cost of £2,000 for ten concerts. Out of the profit, presumably, would come Sullivan's own fees as conductor.

Nothing proceeded from this, but meanwhile Sullivan was broadening his musical experience through private as well as public performance. 'Are you disposed', he wrote to an unidentified friend on a Friday evening, 31 May 1872, 'to hear a cantata of Bach, bits of *Lohengrin*, and other choice morsels tomorrow afternoon? If so, I am charged by an old and dear friend, one Arthur Coleridge by name, to invite you to his house at 4.30 tomorrow afternoon.' Coleridge was a musical amateur who had translated Kreissle von Hellborn's biography of Schubert. By such meetings, informal but evidently well prepared, musical culture was nourished in pre-gramophone days.

10 Fanny

SOMEWHAT before this time – the date, like so much else in their relationship, is veiled – Arthur Sullivan met Mary Frances Ronalds, an American nearly three years older than himself. (Her birth-date was 23 August 1839.) She was to be his companion, outside marriage, till the end of his life.

The story of Fanny, as her friends called her, is linked with that of Jennie Jerome (1854–1921), later Lady Randolph Churchill and mother of Winston Churchill. Named after Jenny Lind, Jennie was the daughter of one of the wealthiest men in New York, Leonard Jerome – racehorse-owner, sailing-ship racer, devotee of music, and a notorious womanizer. His rival in New York society was August Belmont, and one of the objects of their rivalry was a Bostonian beauty separated from her husband and thus described in a male New Yorker's notebook of the time:

Her face was perfectly divine in its loveliness, her features small and exquisitely regular. Her hair was a dark shade of brown – *châtain foncé* [deep chestnut] – and very abundant . . . a lovely woman, with the most generous smile one could possibly imagine, and the most beautiful teeth.[1]

This was Fanny Ronalds. A photograph of about this time discloses an oval face, a high forehead, the hair falling in ringlets at the back. High-spirited, she was a dashing skater and showed a gift for the reins when she took driving lessons from Leonard Jerome.[2] She is said to have studied singing in Italy but she remained an amateur: it would have demeaned a member of 'the four hundred' (as New York's top stratum was already called) to take up the profession.

The magnificent ball which Fanny gave in the early 1860s passed into New York's chronicles of extravagance. Dressed as Music, in a white satin gown embroidered with bars from Verdi's *Un ballo in maschera*, she wore a harp-shaped crown lit up by tiny gas-jets. Twenty years after, Leonard Jerome asked August Belmont whether he remembered that ball.

'Indeed I ought to,' said Belmont. 'I paid for it.'

'Why, how very strange,' replied Jerome, 'so did I.'[3]

Born Mary Frances Carter in Boston, she had married Peter (or Pierre) Lorillard Ronalds of New York in 1859. At the ceremony on 16 November she gave her age as 20; her husband was 33. They separated about 1867 after the birth of three children.[4] Whether or not she had been one of Leonard Jerome's mistresses, Jerome's wife seems to have had no objection to her company. When

Mrs Jerome and her three daughters moved to Paris in 1867, Fanny Ronalds followed them. They were not the only wealthy, cultured Americans to seek the pleasure-loving court of Napoleon III, where the formal presentation at court of *débutante* daughters was easier to obtain than at Victoria's court. Napoleon and the Empress Eugénie, some 20 years younger than her husband, took the Jeromes and Fanny Ronalds into their intimate circle.

It was probably Juliette Conneau, Sullivan's patroness in Paris and a lady-in-waiting to the Empress Eugénie, who introduced Arthur Sullivan to Fanny Ronalds in Paris. When Eugénie fled to the safety of England from the invading Germans, the Jeromes and Fanny Ronalds took the same course. The Jeromes re-established themselves in Paris late in 1871 but displayed themselves at Cowes for the fashionable yachting season in summer 1872 and again in 1873. It was there that Jennie Jerome received a proposal from Lord Randolph Churchill on the third day of their acquaintance: they were married at the British Embassy in Paris on 15 April 1874. France under the new republic was achieving political stability, but for the former emperor there was no return. Napoleon died in exile in Chislehurst (Kent) on 9 June 1873, his faithful Conneau at his side.

Helped no doubt by her position in the Emperor's circle (and perhaps receiving a pension from Napoleon himself),[5] Fanny Ronalds seemingly had no difficulty along with two of her children in establishing herself in London. Her elder son (Pierre, named after his father) remained in America, but her daughter Fannie ('Fanette') and her younger son Reginald ('Regie') came with her. Henry James, in a letter of July 1877, reported a social meeting with 'the once famous Mrs Ronalds of America, who has lately turned up here again, and who, though somewhat "gone off", as they say here, is still as pretty as an angel'. In her new life in London Mary Frances Ronalds continued to cultivate a friendship, though hardly an intimacy, with Jennie Jerome and with Jennie's elder sister Clara, who was to become Mrs Moreton Frewen. Another New York friend who transferred herself to London was Consuelo Yznaga, who in 1876 trumped the social pack by becoming Duchess of Manchester.[6]

In a letter written late in life to his nephew Herbert (30 December 1896), Arthur Sullivan actually dated his first acquaintance with Fanny Ronalds.

You see, my dear Bertie, it is [now] a very trying period of life for her. In '62 when I first knew her, all London ran after her. Later, in '68, all Paris (when I was there) from the Emperor downwards was at her feet.

Sullivan's memory is not absolutely to be relied on. Fanny *may* have crossed the Atlantic and briefly visited London as early as 1862 but no evidence of such a visit is forthcoming. Nor does her name occur in the records of Sullivan and his principal friends (Grove, the Lehmanns, Chorley, Davison) at this date. It was, moreover, in 1867 that Sullivan spent some time in Paris in connection with his duties at the International Exhibition; in 1868 he made, apparently, no visit there. An initial meeting in Paris through Mme Conneau in 1867, followed by a greater intimacy after both Fanny and the Conneaus came to London in 1870–1, seems most probable. On Sullivan's death in 1900, Fanny herself was to refer to a friendship of 23 years.[7]

Fanny Ronalds's liaison with Arthur Sullivan was to remain clandestine and illicit. She was never divorced. Divorce still carried the strong taint of scandal in England: had Sullivan married her as a divorcee, neither of them would have been admitted to intimacy in the aristocratic and royal *milieu* to whose parties they were separately invited. As it was, she moved freely in the circle of the Prince of Wales, in which (as it was phrased by the *diplomate étranger* quoted earlier)[8] 'the dominant principle was not the cultivation of virtue but the avoidance of scandal'.

The *diplomate* described in some detail the changes in the routines of society which the Prince had brought about.

. . . The custom of smoking a cigar or cigarette after dinner when the ladies have withdrawn, and the economy of wine which is the consequence; the diffusion of musical and theatrical taste; the welcome – not merely artistic but personal – given to actors and singers and the way in which use is made of their services at soirées; the custom of serving a large piece of meat – a *pièce de résistance* – immediately after the fish course and before the *entrées*; above all the whole tendency of reducing the menu (even though dinners in London are still excessively long): these are among the reforms which, though trifling in themselves, bear witness to the Prince's powerful initiative.

. . . London society is thus very extended and difficult to grasp as a whole. It has no unity, it is amorphous, a chaos of different parts and divergent classes. . . . Although there are Liberal and Tory houses, etc., this is not a real social division. Unlike its equivalent in Paris, London society, as society, belongs to all those who are admitted to it.

Fanny Ronalds was only one member of an American sisterhood which our *diplomate* observed in action:

Hardly has the Yankee belle made her conquest and led her English aristocrat to the altar than she immediately asks herself what she could do for her fellow-countrywomen by using her marriage as a lever. She has sisters and cousins as beautiful as she; she experiences a conqueror's pride in tempting amorous young Englishmen under the sway of American womanhood and enforcing them under its yoke . . . The Jews, the Germans and the Americans are in a sense a new blood introduced into the veins of English society.

Fanny Ronalds set up house in Chelsea at 84 Sloane Street, afterwards moving to 104 in the same street and later to 7 Cadogan Place in the same area. Here London had acquired a new, much-remarked and generally applauded architectural feature – high, gabled houses in red brick and terracotta. 'Queen Anne is by no means dead,' reported the *Building News* in 1876, 'as the style is about to be employed for the whole of the houses to be erected on [Earl Cadogan's] estate, at Chelsea, where it is said red brick and green trees are to reign triumphant.'[9] Older property on the site was demolished for the purpose, thousands of poorer inhabitants being driven out for the sake of the higher rents. Five years later, 'modern terracottary' was seized on by Gilbert (in *Patience*) as a rhyme for 'pottery' and 'lottery'.

This was 'imperial' London. Disraeli's first ministry (1874–80) not only enacted reforms in trade union rights, housing, the legal system and public health; it also made the Queen 'Empress of India' (1876) and pursued an expansionist foreign policy of which the most celebrated act was the purchase for £4,000,000 of the Khedive Ismail's shares in the Suez Canal Company. The Canal had opened only six years before, in 1869: Verdi's *Aida* had been intended to celebrate the event, but its production did not take place until 1871. Egypt would provide leading issues in British politics within a few years, and Sullivan would visit there in the company of a political journalist friend. But in 1874, it was the war in 'Ashantee' (as that region of West Africa was then spelt) which hit the newspaper-reader for week after week. The 'skill of Sir Garnet in thrashing a cannibal' (*Patience*) alludes to Sir Garnet Wolseley's success as commander both in that campaign and in the Zulu war of 1879.

Aida reached London in 1876 with Adelina Patti in the title-role – queen of prima donnas of her time, as Jenny Lind had been. Such opera stars, when they appeared at concerts, attracted the largest audiences and commanded fees accordingly. At the Liverpool Festival of 1874 – the same festival which performed Sullivan's *The Light of the World* – Patti had contributed four songs to each of two programmes and was paid £400 a night. Compare Sims Reeves' fee of 90 guineas [£94.50p] – or an opera chorister's income of £2 or less *per week*! Patti was engaged because she was profitable. The organizers took pride in announcing that her appearances at Liverpool (with orchestra) had brought in £3,194 at the box office and had cost £2,220.

Sullivan was never asked to conduct opera with Patti and comparable stars at Covent Garden or Drury Lane. That was not a snub: it was not even surprising, since 'international' opera was felt to be an exotic and almost exclusively Italian realm. After Costa, the leading opera conductor in London was Luigi Arditi (1822–1903), whose waltz song 'Il bacio' (The Kiss) was enormously successful in the domestic and 'ballad concert' repertory. Just as *Der fliegende Holländer* had been sung in Italian on its first appearance, so now *Lohengrin* appeared in 1875 in two productions, *both* in Italian, at Drury Lane and Covent Garden. Carl Rosa, emerging as an impresario championing English opera and opera in English showed tactical skill in avoiding London during the 'grand season'. His company, tested out in the provinces, first appeared in London in September 1875 with a production of *The Marriage of Figaro* at the Prince's Theatre.

At the Philharmonic Society Sullivan's *Marmion* Overture was revived in 1874[10] ('retouched but not improved, in its attempt at impossible sound-painting', said *The Orchestra* in August) and next season *The Tempest* returned, or rather six numbers of it. The Philharmonic was going its cautious way. W. G. Cusins (1833–93) had been the conductor since Sterndale Bennett's retirement in 1866. From 1870 until his death in 1893 Cusins was also Master of the Queen's Music – at that time simply implying the superintendence of the Queen's 'private band', i.e. the orchestra engaged as required for state occasions. Like Bennett and unlike Costa, Arditi, Manns and Hallé (all foreigners!), Cusins represented that style of anonymous conducting which enabled reviewers simply to omit from their notices any mention of *how* a piece went. No one ever wrote of 'Cusins'

Eroica'. Hanslick, Vienna's leading critic, came and reported that Cusins 'looks exactly like an English clergyman and conducts also very piously'.[11]

The programmes at the Crystal Palace, where the concerts continued under August Manns' direction, testified to the popularity of Spohr and Raff as well as of Haydn and Beethoven. Joachim was heard in his own Violin Concerto in G, and the increasing interest in Bach's music produced the orchestral Suite in C (BWV 1066) and the cantata 'Ich hatte viel Bekümmernis' (No. 21) – in English, naturally: the quaint notion that an English choir should address an English audience in German was not yet current. Sullivan's share of the repertory was a selection from *On Shore and Sea* and the air 'Refrain thy voice' from *The Light of the World*. Other British-born composers represented were Macfarren, Henry Hugo Pierson, Ouseley, the brothers Henry and Alfred Holmes, and Henry Gadsby – a roll-call which arouses an echo of stunning silence today, not perhaps quite justified in Pierson's case.

New plays of the 1874 season included *Sweethearts* by W. S. Gilbert, unusual in its reliance on long speeches with comparatively little plot. But it was operetta, along with such melodramas as *East Lynne*, which still carried the taste of the town.[12] At the Gaiety, in September 1874, a revived *Cox and Box* opened the season in a triple bill with two of Offenbach's, *Les Deux Aveugles* and *La Princesse de Trébizonde*.[13] Among the shows that followed were Lecocq's *The Island of Bachelors* (it was apparently thought too shocking to translate *Les Cent Vierges* literally as 'the hundred virgins') and Offenbach's recent *The Love Apple* (*Pomme d'Api*). At the Lyceum, the ever-popular *Grand Duchess of Gerolstein* was succeeded by Lecocq's *La Fille de Mme Angot*.

Offenbach was also the choice of the actress Selina Dolaro for the new company which she inaugurated at the Royalty Theatre on 30 January 1875. She was both star and proprietor,[15] in a manner common at the time, of which Henry Irving's career provides the most celebrated example.[15] *La Périchole* was new to London: daringly it allowed the heroine (played by Dolaro herself) to become tipsy. But Offenbach's three acts were insufficient to round out a complete evening, and it was in order to fill the deficiency that Gilbert and Sullivan's *Trial by Jury* came into existence. Its commissioning was due, apparently, to the man whom Dolaro had engaged as manager of her company, Richard D'Oyly Carte (1844–1901). 'D'Oyly' was a forename, not part of a 'double barrel'.[16]

As proprietor of a concert and lecture agency, Carte had recently supervised the farewell tour of the great tenor, Mario; in 1874, in association with Cramer's, the music publishers, he had contracted Offenbach to compose and supervise his operetta *Whittington* as the Christmas entertainment for the Alhambra Theatre.[17] A letter of Sullivan's to his mother as early as 1 April 1874 shows that Carte and he were already negotiating about some (unidentified) proposition. But the story of the birth of *Trial by Jury*, as set forth in various accounts compiled long afterwards, begins only when Gilbert dropped in on a rehearsal at the Royalty in mid-January 1875, and was asked by Carte whether he had anything suitable for the company.

Gilbert sent Carte the manuscript of a skit he had written, set in a court of law and relating a trial for breach of promise of marriage. The right of a woman to financial compensation if she could prove that a promise of marriage had been broken was an apt subject for satire: since the court had actually to assess 'damages' in financial terms, the injured female would gain by persuading the jury that her prospective loss had been immense, while the male defendant would strive to show the opposite. Seven years before (11 April 1868), *Trial by Jury* had appeared in miniature form in the pages of *Fun*, prophetically sub-titled an 'operetta'. Before Carte's inquiry Gilbert had already re-cast it as a stage work, for which Carl Rosa was to have written the music. Rosa's relinquishment was Sullivan's opportunity. Gilbert called on Sullivan and read out his libretto aloud – in a manner later recollected by the composer himself.

He read it through, as it seemed to me, in a perturbed sort of way, with a gradual crescendo of indignation, in the manner of a man considerably disappointed with what he had written. As soon as he had come to the last word he closed up the manuscript violently, apparently unconscious of the fact that he had achieved his purpose so far as I was concerned, in as much as I was screaming with laughter the whole time. The music was written, and the rehearsals completed, within the space of three weeks' time.[18]

Trial by Jury appeared at the Royalty on 25 March 1875 as an after-piece to *La Périchole*, itself preceded by a one-act farce already in the repertory called *Cryptoconchoidsyphonostomata* by Edgar and Collette. In the programme, and in the 18-page printed libretto available to the audience, the name of Arthur Sullivan preceded that of W. S. Gilbert. *Trial by Jury* was a complete success, 'extremely funny and admirably composed' (as the reviewer in *Fun* put it).[19] The composer conducted, and his brother Fred's talent had developed sufficiently for him to take the part of the Judge with particular success, according to the same reviewer:

The greatest 'hit' was made by Mr F. Sullivan, whose blending of official dignity, condescension, and at the right moment, extravagant humour, made the character of the Judge stand out with all requisite prominence, and added much to the interest of the piece.[20]

Oddly enough the 'operetta' of *Fun* was now styled a 'dramatic cantata' – a term normally signifying (as with Sullivan's *On Shore and Sea*, or Sterndale Bennett's *The May Queen*) a work for the concert-hall. Was 'operetta' not quite respectable, a little alarming to potential audiences? This explanation would be more convincing if *Trial by Jury* had been put on by German Reed; but since the presentation was Dolaro's, and *La Périchole* was already in the bill, the term 'operetta' could hardly be thought a deterrent. It is more likely that in Sullivan's mind the word 'operetta' implied spoken dialogue: *Trial by Jury*, all-sung, has none. But, as it turned out, the word *operetta* was never used by Gilbert and Sullivan as a formal description of any of their joint works.

One might suppose that the decision to set the text completely to music, without speech, was Sullivan's own. But the real credit is Gilbert's – assuming (from Sullivan's own account quoted above) that the text was handed to the composer complete and settled. There is no prose conversation. To link the musical numbers, there are only a few brief lines set out in verse style, which were evidently intended as recitative. The actual word 'recitative' was used for such points in the *Fun* prototype.

Indeed, the operatic form is implicit in the literary text. In the original *Fun* sketch, after the Counsel for the jilted girl has swayed the jury, the Judge moves immediately into his solo, leading to the line, 'I will marry her myself!' But in the expanded stage libretto Gilbert not only allows the Defendant and Plaintiff to be heard in solos: he also introduces the ensemble 'A nice dilemma', expressing everyone's perplexity, including that of the spectators in the courtroom. The positioning of this ensemble enables the Judge's intervention, *when* it occurs, to come with a decisive point, just after the maximum tension in the comic plot has been reached simultaneously with the maximum musical load.

Sullivan turned the ensemble into a jest of his own. Earlier in the operetta, he had 'hailed' the Judge in a parody of Handel's grandest oratorio manner, comically burdened with repetitions. Now he made 'A nice dilemma' into a parody of a typical 'dilemma' ensemble of Italian opera – specifically the ensemble beginning 'D'un pensiero' which occurs in the finale of the first act of Bellini's *La sonnambula*, when the heroine's fellow-villagers do not know whether to believe in her innocence. Sullivan uses the same kind of musical figure, the same dominating rhythm, and the same key – and even lets the chorus chop up the syllables nonsensically ('A nice/di-lem/-ma we/have here') in simulation of the *oom-cha-cha* or 'big guitar' effect so characteristic of the Italian opera chorus.

The themes of paradox and the reversal of roles which had animated *Thespis* and were to animate Gilbert's next work for Sullivan, *The Sorcerer*, are hardly present here. Instead, the humour of *Trial by Jury* derives from farcical exaggeration of behaviour and from the sly exposure of self-seeking. It was characteristic of Gilbert to present an attractive young woman as capitulating immediately to a considerably older man, assumed to be unmarried. In *The Pirates of Penzance* and in the first version of *Ruddigore*, the symbolic rape was to be, so to speak, collectivized. One of the less pleasant aspects of Victorian sexuality lurks here. For the older single *woman*, however, there is only derision. So far she is only obliquely mentioned ('that rich attorney's elderly, ugly daughter') but she would not remain off stage for much longer.

The vocal score of *Trial by Jury* was published in May 1875 – not in anticipation of the production but in recognition of its success. On separately numbered pages preceding the music itself, the score prints Gilbert's libretto. The text here includes several short passages not set to music; conversely, Sullivan fills a chorus part (after the Plaintiff's 'Yes, he must pay') with a line that is not Gilbert's. Careless and inconsistent editing of the music itself indicates that the vocal score was hastily prepared. The publication would answer the demands of the public wishing to sing and play the music at home, but it is rash to treat this or later vocal scores as a documented legacy of intentions (in the way a published piano sonata might be) or as a historical record of a particular performance.

But the fact that a vocal score of *Trial by Jury* was published (as had not happened with *Thespis*) testified at least to an expectation of continued public interest. Sullivan's next operetta, three months after *Trial by Jury*, was allowed to sink almost without trace after its first production – its very name virtually unknown to the next two generations of devotees. Not until a century later did *The Zoo* achieve a vocal score (two different editions, 1969 and 1975, revised 1991).[21] It was another one-act work, described this time as 'a musical folly', and again set to music throughout, without spoken dialogue. The librettist was 'Bolton Rowe', the pseudonym of B.C. Stephenson, who later found greater success under his own name.

Produced on Saturday, 5 June 1875 as the concluding item of a triple bill at the St James's Theatre, *The Zoo* was advertised as beginning at 10.15 – information for those who did not wish to arrive at 7.30 in time for *The Dancing Barber* and the theatre's current success, Gilbert's *Tom Cobb*. After 18 performances there (the last on 25 June), *The Zoo* was transferred with some of the same performers to the Haymarket (28 June) and played until almost two weeks later (9 July). The action, with the novel setting of London's Zoological Gardens, presents two pairs of lovers – Aesculapius Carboy (a rather heavy-handed name for an apothecary) and Laetitia, Thomas Brown and Eliza. Thomas Brown turns out to be a duke, and a tongue-tied public speaker whose utterance is wordlessly given out by an oboe while a sympathetic crowd prompts him:

Thomas. Accustomed as I am to public – ah – ah –

Chorus. Speaking . . .

Thomas. (Thank you) speaking, I feel over – ah – over – ah –

Chorus. Overpowered . . .

Thomas. (Thank you, no) overwhelmed upon this – ah – this – ah –

The comic idea here is deliciously worked out in the music, and so is the counterpointing of 15 syllables of a slow, soulful strain against 39 syllables of a rapidly pattering one:

Laetitia, Carboy. Let me gaze upon thy face,
    And lean, and lean upon thy breast.

Eliza, Thomas. $\left\{ \begin{array}{l} \text{You've} \\ \text{I've} \end{array} \right\}$ had four tarts and a couple of pears,

                $\left\{ \begin{array}{l} \text{You've} \\ \text{I've} \end{array} \right\}$ had three buns that were meant for the bears.

Two bags of nuts instead of the apes,
Ten biscuits of various sizes and shapes.

Though other numbers are musically less interesting, the failure of the piece to survive must be principally ascribed to Stephenson's clumsy plot. No sudden happening, like the Judge's decision to marry the Plaintiff, serves to change the situation and thus solve what seemed to be insoluble. The idea of a slow-versus-rapid ensemble was to be taken up again in *The Pirates of Penzance* but it is strange that Sullivan never returned to the tongue-tied orator.

   The Zoo was revived in a London suburban production (at the Philharmonic, Islington) on 2 October 1875. Two years later, when talk of a revival was again in the air, he evidently felt that both words and music needed revision and asked Alan Cole, 'Will you *rewrite* it with me?'[22] But it was never done, and a revival at the Royalty Theatre in April 1879 showed no substantial change. By then Sullivan's preoccupations were elsewhere.

11   A College and an Aquarium

IN gaining Gilbert as a partner, Sullivan gained more than a librettist. Unusually, Gilbert was his own stage director – following an older playwright, T. W. Robertson, the author of *Caste*. Not merely the plots, not merely the lines, but the pacing and staging of the operettas were to be his. His surviving prompt-books indicate his obsession with pictorial grouping and co-ordinated rhythmical gesture. By the use of a model stage, with blocks three inches high for male characters and 2½ inches for females, he created his action in advance. As George Rowell acutely points out, the counter-marshalling of opposed choruses – rapturous maidens and Guards officers, fairies and peers, giggling schoolgirls and stiff Japanese gentlemen – was to provide one of his strongest means of theatrical articulation and effect.[1]

Sullivan's collaboration with Gilbert in *Trial by Jury* brought an exceptionally long and gratifying run of 175 (non-consecutive) performances during 1875. Among those who went to see it was the Lord Chief Justice, Sir Alexander Cockburn, before whom the 188-day trial of the 'Tichborne claimant' (resulting in a fourteen-year sentence for impersonating an heir) had unrolled its complexities in 1873–4. Older than Sullivan by 40 years, Cockburn had become his friend and was a keen amateur musician. With pretended gravity Sullivan later maintained that Cockburn really disapproved of *Trial by Jury* 'as he thought the piece was calculated to bring the Bench into contempt. . . . He would not go again for fear he should seem to encourage it.'[2]

Other work came, and other pleasures. In February 1875 he conducted his *Ballo* overture at the Brighton Festival – since 1870 an event of some importance, apparently the earliest festival to spring up in the growing seaside resorts. He continued to compose drawing-room ballads such as 'Let me dream again' and 'Thou'rt passing hence' (both of 1875, both very successful). The summer and autumn brought three trips abroad. Mrs Grant had evidently been in London and was to go (with her children Adele and Douglas and the new baby, plus a nurse and a maid) to take the waters at the German spa of Kissingen. It had been Sullivan's plan to escort them only as far as Cologne and then to go for his own purposes to Paris.

But Mrs Grant fainted on the journey, no one in their party spoke German, and out of kindness Sullivan re-routed his ticket and baggage and accompanied them as far as Kissingen. He found no room for himself at the hotel except 'a luxurious apartment some few steps above the roof, as far as I could make out'. (Such shafts of dry wit continue to pepper his letters to his mother.) Then 'I had to bustle about, and get good apartments [for the Grants' stay], engage [a tutor] for Douglas, hire a pianoforte, and a thousand other little things, besides having the care of the children'.

What a perfect bachelor 'uncle'! He spent a couple of days with the Grants in Kissingen before going on to Paris – presumably to renew both private and professional acquaintance.

He returned to London, but in less than two weeks he was in Paris again, this time with the Lindsays on the way to the Italian resort of Cadenabbia on Lake Maggiore. From Paris the train took them (11–13 August 1875) to Basle, Zurich and Chur, followed by a two-day road journey over the Splügen pass in an open carriage and pair, with

a capital fellow to drive us. We got to the village of Splügen about 7 in the evening, where we slept, and a capital little hotel it was too. The next morning (Sunday) we were off betimes, and after two hours' zig-zag ascent we got to the top of the mountain and stood for a little – one foot in Switzerland and one in Italy. It is very rugged, very gloomy, bleak and bare, and yet very grand. It impressed me with a sense of loneliness and isolation that I have never before experienced. At the very top there is not a bit of vegetation to be seen, nothing but bleak stones and grim looking rocks. Our descent was very different, for soon we began to feel the warmth of the sunny south and all going down the mountain instead of fir trees as on the Swiss side the ground was covered with beautiful chestnuts. The descent was too beautiful to describe, and at 7 we came to Chiavenna, our halting-place for the night. It is the most Italian-looking of Italian towns, picturesque and like nothing else I have seen. Yesterday we started off again in the morning, and parted with our driver and carriage at Colico, where we took the boat to here. Your letter came this morning . . .[3]

'Here' was Cadenabbia. They were welcomed by Piatti (the cellist for whom Sullivan had written his concerto), who had a villa there. Milan beckoned also. Sullivan stayed there with another old friend from London, the composer Alberto Visetti, and was warmly greeted at the Conservatory by its director, Alberto Mazzucato. Then there was the delight of Lake Maggiore itself and the welcoming warmth of its climate. 'You mustn't mind short letters', he wrote to his mother on 18 August,

for the heat is so great as to render it almost impossible to do anything but sit without movement in a chair until the evening, when we manage to saunter out a little or be paddled about in a flat-bottomed boat. Then it is delicious, absolutely lovely. The stillness of the water – the brilliant moon throwing its glittering light upon the lake and making a long trail of little diamonds, the mountains all round looking grave and calm, little boats filled with men and women, some of them with mandolins singing popular melodies, and the lights from the villages and towns dotted round the lake all contribute to form a scene that is enchanting, and unlike anything one has dreamed of . . .

On the way back – likewise in a carriage, but this time over the Simplon pass to Brig – Sullivan stayed nearly three weeks in Paris. He was anxious to promote performances of his work there, and he had the renewed pleasure of the Grants' company. Sullivan had become Mrs Grant's counsellor. (If there was any closer relationship, it is not ascertainable.) It was felt that young Douglas Grant needed a touch of discipline beyond that of the family circle. Sullivan arranged to bring him back to London, and 'dearest Mum' was expected to 'look after him until I get him to a good school'. In Paris he found time to write in his typical mock-moral style to his 12-year-old niece Amy (Fred's eldest child): 'I am very glad you like your school and I hope you will not waste a moment of your working time in playing nor waste a moment of your playtime by working.' In Paris he found an oboe-player whom he wanted to engage for London, but to do that 'it seems that I must use interest with the French Ambassador at London. I don't know him personally, but I must get at him. The young man is in the army, and the only means of getting him off is for the Ambassador to say he wants him there!'[4] In general he was 'dreadfully disappointed' at the fruitless result of the auditions he gave in Paris. He found an oboist eventually by going to Brussels.

The quest for instrumentalists was part of an enterprise in which Sullivan was placing his highest hopes as a conductor. A Royal Westminster Aquarium was to open as a new place of popular amusement and to contain a sizeable concert-hall. Although the *Musical Times* made a sniffy remark ('We should certainly be puzzled to divine the connection between fish and music')[5] the connection was in fact obvious: it was money. The Brighton Aquarium could attract over 10,000 visitors on an Easter Bank Holiday (as against about 30,000 who went to Epping Forest to see the annual stag-hunt).[6] At the London establishment there was to be a salaried orchestra, as at the Crystal Palace, and Sullivan was to be its musical director. 'I am not going to engage a foreign band', Sullivan wrote to his mother while at Cadenabbia,

[but] it is not unlikely that some of the principal wind will be got from abroad, as the directors will not sanction deputies, and a good English player could not afford to throw up every other engagement for the Aquarium. This is commonsense, and he [Shepherd, the orchestral manager] can tell the profession so.

To occupy the two months preceding the opening of the Aquarium, Sullivan took on the conductorship of the Glasgow Choral and Orchestral Union, under which Glasgow had newly acquired a regular series of orchestral concerts. There was 'such a rattling good band – London men', he wrote from Glasgow to Alan Cole on 25 November. (Evidently the players, like the conductor, had to be brought in!) Frost and fog greeted his arrival in the early hours of Friday morning, 12 November 1875. A new French servant, Sylvain, probably engaged on one of Sullivan's recent visits to Paris, was with him. They eventually found a cab and drove to the private lodging which had been engaged for him.

I was received by the landlady – an elderly spinster lady looking oh! so dirty and slatternly. She got me a cup of tea, and I turned into bed. There was no room vacant until next morning for Sylvain, and so I made him lie on the sofa in the sitting-room before the fire, for he was dreadfully cold. I got up at twelve, ordered breakfast, and had to wait an hour and a half for it. It was only tea and some dried-up bacon. Sylvain had to go and hurry them in the kitchen, which he described as dirty. He had been unable to get anything himself to eat, and so I had to give him half my own wretched fare and pull him together with some brandy and water.

I felt this would not do, and having taken a thorough dislike to the place resolved to clear out at once. The things were packed and we went off to an hotel. The old harpy made me pay two weeks' rent, but I would have paid five rather than stay there longer . . .

He wrote to his mother from the Hanover Hotel two days later, a Sunday:

. . . A Scotch 'Sawbath' is a ghastly thing. However, I didn't get up early this morning, and I have got heaps of letters to write so that the day will be occupied. I tried to find a good Anglican church but they are all dull or else kirks. Cabs are double fares on Sundays, all locomotion and recreation are discouraged, and whisky-drinking encouraged.

Six concerts had been planned, with 'programmes prepared by Mr George Grove of London in consultation with Mr Sullivan'. The first was held on Tuesday 16 November 1875 in the City Hall, Glasgow – used until 1990 by the Scottish National Orchestra, which descends lineally from the orchestra assembled for the 33-year-old Arthur Sullivan. Weber's *Oberon* overture opened the programme, with Beethoven's Symphony no. 7 following. This, too, was reported to 'Dearest Mum', to whom Sullivan sent no less than six letters in his first two weeks in Scotland.

You will see by the papers I send that the concert last night was a brilliant success. The playing of the orchestra and my readings are talked about by everyone today. The directors are delighted. Tonight we go to Greenock and give a popular concert – we leave at six and shall be home by midnight, I hope – we have been rehearsing this morning, amongst other things the *Ballo* overture which will go very well, I think. . . . Tomorrow we have nothing to do (I have much writing) and on Friday we go to Hamilton and repeat tonight's programme.

Sullivan had other work pressing him, including 12 church chants promised to Novello: if composed, they were never published. Time to spare, if not Sullivan's lot, was enjoyed by his servant, since they had moved to an hotel. Sullivan now re-named him Silva rather than Sylvain.

Silva is very steady and extremely attentive but I wish he had more to do. I make him do all I can, and he attends rehearsals and concerts with me. It keeps him occupied and I find he is passionately fond of music. He sings in a rich baritone voice fragments of the symphonies, overtures, etc., whilst he is varnishing my shoes!

The Grants' son, Douglas, had now been placed with a private tutor (Waterfield). Mrs Sullivan of course had to run the errands.

Will you also send *this week* a bottle of eau de cologne and some pommade to Douglas Grant. He wrote to me for it. Keep a separate account of all that is spent for him and I must get it at Christmas from his mother.

In a subsequent letter dated merely 'Sunday', perhaps 5 December (written from 144 Holland Street, Glasgow, presumably while dining at a friend's house) he detailed for his mother the coming week's activity:

Monday, rehearsal, Tuesday, rehearsal and concert Glasgow, Wednesday, rehearsal and concert Greenock, Thursday, rehearsal and concert Perth (start at 9 in the morning and sleep there), Friday, rehearsal and concert Dundee (and sleep there), Saturday, return to Glasgow, rehearsal at 2, concert at 7. . . . We do our work valiantly and the band and myself work well together and are covering ourselves with glory – but not money. . . .

There is a wretched creature on the floor above (in the hotel) who plays the piano a little. He or she has been playing *my* hymn tunes all this afternoon. I hope they don't do it out of compliment to me, for they put their own harmony, which to say the least isn't as good as mine.

At the fourth Glasgow concert on 14 December, Sullivan's programme included the music to the masque in *The Merchant of Venice* and his partsong (to Sir Walter Scott's words) 'Oh hush thee, my babie'.

His letter of 17 December not only reported enthusiastically on his concerts but showed that his social circle was developing apace. His friend Nina Lehmann had evidently recommended him to her younger sister living in Glasgow, a Mrs Ziegler. Meanwhile Sullivan's London home was being redecorated and he was insistent that his mother move out, recommending her to the Grosvenor Hotel which had been built in the previous decade to accommodate travellers arriving at Victoria Station.

Shepherd [orchestral manager] has been here this morning to have a chat. He says the band think I am the best conductor living. We had *such* a performance on Tuesday. It was really superb, and my compositions came in for more than their share of the applause. I send two papers. At Greenock on Wednesday, the same programme went also wonderfully well. Last night I dined at Bunting's, a nice fellow who lives with his sister, and tonight I dine at Ziegler's, with exactly the same party as last night. I do hope you will leave the house next week. It is useless to press you upon it, I fear but it is dangerous to stay longer, as soon as painting, whitewashing and breaking outer walls begin.

I hope you will let me hear on Tuesday that you have got comfortable rooms close by – indeed, as it is only bedrooms you want now, the Grosvenor would be as cheap as any other place I believe. Next Tuesday we do *In Memoriam* here, and the following day at Greenock it is a curious coincidence that accidentally the performances take place on the *21 and 22*. I look forward to a very good performance, as I have already begun to rehearse it.

Thomas Sullivan had died in the early morning of 23 September 1866, but the two previous days were obviously remembered as those of the family's vigil. The *In Memoriam* overture must have made a good effect at this, the fifth concert of the series; it was repeated 'by desire' (as the programme-books put it in those days) at the next concert of the season on 28 December 1875. An extra concert on 1 January 1876 gave Glasgow the *Ballo* overture and one of Sullivan's most popular songs, 'Once again', with William Shakespeare (a popular tenor) as soloist.

Glasgow was near enough to Balcarres for him to pay a weekend visit to the Lindsays, and also to spend Christmas there. His mother received a cheery report.

Christmas day was beautiful and we had a tree in the afternoon for the servants. You have got a paper-knife off it, and Bertie [Fred's third child Herbert, now seven years old] a top, Amy a thimble. . . . Yesterday Lindsay and I went for a long walk along the seashore. The view of the Firth of Forth at this moment is divine from my window. The sun, first red, then white, makes it look like a gold and silver sea alternately. Silva says there is no such 'propriété' in France! 'C'est magnifique, Monsieur!'

At the beginning of his Glasgow season Sullivan welcomed the company of Christine Nilsson (Rouzeaud) with her husband. A company promoted by the

London impresario J. H. Mapleson had just given Glasgow its first-ever Wagner opera, *Lohengrin*, with conspicuous success. (At the Theatre Royal, then the largest theatre outside London, with 3,000 seats, many were turned away.) Now Mapleson had sent Nilsson as the star of another ensemble which performed *Faust, Lucia di Lammermoor, Il trovatore, Les Huguenots, Il barbiere di Siviglia, Rigoletto* and *Martha*: the Swedish soprano sang in the first four of these, all within ten days!

Sullivan's Scottish season, short as it was, had won him decisive approval as conductor and bore the seeds of his future re-engagement. The directors of the Glasgow Choral Union, the organization which had promoted the series, gave a banquet in his honour on New Year's Eve. Early in January he was back in London – in temporary quarters at 2 Albert St (the house was still being redecorated). It was his responsibility to prepare for the opening of the 'Royal Aquarium and Summer and Winter Garden' by the Duke of Edinburgh on Saturday, 22 January 1876.

It was doubtless Sullivan's ducal friend who secured the royal title for the place. The Scots Guards and Coldstream Guards bands played an inaugural programme which included the Duke's own composition, a waltz called *Galatea* (named after the naval ship he had commanded). Later that day Sullivan conducted an orchestral programme which consisted entirely of British music. It opened with a *Festival Overture* by Macfarren to which military band parts had been specially added and closed with Sullivan's *Procession March* (an alternative title for the Royal Wedding March of 1863). The minuet and trio from Sterndale Bennett's Symphony in G minor were sandwiched into the middle, and such favourite songs as Balfe's 'Come into the Garden, Maud' and Clay's 'She Wandered down the Mountain Side' were delivered by Sims Reeves, Edith Wynne and 'Madame Patey', as the favourite British contralto was always described.

Apart from music, and apart from the exotic creatures of the aquarium proper, the other attractions included a theatre, an art gallery, restaurants, a billiard-room and – serving a newly popular pursuit – a roller-skating rink with a band in attendance. (A return ticket priced at 2s. 6d. giving admission to all these was available from any station on the District Line, the passenger alighting at St James's Park.) The intention was evidently to present a compendium of entertainment under a single roof – such as had been demonstrated on a vaster scale by the Crystal Palace on London's southern suburban fringe. The recently opened Alexandra Palace (1875) in the northern suburb of Muswell Hill was another example. Here Gilbert's play *Creatures of Impulse* was given, with music by Alberto Randegger, and in 1876 *La traviata*, with singers and conductor from Covent Garden, and a revival of *Trial by Jury* (13 and 23 May) 'with the original cast'.

The Aquarium was less ambitious. Its resident orchestra played a twice-daily popular programme, with a more weighty concert on Thursdays at 4 p.m. (those leisured audiences!), which it was Sullivan's normal duty to conduct. On 3

February at the first of these concerts the overtures to Schubert's *Rosamunde* and Wagner's *Tannhäuser* were on the programme, along with two movements (only!) of Mendelssohn's Violin Concerto, and vocal items. The venture was, musically, a failure. Readers of the *Musical Times* in August 1876 learnt that Sullivan had resigned his post as musical director. (His deputy, George Mount, succeeded him.) He may have sensed the failure of the Aquarium to maintain its tone. The attractions of the place 'soon began to be very fishy indeed. Ladies promenaded there up and down o'nights without the escort of any gentleman friend (till, maybe, they found one) . . .'[7] Such was the later recollection of an old habitué of London theatres, Erroll Sherson.

Sullivan's withdrawal must have been prompted also by the prospect of a strikingly different and important role. He was to be nothing less than the head of a new conservatory of music.

It was a testimony to his standing that he should be chosen, at 34, to guide the National Training School for Music, which was to be added at last to the complex of arts buildings in South Kensington. (The building, adjacent to the Albert Hall, later accommodated the Royal College of Organists.) Sullivan was already teaching at his *alma mater*, the Royal Academy of Music, and indeed continued to do so for a while after taking up his new post.[8] Those who urged, in national terms, the importance of the new foundation tended simply to ignore the Academy, as the *Musical Times* rather petulantly pointed out in July 1875. But it could be legitimately argued that the Academy was too small and had failed to produce a sufficiently talented orchestral profession. It was so uncertainly financed that it almost had to close in 1867–8. Moreover, instead of being freely and competitively open to talent, it was a fee-paying institution – save for a highly exceptional scholarship such as had supported Sullivan himself.

The comparison was with state-supported Continental conservatories such as that of Paris, where merit alone governed admission and no fees were charged. Such a comparison was made by John Ella, the veteran violinist, concert-promoter and writer (1802–88):

Within a few weeks lately in Paris I have heard splendid orchestral concerts, of 80 to 100 musicians, besides those of the Grand Opéra and Opéra-Comique, composed entirely of native talent, well-educated musicians. For unity of style, taste and feeling, the tenet of national schools, we have nothing in London to compare with the first-class orchestras of Paris and, for the same reason, those of Vienna. Our cosmopolitan London orchestras are composed of the surplus talent of the Continent, some educated, some uneducated, and no two of the same style of playing. With the immediate prospect of a national school for the gratuitous education of the musically gifted youths of this country, let us hope that eventually we may have our orchestras complete of well-educated native musicians.[9]

But how could free admission to the new institution be provided? State subsidy on the necessary scale was not to be had. (The government granted a mere £500 annually to the Royal Academy of Music.) The plan was that local authorities, the City of London livery companies and other bodies would endow sufficient scholarships. To encourage such endowments the Society of Arts had convened a meeting in June 1875 addressed by the Prince of Wales (the society's president) and by the Duke of Edinburgh, chairman of the school's committee of management.[10] The power of royal exhortation was evidently limited, for within a year only 82 scholarships out of the hoped-for 300 had in fact been endowed. But that was sufficient for a first intake of students, and Sullivan agreed to take on the direction.

Henry Cole (now Sir Henry), though retired from government service, had a chief role in the establishment of the new institution – a part of his grand plan for the utilization of the Kensington exhibition area. His son, as a friend of Sullivan's, proved a useful informal intermediary. On 10 January 1876 Sullivan wrote to 'my dear Alan':

Against my own inclination and judgement I have accepted the position of director of the new school. Don't think me ungracious. I never wanted it, but now I have taken it I will work for it loyally and earnestly. I still object very strongly to be clothed with such a verbose title, 'Professional Director' – of course I am professional, but the term would imply that there is another director who is *not* professional. Is this the case? If not, is there any objection to my being called simply 'Director'?

Before you make the announcements, I wish I could see you. I have a meeting at the R.A.M. at *3 o'clock* and am hard at work until then. I suppose you couldn't run up here in a hansom just for ten minutes? . . . If you can't, come to the Opera Comique (stage door) at *5*. There is a rehearsal of *Trial by Jury* [evidently for a change of cast].

A compromise was evidently reached over the title – he was called principal, like the head of the Royal Academy of Music. The post itself and its terms were evidently also the subject of dispute. On 13 January Sullivan wrote both an official and an unofficial letter to the Duke of Edinburgh, his mother making copies for him to keep. 'Sir' (the unofficial letter begins)

I had conversations on Sunday which made me, at the risk of incurring your Royal Highness's displeasure, pause before sending in my official acceptance of the post offered to me on Saturday. I felt that it would be impossible to enter into a position of authority unless I were supported by the unanimous goodwill of the committee and I learned that not only was it not unanimous but that a protest and strong opposition would be offered to my appointment on the terms which have been arranged.

No school could be carried on successfully with the element of discontent already there at the very beginning and yet I could not well withdraw again after my promise had been given to Your Royal Highness. So I thought the best thing was to see where the cause for the dissatisfaction lay and if possible to endeavour to remove it. So I went straight to Sir H. Cole and yesterday discussed the whole matter in the fullest possible manner. The whole scheme . . . was placed before me and I must honestly confess that many things assumed a totally different aspect to what they had hitherto borne. The result is that I have sent to your Royal Highness the accompanying letter which I trust may be more acceptable to the committee as being planned on a more suitable basis than my former one. Whilst I still reserve my private judgement as to the expediency of certain details, I will, now I have made my choice, act loyally and energetically towards the new institution in the hope that neither the committee nor myself will have cause to regret the appointment.

The official letter, evidently making some concession, ran:

Sir,

On reconsideration of the subject and having had many of the misapprehensions which I was labouring under cleared away, I request Your Royal Highness's permission to withdraw my letter and memorandum . . . and to say that I am ready to accept the Professorship of Composition and the Office of Principal acting in concert with the Board of Principal Professors, devoting my best energies to the School in the hope that it may become recognized by the State. I am also willing to receive the fee of £400 for my services during the first year as Principal and Professor of Composition. I have the honour to be, Sir, etc. . . .

An editorial of February 1876 in *The Orchestra* wondered whether it was not a waste of his gifts – and Sullivan, reading it as he continued to read assiduously everything in the press that concerned him, might himself have shared some of the sentiments:

The first effect of the new school at South Kensington would seem to be to deprive the world of the services of the only English composer we have who has made his mark in what he has done, and who might certainly far surpass himself in the future, and possibly leave behind him a great name and really great works. Mr Sullivan might conduct concerts at Glasgow, he might have a class at the Royal Academy, he might occasionally attend festivals at the Alexandra and Crystal Palaces, and at the Royal Albert Hall, and constantly superintend the musical arrangements of the Royal Aquarium and Winter Garden; he might attend to all this, produce his usual supply of pot-boilers, and conform to the requirements of royal and aristocratic patronage – and yet in his leisure intervals might find means for producing from time to time a symphony, an oratorio, or an opera. But to superadd to Mr Sullivan's routine occupations the duties of principal of the new school augurs well neither for art, for the school where it is to be taught, nor for the principal himself.

It will be sad if Mr Sullivan's acceptance of the appointment involved the loss of opportunity of becoming a great composer: one who might be mentioned by posterity in the same category as Handel, and Haydn, and Mozart, and Beethoven, and Spohr, and Mendelssohn. The notice from high places which is so conspicuously awarded to Mr Sullivan should be directed to furnishing him with means and opportunity for cultivating his peculiar talent, instead of forcing on him an occupation which will prevent him exercising it at all.

The school began its operations not at the beginning of an academic year but on 17 May 1876. Four days before, but with the students already present, the Queen paid a formal visit with her eldest daughter Victoria (now the Crown Princess of Germany). On the previous evening she had given a party for her daughter, at which the Grenadier Guards Band had played a selection from *Trial by Jury* as well as one from Gounod's *Faust*.

So 'the most conspicuous musician we have', as *The Orchestra* called him in February 1876, was installed at the head of a training establishment. He was to remain at the school for five years of its six-year existence: in 1882 the school would close its doors, to be absorbed in the new Royal College of Music. Sullivan's reign was conscientious but not influential as either administrator or teacher of composition. Ironically, the forced abandonment of the 'scholarships only' basis plus an improvement at the Royal Academy of Music brought the two institutions closer together in purpose. London acquired an approximate doubling of its higher educational facilities in music, but not a sharply differentiated, alternative curriculum.

In March and April 1876 Sullivan was again in Paris. Jules Pasdeloup, who was still running his own series of orchestral concerts, had accepted Sullivan's symphony for a rehearsal – or as we should now say, a run-through, no performance being promised (or, in fact, eventuating). Sullivan also took the opportunity of visiting the recently opened Opéra, which had taken 14 years to construct at a then unparalleled cost of £1,450,000 and was shortly to be styled by the *Encyclopaedia Britannica* 'the finest theatre in the world'. The report to his mother said nothing of the magnificence of the house, but dealt with the play by Jules Barbier to which Gounod had written extensive incidental music: 'Last night I went to the new Opéra to see *Jeanne d'Arc* and in my most sanguine moments I never expected to see such rubbish.'

In London, the Bach revival continued. The *St Matthew Passion* had been given under Sterndale Bennett as early as 1854, but the more abstract *Mass in B minor* had remained untackled.[11] Otto Goldschmidt had formed the Bach Choir specifically to remedy that deficiency. The performance at St James's Hall, on 26 April 1876, was followed by a repeat performance on 8 May which won a laudatory notice of quite exceptional length (more than a column of tiny print) in *The Times*. The writer, presumably Davison, did not fail to remark the presence of the conductor's 'distinguished lady' (Jenny Lind) in the choir, which she had helped to train. Though 'complete', i.e. with all movements, the Mass was performed with some abridgement and some changes in orchestration, the *obbligato* to 'Qui sedes' being played on a clarinet instead of Bach's 'oboe da caccia'. Sullivan was almost certainly present at one of these performances of Goldschmidt's and was himself to introduce the Mass – in more 'faithful' form – to the Leeds Festival ten years later.

At the opera Wagner's cause could be considered as won, no matter how much the conservative critics railed. At Covent Garden in 1876 there were eight performances of *Tannhäuser* and three of *Lohengrin* (given, as ever, in the language of the Royal *Italian* Opera House) as against five of the new *Aida*. Joseph Bennett, dispatched to Bayreuth that summer to cover the first performance of *The Ring*, filled seven pages of the *Musical Times* with a mixture of admiration and revulsion. The work 'teems with evidence of genius', but Wagner's perversity makes his art 'powerful chiefly for evil. Let us take care that neither in toad-form nor in any other does he sit at the ear of the fair art-world, pouring therein sophistries to work inevitable ruin.'

Arthur Sullivan and Christine Nilsson appeared together at St James's Hall on a weekday afternoon, 24 May 1876: it was a charity concert, organized by the singer, in aid of the building fund for the Hospital for Diseases of the Throat. Tietjens, Sims Reeves and other fellow-singers were also to participate, and Hallé as solo pianist, but Reeves failed to show up. His messages pleading vocal ill-health on such occasions had become notorious. *The Orchestra* suggested that promoters resort to a new form of advertisement:

ON THIS OCCASION THE AUDIENCE WILL

POSITIVELY HAVE A * CHANCE OF HEARING

MR SIMS REEVES

---

* Here insert "good," "fair," "small," or
"poor" as the case may be.

Afternoon concerts were for the few and the moneyed; summer evening promenade concerts at Covent Garden continued the Jullien tradition of appealing to a broader audience who paid an admission charge of as little as one shilling.

The floor of the auditorium was raised to the level of the stage, and a square bandstand, something like a broad, ancient hustings, was erected immediately below the proscenium to accommodate solo artists, a full orchestra, a military band, and frequently a numerous choir as well.

So Hermann Klein described the transformation of the theatre. An editorial in *The Orchestra* (September 1874) made the point that the atmosphere, sufficiently informal and inexpensive to attract the clerk or shopkeeper, might also attract the gentry of such a well-to-do suburb as St John's Wood.

Nine-tenths of those who go scarcely know what music is being played; the appreciation comes from the other tenth. But the place is a great mart for flirtation. Venus meets her Adonis there; . . . Jove, fat and pursy of build, carries off Europa, nothing loth, in his hansom, to sup with her in sylvan shades in the Groves of St John.

Favourite performers at these concerts included

Mr Levy the cornet, looking as if not a cornet but a coronet were in his grasp, and as if that theatre and all its contents belonged to him. . . . Or M Wieniawski appears, called variously 'Wine and whiskey', and 'Wiry whiskers' by the audience. But M Wieniawski's violin has nothing wiry about it, as he entrances his hearers by some charming concerto or *air varié*. There is no other capital can show a sight like these promenade concerts.[12]

At these concerts in 1873 and 1875 Sullivan's music to *The Merchant of Venice* was played: on the latter occasion the weekly *Hornet* described it as 'exquisitely graceful and full of melody'. Two years later Sullivan would himself appear as conductor at these concerts, where the cheerful, undemanding nature of the musical occasion proved a fit home for his deft operatic numbers in orchestral guise.

12 Collaborators

THE gossip-writer's trade throve then as now on the foibles or scandals of the famous. The weekly *Hornet* had been permitted a peep inside 8 Albert Mansions, Victoria Street:

Visitors to the studio of Mr Arthur Sullivan have been struck by the sight of a very primitive ornament over the mantelpiece, elevated to the highest place of honour. It is a butterfly net, such as schoolboys use and love, but one of the simplest pattern imaginable, its value being that it was the work of the Duchess of Edinburgh. Mr Sullivan, being some time ago one of a party of guests at the Duke's country seat, was setting out one day with some enthusiastic naturalists who were anxious to collect cabinet specimens of moths and butterflies. Observing that of all the party Mr Sullivan was the only one unprovided with the means of capture, the Duchess inquired the reason. A frank admission that he had not a net was enough; for the Duchess, courteously requesting the party to delay for a few minutes, ran to her boudoir, and before the ladies-in-waiting could come to her assistance, had improvised a net, attached it to a handle, and was back on the hall-door steps presenting it to the favoured owner. No wonder the net was used carefully, and brought home in triumph, to be preserved as a souvenir of the visit and the kindness shown by the royal hostess.

Such was celebrity, with royal connections duly noted. (That the 34-year-old composer of *Trial by Jury* should still be unmarried gave the gossip-writers a further field of speculation.) He was now to undertake two theatrical collaborations with Gilbert which, unlike *Trial by Jury*, were to be of full length. The *Sorcerer* (1877) and *HMS Pinafore* (1878) were landmarks. They brought the librettist and composer into a lasting relationship with Richard D'Oyly Carte and, as we shall see, they were created under a business arrangement newly advantageous for the creative parties: cash down on delivery of the material, in advance of production.

Before this, in the closing weeks of 1876, Sullivan had fulfilled another Glasgow season as conductor – a five-week season only, the reduction presumably indicating financial difficulties on the promoters' part. At the third concert on 5 December the ballet music from *Rienzi* and Siegfried's Funeral March from *Götterdämmerung* paid tribute to the vogue for Wagner.[1] The programme on 5 December also included Sullivan's own *Sapphire Necklace* overture, and he conducted more of his own music at other Glasgow concerts. On 21 November and 12 December he gave extracts from *The Light of the World*; on 19 December Hélène Arnim sang 'Thou art weary' to the composer's piano accompaniment, and two days later came the seven-movement suite from *The Tempest*.

Early in the following year Sullivan experienced a loss which shifted his manner of living and burdened him with permanent new responsibilities. His brother – 'dear old Fred, dearer to me than I can express' – died on 18 January 1877, aged 39.[2] For two years he had been suffering from disease of the liver, and his death certificate also mentioned phthisis, i.e. pulmonary tuberculosis. He left seven children aged between 13 and two.

Arthur Sullivan assumed immediately the position of breadwinner. He was already good-naturedly fond of his sister-in-law Charlotte ('Muff') and the children. His mother now joined the fatherless family at Northumberland House, Fulham; and at the end of June Sullivan himself – still living as a bachelor on his own – moved from no. 8 Albert Mansions to no. 9. He kept a housekeeper and apparently two manservants, Jack as a valet and Godfrey who could act as coachman. The four daughters of his brother Fred and the two very young sons (in order of age Amy, Florence, Edith, Maude, Frederic Richard, and George) remained with their mother and grandmother at Fulham, but Sullivan himself took charge of his eldest nephew, Herbert. Born 31 May 1868, in age between Edith and Maude, Herbert ('Bertie') henceforth lived as Arthur Sullivan's son, though not formally adopted. Charlotte was pregnant with another son, to be named William Lacy Sullivan. One of the daughters, Edith, was to die (aged 10) on 2 September 1877.

His habitual Sunday afternoon visits to his mother were happily anticipated.

Tomorrow Grove and I are coming out to see you . . . Order a nice open carriage at *five* and we will drive for an hour or so, and come back and have a frugal dinner with you at 6 or 6.30. Let us have cold beef and salad and fried ham and peas. I will bring or send Jack to wait. Don't let anybody else come.[3]

If there were a sudden need to change arrangements he would send his servant with a note:

I fear I cannot come down today, as [Sir Coutts] Lindsay is so pushed with [Grosvenor] Gallery business at the last moment and I am helping him. He has been so good to me that I am bound to do all I can for him, and am making myself *very useful*. . . . I shall be at the Grosvenor Gallery tomorrow afternoon at 3: you will come of course and, I hope, Charlotte too. You needn't go to Albert Mansions as no one will be there, and you must be *smart* as the whole fashionable world will be at the Gallery.

When planning a short visit to Paris in June 1877, he again urged his mother to 'have the open carriage' (that is, to take one under his regular arrangement for hiring) and on 17 May he told her to order a brougham (a type of closed carriage) 'for Amy tomorrow for confirmation, which I will treat her to'.

By the standards of the social class into which Arthur Sullivan had raised himself, his nine-year-old nephew was now ready to be sent to boarding-school. Prior to that he was placed with a tutor in Brighton.

Dearest Mum . . . I will take Bertie down tomorrow (Sunday) [9 September 1877] by the 5.50 train from Victoria. I should like you and Charlotte to have the carriage and drive up here when you have finished dinner and bring his clothes and books. We can have tea here. . . . You can be here between 3 and 4. I have to see my doctor again at 2.

His mother was called on to help in preparations (and was sometimes asked to bring Charlotte too) when Sullivan had an unusually grand dinner. From such occasions she must have guessed, if she had not been told, the status of Fanny Ronalds in her son's life.

Dearest Mum,

In for a penny – in for a pound. My Princess Louise is coming tomorrow [6 July 1877], so I had better do all I can to make her happy!

Bring a *lot of roses* – never mind what it costs – I don't get her every day. I want nothing but roses about the rooms – masses of them, and one in every single thing I have got. Hooray! Blow the expense. Godfrey [coachman] will be with you at 10.30. I hope neither you nor Charlotte will be late as there is a good deal to do.

A postscript follows: 'Don't forget the tea-spoons.' Preserved with this letter is a guest-list in his mother's own hand, headed by Princess Louise and her lady-in-waiting, followed by the Duchess of Westminster (or rather 'Dutchess': Mrs Sullivan's spelling was not immaculate and on other occasions Sullivan sometimes felt obliged to correct it). Other names included those of Mrs Ronalds, Lady Lindsay, the Lord Chief Justice (Cockburn), Santley, 'Signor Tosti' and 'Signor Visetti'. Like Alberto Randegger and Alberto Visetti, previously mentioned, Paolo Tosti (1846–1916) was an Italian composer who eventually settled in England – becoming a royal singing-teacher, a knight, and a celebrity.

Princess Louise (1848–1939) was Queen Victoria's sixth child: it was a sign of the gap between the queen's outlook and her children's that the princess (who had married the Marquess of Lorne in 1871) should dine at a commoner's home in this informal way. In four years' time, when Lorne had become Governor-General of Canada, the princess was to reciprocate with rather grander hospitality to Sullivan in Ottawa. Sullivan was also received by the Prince of Wales. 'The party at Marlborough House was small and very swell', wrote Sullivan to his mother:

The Prince and Princess were both very kind and nice to me and Mrs Ronalds sang *The Lost Chord* splendidly. I suppose if it is fine you will go and see the Boat Race. [Her home lay within a few hundred yards of that part of the Thames where the annual Oxford and Cambridge University contest was rowed.] I can't afford the time . . .

The Lost Chord, to words by Adelaide Procter, was the song particularly associated with Fanny Ronalds. Her singing of it, usually at private 'society' functions but on at least one informal public occasion (see p. 162), was famous. The Prince of Wales is said to have declared that he would travel the length of his future kingdom to hear her sing it. There is contradictory 'information' about the origin of *The Lost Chord*: that it was written 'in sorrow at my brother's death' *and* while watching by the bedside during Frederic Sullivan's last days.[4] It was published in the year of that death (1877). The obsessive repeated notes at the opening no doubt conveyed solemn intensity then as surely as they seem now to be a cliché of such emotion. Similar though not identical formulas, already remarked in connection with *In Memoriam*, may be found at 'How many hired servants' in *The Prodigal Son*, 'I hear the soft note' in *Patience*, and 'Now to the sunset' in *The Golden Legend*.

In outline form *The Lost Chord* follows a ballad convention – stanza [A], repeat of stanza with slightly different accompaniment [A¹], new strain [B], heightened version of first stanza [AX]. But several novel features, beginning with a harmonic change and an extra line at the end of [A], must have helped (apart from the sentimental religiosity of the words) to establish its individual flavour. Over-familiarity caused it to be derided, parodied and abused, and it was more than a century before a leading scholar, Nicholas Temperley, dared to reclaim it as 'Sullivan's maligned masterpiece'.[5] The oddest tribute to its popularity was to be Caruso's writing-out of the English words ('Seated one day at the organ . . .') in his own Italian phonetics so that he could please his British and American audiences: 'Sit-ed uan dei at dhi or-gan/Ai uas uiri and il at üz . . .'[6]

'Pot-boiler' it might be called (in the *Daily Telegraph*'s obituary of the composer, a sale exceeding 200,000 copies was noted), but there is no record that Sullivan felt such work as degrading. Why should he? Was not an even more eminent composer exploiting the ballad market, including that for the 'sacred song'? In the spring of 1876 a compound advertisement in *The Times* hammered home the point:

'There is a green hill' (Gounod's favourite song) will be sung by Madame Patti at the Royal Albert Hall on April 18

'There is a green hill' (Gounod's favourite song) will be sung by Madame Antoinette Sterling at the Alexandra Palace on Good Friday [April 14]

'There is a green hill' (Gounod's favourite song) will be sung by Mr Santley, at Liverpool, on Good Friday.

It was Gounod's publishers, Novello, who placed this and similar advertisements. The singer, in such a case, profited from a royalty on each song-copy sold. Gounod, who had involved himself in a scandalous *ménage à trois* with the singer and author Georgina Weldon and her husband, knew what his English public would buy. *There is a green hill*, to the words of the hymn by Mrs C. F. Alexander, was only one of dozens of his songs and part-songs written or adapted to English words at this period. The two-part, non-repeating form of the song – minor, then tonic major – was unusual in the English ballad context, though the 'obsessive' repeated notes in the melody and the throbbing triplet accompaniment were familiar. Indeed in Sullivan's own scornful attitude to Gounod's music one cannot help suspecting jealousy of the invasion of his own ground by the successful foreigner.

Sullivan's new commitment to the National Training School for Music took much time. To Sir Henry Cole he wrote in July 1877 that he was 'in the midst of a week's examinations, hard at work from morning till night, as I want a thorough overhauling of the school'; three months later he told his mother he was 'writing and "schooling" every day'. In November his insistence that additional funds be raised immediately, without waiting for more scholarships to be endowed, evidently involved him in acrimonious dispute. But 'we cannot go on as we are' (he wrote to Cole), 'because we are not keeping the promises we made in the Directory and are missing the essential elements of an Academy or Conservatorium'.

From Christ Church, Oxford, in March 1877 Sullivan received a letter: 'I am the author of a little book for children, *Alice's Adventures in Wonderland* . . .'. Lewis Carroll was meditating the possibilities of dramatizing the book:

If that is ever done, I shall want it done in the best possible way, sparing no expense, and one feature I should want would be good music. So I thought (knowing your charming compositions) it would be well to get two or three of the songs in it set by you, to be kept for the occasion (if that should arrive) of its being dramatized, so that we might then arrange for publishing them with music.

The proposal did not appeal to Sullivan. He told Carroll that he would have to charge an 'absurdly extravagant' fee if such settings were to be bought as copyright works and held for possible use; but he was willing to reconsider the matter if an actual proposal for a stage presentation were made. It came to nothing. Meanwhile there was an immediately lucrative stage task ahead – another commission to provide Shakespearean incidental music for Charles Calvert in Manchester. The Prince's Theatre had passed out of his hands, but at the Theatre Royal he produced *Henry VIII*, then as now among the most rarely staged of the plays.

'I do nothing but write, write, write. I think I shall get it finished by Saturday. I hope so – if not I must work all Sunday at it.' Sullivan's letter is dated only 12 days before *Henry VIII* was due to open: his psychological disposition was to wait until the pressure of an impending event built itself up. On the Saturday he was still writing but now thinking of a completion three days later still. The opening was postponed by two days from 27 to 29 August. Sullivan's contributions to the play were for the fifth act only, according to the *Manchester Courier* (31 August 1877), in a notice implying that pre-existent music had been selected for the rest of the play. Along with a *March*, a *Graceful Dance*, and *Water Music*, there was the interpolation of a song for the king, with chorus, to a text attributed to Henry himself ('Youth must needs have dalliance'). The *Manchester Courier* called Sullivan's music 'exquisite'.

From early 1877, kidney disease subjected him to increasingly violent attacks. One such attack occurred at Balcarres, on the occasion of another house-party where the Lindsays' guests included J. Comyns Carr (later to become a librettist for him),[7] Prince Leopold, and 'Mrs Ronalds and myself' (as he reported to his mother). A manservant surnamed Wren went with him, Jack having left him for another employer: 'I can't go without a servant, as the house will be full and the Prince will give extra work [to the Lindsays' own servants]'. At the end of his 11-day stay

my things with Wren had gone to the station yesterday afternoon and I was following them, when I had a violent haemorrhage suddenly come on and it left me so weak that Lindsay would not allow me to go, so here I am. I am much better today and I fancy it will have done me good and I got rid of bad blood. I think the change of air and violent exercise which I took on Saturday brought it on. I had to telegraph to the school and to Mrs Dockett [his London housekeeper], also to Grove. I hope to leave here on Wednesday and be in town early Thursday morning. I am very shaky still but know I am getting better. God bless you.

Detained at Balcarres by the Lindsays' solicitude, Sullivan superintended a musical evening for his hosts. He was a piano duettist in the Grand March from *Tannhäuser*; he accompanied Fanny Ronalds (who was likewise still a guest!) in *The Lost Chord*; he himself apparently sang in a trio. The song from *Henry VIII* (with a quartet to replace the chorus) was heard too.

If he had cut it fine in timing the composition of *Henry VIII*, he cut it even finer with the much larger undertaking of *The Sorcerer*, due for production at the London theatre oddly named the Opera Comique and located off the Strand. On 21 August 1877 he wrote to Visetti that he was 'going to work now on a new 2-act piece with W. S. Gilbert, to come out on 1 November, so I have not *too* much time to spare!' It would seem that Gilbert's complete libretto had been in Sullivan's hands since April and that Sullivan had postponed all work on it for three months – a truly remarkable procrastination, but one which became characteristic of him. The piece was not in fact ready until mid-November.

In order to finance it, Carte had set up a public company, the Comedy Opera Co. Ltd, in the previous year. The four directors included Frank Chappell and George Metzler, partners in Metzler's publishing house, which was to issue *The Sorcerer*. (Frank Chappell, it is important to note, was unconnected with the Chappells who ran the rival publishing house of that name.) According to Reginald Allen's account, Gilbert had insisted in March 1876 that he and Sullivan must 'receive a sum down, before putting pen to paper'. But in fact the contract as proposed in a letter from Sullivan on 5 June 1877 suggests that the first money would be paid only on delivery, not on commissioning.

On Gilbert's part, it was characteristic of him to offer a plot based on something he had already written – a story which had appeared in the previous Christmas number of *The Graphic*. The title of the story, with a strange echo of Donizetti and of an earlier Gilbert play (see p. 65), was *The Elixir of Love*. In his new libretto the love-potion was called not an elixir but a 'philtre' – with the inevitable pun:

Well, dear, of course a filter is a very useful thing in a house – quite indispensable in the present state of Thames water – but still I don't quite see that it is the sort of thing that places its possessor on the very pinnacle of earthly joy.

So says Aline on learning that her Guards officer fiancé, Alexis, proposes to put a dose of the potion into the communal teapot at a village fête to make sure that all the villagers are set on a course of love and matrimony. Such is the efficiency of the potion, as made by the firm of John Wellington Wells and Co., that each one will fall in love with whomever he or she first sets eyes on after awakening from a magic sleep.

Aline. But bless me, Alexis, many of the villagers are married people.

Mr Wells. Madam, this philtre is composed on the strictest principles. On married people it has no effect whatever.

The absurdity of an all-powerful magic limited by Victorian decorum brings us near to the fundamental humour of *The Sorcerer* and of other pieces to come. Suppose sorcery *were* a family business, with reductions for buying in quantity! Later there were to be other such clashes of conventions: suppose that the power of fairyland extended to the House of Lords, suppose that social equality were applied within a royal palace . . .

As in Shakespeare's *A Midsummer Night's Dream*, the personages under the enchanted influence see first (and fall in love with) the 'wrong' people, Aline herself becoming infatuated with the elderly rector, Dr Daly. The spell is undone by the gratuitous suicide of the Sorcerer himself – in a sufficiently stagy fashion (disappearing through a trap-door) to be accepted within the comic context. With the restoration of all to their former lovers, the opera ends with the resumption of the chorus and dance from the first act which Gilbert called 'the tea-pot *brindisi*' (drinking song). Here was another self-borrowing. A carousal on tea, making fun of the operatic drinking-chorus, had occurred in Gilbert's parody on *The Bohemian Girl* nine years before.

A different operatic model was in Sullivan's mind – the preparation of the magic brew is accomplished in an incantation scene which evokes (rather than mocks) the casting of the devil's bullets in Weber's *Der Freischütz*. As in that model, the spells are called by number; an off-stage chorus sings in 6/8 time; 'spooky' diminished seventh chords are heard, with shrieks from the woodwind. As the potion begins to take effect Sullivan writes an impressively sonorous ensemble for all soloists and chorus: 'Oh, marvellous illusion, oh, terrible surprise'. Here the basic four-bar period is stretched so that an extra bar leads to an exciting harmonic change at the climax – as thrilling a musical stroke as any which Sullivan was to produce in any later operetta. Because this section is couched in B (after previously prevailing keys of A, D, and G) the effect of strangeness is accentuated. Considerations of traditional form then led Sullivan to return to D major (which may be said to be the basic key of the whole act). But for a revival of the opera in 1884 this last section was dropped (it is one of Sullivan's most significant revisions) and a formal rounding-off was sacrificed for the greater effectiveness of the big sonority – even in a 'wrong' key.

The score as a whole displays, if not in fully developed form, Sullivan's basic operatic 'armoury'. A gavotte for the elderly Sir Marmaduke and his adored Lady Sangazure not only represents the 'old English' style but exploits the combination of previously separate tunes – the stately measure of one voice being contrasted with the other's rapid, passionate avowal. In Dr Daly's reminiscence, 'Time was when love and I were well acquainted', Sullivan's illumination of a single syllable is seen by comparing identical points of the two stanzas at the following lines:

> (verse 1) 'A saintly youth, by wordly thought untainted'
> (verse 2) 'Did I look pale? Then half a parish trembled'

Apart from a variation in musical metre to accommodate the altered poetic scansion, the optional high note on '*trem*bled' is perfect. The 'serious' pastoral recitative preceding this song has an orchestral background of nature-painting including bird-song, while Dr Daly's second-act song allowed the audience to witness an English clergyman interspersing his musings with flageolet solos – apparently played 'live' in Rutland Barrington's original performance.

More obviously tuneful in appeal are the ballads ready for transfer to the drawing-room, such as Alexis's 'It is not love'. It is significant that *The Sorcerer* displays not only what became recognized as Sullivan's typical range of musical devices and structures, but also a range of stylized character-personalities which were likewise to become familiar. We meet a tenor and soprano as young lovers; a second young woman (mezzo-soprano) and her lover (baritone); a comic character, of a jesting and perhaps morally ambiguous nature (baritone); an elderly, or in some other sense authoritarian, man – and, not necessarily linked to him, an elderly woman (bass and contralto). These types can be easily traced back to Italian comic opera and, behind it, the *commedia dell'arte*.

In the Gilbert and Sullivan pieces the gallery of characters just described is not always literally on view: but it is a basic theme on which dramatist and composer worked their variations. It is surely no casual neglect that the voice-types themselves (soprano, tenor, etc.) are not specified in the score of this or the later operettas; they may be deduced, but the roles are specified as if they were those of a spoken play.

The impersonators of these types were recruited only partly from the ranks of opera proper. George Bentham, the tenor who first sang Alexis in *The Sorcerer*, had performed with 'Her Majesty's Opera' – that is, not at Covent Garden or Drury Lane but at one of the international opera seasons promoted at Her Majesty's Theatre in the Haymarket. Giulia Warwick, who took the mezzo-soprano role of Constance, had sung with the Carl Rosa Opera. But a search for suitable talent was also made elsewhere.

There was strolling about the kingdom a small army of quasi-theatrical entertainers, who had won reputations in town halls, mechanics' institutes, and other such places as might aptly and without disrespect be styled chapels-of-ease to the theatres.

That was the recollection of François Cellier, who was to succeed his brother Alfred in 1878 as musical director at the Opera Comique and to remain Sullivan's closest musical associate. One of that 'army' was George Grossmith, whose appearance as John Wellington Wells was his first on the professional stage, and who was nervous lest his new connection with the theatre should prejudice the Y.M.C.A. against ever engaging him again. He came on the recommendation of Isabella Paul (Mrs Howard Paul), an experienced actress who managed her own theatrical company and herself sang as Lady Sangazure. From that company also came Rutland Barrington to play the role of Dr Daly. The two men were to become stalwarts – and public favourites – of the Gilbert-Sullivan-Carte team, Grossmith always in the comedians' parts.

With the last-minute haste which was characteristic of him, Sullivan left no time for writing an overture. As a substitute at the opening performance of *The Sorcerer* on 15 November 1877 he adapted the 'Graceful Dance' from *Henry VIII*; later an overture was compiled (from the tunes of the opera) – apparently by Hamilton Clarke, with revision by Sullivan himself.[8] The orchestra at the first night numbered 28: 14 strings (4/4/2/2/2), 2 flutes, 1 oboe, 2 clarinets, 1 bassoon, 2 horns, 2 cornets, 1 trombone, and 1 player of 'drums, cymbals, etc'. This opening night was a decided success, with liberal encores, and five days later the composer could write to Alan Cole:

They are doing tremendous business at the Op. Comique, I am glad to say: I was on the stage [i.e. behind the scenes] last night and heard *three* encores before I left. If it is a great success it is another nail in the coffin of Opéra Bouffe from the French.

The report to his mother mingled professional elation and filial solicitude ('Woodhouse' being the family doctor in Fulham):

Our piece goes very brilliantly every night and is I think a great financial success for the management. I went Monday and last night. . . . Have you seen Woodhouse as I told you? If not, please send for him *at once*. Never neglect a cold. I am working hard at the pianoforte score of the work for the printer. It ought to be out now. Metzler [publisher] anticipates a large sale for it. Tomorrow night I dine with the Chief Justice, tonight Gilbert and I have a long business talk. . . . God bless you. Now, mind you see Woodhouse. You will have your claret tomorrow.

The Sorcerer was preceded, at each night's performance, by a short one-act piece, *Dora's Dream*, to words by Arthur Cecil and music by Alfred Cellier; it was replaced, from 9 February 1878, by Cellier's new work, *The Spectre Knight* (words by James Albery).

The welcome which Sullivan found in the theatre was, however, already countered by a critical comment which in various forms was to follow him all his life. The London *Figaro* voiced

a sense of disappointment at the downward art course that Sullivan appears to be drifting into. . . . [He] has all the ability to make him a great composer, but he wilfully throws his opportunity away. A giant may play at times, but Mr Sullivan is always playing.[9]

13 'Pinafore' and Piracy

THE impact of Gilbert and Sullivan's work on London theatregoers of the 1870s was recalled by the critic Hermann Klein 50 years later:[1]

If *Trial by Jury* gave an inkling as to the possibilities of the new combination, *The Sorcerer* made manifest what skill and dexterity could do with clever people who were not stars; with actors who were not too 'distinguished' to be moulded into their parts or to yield to the fancies of tutors who knew exactly what they wanted, odd and unusual as these fancies might seem to them. Hence, whilst smiling at the 'topsy-turvydom' and laughing over the quips or the witticisms, we secretly marvelled at the naturalness and ease with which these quaint things were said and done.

For until then no living soul had seen upon the stage such weird, eccentric, yet intensely human beings, or listened to such voiceless, yet not unvocal singers, as the 'pale young curate' of Rutland Barrington or the 'dealer in magic and spells' depicted by George Grossmith. Their strangeness was disconcerting but irresistible; they conjured into existence a hitherto unknown comic world of sheer delight. The novel fascination and attractiveness of what they said and sang, whether in solo, ensemble, or chorus, fell upon the ear with a tickling lilt or a soothing balm that was irresistible. Their dances, like 'their exits and their entrances', were models of eloquent, fantastic movement.

In December 1877 the publishing house of Metzler had a success on its hands. The appearance of *The Sorcerer* in print did not take the form only of a complete vocal score. Individual songs, dance arrangements, and other selections augmented the publisher's and the composer's revenue, just as in the cases of Auber, Donizetti, Verdi and other composers of successful operatic works. By such means, and by the selections specially arranged for military bands, the music of 'serious' composers had a popular diffusion. Another channel, though it put nothing directly in the composer's pocket, was in the performances of itinerant street musicians – then as common a feature of town life as the vendors who 'cried' muffins, vegetables and other household staples.

The Victorian invention of the street-organ (or 'piano-organ') created a new type of street-purveyor, often Italian. A handle-turning gesture would long be preserved in D'Oyly Carte productions of *HMS Pinafore* to accompany the words 'or perhaps I-ta-li-an'.

Basso Giuseppe, aged 56, living at Saffron Hill, a musician, was charged before Mr D'Eyncourt with playing an organ at Bryanston St, Marylebone, to the annoyance of Col. Henry A. Ouvry, [who] went to the defendant and told him to go away, and he moved about five yards and then started playing. . . . [Defendant was found guilty and] would have to pay a fine of 10s, and 5s, the cost of the interpreter, or in default to be imprisoned in the House of Correction for 14 days.

Sullivan, if he read that report in *The Orchestra* (the offender's Italian surname and forename had evidently been reversed), would have shared the feelings not of the 'musician' but of the colonel. He referred in letters to 'horgins' (his own comic spelling) as a menace to his concentration, and must have concurred when 'the piano-organist' was put on the list of Ko-Ko's victims in *The Mikado*. Of predominantly German origin, however, were the groups of wind-players who paraded the streets. They, too, could be accounted a nuisance. In *Princess Ida* (1884) Gilbert made King Gama complain that he had 'nothing whatever to grumble at' because

> When German bands
> From music stands
> Played Wagner imper*fectly* –
> I bade them go –
> They didn't say no,
> But off they went directly!

But what was a nuisance in a well-to-do area was welcome elsewhere. In *The Graphic* at about this time is an illustration – reproduced in the observant pages of Alan Bott and Irene Clephane's book, *Our Mothers* (1932) – of an improvised open-air dance in a working-class street to the music of an organ-grinder. Half an hour's entertainment was no doubt provided for the cost of a few pennies thrown in the hat.

Sullivan's tunes were to nourish that kind of entertainment as well as others. He did not – how could he? – despise popularity. No less pleased than Mozart on discovering that the populace of Prague was singing 'nothing but *Figaro*', Sullivan noted that his music was to be heard at Nice while he was there in early January 1878. His pleasure is clear beneath the mock-pompous style of his letter to his mother.

I go [daily] to show myself on the promenade to the eager and expectant crowd, who rise to their feet as I pass while the band plays *Sweethearts*. . . . I went to Monaco the other day to have a look at the gaming tables. I staked a few five-franc pieces and came away the winner of 100 francs! . . . Tomorrow I shall make a colossal effort and go to church to counter-balance the wickedness of gambling.

While on the Riviera he received from Gilbert the draft of a new plot – the plot of *HMS Pinafore*, as it was to be named.

I hope and think you will like it. I called on you two days ago (not knowing that you had gone abroad) to consult you about it before drawing it up in full. I have very little doubt whatever but that you will be pleased with it. I should have liked to have talked it over with you, as there is a good deal of fun in it which I haven't set down on paper. Among other things a song (a kind of 'Judge's Song') for the First Lord – tracing his career as office-boy in cotton-broker's office, clerk, traveller, junior partner and First Lord of Britain's Navy. I think a splendid song can be made of this. Of course there will be no *personality* in this – the fact that the First Lord in the Opera is a *Radical* of the most pronounced type will do away with any suspicion that W. H. Smith is intended. Mrs Cripps will be a capital part for [Harriet] Everard.[2] I propose to have no *comprimaria* and to make Hebe, the First Lord's cousin (a more important part than appears in the sketch) the contralto. Barrington will be a capital captain, and Grossmith a first-rate First Lord. The uniforms of the officers and crew will be effective – the chorus will look like sailors, and we will ask to have their uniforms *made for them* at Portsmouth.

I shall be anxious to know what you think of the plot. It seems to me that there is plenty of story in it (*The Sorcerer* rather lacks story) with good musical situations. Josephine can have two good ballads and so can Ralph.

As soon as I hear from you that the plot will do, I will set to work, sending you the first act as soon as it is finished.

As for 'doing away' with any suspicion of making fun of W. H. Smith (Disraeli's First Lord of the Admiralty), the remark was probably ironic: of course the satire would hit its mark. The letter is notable because once again it shows how dominant was Gilbert's role in determining the structure of such a theatrical work. His proposal to have 'no *comprimaria*' (i.e. no second principal female singer *with her own solos*, corresponding to Constance in *The Sorcerer*), means that Gilbert had taken a *musical* decision and was submitting it to Sullivan's approval.

Gilbert's decision on the *comprimaria* shows him to be thinking, as Carte always did, of a company on long-term contract and of what would later be derogatorily called 'type-casting'. But the specialization of actors and actresses to particular types of role was the basis of the Victorian theatrical company. Harriet Everard, who had been Mrs Partlet in *The Sorcerer*, was to find a much more prominent role as Mrs Cripps (Little Buttercup), but it was the same kind of part. Barrington and Grossmith reappeared (as Captain Corcoran and Sir Joseph Porter), and also Richard Temple – a genuine bass, formerly Sir Marmaduke Pointdextre and now Dick Deadeye. A newcomer, Emma Howson, would sing Josephine, with George (later Sir George) Power as Ralph.

The role of Hebe did not turn out to be as important as Gilbert had forecast and was allotted to a newcomer, Jessie Bond – who began here her celebrated involvement with Gilbert and Sullivan's works. Her autobiography, written some 50 years later and not always reliable in detail, nevertheless vividly evokes the memory of being summoned from Liverpool by Carte's telegram: 'It was like a trumpet-call.' In her mind, ambition fought with the proprieties:

I had been trained in the strict conditions of concert and oratorio singing. Would not such a change in my life mean social downfall, and would not my parents think I had gone to perdition? I dared not tell them of Carte's offer. I knew too well beforehand how strong their objections would be. But in my eyes the prospect was too dazzling, I could not turn away from it. I made some excuse about a pressing engagement in London, packed in hot haste, and caught the first possible train. At eleven o'clock on the appointed morning I was in Mr D'Oyly Carte's office. He offered me an engagement in his company, and without hesitation I signed a contract for three years, at the princely salary – for me – of three pounds a week.

Grossmith, as a star, received at this time a weekly salary of 18 guineas (£18.90).[3]

'I think the new piece ought to be very funny', Sullivan wrote to Carte from the Hotel Chauvain, Nice, on 5 February 1878, noting also that *Cox and Box* had been performed at 'the Philharmonic' – meaning the London music-hall of that name. In the same letter the remark, 'I have lost all my money gambling – a regular facer' was characteristic. His work was not allowed to disturb his holiday mood. At Nice he lived a relaxed life, attended by his manservant Silva: 'I do literally nothing. I can't even get Boosey's two songs finished' (probably 'Old Love Letters' and 'St Agnes' Eve', published in 1879). He even resented the telegram which had summoned him to Paris for a mid-January meeting to discuss the British contribution to yet another international exhibition due to open in May. 'So I must leave my beautiful sunshine and travel 22 hours into the cold again.' To his joy, his kidney pain had suddenly left him on New Year's Day ('after one year and seven days of it'). Mme Conneau put on a concert for him in Nice on 18 February, at which he conducted the *Merchant of Venice* music complete, the *Overtura di Ballo* (again, his own spelling) and the 'Graceful Dance' from *Henry VIII*.

He was ill again just before the concert ('a violent crisis – racking rheumatic pains all over me, my head like a furnace and my throat closed up') but managed to conduct it with success. In a vein of sarcastic humour he sent back to his friend Davison of *The Times* a local review to show that

we Niçois are not behind the world in either performance or criticism. . . . What do you think of the Trio in the *Bourrée* (*Merchant of Venice*) 'containing trumpet-calls of quite a London colour which carry us back to the chimes of the Horse Guards of yore'? It is a pity that there is no Trio, nor are there any trumpets in it. Never mind, the concert was a brilliant success . . .

Mme Conneau's own singing of 'Pensa alla patria' from Rossini's *L'Italiana in Algeri* was 'as fine a work of art as I have heard for years. The phrases were so largely and nobly formed, the [rapid] passages sung with a perfection of technical power such as few singers possess now.'

In the same letter to Davison he wrote glowingly about his journey along the cliff road – Napoleon's celebrated Route de la Grande Corniche – eastward into Italy.

What a paradise from here to San Remo! Is anything more beautiful than the Riviera? My Italian blood warms and runs sympathetically all the quicker as I wend my way along the road amongst the palms, olives, and oranges. Blue sky, blue sea, and such a picturesque people. I should like to live in Italy.

Further east, lay his homeward route – via Genoa, another hundred miles along the coast road past San Remo. 'Here I am in "Genoa the proud",' wrote the adventurous traveller to his mother on Monday 25 February 1878,

having arrived here late last night. I took an affecting farewell of all my friends at Nice on Friday and on Saturday morning started off with a very nice fellow, Ernest Dresden, in a little carriage with two capital little horses. Silva went by train with the luggage and we drove along the famed Cornice road which runs all along the Riviera from Nice to Genoa. It was a heavenly day and I never enjoyed anything so much in my life. I cannot give a description but refer you to 'Doctor Antonio' for it. We stayed an hour and a half at Mentone for lunch and then resumed our journey as far as Bordighera where we stayed the night. Yesterday morning we were up betimes and on our way again, winding for miles along the picturesque route, mountains on one side of us, the Mediterranean on the other, through the quaintest, dirtiest, most picturesque old towns and villages as far as Albenga.

There we parted from our carriage, it being late in the evening, and took a parliamentary train which seemed to be wandering about listlessly on to Genoa. [A train which stopped at every station is meant, as in the penny-a-mile daily trains which Parliament had imposed on British railways (see p. 17).] We could find no good place to eat at Albenga so we went into a little tumbledown place near the station – got some eggs boiled hard with a little bread, salt and pepper, and took our hearty meal in the train. We are very comfortably lodged in this hotel and have been sauntering about all the morning looking at the town. The thing that most interested me was the Church of San Lorenzo – the finest here. It was shut up but we got in at the side door and found the interior magnificently prepared for the funeral mass of the Doge the day after tomorrow. All the pillars and other stonework was covered with red satin damask and gold – a great catafalque in the centre draped in scarlet, black, white and gold and nothing but scarlet, black and gold everywhere. The effect was magnificent.

The route he planned, and presumably followed, was from Genoa by train to Turin, Paris, and thence to London.

'D'Oyly Carte keeps worrying me to begin a new piece for the Opera Comique', he had written to his mother from Nice on 20 February, as though that were an annoyance to be brushed aside, and as though he had not had Gilbert's sketch to hand for almost two months. It was in his nature to postpone until pressure became irresistible. He may have begun work in March 1878 (evidence is lacking) but he had a smaller commission to fulfil first, promised for his friend John Hare's *Olivia*, a stage adaptation of Goldsmith's *The Vicar of Wakefield*, at the Court Theatre. From his London home on the Sunday preceding the opening night (it was to be 30 March 1878) he sent a regretful note to 'Dearest Mum':

The violence of the storm kept me away today as you probably judged. I would have come after it was over (about 6.30) but I feared the getting back as the roads would be so bad. The park tonight is nearly impassable and only two or three cabs are out. So I stayed at home and worked, then went to the Beef Steak Club and got dinner and now am home again, having relit my fire with a wheel. I have nearly finished a trio I am writing for Johnny Hare's new piece (the *Vicar of Wakefield*) next Saturday. I shall finish it before I go to bed, so that he can have it in the morning. Shepherd came today and asked after you, also two or three business callers, otherwise I have been undisturbed in my work.[4] I had a beefsteak, salad and cheese and a pint of light claret for dinner and now I am going out into the snow to post this.

Not until Good Friday (19 April) did he write to his mother that he was 'in the full swing of my new work. . . . It will be bright and probably more popular than *The Sorcerer*, but is not so clever.' His illness recurred: in later years he recalled the agonies experienced while composing music which was 'thought to be so merry and spontaneous . . . I would compose a few bars, and then lie almost insensible from pain. When the paroxysm had passed, I would write a little more . . .'

Other professional and social commitments had to be reduced. 'I must go to the [National Training] School for a couple of hours – that is all my outing this week', he had written to his mother on 18 April. On 23 April, preparing to begin rehearsals next day, he wrote requesting that 'the present chorus' (for *The Sorcerer*) be augmented in the male section to '*six* tenors and eight basses'.

HMS Pinafore was produced under the composer's baton at the Opera Comique on 25 May 1878 – *not* with a preceding piece, as in the case of *The Sorcerer*. The 'entirely original nautical comic opera' bore the subtitle, *Or, The Lass That Loved a Sailor*, recalling the refrain of a song by Charles Dibdin (1745–1819): '. . . the wind that blows, the ship that goes and the lass that loves a sailor'. As Burnand had already done, in a long-running burlesque called *Black-Eyed Susan*, Gilbert parodied an old theatrical tradition involving the clean-limbed young Jack Tar whose patriotism guarantees his virtue ('I am an Englishman, behold me!'). The villainy of the hunch-backed Dick Deadeye (the name is that of a block used as nautical equipment, but has a Dickensian suggestion of malevolence) is likewise that of melodramatic tradition. Gilbert had already, in one of the *Bab Ballads*, introduced a naval captain whose 'few female cousins and a niece, six sisters and an aunt or two' could suitably be matched with 'the unmarried members of the crew'. A further comic idea – of children mixed up in infancy and later taking each other's social position – had likewise been exploited in another *Bab Ballad*, in which a lowly soldier convinced his general that the two of them 'were cruelly changed at birth'.

> So General John as Private James
>   Fell in, parade upon;
> And Private James, by change of names
>   Was Major-General John.

The 'baby-farming' to which Little Buttercup confesses in *HMS Pinafore* as the cause of the mistake was no innocent child-minding: the placing of 'unwanted' infants in unskilled custody (sometimes to be drugged, underfed, and even allowed to die) had been a source of scandal.

When applied in the opera to Able Seaman Ralph Rackstraw and Captain Corcoran, the baby-swapping exposes a logical weakness on Gilbert's part: Ralph, hitherto presented as a conventional young suitor for Josephine, must in fact be as old as her father. But the plot, stronger than that of *The Sorcerer* in incident and motivation, admirably sparked off Sullivan's genius, not least in the trio 'Never mind the why and wherefore' (which begins with a melody-note which is not in the key at all, but serves to emphasize the phrase like a Johann-Straussian grace-note). The apt hint of a canon illustrates the duet in which Captain Corcoran and Deadeye circle round each other's meaning. The part-song supposedly composed by Sir Joseph Porter for the edification of the Fleet, and sung by Ralph with the Boatswain and Boatswain's Mate, takes the suitably old-fashioned form of a 'glee' in 'Old English' style – a 'set' effect paralleled in later operettas by the so-called madrigals.

Serious opera (and oratorio) is parodied. The big Handelian manner emerges in absurd mock-patriotic context of 'For he is an Englishman', where portentous music is harnessed to dramatic triviality. The 'mystic' revelations of Little Buttercup ('Things are seldom what they seem . . .') are unfolded to a mixture of confidential whispers and unnerving bangs; such commonplace expressions as 'But for some reason she does not seem to tackle kindly to it' are declaimed in Donizettian recitative. But Sullivan has his own seriousness. Approaching the emotional climax of Josephine's appeal to 'God of love, god of reason', or subtly shifting the rhythms and bar-groupings of 'This very night, with bated breath', he is composing 'straight', and well.

The ballads carefully placed by Gilbert were composed by Sullivan without undue effusiveness; he stooped to obvious tune-trundling only in 'I'm called Little Buttercup' – which, Offenbach-like, returns as an entr'acte so as to imprint itself even on the least musically minded of the audience. He unerringly found the right musical setting for Gilbert's 'What never? – Hardly ever!' – an exchange that later won proverbial familiarity – and even such an obviously verbal point was cunningly sharpened in music through the chromatic touch on the bassoon.

It was not surprising that *HMS Pinafore* greatly pleased its first-night audience and went on to win a favoured place in the affections of later admirers of Gilbert and Sullivan. What was surprising was that the press gave it a notably grudging welcome. The plot was said to be thin and the comic material 'not of the sort to allow a musician much chance of distinction' (*Sunday Times*): the music was 'disappointing' (*Daily Telegraph*) and 'feebler than anything that Mr Sullivan has given us' (the weekly *Figaro*). So strong was the adverse current that on 6 July the *Saturday Review* devoted an article to the contrary view, maintaining 'our conviction that there is no ground for the disappointment which some people have felt in *HMS Pinafore* at the Opera Comique. The play seems to us brisker than *The Sorcerer* and certainly not inferior to it in humorous qualities, and Mr Sullivan's music is throughout bright and pleasant.'

As with *The Sorcerer*, the observation was heard that such a type of comic opera was unworthy of Sullivan – unworthy in a moral sense, almost. *The Times*, even when noting the first night and recording 'the decided success of Mr Sullivan's new work', regretted 'that the composer on whom before all others the chances of a national school of music depend should confine himself, or be confined by circumstances, to a class of production which, however attractive, is hardly worthy of the efforts of an accomplished and serious artist'.

On the day after opening the composer and librettist decided to cut a hornpipe from the first act and Corcoran's 'serenade' ('Fair moon, to thee I sing') from the second – the latter afterwards restored. It is perhaps curious that Sullivan did not re-design and rewrite the second-act finale, a chain of reprises of five principal tunes (including, yet again, the 'Buttercup' waltz). That sequence is surely too long and 'not sufficiently welded together', as *The Times* put it.

In Paris, the International Exhibition was now open and Sullivan's presence as one of England's Commissioners was demanded. He wrote to his mother from the Hôtel du Rhin on 2 June:

I suppose you read about the awful shipwreck in the Channel. [The German warship *Grosser Kurfurst* sank with the loss of 284 men after colliding with the flagship of her own fleet.] Well, I saw it all – saw the unfortunate vessel slowly go over and disappear under the water in clear, bright sunshine, and the water like a calm lake. It was too horrible – and then we saw all the boats moving about picking up the survivors, some so exhausted they had to be lifted on to the ships. We were late arriving in Paris of course and I soon went to bed. Yesterday I spent at the exhibition and shall be obliged to do the same every day now as there are so many details to be settled . . . Last night I went to the great ball of the Minister of Finance in the Louvre, all very magnificent except the people who were rather dowdy. No good toilettes, no pretty women. . . . The Prince of Wales arrives here next Saturday for an official reception at the exhibition and Owen [Sir Philip Cunliffe-Owen, the Prince's secretary] very much wants me to stay for it. But I am not inclined as I am rather bored in Paris. It is very full and the exhibition is a great success. Things are not so dear as I expected.

He returned to London, only to be summoned back to Paris by telegram on 5 June; came home a second time and returned yet again on 13 July. He was so busy that, in order to have time to talk with him, 'D'Oyly Carte in despair got into the train and accompanied me to Dover'. In Paris he busied himself 'writing many letters and seeing people', including Prince Leopold, who evidently helped to establish a British royal presence. A pleasant duty was to arrange a choral and orchestral concert, attended by the Prince of Wales, which brought cordial press comment on his gifts as conductor and composer. The programme included Sterndale Bennett's Fourth Piano Concerto (Arabella Goddard being the soloist), an *Intermezzo* by Sullivan's former fellow-student J. F. Barnett, and Macfarren's *Chevy Chase* overture. Sullivan himself was represented by an extract from *The Light of the World*, by the song which was entitled 'L'accord perdu' in the printed programme, and by the 'Domine salvam fac' from the *Festival Te Deum*. This last-named item was a late substitution for the *Ballo* overture – to the confusion of one French newspaper critic, whose comments on the choral piece under the impression that he was hearing the overture occasioned some mirth in the *Musical Times*.

Sullivan stayed, as on a previous occasion in Paris, at the 'New Club'. An informal letter from there to 'Dear Miss Anna' (unidentified),[5] a new young acquaintance who had evidently left Paris for Berlin, sounds a note of tenderness not often found in Sullivan's correspondence.

Our concerts are over and I send you two newspapers to show you how we got on. We had one great drawback to a financial success, namely the absence of all the best Parisian families from Paris, so that all the smart people who would have flocked round the Prince of Wales were away and that made a great difference. Nevertheless, we were musically very successful and everyone speaks very highly of us. I am very tired and awfully hot, but am obliged to stay on as there is a *concours international* tomorrow and I must be present. On Wednesday I go back to England and shall not move again for some time.

How are you, and your Uncle and Aunt? When I came back on the Thursday and found you gone, everything seemed very *triste* and I missed you immensely. I had a sort of lingering hope that you would not go after all but that was soon dispelled. How awfully hot you must be in Berlin. I remember those long, white shadeless streets and shudder at them. Of course, in your pretty house and garden you can luxuriate in a cooler atmosphere, but if you go out – *Weh ihnen!* [Woe to you!]

. . . Write me a little note to London when you have time, and tell me you still think of me and, I hope, kindly. Tell me also, if you have any plans for the autumn and winter yet.

Goodbye, give my love to your Uncle and Aunt and accept – well, it is more proper of course to send you my kind remembrances, which I do with all my heart.

Back in London, he wrote to Carte on 12 September 1878:

My dear Carte,
I regret to say that on my visit to the Theatre last Tuesday I found the Orchestra both in number and efficiency very different to what it was when I rehearsed the *Pinafore*.
There seemed two second violins short and the whole band is of very indifferent quality. I beg to give you notice that if the deficiencies are not supplied by Saturday and the efficiency of the orchestra increased by engaging better players both of the wind and the stringed instruments I shall withdraw my music from the theatre on Monday night.
You know perfectly well that what I say I mean.
Kindly inform the Directors of this and oblige,

Yours very truly,
Arthur Sullivan[6]

The formality of this letter (Sullivan usually addressed correspondence to 'My dear D'Oyly') probably shows its purpose – to place in Carte's hands a weapon which *he* could sternly show to the economizing directors of the Comedy Opera Company.

He had received an honorary doctorate in music from the University of Cambridge in 1876 and would be similarly honoured by Oxford in 1879. In November 1878, as a British Commissioner at the Paris Exhibition, he was made Chevalier of the Legion of Honour. Another distinction was granted him before he left Paris that summer. At the city's leading concert series, the Société des Concerts du Conservatoire – in whose programmes no British-born composer had ever appeared – a morning try-out was arranged of the *In Memoriam* overture.

I was at the Conservatoire at a quarter to 9 [a.m.]. No one there but the orchestra, the conductor [Edouard Deldevez] and Ambroise Thomas and two officials. They tried the overture twice and when it was over the band applauded me loudly and enthusiastically. The Committee met immediately afterwards and sent me a letter last night to say that they had decided to perform it at an early date. So I have the distinction of being the first English composer performed at the Conservatoire!

Two performances accordingly took place to Sullivan's approval, and a further Paris performance in a different series on 8 February 1879, conducted by Pasdeloup – 'a duffer; he cannot enter into the spirit of a composer and his work and cannot reproduce it', as Sullivan reported home. There was no sequel, no general French acceptance of his 'serious' compositions.

It was probably on return from this visit that Sullivan penned a letter to Davison: 'Yes, *mon cher ami*, you may rely upon having the *compte-rendu* on Thursday morning. I got your letter in Paris.' By making sure that such accounts of his work abroad reached the desks of London critics he helped to keep publicity going. But *HMS Pinafore* was doing less well than expected at the box-office. Freakish hot weather in May and June, making theatres unbearably stuffy, is blamed by Jessie Bond and others, but the criticism voiced by London reviewers must also have had its dissuasive power. 'Business was so unsatisfactory, in fact' (wrote Sullivan himself much later)

that in July it was determined to put up the notice, and bring the piece to an end. Just then, however, a sudden change took place, and the theatre began to fill so well that the notice was withdrawn. At this time I was conducting the Promenade Concerts at Covent Garden, and every night I played a most spirited arrangement of the *Pinafore* music, which had been prepared for me by Mr Hamilton Clarke. It always went exceedingly well, and proved, I think, an excellent advertisement for the piece.[7]

Recollected at a 21-year distance, this account needs to be treated with some caution. In Davison's long article devoted to Sullivan's Promenade concerts (*The Times*, 19 August 1878), discussing the programmes in detail, there was not one word about the *Pinafore* selection (nor indeed about any of Sullivan's own music). It is inconceivable that had this selection been played 'every night' the fact should not be reported by such an admirer of Sullivan as 'old Jimmy' was. Apparently first given on 19 August (being greeted then as a novelty by the *Illustrated Sporting and Dramatic News*),[8] it could not have 'rescued' the operetta in July. There is no hint of such a rescue in the letter which Sullivan wrote to his mother on 16 August 1878 – though it does refer to the Promenade Concerts, to Gatti's as their proprietors, and to Alfred Cellier as Sullivan's assistant conductor.

Today is an off-day. No rehearsal and nothing to do till 3 o'clock at the theatre. So I polish off a few lines to you.

The concerts are brilliantly successful, they never had such houses before and the Gattis are delighted. But we work precious hard, and Cellier is a model! He is indefatigable. J. W. Davison comes regularly, and detains everyone at every corner, and tells long stories which he never finishes – but no one minds as he is so kind. Last night we did the *Overtura di Ballo*, and tonight the *Merchant of Venice*. The band is getting into splendid order, and some of our performances are very fine.

What extraordinary weather we are having! It has been beautiful sunshine all the morning, and now suddenly there comes on heavy rain and thunder. The coolness however is good for the concerts and the *Pinafore*.

Look at today's *Times*, about poor old Scott Russell. [He had been financially unfortunate and there was an attempt to foreclose the mortgage on his house.][9] I am dreadfully grieved, but I fear they can hold out there no longer. The marvel to me is how they have stayed so long. *She* will never leave the place except by force, I believe. Everyone is out of town, except Mrs Chichester next door, there is no one left at any of the clubs, and so my evenings are solitary after the concert is over, but as I am always pretty tired, it doesn't matter. Edward Dicey came up last Saturday, and we had a furious bout at cribbage (my first for many months!). I beat him by 177 holes on the night! You get the papers regularly I hope, as they are sent off early always.

Edward Dicey (1832–1911, ten years older than Sullivan), editor of the *Observer* from 1870 to 1889, was to become one of the composer's closest friends and companions. Sullivan had, indeed, contributed a single (anonymous) musical review to the *Observer* in June 1870, in such a forthrightly critical vein that his first article became his last.[10]

Arthur Sullivan's family responsibilities continued, especially towards Fred's children. 'Bertie', at boarding-school, remained his special care. On one occasion a letter from Mrs Sullivan tells him that 'Bertie' required a day's leave from school, presumably so that he could stay longer with her on holiday near Newbury (Berkshire).

My shorthand writer shall write to Christ's Hospital tomorrow about Bertie's leave. . . . I wouldn't bring him up [to London on the way back to school] next week if I were you, as it is a needless fatigue . . . Take Bertie yourself to Newbury Station, put him in charge of the guard (1st class), and I will send Godfrey (and Knight) [Sullivan's coachman and another manservant] to Paddington to meet him.

Later, when Amy was travelling on the continent and intended to visit Coburg, her uncle would send a note to the Duke of Coburg (see above, p. 82) to tell him so. Florence now found work looking after her uncle's bachelor household, replacing the ailing housekeeper, Mrs Minnie Dockett.

It was presumably at this time (that is, while his mother was at Newbury and *HMS Pinafore* was playing) that Sullivan wrote an undated letter to her:

Are there flys [light carriages for hire] at Newbury Station? Because if it is a fine day on Thursday, and I can get off rehearsal, I should like to run down there by the 9.0 train from Paddington returning by the 5.15 in time for the concert [one of the promenade concerts at Covent Garden Theatre]. Then I will bring some salmon and a piece of green paper with me unless you want the latter sooner. Old Jimmy [Davison] is a trump. He comes regularly to the theatre every evening.

The London success of *HMS Pinafore* continued. It was to extend even to the production of a *Children's Pinafore* (as matinées at the Opera Comique, beginning 16 December 1879), the entire cast being boys and girls. The revised vocal and orchestral arrangement was by François Cellier. There were repetitions in later seasons – one of which, after Sullivan had received his knighthood, aroused the pained expostulation of Lewis Carroll. One passage he found sad beyond words:

It occurs when the captain utters the oath 'Damn me!' and forthwith a bevy of sweet, innocent-looking girls sing, with bright and happy looks, the chorus 'He said, Damn me! He said, Damn me!' I cannot find words to convey to the reader the pain I felt in seeing these dear children taught to utter such words to amuse ears grown callous to their ghastly meaning. Put the two ideas side by side – Hell (no matter whether you believe in it or not; millions do) and those pure young lips thus sporting with its horrors – and then find what fun in it you can! How Mr Gilbert could have stooped to write, or Sir Arthur Sullivan could have prostituted his noble art to set to music, such vile trash, it passes my skill to understand.

Six months exactly after *HMS Pinafore* was born it crossed the Atlantic to Boston. The performance at the Boston Museum on 25 November 1878 drew the verdict of the *Boston Advertiser* that it was a long time since the city had seen 'an entertainment at once so novel, droll, decent and delightful'. The Boston version, apparently more or less faithful to the original, was the forerunner of a positive rash of *Pinafore* productions in New York, all taking various liberties of treatment and interpolation and making tidy profits. All (including Boston's) were necessarily based on the published vocal score, locally orchestrated; Sullivan's orchestrations existed only in his manuscript copies.

Neither Gilbert nor Sullivan could draw a cent from these productions. Under United States law, it was generally understood that the publication of a theatrical work made it public property, freely usable. The free-enterprise American promoters of *Pinafore* were exercising their rights – as London theatrical managers had put on French plays in translation without paying their authors. The promoters were infringing no law, no international convention (there were no international conventions on copyright in those days). It is usual to refer to them as pirates but they were not so in any strict sense.

Sullivan might, perhaps, have gone over on his own to conduct the operetta – he told Carte he had been offered a thousand pounds to conduct it for a fortnight in Philadelphia (bringing, it must be supposed, his own orchestrations).[11] Instead, Carte determined to take over a whole company – that is, a group of leading soloists, not a complete cast with chorus – and to present the work in its authentic London guise. Carte sailed in July 1879 on what is usually described as a reconnoitring of the pirates' ground. But in fact the decision that Gilbert, Sullivan, and the company should go must have already been taken. On Whit Monday (2 June) the composer had written to Prince Leopold: 'I am going to America in October.' In July he underwent a medical operation on the kidneys, perhaps expressly to make himself fit for the trip. For Gilbert, it would not be a first trip: he had briefly set foot in New York a few years before, an episode on which he did not care to dwell. He had an additional reason for a visit: the operetta *Princess Toto*,[12] in which he had collaborated with Frederic Clay, had been successfully produced in London and was now to be given in New York. Clay was already there.

Sullivan's plans to visit America naturally involved Fanny Ronalds. In the previous winter she had changed her London address, and on her behalf Sullivan had asked a favour from his friend A. J. Hipkins of the firm of Broadwood:

Will you kindly give directions for Mrs Ronalds' piano (84 Sloane St.) to be taken away tomorrow, as she and her family are moving to 104 in the same street, and she would like it back after it has been tuned, etc. . . . [P.S.] Did you see the notice of Grove's *Dictionary* in today's *Times*? [27 December 1878]

Perhaps it was at the time of this move to presumably larger premises that Fanny Ronalds brought Mr and Mrs Carter, her parents, from America to live with her and the two children, 'Fanette' and 'Regie'. Her roots were now where Arthur Sullivan was.

Two months later (11 February 1879) Sullivan pursued the matter.

My dear Hipkins . . . *I* want to pay for Mrs Ronalds' piano – the hire, I mean. She is a *very* old friend of mine, and not well off, the best amateur singer in London, and has sung my songs in London, Paris, and New York as if she had a royalty upon them! – and I should like to give her this musical little attention. Send me her bill like a good fellow and I will send you a cheque. I can easily afford it, for I have had a very good year with the *Pinafore* and *The Lost Chord* . . .

That sense of well-being must have been conspicuous on 13 May 1879, when Sullivan celebrated his birthday with a dinner-party at the Garrick Club, Gilbert and the Duke of Edinburgh being among the guests. He had already been marked as a successful composer; he was now to be a prosperous one.

14 Transatlantic

FOR Carte to take his leading performers and his two creative spirits to America was adventurous, but it was far from pioneering. 'Grand opera' performed by European stars had been firmly established in New York's social season since 1854, when Grisi and Mario appeared in Bellini's *Norma* at the opening of the Academy of Music, as the city's opera house was called. Four years before, Jenny Lind, with Julius Benedict as her accompanist and conductor, had been promoted on an American tour by the famous showman P. T. Barnum, at an unprecedented fee of $1,000 per concert, plus all expenses. In 1859 the career of Adelina Patti, who had been brought up in New York, was launched at the age of 16 when she sang there the title-role in Donizetti's *Lucia di Lammermoor*. (An intimate patron of hers was the wealthy Leonard Jerome, soon to transfer his attentions to Fanny Ronalds.) *Aida* had reached New York as early as 1873, before being produced either in London or Paris, and in 1878 J. H. Mapleson (London's leading operatic impresario at Covent Garden and elsewhere) began regularly to take a European company to New York.

Carte, on his advance trip prospecting for his New York enterprise, sensed a difference between New York and London tastes. It would be necessary (he wrote to Sullivan on his return)

to give a much more *prononcé* performance than we do here. They like 'emotional' singing and acting. The placid English style won't do and I assure you that if we took out such a company as [the one currently performing at] the Opera Comique we should make a big failure as likely as not . . .[1]

While Carte was in America, Sullivan had departed on a further holiday to Switzerland and Italy. He had undergone a 'very successful' operation for crushing the stone in the kidney and on 30 July wrote from Paris to Michael Gunn (Carte's assistant manager) that he was 'free from all pain and only want[ing] rest and fresh air.[2] Tomorrow morning I start for Pontresina in the Engadine . . .' There he was to be in the congenial company of Arthur Cecil, Joseph Barnby and his wife, the actor Squire Bancroft and his wife, and Otto Goldschmidt.[3] On 26 August, in aid of the English Church at Pontresina, Sullivan himself sang the part of Cox in a performance of *Cox and Box* with Cecil as Box, Barnby as Bouncer, and Goldschmidt at the piano.

But while Carte and Sullivan were both absent from London, and Michael Gunn was supervising the *Pinafore* production, there was upheaval at the Opera Comique. The lease of the theatre to the Comedy Opera Company ran out on 31

July 1879. After that Carte would be independent of the company and the proceeds of the production would be divisible only between himself and the composer and librettist. But the directors of the Comedy Opera Company, claiming that the right to perform the work was theirs and no one else's, sent in a gang of men to carry off the Opera Comique scenery in the middle of the performance.

Gilbert, in a letter to Sullivan, reported that the attack had been directly urged on by Frank Chappell of Metzler's and his brother Cecil, a solicitor: 'Barker [licensee of the theatre] resisted their approach and was knocked down and seriously hurt. There was an alarm among the audience who raised a cry of 'Fire!' – appeased, however, by Grossmith, who made them a speech from the stage . . .' The dispute turned partly on whether Sullivan had retained complete rights to his music and thus could withdraw score and orchestral parts from a theatrical management. He relied on the advice of his friend George Lewis, 'the subtlest, cleverest and most likeable of English solicitors', and a prominent figure in theatrical circles.[4] On Sullivan's behalf, Lewis announced the composer's intention to withdraw his material on 31 July. The company, however, gave notice as early as 9 July that they contested this position and intended to transfer the piece to another theatre. An injunction was granted which restrained the company from doing so, but because of Lewis's delay (he should have applied for the injunction immediately on receiving the letter of 9 July, but did not do so until 1 August) the injunction was dissolved by the Court of Appeal.

The directors of the Comedy Opera Company profited from their temporarily advantageous position. On 21 August they successfully brought an action against Carte (who had returned from America) and secured their right to go on presenting the rival performances at the Aquarium, otherwise known as the Imperial Theatre. 'Business is fairly good at the Comique', reported Carte in a letter to Sullivan on 26 August, 'but seriously damaged no doubt by the performances at the Aquarium.' The legal wrangle with the Comedy Opera Company would not be finally put to rest until 1881.

Carte's plan in America was not merely to present the authentic version of *Pinafore* in New York and other American cities. He would launch a new operetta by Gilbert and Sullivan. As usual, Gilbert would be the stage director and Sullivan would conduct the opening performance. Since it would be first produced in America, the hope was that it could claim the protection of American copyright and earn fees for its begetters, instead of being freely grabbed by 'piratical' rivals. Gilbert, Sullivan and Carte were to divide the box-office receipts equally, after payment of expenses, and in addition Carte was to give each of the others one-sixth of his net profit from the whole tour. (This was demanded in a letter of Sullivan's to Carte, 4 October 1879, and was presumably conceded.)

While in America, Sullivan was ambitious to promote his concert works too. The *Ballo* overture had been given in New York as early as 1870 by Theodore Thomas's orchestra, and Thomas had also conducted the cantata *On Shore and Sea* in Chicago in 1877. Now Sullivan had the prospect of going to Boston to

conduct *The Prodigal Son* – an engagement pre-arranged for him by Carte.[5]
Sullivan left London on Saturday 25 October, taking the boat-train in order to
embark at Liverpool, accompanied by his manservant, Joseph. His last day at
home was crammed: in the course of it he had seen 'at least 30 people' (as he wrote
to his mother at 1 a.m. on that Saturday).

> I dined with the Lindsays at 7, the only time I have seen them for months, and was home
> to meet [Tom] Chappell at 9.15. I was writing and working all last evening [i.e. 24
> October] and finished a song, 'Edward Gray', which I had promised for a Tennyson
> collection. Joseph has gone off this evening with the luggage. I am very glad now you
> didn't come today – I couldn't have spent two minutes alone with you . . .

He had to part also from Fanny Ronalds, but did not refer to it.

W. S. Gilbert and Arthur Sullivan were fellow-passengers aboard the Cunard
Steamer *Bothnia* along with Alfred Cellier. His brother François was now in
charge at the Opera Comique, so Alfred would take over from Sullivan as the
regular conductor for Carte's New York season. Also on board was a 25-year-old
American soprano, Blanche Tucker Roosevelt (she sang in Italian opera under
the surname Rosavella), and her husband.[6] She was to sing the heroine's roles in
both *HMS Pinafore* and the new work. Six other principals came with Carte
aboard the *Gallia* a few days later, Carte himself almost missing the boat after the
directors of the Comedy Opera Company had tried to detain him by legal process.
The remaining artist from England, R. Furneaux Cook (he was to play Dick
Deadeye in *Pinafore*) arrived in the following week.

Gilbert and Sullivan landed on 5 November and were immediately received in
New York as celebrities. Frederic Clay was at the dock to greet his old friend
Sullivan. On 13 December *Princess Toto* would open at the Standard Theatre,
billed as 'the new opera by W. S. Gilbert and Frederic Clay'. Note the order of
the names (the 'G. and S.' coupling was not unique) and the preference for
'opera' rather than 'operetta' as the description of this light, fanciful comedy.
Sullivan found himself most happily lodged at 361 West 23rd St, the home of
David Beach Grant and his wife. 'The house is as pretty as it can be – unlike a
street house, more like a country cottage', as he reported on 10 November to
'dearest Mum'.

Carrying out a procedure which afterwards became habitual, Gilbert and
Sullivan left till late the determination of the name for their new piece and kept it
concealed from the public (and rival theatrical managements) as long as possible.
On landing, they had given an interview to the *New York Herald* which took up
nearly 2½ columns of print in next day's 12-page paper. The reporter asked
about 'your new opera – *The Robbers*, it is to be called, I believe?' Gilbert replied
that the name was at yet undecided, and sidestepped a query about 'the story of
the six burglars making love to the six daughters of the proprietor of the house
they break into'. Sullivan, referring to an opera of Hérold's about a sixteenth-
century pirate, vouchsafed the information that 'it's the story of a modern *Zampa*
– of pirates and escapades of 200 years old, which, if dressed up in our modern
clothes, must seem very absurd'.

Journalism in New York was much more free in comment on personal appearance than Sullivan had been used to in London. He did not like the New York approach and probably read the *Herald*'s description of himself with some distaste.

In his appearance gentle feeling and tender emotion are as strongly expressed as cold, glittering keen intellect is in that of Mr Gilbert. He is short, round and plump, with a very fleshy neck, and as dark as his *collaborateur* is fair, with a face of wonderful mobility and sensitiveness, [on] which the slightest emotion plays with unmistakable feeling, with eyes which only the Germanic adjective of 'soulful' would fitly describe and the full, sensuous lips of a man of impassioned nature. With all this Mr Sullivan, who keeps a monocle dangling over one eye while the other twinkles merrily at you, and whose dark whiskers and hair have an ambrosial curl, is also something of a polished man of fashion.

With a population just short of one million, New York was effectively confined to what would now be called Lower Manhattan. The Brooklyn Bridge, though begun, had not yet opened for traffic, and Brooklyn, with its own 'Society', was not part of New York City at all. Theatrical life was vigorous. At least 20 theatres advertised in the press, and farces and musical plays (of American, British or continental origin) were popular. Maurice Grau's French opera company was due to open at Booth's Theatre on 24 November. Its programme would be mainly of operetta (including Offenbach's *La Belle Héléne* and *La Grande-Duchesse de Gérolstein*) and would include Ambroise Thomas's *Mignon*, which Sullivan took the opportunity of seeing.

He became particularly friendly in New York with David Beach Grant's youngest brother R. Suydam Grant (they were familiarly addressed by their middle names as 'Beach' and 'Suydam'). A prominent society bachelor, Suydam Grant was one of New York's best-known brokers and a member of the New York Stock Exchange from 1865 until his death in 1912. Sullivan met warmth everywhere. At a dinner given in his and Gilbert's honour at the Lotus Club,

the Judge of the Police Court said that to show his hearty goodwill and to mark his feeling of gratitude for the many happy hours we had given him, he hoped we might soon be brought before him as drunk and disorderly, so that he might have the pleasure of letting us off! Everyone is most kind, and most anxious to show us every attention. The first impulse of an American when he is introduced to you is to try and do something for you – something agreeable.

His mother was kept abreast of his friendships:

. . . Mrs Grant is quite unchanged, a shade stouter perhaps. Beach Grant I like immensely – he is the kindest host possible and we are great chums. . . . Shall I say that Suydam is an angel? No, he is better than that, because he *practises* goodness, and don't sing about it with a harp. He is the dearest fellow in the world, so thoughtful and so unselfish. Mrs Grant is just as sweet and dear as she always was. She sends her love to you and says that she does her best to make me feel I have a mother here. . . . Joseph is a great comfort to me – he is a most admirable servant and is a kind, good-hearted lad: he is very popular downstairs [i.e. among the house servants].

. . . The papers tell me every morning what is doing in England, and then I think the blankness of the ocean really destroys the idea of distance. You leave one town and arrive at another just like it – same language, habits, etc., and the water in between prevents any diversion of one's thoughts – no scenery or variety or change to distract one. I assure you I don't feel nearly so far off here as I did at Nice. How is everyone? Charlotte, children, the Dremels,[7] yourself? Don't ever telegraph unless a quick answer is required, as it is costly.

Sullivan had nevertheless registered for himself the telegraphic address of 'Pinafore, New York', corresponding to 'Pinafore, London' which he used at home.

His state of excitement and well-being continued when he arrived by train in Boston to conduct the Handel and Haydn Society – as prestigious a choral body as any in America – in *The Prodigal Son* on 23 November. His hotel was Tremont House. He met the music publisher Oliver Ditson and found the Society's orchestra 'very good indeed'. Carte's opening night was scarcely a week away. 'We have engaged a first-rate chorus,' (wrote Sullivan to his mother on 21 November) 'and the principals are the best who have ever been got together for the immortal *Pinafore*.' On Monday 1 December he conducted the opening at the crowded Fifth Avenue theatre – the first 'authentic' Gilbert and Sullivan production (with the composer's own orchestration) to be heard in the United States. Exceptionally, Gilbert himself took part on stage – in the chorus, doubtless to give precise leadership in stage movement.

But neither the *New York Herald* nor the *New York Mirror* (a weekly theatrical newspaper) treated the event as a revelation. Neither did so much as mention the new orchestration, and even Gilbert's stage direction did not deter the *Mirror* from the observation that this production 'did not materially differ from the *Pinafore* we are familiar with'. It almost looked as if the purveyors of the *Pinafore* had missed the boat. A printed form detailing box-office receipts, completed day by day in Sullivan's hand, shows that gross receipts of $1,337.25 on the first night went down to $925.50 on the next and (with the note 'very wet day – thunderstorm at night') went as low as $624.50 on Saturday matinee and $717.25 on Saturday evening: total revenue $6,194.50. The company's salaries took $1,310.00, which with other expenses mounted to $2,291.58, and the lessee of the theatre was entitled to $2,478. A profit of $1,324.92 remained to be divided between Sullivan, Gilbert and Carte – $441.80 to each. That was little more than £110 at the current rate of exchange of 4s. 1d. [just over 20p] to the dollar. Moreover Sullivan found New York prices outrageous, telling his mother that 'a dollar is about a shilling, for all practical purposes'.

On 4 December Sullivan moved into lodgings at 45 East 20th Street, paying $28 weekly for his and Joseph's rooms 'and $2 a week for fires if I have them'. Mrs Grant supplied him with cutlery and crockery. No meals were provided, so 'Joseph has bought a little gas stove, and cooks my breakfast every morning in the bathroom'. A further letter to his mother (12 December) told of further disappointment at the box-office:

All the theatres are doing badly, and we still have no profits until the new piece comes out. So Gilbert and I are reducing our expenditure. We shall begin by not paying the postage of our letters home! We hope to have the new opera out on the 27th or the 29th. It is called

The Pirates of Penzance, or *Love and Duty*. I can't help feeling sanguine of success, though one ought never to be sanguine . . .

In the same letter he asked his mother to send out urgently 'some plum puddings, good English ones, as many as you think judicious', as well as a dozen bottles of Brown's boot-polish, some tea and other things, suggesting that she could consult 'Mr Carter (104 Sloane Street)' – i.e. Fanny Ronalds's father – about the best way of packing and shipping.

In the same letter, in an astonishing reversal of his former praise for the generality of American life, he wrote:

I wish I were in England. If anyone wants thoroughly to appreciate England let him come to America. That will show him what England is worth. I will not put on paper my feelings with reference to many things in this land of liberty and freedom, but I will give them to you freely when I return.

And, more explicitly, on 20 December:

Dearest Mum,

This is to wish you and all around you at home a Happy New Year, and the most heartfelt wish I can venture is to hope that next year I may spend it with you. I am sick of the place and the people. It is like a provincial English town – only ill-bred, rough and swaggering – I am bitterly disappointed in everything around me. The people in the street and shops are insolent and ill-mannered and with the exception of a circle like the Grants, Barlows, etc. [Samuel Barlow was a lawyer friend of Gilbert's] there is no real lady or gentleman to be found. I of course accept them if they are pleasant in any way but for the rest I don't care a straw. This is only New York I am speaking of as I don't know what the other towns are like (except Boston) but I suspect they are all pretty much alike but perhaps the South is different, I hope it is.

Don't show this letter to anyone as it might get about and I shall probably read in the newspapers in the morning the large heading 'Arthur Sullivan's opinion of Americans' and I am obliged to be very careful. It is like walking on stilts, every word I utter I have a feeling will appear in a paper the following day. The pressmen are an unscrupulous, lying, inquisitive, and mischievous set, who will do anything and print anything. Eight weeks tomorrow since I left England and I wish myself back already.

Republicanism is the curse of the country. Everyone is not only equal to but better than his neighbour and the consequence is insolence and churlishness in all the lower orders. Well, it won't last very long for me. So, having opened my heart, I will leave the subject.

Sullivan had begun work on *The Pirates of Penzance* before he left England. He had completely 'sketched' the first act (the next stage would be to transform this into a skeleton score with all the vocal work complete) and had then gone on to sketching the second act. But, as he wrote to his mother on 10 December,

I fear I have left all the sketches of the first act at home,[8] as I have searched everywhere for them. I would have telegraphed for them but they would not have arrived in time. It is a great nuisance as I have to rewrite it all now, and can't recollect every number I did.

Meanwhile he had proceeded with the actual composition of the second act which was now 'done and is in rehearsal'. Probably not yet 'done', however, was the writing-out of the end of the act, which involved no new composition but only a reprise of previous music.

It is not only Sullivan's letters home that reveal much of his habits of work at this vital moment and later. From the beginning of this American trip Sullivan kept a diary: he was to continue it, with varying assiduity, until his death. Twenty leather-bound volumes (1881–1900) now repose at the Beinecke Library, Yale University, and a preceding volume (covering the end of 1879 and the year 1880) at the Pierpont Morgan Library, New York; they form a basic source of biographical knowledge. Metal locks on the volumes afforded the diarist a measure of secrecy and he further protected himself by the use of initials and code-signs – generally in alluding to a sexual relationship. But most of the material in the diaries is open in form and vivid in expression.

Not the first entry in the diary, but the first to describe his work on the new opera, may be quoted. Typically, the transcription in the Flower biography (see Preface) not only shortens the entries but transcribes them faultily. It was not 'Cecil Clay' but, of course, his old friend Frederic Clay who gave assistance in copying out the overture – written not by Sullivan but by Alfred Cellier, whose invaluable role was to rehearse the cast in what the composer had *already* written while Sullivan himself was getting another instalment ready. Cellier, it will be noted, also 'finished second act' – presumably writing out the last number as a reprise under Sullivan's instruction.

[10 December] Writing all day. Gilbert, Cellier, Rosavella [i.e. Blanche Roosevelt], Clay called. Cellier stayed and finished second act . . . I wrote till 4.30 [a.m.].

[13 December] Conducted matinée at theatre [i.e. of *Pinafore*]. Came home and wrote. Had no dinner.

[14 December] Wrote all day. Went to the Grants afterwards. Came home and wrote.

It was in rewriting the first act, without his missing sketches, that Sullivan adapted a chorus from *Thespis* (see p. 73) into 'Climbing over rocky mountain'. Inspection of the *Pirates* manuscript shows the relevant part of the *Thespis* score inserted with altered words. (Evidently the composer had a *Thespis* manuscript with him – in a copyist's hand – which he raided.)[9] By 15 December enough of the first act had been written, and copies of the vocal parts made, for rehearsals to begin.

Rehearsal of music of 1st act at theatre. Wrote afterwards. Dined at the Manhattan Club with Gilbert. Went round to theatre. Then home to work.

[16 December] Wrote in the morning. Interrupted by constant callers. No dinner. Went to concert of the Mendelssohn Glee Club; heard *The Long Day Closes*. Admirably sung and encored.

[17 December] Went to rehearsal 11–4. Came home tired. Couldn't work. Dined at the Betts. Then home. Wrote Trio (2nd Act) and [re-wrote] Ruth's Song (1st Act) and went to bed at 5 [a.m.].

In the margin opposite 18 December (not 17th, as given in Flower), occurs the remark 'Began scoring of the opera' – i.e. the writing out of the full score, necessary for the orchestral but not the singers' rehearsals.

[18 December] Rehearsal at my own rooms of principals, 11.30 till 3.30. Very tired. Went to bed at 5.30 till 7. Then up, had a walk, dined with Gilbert. Came home; scored 2 numbers of 1st Act. Went to bed at 4.

[19 December] At work all day, scoring. Went to *Pinafore* afterwards. I conducted. Came home with Cellier; stopped at Dorlon's [restaurant] to have a chop; saw Sothern [Edward Sothern, the celebrated actor] there. Wrote till 6 a.m.

[20 December] Conducted at matinée. Came home at 9.30 and wrote till 4 a.m. The roysterers (Gilbert and Clay) came in of course about 1.

[21 December – Sunday] Went to Grace Church at 11 to hear my *Te Deum* and *Jubilate* and *Kyrie in D*. Came home and worked till 5.30 [a.m.]

[25 December] Worked all day. Dined at the Grants'. Came home and worked till 5.30 [a.m.]

[26 December] Writing. First act rehearsed with band only.

[27 December] Finished full score at 7 a.m. on morning of 28th, Sunday.

[29 December] Full band rehearsal 10.30, 2nd act. First act, full dress [in the afternoon?]. Rehearsal at night again, 8 o'clock, of 2nd act. Full dress. In despair because it went so badly. Finished at 1 [a.m.].

[30 December] Full band rehearsal of 2nd act at 10.30. Went much better – lasted till 1.30 only . . . Full dress rehearsal at 8. Press and some friends there. Excellent rehearsal; everyone enthusiastic. Over at 1. Came home with Cellier, Clay and Gilbert; all set to work at the overture, Cellier finishing the score, and me and others copying parts. Gilbert and Clay knocked off at 3 a.m. Cellier and I wrote till 5 and finished it.

So, thanks to Sullivan's assiduity in working through Christmas Day, *The Pirates of Penzance* was at last ready – not for 27 or 29 December, as had been hoped, but for New Year's Eve. Its subtitle had been changed to *or, The Slave of Duty*.

[31 December] No rehearsal, except band at 11 for overture. Went to Brunswick [Hotel] to have my hair cut. Home at 1.45 to breakfast. Too ill to eat. Went to bed to try and get sleep, but could not. Stayed in bed till 5.30. Gilbert came. Got up feeling miserably ill, head on fire. Dressed slowly and got to New York Club at 7.30. Had 12 oysters and a glass of champagne. Went to Theatre. House crammed with the élite of New York. Went into the orchestra, more dead than alive, but got better when I took the stick in my hand – fine reception. Piece went marvellously well. Grand success. Went to Frank's afterwards, driving Adèle [the Beach Grants' daughter] home. Mr and Mrs Woolsey there, to see Old Year out. Went afterwards to Mrs Murray's (72 Fifth Avenue) to reception. Then home – could not sleep, so did not go to bed till 3.30. Felt utterly worn out.

There were nine encores. Sullivan telegraphed to his mother next day: BISCUIT BLOOD CANDLESTICK CARICATURE LAUNDRESS FORGERY MALEDICTION. A long list of code-words had been drawn up in advance – and with an arbitrary humour – by Gilbert.[10] The seven-word message meant: 'We played new piece last night/ piece enormously successful/both [i.e. words and music] equally successful/both called [on stage afterwards]/under £270 in the house/notices generally magnificent/send this to Mrs Gilbert.' The success of the piece was assured, and financial worries were at least temporarily over.

Writing to his mother on 2 January 1880 ('At last I am out of my penal servitude'), Sullivan was confident of

immense business for the next few weeks. At the end of the 8th week from now we leave
New York and go to the big towns west – Chicago, Cincinatti [sic], St Louis, etc., where
good business is to be done. We also send another company with it [the opera] as soon as
we can get it ready, to the smaller towns in New England first, then South. Strike whilst
the iron is hot.

The last sentence must have been a family catch-phrase: he used it three times
in writing at this time to his mother. Carte in fact was to find it worth sending
three companies on tour. The letter of 2 January continued:

What do I think of the piece myself? The libretto is ingenious, clever, wonderfully funny
in parts, and sometimes brilliant in dialogue – beautifully written for music, as is all
Gilbert does, and all the action and business perfect. The music is infinitely superior in
every way to the *Pinafore* – 'tunier' and more developed, of a higher class altogether. I
think that in time it will be more popular. Then the *mise-en-scène* and the dresses are
something to be dreamed about! I never saw such a beautiful combination of colour and
form on any stage. All the girls dressed in the old-fashioned English style, every dress
designed separately by Faustin, and some of the girls look as if they had stepped bodily out
of the frame of a Gainsborough picture. The New York ladies are raving about them. The
'policemen's chorus' is an enormous hit and they cheered tremendously when they march
on with their Bulls-Eyes [lanterns] all alight, and are always encored. I am sanguine of its
success in London, for there are the local allusions etc. which will have twice the force they
have here . . . I send you all the morning papers except the *Sun*, which is excellent also –
there is not a copy to be had. You will see that they don't go into the music much as
they don't know much about it and it isn't printed. So the New Year opens auspiciously
for me . . .

15 'We select an Englishman'

IT was fitting – though it was none of Sullivan's doing – that the operetta chosen for prior production in the United States should eventually engender an American national song. 'Come, friends, who plough the sea' (part of the pirates' chorus on their burglarious enterprise) was transformed in or before 1908 into 'Hail, hail, the gang's all here'. How and by whom the transformation was effected – the tune being modified and the new words fitted – remains a mystery.[1]

In New York in the first days of 1880, Arthur Sullivan could rejoice in the general success of *The Pirates of Penzance* more than in any recognition of his specific contribution. In those days as now, light theatrical entertainments fell to the scrutiny of drama critics rather than music critics. The reviewer in the *Mirror* was condescending. 'Of the music there is little to say. Mr Sullivan's compositions can hardly be other than graceful scores, and his handling of the orchestra is always good, if not masterly.'

In the *Mirror* and elsewhere, the similarity of the plot and characters to those of *HMS Pinafore* was noted – the parodied, patter-singing First Lord of the Admiralty had been metamorphosed into a parodied, patter-singing Major-General (the father of the heroine in this case), and the First Lord's 'sisters and his cousins and his aunts' had become the Major-General's bevy of daughters. Little Buttercup was transformed into 'Little' Ruth (for so the matronly nursemaid describes herself). Similarly with the hero's and the heroine's roles. Gilbert had even permitted himself a direct allusion from the newer to the earlier work. The Major-General's accomplishments include the ability to 'whistle all the airs from that infernal nonsense, *Pinafore*'. Once the pirates are captured, the girls plead on their behalf because 'they are all noblemen who have gone wrong'. 'What, *all* noblemen?' 'Yes, all noblemen.' 'What, all?' 'Well, nearly all' (and so on). Sullivan's music is obliged to join in the reminiscence of 'What never? Hardly ever'. But the point seems laboured, and the passage is customarily and not surprisingly omitted from modern performances.

At this precise point, however, Sullivan found the opportunity for one of his sly musical jokes. The words 'Who have gone wrong' are set with clumsy, 'wrong' emphasis in rhythm and harmony. A more substantial stroke of musical skill is the combination of lovers' duet and female chorus in the first act. Such a presentation of two dissimilar tunes, at first separately and then together, has already been noted as a Sullivan 'trade-mark', but this is unique in setting a chattering 2/4 (the girls' 'How beautifully blue the sky') against the 3/4 of the lovers' ardour, the whole presented with a Schubertian shift of keys from B major to G major and back again.

In the second act Sullivan touched the height of operatic parody. Two male choruses lie concealed – the police ambushing the pirates, the pirates waiting to entrap the Major-General. Though concealed they are fully vocal, even providing an accompaniment for a solo by the Major-General – who, placed only a few yards away, is supposed neither to hear nor see them. This scene, taking place outside a chapel, mocks the abduction scene in *Il trovatore* – in which a chorus of warriors lie similarly concealed and manage to sing without being detected. On this level (where the fun is equally Gilbert's) the parody is clear enough. But Sullivan goes further. The Major-General's song is a conventionally poetic address to Nature, 'River, river, running river', to which Sullivan supplies a rippling orchestral accompaniment, as in Schubert's song 'To be sung on the water' ('Auf dem Wasser zu singen'). This whole number is absolutely straight; it is in no sense 'funny' music. Its comic point is one of pure irony, and doubly sophisticated at that.

Another stroke of parody fails of full effect because of the restrictive canons of Victorian taste. The pirates have conferred honorary membership on the Major-General for sentimental reasons – 'For what is life, we ask, without a touch of poetry in it?' Pirates and girls then launch into a brief but richly-scored, intense salutation: 'Hail, Poetry! thou heav'n-born maid . . .'. It is, in miniature, a burlesque of an operatic prayer scene, such as was liable to intrude with breathtaking irrelevance into a serious operatic plot: that in Balfe's *The Bohemian Girl* is famously ridiculous, and that in Verdi's *La forza del destino* only just escapes the charge. But the words of prayer could not be burlesqued, nor could the Deity be invoked in satire. So the abstraction of 'Poetry' takes its place, an awkward substitute.

But if religion, even the semblance of religion, could not be mocked, the parrot-crying of patriotism and duty could. In *HMS Pinafore*, patriotism triumphed 'in spite of all temptations/To belong to other nations . . .'; in the newer operetta, the pirates make a sudden capitulation not to superior force but to 'Queen Victoria's name'. The hero's 'duty' obliges him at one moment to fight for the pirates, at another moment against them. Mabel similarly cites a supposed obligation as a mask for self-interest. Her sisters are not deceived:

> The question is, had he not been a thing of beauty
> Would she be swayed by quite as keen a sense of duty?

Time and again, from the self-doubts of the dairymaid heroine of *Patience* to the intrigues of Julia in *The Grand Duke*, Gilbert would continue to expose his characters on this particular rack – whether as hypocrites or merely deluded. In *Ruddigore* Gilbert would put the point with greatest comic force and Sullivan would puncture the sanctimonious sentiment ('Duty, duty must be done') with the dance-rhythms of his gayest, most impudent music.

From New York, Sullivan wrote frequently to Fanny Ronalds ('L.W.' in the diary) as well as to his mother. Through Mrs Sullivan he also kept in touch with George Grove, to whom she passed on a letter which included a diagrammatic sketch Sullivan had made of his New York rooms. 'Dear Mrs Sullivan', came Grove's reply on 30 December 1879,

I am very much obliged to you for the letter. I am delighted to find him so [illegible] and well. I can sympathize with him on the loss of his sketches but I should not have been so brave and should have howled much louder – but then I am 59½ and he only 37½ which makes a difference. The rooms are just like what Clay had. I am going to write to Arthur on New Year's Day and shall ask him to try and bring in my Dictionary into some of the 'gag' [sic] in The Pirates of Penzance. A good idea! You might mention it too.

There were indeed some alterations made to The Pirates (Sullivan's diary speaks of a 'rehearsal at theatre for cuts' on 5 January 1880) but this was not one of them. Minor changes in Gilbert's text were made both in dialogue and in musical numbers, the latter requiring the composer's attention, if only to sanction a cut. Such revisions were common after Gilbert and Sullivan first nights. But the task of discovering today exactly what was performed, and when, is particularly difficult in the case of The Pirates. Not only did differences exist between the first British version (see p. 143) and the first American. The librettist and composer also abstained at first (in order to deter unauthorized copying)[2] from publishing either vocal score or libretto. Only on their return to London did Gilbert and Sullivan make their biggest change – a new ending to the opera.

Meanwhile their American tasks were by no means done. There was much labour in rehearsing the three touring companies, with the possibility of a fourth:

But we don't mind it, we all work like slaves – D'Oyly, Cellier, Gilbert and myself. Cellier is at Philadelphia this week rehearsing the chorus out there, and I am doing the rehearsals here. The houses here are still excellent, and I believe will keep up well through Lent [i.e. for another two months]. . . . In the meantime the excitement is kept alive by articles and correspondence in the newspapers about conspiracies to pirate the opera.

So he wrote to his mother on 28 January 1880. He discussed a visit to Baltimore earlier that month. A 'Great Sullivan Concert' at the Academy of Music was advertised for 8 January, with the 'largest orchestra heard in Baltimore' (some 45 players, with a chorus of over 200) and 'Rare Music – Never Before Played in America'. The music had been rehearsed by 'Prof. Hamerik' (the Danish-born composer Asger Hamerik, 1843–1923, then resident in Baltimore) and the programme included choruses from Beethoven's The Mount of Olives and Wagner's Tannhäuser as well as Sullivan's Ballo overture and music to The Tempest and The Merchant of Venice. The conducting was perhaps less energetic than the polite reviewer of the Baltimore Sun (9 January) expected:

Mr Sullivan directed throughout in a quiet and artistic manner, and in the Beethoven and Wagner selections kept chorus and orchestra well together.

There were songs, too – including, inevitably, The Lost Chord with Sullivan at the piano and 'Mr [Otto] Sutro' at the organ.

He was entertained in Baltimore at the Maryland Club that night and on the following day he set out for Berryville, Virginia. He was to visit Leonidas Polk Wheat, known as Leo Wheat, a pianist and composer five years his junior who had been a fellow-student at Leipzig and whom he had introduced to his mother in their Pimlico days.

From the river we wended our way up the Blue Ridge mountains, and then down to our station (Round Hill). The country was all along beautiful, and we had a superb view of the Shenandoah valley from the summit. I never enjoyed anything more in my life.

A souvenir album of Wheat's, now in the Library of Congress in Washington, DC, contains a leaf with a vignette of Sullivan (pasted on) and a theme from *The Tempest* in the composer's hand with the following inscription.

> Leipzig 1861
> Berryville, Va 1880
> After twenty years, my dear Wheat, a friendship begun in Leipzig is renewed and strengthened in this lovely Virginian valley.[3]

It is signed 'Arthur Sullivan' and dated 10 January 1880.

Sullivan had moved his New York quarters and was now living at a hotel, Hoffman House – 'on Madison Square', the centre of New York. He thanked his mother for sending the plum-puddings and other things. 'The tea is winning me enormous social popularity. I took some to Mrs Belmont yesterday and made it there . . . The boot varnish is granted in bottles to highly favoured individuals.' This was the first wife (née Caroline Perry) of August Belmont, formerly the society rival of Leonard Jerome. (See p. 88.)

Through his friend Suydam Grant, he paid into his account $3,129.50 and $1,208.60 at dates only a week apart. His return to England was already determined, but there were two trips still to be undertaken. At Philadelphia on 9 February he conducted the opening performance of the company Cellier had been rehearsing, and then headed north for Buffalo, Niagara and Ottawa. At Buffalo, on Saturday 21 February, he conducted both the matinées and evening performances of *The Pirates of Penzance* given by another of Carte's companies. Niagara was conveniently on the route to Ottawa, where he had been invited to Government House by Lord Lorne, the Governor-General.

In a hotel (Prospect House) on the Canadian side of Niagara Falls he sat down to write to his mother while gazing at the torrent 'dashing and fuming within 50 yards of me'. The river nearby had frozen over for the first time since 1865,

and yesterday we walked over it. We also went *under the falls* with guide and proper tarpaulin dresses! What do you think of that? Fancy your boy being underneath at the foot of Niagara with the great foaming, tumbling cataract falling just in front of him! You wouldn't have slept, would you?

Two days later he was in snow-covered Ottawa, a sleigh waiting at the station to take him to Government House. Princess Louise, the Governor-General's wife, was unwell and suffering as the result of an accident and Sullivan was able to have less of her company than he had hoped. But in a letter to his mother he was able to describe the thrill of 'toboggoning' (so he spelt it) and to leave a sketch of himself doing it – in which he lies on his stomach, facing forward, with his British bowler or something very like it firmly perched on his head.

His mother had retrieved for him the music of a national hymn for Canada which he had sketched in England but left at home, along with the sketches for *The Pirates of Penzance*. He was now able to write it out while still in Ottawa. The words were by Lord Lorne himself (beginning 'God bless our wide Dominion, our fathers' chosen land') but the Governor-General's authorship was left anonymous when the hymn was published in Montreal and London. It was *not* adopted as a national anthem. From Ottawa Sullivan himself took the trip to Montreal, 101 miles away. When he was back in New York, preparing for his journey home, one of his last letters (on the notepaper of the Beach Grants, with whom he may have spent his last few days in America) was to thank Lorne for his hospitality.

In company with Gilbert, Sullivan sailed on the *Gallia* on 3 March. His hope of a trip to Cuba and to America's Pacific coast had to be abandoned, 'as we *must* produce the *Pirates* in London without delay, otherwise the best part of the season will escape us'.[4] Having landed at Liverpool, he was soon at home and busy – though he had already indicated to his mother, in a letter from New York (13 February) that he now felt the need of a more spacious London apartment, 'with a place for a writer and secretary: I can't get on without one much longer'.

The Pirates of Penzance as presented to London audiences at the Opera Comique on 3 April 1880 was not actually the first British performance.[5] For reasons of copyright a touring company of Carte's had given a performance at the Royal Bijou Theatre at Paignton, Devon, on 30 December 1879, the day before the American unveiling. But, since Sullivan was still working on his score, the version presented there was partial and provisional. (It contained neither 'Poor wand'ring one' nor 'Come, friends, who plough the sea'.)[6] As compared with New York, the London first performance had the decisively advantageous presence of George Grossmith (as the Major-General), whose 'mixture of dry, quaint humour and caricatured military sternness' was particularly liked by *The Times*.[7] Rutland Barrington as the Sergeant of Police was, according to the same critic, 'absolutely sublime'.

Moreover the score itself was not quite the same. The finale to Act 2 was rewritten, a change with a stronger musical than dramatic reason: the audience was now sent away on the wings of a tuneful waltz (a reprise of Mabel's 'Poor wand'ring one') instead of on a reprise of the Major-General's song, amusing but hardly hummable. Sullivan himself conducted the first night (though the theatre programme failed to mention the fact), and he and Gilbert took curtain-calls at the end of each act. The success of the work was complete.

Having 'just finished the scoring (4 a.m.)' on the night of 31 March/1 April he put in an envelope the tickets for his mother and others of the family: 'Here are the four stalls – the *best in the house* for seeing and hearing'. In the same brief note he spoke of having 'only an overture' still to do, presumably an indication that the

New York overture written by Cellier was replaced or at least revised for London by Sullivan himself. The point is of some importance because it has long been recognized that few of the published overtures to Sullivan's operettas are his own work. In the case of *The Pirates* there is one passage in the newer and still current overture which is so original (it does not occur in the operetta itself) that no helper would have dared to impose it: just before the final *stringendo*, the tunes of 'How beautifully blue the sky' and 'A paradox, a paradox' suddenly meet in witty counterpoint.

There was counterpoint in a more expected context in the next (and the oddest) collaboration of Sullivan with Gilbert. Sullivan called on his partner to help turn Dean Milman's poem *The Martyr of Antioch* into the 'book' of a cantata. As far back as 12 March 1878 Sullivan had accepted the Leeds Festival commission for a new work, but had proposed the biblical theme of David and Jonathan.[8] The switch to Milman's subject was not announced to the public until June 1880. On 19 May a performance of Sullivan's symphony at the Philharmonic under Cusins (it was the only time the society ever gave it) marked the composer's continuing reputation in the concert-hall. The symphony had suffered 'unjust neglect', declared *The Times* two days later.

On 30 June Sullivan and 19 of his fellow-composers met at his flat to organize a united defence of their professional rights – a matter on which Sullivan had already expressed himself strongly (p.85). The gathering included Barnby, J. F. Barnett (Sullivan's colleague of Leipzig student days), and Frederic Hymen Cowen (1852–1935), who was already noted among the country's most promising 'serious' composers. Others present were mainly writers of popular songs such as J. L. Molloy (1837–1909; 'Love's Old Sweet Song') and Stephen Adams, real name Michael Maybrick (1844–1913; 'The Holy City'). The concern of the meeting was not with international 'piracy' such as Sullivan had experienced, but with the protection of the composer's rights against the power of his publishers. Under Sullivan's chairmanship it was formally resolved that it was 'desirable for the composer to keep his interest, present and future, in the copyright of his works'. (That is, he should resist the pressure to part with the copyright as such in return for a lump sum.) Concern was expressed, without any action proposed, on the publishers' practice of paying to singers, in return for 'pushing' a song at concerts, a royalty on every copy sold. It was proposed to set up a composers' society to negotiate with publishers. Nothing eventuated. It was not until 1913 that discussions leading to the present Performing Right Society took place.

The commitment to Leeds proved to be a double one. Sullivan was invited not only to contribute a new work but to be the conductor of the whole festival, and had written his acceptance from New York. There was no more important event in the British musical calendar than the triennial affair at Leeds, at which the celebrated local chorus was joined by an orchestra raised almost entirely from London. The four-day programme (in a pattern established at the previous festivals, 1874 and 1877) was almost entirely vocal, with a morning as well as an evening concert each day, and an afternoon organ recital for those whose musical appetites demanded more. As always, leading singers from London lent glamour to the performances and demanded fees in proportion. After the 1877 festival the Committee had ventured to send to 'Mme Albani' (the Canadian-born soprano Emma Albani, wife of the London impresario Ernest Gye) her fee of 550 guineas (£577.50) reduced by the sum of 50 guineas (£52.50) she had promised to festival charities.[9] The cheque was rejected. The committee was obliged to pay the full fee, the soprano then with strict propriety sending the amount of her promised donation.

The acceptance of the conductorship was a major step for Sullivan. With his later conductorship of the Philharmonic Society in London, for the three seasons from 1885 to 1887, it marked the highest point in this branch of his career. At Leeds, moreover, he succeeded the mighty autocrat, Costa, who had officiated at the two previous festivals. The festival committee indeed invited Costa again but in restrictive terms which they must have known he would scorn: 'The committee also desire to know if you will undertake to conduct the works which will be selected by the committee, and will furnish for their approval a list of the band.' Charles Hallé in Manchester had been informally approached as Costa's possible successor, but had wanted to bring his own orchestra whereas the committee insisted on London players. Thus Sullivan got the post as a convenient third-best. As a conductor he was, and remained, below the professional level represented by Costa, Hallé and Hans Richter (1843–1916) – who had been Wagner's chosen conductor for *The Ring* (Bayreuth, 1876) and had made his London debut in the Wagner Festival of 1877 at the Albert Hall. If Sullivan's appointment was not exactly 'managed by a job' (like the Judge's in *Trial by Jury*), it was no doubt supported in the non-musical terms as expressed by a local columnist:[10]

There is one point, however, in the election of Mr Sullivan about which I am particularly pleased. It is the fact that for an *English* festival we are to have an *English* conductor. Too long have we in this country bowed down to foreign talent, even when it has been far inferior to English talent. On the selection of an Englishman over Costa and Hallé as conductor, an admirer of *Pinafore* sends me the following from that work, slightly altered:

> We might have had a Russian – a French, or Turk, or Prussian,
> Or else I-ta-li-an.
> But in spite of all temptations to go to other nations
> We select an *Englishman*!

Arthur Sullivan himself, who later did not disguise his resentment of Richter's appointment as conductor of the Birmingham Festival, may have considered the sentiment entirely just. To have it expressed in terms of one of his own operettas affords an irony to a later age which sees those operettas as his great achievement, the conducting as a lesser matter altogether.

16   The Martyr and the Dairymaid

SULLIVAN was not alone in providing a new work for Leeds in 1880. As an alternative to a religious subject, a text in praise of valour, industry, patriotism or other secular virtue was highly acceptable at such a festival and John F. Barnett had seized on Longfellow's poem *The Building of the Ship*, in which 'the compass in its brazen ring/ever level, ever true' was extolled as a model for human steadfastness. The political climax of the poem, beginning 'Sail on, thou, too, O ship of state', was omitted. Conducted by Barnett himself, the work was greeted as pleasant, transparent, unproblematic: indeed some of the compliments were decidedly double-edged, the *Athenaeum* declaring that 'the greatest charm in Mr Barnett's work is its perfect freedom from any suspicion of labour'.

To choose a 'sacred' subject, however, allowed the composer to reckon on a ready-made receptivity from his audience. There might be an opportunity (such as Sullivan had already seized in the *Festival Te Deum*) to raise a 'stock response' by quotation of well-loved hymn or ancient chant. Strictly, the title *oratorio* was reserved to works based on a biblical story and using biblical words. Otherwise some variant label might be devised. *Rebekah* (1870) by Sullivan's friend Barnby, in which the episode is biblical but the words entirely new, was called a 'sacred idyll'. Where not even the story itself was biblical, the same necessity for invention arose: *The Martyr of Antioch* was described on its title-page as a 'sacred musical drama'. It would not be far-fetched to call it an opera in concert form. The 'moralizing' quartet or chorus – coming, as it were, from outside the action – no longer had a place.

On matters of text and musical setting Sullivan consulted Grove, who was now at the apex of his fame; the second volume of the *Dictionary of Music and Musicians* (eventually there were four) had recently been issued. To the first edition of that *Dictionary* Sullivan contributed the articles on Fred Clay and on Louis Plaidy, his Leipzig piano teacher, initialled (in his old form) 'A.S.S.'. On 29 July 1880 Grove was saluted by the presentation of a gold chronometer and a purse of 1,000 guineas at a function in St James's Hall: his services to music were eulogized by Sullivan, and to biblical research by the elder figure of Arthur Stanley, Dean of Westminster.

Just who was the 'martyr of Antioch', Sullivan's titular figure? It was not a familiar allusion even in that age, which recognized a special category of devotional verse, often the product of under-employed clerics. Henry Hart Milman (1791–1868), Dean of St Paul's, had published his poetic drama as far back as 1822. Some celebrity had already been won by the 'funeral anthem' contained within it, 'Brother, thou art gone before us', each stanza ending with a line adapted from Job, 'Where the wicked cease from troubling, and the weary are at rest'. Perhaps it was on Helmore's shelves that the young Sullivan had come across the poem. Its heroine was St Margaret of Antioch in Syria ('Margarita' in the poem), whose reputed martyrdom took place under Roman persecution in the fourth century. A pagan priest's daughter, she became a convert to Christianity and, rejecting her lover (the Roman prefect, Olybius), suffered execution – by the headsman in the poem, by the more operatic convention of the funeral pyre in the cantata.

The composing of a work intended for a festival performance could not be left, like an operetta, till the very latest moment with the possibility of a theatrical postponement. The tight festival schedule was fixed and, no less tight, the schedule of weekly rehearsals at which the choir would be drilled over a period of months. (James Broughton was its seasoned choirmaster.) The choral sections of the score, at least, had to be completed in sufficient time to be printed for these rehearsals. Sullivan, whose assignment was to conduct virtually the entire festival programme of eight concerts and not just his own work, made his first appearance at a choral rehearsal on 4 June 1880. A force of 306 choral singers had been selected including 34 male altos as well as 41 (female) contraltos:[1] the high falsetto male voice, surviving in glee clubs and church choirs, was evidently a reckonable constituent of the famous Yorkshire sound. Moreover, Sullivan wrote especially for it in *The Martyr of Antioch*: the male altos are allocated their own stave in the score and are strictly enjoined *not* to sing with the contraltos where the female populace is represented.

Sullivan knew how to handle a choir and to inject the right note of flattery when a local newspaper came to interview him at rehearsal:

Mr Sullivan was evidently astonished at the excellence of the chorus. After the Choral Symphony he could not refrain from expressing his admiration of the manner in which it was rendered; and he added that if they only sang it at the festival as he now expected they would, it would be the finest performance of Beethoven's Symphony that had ever been heard.[2]

He next appeared at rehearsal on 31 August to rehearse *The Martyr of Antioch*, the choral parts of which were available for the first time. Nine days later he had 'finished my work, thank God, but am now in the midst of proofs, copyists, etc.' he wrote to his mother from 9 Albert Mansions. There was a significant change at that establishment: a male secretary had been engaged in the person of the efficient but humourless Walter Smythe, who attended Sullivan daily to deal with his correspondence. On 15 September the composer left for the Belgian health resort, Spa ('to rest and drink a little water for my digestion and liver') but was annoyed to find that the prescribed 'course' of the waters there would take a week, and he could not spare as long. He paid a visit to Paris on the way back, probably to see his niece Amy, who was at school in nearby Neuilly. His mother had preceded him to France and had received advice in a letter written by him from Spa:

A pint of *good wine* every day you ought to have. English beer never agrees with people abroad as the climate is so much lighter.

The 'band' for the festival, being recruited from London orchestral musicians, rehearsed in London. Sullivan insisted, apparently against precedent, that no visitors were to be allowed into rehearsal save 'on production of a card signed by myself'. A few Leeds instrumentalists were added and probably took their places only at the combined choral and orchestral rehearsals in Leeds immediately before the festival. The selection of the orchestral players was left to the conductor, but the total number was fixed at 111, to include what Sullivan (in a letter to the festival committee) called 'double wind' – i.e. quadruple wind, with a doubling of each of the two flute parts, two oboe parts, etc., of the classical orchestra. Sullivan's request for ten more strings was rejected. The antiquated ophicleide, not the tuba, was still the bass instrument of the brass section.

Staying at 13 Lyddon Terrace, Leeds, Sullivan wrote on Sunday 10 October that he was 'resting before the battle begins tomorrow – we commence rehearsal at 10 sharp and rehearse all day and all the evening, and again on Tuesday . . . You come down on Thursday, and you shall be made comfortable.'

Elijah, on Wednesday morning, was the safe opening work. On Thursday Sullivan assumed the almost incredible load of Mendelssohn's Psalm 114, Beethoven's Ninth Symphony and Bennett's *The May Queen* in the morning and Handel's *Samson* ('abridged, and with additional accompaniments written for this festival by Ebenezer Prout') in the evening – all this on the day before launching his own new composition.

On Friday morning (15 October) a proud mother heard *The Martyr of Antioch* performed in the presence of the Duke of Edinburgh (the 'president' of the festival, and dedicatee of the work). It formed the first part of a programme which continued with Beethoven's Mass in C and Schubert's *Song of Miriam* (*Mirjam's Siegesgesang*). The new work had the best possible soprano, contralto and tenor – Albani as Margarita, Patey as one of Apollo's worshippers, and Edward Lloyd as the Roman prefect. But Santley had turned his back on the festival after being subject to what he considered offensive treatment over his fee, and the principal bass (or baritone) role of Callias, the priest of Apollo, went to a young singer, Frederic King. Henry Cross took the secondary bass part of Fabius, bishop of Antioch.

Sullivan was doubly under test. As a conductor he achieved signal success in the eyes of press, performers and public. (That some under-rehearsal was noted in Mozart's Symphony no. 40 and Beethoven's Ninth was not surprising.) The composer, however, was but moderately praised. The reception for *The Martyr of Antioch* may well have signalled to him the first of a series of disappointments that he was to win less acclaim for his 'serious' work than for his operettas. The verdict of his friend and admirer Joseph Bennett in the *Daily Telegraph* (18 October 1880) is worth quoting precisely because he *was* an admirer, and had written the programme-note for this as for most other works of the festival. He found Sullivan's treatment too lyrical, not dramatic or forceful enough:

Seven-ninths of the pages devoted to it [the first scene] are taken up by the pagan chorus ['Lord of the Golden day']: whence it follows that the real action is treated in a somewhat sketchy manner. As here, so throughout the drama; and as throughout the drama so here, few music-lovers will feel inclined to visit the composer with censure. Our judgement may warn us of too much lyricism, and that the dramatic element is being hurriedly passed by, but our feelings are likely to override our judgement, since Mr Sullivan is most charming when represented by the incense, flowers and songs of Apollo's maidens. With these are all his sympathies, and he invests them with such musical beauty of form and colour that they command our sympathies likewise, and make the poor Christians and their lugubrious strains appear as uninteresting as they are sombre.

Later in the first scene, Olybius's song to his intended bride, 'Come, Margarita, come', was found to be 'a perfect gem in its pretty, yet withal artistic way'. (It was encored, as was 'The love-sick damsel', a contralto solo within the pagan chorus.) But in the third scene Sullivan 'has again treated his drama with scant respect' and the quartet in the fourth scene 'though pleasing, lacks the intense feeling natural to the situation'. In conclusion, after some 3,000 words:

Taking *The Martyr of Antioch* as a whole, I do not question its chance of the popularity for which Mr Sullivan has striven. It is a work that no one, be he musician or not, can hear without interest and admiration. At the same time criticism will always point to the fact that the drama is treated substantially as a pretext for charming choruses and airs . . .

The *Athenaeum* led its readers by a different route to the same verdict, commenting (25 October 1880) that part of the work

already sounds strangely old-fashioned, owing to the rapid growth of the dramatic at the expense of the lyrical cantata during the last decade. . . . It might be wished that in some portions Mr Sullivan had taken a loftier view of his theme, but at any rate he has written some most charming music, and orchestration equal, if not superior, to any that has ever proceeded from the pen of an English musician. And, further, it is an advantage to have the composer of *HMS Pinafore* occupying himself with a worthier form of art.

The opinion that in his 'serious' work he lacked a sense of the dramatic and appealed mainly by charm was to pursue Sullivan's career from this time on – right up to *The Golden Legend* and *Ivanhoe*.

The audience at the Victoria Hall (as the auditorium within Leeds Town Hall was named) were not the only listeners to the festival. Three 'telephonic transmitters', all attached to one wire, were set up in the hall by the Yorkshire Telephone Company. Handel's *Samson* was thus relayed to seven men seated in the company's offices, each listening to an individual receiver. The greater part of the work came over 'with wonderful distinctness and fidelity' according to the *Yorkshire Post* (15 October). The experiment went on at later performances, with another listening post at Bradford. There is no evidence to show whether *The Martyr of Antioch* was so heard, but the reports obviously inspired *Punch* (23 October). Sterndale Bennett is referred to as composer of *The May Queen* and

likewise Aline Osgood, soprano soloist in that work.[3] The italics of '*tell of one*'
form an indication of a (strained) pun. The contribution was signed 'Bouncer'
(surely Burnand).

Sir, – You told me to go to Leeds, and I told you to go to Jericho. You didn't go to
Jericho, and I didn't go to Leeds.

Who needs
To go to Leeds?

when he can do as I did, and always intend to do in future. I simply – very simply – sat in
my little second-floor back-room, with one end of a Telephone fitted up to my study-table,
the other being attached to Dr ARTHUR SULLIVAN, who went off with it to the Leeds Festival,
and took it with him on the platform. Did you ever hear of a Telephone being attached to a
person? They do, I assure you, become deeply attached – like cats, however, more to
places than persons. Of course it was a brilliant idea of mine – (you, Sir, never thought of
it) – to put the Telephone into ARTHUR SULLIVAN's head – in at one ear and out at the other –
because, as everyone knows, he is such a perfect Conductor of sound. It succeeded
marvellously. I heard everything; and was charmed with BARNETT and BENNETT, and *April
Fool* and *Shipping the Builder*, and that ancient Conservative musician, the *Hoary Tory O!*
Where all was so good, and so much was OSGOOD, and where one thing was so good as
another, as the Telephone said – (I heard by Telephone all the jokes, made *sotto voice* on
the platform, but shan't *tell of one* of 'em) – it is impossible to discriminate. Dr SULLIVAN's
prescriptions, for an opening symphony to a tonic, were most successful. The learned
author of *Pinafore* did the words of the *Martyr of Antioch*, and the Telephone gave me a few
particulars which the general public was not privileged to hear.

The great song rather reminded me of something in *Trial by Jury* and *Pinafore*; it is
called *I'll tell you how I came to be a Martyr*, with chorus. The refrain of the next most
popular number is

In spite of all temptations
From some denominations,
I remained a Chris*tian*.
(*Triumphantly*) I remained a Chris*tian*.

This, with the magnificent accompaniment to which it is set, created a profound sensation –

A most profound sensation
From the grand instrumentation
Of Doctor Sulli*van* –
Of D-o-o-octor Sul-ul-ul-*i-van*.

Well, if Sir ARTHUR – (is the Telephone correct, or did it say Dr ARTHUR? Odd! I thought
it whispered 'Sir,' – but perhaps it said 'Sir' to me) – if Dr ARTHUR SULLIVAN isn't satisfied
with the result of our spirited telephonic experiment, he ought to be. But if everyone can
hear musical festivals by Telephone, why go to Leeds, or anywhere else? – except as an
excuse for an outing – out on the Leeds. Adoo!

George Grove had also travelled to Leeds for the performance. Diplomatic-
ally, as it would seem, he reserved his comment until he took pen in hand six days
later to address his 'Dearest A'. Writing on 19 October, on notepaper bearing the
joint printed headings of the *Dictionary of Music and Musicians* and *Macmillan's
Magazine*, of which he was still editor, he alluded to Francis Hueffer, who was
now music critic of *The Times*, and to J. W. Davison ('old Jimmy'), who had

retired from that position but had nevertheless attended in his capacity as editor of the *Musical World*.

There was such a crowd waiting round your door after the cantata that I felt I should not get a word: and I was obliged to go back in the middle of the Beethoven Mass. I heard the work downstairs standing against the wall with old Jimmy and we were both as happy as we could well be all through. Jimmy thought that the coda to two of the numbers wanted extending – and made one or two other small criticisms – but nothing of any moment. The chief point on which I felt uneasy was one which regarded myself. Margarita's words "tis made; the funeral pyre' are not enough to warrant the shout of 'Blasphemy . . . she doth profane our faith' and I wish that some more pronounced confession could be found for her at that place. It surely would not be difficult. – I thought the Introduction too light in character. – As a part of the first chorus nothing could be better but as an introduction to the whole work my feeling was as I have said – though possibly that would be modified on a second hearing. Also I think, for the interests of the whole piece, it is almost a pity that Margarita's first scene is so splendid and important: it makes her subsequent solo sound like an anticlimax. *How beautiful her first solo is!* – the expression and sentiment and suitability of the music to the words *could not by any possibility be better*, and the music was so lovely to hear – the beautiful modulations and the cleverness of the escapes – that really I could hardly contain myself now and then. I think the funeral hymn *surprised* me more than any other part. I was not prepared for its very great pathos and beauty.

The singing struck me as wonderfully good, especially Lloyd and Patey.

The criticisms none of them seem to me at all equal to the subject and in both *Times* and *Telegraph* there is a sort of bantering tone (only banter without fun in it) as if it was a sort of joke not fit to be criticized seriously. I am very much disgusted with Hueffer: there never was a better illustration of the beggar on horseback. Still, he pulls the strings of the *Times* and I think that with reference to the Training School it might be well if you saw him. He's going to treat the subject before long and if you could write him a civil note and propose to call upon him it would not do harm . . .

Goodbye, old man. What can be better than to know that your last work is your best? and there can be no doubts about in this case . . .

On his return to London from Leeds, Sullivan made a gesture no doubt expected of him (but a gesture of substance, none the less) in sending a cheque for £25 as a contribution to the city's hospital funds – the benefaction which, in name at any rate, was the reason for holding the festival. In November the committee reported that the hospitals had benefited by £2,000, leaving a surplus of £329.0.10 after the payment of expenses. Fees to conductor, soloists, organist, chorus-master and accompanist came to £1,829.7.0. The engagement of the orchestra, including rail fares from London, came to £1,915.9.8. Sullivan's fee was not separately announced, but was listed in his own accounting (see next chapter) as £315 – doubtless formally agreed as 'three hundred guineas'.

To Gilbert the grateful composer presented an engraved silver cup. His letter of acknowledgement bears witness to the formality of their relationship – never to ripen into intimacy.

Dear Sullivan,

It always seemed to me that my particularly humble services in connection with the Leeds Festival had received far more than their meed of acknowledgement in your preamble to the libretto – and it most certainly never occurred to me to look for any other reward than the honour of being associated, however remotely and unworthily, in a success which, I suppose, will endure until music itself shall die. Pray believe that of the many substantial advantages that have resulted to me from our association, this last is, and always will be, the most highly prized.

Very truly yours,
W.S.G.

A different kind of account is revealed by Sullivan's list of his gains and losses at cards, at the Orleans and Argus clubs and elsewhere, in November 1880 (he wrote it on the opening page of his 1881 diary).

		[£]	[£]
12 Nov	Orleans	+ 40	
13 Nov	Argus	+ 565	
15 Nov	Orleans – Ricketts	+ 80	
17 Nov	Argus	–	100
18 Nov	Mrs Chaine's – poker	+ 12	
19 Nov	Leslie Ward	+ 8	
20 Nov	{ Bramston	–	12.10
	{ Argus	–	90
22 Nov	Orleans	–	50
ditto	Argus	+ 180	
24 Nov	Fendall	–	7.10
ditto	Argus	+ 130	
26 Nov	Orleans – Ricketts	–	90
27 Nov	Argus	–	30
28 Nov	At home – loo [game]	–	65
29 [Nov]	Argus	+ 35	
30 [Nov]	Mrs Chaine	+ 7.10	
		1057.10	445.0
		445	
Profit. Balance on the month: [£]		612.10	

The Pirates of Penzance was still running at the Opera Comique (it was to achieve 363 performances, as against the 571 of *HMS Pinafore*) but Sullivan's prudent partners were already planning its successor. 'Carte and Gilbert have given me three hours of their company today,' he noted in a letter to his mother on 21 November, 'and I have tried in vain to write a song.' The new work was to be *Patience*.

This subject, when Gilbert first began work on it, was the comic rivalry of a contrasted pair of clergymen – a theme he had already explored in the *Bab Ballads* ('The Rival Curates'). But satire on the church, agreeable enough to the readers of *Fun*, was judged to be dangerous ground for Carte's respectable family audiences. As Gilbert had put it in a letter to Sullivan:

I don't feel comfortable about it. I mistrust the clerical element. I feel hampered by the restrictions which the nature of the subject places upon my freedom of action, and I want to revert to my old idea of rivalry between two aesthetic fanatics, worshipped by a chorus of female aesthetics, instead of a couple of clergymen worshipped by a chorus of female devotees. I can get much more fun out of the subject as I propose to alter it. . . . I entertained this idea at first, as you may remember, but abandoned it because I foresaw great difficulty in getting the chorus to dress and make up aesthetically – but if we can get Du Maurier to design the costumes, I don't know that the difficulty will be insuperable.

The very word *aesthetic* had undergone, as Eric de Maré points out, a change of meaning.[4] It had become 'almost a synonym for fashionable'; no longer pertaining to considerations of the beautiful in the abstract, it came to mean 'in accordance with the principles of good taste'. The 'aesthetic movement', even though its supposed motto was 'art for art's sake', was an attitude not just to art but to life. In the cartoons which George du Maurier contributed to the pages of *Punch*, 'Postlethwaite' and 'Maudle' (a splendid back-formation from *maudlin*) were the two caricatured apostles of the cult whose affected conversation was larded with such expressions of approval as 'too jolly utter'.

The visual model was Oscar Wilde – who, at 24, without having published more than a few poems, was the dazzling incarnation of the cult. He had become celebrated even while an undergraduate at Oxford, where he declared that he hoped to be able to live up to his blue china, and where he chose to appear at a fancy-dress ball as Prince Rupert, in a velvet coat edged with braid, knee-breeches, buckle shoes, a soft silk shirt with a wide turn-down collar, and a large, flowing green tie. For the dress of his female aesthetics, typified by the earnestly adoring 'Mrs Cimabue Brown', Du Maurier may have taken as models the nymphs of Burne-Jones's paintings, of which *Merlin and Venus* and eight others had been exhibited at the opening of the Grosvenor Gallery three years before. That Sullivan's friend Sir Coutts Lindsay was the gallery's proprietor lent a private irony to the situation. But if Sullivan was ever troubled by a conflict of loyalties between Lindsay's principles and Gilbert's mockery, he left no evidence to say so.

'Grosvenor' was indeed the name of one of Gilbert's two poets in his 'aesthetic opera'. According to H. Montgomery Hyde, Wilde's biographer, some of Wilde's peculiarities were portrayed in both Archibald Grosvenor the 'idyllic poet' and Reginald Bunthorne, the 'fleshly poet'. It is Grosvenor who proclaims himself 'aesthetic and poetic', but it is Bunthorne who counsels:

> Though the Philistines may jostle,
>   You may rank as an apostle
>   In the high aesthetic band
>   If you walk down Piccadilly
>   With a poppy or a lily
>   In your medieval hand.

'Contrary to the general opinion at the time', Hyde comments,

Wilde never walked down Piccadilly thus adorned. Anyone could have done that, he used to say. 'The difficult thing to achieve was to make people think I had done it'.

The poets in *Patience* are hypocrites, their poses 'born of a morbid love of admiration'; in contrast with them, the three Dragoon Guards officers (with supporting chorus) represent 'normal' male behaviour. Similarly the lovesick,

high-born maidens who swoon first for Bunthorne, then for Grosvenor, are
exposed to the commonsense commentary of the dairymaid who gives her name
to the work.

A portion at least of *Patience* was in Sullivan's bag when he set out for France
once again. His companion was Edward Hall, a stockbroker friend who advised
him on investing his considerable income. On 24 December, staying at the Hotel
du Rhin in Paris, he dutifully visited his niece Amy at her school, and on
Christmas Day ('after church' as he noted in a letter to his mother) Amy and some
of her school friends visited him. Then he and Hall were off to the warmth of
Nice (the Hôtel des Anglais), where his journalist friend Edward Dicey joined
them on 2 January 1881.

Ten miles eastward from sedate Nice stood the more daringly attractive Monte
Carlo. Under the laws of the principality of Monaco (separate from those of
France) it had risen to prosperity by the availability of its gambling facilities. In
1879 the jewel of a theatre within the sumptuous new casino had been opened by
Sarah Bernhardt – who had herself acted as model for a statue of Song on the
exterior. While Nice remained the larger and smarter place to stay, 'the winter-
rendezvous of invalids and others from all parts of Europe, for whose comfort or
entertainment every provision is made' (Baedeker), Monte Carlo had an
irresistible attraction for such a gambler as Sullivan. He and his friends often
took the train there to 'tempt fortune with a few louis – winning one day, losing
the next', as he wrote to his mother.

While at Nice he composed the song 'The particularly good young man',
which (with words subsequently altered) was to become Bunthorne's self-
describing solo in Act I of *Patience*; but otherwise 'my natural indolence aided by
the sunshine prevent my doing any real work. I enjoy myself in the *dolce far
niente*', as he himself wrote. He and Hall, prompted by a business interest of the
latter in Italy, then went to Turin and returned home via the Mont Cenis rail
tunnel through the Alps ('take the right-hand side of the carriage for the scenery',
he noted) and Paris.

He was back in London on 16 January 1881 – a week when an explosion at a
barracks in Salford killed a boy in a recurrence of 'Fenian' (Irish nationalist)
violence. Fanny Ronalds was away, but her daughter Fanny (otherwise Fanette)
was still at the house in Cadogan Place in the care of her grandparents. Sullivan's
diary records that on 26 January he took 'Mother, Fanny Ronalds, and Dickie'
(his young nephew, now aged 8) to see *Mother Goose*, the pantomime at Drury
Lane Theatre.

Patience was not his only preoccupation. He conducted *The Martyr of Antioch*
thrice more – at St James's Hall on 11 February (describing it as the first
performance 'in London' – a previous hearing at the Crystal Palace being
reckoned as suburban); again there on 18 March; and again, in the presence of
the Prince of Wales, at the Albert Hall on 7 April. He was required in the
preparation of the law-suit (though he was not called as a witness) which he,
Gilbert and Carte had brought against the Comedy Opera Company, who

had continued to present *HMS Pinafore* (see p. 131). With Charles Russell as their leading counsel – he was later to be Sir Charles, and then Lord Russell of Killowen and Lord Chief Justice – Sullivan and his colleagues won their case and were awarded full costs, 'but we never got a penny, as the company in order to avoid paying went into liquidation'.

At the National Training School, Sullivan received an eminent visitor in the great Anton Rubinstein – a giant among pianists who was compared to Liszt, and a composer of operas and orchestral works then much admired. Rubinstein was greatly taken with the gifts of a young student, Eugène d'Albert, son of Charles d'Albert, a musician whom Sullivan sometimes used as an arranger. The son, later germanizing his forename as Eugen, was himself to become celebrated as a composer and as director of the Berlin High School for Music. But Sullivan, evidently strict in academic discipline, refused to let young d'Albert break his study to appear at one of Manns's concerts at the Crystal Palace.

The funding of the School, which had been troublesome from the start, was still a source of worry. As Sullivan later recalled, 'My hand was always in my pocket to help some poor student to get daily food. Oh, the curse of this free education bringing up a class of educated, helpless paupers!'

Moreover he considered that he had been unfairly treated in a report by the eminent musicians who served as visiting examiners in the summer term of 1880.

It was a 'backstairs' intrigue against me led by Hallé, who could not forgive my being appointed conductor of the Leeds Festival instead of himself. So he led the other examiners (Costa, Goldschmidt, Henry Leslie and Hullah) entirely with him, and besides revenging himself on me, was enabled to give his rival E. Pauer [Eduard Pauer, a principal piano teacher at the school] a nasty dig also.

Sullivan's imputation of cowardice and venality to his old friend Goldschmidt, his old mentor Costa, and two such strong-willed men as Leslie (a famous choral conductor) and Hullah reads unconvincingly, but it is not surprising that at the beginning of 1881 he decided this would be his last term. The formal consent of the Duke of Edinburgh as chairman of the committee of management was necessary. It was a big decision (never again was he to have a 'permanent', salaried post), but Sullivan's diary dealt with it tersely:

[31 January 1881]: Tooth very bad. Slept a little from 10 [a.m.] to 1.30; got up at 4. Miss de la Motte came to see Mother.[5] Duke of Edinburgh called; told him again of my wish and resolve to leave the School at Easter. He assented. Tooth still aching . . .

His mother at this time had temporarily left her Fulham home and was in lodgings at 124 Buckingham Palace Road, not far from Sullivan's own quarters – perhaps in order to assist him in looking for a new house. In this quest he was unsuccessful, though he showed some interest in acquiring a house in Queen's Gate (near the Albert Hall) from his friend Henry Labouchère, the Radical M.P. He kept up his convivial club life, gambling at the Argus, dining at the Beefsteak in King William Street and adding membership of the Fielding Club (an offshoot of the Beefsteak) and of the Marlborough Club in Pall Mall. The latter was named after (and situated opposite) Marlborough House, residence of the Prince of Wales, and the Prince himself was its most illustrious member.

In his application to join the Marlborough Club he could have had no more illustrious proposer and seconder than the Duke of Edinburgh and Prince Christian (the Danish husband of Queen Victoria's third daughter, Princess Helena). The entrance fee and first year's subscription cost him the substantial sum of £42. When he dined there for the first time, on 23 January, he noted 'Prince Teck [father of the future Queen Mary] at the next table'. He was now moving at ease in an exalted circle, and of 500 names culled from his daily diary entries in 1881 more than one-sixth were titled. Princess Louise and Prince Leopold were his guests in January at a performance of the 'Children's *Pinafore*' which was playing at matinées at the Opera Comique for the third season.

Patience became pressing.[6] Carte had planned the production for April and resisted Sullivan's plea (as late as 6 March!) for postponement. Gilbert himself, not Du Maurier, designed the costumes. The operetta was, as usual, well into rehearsal with piano before he turned to the orchestration on 13 April. His diary shows him sometimes composing through the night until dawn, after a heavy day which might include the conducting of two rehearsals.

[20 April]: Rehearsal at 12, then home to write tenor song, afterwards cut out [probably the Duke's 'Though men of rank may useless seem']. Duke of Edinburgh called to see me, stayed whilst I wrote and dined. Went to the theatre at 7.30 to dress rehearsal. Came home late. Scored tenor song and sketched out overture. To bed at 5.30 a.m. Finished all the scoring of the opera.

[21 April]: Full rehearsal with band [i.e. orchestra only – probably the first orchestral rehearsal] at 11. Everything except the overture. Afterwards band and singers on the stage. Everyone sang flat. Heated discussion with Gilbert about things generally. Dined at home, finished some odd jobs in writing. Gave d'Albert my sketch of the overture to score. He finished it next morning in time to have the parts copied and rehearsed at night. Went round to Cadogan Place, then to Argus – minus £450. D.C. [D'Oyly Carte] came in the afternoon.

A 'sketch' for the overture – indicating what tunes from the opera were to be used, and in what key and at what length – would be, as in this case, sufficient for a competent associate to work on. In this case the musical handwriting suggests that the arranger was the younger (Eugène) D'Albert, not his father.[7]

[23 April]: Crammed house at Opera Comique. Enthusiastic reception on entering the orchestra. New piece (*Patience*) performed for [the] first time.[8] Went splendidly. Eight encores. Seemed a great success. Very tired afterwards, refused all invitations to supper. Called at the Fielding for a lemon and soda. Talked a little to Randegger, Hare, Aidé, etc. Then to Argus + £300. Spät [late].

The last half-dozen words, characteristically suppressed from the entry as reproduced in the Flower biography, reveal the man. Too tired for an after-the-show supper, he none the less needed a touch of sociability before retiring. (Alberto Randegger was a composer [see p. 102], John Hare a theatrical manager and Hamilton Aidé both a playwright and composer.) Then, stimulated, he went gambling. This time at the Argus Club he won £300; on 21 April (see above) he had lost £450. He was staking, more or less, a sum equivalent to his annual remuneration as principal of the National Training School for Music (£400). The annual wage for living-in maidservant was still about £20.

Next day the press began its chorus of welcome to *Patience, or Bunthorne's Bride* – the subtitle is a neat joke, for the poseur of a poet gets no bride at all. Grossmith played the role in a make-up which might have been modelled not on Wilde but on the painter James McNeill Whistler, then 45; he too was known for his eccentricities of dress as well as for his association with the Grosvenor Gallery. (His exhibits there in 1877 led to Ruskin's accusation of 'throwing a pot of paint in the public's face' and to the artist's libel action.) Rutland Barrington was Grosvenor and a newcomer, Leonora Braham, carried her milking-stool as Patience. The 'aesthetic dresses' – as the audience learned from their painted programmes – were themselves 'designed by the author', using 'art fabrics' from the fashionable London store of Liberty's, who took an advertisement in the programmes to emphasize the fact. The 'aesthetic' poses contrived by Gilbert as stage director were reproduced in the many line-illustrations and photographs of the time. The height of comic mockery was reached when such poses were clumsily attempted by the three officers (Richard Temple as Colonel Calverley, Frank Thornton as Major Murgatroyd, Durward Lely as Lieutenant the Duke of Dunstable) in a desperate attempt to win back their fiancées.

For that tableau, with its marionette-like gestures ('You hold yourself like this – you hold yourself like that') Sullivan provided a deliberately jerky musical setting, based on a melodic line identical with that of the entrance of Sergeant Belcore in Donizetti's *L'elisir d'amore*. The military identity can hardly be accidental, especially as the military music throughout the operetta finds Sullivan in such splendid and exhilarating form. Drum-rhythms tap through the entry-chorus, 'The soldiers of our queen', leading to Colonel Calverley's patter-song 'If you want a receipt for that popular mystery/Known to the world as a Heavy Dragoon . . .', and later through the Colonel's song 'When I first put this uniform on'. There is no need to postulate a surge of the composer's boyhood memories, since the military idiom was one of the most common ingredients of opera.

In the patter-song, the 'receipt' (an old alternative for 'recipe') turns out to comprise a fantastic catalogue of attributes. Real and fictional characters and types jostle for position in Gilbert's trisyllable rhymes:

> A smack of Lord Waterford, reckless and rollicky –
> Swagger of Roderick, heading his clan –
> The keen penetration of Paddington Pollaky –
> Grace of an odalisque on a divan –
>
> . . .
>
> Take of these elements all that is fusible
> Melt them all down in a pipkin or crucible
> Set them to simmer and take off the scum –
> And a Heavy Dragoon is the residuum.

The rhythmic stimulus to a composer is obvious, but Gilbert's list left a legacy of references to puzzle later audiences. 'Roderick' was Roderick Dhu in Scott's *The Lady of the Lake*; Ignatius Pollaky was a private inquiry agent operating from an address in Paddington, as advertisements in newspapers show.[9]

Some of the music in *Patience* does not escape the charge of banality – though in the case of the duet for the rival poets, 'When I go out of door', an ingenuous defence would be that the banality deliberately meets the situation. The sextet 'I hear the soft note' (much admired at the time) now can hardly help but seem over-sentimental in its cloying chords and repeated melody-notes. The sextet occurs within the long finale to Act 1, which as usual focuses the drama by assembling all the main characters at a point of tension.

The brightest musical sparkle comes in the quintet of Act 2, in which – by changing partners in a dance on stage – Angela and Saphir and the three officers exemplify their matrimonial options. Here there are two touches of rhythmic brilliance, worthy of the *Ballo* overture itself, both occurring not in the voices but in the orchestra. The introductory melody is strongly syncopated and 'chopped' within a 6/8 beat, to an irresistibly merry effect; later ('In that case unprecedented') a clarinet pipes up a dance-like tune in another syncopation above the voices. With entire justification this number returns to end the work.

The middle-aged spinster incurred Gilbert's cruel mockery, as usual. 'Silver'd is the raven hair', sang Alice Barnett in the role of the corpulent Lady Jane in Act 2. It was a grimly humorous text about an ageing figure, with successive refrains 'Little will be left of me' and 'There will be too much of me'. What raises this number to a high level of comedy is the caricature of its preliminary recitative, punctuated by doom-like declamations in octaves from orchestral cello and double-bass: the singer pretends to play (or, in at least one London production since World War II, has actually played) such an instrument on the stage. The parody is probably not specific, but similar interjections in octaves on the strings could be remembered from anguished recitatives in Verdi – at 'Pari siamo' in *Rigoletto*, for instance. Or perhaps there was a sly allusion to the cello-and-bass recitative in the finale of Beethoven's Ninth!

For the words of the song following the recitative, Sullivan was content to provide a straight setting. So straight, indeed, that it was worth reissuing as a separate ballad. But who, off stage, would wish to sing such lines as 'Stouter than I used to be'? (It was the situation which had already occurred with 'Hush'd is the bacon' from *Cox and Box*.) A new lyric beginning 'In the twilight of our love' was concocted and the song went forth to be warbled in many a decorous drawing-room. *Patience* itself would prove durable even when the artistic target of its satire had receded from public view.

17   Diarist and Traveller

FROM this time onwards, thanks to the details noted in his diary, much more is known about Sullivan's inner thoughts and private activities. Its pages have many references to his sexual life, the one thing he naturally chose not to reveal in all the correspondence with 'Dearest Mum'. The diary has gaps – no entry, for example, between 1 and 11 January 1881 – but its layout of three days to a page (Sullivan yearly ordered the same size of locked volume) evidently challenged him to a brief daily reporting. It was usually compiled *after* the day in question, as is clear from his notes of the hour of going to bed. For 1881, though for no other year, there also survives a kind of 'summary diary' in a separate volume. This excludes sexual references and (since it includes an obituary mark against the names of individuals still alive in 1881 and subsequent years) must have been compiled much later, probably for the benefit of a biographer. While based on the 'original' diary, the summary is obviously valuable in reproducing Sullivan's later perspective of importance – and sometimes a sharp recollection:

Went occasionally to dine and play poker at Spencer Brunton's – then living with his wife and family at 84 Brook St [Mayfair]. She was always very pleasant and friendly to me, but then I wasn't her husband.

The summary diary for 1881 begins with Sullivan's calculation of his income for the previous year – with an overwhelming share contributed by his collaboration with Gilbert. The firm of Metzler had published *The Sorcerer* and *HMS Pinafore*, but there could be no question of remaining with them after the *fracas* at the Opera Comique in which Frank Chappell and other directors of Metzler's were involved. Sullivan went over to the firm of Chappell's (directed by Thomas Chappell, brother of Arthur of the 'Monday Pops') for *The Pirates of Penzance*. From this, published in 1880, Sullivan as yet had drawn no royalties – which, in respect of stage works, arose only from sales of printed music (vocal scores, piano scores, selections and dances). Sullivan's share of box-office profits (under the agreement with Carte) is separately listed. Carte had initially acquired only the right to theatrical performances in London, and now had to pay additionally for the 'country' [provincial touring] rights. The item 'Tennyson song' refers to Sullivan's duet-setting of *The Sisters*, published by Kegan, Paul & Co. in the periodical *Leisure Hours*.

		£	s	d
Metzler & Co., royalties				
Christmas 1879	£900			
Midsummer 1880	£824.15	1,724.15.0		
Boosey & Co., ditto				
	£373.11.3			
	£304.12.11	678. 4.2		
America, 'Pirates of Penzance' (net)		2,637. 9.0		
Opera Comique, 'Pinafore'		655. 4.0		
Ditto, 'Pirates of Penzance'		2,517.11.0		
Ditto, balance of 'Pinafore' and children		100.16.0		
[i.e. performances of 'Pinafore' by the children's cast]				
Country right of pieces – half paid Xmas		725. 0.0		
Australian ditto		150. 0.0		
India ditto, and 'Cox and Box'		41. 0.0		
School of Music: 2 terms		266.13.4		
Tennyson song, Kegan, Paul & Co.		42. 0.0		
Leeds Festival		315. 0.0		
Australian rights, 'Pinafore', 2nd year		135. 0.0		

£9,988.12.6

An income of virtually £10,000 a year was an extraordinary level for anyone in the arts to attain. (Gladstone's salary as prime minister was £7,500.) To maintain such an income, what alternative was there but to continue his output of operettas? To compose and conduct for the concert-hall could not have brought him near that level. 'Grand Opera' might do so, if only it were internationally successful – as successful as it was for Gounod and Ambroise Thomas, not to mention Verdi and Wagner. That was where Sullivan's ambition lay. After *Patience* he wrote to Carte that he would deliver only one more operetta 'as I want to write an opera for Covent Garden'. But to find a subject and a librettist was difficult enough; to reorder his schedule of work, to plan the necessary 'investment' of time, to risk the uncertainty of such an enterprise against the well-tried formulas of operetta – this was even more difficult for a man who so much enjoyed his leisure and luxuries. Sullivan and Gilbert were now able to impose on Carte slightly more advantageous terms: the *entire* profits (without a reserve of £3,000, as previously) were to be divided every three months, and Carte undertook to pay the composer and librettist '£2,000 each for the American rights of any new piece, and £500 each for personal expenses, if we go over'.

The year 1881 not only saw the production of *Patience* at the old Opera Comique theatre in April and its transfer to Carte's magnificent, newly-built Savoy Theatre in October. For Sullivan it was also the year of three of his longest pleasure-journeys. A cruise in the Duke of Edinburgh's flagship took him to northern Europe and Russia in June and July, which was followed by a 45-day holiday in Germany and France in August and September. Then on 21 December began a winter trip to Egypt from which he did not return until the following April. In the 16 months beginning January 1881 he was away more than seven months, and made on these absences some of the liveliest descriptive entries in his diary.

The names of Gilbert, Carte and other professional collaborators mingle in the diary with those of royal patrons, family friends, tradesmen, servants and casual acquaintances. In addition there is the constant reference to his mistress, 'L.W.'. Entries of the type 'Two letters from L.W. Wrote to L.W.' [20 January 1881] testify to the close frequency of correspondence when he was away from home. What the letters 'L.W.' stand for is open to speculation (perhaps 'Little Woman', a Victorian endearment by which Louise Scott Russell had long ago signed herself), but there is no doubt that this 'L.W.' was Fanny Ronalds. As the entries of successive years show, the birthday of 'L.W.' and the birthday of Fanny Ronalds were the same (23 August) and there are frequent links between 'L.W.' and 'Cad. Pl.' – Fanny Ronalds' address being no. 7 Cadogan Place. Moreover, 'L.W.' is identified as the daughter of a 'Mrs C.' [Carter] and on a much later document (p. 373) Fanny Ronalds herself used the identification 'L.W.'

But the diary also has many references to her as 'Mrs Ronalds' (and its abbreviation 'Mrs R.'). Why, if she can be named openly, should the same person also be mentioned in coded form? The reason is exactly because Fanny Ronalds and Arthur Sullivan had a double relationship. They met openly, mixing at society's musical gatherings, at dinner-parties, at house-parties; in recording such meetings the diary uses the conventional and formal description. (It is always 'Mrs', never the forename.) Their relationship as lovers had the coded reference. It was a safety precaution lest prying eyes should scan those pages, locked though they were. The precaution was the more necessary because, as we shall see, Sullivan added a simple numerical code to indicate the sexual act – and that, once noticed and understood, would be fatally compromising.

On 5 April the one-line entry 'L.W. returned' put an end to the stream of entries noting the arrival of her letters. Naturally she went to the final rehearsal of *Patience* (and brought her daughter) – and since that occasion was public, she is openly identified, along with Tom Chappell (publisher) and others. Here the parentheses indicate numbers of people. Chappell and his wife evidently brought three other members of their family.

[22 April]: Rehearsal very smooth. Oyster supper afterwards at Smiths. Tom Chappells (5), Ionides (2), Gilberts (2), Mrs Ronalds, Fanny [i.e. daughter], and Mr Carter [Mrs Ronalds's father], and self. Then home, very tired.

But who was 'D.H.', a woman so imprudent as to call on him at almost midnight? As later evidence will show, these initials, perhaps standing for 'Dear heart', very likely represent yet another concealment of the identity of Fanny Ronalds herself.

[8 May]: Got up late, stayed at home all the afternoon. Called at Cad. Pl. en route for Fulham [visiting his mother]. Came home 10 [p.m.]. D.H. came in for a few minutes at 11.30.

[12 May]: D.H. breakfasted with me. Walked up to the Marlborough Club to look after dinner arrangements.[1] Met the D[uke] of Edinburgh; Duke of Connaught [third son of

Queen Victoria] joined us. Gave my annual birthday dinner at the Club. Present – Duke of Edinburgh, Costa, Alfred Rothschild, Reuben Sassoon, Fred Clay, Edward Hall, George Lewis, J. E. Millais, W. S. Gilbert, Tom Chappell, John Delacour, Charles Hall, Alfred Cooper, Harvie Farquhar and self. Very pleasant – good dinner . . .

[13 May]: My birthday – 39, alas! Mother and all the family came bringing flowers, etc. Also Mrs Dremel [his mother's friend], likewise Carte and Gunn. Went to the School at 1.30. Committee at 3. Formally gave up office of Principal. Called at Cadogan Place on my way home. Mrs R. not very well. Dined at the Marlborough with Duke of Edinburgh . . . Gave L.W. share of earnings £300.

The 'share' of earnings seems to denote a *regular* apportionment of his income (as one would expect) to his mistress. But all was not well. A strong suggestion of another sexual liaison is conveyed by the record of a day when a late sleep was followed by a late breakfast. But it will be noted that this rival to L.W. is not identified as D.H.

[17 May]: L.W. to breakfast 1.30. A telegram on my table was seen – painful scene in consequence. At 4, went to Gloucester Place – another painful interview – confirmed what I had said the night before. Came home – sent a bouquet. Dined at Millais' – only men: Anthony Trollope, Lethbridge, Crabb, F. Clay, Eden, [Thomas] Hardy, Lambton, Sir Henry Thompson.[2] Won £6 from Trollope, drove F.C. [Clay] to St James's Club, then home.

[18 May]: L.W. came at 12.30, stayed till 2. Storm over. Drove Dick [his nephew] (at 3) up to St Paul's. Went into the Cathedral to hear *In Memoriam* – Sons of the Clergy [Festival], very fine. Then to Hobbs [shop] to choose a safe with Smythe. Sent the brougham for Mrs R and Fanny [daughter] – called later at no. 7 [Cadogan Place] . . . Added metronome marks in proof of *Patience*. Opened account (£458) at [?] Coutts Bank, Victoria St.

Sullivan had much work for Walter Smythe as his secretary, one of whose tasks would be to deal with the composer's correspondence during his absence abroad. He spent a few days (19–25 May) in Paris with Clay, then came home.

[27 May]: . . . To Cad. Place: accès! Dined at [Edward] Hall's – J. B. Martin, Mr & Mrs Ed[mund] Gurney and Cecil Clay [Frederic's brother] and wife, Freddie [Clay] and self. Ran away to play *Lost Chord* at St James's Hall for Mrs Ronalds: sang well, great success. Back to Hall's. Then to Lady Molesworth's – party for Princess Louise.

The sexual satisfaction denoted by the French *accès* was to be paralleled later by German words. Sullivan also indicated his sexual acts numerically, as 'L.W. (2)' on 2 June and 'L.W. tea (1)' on the following day. A few days afterwards the couple joined a house-party some 35 miles north of London at Luton Hoo, the mansion owned by the widowed Mrs Dudley Leigh.

[6 June]: At Luton Hoo. All went to Luton. Mrs Leigh opened a bazaar. I gave £5 . . . and accompanied Mrs R. in *The Lost Chord* in the middle of the bazaar. Great enthusiasm.

The guest-list (above) for the all-male party of 17 May links Sullivan not merely with his close friend Millais (aged 51) but with two leading novelists of different generations. Trollope, secure in his reputation, was to die in the following year at the age of 67, but the 40-year-old Thomas Hardy had as yet written only two of the novels (*Far from the Madding Crowd* and *The Return of the*

Native) on which his fame rests. No less fascinating as a dinner guest must have been the eminent surgeon, Sir Henry Thompson, whose wide range of interests (he was a novelist and painter) would lead him to write, at the age of 82 in the new century, one of the first manuals of the motor-car. Thompson's professional speciality was the treatment of stones in the kidney – Sullivan's own malady.

Millais, on whom a baronetcy was to be conferred in 1885, had moved to a spacious, newly-built house in Kensington – reflecting a prosperity as exceptional among painters as Sullivan's was among musicians. It was there, on 2 June, that Sullivan unexpectedly met his old love again:

John Millais gave a splendid ball at his new house in Palace Gate and there I ran up against Chenny! (R.S.R.) – whom I had not met since her marriage [in 1872] and departure for India. We sat on the stairs talking for three hours! She is as handsome as ever.

The initials of Rachel Scott Russell are as given in the diarist's hand.

His friendship with the Duke of Edinburgh gave him, in summer 1881, the opportunity of a sea cruise and a visit to Russia. Making his own way to Copenhagen (via Calais, Hamburg, Kiel and the night boat across to Denmark), he joined the naval exercises proceeding under the command of the Duke in his capacity as Rear-Admiral superintending the Royal Navy's reserve squadron. The Duke had ensured congenial off-duty music-making by inviting both Sullivan and Frederic Clay to be his guests aboard. The goal of the cruise was Kronstadt, the port of St Petersburg. As well as naval manoeuvres on the way, there were royal ties to be strengthened on arrival. Tsar Alexander II (the Duke's father-in-law) had been assassinated the previous March. His successor was his son, Alexander III, who was married to a Danish princess.

The Duke's flagship was *HMS Hercules*, a modern ironclad (most of Britain's naval ships still had wooden hulls) and one of the biggest vessels of the fleet, 8,677 tons. On his arrival at Copenhagen Sullivan found himself involved straight away in high-level festivities: that very evening (Friday 24 June) he went with the Duke of Edinburgh to dine with King Christian IX of Denmark and his Queen, bringing to her a package of photographs which he was carrying from her daughter, the Princess of Wales.

She said: 'The Princess says you will tell me all about the little monkey'. I said: 'I have no instructions about any monkey, your Majesty'. 'She means herself,' said the Queen, laughing heartily, and we both laughed.

After dinner Sullivan drove with his companions to the Tivoli Gardens and approved the sight: 'About 10,000 people were there, all perfectly happy, perfectly sober, and perfectly well-behaved. There was an orchestra, a military band, swings, rifle galleries, performing fleas, a fat lady, and [a] good restaurant.'

Next day they lunched aboard the *Lively* (a small ship which served as tender to the flagship) and joined the *Hercules* at 4. The whole squadron left at 5.30 and passed Elsinore ('Hamlet's home', as Sullivan carefully observed in writing to his mother) with a salute of 21 guns from the shore. Sullivan found life aboard most agreeable.

We breakfast at 8 (I am afraid I shall get into the habit of getting up early), lunch at 12, and dine at 7. After dinner we make music, etc, and go to bed at 12. Yesterday being Sunday [26 June 1881], there was Church service, and I played the harmonium. I was greatly delighted with the singing of the crew. They roared out the chants and hymn-tunes lustily and loved to dwell on the high notes.

I have a lovely cabin in the Admiral's quarters at the stem of the ship, and am very luxuriously lodged altogether. Sir William Hewitt V.C. (admiral) is the Duke's other guest and is a most delightful companion. The officers seem most pleasant fellows and the ship is splendid, the sea like glass, and the weather heavenly, and I have nothing to do.

Our squadron consists of eight ships, and we move along in double Indian file, so that the nose of the *Warrior* is close to our stern [a drawing accompanies this]. Today we have been exercising the fleet in fog signals – guns and hideous steam whistles. Tomorrow, gunnery practice; Wednesday, manoeuvring . . . L'Estrange, who is captain of the *Lively*, meets us tomorrow to bring letters from Copenhagen and to take our letters to Reval to post them . . . I am finishing this letter after dinner, HRH the Admiral having gone down to the officers' wardroom to play a rubber of whist. I must join him now, so will drop my anchor (I am full of good nautical phrases).

While on the cruise he posted letters not only to his mother, and his secretary Smythe, but also to 'L.W.' and the mysterious 'D.H.' after receiving one 'from D.H.'

Before the fleet arrived at its Russian destination there was an entertainment got up for the benefit of the crew of the *Hercules*:

Artists: HRH the Duke of Edinburgh, three sailors, Major Welch (commanding the Marines), Mr F. Clay and Mr Arthur Sullivan. It went off splendidly, and to finish with I sang 'the Englishman' from the *Pinafore*, and the whole crew to my astonishment sang the chorus!

Arriving at Kronstadt on Saturday 2 July they disembarked next day and were taken by launch up the River Neva to Peterhof –

. . . a village about 15 miles (I think) from St Petersburg. Here are all the summer palaces of the Emperor and all the Grand Dukes. It is like an enormous park, with a mixture of the Bois de Boulogne and Virginia Water. . . . Close to the [Imperial] Palace is our villa, a spare one belonging to the Emperor, where he puts up stray royalties and relations when they come to see him. It is very comfortable but plainly furnished – the bedrooms like an alpine hotel, polished floors and no carpets. . . . [Next day] in the evening we dined at the royal palace with the Emperor and Empress. . . . The former shook hands and said 'Nous nous sommes souvent rencontrés à Londres' [We often met in London] and the Empress said her mother [the Queen of Denmark] had written to her about me, and told her I was going to give her some music.

In St Petersburg itself he was impressed by the Winter Palace – 'certainly the finest in Europe', declared the seasoned traveller to his mother – 'with its magnificent suites and not one but five or six ball- and concert-rooms!' It was there on Wednesday 6 July that the Imperial Chapel Choir were paraded for the visitors:

all in full dress – red and gold . . . The Duke said to me: 'Doesn't it remind you of when you were in the Chapel Royal?' And it did rather. There were about 80 and, blasé as I am with music, I confess to a new sensation at hearing them. It is like nothing else. They have basses with the most wonderful voices going down to the *low A* and the effect of their singing their church music was thrilling. Sometimes it was exactly like an organ, only more beautiful. They sang for an hour, and I could have heard them for a couple of hours more . . .

The other things besides the Choir which have impressed me most are the caviar and the sterlet [a small species of sturgeon] . . . it is an etherealized eel, it melts in your mouth.

Of Russian composers Sullivan reported nothing – perhaps because it was not then the season for concerts. The most active of the St Petersburg musicians was Rimsky-Korsakov (1844–1908), who had just completed his opera *The Snow-Maiden*. The 41-year-old Tchaikovsky (who lived in Moscow, not St Petersburg) was at the time in the West.

Disappointed that he had not heard from his mother, Sullivan made his next letter (11 July) a short one, 'to punish you'. It was written at sea, on the homeward journey, with a memory of the British ships' festive departure from Krondstadt, prior to which the Russian Emperor and Empress came aboard the *Hercules*.

Oh, my stars! Wasn't it splendid to see the yards all manned – the guns all firing royal salutes! It was a grand sight. Then we weighed anchor and here we are in a thick fog & all the signals going like Blackwater Fair, guns, steam-whistles and bell-buoys. If we don't all run each other down we shall arrive at Kiel on Thursday [14 July].

At Kiel it was the turn of the German royal family to behave in a pleasantly friendly fashion. Sullivan dined with Prince William (now 22) and Prince Henry (18), sons of the German Crown Prince and his wife Victoria (Queen Victoria's eldest daughter). It was not only the sailors of the Royal Navy who knew their *Pinafore*, as the composer discovered: 'When I got into the carriage Prince William bowed to me and sang: "He polished up the handle of the big front door". I burst out laughing and so did everyone. It was too funny.'

The future William II ('Kaiser Bill' of the First World War) would continue to show a high regard for Sullivan and his music right up to the year of the composer's death.

Sullivan was back on native soil on 26 July (having landed at Leith and taken the train from Edinburgh to London) and at last found the new home he had been looking for. On the same street (Victoria St) as Albert Mansions, a new block of flats called Queen's Mansions was opened. He took no. 1 (at first only the ground floor, later renting a basement also). It was to be his address for the rest of his life. Smythe, his secretary, was to occupy no. 2. His occupancy took effect only from the New Year, but on 2 August he 'took L.W. to see Queen's Mansions'. The sexual act continued to be recorded numerically in his diary, the partner being indicated variously as 'L.W.', 'D.H.', or simply 'Cad. Pl.' – Cadogan Place, Fanny Ronalds's address.

1 August . . . Afterwards Cad. Pl. (1)
2 August . . . Dined at home. D.H. (2)
4 August . . . Home L.W. (1)
5 August . . . Dined at Cad. Pl. (2), then home.

On 8 August, during the annual Cowes yachting event on the Isle of Wight he went to stay for a night as the Prince of Wales's guest at the royal residence, Osborne, 'to discuss the question of a knighthood. I firmly and strongly declined it – or rather would decline it if it were offered to me. I don't want to be one of a batch – nor do I care for a knighthood at all.'

On 11 August his daily diary noted the sending of £861.15s. to his friend and broker, Edward Hall, for investment in gold-mining shares. (A disastrous decision, as was to become clear.) On that same evening, in the company of Dicey, Fanny Ronalds, and her mother Mrs J. B. Carter, Sullivan left by the 7.40 p.m. train to catch the night ferry from Dover to Calais. The ladies and Sullivan (who took a servant with him) were bound for separate German spas – they for Ems, Sullivan for Homburg, eight miles north of Frankfurt-am-Main. There Dicey would leave him and he would take the 'cure' – that is, drink the waters under medical supervision. (There had evidently been a recurrence of his kidney trouble: a later letter to his mother refers to the Homburg treatment as a 'patching-up'.) The spa waters and the restricted diet were supposed to be accompanied by rest, but Sullivan nevertheless twice took the train to Frankfurt to see *Fidelio* and *Rigoletto*. He also visited Schwalbach, yet another spa, where his Paris-based American friend Mrs Beach Grant was taking *her* 'cure'; and on 23 August he drove the 30 miles to Ems 'to wish Mrs Ronalds many happy returns of her birthday'.

Why the separation in different spas? It may be conjectured that the 'rest' accompanying the treatment included a prescribed sexual abstinence. As for the 'cure' itself, 'ink and Lucifer matches seem to be the principal ingredients of the waters, judging by the taste', complained Sullivan in a letter to his mother from his lodgings at 47 Untere Promenade. He found a few British friends and acquaintances – including Lady Coutts Lindsay, 'very weak' – but called it 'a miserably dull existence'. On 4 September he complained in his diary of 'bad headache all day' but the period of the 'cure' was over. Next day he hastened to join Fanny Ronalds and her mother for a rendezvous at Kassel.

Went to Hotel König von Preussen. Found my friends there. Our rooms are 5, 6, 7. Very comfortable. Mrs R. looking much better. Mrs C. also better. After lunch drove out to Wilhelmshöhe. Visited park and castle – the latter has most beautiful furniture, wall-hangings, etc, all in the style of the First [Napoleonic] Empire. Much interested in the account of Napoleon III's stay there. Drove back and shopped. Nothing to do in the evening. L.W.2.

The intensity of the lovers' reunion at Kassel is indicated in his diary not only by Arthur Sullivan's customary numerical sign but by the recurrent expression 'Himmelische Nacht', meaning 'heavenly night' (he mistakenly writes *himmelische* for *himmlische*), sometimes shortened to 'Him. N.'

[6 September] . . . Tel[egraphed] to Smythe for letters, etc. Drove out after lunch to Wilhelmsthal – an hour's drive – a hunting-box in a picturesque park belonging formerly to the Landgraves of Cassel – now Prussian, but unused. In the park is an interesting old tower, built 1754 with fine view of surrounding country. L.W. (1) *straight up!* Coffee at the restaurant. Shopped a little. V.S. [meaning unknown] Stayed at home and played poker all evening. Beautiful moon. Himmelische Nacht! (1).

[7 September] . . . After dinner went to Dreike's Circus with L.W. So cold we came in again at 9. Himmelische Nacht (2). [Letters] to and from Dicey.

Their idyll continued when they (accompanied by Mrs Carter) travelled on to north-eastern France, staying with the Marquis d'Aoust at his chateau of Cuincy near Douai.[3] The Marquis was an amateur composer some years Sullivan's senior.

[15 September]: *Cuincy*. Wet. Played besique the greater part of the day. [This, rather than *bezique*, was Sullivan's habitual spelling for the card-game.]

[16 September]: *Cuincy*. Fine day. After breakfast drove into Douai to try the organ at St Jacques. New organ by a Belgian builder – three manuals, pedals, etc. Good mechanism, but poor tone – diapason work thin and reedy – reeds too powerful. Introduced to the organist, M. Delahaye. Accompd. Mrs Ronalds in *The Lost Chord* and [Mendelssohn's] *Oh for the wings*. Him. N. (2).

On his way home Sullivan stayed briefly in Paris, arriving back in London on 25 September with a festive event ahead of him. The new Savoy Theatre, built by Carte from the profits of the partnership was ready. It was designed by C. J. Phipps (1835–97), the leading theatrical architect of the day. Seating just under 1,300 (including 18 private boxes), it was the first London theatre to be lit entirely by electricity.[4] On 1 October Sullivan inspected the orchestra pit and 'gave directions to have it raised 8 inches'. On 11 October the theatre opened with *Patience* (transferred from the Opera Comique), the conductor on this special occasion being Sullivan himself.

[10 October]: Rehearsal at Savoy at 11 – lasted till 4.30. Lady K[atherine] Coke, Mrs R. etc. there. Came home. L.W. tea (1). Dined at home with Smythe. Went to conduct the first performance of *Patience* in new theatre. Great house, enthusiastic reception for all. Went back to sup at Gilbert's, returned home at 3 a.m., changed my clothes, had coffee and drove to Liverpool Street to take the 5.10 a.m. train to Norwich.

There was a rehearsal at Norwich the next morning of *The Martyr of Antioch* which Sullivan was to conduct on 12 October as part of the Norwich Festival. 'Great reception. Very fair performance. Chorus toneless and weak,' his diary reported.

Lady Katherine Coke had been a friend since the time when the youthful Sullivan had been courting Rachel Scott Russell.[5] A dispassionate entry notes a visit from Rachel herself after that unexpected meeting at Millais's ball:

[5 October]: Chenny came at 4.30 – stayed till 6.15. Had a long talk. She is very little changed.

On 24 October he went to hear his protégé, Eugène d'Albert, play his own piano concerto at St James's Hall – 'a brilliant success, reminding me of my first appearance with *The Tempest*. This was one of the 'Richter Concerts', which had been an important part of London's musical season since 1879, reflecting the conductor's immense prestige in England. Hans Richter was the 'true artist and true friend' to whom Elgar was to dedicate his First Symphony in 1908; but to the resentful Sullivan, who never acknowledged that the master of Bayreuth was of a superior *class* of conductor to any British product, Richter was the pre-eminent example of the foreigner unfairly preferred above the native artist.

Sullivan was again the Duke of Edinburgh's guest – this time at his home, Eastwell Park, near Ashford, Kent – in late November. 'After dinner, H.R.H. [i.e. the Duke], Thring [Sir Henry Thring, 1818–1907, an eminent lawyer], and self discussed Manchester speeches': this (26 November) is one of the rare allusions in the diary to domestic politics. Richard Assheton Cross, Home Secretary in the late Conservative government, had made a number of prominently reported speeches at Stockport and elsewhere in the Manchester area, denouncing the present liberal govemment's policies in Ireland and elsewhere. *The Times* had commented on 22 November:

The conditions under which political controversy is conducted in these days impose upon public men tasks unknown to their forerunners in party leadership. . . . It is considered indispensably necessary for a party to keep its claims before the public in the [Parliamentary] recess as well as during the session.

Ireland was the sore point of government policy. Gladstone's liberalizing measures in matters of land tenure had not stopped the outbreaks of 'Fenian' violence in England. It was not the Irish disturbances, however, but those of Egypt which impinged on Sullivan's life for an extended period in 1881–2, through his friendship with Edward Dicey. Not only as editor of the *Observer*, but as the author of a recently published book, *England and Egypt*, Dicey was prominent among those urging a British annexation of Egypt, after it had become clear that joint Anglo-French supervision established in 1876 could barely contain the rise of Arab nationalism. Dicey had several times visited Egypt and was to do so every winter up to 1885. He was a director of the Ottoman Bank in Cairo and the intimate acquaintance of Nubar Pasha, who had been Prime Minister until deposed by an officers' revolt.

With *Patience* firmly established at the Savoy, Sullivan had every reason to allow himself a lengthy holiday. A trip to Egypt would take him out of England's miserable winter and would offer him an acquaintance with an exotic landscape, an ancient culture and a cosmopolitan 'society'. Guide-books were available in English, and Thomas Cook & Son had already placed Egypt on the list of its tourist destinations. But Sullivan would not need Cook's: Dicey would be the best possible personal guide. Travelling across France by rail, the two friends embarked at Marseilles to cross the Mediterranean on the French steamer *Irraouaddy*, Sullivan 'thinking what a curious way it was of spending Christmas Day!' He had engaged two cabins to Dicey's one, having with him a new manservant, Finch, who probably waited on both the distinguished travellers.

There is one rather pretty girl on board. She asked me yesterday if I had heard *Patience*. I said yes, I had. Then she began to quote it and rave about it. I let her run on for some time, then told her she would be glad to know that I had written the music. Tableau!

The last word is significant. The direction 'tableau' or 'picture' at the end of the act in many Victorian theatrical works indicates a carefully balanced, pictorial grouping of the characters, held for an appreciable moment in order to gather applause. The *tableau vivant* or 'living picture' as a public or private exhibition was likewise favoured – and Sullivan himself would be involved (p. 257) in such an activity at the imperial German court.

On 31 December they disembarked at Port Said, a 'new ramshackling place, rather like a Californian "city" in its insubstantial character', he wrote to his mother. 'Dicey and I will have to see the old year out in this heaven-forsaken place all alone. We shall get a bottle of champagne and try to think we are rollicking dogs.' By 7.30 a.m. on New Year's Day, after a night's sleep at Port Said, they were aboard the steamer which would take them through the Suez Canal to Ismailia. There they would sleep for a further night (at the Hôtel des Bains) before catching a train to Cairo and the luxury of the celebrated Shepheard's Hotel.

Dicey's familiarity with the Cairo scene soon introduced Sullivan to Sir Edward Malet, the British Minister, and to Sir Auckland Colvin, the chief British financial adviser, and his daughters. On a visit to the Pyramids he 'crawled in and out of different tombs on my hands and knees, and swallowed a lot of dust, lunched on the sand in the Temple of the Sphynx [*sic*], and felt I had done the Pyramids and my duty also'.

The European and Europeanized upper society of Cairo kept up its conventional gatherings and entertainments. Both the Opera House (for which *Aida* had been composed) and a French theatre received state subsidies. Sullivan saw *Carmen* ('the female chorus execrable, the Carmen bad – awkward, ungraceful and ugly') on 7 January 1882, followed by Flotow's *Martha* on 28 January and Offenbach's *Les Brigands* on 20 February.

A greater stimulus to his interest was the novelty of Arab music with its associated dancing and ceremonies, reported at length in his diary and in letters home. The Friday afternoon ceremonies of the 'Howling Dervishes' and the 'Dancing Dervishes' were public (the current Baedeker advised that 20–25 minutes would be enough for each). But Sullivan's special interest demanded a private after-dinner session with Arab musicians at the house of a leading official, Tigrane Bey, in the company of Osman Pasha.[6]

[Diary, 14 January 1882]: Six musicians were in waiting for us, and Osman said they were the best in Cairo, that there were none so good anywhere. Only one, the chief singer, was in Arab dress. They all sat cross-legged on a divan. Four played and two sang; occasionally they all joined in the chorus. The instruments were the *out*, a kind of large mandolin, six bichord strings tuned . . . and played with a quill, the *kanoun*, a kind of trichord zither, with a scale of three octaves, quills on both hands, and the *ney* or *ni*, a perpendicular flute from which I could not elicit one single sound. I can't understand how it is blown, although I watched and tried frequently. There was also a tambourine which was only tapped very gently to help the rhythm. The music is impossible to describe and impossible to note down. We had three hours and a half of it – refreshments and smoking all the time. I came away dead beat, having listened with all my ears and all my intelligence.

He did, however, set down in musical notation the tuning of the *out*. Modern scholarship transcribes the names of the three instruments as *'ud, qanūn, nāy*.

On 23 January a jovial letter to his mother told her how he and his friends got about on donkeys: 'I often ride a capital white donkey who is called Prince of Wales. Mrs Langtry and Mrs Cornwallis West are also favourite donkeys.'

Conspicuous as a favourite of the Prince of Wales, and equally conspicuous as a woman of 'society' who went on the stage, Lillie Langtry had recently made her London theatrical debut; the other reference is presumably to the wife of William Cornwallis West, whose residence was in Eaton Place near that of one of Sullivan's friends and hostesses, Lady Andalusia Molesworth. In the typical mock-pompous style he loved to employ in letters to his mother, Sullivan wrote that 'the great historical event of the week' was his playing the organ for morning service that Sunday at the English church – but as it obliged him to get up at 8.30 a.m., 'I told Dean Butcher (the parson) he must not expect it again. He of course saw the "justice" of my remark.'

As to work, he had done little – but

I find now, from the experience I have already made, that it is useless to try to write whilst you are in the midst of new scenery and people, habits and emotions, but that afterwards the effect is very great and one's power is redoubled and freshness restored . . .

Dicey is very well and sends his love to you. His intellect is feeble, but he is not dangerous. [In Dicey's hand is the marginal mark, 'Impudence'.] He passes the greater part of his time in writing letters to important personages – Lord Granville [British Foreign Secretary], the Khedive [nominal Egyptian ruler], Gambetta [French Prime Minister], Rothschild [Alfred or Leopold?], etc., but of course Finch has strict orders not to post them! His appetite is good, I am glad to say.

Grove is an imposter. He sends a message by Smythe every week to say he is going to write but he doesn't write . . .

The Egyptian trip indeed brought out Sullivan's genius – it is hardly too strong a word – for letter-writing. Lively observation of unfamiliar scenes, witty and sometimes self-depreciating accounts of his activities, shrewd professional assessment – all are there, but always with a caring remembrance of those at home. On 29 January he took up his pen again to write to his mother at Fulham.

This is the most enervating place in the world, I think – if you once begin to be lazy you can never stop, but are carried on with a mad impetus until from sheer exhaustion at doing nothing you write a letter or read one.

I can't do any proper work here, but it doesn't matter. On Friday [January] I went to see the Howling Dervishes, and a pretty sight they were! I drove with the Colvins to a small mosque in the midst of a lot of ruined and half-completed structures at Old Cairo. We were shown into the mosque by an attendant, sat down on chairs and looked at our friends the Dervishes. It was not a pleasant sight, or one calculated to make one say proudly, 'I, too, am a man like these,' but it was interesting. They stood in a circle, one boss Dervish in the middle, a sort of conductor whose motions they followed, and at one side were one or two gifted vocalists who sang real Arab music accompanied by tom-toms. This collection of human beings then howled and gasped (breathing 'Al-lah') and swayed their bodies backwards and forwards and sideways, their long hair waving in the air, giving them a wild and mad appearance. They went on for twenty minutes without stopping, then a minute or two quiet while a verse of the Koran was read, then off they went again. It lasted two hours but I was only there an hour. At the end they all quietly did up their hair and resumed their turbans and then smoked cigarettes as if nothing had happened. These were the Howling Dervishes. Next Friday I am going to see the Dancing Dervishes! After all, it was very interesting and not much worse than some of the performances by the Shakers [Protestant sect] in England and America.

The letter also describes Sullivan's visit, after dinner one night to 'the great fair at Abbasiyeh', a short drive from Cairo into the desert:

a most extraordinary gathering – a great collection of tents, some of enormous size, erected in a circle, all brilliantly illuminated and each containing the representatives of some sect or the Sheik of the district or guild. In every tent there were a number of worshippers, in some they were reciting the Koran, in others howling like the dervishes; indeed in one big tent there was a circle of a hundred howlers all swaying their bodies and prostrating themselves. One tent contained a devotee who was dancing exactly like the figure the children have got at Fulham. Then there was a tremendous procession of about a couple of thousand men carrying torches and candles, playing pipes, beating drums and singing in the most hideous fashion, the Sheik walking gravely in the middle. They walked round the circle twice then stood in front of a large and splendid tent wherein sat a chief eunuch who was a 'Hadji' or sacred man because he had been to Mecca, and also two important Sheiks.

They chanted something in honour of these 'prominent citizens', as the Americans would say, and then retired. The whole scene was one of the most striking things I ever saw.

A visit to Heliopolis on Sunday 5 February enabled him not only to see its famous obelisk, 66 feet high ('the oldest but one in Egypt') and the 'Virgin's Tree' – a large sycamore under which, according to tradition, Mary and her son rested during the Flight into Egypt – but also to call on Wilfrid Scawen Blunt and his wife, who had been

bitten by the Arab mania, and live in tents, ride on camels, dress like Arabs, and generally behave like maniacs. There they were – in tents pitched in the desert, just like two children playing at being Arabs. She was Lady Anne Noel, a grand-daughter of Lord Byron. We were entertained with pistachio nuts, sweet-meats and coffee.

It was typical of Sullivan's conservative outlook that he should dismiss Blunt (1840–1922) in these terms, or as 'a fatuous prig'.[7] Already known as poet and oriental traveller, he was to show a passionate political radicalism which earned him two months in prison for exhorting Irish tenantry to resist eviction. In April 1885 Lord Randolph Churchill, trying to establish a 'Fourth Party' in the British parliamentary system, would ask Blunt for an inspiriting poem which Sullivan might set to music. Blunt's scathing response was 'With something about a primrose in it?' – an allusion to the Primrose League, set up in Disraeli's memory in 1883.[8]

Six days after his meeting with Blunt, Sullivan bestirred himself to rise before seven in order to watch from a merchant's house the procession which brought to Cairo the sacred carpet from Mecca.

First came all the soldiers, cavalry and infantry, with their bands playing, then some of the sects singing, reading the Koran, and their banners flying and finally the camel with an enormous palanquin of gold cloth on his back containing the sacred carpet itself. Behind this came the Sheik of the caravan which had brought it from Mecca – an old man on a camel with long grey hair, stark naked down to the waist, drunk with opium or 'hashisch' and nodding his head from side to side all the way. He is supposed to go like that all the way to Mecca and back but I have no doubt directly he gets well into the desert he puts his clothes on and stops nodding and behaves like any other respectable Arab. Behind him came several Sheiks, drummers, etc., on camels and that completed the procession. We moved off then and drove to the citadel where the Khedive was to be and I have never seen such a picturesque or striking sight. Thousands of people lined the streets, in the houses, on walls and on the steps of the mosques, every corner where they could obtain standing room and the large square in front of the citadel was a sea of heads, [?] and all Arabs together, not chimney-pot hats but turbans and fezzes together with the most striking costumes in beautiful colours. We got out of our carriage and joined the Colvins who were just near us and through them we got into the large portico where stood all the ministers and officials waiting the Khedive. At last the guns proclaimed his arrival. The roads were lined with troops as he drove through them in an open carriage, outriders, scarlet [words illegible] and up to where we were. Then the procession passed before him – first a regular march-past of the troops who all saluted him and cried out something as each company went by, then the camel and carpet, and then the old Sheik again. The Khedive touched the carpet, I think (I couldn't quite see) and the procession went by, then all was over. More guns and the Khedive left and we came home to lunch . . .

Friday I went for a picnic to the Caves of Tourah [Turra] . . . We filled the little train nearly, 17 of us rowdy young people, 20 donkeys (three for the luncheon), ten donkey boys and two Arab servants. My own particular dragoman, Ali, who is devoted to me, couldn't go, so I took another and this other had got no head on his shoulders, for when we got out of the train at Fourah and were halfway to the Caves I discovered that my idiot had let all the luncheon go on in the train to Helouan. Here was a pretty to-do. We held a consultation in the desert and I dispatched two donkey boys off to Helouan about four or five miles off to bring it over. We waited and toiled in and out of the caves and clambered up and down. Still no luncheon came and at last we had to leave without it to ride to Massourah [Masara] to take the train home. Near Massourah we met it! And we sat down in the wilderness to eat the manna and locusts and wild honey in the shape of cold turkey, ham, potted meats, cakes, etc. Although Moses did *not* strike the rock and produce water for us to drink, Ali did open a bottle and produce wine and soda water, likewise beer. We were famished and gobbled for ten minutes. Then we saw the train approaching so we bolted ourselves as well as our food and left donkeys, donkey boys, food, drink, knives, forks, glasses and my idiot to get home how they liked. They turned up all right in the evening. The same evening we had a 'children's party' at Sir William and Lady Gregory's with whom we shared our hotel. Only unmarried people invited. We played wild games till one o'clock in the morning and yesterday I was so stiff again I couldn't move.

The political situation, of which the newspapers kept the British public aware, was dangerous. Later in 1882 it would reach a violent climax: faced with an armed Arab revolt, the British bombarded Alexandria and a British army under Sir Garnet Wolseley defeated the rebel force at Tel el-Kebir. The British imperial dominance of Egypt brought in its train a bitter Anglo-French antagonism.

Meanwhile Sullivan lightly pooh-poohed the fears to which his mother had presumably given voice:

I am still alive. So are all my friends here – no one has been massacred! – and I only hope that they mean to leave us in safety. Indeed I have spoken with several leading men here, some of the most prominent massacrers, and they have kindly promised not to touch any of us, so that I may go out into the bazaar, mosques and among the crowds without any fear.

Later there was another much-enjoyed session of Arab music to report: 'I again tried my old friend the *nei* or flute, and in five minutes succeeded in not being able to elicit a single sound from the instrument.'

There was also a visit to the dancing dervishes, which Sullivan reported as if he had forgotten telling her about the earlier one. He had by this time been prodded to start working on setting the new libretto Gilbert had sent (it was to be *Iolanthe*) and had several days of bad headaches which he ascribed to 'bile, liver, and weather'. Then there was another worry:

My treasure of a servant that I brought with me (Finch) is a failure . . . lazy, light-headed and worst of all a tendency to drink. This last is quite enough so we part when we reach English soil again.

Oh, the bother of servants! – and I shall have to get a cook also, besides a man. It is enough to make one marry – but the cure would be more awful than the disease. I can get rid of servants but not of a wife – especially if she is *my* wife.

The bantering tone was typical, but did Sullivan's mother receive such a message entirely in jest? Sullivan's references to himself in another letter as one of the 'rowdy young people' – when he was approaching 40! – must have been written and read with wry understanding.

It may be surmised that Fanny Ronalds, back in London, was by no means pleased at her lover's prolonged absence.

[Diary, 2 March 1882]: Letters from L.W. (nasty), Smythe, Mother, Spark [Secretary of Leeds Festival] and Carte from America. . .

18 Loss

HE had not intended to stay so long in Egypt, but Dicey's business was not concluded in time for them to leave before mid-March. The delay led Sullivan into one of the most bizarre episodes of his life – an involvement in what was very nearly a duel. His mother learnt in a letter of 5 March 1882 of the quarrel between a young English Guards officer named Farrer and a German baron, de Malortie.

Malortie challenged him and Farrer put his case into Sir Frederic Goldsmid's hands (an old general officer) and whose else's do you think? *Mine!* I, a man of peace who can hardly load a pistol. It flew all over the town directly – at the hotel, in the theatre, everywhere, people talked of nothing else. However, I put my head together and used my best judgement and discretion and settled the whole matter without bloodshed.

But more was to come. Baron D'Atzel – described by Sullivan as 'an Austrian swashbuckler' and 'a swaggering, half-witted, vulgar idiot' – insulted Farrer on club premises with an imputation of ungentlemanly behaviour.[1] A British civilian, Oliphant, responded by hitting D'Atzel in the face – while Farrer looked on. 'That was the worst episode of the lot,' wrote Sullivan in his diary of 8 March. Further entries continued the account. (The 'Sala' mentioned, sometimes as 'Della Sala', is unidentified but was not the well-known London journalist, George Augustus Sala.)

[Diary, 9 March 1882]: All Cairo wild with excitement. Oliphant refused to apologize or to fight, saying D'Atzel had called him a *poltron* [coward] and that he would hit him again, but not fight a duel. Farrer again came to my room with [Lord] Dungarvon to ask whether he should challenge D'Atzel or not. I said [that] after the discreditable scene of last night I could offer no advice. He told me he had been advised to go away. Dicey and I then *both* said separately: 'I take it for granted that no further action will be taken on your part, therefore you had better leave Cairo.' This was said so pointedly there was no mistake in the meaning, which was 'Fight or run'. To my amazement he coolly said: 'I think I had better consult Sir F. Goldsmid' and left.

[Diary, 10 March 1882]: Sala showed me a note he had received from Farrer dated 9th; 'I have determined to ask Baron D'Atzel for an apology or call him out: will you act for me?' [i.e., be his second if a duel were fought]. Sala had declined, having refused Malortie in the previous quarrel. The whole town talking about Oliphant and Farrer and sneering at the English *courage*. My blood boiled. Oliphant hung about the hotel all day and eventually asked me whether he ought to leave Cairo for a time as he had been advised. I replied that I could give no advice and afterwards said: 'If, as I presume, no further action is to be taken in this matter, you had better go.'

A letter to his mother on 13 March sums up:

It has been a humiliation to all of us English here and the ruin, I should think, of a young English officer. An officer is insulted and wantonly provoked to a duel. He takes no notice of it, beyond asking everyone's advice as to what he should do. He allows another man, a civilian, to take up his quarrel and this in the most discreditable way. After five days waiting and submitting to fresh insults he at last resolves to demand an apology or call the man out and in the meantime gets a friend to swear information before the Consul that a breach of the peace is imminent, gets a warrant issued against him of course and goes off by the next train to Alexandria – in fact bolts! Isn't it enough to make one's blood boil. . . . The whole town has been in the fever-heat of excitement and our room has been a sort of general office for juries of honour, seconds, etc. I suppose the whole details of the case will appear in the English papers before long and so I won't say any more about it. A little dean (Butcher) was admirably funny this morning: 'As a Christian, Sir, and Minister of the Gospel, I abhore duelling but as a man and an Englishman I' – and here he shook his fist in my face and looked like business.

Festivities continued. Sullivan joined parties which took the form of chartering a steamer to cruise on the Nile in two successive days – to Sakkara and to the Nile barrage ('a huge, unsightly engineering failure'). The first of these parties had a band on board which played Sullivan's *Sweethearts* 'and dancing went on vigorously' before the ship returned to Cairo.

Sullivan confided to his diary some days of 'great pain'; on 17 March he 'feared it was another kidney attack'. But his imminent departure spared him the discomfort of the coming hot season. A letter to his mother, two days later, shows that those like Sullivan who could afford to voyage in individual luxury were already disparaging the 'tourists'.

. . . They have had awfully hot weather up the Nile, I am told. Everyone is returning rapidly now as it is getting too hot to stay. The consequence is, Shepheards is crowded with Cook's tourists, including of course a lot of parsons who all sit together at the table d'hôte[2] . . . I wish they wouldn't wear black coats, they look so dirty and disreputable. One man I know did disguise himself coming out in a suit of dittos [a plain, matching suit], top hat and a pipe, but it was recognised by a brother parson who split upon him and made him read part of the service on board. . . . Next week begins the great exodus from Cairo. All the tourists rush away together and the Brindisi and Marseilles boats will be unpleasantly crowded for the next two or three weeks. That is why Dicey (who is as cunning as he is heartless and unscrupulous) and I are going by the Orient Line to Naples. We shall miss the mob and get a larger, freer boat.

On 28 March Dicey and he (and his servant Finch) left Alexandria in 'a beastly, small, inconvenient French boat belonging to the Messageries Maritimes called the *Tage*'. They landed in Naples when Sullivan saw 'half a feeble opera by Mercadante' [*Gli Orazii e gli Curiazi*] at the San Carlo Theatre. The rooms allotted to him at the Hôtel des Etrangers were those just vacated by Sarah Bernhardt. 'Mirrors and blue velvet in the sitting-room, and beautiful white muslin linings on the walls of the bedroom, covered with bunches of artificial white flowers. I have no doubt I shall look lovely in bed tonight.'

He not only wrote to his mother from Naples but telegraphed his safe arrival. He also (according to his diary) telegraphed 'L.W.' and 'Rem. and Miss Mason' – the first time these names are so coupled. A family called Mason had been staying at the same time as he at Shepheard's Hotel and 'Miss Mason' would normally indicate an elder daughter. (Another reference, in a letter home, mentions a Miss Mason as a sister of Mrs Spencer Stanhope.) A Cairo diary entry of 10 March, above which stands by itself the single word 'Lonely', begins: 'Charlotte C. and Tootsie came whilst I was in the Masons' rooms' – both these names suggesting a link with later love-episodes. The enigmatic form of 'Rem' seems also to indicate an amorous relationship begun in Egypt.

With a tourist's assiduity Sullivan ascended Vesuvius and visited Pompeii before leaving Naples, describing the first experience to his mother but not the second (perhaps for fear that its erotic element might give offence). At Rome he was disappointed that a change in the customary papal arrangements for the week preceding Easter deprived him of the opportunity to hear Allegri's celebrated *Miserere*, a work reserved to the Sistine Chapel. Via Turin and (as in 1881) the Mont Cenis tunnel through the Alps, he reached Paris on 10 April. The timing of the day is noted in the diary – the three rooms at the hotel being those of himself, his servant, and Dicey. 'Adèle' was a former French servant of his from London, who was to return to his service. An amorous rendezvous had been arranged in Paris.

[Diary, 10 April 1882]: Arr. at 6 a.m. Descended at Grand Hotel – rooms 197–199. Adèle came at 9. Breakfasted at Voisin's at 11. At 12 went to keep appointment at no. 4, rue M.T. Stayed till 5.30 (2). Dined with Dicey and D.H. at Restaurant Poissonnière. Took Dicey home, then D.H. (1). Then home myself, very tired.

'Very tired' is hardly surprising. The figure '2' in parenthesis indicates that 'no. 4' as well as 'D.H.' gave satisfactory sexual experience. It is tempting to suppose that 'no. 4' was a brothel since Sullivan's successive diary references to it are unusually indicated by the length of time spent there.

[11 April]: Dined at Véfours [a celebrated restaurant] with D.H. Then went to no. 4 till midnight (2).

[13 April]: Spent a couple of hours at no. 4 (1). Dined at Véfours with Mrs R. and Fan.

[14 April]: Spent an hour and a half at no. 4. Then called on the Duke of Edinburgh and had a chat; dined at Voisin's, and spent the evening at Prince Leopold's with Mrs R. and Fan. Went to the club [the New Club]. Chemin-de-fer, minus £720 [perhaps his biggest-ever gambling loss].

[15 April]: Spent an hour at no. 4 till 12.30 (2) [i.e. till 12.30 a.m. on 16th]

[16 April]: Spent an hour and a half at no. 4.

[17 April]: Spent a couple of hours at no. 4 (1).

Such a succession of entries reinforces the suggestion that 'D.H.' and Fanny Ronalds (alias L.W. or L.) were in fact the same. That Sullivan should have arranged for the company of *two* mistresses in Paris, on his way home from Egypt, seems almost inconceivable. ('Fan' is, as always, Mrs Ronalds' daughter.)

And so, finally, to London (18 April) 'to sleep for the first time in my new house' (the flat at 1 Queens Mansions, Victoria Street). He maintained his relationship with 'L.W.' As before, some of the amorous entries in the diary give an identification by using the address, as on 20 April: 'Dined at Cad. Pl (1)'. For gambling he was back in his old clubland haunts, as noted in a diary entry which also refers to the first anniversary performance of his latest operetta and again to the unidentifiable but surely female Rem.

[Diary, 24 April 1882]: . . . Called at Clarence House [residence of the Duke of Edinburgh]. L.W. came (1). Wrote to Rem. Conducted 366th performance of *Patience* – fine house, splendid performance. Afterwards walked with George Lewis to Argus – minus [£]500.

Was it in a self-disciplined effort to curb his own potentially ruinous gambling that next day he 'took my name off Argus'?

The performances of *Patience* at the Savoy had gone well. The transfer from the Opera Comique in the previous October had been encompassed with new scenery and costumes and an augmentation of the chorus.[3] 'It was natural and foresighted of Carte', as Reginald Allen remarks, 'to recognize that a production mounted for the dim illumination of gaslight would need something quite different when exposed to the bright glare of electricity.' But, as a memorandum in Sullivan's hand shows, the weekly takings decreased dangerously in the New Year – from a peak of £1,681.6s.6d. in the week ending 20 January to £883.2s.0d. in the week ending on 24 March. The quarterly payment which Sullivan received from Carte in April, £2,500, represented a marked fall from the previous payment of £3,666.13s.4d. The necessity to speed the next operetta must have weighed more and more heavily on Carte – particularly because, again in the hope of foiling American 'piracy', he resolved that the next Gilbert and Sullivan production should be presented *on the same day* in New York as in London, by a company which would have been sufficiently rehearsed in London and shipped out in advance.

But Sullivan did not settle down to any sustained work. Other matters occupied him. He engaged a new cook on 9 May and gave her notice six days later. The operatic sensation of that month was the first performance in London of Wagner's *Ring* (in German): he went to Her Majesty's Theatre 'to see the new *Götterdämmerung* with Mrs R. and Fanny: got the most splitting headache from it'. (No other comment!) On 12 May he 'received a telegram from Cairo' – a diary entry which he underlined, adding in Gothic letters and with a curious misspelling, 'schnel' [*schnell*, quick]. Next day there was a 'letter from Ramle' (Ramleh, Egypt). Within his family circle, his responsibility had changed. Charlotte, his brother's widow, had remarried in the previous December. She was now the wife of a Captain B. C. Hutchinson, a clergyman's son – in Sullivan's own description 'a good-natured, dull, useless, gentlemanly fellow', and thirteen years her junior.

On his 40th birthday (13 May) his mother and his sister-in-law with her children were among those who called on him. Then he went off to play at an afternoon concert in aid of the Royal College of Music – which had just opened its doors, with the ageing Grove at its head, as the successor of the National Training School for Music. On that occasion the Duke of Edinburgh provided the violin obbligato and Sullivan played the harmonium when Albani sang the Bach–

Gounod *Ave Maria*. It was perhaps to reciprocate Albani's gesture that Sullivan attended her performance in Ambroise Thomas's *Mignon* (or rather, he attended one act of it) three nights later.

In mid-May Clementina Sullivan became severely ill and on the 25th 'restless and nearly unmanageable'. Arthur Sullivan was about to lose a mother who – now past her 70th birthday – had been the confidante of every stage and every aspect (save one) of his life. Her illness was accompanied, as fate would have it, by a terrifying further anxiety. The diary entries, with abbreviations as usual, seem open only to one interpretation – a fear that he had made his mistress ('Mrs R. and 'D.H.' being the same) pregnant. 'M.' was evidently a doctor or abortionist.

[Diary, 25 May 1882]:. . . L.W. here 12 to 2. Drove at 4.30 to Roberts', butchers, etc, then to Fulham in a pelting shower. Stayed an hour and found Mother still restless but a little more patient. Left her at 7.15 to return home to dinner. Important business with Mrs R. Drove after dinner with D.H. to M., who advised a delay in taking action until 20 June. Submitted to this advice (fee £1.1s.), returned home (2). 'Soldier' at 1 . . .

The final words, often paralleled in later entries, may indicate that the visitor was driven home by an ex-soldier cabman whose services Sullivan regularly used.

[Diary, 26 May]: Mother very weak. Sent Louis [new manservant] down to inquire. She had morphia injected during the night which, with a hop pillow, gave her 3 hours' sleep. Silva came [formerly in Sullivan's service, now apparently in Hall's]. Gave him a cheque for £1,000 for E.A. Hall – a loan which he promised to repay 14 June. Carte called.
    Drove to Fulham in the afternoon. Found Mother still in a weak state – great difficulty in giving her nourishment. At night when [Dr] Woodhouse came, I urged him to fetch [Sir Henry] Thompson . . . They returned at midnight, and after a long examination Thompson told me there was little hope as her strength was failing her . . . [later] her breathing was better and her sleep was calm and natural. I returned to Town at 3.30 [a.m., 27th] to get into bed for a few hours – and regretted it afterwards.

[Diary, 27 May]: I got into bed at 4 and was awoke [sic] by Amy at a quarter past eight, who had been sent [from Fulham] to fetch me immediately. I knew the worst was at hand, if not already over. I put on my clothes rapidly and was at Fulham before 9. The blinds were all down – Charlotte opened the door – I rushed upstairs, and was alone in the room – alone, that is, with dear Mother's lifeless body – her soul had gone to God.
    . . . Thompson and Woodhouse came. I sent for Wilcox the undertaker to make all arrangements and came back home at 11.30. Mrs. R. came. Then Mrs Dremel. I sent for Poole's man for mourning [i.e. to be measured for mourning clothes]. Wrote to Mrs Grant, the Duke of Edinburgh and a few near friends. Mrs R. dined with me. Soldier took her home, and I went to bed, 12.30.

The suspected pregnancy of his mistress was evidently a false alarm.

[Diary, 2 June 1882]: L.W. came. Had seen A.C. [Dr Alfred Cooper]. Symptoms beginning.[4]

Next day she was 'suffering a good deal but thankful for the cause', and on 5 June, when she left for a few days away, the diary recorded 'Things going well'.
    But in another matter they did not go well. On 9 June 'Rem and Tootie dined here'. Was 'Tootie' the same as 'Tootsie' who had called on him in the company

of 'Charlotte C' at Shepheards' Hotel in Cairo? And indeed was 'Rem' perhaps 'Charlotte C' herself? The diary entry continues, with the dots which in this case are Sullivan's own: 'Long talk with Rem . . . Settled "all off".'

That 'Rem' was indeed a 'Miss C' seems confirmed by the diary entry of 13 June.

Sent letter to L.W. telling her to be happy . . . All over about Miss C. Awful letter back – completely staggered and upset me. Couldn't do any work all day.

What a naïve reaction! Sullivan had evidently underestimated the fury of a middle-aged mistress faced with the rivalry of a younger. The assurance given that the rival had been shown the door mattered less, evidently, than the confirmation of what *had* been happening. However, the fury was soothed in lovers' fashion next day: 'L.W. dined here (1). Left much better than when she came'.

At a dinner party he gave on 25 July his guest-list included not only Fanny Ronalds and Christine Nilsson but Captain Eyre Massey Shaw, who had been for 20 years chief of the London Fire Brigade and was to be immortalized in *Iolanthe* – as yet unnamed, and referred to by Sullivan simply as 'the new opera'. Evidently he had not been quite satisfied with the libretto: it was the 'first act revised and completed (except bit of finale)' which Gilbert brought to him on 25 July. Two days later he left for Pencarrow, his friend Lady Andalusia Molesworth's home in Cornwall, and stayed till 7 August, working at the 'framing' of the finale.

Sullivan's terms here allow an insight into his methods of composition.[5] The actual invention of music is denoted as 'sketching' and 'writing'; the ensuing process of 'framing' entailed the drawing-up of a 'skeleton score' in which all the vocal parts were set down, with an indication of all the rests or vacant bars where only the orchestra was to be heard. At this point (as he was to explain later for the benefit of his biographer Arthur Lawrence), the written page was 'without a note of accompaniment or instrumental work of any kind, although, naturally, I have all that in mind'. From that stage, the copyists could copy the voice-parts and the rehearsals could begin, with Sullivan or a theatre accompanist 'vamping' a piano accompaniment. 'It is not until the music has been thoroughly learnt, and the rehearsals on the stage with the necessary action and "business" are well advanced, that I begin orchestration'. This account is somewhat simplified: Sullivan's 'sketches' often *do* contain hints of instrumental work, and when time was pressing he might have to proceed with orchestration even before stage rehearsals were 'well advanced'. On 17 August, in London, he 'wrote the first chorus of new opera and framed it'.

His health still troubled him occasionally and he seems to have suspected a malady of the liver as well as of the kidneys. He consulted a Dr Gordon Powell, who said there was 'nothing organically wrong in my liver' but 'was very urgent on the subject of diet'. That advice was apparently enough to send him off to Germany on another 'cure'. This time he would take the waters at Bertrich (a tiny but renowned spa near the Mosel valley). Sexual abstinence was this time not prescribed: on 19 August in the company of 'Mrs C. and daughter [i.e. Fanny Ronalds and her mother, Mrs Carter], Louis and Adele [servants]', he began the two-day journey via Dover, Calais and Cologne. He had previously spent a day with Gilbert at Exeter – Gilbert was holidaying in a locality which made that rendezvous convenient – to discuss a further modification of the text, so that Sullivan could carry on his composition while undergoing his treatment.

'After lunch, long walk. Saw wonderful rainbow. Home, stroll, bath, dinner, euchre': the relaxing routine ('euchre' being a popular card game) was recorded in the diary at Bertrich. So was the arrival of a hired piano which he had ordered from Koblenz; likewise his correspondence. The remarks 'L.W. 0!' and 'L.W. (0! disappointed ambition)' tell a tale of frustration, but at length (30 August) there was a 'Him. Nt! (2), 11.30–1.30', followed by other similar indications, one (5 September) with the remark 'Long, Circassian'. For one such reference at Bertrich he used the symbol 'D.H.' – a clear indication that it must be the same as 'L.W.' He can hardly have brought another mistress to stay in a small resort where he was every day in the company of Fanny Ronalds and her mother.

Work on the operetta made leisurely progress. The entry of 24 August recorded that he had 'framed' the Lord Chancellor's song and sketched the love-duet which he referred to as 'He the tree, I the flower' (the words were later improved), no. 5 of the first act. On 4 September he 'framed no. 11, 1st act' (the ensemble, 'My lords, it may not be'), and on 7 September filled in the words of this and two other numbers (nos. 9A and 10, i.e. Phyllis's recitative and Lord Tolloller's 'Spurn not the lordly born') and posted them off to Smythe, who would deliver them to the copyist.

Once back in London, the pressure was on him. He arrived on 12 September at Victoria Station at 6.30 a.m. His apartment being so near, he was in bed by 7 – but up again at 11, when he received both Carte and François Cellier before proceeding to a rehearsal of the first act at the Savoy. (As usual, Cellier would be the conductor of the London performances after the composer himself had conducted the opening night.) On 15 September he worked till 5.30 p.m. then went to call on Fanny Ronalds and found 'the Grants' there. David Beach Grant, his wife and their daughter Adele, visiting London, were his guests for dinner that night along with Fanny Ronalds and her daughter, W. S. Gilbert and his wife, and Edward Hall. After his guests had departed, he wrote again till 3 a.m. In this fashion, time and again, a sociable evening re-stimulated his desire to work. His diary recorded that he went to bed at 4.30 a.m. on 27 September, at 4.30 again on the 29th, at 4.45 on the 30th, at 4.45 again on 3 October (when he 'finished scoring of first act' – though he 'touched up' the finale of that act the next night).

Having made a new arrangement with a horse-stabler (Daines) to assure himself the hire of carriages as he wished, he was able on 4 October to write:

Sent victoria [a type of four-wheeled carriage] to Cadogan Place. Drove to Garrick [Club] at 6, read papers, walked home. Dined *at home*, 7.30. L.W.2. Soldier [took her home].

Sketched second act. Did the following numbers: 'Fold your flapping wings', 'Heigh-ho, love is a thorn', 'He loves', 'When Britain *really* ruled' – to bed at 5 a.m.

'Fold your flapping wings' (sung by Strephon) was duly sung on the opening night, but was soon cut; 'Heigh-ho, love is a thorn' is not identifiable and did not survive into either the London or the New York production. By 20 October the actual composition of the second act was done – save for a 'new quartet' which Gilbert supplied as no. 7 of the second act. (The numbering is different in the score as eventually printed.) The labour of the orchestration likewise kept Sullivan working through the night – till 6 a.m. on both 25 and 26 October. At 4.30 a.m. the next morning the necessary scoring of the operetta was completed – 'only the finale (repetition of Trio, no. 9) and the overture to do now'. The copyist (or copyists) followed on the composer's heels and a 'full band rehearsal' of the second act was possible at the Savoy on Monday 30 October.

In New York, Alfred Cellier had been put in charge of a company of Carte's at the Standard Theatre, which was not only to give *Iolanthe* but had a repertory of various non-Gilbert, non-Sullivan operas as well.[6] A letter of Sullivan's to Cellier, dated 29 October, gives the instruction: 'Overture. Write one yourself' (since the composer's own could not be despatched to New York in time). So the New York première on the same night as that in London differed in that respect – though the same vocal numbers were given throughout. J. H. Ryley, a reputable American comedian, was the Lord Chancellor, and the part of the Fairy Queen was allotted in New York to Selina Dolaro – under whose management, in London, *Trial by Jury* had first been given.[7]

A visit to his mother's grave on 2 November (her birthday), and a rehearsal and performance at which he conducted *The Martyr of Antioch* in Brighton (6 and 7 November) were among the few obligations that Sullivan now allowed to distract him from the preparation of the operetta. The love-duet of the first act was rewritten on the night of Sunday/Monday, 5/6 November. Daily stage rehearsals demanded his presence – and still, three days before the appointed first night, the overture remained unwritten. Sullivan finished it at 7 a.m. on Friday 24 November. On that evening a full dress rehearsal ('very satisfactory') occupied him and the cast from 7 p.m. till 1.30 a.m. after which he and Tom Chappell went for supper to Rule's, the celebrated restaurant situated five minutes away from the theatre, in Maiden Lane.

The 25th dawned. Gilbert and Sullivan's first *new* work in Carte's new theatre was eagerly awaited. Programmes had been printed in which the theatre's incandescent bulbs were worked into the floral pattern surrounding the cast-list. Below the list Carte proclaimed (as he had done since the theatre opened) his own brand of service, unique in London at the time:

NO FEES OF ANY KIND

PROGRAMMES are provided, and Wraps and Umbrellas taken free of charge. Any attendant detected in accepting money from visitors will be instantly dismissed; the public is therefore requested not to tempt the attendants by offering them gratuities.

It was a day which was to bring artistic triumph to Sullivan – and financial disaster. The diary tells the story with a coolness which must be wondered at.

[25 November]: At home all day. L.W to tea. Received letter from E. A. Hall saying that he was ruined and my money (about £7,000) lost, just before starting for the theatre. Dined with Smythe at home. 1st performance of *Iolanthe* at the Savoy Theatre. House crammed – awfully nervous, more so than usual on going into the orchestra. Tremendous reception. 1st act went splendidly – the 2nd dragged and I was afraid it must be compressed. However it finished well and Gilbert and myself were called and heartily cheered. Very low afterwards – came home.

The disaster was not total. The sum lost did not represent the shares Sullivan kept at his bank, nor his bank deposits, but only the amount currently entrusted to Hall for investing. Nevertheless it was a misfortune which Sullivan might have allowed to mar the opening night; and he might have broken for ever with Hall. Even-tempered, professionally assured, loyal in friendship, he did neither. He had composed a brilliant new score (his most subtle yet) to a scintillating libretto: now he delivered it to an avid public. With some sense of irony he must have heard the merry waltz-tune to which he had set Gilbert's encapsuled proverbs: 'Nothing venture, nothing win . . . dark the dawn when day is nigh . . .'

In a letter sent next day it was Sullivan who assured 'my dear Edward' of his 'deepest sympathy', and next year he was a guest in Hall's home. Sullivan evidently accepted his friend's good faith and promises to repay, though it is not clear when (if ever) that repayment took place.

19 With Electric Light

PRESENT in the first-night audience of *Iolanthe*, the chief of the London fire brigade heard himself addressed by the plump Queen of the Fairies:

> Oh, Captain Shaw
> Type of true love kept under!
> Could thy brigade
> With cold cascade
> Quench my great love, I wonder?

In this role, played by Alice Barnett, Gilbert had for once treated sympathetically and without a sneer the elderly female in love. But the most important role was not hers, nor the title-role (played by Jessie Bond), but that of the Lord Chancellor. At first merely the caricatured holder of high office in the mould of Sir Joseph Porter or Major-General Stanley, he is later the participant in the crucial serious scene of recognition with its threat of mortal penalty. George Grossmith carried it off within what the *Era* called 'one of the drollest impersonations imaginable'.[1]

Iolanthe was subtitled *or, The Peer and the Peri*. Until late in rehearsal, evidently in the belief that to divulge the true title might assist potential pirates, the pretended title *Perola* was used and sung, with necessary reallocations of words to notes when the four syllables of 'Iolanthe' were replaced by three.[2] (The marks in the composer's autograph score, later in the possession of Dame Bridget D'Oyly Carte, make it quite clear that 'Iolanthe' was the originally chosen name, and 'Perola' – not 'Periola' – the cover-up.) Thanks to Thomas Moore's *Paradise and the Peri*, the term *peri* was not so strange then as now. Nor were fairies themselves unknown as stage characters, even in an adult context. A supernatural hovering creature called Rebecca had the title-role in Gilbert's farce of 1881, *Foggerty's Fairy*, and in 1870 he had set the action of *The Palace of Truth* entirely in Fairyland.

As the fairies in *Iolanthe* replace the love-sick maidens of *Patience*, so the peers take over from the swaggering officers of the earlier work: their lordships have a vigorous march-tune for their entrance and retain a military musical tone thereafter. The fairies' music is recurrent, just as the chorus 'Twenty love-sick maidens' was recurrent – but now the reappearance is musically varied, instead of being identical. Indeed, *Iolanthe* is the work in which Sullivan's operetta style takes a definite step forward, and metamorphosis of musical themes is its characteristic new feature. The fugal tag in the orchestra which marks the Lord Chancellor's entrances changes from 6/8 time to 4/4; the very name of *Iolanthe*, invoked by the other fairies and their Queen, becomes thematic. As well as providing a swiftly telling orchestral stroke for 'I'll stick to my pipes and my tabors', Sullivan gives to Strephon ('an Arcadian shepherd') and his Phyllis a repeated shepherd's-pipe theme over a 6/8 pastoral pulse. The orchestral music which is heard in the opening scene, when Iolanthe's punishment is lifted, returns when punishment is again threatened towards the end of the opera.

Such recurrences to make a dramatic point were no new thing in opera – or oratorio either, Mendelssohn having used the procedure nearly 40 years before in *Elijah*. They were not, in any exclusive or special sense, 'Wagnerian'. The harmony underlying the 'punishment' motive, though unusually chromatic within the context of the operetta, could not be called Wagnerian either. But Gilbert (as always, stage director in addition to his role as librettist) seized on the topicality of the London performances of *The Ring* to make the Queen of the Fairies into a caricatured Brünnhilde with breastplate, winged helmet, and spear. Perhaps this is what deluded W. Beatty-Kingston, the influential critic of *The Theatre*, into supposing that he could hear Wagner in the score:

The parody of 'Die alte Weise' (*Tristan and Isolde*, Act 3) played whilst Iolanthe is rising from her watery prison, struck me as being uncommonly clever, and so did the 'Rhinedaughter' and 'Walküre' reminders in the last scene . . .[3]

By recurrence and metamorphosis of themes Sullivan made the score more fluid; but the single song remained the unit, and never was character and dramatic point more vividly put over than in the Lord Chancellor's 'Nightmare Song' and in the Sentry's soliloquy while on duty outside the Houses of Parliament. The Sentry's observations on 'ev'ry boy and ev'ry gal' becoming 'either a little Liberal or else a little Conservative' were to acquire proverbial force – though few of the public, and indeed not all performers of the role, realize that 'gal' rhymes with 'liberal' in Gilbert's ever-ingenious versification. The mere generalized ballad, so deliberately placed in earlier works including *Patience* ('I cannot tell what this love may be') has gone. Instead, the lovers express their love only in duets – in one of which, 'None shall part us', occurs one of the most exquisite of Sullivan's chromatic modulations (at 'I to thee, and thou to me'). Equally distinctive is the overture – no routine compilation of tunes by an assistant but a thoroughly worked-out composition. Here the 'Captain Shaw' melody is uniquely set against a counter-melody of Mendelssohnian grace which does not appear in the operetta at all.

On 4 December 1882, within ten days of the opening of *Iolanthe*, the Prime Minister attended a performance as Sullivan's guest and expressed himself delighted:

. . . Nothing, I thought, could have been happier than the manner in which the comic strain of the piece was blended with its harmonies of sight and sound, so good in taste and so admirable in execution from beginning to end.

I remain, my dear Sir,
Faithfully yours,
W. E. GLADSTONE

The suggestion made by Kenneth Baker M.P., in 1981, that the Lord Chancellor is a satirical representation of Gladstone (with the Fairy Queen as a hostile Queen Victoria) seems not to have occurred to Gladstone himself.[4]

Characteristically going abroad for diversion as soon as possible after launching a major work, Sullivan left for Paris on 3 January 1883. His servant Louis had been sent ahead the previous day. He joined the crowds in watching the funeral (perhaps the biggest Paris had ever seen) of Gambetta – whose premiership had lasted only three months but who was a political hero of the radicals and who had died at the age of only 44. The husband of Sullivan's new housekeeper Adèle had been Gambetta's valet, and personally told Sullivan of the circumstances of his master's death. According to this account, the revolver shot in the arm which led to his fatal illness had been fired by Gambetta himself by accident – not, as scandal had it, by his mistress.

Gilbert was soon ready to propose a successor to *Iolanthe*. On 8 February 1883, at the Savoy, he read to Carte and Sullivan the prologue (corresponding to what is now known as the first of the three acts) of *Princess Ida, or Castle Adamant*. At the same February meeting, Sullivan and Gilbert signed a new type of agreement with Carte to run for five years and 31 days. Composer and librettist were each assured of one-third of the takings on *Iolanthe* and future operas ('after deducting all expenses and charges of producing the said operas'); and Carte was empowered to *demand* a new work of the collaborators at six months' notice. What induced Sullivan to bind himself so? Had he not declared to Carte, even before composing *Iolanthe*, that he wanted to turn aside from operetta? Habituated to luxury, he evidently lacked the nerve to say no to Carte's proffer of a goldmine. His assent was later to place him in a barely defensible position.

In the following May another letter arrived from Gladstone, offering knighthood. Sullivan's earlier objections had apparently flown – and indeed if there were some value in standing aloof, as an artist, from the pomp of state, then Sullivan's career could no longer pretend to it. At the same ceremony in Windsor Castle a knighthood was also conferred on George Grove and George Macfarren, the 70-year-old blind composer whose new oratorio was to be conducted by Sullivan at the coming Leeds Festival. Macfarren had apparently been reluctant to accept state honours, but, on the Prince of Wales's urging, Sullivan persuaded him.

[Diary, 22 May 1883]: Went down by special train with some of the Ministers [as part of the Privy Council] to Windsor to be knighted with Grove and Macfarren. Met by royal carriages and driven to the Castle. Had lunch with the [Royal] Household – Sir H. Ponsonby [private secretary to the Queen], Sir John Cordell McNeill, etc. Council meeting and separate audiences of Ministers till 3.30. Then Grove and Macfarren entered the presence; and lastly myself. The Queen was seated, with the equerry (McNeill) just behind her, Princess Beatrice, Sir H. Ponsonby, and one or two others. I bowed low – then knelt down – the Queen took the equerry's sword and laid it first on right then on left shoulder – said softly 'Sir Arthur' and gave me her hand to kiss. Then I rose, bowed low again, and backed out . . .

Though such a knighthood fell then (as now) under the initiative of the Prime Minister, there was no doubt that Queen Victoria gave it an unusual personal approval. She had cut herself off from public theatre-going since the Prince Consort's death in 1861 (and was not to initiate her private 'command performances' until 1887) but had surely heard, and possibly sung, Sullivan's operetta songs in her drawing-room. A hint dropped by the Duke of Edinburgh or the Prince of Wales to Sullivan led to his writing to Sir Henry Ponsonby in the preceding January:

I have been fortunate enough to obtain Her Majesty's acceptance of all my serious works, but I have hitherto never ventured to send those of a lighter character. I am encouraged to do so now, since I have heard that Her Majesty has frequently expressed herself with regard to them on kindly and favourable terms. The favour I would therefore ask of you is that you would beg Her Majesty's acceptance of the accompanying volumes of my comic operas, six in number [i.e., those published: *Cox and Box* plus the five with Gilbert from *Trial by Jury*].

A pleasant irony placed Sullivan's knighthood in the period when *Iolanthe*, with its reduction of the peerage to lovelorn boobies, was running at the Savoy.

The Savoy programmes, in acknowledging various contributions to *Iolanthe*, mentioned 'telephones on the stage' – that is, *behind* the scenes, to facilitate control. To celebrate his 41st birthday (one day late, on 14 May 1883), Sullivan arranged that multiple telephone apparatus should be installed at his home to enable his dinner guests to hear selections from *Iolanthe* at the Savoy Theatre, where the company had been specially engaged by him for the occasion. For business purposes both Sullivan and Gilbert now had their own direct telephone lines to the Savoy.

The guests at that dinner included Gilbert, Burnand, Millais, and Sullivan's faithful old patron the Duke of Edinburgh. As a mark of still higher favour, the Prince of Wales was also present. So was Baron Ferdinand de Rothschild, who had created in Waddesdon Manor (near Aylesbury, Bucks) one of the most magnificent of private Victorian 'palaces'. Baron Ferdinand, though settled in Britain, was of the French branch of the family. With the members of the English branch Sullivan continued his friendship: between November 1883 and the following February he was twice house-guest at Alfred de Rothschild's (Halton, Tring, Herts) and once at Leopold de Rothschild's (Ascott, Leighton Buzzard, Beds). Between Leopold and Sullivan there had developed a particularly warm friendship, as denoted in the diary by the name 'Leo' (without surname).

Princess Ida, on which Sullivan was now working, represented a step backwards on Gilbert's part. It was a re-working of his burlesque entertainment called *The Princess* (1870), parodying the long narrative poem of that name which had helped to establish Tennyson's fame 20 years before that. Mock-

Tennysonian blank verse (instead of the customary prose dialogue) survives in the new form, which was now tailored for Sullivan's purposes. Tennyson had prophesied and welcomed the emancipation of women: Gilbert's sneer at that ideal, far from being topical, now recoiled on itself. His presentation of a women's college as the 'maddest folly going' was itself ridiculous in the 1880s, when colleges for women had already been established at both Oxford and Cambridge.

Yet Sullivan must have relished the unflagging cleverness of Gilbert's lyrics. 'The ape and the lady' (sung by Lady Psyche, the 'professor of humanities' at the women's college) fantastically supposes that only the male of the human species needed to evolve from the lower creation: woman in her essence is 'a radiant being,/With a brain far-seeing' while 'a man, however well-behaved/At best is only a monkey shaved'. (These verses, with their reference to 'Darwinian man', reflect the controversy which had raged since the publication of *The Origin of Species* in 1859.) Part of the new libretto was in the composer's luggage when he once again set out for a continental spa on 31 May 1883. This time his destination, reached through Cologne and Frankfurt, was the elegant Austrian resort of Carlsbad (now Karlovy Vary, Czechoslovakia).

Goethe, Beethoven, Chopin and Smetana had visited the place, and it was now a summer resort boasting the richness of its mineral springs and geared to the care of the rich from all over Europe. On 4 June Sullivan 'began the cure at 7.15 a.m.' as his diary put it – that is, began the regimen of several weeks of taking the waters – finishing off the day with 'supper at 7, euchre and bed at 10'. The entries for 6 and 8 June show him working on *Princess Ida*, while on the 15th Dr Seeger, his medical superintendent 'came again – all well – advised me to discontinue boiled ham and eat raw ditto'. He had the company of Frederic Clay and Clay's sister, Mrs Gertrude Clay Ker Seymer. His diary shows a busy register of correspondence (often using a plus sign for letters sent, minus for letters received). As well as Smythe, from whom he received business communications almost daily, the correspondents included 'Mrs R.', 'L.W.', 'L.' and 'D.H.'. The social need – or was it a psychological need? – for secrecy is indeed remarkable if (as seems the case) these references were all to Fanny Ronalds. Correspondence continued as he returned via Paris: '[9 July] To Smythe, L.W. Tel[egraphed] D.H.'

During his time at Carlsbad he recorded his impression of the Good Friday Music from *Parsifal*: 'I think it hideous – four bars of beauty towards the end, but the whole confused, harmonies forced, restless and unnatural'. It seems likely that he can have heard only a reduced-orchestral version. Performances of the opera itself were at this time reserved to Bayreuth, and London was to hear only a concert performance during Sullivan's lifetime.

Back in England on 12 July, he went to Waterloo Station to meet 'Helen and her niece Helen' (mentioned in later entries as 'the two Helens'). A sister of his maternal grandmother had married Edward Philipps, who was settled in Barbados, and the arrivals (off the boat-train from Southampton?) were presumably Edward Philipps's daughter Helen Maria Philipps (unmarried, 17 years older than Sullivan) and her niece Helen Sarah Philipps. (See the Family Tree, pp. 452–3.) Arthur Sullivan maintained such family connections on both sides: on 14 April he received 'Uncle John' (his late father's brother) and 'promised him £50 a year towards his rent'. But his closest feeling remained directed towards Fred's children. What would become of them now that their mother was married to her shiftless second husband?

The husband could show no prospects at home. But Charlotte's brother William had emigrated to California, where gold and oranges (and, later, oil) dangled hopes of prosperity as the reward for initiative. Urged by her brother's invitation, Charlotte resolved to join him with her family. They – 'my little brood', as Arthur Sullivan affectionately called them – left London on 14 December to sail to New York from Liverpool next day. Herbert, the eldest boy, remained behind in his uncle's care.

As so often, Sullivan found it pleasant – and less distracting – to work away from London. From 8 August to 14 September 1883 he was in 'lodgings', as he put it (with two of his own servants, Delphine and Elizabeth) at a house called Stoneham in an unidentified location – but convenient for Smythe to come with mail occasionally and for Sullivan to go occasionally to 'town'. *Princess Ida* was causing him some frustration, and he had also to attend to the composition of an anthem for Novello. The bare phrase 'trio in second act' (whereas there were eventually to be *two* male trios in succession, 'Gently, gently' and 'I am a maiden'), shows that the libretto was still in process of change. Indeed in a letter of 22 September Gilbert was suggesting that the first act should end after 'Oh, dainty triolet' with a wordless acted sequence 'done to symphony' (i.e. to orchestra alone) – a notion evidently rejected.

[Diary, 11 August]: Composed trio second act

[12 August]: Wrote – no good

[13 August]: Wrote – no good

[14 August]: Wrote beginning of Finale (second act) including love-song [Hilarion's 'Whom thou hast chain'd']

[16 August]: Began anthem, 'Who is like unto thee?'

[17 August]: Working at anthem

[18 August]: Working at anthem

[19 August]: Finished anthem. Smythe came – wrote 13 letters.

[20 August]: Began again at new opera.

[21 August]: The Governor's birthday. Walked to shrubbery [a tick follows]

[22 August]: Shrubbery [tick]

[23 August]: L.W.'s birthday. Finished finale, 2nd act, except last movement

[24 August]: To London by 10 [o'clock] express . . . Took anthem to Novello's and gave it to Littleton [Alfred Littleton, managing director of the firm]

From London he went to pass a weekend with friends at Withyham, Sussex, and then was back at 'Stoneham'.

[28 August]: Very bad headache. Wrote four numbers – first chorus, second ditto, trio 'I am a maiden' and 'The Ape and the Lady'.

The 'shrubbery' followed by a tick (which recurs in September entries) seems likely to denote a sexual encounter. The reference to 'the Governor' (in later entries more often 'Guv'nor', in the traditional cockney style) is to Fanny Ronalds's father, Joseph Carter. Were Fanny and her father staying 'with him on that occasion? If not, why should he suddenly recall 'the Governor's birthday'?

The Leeds Festival, to which the committee had renominated Sullivan as conductor (it was not automatic) did not present him in 1883 with the excessive labour of 1880. There was no new work of his: he had been asked to write a symphony but had declined. Once again the fee for his conducting the whole or part of all the concerts was 300 guineas (£315). Once again the committee exerted some authority in selecting the programmes: the conductor's consent, rather than preference, was sought. Sullivan declared that Raff's *Weltende* ('The World's End') was 'not sufficiently effective to suit the taste of a British audience – it is wanting in character and brightness', but it was nevertheless selected and it was Sullivan's task to conduct it. Other unfamiliar works which he conducted included *The Crusaders* by the Danish disciple of Mendelssohn and Schumann, Niels Gade, and Macfarren's new oratorio *King David*: the blind composer could participate only by acknowledging the applause. Joseph Barnby conducted his own setting of Psalm 97, under the title *The Lord is King* – his vigour with the baton (in comparison with Sullivan's style of conducting) arousing some pointedly favourable comment from the choir at rehearsal.

Sullivan's friend Frederic Clay had let him down (and alarmed the festival committee) by failing to complete the commission he had accepted for a completion of a cantata on Byron's *Sardanapalus*. In its place was heard a setting by Alfred Cellier of Gray's *Elegy* which dug its own grave. What pleased Sullivan particularly was the opportunity to bring to the festival, for the first time, Beethoven's *Grand Mass in D*, as it was called. As if that huge work were not long enough, the morning programme on Saturday 13 October was made up by Mendelssohn's *Hymn of Praise*. Beethoven's mass (the *Missa Solemnis*) was far from a familiar work: two performances given under Barnby's conductorship in London in 1870 were advertised as the first in Britain to give the work 'without alteration or curtailment'. Every seat was sold for the Leeds performance and consequently the takings for this concert were the highest of the festival, even higher than those for the opening *Elijah*.

'Stupendous performance!' Sullivan noted afterwards in his diary. '. . . Great cheering for me afterwards.' *The Times* (presumably Hueffer was the writer) considered this the greatest occasion of the festival but failed to particularize Sullivan's part in it. The critic complained that the choral difficulties, especially those of the sopranos' high notes, were exacerbated by the prevailing high pitch:

'If our legislature declines much longer to give us an equivalent of a *diapason normal* [the lower French pitch], the Mass in D will have to be transposed half a tone lower to bring it within the bounds of physical possibility.'

Sullivan no doubt recognized the difficulties; he did not, however, exert any decisive power at Leeds to remedy the matter, perhaps because of the alterations to the organ which would have been entailed. Not until the 1898 festival was the lower pitch adopted.

In London, the Savoy was still advertised as 'the only theatre lighted entirely [i.e. on stage as well as in the auditorium] by electric light, securing perfectly PURE and COOL air in all parts. Electric star lights in the hair are worn by the Principals and the whole of the chorus ladies in the last scene.' *Iolanthe* reached its 323rd performance on 13 October, when Sullivan was conducting the final concert of the Leeds Festival, and was now preceded by *Private Wire*, a one-act farce composed by Percy Reeve, with words by A. Felix and F. Desprez. The town's other long-running theatrical success was scored by Henry Arthur Jones's melodrama, *The Silver King* (over 250 performances), while operettas by Offenbach (*Bluebeard* and an adaptation of *La Vie Parisienne*) and Planquette (*Rip van Winkle* and *Les Cloches de Corneville*) showed that Gilbert and Sullivan's native product never swept away the appeal of the original imported article.

As usual with his operettas, *Princess Ida* was put into rehearsal while the composer was still working on it. 'Began scoring of opera – heavy work' runs the diary on 15 December 1883, with the first night only three weeks away. 'Penal servitude' was how he described his condition in a letter to his much-loved old friend Nina Lehmann when he found himself with '320 pages to score by this day fortnight'. To 'score' meant to orchestrate, but even the actual composition was not finished: Gilbert and he were still making changes. On 24 December Gilbert brought him the words of a new quintet ('The woman of the wisest wit'): between midnight and 5 a.m. on Christmas Day he 'composed, and wrote out in full score, new quintet'. The evenings were his time for sociable relaxation. On 29 December he went to *Jack and Jill*, the 'very amusing' pantomime[5] at the Surrey Theatre, came back and 'finished scoring of opera (except 3 numbers to rewrite)' at 5 a.m. Next day he was 'at home all day, writing and scoring' (note the different terms). On 31 December he found time to attend a rehearsal, to write 'a new number', and to call on the Lehmanns before returning to sit the night through at his desk. 'Servants came at midnight to wish me Happy New Year.'

Two of the new numbers were Ida's 'I built upon a rock' and King Gama's 'Nothing whatever to grumble at': Sullivan scored them on 1 January 1884. Next morning there was a full music rehearsal (all cast and orchestra but without action – therefore solely under the conductor's control), and that evening a full-dress rehearsal from 7 until 2 a.m. Two days later another, even longer dress rehearsal lasted from 6.30 till 2.30 a.m.

Such a strain must have taken toll even of a man in better health. Sullivan's broke that very night, when he had retired to bed after that late rehearsal. In the early morning hours he was seized with violent pain which even an injection of morphine did not relieve. With the curtain due to rise that evening and the composer seriously ill in bed, Carte hastily had new programmes printed with François Cellier's name as conductor, putting aside those already printed which bore Sullivan's. But even Carte had not reckoned with the strength of Sullivan's will.

[Diary, 5 January 1884]: Resolved to conduct the first performance of the new opera *Princess Ida* at night, but from the state I was in it seemed hopeless. At 7 pm had another strong hypodermic injection to ease the pain, and a strong cup of black coffee to keep me awake. Managed to get up and dressed, and drove to the theatre more dead than alive – went into the orchestra at 8.10. Tremendous house – usual reception.
     Very fine first performance – not a hitch. Brilliant success. After the performance I turned very faint and could not stand. Was brought home by Smythe, Cellier, Carte etc. and put to bed in dreadful pain.

He fainted after appearing on stage with Gilbert to acknowledge the applause. So unexpected to Carte had been his arrival in the theatre that the new programmes with Cellier's name as conductor *were* distributed in the theatre that night – and the programmes with Sullivan's name thriftily (but misleadingly) used on later occasions when he did *not* conduct.[6] In its issue of 12 January 1884, the *Era* reproduced the bulletin issued from Queen's Mansions on the day after the opening: 'Sir Arthur Sullivan has passed a good night and, although suffering much pain from a muscular affection of the neck, is on the whole much better. Absolute rest and quietude are enjoined by his medical attendant, Dr Lynch.' On the following Friday another bulletin announced that he was 'almost free from pain', and the journal's issue of 2 February proclaimed him 'quite recovered'.
     The title-role of *Princess Ida* was to have been sung by the American operetta star, Lillian Russell, whose beauty and talents were seasoned by reports of scandal off stage and on.[7] Her career had begun, ironically enough, in one of the 'pirate' companies playing *HMS Pinafore* in New York in 1878–9. By 1883, at the age of 21, she was a celebrity. She had eloped from New York with the English operetta composer Edward Solomon (she took him as the third of her four husbands, but the marriage was found to be bigamous on his part) and appeared in London at the Gaiety in Solomon's *Virginia and Paul* in July 1883. ('Utter rubbish' was Sullivan's description of the piece, which failed.) Engaged as Princess Ida, she fell foul of Gilbert by missing a rehearsal. In the reminiscences published in *Cosmopolitan* magazine some 40 years later (February–September 1922; she died in June 1922!), she quoted him as saying (with obvious sexual implications): 'You can't play it the way I want it played unless you come down to my room every night and rehearse the part with me'.[8]
     The imputation of that kind of conduct seems far-fetched in Gilbert's case, especially on Lillian Russell's word. Sullivan's diary (23 December 1883) records the failure to turn up for rehearsal and Gilbert's subsequent remark: 'I won't speak to her and she shan't play in any piece of mine'. According to the diary, she sent an apology next day. To no avail: she was dismissed, and she thereupon sued

for breach of contract. The action was not settled until November 1884, when Michael Gunn as Carte's deputy was apparently given discretion to make an out-of-court payment to the solicitors of 'airy, fairy Lillian', as her fans admiringly called her, quoting Tennyson.

In her place the Princess was sung by Leonora Braham. Durward Lely was again a useful tenor (Cyril) and Grossmith played the nimble, spitefully written part of King Gama which had been designed for him. The two songs for Ida (her invocation to Minerva, 'Oh, goddess wise' and her remorseful 'I built upon a rock') are rather emptily earnest and too much resemble each other; but there are many touches of Sullivan at his most attractive. Notable in Act 1 is the perfumed, sensuous chromaticism following the words 'Oh, dainty triolet! oh, fragrant violet!'; in Act 2, the swing of the quintet recaptures that of the quintet in *Patience*, in the same quick 6/8 dance-rhythm. No less effective is the deliberately clumsy stamping gait for Ida's three warrior brothers, Arac, Guron, and Scynthius, in which Sullivan mirrors Gilbert's depiction of their martial stupidity. Handelian pomp is once again felicitously parodied when Arac laboriously takes armour *off* before battle ('This helmet, I suppose/Was meant to ward off blows . . .').

All this was sufficient to win considerable praise for Sullivan. 'The score of the new opera at the Savoy may be summed up in a sentence – it is the best in every way that Sir Arthur Sullivan has produced, apart from his serious works . . .' Such was the verdict of Hermann Klein of the *Sunday Times*, who had become one of the composer's most enthusiastic advocates.[9] As a drama critic, however, Edmund Yates (of the *World*) seized on the longueurs of the 'desperately dull performance', and the public probably seconded him in reacting against both the unusual three-act form and the obsolescence of the satire. The production notched up the moderate total of 246 performances and no work was ready to replace it. Instead, on 11 October 1884, the Savoy saw a revised version of *The Sorcerer* with the shortened finale of Act 1 already referred to (p. 114) and with a rewriting of both words and music of the opening number of the second act. To form a double bill, *Trial by Jury* was revived: the manuscript full score having temporarily disappeared, Sullivan had a new score constructed by a copyist from the orchestral parts.

Long before this, however, the collaborators should have embarked on their next joint venture. A new work, not a revival, was what Carte wanted. Gilbert was willing, indeed expected, that the collaboration should proceed in the same vein. Sullivan was not. The first serious rift opened between them – and it was a rift over the essential difference in their approach. Gilbert, no longer very successful in non-musical plays, was fulfilling himself at the Savoy. It was with every right that his name preceded Sullivan's. His was the basic idea, as well as the book and lyrics, of each succeeding piece. He was the director, or 'stage manager' as it was still called, of the spectacle. Sullivan, however, did not consider himself fulfilled – except financially. He found the operetta convention constricting, and continued to believe that success in 'grand opera' was open to him. On 29 January 1884, barely three weeks after the opening of *Princess Ida*, he received Carte at his home and 'told him of my resolve not to write any more Savoy pieces'.

As soon as he could consider himself convalescent he left (on 4 February) for the Riviera. He stayed at the Grand Hotel in Monte Carlo, seeing Ambroise Thomas's opera *Hamlet* there on 16 February, and then extended his holiday to Pisa, Florence, Lucerne (19 March), Basle, Paris, and Brussels. At Brussels he received the letter which invoked the terms of the agreement by which he had bound himself a year since. Carte wrote from the Savoy Theatre on 22 March:

The business here, as you will have observed, shows signs of dropping. It may of course pick up again after Lent, but it may not, and in any case it seems probable that we shall want a new piece for the autumn.

By our agreement I have to give you and Gilbert six months' notice in case of a new opera being required.

Will you please accept this note as fulfilling the required formality? I am sending a duplicate of this note to Gilbert.

The conflict was about to begin – nor did Sullivan have a helmet 'to ward off blows'. On the contrary, his hands were tied by the five-year contract which he himself had signed. If he felt that the path to his artistic self-expression could be found only in a new direction, he would find the path rough.

20 Conflict

SULLIVAN to Carte, 28 March 1884:

Your letter of the 22nd inst. has reached me, in which you give me formal notice that you may require a new opera in six months' time. I ought therefore to tell you at once that it is impossible for me to do another piece of the character of those already written by Gilbert and myself. The reason for this decision I can give you verbally when we meet. When I return to town, I must, of course, talk the matter over with Gilbert and hear what his views on the subject are.

P.S. I have not written to Gilbert as I much prefer talking it over with him.

Gilbert to Sullivan, 30 March 1884:

I learnt from Carte yesterday, to my unbounded surprise, that you do not intend to write any more operas of the class with which you and I have been so long identified. . . . You are of course aware that by our agreement entered into on the 8th February, 1883, and extending over five years, we are bound to supply Carte with a new opera on receiving from him six months' notice, and, if from any reason, we fail to do so, we are liable with him for any losses that may result from our default . . .

During your absence I have busied myself with constructing a libretto; I have even gone so far as to write some of the numbers and to sketch out portions of the dialogue. I have written twice to you, reporting progress and urging upon you the advisability of getting the piece well in hand. . . . In all the pieces we have written together I have invariably subordinated my views to your own. You have often expatiated to me, and to others, on the thorough good feeling with which we have worked together for so many years. Nothing, as far as I am aware, has occurred to induce you to change your views on this point, and I am, therefore, absolutely at a loss to account for the decision . . . which, I hope and believe, your good feeling and strong sense of justice will induce you, on consideration, to recall.

Sullivan to Gilbert, 1 April 1884:[1]

I will be quite frank. With *Princess Ida* I have come to the end of my tether – the end of my capability in that class of piece. My tunes are in danger of becoming mere repetitions of my former pieces, my concerted movements are getting to possess a strong family likeness and I have rung all the changes possible in the way of variety of rhythm. It has hitherto been word-setting, I might almost say syllable-setting, for I have looked upon the words as being of such importance that I have been continually keeping down the music in order that not one should be lost.

And this very suppression is most difficult, most fatiguing, and I may say most disheartening, for the music is never allowed to rise and speak for itself. I want a chance for the music to act in its own proper sphere – to intensify the emotional element not only of the actual words but of the situation.

I should like to set a story of human interest and probability, where the humorous words would come in a humorous (not serious) situation, and where, if the situation were a tender or dramatic one, the words would be of a similar character. There would then be a feeling of reality about it which would give a fresh interest in writing, and fresh vitality to our joint work. . . . I hope with all my heart they [our views] may coincide so that there may be no break in our chain of joint workmanship.

Sullivan moreover protested that Gilbert had *not* written 'reporting progress', and Gilbert withdrew that point, but none the less replied as if under personal attack.

Your reflections on the character of the libretti which I have supplied you have caused me considerable pain. However, I cannot suppose that you have intended to gall and wound me, when you wrote as you did. I must assume that your letter was written hurriedly.

When you tell me that your desire is that I shall write a libretto in which the humorous words will come in a humorous situation, and in which a tender or dramatic situation will be treated tenderly and dramatically, you teach me the ABC of my profession. It is inconceivable that any sane author should ever write otherwise than as you propose I should write in future.

The rift, which had hitherto turned on Sullivan's statement that he would write no more of the Savoy *type* of pieces, then shifted to the composer's rejection of the particular plot Gilbert proposed to him. Sullivan's next letter (7 April 1884), one of the most important statements of his artistic position, survives in draft and is reproduced here in full for the first time:

It is I who feel hurt that you should put such a construction upon my words as to make them even seem to cast a reflection upon your works. I yield to no one in admiration of their matchless skill and genius and, as I am not compelled to set anything I don't like, it is not very likely that I should have worked so long with you if I hadn't done so with real pleasure. If you will read my letter again carefully, you will see that there is not the faintest trace of reflection on past work – only the strongly expressed wish to do something in the future of a different character – partly caused by the great distrust I have of my own power of doing anything more in the same way. In fact I feel that I cannot. You yourself on more than one occasion have suggested that we might do something from which the element of burlesque (as the term is generally understood) should be absent, and it is nothing more than this I am now proposing we should carry out. Apart from my own personal feeling in the matter, I am convinced that popularity of our joint work will rapidly decline, as people will say and do say already that we are only repeating ourselves.

There is so much that I like in the sketch of your proposed new piece that I am loth to say I must give it up. But the more I study it, and think about it, the more does my dislike [*the word 'antipathy' was crossed out*] to the device of the charm increase. Moreover, I am quite concerned that everyone will be struck by its similarity to *The Sorcerer* (in so far as the same device (lozenge or potion) is used to bring about the same result, viz., people falling in love with each other against their wills), and, like *The Sorcerer*, things returning to their original conditions when the force of the charm is removed. And of course they will say that we are repeating ourselves. At the same time, as this device is the pivot upon which the action of the piece turns, I quite see the difficulty you would have in modifying it, if you were disposed to do so.

Now, in dealing with your libretto, I like to enter upon the work with interest, even enthusiasm. This new subject I feel is not congenial to me, and it is of no use my arguing either with you or with myself about it. That is why I write this instead of saying it, as each conversation only leaves things just as unsettled as they were before. After 20 years' hard work in my career, I am not going to depart from a principle I have always acted upon, viz., never to force myself to try to do that which I feel I cannot do well.

This is a matter of financial interest to both of us – we both want the piece to succeed. So far as I am concerned, my share of the success will lie in my having to deal with a subject which is thoroughly congenial to me, and which hitherto you have had no difficulty in giving me.

Now pray do not say again or think that I cast reflection on the pieces you have already written. I have enjoyed doing them with you and know of no one with whom I can write so sympathetically, but I don't want my interest in our joint work to flag, and that is why I sincerely trust you will see your way to do something which will give me fresh vigour and energy. A piece of the character and treatment of *Pygmalion and Galatea*, *The Wicked World* or even of a lighter stamp, I feel that I could do with interest and confidence of success. I am still uncertain which day I shall be in town, but I will telephone you directly I arrive [from Paris].

But Gilbert did not take the bait. Of all his plays, *Pygmalion and Galatea* was the most highly regarded and had just been successfully revived in London, with the distinguished American actress Mary Anderson. But he might well have considered it a debasement to convert a serious play into an operatic form.

[Diary, 10 April 1884]: Gilbert came at 2. Two hours' conversation. He proposed to me as subject of new piece, the same idea that I had already declined two years ago, based on the notion that by means of a charm (formerly a coin, now a lozenge) a person would really become the character he or she represented themselves to be. Thus a young woman playing an old woman's part would, by taking the lozenge, really become an old woman for the time, and so on. I was obliged to reject the subject, as it makes the whole piece unreal and artificial. Long argument on his part – no concession on either side – complete deadlock, though quite friendly throughout.

The 'deadlock' would have been resolved if Sullivan had accepted Gilbert's next suggestion – that the composer should choose another librettist: 'I will willingly retire for one turn, our agreement notwithstanding'. But Sullivan knew that there was no second Gilbert waiting in the wings. He wanted the same valued collaborator but a new kind of work.

[Sullivan to Carte, 12 April 1884]:
The case stands thus: Gilbert gives me the outlines of a piece. I do not like it.
1st: because it is going back to the elements of topsyturvydom and unreality which I had hoped we had now done with, and about which I had written most earnestly in my letter to him of 2nd April.
2nd: It bears a strong resemblance to *The Sorcerer*, inasmuch as in both pieces by means of a charm, people all fall in love with each other *à tort et à travers*, and if, as is probable, we revive *The Sorcerer* after the new piece, people will not fail to observe the resemblance.
3rd: Any element of romance and tenderness which Gilbert might introduce must, by its surroundings, be unreal and artificial, and this reacts on me most disadvantageously. I cannot do any more of that class of work.

In answer to all this G. says that he cannot look for another subject, as he fails to see what I want, that if this does not suit me, it is impossible for him to find one that will. And so there we are.

[Diary, 15 April 1884]: Home to meet Gilbert. Long talk. He sketched out the piece (in dispute) with considerable modifications, proposing to give it a very serious and tender interest in addition to its grotesque and humorous elements, and to keep the two elements totally distinct. There still remains the machinery of the 'charm' which is to me so objectionable musically. It was arranged that he should send me a sketch of 2nd Act, and that then, after giving it my most earnest consideration, [if] I still found the subject uncongenial to me, I should say so, and he would then look about for another idea altogether . . .

Eleven days later Gilbert brought his revised version and left it with Sullivan. The diary records his promise to consider it carefully – but 'I don't think I can ever get over my distaste for the charm'. Gilbert, however, thought – or later convinced himself that he thought – that at this meeting Sullivan had in principle accepted the new treatment.

By half past midnight on 2 May Sullivan had made up his mind to reject the plot. He wrote a 'long letter to Gilbert begging him to put aside the plot he prepared, and give me another'. Next day he 'received a letter from Gilbert, absolutely refusing'. This refusal was elaborated by Gilbert in a six-page letter two days later, in which the accusation of hurtful, unprofessional conduct on Sullivan's part was clearly – but unconvincingly – made.

After the lapse of a week during which I wrote three lyrics and a considerable amount of dialogue, I received a letter from you to the effect that you could not bring yourself to like the plot, and that you wished me to construct a story in which there should be no supernatural or improbable element. This specification of your wishes, expressed as it was, for the first time, some four months after the production of *Princess Ida*, seemed to me to be so wholly unreasonable that I had no alternative but to express my regret that it was impossible for me to agree to your suggestion. Upon this you wrote to me that you felt convinced that my decision was final, and that therefore further discussion was useless. And so ends a musical and literary association of seven years' standing – an association of exceptional reputation – an association unequalled in its monetary results, and hitherto undisturbed by a single jarring or discordant element. In justification of the course that I adopted in declining to construct a new libretto, I must point out to you that your own course of action in desiring me to do so, can only be justified on the assumption that, by the terms of our agreement, I am bound to go on constructing new libretti until I hit upon one which meets your views as to what a libretto should be. That you regard my relation towards yourself as of this servile nature, I do not for one moment believe. As reasonably might I assume that a composer of your distinction is bound to set to music any words with which I might think fit to supply him. The plot of the piece, for which, you must remember *I alone am responsible to the public*, I take to be a matter in which I am entitled to a casting vote: the subjects of the lyrics – questions of metre and rhythm – construction of duets, trios and concerted music, and, in short, all points bearing on the musical requirements of the piece are matters in which I hold that your decision is final. You must remember that we are not absolutely free agents – that I am not in the position of an author who comes to a composer with a suggestion which the composer is at entire liberty to reject – this would be our relation to one another if no agreement existed. But as a matter of fact, an agreement *does* exist – an agreement entered into presumably on the assumption that we have, from long experience of the other, sufficient confidence in each other, to bind ourselves – you to accept my plots as belief to be good enough for your purpose, I to accept your musical setting as adding an invaluable element of attraction to my libretto. That my duty is to supply you with a series of pieces 'on approval' I cannot for one moment admit. At the same time I, of course, hold myself bound, in common courtesy towards a composer of your eminence, to give every practical value to your wishes in putting together the plots of my libretti. This I have invariably done – this I took infinite pains to do in the present case. And on Saturday week last you told me, in unmistakeable terms, that you were satisfied.

I should be grieved indeed if it were supposed that I desired, on the strength of our agreement with Carte, to fetter you to a class of composition in which your musical genius could not find adequate expression. If you desired to devote a year to the composition of (say) a grand opera, I should, with Carte's consent, have been most willing to forgo, for such a period, the agreement by which we are bound. I would even have accepted the subordinate position which the librettist of such an opera must necessarily occupy, if you considered that a work of an ambitious class would, in any way, be furthered by my co-operation. But I need hardly remind you that such a work would be wholly and ridiculously out of place at the Savoy Theatre. We have educated our audiences to expect pieces of a light and entertaining character, and moreover our company does not possess the vocal resources which would enable them to deal with work of an ambitious class. Such a piece must be produced at another theatre, and the libretto of such a piece I have more than once expressed to you my readiness to construct, if my doing so would in any way serve your purpose . . .

Next day (6 May), according to a surviving draft, Sullivan denied Gilbert's assertion that he (Sullivan) had in principle accepted the plot in its revised version. He had examined the new treatment but 'eventually I found I could not reconcile myself to the charm and, distasteful as was the task, I was compelled to tell you so'. Moreover,

All that you say in reference to the respective positions of author and composer, and the responsibility which they individually and jointly hold, I cordially agree with, and I should be humiliated and grieved if anything in my words or manner had ever indicated that I claimed to see your librettos 'on approval'. This constitutes a striking difference between us and other writers. Another composer would concern himself with all those things. . . . That you are responsible for the plot is indisputable, but you cannot blame me if my interest extends even to that for which I am not directly responsible. I felt uneasy about the subject you proposed, and concealed dissatisfaction on one side is a bad element in joint workmanship.

Now, if, as you say, our collaboration is to end, I am bound in self-defence to put on record my own view of the cause of the disaster, and for this reason I have endeavoured to explain to you where there has been error and misapprehension. But whatever may be the result, it would be a source of unmixed pleasure to me to think that we can conduct an argumentative correspondence and differ on the most important points without our friendly relation being disturbed.

Never were the attitudes of the two men – their mutual relationship as artists, as well as their approach to their material – most vividly set forth than in this lengthy correspondence. Neither 'won' the quarrel, but Sullivan started from a weak position and ended in one. Having bound himself under the agreement with Carte to produce a new work with Gilbert on six months' notice, he was ill qualified to claim a right of veto on a plot – a right which he had never before asserted. Yet it was Gilbert who gave way, belying the self-willed rigidity often associated with him. He dropped the 'charm' plot (more often known as the 'lozenge' plot) – or rather, he put it in storage, only to bring it out eight years later for his unsuccessful opera with Alfred Cellier's music, *The Mountebanks*. For Sullivan he would construct a new plot.

Gilbert's gesture drew an immediate, heartfelt reply:

Your letter of today [8 May] is an inexpressible relief to me, as it clearly shows me that you, equally with myself, are loth to discontinue the collaboration which has been such a pleasure and advantage to us.

If, as I understand you to propose, you will construct a plot without the supernatural and impromptu elements, and on the lines which you describe, I gladly undertake to set it without further discussing the matter, or asking what the subject is to be.

The subject, Sullivan was to discover, was Japanese. A pleasing but unsubstantiated anecdote has it that a Japanese sword suddenly fell down from the wall of Gilbert's study, setting off a train of thought which led to *The Mikado*.

During its literary gestation Sullivan had other matters both professional and private to occupy him. The appointment of Hans Richter to conduct the Birmingham Festival (the chief rival to Leeds) incensed him. To Joseph Bennett, in his capacity as editor of a short-lived monthly musical journal called *The Lute*, he dispatched a letter calling it

an affront – a bitter humiliation for all of us English. Royalty takes us by the hand, pats us on the back, says that music is an admirable pursuit that we must be properly taught at special colleges, that we cannot do anything for ourselves and therefore kindly hands us over to committees and councils for guidance and educates hundreds of future paupers. After all this cry about English music and English musicians, Royalty will probably patronize the festival and so set its approval on the greatest and most insolent kick that the English musicians have ever had. You will probably say that this is all personal disappointment. But it isn't. I should certainly have considered it an honour if they had offered me the festival, whether I could have undertaken it or not. But it is not entirely selfish. For not a thought of envy or regret should I have felt if Cowen, Stanford, Barnby or Randegger (who is one of us, to all practical purposes) had been selected. They would all have done the work well – a hundred times better than a German who cannot speak the language, who had never had any experience in dealing with English choruses, and who knows none of the traditions of those choral works which form a large element in the Festival. Would I had your pen and your power – I would use the one to make the other felt. Excuse this little outburst. *Libravi animam meam* [I have released my feelings].

Bennett sent a soothing reply (14 May 1884) to the effect that the Birmingham committee 'would not play second fiddle to Leeds and take the conductor approved of by the rival festival': this was why 'the blonde [*sic*] Teuton' had been able to step into the vacant place. Hermann Klein, to whose advocacy Sullivan also appealed, took the opportunity to call on him personally. He later recalled it as

the first of the many Sunday-afternoon chats that I enjoyed in the library of his comfortable apartment in Victoria Street. He was an inveterate cigarette-smoker, and from the moment I entered until the time I left, a cigarette was scarcely ever out of his mouth. He was a bright, interesting talker, full of genuine Irish mother-wit, yet withal earnest, emphatic, and impressive when he wished. He was devotedly attached to a parrot that was also a good talker, and would amuse him by insisting on spelling Polly with only one 'l'. At the period to which I am referring he was already a sufferer from the painful malady which eventually carried him off; but his hair had not yet turned gray, he still wore the familiar bushy whiskers shown in his early portraits, and he was robust enough to indulge frequently in his favourite pastime, lawn-tennis.[2]

Sullivan's ambition to write a 'grand opera' found an unexpected stimulus. By chance he rediscovered, on 20 April, a scenario or outline-libretto of *Guinevere*, written for him in the 1860s by his friend who died young, Lionel Lewin. He sought the aid of the author and journalist Andrew Lang (1844–1912) in re-working this or at least in re-working the theme; but it came to nothing. He must have felt the prick of rivalry when, on 23 April 1884, Stanford's *The Canterbury Pilgrims*, with a libretto by Gilbert Arthur A'Beckett, was produced by the Carl Rosa company at Drury Lane Theatre. Sullivan was otherwise engaged: he conducted his *In Memoriam* at the Philharmonic (John F. Barnett conducted the remainder of the concert) to mark the death of the young Prince Leopold. Nor does Sullivan seem to have seen one of the later performances of Stanford's opera, though on 14 June he 'looked in' at Covent Garden to see Adelina Patti's first appearance that season in the title-role of *La traviata*. Typically his diary records the visit with no comment at all.

Five days later at a quiet wedding at Holy Trinity Church, Sloane Street, Fanny Ronalds's daughter 'Fanette' became Mrs Thomas Ritchie: 'Mrs Ronalds gave the bride away, I played the Wedding March, only families and a few old friends present'. Next day Sullivan withdrew £10,000 of securities kept at his bank to deposit them as security with Rothschilds 'on account of loan of £5,000'. The purpose of such a large borrowing is not known. A mere 180 guineas (£189) would suffice for his rental of a country house that summer.

The search for a suitable summer residence occupied him intermittently for two months and it was not until mid-August that he made an offer for Stagenhoe Park near Hitchin in Hertfordshire.

[Diary, 15 August]: Preparing to move out of town . . . Louis [valet], chef, Jane, Harriet (housemaid), William (boy) left with luggage for Stagenhoe Park. Dicey and I dined at the Portland.

Next day, with two more maidservants (Delphine and Theresa), the master of the household himself made his removal and 'found clerks still at inventory. Hurried them up. Mr and Mrs Carter [Mrs Ronalds's parents], Mrs Ronalds and Reggie [her son] arrived at 6. Dicey came after dinner.'

Stagenhoe entailed only an hour's journey (32 miles) northward from London to Hitchin. On 11 October, after he had conducted the revival of *The Sorcerer* and *Trial by Jury* in London ('magnificent house, most brilliant and enthusiastic reception') he returned to Stagenhoe by a midnight train which was supposed to go only as far as Hatfield but ran the extra 14 miles to take Sullivan and his party to Hitchin for a fee of 14 shillings.

After many years of attending other and richer people's country-house parties, Sullivan was now in a position to invite his own friends similarly – not, of course, on the grand scale of a country landowner. Earlier in the summer on 8 June he had given, in his own apartments, a small dinner party with an almost wholly aristocratic guest-list, after which a much larger company arrived. It was a Sunday, so he went first 'to Mrs Ronalds' music' – the regular Sunday 'salon' at which Fanny Ronalds brought gifted musicians and discerning patrons together. At dinner were

Lord and Lady Castlereagh, Lord and Lady Hothfield, Lord Brooke (Lady Brooke ill and sent [to say so] at the last moment, so I sent off hastily to Mrs Ronalds who came instead), Mrs Pereira and self. After dinner Mrs F. Post, Mrs [Beach] and Miss [Adele] Grant, Mrs Scott, Mr [Moreton] Frewen and Miss [Leonie] Jerome, Lady Shrewsbury, Mr Sterling, Lord Hopetown, Lady Mandeville, Lady Ch[arles] Beresford, Lady Kath[erine] and Miss Coke, Mr Belmont and Miss Whiting, Lady Marg[aret] Browne, Miss Fitzherbert, Mr and Mrs Gilbert, Mrs Ronalds and Mrs Ritchie [Fanette]. . .

Lord Castlereagh, later the Marquis of Londonderry, was a prominent Conservative politician. Among the other after-dinner guests was a dignitary Sullivan had met in Egypt, Blum Pasha, as well as a sprinkling of his fellow-artists – the composers Paolo Tosti and Isidore de Lara, Brandon Thomas (author of *Charley's Aunt*) and Alfred Cellier. There was 'music, supper, music: general exit at 2.30' [a.m.]

Four weeks later (Sunday 6 July) there was a larger dinner and an equally large after-dinner assembly. Once again his American friend from Paris, Mrs Beach Grant, was present. George and Weedon Grossmith were among those engaged to entertain.

Dined here: Duke of Edinburgh, Count and Countess de Florian, Lord and Lady Wharncliffe, Lady Hothfield, Lady Sykes, Mr and Mrs W. Oppenheim, Mrs Ronalds, Mrs Grant, Corrêa [a Brazilian diplomat], Sir A[lgernon] Borthwick, and self. (First time I have had 14.) After dinner Miss [Gertrude] Griswold, Edward Lloyd and [Pasquale] Costa sang, Lebano and Albanesi played [Felix Lebano, harpist; Carlo Albanesi, pianist], [George] Grossmith and his brother [Weedon] – and a conjuror (Cherry) who was marvellous. . . . Supper, and everyone went about a quarter to three.

The after-dinner guests included Lord Wolseley (as General Sir Garnet Wolseley had become) and Lady Wolseley; Tigrane Pasha (who had entertained Sullivan in Egypt) as well as Blum Pasha; Carte, but not the Gilberts; the lawyer George Lewis and his wife, Mrs Ronalds with her daughter and new son-in-law, Adele Grant, Ernest Dresden (the friend of his 1878 Riviera journey), the composer-playwright Hamilton Aidé, the Earl and Countess of Denbigh, and Isabella, Countess of Wilton, the stepmother of Sullivan's old friend, Seymour ('Sym') Egerton. Sullivan's dinners were not to have the gastronomic and social uniqueness of the 'octaves' (eight-course dinners for eight men) held by his friend Sir Henry Thompson, but there can have been few gatherings to rival his in mixing royal and noble guests with leading personages of music and the stage.

This was also the summer of Marie van Zandt. In 1879, at the age of only 18, the American-born soprano had appeared at Her Majesty's Theatre in the leading role of Bellini's *La sonnambula*; she then joined the company of the Opéra-Comique in Paris, where in 1883 she had created the title-role in Delibes's *Lakmé*. That she had turned down an invitation from Sullivan is suggested by his diary entry for 11 July 1884. It may be presumed that the Prince of Wales's interest in her was not purely artistic.

[At] 4.30 went to Costa's concert [the Italian composer Pasquale Costa, already mentioned] at Mme Santurca's house. Prince of Wales came directly after I arrived. He had lunched at Mrs Arthur Paget's to meet Marie van Zandt (!) who stayed in London on purpose. This is too bad and after such behaviour to me I can't have anything more to do with her. Miss van Zandt had also asked Mrs Paget to invite her mother to lunch. Mrs P. declined and said she could come after lunch! In spite of this insult Miss van Zandt went.

Ten days later after a long talk with Burnand (about a renewed collaboration?) Sullivan encountered the political demonstration in favour of Gladstone's Parliamentary Reform Bill, which was in effect to establish adult male franchise in the country as it had already been established in the towns. *The Times* estimated that between 125,000 and 150,000 men marched in the procession and that anything up to a million 'took part in the day's proceedings' on 21 July. Presumably Sullivan had just left Burnand's Bloomsbury home at 64 Russell Square: 'Walked all down to 139 Piccadilly [home of Sir Algernon Borthwick] through the demonstration. Good-humoured crowd – no fixed political principles. Took refuge at Borthwick's.'

'No fixed political principles' was perhaps a better label for Arthur Sullivan than for the demonstrators whose aspirations he so amiably dismissed.

He had sufficient leisure in November to journey with his nephew and ward, Herbert (usually 'Bertie' in the diary), via Paris to Zurich, where the intention was to enrol him in the Polytechnikum for training as an engineer. But having arrived there and discussed the matter, Sullivan decided that his nephew should first spend some time in Germany to learn the language. So they went on to Freiburg (Breisgau) where the young man was put in the care of a tutor: 'I left him there (£90 a year) paying first quarter in advance.' Five days later, back in London, he heard Barnby conduct the first London performance (15 November 1884) of Wagner's *Parsifal* in a concert version at the Albert Hall:

Finale to first act impressive and noble. 'Flower' scene graceful and scored with delicate charm – other little bits here and there of great beauty and originality. But the whole is heavy, gloomy, dull and ugly – very undramatic, as except by means of the outworn *leitmotiven* trick, there is nothing *characteristic* in the music sung by each individual. The music of one individual would do just as well for any other.

Barnby was one of the musical friends with whom he remained on the most informal and jolliest of terms, often visiting him and his family at Eton College, near Windsor. Barnby was 'precentor', i.e. director of music, at the College. In her recollections more than 40 years later (*Strand Magazine*, January 1927) Muriel Barnby recalled herself as 'a little thin-legged girl in red stockings', curled up in an armchair as 'Uncle Arthur' walked across the room to the piano with jovial comments to her father on the difficulty of setting such-and-such a 'teaser' as Gilbert provided. He 'never missed slipping a bright new half-sovereign into my hand on leaving'.

At last the libretto of *The Mikado* – or at least some of it – was ready for the composer's consideration. It was only the first act which Sullivan was shown when he dined with Gilbert and his wife on 20 November. 'Made several important suggestions with which Gilbert agreed. Act still in an incomplete and somewhat crude condition, but will shape out well.' A week later Gilbert sent 'seven numbers – all that don't require rewriting' and on 2 December Gilbert hoped 'to have Act I ready for you tomorrow in every detail'. On 8 December Sullivan's diary records that he 'wrote "For he is right" ' – the number that was to become no. 3 (Pish-Tush's solo with chorus) in the eventual score. On the same day 'Gilbert brought new finale [to Act I] and chorus of girls [the eventual no. 6], both excellent'. The indication of a *new* finale presumably refers to the modifications Sullivan had urged on his partner.

A letter sent next day by Gilbert reflects his share in what was to be the *musical* shape of the numbers.

I send a trio for Ko-Ko, Pooh-Bah and Pish-Tush. I think it might be quaint and effective. I have put the three verses side-by-side for convenience' sake, but of course they would be sung separately. I fancy the metre admits of each verse being set differently, but I may be wrong in this.

Gilbert's tone here was suitably deferential but his suggestion was indeed adopted: the verses were set differently and separately. Then, with brilliant musical skill, Sullivan brought all three tunes together in contrapuntal combination. His creative impulse was vigorously stirred by the new challenge. On 6 January 1885 he 'went to see A. B. Mitford, got some Japanese musical phrases from him'. Algernon Mitford, the future Lord Redesdale (1837–1916) had been on the staff of the British Legation in Tokyo. In the event Sullivan made only two borrowings. For the entrance of the Mikado there was a quotation of both words and music from a patriotic song ('Miya sama, miya sama'); and a repeated Japanese phrase 'O ni! bikkuri shakkuri to!' (apparently the words, and perhaps the music, of a children's song) became the protesting shout of the crowd in the finale of the first act.

Amid the immersion in the creative process came a crisis in December 1884 similar to that of May 1882 – and, like that one, set down in the diary in a form that makes a comprehensible sequence only if it is assumed that 'D.H.' is the same person as 'Mrs R.' and 'L.W.' Again 'M.' is the consultant.

[11 December]: Uncertainty changed to conviction. [That is the complete entry for that day.]

[12 December]: Went to M. alone . . .

[13 December]: Things very bad. Took D.H. to M. Usual course advised.

[16 December]: Dined Cad[ogan] Pl[ace].

[19 December]: Signals of safety began. Attended performance of *Prodigal Son* by R.A.M. [Royal Academy of Music]. Very well done. Walked home with Mrs R. *L.W. to see A.C., important.*

[20 December]: Signals of safety. Things going well. Dined at Cad. Place.

[21 December]: Out of the wood.

'A.C.' was presumably Alfred Cooper, a physician whom Sullivan often consulted. Those four words of relief entered on 21 December were preceded by a description of work and sociability in sequence:

Worked at home all day. Wrote two numbers, *Three Little Maids* [the Trio, no. 7 of Act 1] and quintet [probably later converted to the quartet, no. 8] in new piece [as usual, not yet named]. Called at C[adogan] P[lace]: Mrs R. told me about Louise. Dined at Ferdinand Rothschild's [143 Piccadilly]: Prince of Wales and Princess Louise there. Portland [Club].

In working on a Japanese subject, Gilbert and Sullivan knew that they were tapping a vein of acknowledged public interest. A vogue for Japanese design had been manifested in the 'Aesthetic' movement, had been exploited by Arthur Lazonby Liberty's famous London shop (see p. 157) and had been ridiculed in *Patience* through the mouth of Bunthorne, who did *not* long for

> . . . everything one sees
> That's Japanese.

But the interest was re-stimulated early in 1885 by a 'Japanese village' exhibition at Humphrey's Hall in the Knightsbridge area of London, which advertised 'five streets and shops showing the manufactures and daily life of Japan – one hundred men, women and children'. The issue of the *Era* (17 January) which drew its readers' attention to the exhibition also informed them that Gilbert had enlivened his recent party

by having the second act of *Patience* performed on a charming little stage expressly fitted up in the drawing-room of his house in Kensington. Few more artistic and elegant residences are to be seen in the metropolis than the abode of this distinguished author [at 39 Harrington Gardens], and the guests enjoyed the performance thoroughly. Sir Arthur Sullivan presided at the harmonium and Mr [François] Cellier at the piano.

The exhibition would heighten the topicality of the new operetta and would even provide Gilbert with a joke: 'Knightsbridge' is the address for Nanki-Poo which the trembling Ko-Ko gives to the Mikado.

Sullivan had taken on an additional role, at the very centre of London concert-giving: the conductorship of the Philharmonic Society. His practical experience at Leeds, apart from his national reputation in a more general sense, made him naturally attractive to a conservative musical organization which had recently been in difficulties both musical and financial. Joseph Bennett's journal, *The Lute*, spoke of the society as 'fast lapsing into dotage'. The staid Cusins, who had succeeded to Sterndale Bennett's place in 1867, had resigned in 1883 and the 1884 season had a stop-gap of five different conductors including Frederic Cowen, ten years Sullivan's junior. In accepting for the 1885 season, from February to May, Sullivan had stipulated that he should be allowed a deputy 'if my engagements took me out of England during the earlier concerts of the season'. That proviso, perhaps, would permit him to continue to winter on his beloved Riviera! By the standards of his theatrical earnings, the fee offered was puny: £100 for six concerts.[3] A celebrity soloist might command a better rate: to the violinist Wilhelmj the Society offered £40 for one concert or £60 for two.

Sullivan was to hold the position for three seasons, after which Cowen succeeded to the post. Shortly after the beginning of his first season he asked the Philharmonic committee to permit students of the Royal Academy and Royal College of Music to have free entry to rehearsals:

The opportunities for hearing orchestral music are not very numerous, and as it is a most important element in the education of music students I think it almost incumbent on a leading society like the Philharmonic to afford this chance.

As the date of his first concert approached his work on *The Mikado* was (as usual with the composition of the operettas) reaching an ever-intensified pace. While the music was being composed, and while Gilbert was still making alterations in the libretto, the Savoy company was already at rehearsal.

[Diary, 9 February]: Rehearsal: Finale to 1st Act complete. Home, dined early (5.30), wrote from 9 till 3 [a.m.]. Composed and framed Entrance of Mikado and following [Mikado's] song.

Sullivan's diary for 1885 contains an account of domestic and other expenses for February: at least it may be presumed to belong to that month, since it occurs on the page allotted to February in the specially ruled accounts pages at the end of the volume. Its particulars are of special interest since for no other month did the composer set down a similar calculation.

		[£ s]	[£ s d]
	Sm.		25.0.0
	Ser.	8	
		5	
		2.10	
		2.10	
	Beer	1.6	
		——	19.6.0
Rent and gas			46
	L.		100
	L.A.		42
	Books		110
	Sundries		50
			——
			392.6.0.

The interpretation does not admit of much doubt. Walter Smythe as his secretary received £25 a month. He had four servants of whom his personal valet received £8 a month, the remainder less. Beer was commonly itemized (for instance in newspaper advertisements) as a separate prerequisite for servants in addition to wages and is so treated here. The regular provision for Mrs Ronalds is itemized 'L.'; and the provision for his late brother's family in Los Angeles (L.A.) is noted. The item of £110 allotted for 'books' plainly does not refer to reading matter at a time when a new novel such as H. Rider Haggard's *King Solomon's Mines* cost 5s. (25p.). The most plausible interpretation is that it was a net gambling loss, perhaps not at the (racing) 'book-makers' but at cards. Gambling remained one of the obsessions, and the Portland Club at 9 St James's Square remained one of the fixed institutions, in Arthur Sullivan's life.

21   At the Centre

THE method by which Arthur Sullivan and W.S. Gilbert put their work on stage was by now well established. Musical rehearsals were first begun. Then Gilbert, normally seated on a stage 'bridge' (a structure spanning across the orchestra pit), would initiate the dramatic rehearsals by reading his complete text aloud to the company. It was a vital step in the proceedings, beginning that shaping and refining of the production in which Gilbert, not Sullivan, was in charge. Sullivan would attend whenever he could, but not constantly. Musical matters would in his absence be left under the direction of François Cellier.

On 15 February 1885 Gilbert called at Queen's Mansions 'with many alterations'. Next day Gilbert's 'reading' took place. Then Sullivan faced a schedule which embraced his Philharmonic debut as well as rehearsals at the Savoy *and* the completion of those parts of *The Mikado* which had not yet been written, or not yet orchestrated.

[17 February]: First rehearsal on stage. Could not go: writing all day. Dined at Cad. Pl. Mrs R. arrived home from Belfast. [*tick*]

[20 February] Reh[earsed] Phil[harmonic] at 10: Brahms Sym. [in] F [no. 3] Reh. Savoy 12.30, finale first act. Returned home at 4.30 dead beat. Went to Whistler's '10 o'clock' [party] with Mrs Chappell [wife of his publisher] and Mrs Ronalds. Home.

[22 February]: Made alterations in finale (1st act) and gave new score to Baird [copyist]. Wrote 'The Flowers that bloom' [i.e. still composing, not yet orchestrating, the second act]. Dined at home, 10 o'clock. Portland + [£]20.

[26 February]: My first appearance as conductor of the Philharmonic Society. Great reception.

The programme, at St James's Hall, had the distinguished participation of Sullivan's old friend Joachim, the almost inevitable garnish of vocal items being provided by a soprano, Elly Warnots. Brahms's symphony, his latest, was receiving its first Philharmonic performance.

Overture, 'Athalie'	Mendelssohn
Aria, 'Sweet bird' (*L'Allegro*)	Handel
Violin Concerto	Beethoven
Symphony no. 3 in F	Brahms
Aria, 'Come per me sereno' (*La sonnambula*)	Bellini
Overture, 'Ruler of the Spirits'	Weber

The two weeks preceding the Savoy's opening allowed no slackening of pace the usual two full rehearsals of the next Philharmonic concert had somehow to be fitted in. The diaries reveal the ardours both of rehearsal and of lonely, night-long work at his desk.

[3 March 1885]: Worked all night at Finale, 1st act. Finished at 5 a.m. 63 pages of score at one sitting!

[6 March 1885]: Finished scoring 2nd act at 5.45 a.m. [of 7 March, a Saturday].

[9 March 1885]: First band rehearsal [of] new opera. Everything complete except finale 2nd act [presumably the parts were still at the copyist's] and Brandram's song [Katisha's 'Hearts do not break', also towards the end of the second act], 11.30 to 5. Home to work.

[10 March 1885]: Rehearsed Phil[harmonic] – then to Langham Hall for full music rehearsal [of *The Mikado*], band and voices. Great enthusiasm. Home to work.

The use of Langham Hall for a purely musical, non-acted rehearsal (what modern British performers call by the German name *sitzprobe*, a sitting rehearsal) was necessary because by that time the Savoy stage would be occupied for scenic preparations. Hawes Craven, the stage designer, had his own work to do, and it was evidently necessary even for an *acted* rehearsal to be transferred to another location.

[11 March 1885]: 10 a.m. rehearsal for Phil – till 12.30. Then to Lyceum for stage rehearsal for new opera. (Craven wanted Savoy stage.) Row with Gilbert about 'business'. All right afterwards. Wrote till 10, then took MS to theatre [where the copyist would receive it].

[12 March 1885]: Full dress rehearsal, 11.30. Left at 5.30 to get ready for – Phil. concert. B flat Symphony (Beethoven) went divinely. Duke of Edinburgh present. Smoked a cigarette with him at Clarence House afterwards.

The second Philharmonic programme on 12 March included the prizewinner (out of 88 entries) in the society's competition for a new overture. Its composer, who conducted his work, was a German who had recently taken up residence in England.

Overture to the 'Occasional Oratorio'	Handel
Piano Concerto	Schumann
Scena, 'Me voilà seule' (*La Reine de Saba*)	Gounod
Dramatic Overture	Gustav Ernst
Symphony no. 4	Beethoven
Recit. and aria, 'My strength is spent' (*The Taming of the Shrew*)	Goetz
Hungarian Rhapsody no. 4 in D	Liszt

Clara Schumann herself, still active in her mid-sixties, was to have been the soloist in her husband's concerto, but had withdrawn and was replaced by Oscar Beringer. (Thus Sullivan lost his only opportunity to conduct for the great artist whom he had sought out in Baden-Baden 18 years before.) The soprano soloist was the American, Minnie Hauk (1851–1929), a famous Carmen, who was also a celebrated Kate in *The Taming of the Shrew* – an opera by the now forgotten Hermann Goetz (1840–76). Bernard Shaw considered that this opera and his symphony in F placed Goetz 'securely above all other German composers of the last hundred years, save only Mozart and Beethoven, Weber and Wagner'.

On the day before the production was to open at the Savoy, he found time to call at Cadogan Place: Fanny Ronalds had not been well and he found her 'still v. seedy'. A six-hour dress rehearsal did not end until half-an-hour before midnight, but Arthur Sullivan still made his way to the Portland Club after it.

On the opening night, which Sullivan conducted, the Duke of Edinburgh was again his faithful patron. Princess Louise was there too, and Prince Louis Alexander of Battenberg (who had married a granddaughter of Queen Victoria's in the previous year). So was Sullivan's old collaborator Burnand. The diary mentions the name of the work (previously just 'the new opera') for the first time. The inadvertent omission of 'the' from 'The Flowers that bloom in the spring' is Sullivan's.

[14 March 1885]: New opera, *The Mikado or The Town of Titipu* produced at the Savoy Theatre with every sign of real success. A most brilliant house. Tremendous reception. All went well except Grossmith [as Ko-Ko], whose nervousness nearly upset the piece. A *treble* encore for 'Three Little Maids' and for 'The Flowers that Bloom in Spring'. Seven encores taken – might have taken twelve. Duke and Duchess of Edinburgh present. Portland.

The seven last words of the entry with the inevitable 'Portland' (once again that lure of gambling!) are omitted not only from the Flower biography, but from Reginald Allen's invaluable documentation, *The First Night Gilbert and Sullivan*.

Grossmith later acknowledged his nervousness: 'I lost my voice, the little there is of it, my confidence, and – what I maintain is most valuable to me – my individuality.' But Richard Temple's Mikado, Rutland Barrington's Pooh-Bah, Durward Lely's Nanki-Poo, Leonora Braham's Yum-Yum, and Rosina Brandram's Katisha gave great satisfaction – and so did the Pitti-Sing of Jessie Bond, who with characteristic devilment had secretly persuaded the wardrobe-mistress to make the *obi* of her Japanese costume twice as big as that of the other 'little maids'.

I made the most of my big, big bow, turning my back to the audience whenever I got a chance, and waggling it. The gallery was delighted, but *I* nearly got the sack for that prank. However, I did get noticed, which was what I wanted.

On the next day Sullivan 'got up at 1.30! [p.m.]'. Helen Lenoir, Carte's trusted secretary (later his second wife) was among his callers that Sunday.[1] He himself paid a call on the Duke of Edinburgh, then dined at the home of his friend E.J. Sartoris, 'played two concertos with Joachim after dinner' and went on to the Portland. Each of the three following days' entries in the diary refers to alterations which Sullivan now made in the music of *The Mikado*, needing a further rehearsal on the Wednesday. Ko-Ko's song about his 'Little list' of potential victims was advanced within Act I and Yum-Yum's song 'The Moon and I', originally placed in Act I immediately after 'Three Little Maids', was moved to its present place shortly after the second act opens. The reasons for the shift differ between the two cases and exemplify the different motivations of librettist and composer. The new place for Ko-Ko's song is better because it gives an earlier exposition of the character, instead of interrupting the new train of events started by Pooh-Bah's delivery of the Mikado's message. The shifting of Yum-Yum's song lessens the musical strain on the performer who otherwise must take this solo directly after participating in a vivacious trio, quartet and dance.

These alterations required, naturally, a modest rewriting of dialogue on Gilbert's part. It is odd to reflect that the Mikado's Song was nearly cut out before the opening: Gilbert had decided that it held up the action, and only a deputation of members of the chorus persuaded him to retain it. The supernumerary character of Go-To was a later invention and does not appear in Gilbert's libretto as printed: he merely supplies a bass voice in the madrigal in place of the baritone of Pish-Tush.

The Mikado was to be recognized, by public and connoisseurs alike, as among the best – perhaps indeed the best – of Sullivan's operettas. It is also a *tour-de-force* of Gilbert's, because the whole piece uniquely wears a kind of comic mask. Though billed as 'a Japanese opera', it does not present Japan: under the pretence of doing so it presents England. The picturesqueness of setting, of costumes, of manners (the colourful display of costumes and fans, the girls' giggling, and the parade of supposed oriental despotism) forms a licensed disguise for action and characters as English as they can be. As English, indeed, as the Mikado's references to 'parliamentary trains' (see a mention in Sullivan's own letter, p. 121 above), 'Monday Pops' (the London concert series, mentioned also in *Patience*) and the 'advertising quack'. It is not difficult to see the English origins of the names of Ko-Ko (cocoa) and Yum-Yum, though 'Pitti-Sing' is not so recognizable as baby-talk for 'pretty thing'. Even 'Katisha' was perhaps a variant of 'Atishoo!'. Pooh-Bah is the *English* functionary who knows – like the Judge in *Trial by Jury* – how things are 'managed by a job'. The long-gowned lords of the Japanese court assist the hero to 'heave the capstan round' in the manner of English sea-songs from the days of Storace and Dibdin almost a century past.

The mask is not only present: it is shown by being slipped on and off in dexterous verbal play, prefiguring such a later dramatist as Pirandello.

Ko-Ko. It might have been on his pocket-handkerchief, but Japanese don't use pocket handkerchiefs!

or:

Ko-Ko. Congratulate me, gentlemen, I've found a volunteer!
Chorus. The Japanese equivalent for 'Hear, hear, hear!'

To the composer, the happiest stimulus must have come from the sheer variety of the lyrics and their adaptability to character. More than this: Sullivan was able to model musical shapes on Gilbert's poetic ones. In 'There is beauty in the bellow of the blast/There is grandeur in the growling of the gale' (the duet for Katisha and Ko-Ko), the insistent alliteration of the words gives rise to the alternation of adjacent notes. Later, at

> If that is so,
> Sing derry-down-derry,
> It's evident, very
> Our tastes are one

the rhyming second and third lines are set to the same repeated musical phrase. *The Mikado* is full of such felicities. Never did Sullivan show more musical resource than in the contrapuntal interlocking of three different melodies already referred to in the previous chapter – Pooh-Bah's 'I am so proud', Ko-Ko's 'My brain it teems', Pish-Tush's 'I heard one day'.

In the Mikado's Song, the reference to

> . . . Masses and fugues and 'ops'
> By Bach, interwoven
> With Spohr and Beethoven . . .

prompted Sullivan to throw in a soft-spoken quotation from Bach's 'Great G minor' fugue on clarinet and bassoon: it is not so much the idea which is remarkable but the rhythmic and harmonic deftness of the interpolation.

The orchestration remained that which Sullivan had adopted as standard (a 'theatre orchestra' reduction of conventional symphonic scoring): 2 flutes, 1 oboe, 2 clarinets, 1 bassoon, 2 horns, 2 cornets, 2 trombones, 1 drummer, and strings. Cornets were still standard in the theatre, though trumpets were used in symphony concerts.

Sullivan's manuscript score of *The Mikado* (its publication in facsimile in 1968 marked the first issue of any of his operettas in authoritative full score) shows that Gilbert revised the words of the Mikado's Song at a later stage. Amid the list of social offenders and penalties, the manuscript has:

> And ev'ry big and bulky fellow of elephantine weights
> Is made to run races on gravelly places in eighteen-penny skates.

('On' and 'in' were presumably transposed in error by Sullivan while copying.) In dropping this Gilbert must have rightly sensed that people who *look* odd were not to be coupled with those of irritating behaviour. In performance one scarcely notices the curiosity that *both* Ko-Ko and the Mikado have songs about punishing social offenders.

Reviewing the first night, *The Times* on 16 March 1885 complained at the presence of 'the inevitable "old English" madrigal (sung by Japanese!)'. It is difficult to cite a better example of the obtuseness of the music critic – here presumably Hueffer – since the whole point of the work is precisely this comic anomaly. This particular review, lukewarm or disparaging throughout (Gilbert's plot was 'extremely slight' and 'childish', and Sullivan's music to 'Were you not to Ko-Ko plighted' was 'as feeble as can well be imagined') is none the less significant because the critic was finally forced to throw up his hands: 'The popularity of the two collaborators has reached the point where success depends no longer on intrinisic merit'. History and Hueffer might disagree on where 'intrinsic merit' lay, but the result was that *The Mikado* ran for 672 performances – a record which Gilbert and Sullivan never surpassed.

Reigning equally at the Savoy and at the Philharmonic concerts in St James's Hall, Sullivan was now at the height of his fame and of his earning power. In his early days £5 might have bought from him, as from many another composer, the copyright of a song. Now the *Musical Budget* reported in February 1885 that Sullivan had sold the copyright of *Sweethearts* outright to Chappell's for £700 – 'this, we presume, when it had achieved a success and was selling largely'.[2] The outright payment would replace the few pence per copy which the publishers must otherwise have agreed to pay Sullivan as a royalty.

His health again gave him anxiety in mid-April. On the 14th he

felt pain coming on about 2.30 a.m. when it got very violent. I called up the servants. Louis went for Dr Lynch. He did not arrive till 6. My agony all that time was intense – hypodermic injection and hot flannels gave me relief at last – quarter to 7!

He was well enough two days later to get up from his bed and attend the first performance of *Nadeshda*, the new opera by Arthur Goring Thomas, at Drury Lane Theatre. (Typically, his diary makes no comment on qualities of the work or its performance.) Home by midnight, he did not manage to sleep till after 5 a.m.

But this time he did not seek a 'cure' abroad. Another, sadder errand beckoned him. On 21 January a telegram from Charlotte's brother William Lacy in Los Angeles had arrived at 4 a.m.: 'Charlotte dying: cannot live much longer'. 'Those poor little children!' Sullivan exclaimed to himself in his diary. His nieces and nephews would have the kindly Lacy to turn to, but no one else. A further telegram announced Charlotte's death on 29 January. In a letter Sullivan advised Lacy against his proposal to bring the family to England: America would offer them better social opportunities and 'Amy and Florence are old enough to guide and look after the others'. Instead Sullivan undertook to visit them in May. He had never stopped sending a yearly allowance of £300 (on top of a lump sum of £2,000) to Charlotte, and had sent a further £200 to meet the expenses of her final illness.

A letter from Lacy must have gone straight to his heart. It confirmed his own assessment of the inadequacy of Hutchinson ('Ben'), whose first child Charlotte had but recently borne.

[2 February 1885]

Dear Arthur,

Of course the death of our dear sister has been a sad blow to you and I am not going to write a letter of condolence. I know how you must feel. I know how deeply it has affected me and how everyone who knew her loved her and with all her faults she was the dearest, best and most lovable woman that ever lived and she died a beautiful and lovely death. I was with her a great deal during her last illness and how patient and kind she was during her long suffering, so good, always greeting me with a smile and never complaining. She had a perfect and abiding faith and not the least fear of death. We took the sacrament together with Amy and Florence and Ben [her two eldest daughters and her husband] a few days before she died and she told me she was perfectly happy. She shortly afterwards became delirious and remained so until the day of her death when she became insensible and did not again rally. Some two weeks before she died and from that time until she became unconscious, she imagined Fred [Sullivan's brother, her first husband] was with her. She would sometimes call him, and often mistake Ben and called him Fred. Amy and Florence are the bravest and best of girls. I never in my life saw so much devotion and care as these two girls gave to their mother. During all her long illness one of them was *never* absent from her room . . .

I wired you today that I intended to take the children to England to you and ask you to answer if it was right for me to do so. I have not received your answer but I think it best to write and tell you my reasons for wishing to do this. I telegraphed because I thought it would give you time to think over it as I intend to do nothing that does not meet with your entire approval and by the time you get this letter you will be able to decide quickly what I had better do, and if you then wish me to bring them I can do so on any day on receipt of a message to that effect. Now I want you to understand that I do not wish to shirk my responsibility in this matter. I want to do what is right and intend to do so if possible. They have a comfortable home here and I think like living here very well, but they have lost their great friend and counsellor and who can replace her here? It is their future life that I am thinking about and it is impossible for them, left alone as they are, to receive that amount of care and attention to all the small details of life that they require.

Ben has decided to return to England and will take the baby with him and I think it is as well that he should separate from them now if he wishes to do so. He has been good and kind and most attentive and patient nurse, is honest and good, but I suppose you know him well enough to understand that he is not capable of taking charge of this family and utterly unfit to lead and advise them. Besides he tells me that he is afraid to undertake the responsibility of doing this and would rather go back to his father. Of course you know they must have someone to take charge of the house, someone whom they know and love and respect. If they stay here they will have *no one* for I do not count in the matter at all – only to say that I will do all that man can do for these dear children, but I am not fitted for it. And while I love them as much as I do my own children and am willing to do all I can to make their life happy, we should always be in the position of occupying separate houses and having a separate family. We are only human and little things might occur – small jealousies crop up and perhaps cause an estrangement between them and my own family . . .

I tell you, Arthur, that I have thought over this night and day and when I knew that our poor darling was to be taken from us this problem confronted me, I asked Charlotte about it and she said I was to do whatever I thought best but to do nothing that did not meet with your unqualified sanction and approval. I will do whatever you think I can best . . .

I will say nothing about business in this letter but will leave that either to a personal interview or a future letter. I will add that if you can spare the time to come over here, I should like it very much. I do not want to see England *any more* and you could judge better for yourself if my stewardship has been a faithful one.

Very truly yours,
William Lacy

Sullivan deferred his American trip from May to June, probably so that it would also enable him to participate in D'Oyly Carte's New York launching of *The Mikado*. Before then there was other work to be done. Obliging his old friend Grove, Sullivan did a session of examining at the Royal College of Music, reporting on 30 April that 'Madame [Arabella] Goddard's pupils played octaves with a stiff wrist – this is going back to muzzle-loading rifles'.

There were four more Philharmonic concerts at St James's Hall that season, one of them historic. Dvořák's Symphony in D, opus 60 (at that time known as no. 1) had been acclaimed in London performances by Manns at the Crystal Palace in March 1881 and by Richter two months later. Now on 22 April 1885 the composer himself conducted the first performance of his Symphony in D minor, opus 70 ('no. 2'), commissioned by the Society. It was an occasion of conspicuous success. Dvořák was feted by London musicians and his meetings with Sullivan can hardly have been confined to this concert or their later joint appearance (see the programme for 6 May, below). Yet no record of their acquaintance apparently survives on either side. Did jealousy of foreigners overcome Sullivan's natural sociability?

The Serenade by Thomas Wingham (1846–93), who was to leave no lasting reputation, was the sole new British work admitted that season by the Philharmonic committee.

Third Concert, 26 March 1885

Joseph Joachim, violin; Giovanni Bottesini, double-bass

Symphony no. 2 in C	Schumann
Sextet, 'Sola, sola' (*Don Giovanni*)	Mozart
Violin Concerto in D	Brahms
Serenade for orchestra	Thomas Wingham
Elegy and Tarantella for solo double-bass	Bottesini
Septet, 'O gracious power' (*La Reine de Saba*)	Gounod
Overture, 'Chevy Chase'	G. A. Macfarren

Fourth Concert, 22 April 1885

Clotilde Kleeberg, piano; Marie Etherington, soprano; Edward Lloyd, tenor

Overture, 'Faust'	Spohr
Konzertstück for piano and orchestra	Weber
Duet, 'How sweet the moonlight' (*Kenilworth*)	Sullivan
Overture, 'Leonora' no. 1	Beethoven
Symphony in D minor	Dvořák
Prize Song (*Die Meistersinger*)	Wagner
Overture, 'Don Giovanni'	Mozart

Fifth Concert, 6 May 1885

Franz Rummel, piano; Carlotta Elliott, soprano

Overture, 'The Wood-Nymphs'	Sterndale Bennett
Adagio and 'Queen Mab' Scherzo from *Roméo et Juliette*	Berlioz
Aria, 'Wie nahte mir der Schlummer' (*Der Freischütz*)	Weber
Piano concerto in G (*conducted by the composer*)	Dvořák

Symphony no. 5 in C minor	Beethoven
Aria, 'There's a bower of roses' (*The Veiled Prophet of Khorassan*	Stanford
Piano solos: Nocturne in D flat (op. 27) and Polonaise in A flat (op.53)	Chopin
Overture, 'La Sirène'	Auber

Sixth Concert, 20 May 1885

Franz Rummel, piano; Charles Santley, baritone

Overture, 'Der fliegende Holländer'	Wagner
Ode, 'I wish to tune my quiv'ring lyre'	Sullivan
Symphonic poem 'Johanna d'Arc'	Moszkowski
Piano Concerto no. 5	Beethoven
Recit 'O voi del mio poter' and aria 'Sorge, infausta' (*Orlando*)	Handel
Overture, 'Mireille'	Gounod

Moritz Moszkowski (1854–1925) was a German composer who enjoyed considerable popularity at the time. The Sullivan item in the last concert was a curiosity among his songs, a quasi-dramatic scena which Santley (now 51) had commissioned. Reviewing the third concert, *The Times* on 30 March complained that the promised extracts from Berlioz's *Romeo and Juliet* symphony had not been given, whereas the entire work had been performed 'under Mr Cusins's energetic leadership'. This – and the comparison with Cusins, of all people! – was the type of press criticism which Sullivan cited as a reason for his later resignation from the Philharmonic post.

On 7 May, six days before his 43rd birthday, Sullivan held one of his grander parties. The guests included Algernon Mitford, who had advised the composer of *The Mikado* about matters Japanese. Princess Louise and her husband the Marquis of Lorne were the guests of honour, and others present were Lord and Lady Randolph Churchill, Lord and Lady Hothfield, Lady Borthwick, Fanny Ronalds, the Earl of Cork, Colonel Arthur Ellis, and Alfred Rothschild. 'Very good dinner', Sullivan noted in a diary entry which divulges the standard to which he maintained his apartment. 'Table decor: mass of yellow tulips, violet boutonnières, Worcester service, Sèvres dessert – ice plate of latter broke.' Other guests came after dinner and the company were entertained by Edward Lloyd, the pianist Clotilde Kleeberg, the distinguished Welsh harpist John Thomas, the Grossmith brothers and other performers.

Once again a visit to London by Marie van Zandt created friction. The Prince of Wales, whose interest in her had evidently not diminished, indicated that he would like her to sing at another party of Sullivan's on 7 June. Sullivan duly asked her, but to his anger she declined, blaming it on her agent (who himself said the decision was van Zandt's, not his). On 5 June Sullivan had a 'long talk over a cigarette with the Prince of Wales about the van Zandt incident. She is a little fool and has done herself much harm' (*diary*).

Snubbed as he was by the incident, Sullivan nevertheless attended the opening of *Lakmé* on 6 June, noting it simply as 'great success for van Zandt'. At his flat next evening the 12 who sat down to dinner included not only the Prince of Wales, the Duke of Edinburgh and the French Ambassador (French despite his name, William Henry Waddington) but Sir Henry Irving and Fanny Ronalds. 'Decorations – bed of arums [lilies]; service – Worcester, Sèvres – some of latter missing'.

As usual there was a larger company of guests (56) who arrived after dinner, entertainment being provided by a quartet of stars: the soprano Albani, the contralto Antoinette Sterling, the tenor Carpi, and the baritone (also composer and conductor) Georg Henschel. Sullivan moreover provided something else, as his diary noted:

'Three little maids' from the Savoy sang their trio and the quartet in costume. Compressed version of *Cox and Box* by Arthur Cecil, [George] Grossmith and [Rutland] Barrington. Prince went at 10 minutes to 3. Everyone said the party was a brilliant success.

Carpi and Grossmith, along with the distinguished Spanish violinist Pablo Sarasate and the American soprano who called herself Emma Nevada, also performed 'under my direction' (as the Diary puts it) at the Prince of Wales's dinner which Sullivan attended at Marlborough house on 14 June. Sullivan kept the menu, the extent and layout of which is typical of banqueting in such circles. Perhaps the mistakes in French (*chaux-froix* for *chauds-froids* [of quails], and a singular *poulet* followed by a plural *nouveaux*) were typical also:

> Consommé printanière
> Purée de pois verts
> Whitebait
> Saumon à l'épluche
> Filets de turbot au vin blanc
> Côtelettes d'agneau
> Chaux-froix de cailles
> Bœuf rôti
> Poulet nouveaux
> Asperges
> Plum pudding
> Timbale gauffres à la crême
> Pailles au fromage
> Glaces de fraises

Two days before, he had dined at Alfred Rothschild's and accompanied Christine Nilsson's singing. To undertake such a performance for friends would no doubt be a pleasure, but woe betide the casual cadger. Algernon Mitford was later to write in his memoirs:

Arthur Sullivan once told me how at an evening party the hostess went up to him and said: 'Oh! Sir Arthur, it would be so sweet of you if you would play us something'. The answer was characteristic: 'My dear lady, there is John Millais. If he will sit down and make a sketch for you, I will play. He has been painting all day, I have been working at music all day, so we are both in the same boat.'

Such was the social round on which he now turned his back in departing for the United States on Saturday 20 June, accompanied by his new manservant, Louis Jaeger. A more solemn engagement had been the funeral (9 June 1885) of Sir Julius Benedict, who had led an active musical life in England for 50 years. On the same evening he was present at an 'American concert' in St James's Hall – a charity event, in aid of the National Relief Fund for Sick and Wounded British Soldiers. (General Gordon and his forces at Khartoum had been slaughtered in the previous January and fighting in the Sudan continued.) The concert, in which Fanny Ronalds's organizing role may be inferred, was attended not only by the Prince and Princess of Wales but by Princesses Louise, Victoria and Maud.

His journey would take him away from London (though not from Fanny Ronalds) for almost three and a half months. Its driving force was solicitude for Fred's family: professional interest was to occupy him only at the end. But business pursued him almost up to the moment of the ship's departure from Liverpool:

Up at 5.30. Herbert went with Louis to [Euston] Station at 6.15. Said goodbye to Delphine [maid] and Tommy [dog], both very sad. Left Euston at 7.30 with Smythe [his secretary]. Carte joined us and came [in the train] as far as Rugby and then returned to London, taking a letter to L.W. from me. Arrived Liverpool 12.40. Went with Smythe to buy a hat and rug. Gunn [D'Oyly Carte company manager] came on from Manchester, lunched with me at hotel, and with Smythe accompanied me on the tender to the ship *Etruria*. Blowing hard and very wet and cold. I said goodbye and we sailed at 4 p.m.

22 To California

Two months before, his secretary had inquired on Sullivan's behalf whether his life-insurance company would require a modification of his policy, since he was to travel as far as Los Angeles. The insurance company's reaction can be deduced from Smythe's further letter (17 April 1885):

I am somewhat astonished that you cannot find Los Angeles, California, which is one of the most important places *in the United States*. I have not the time to spare to look up the latitude and longitude of Los Angeles, but it is near San Francisco – about 200 miles distant.

Perhaps the insurance company's ignorance may be excused, since in 1895 the *Los Angeles Herald* itself was to write that, ten years before, 'the major part of our [U.S.] population hardly knew there was such a town as Los Angeles on the Pacific end of the United States'. In the 1880s the city developed at an explosive pace: land-values rose from $100 to $1,500 an acre and the population quadrupled to over 50,000 in 1890. The westward migration in search of land was facilitated by the furious competition between the newly opened Santa Fe Railroad to the Pacific coast and the earlier Southern Pacific Railroad. At one time an outward ticket from Kansas City to San Francisco (over 2,000 miles) could be had for one dollar. The wealthier traveller could be assured of comfort and service, with sleeping-cars (ahead of British usage), dining-cars and parlour-cars to help cover the vast distances.

As the *Etruria* made its way across the ocean, Sullivan's diary recorded the ship's daily mileage. As usual with the Atlantic crossing, there was a call the day after leaving Liverpool (21 June) at Queenstown (modern Cobh) in southern Ireland, where he 'received letters from L. (2), Dicey, Fanny. Sent telegrams to Carte, Fanny, L.' 'Fanny' refers to Mrs Ronalds's daughter ('Fanette'), now Mrs Ritchie; Fanny Ronalds herself is 'L.'. The journey was scheduled to take seven days, but the intended disembarkation in New York on Sunday 28 June was held up by thick fog in stifling weather. 'Passengers sang hymns in the music-room in the evening. I accompanied some of them.'

Next day the fog lifted, and the passengers transferred to a tender for the eight-mile transfer to Customs House where 'I waited in a private room to avoid the interviewers'. Suydam Grant was among those to greet him. Sullivan's quarters were at the Brunswick Hotel, familiar to him from his 1879 visit, but on the day of his arrival he 'dressed and dined at 23rd Street [the Beach Grants' house] with Suydam, Mrs Grant and Adèle. Poor little Edith very ill, just recovering from scarlet fever. Had a drink at Delmonico's with Suydam, then to bed.' Adèle and Edith were the Beach Grants' daughters. Domesticity was evidently very welcome to him and the fashionable restaurant called Delmonico's (or 'Del's') at 56 Beaver St was to be a favourite rendezvous.

New York had seen significant changes since his last visit. The Brooklyn Bridge now linked Brooklyn to Manhattan Island. In October 1883 the Metropolitan Opera had been set up in rivalry to the old Academy of Music. It was not merely a battle of music or managements. The Academy was run by the old New York ruling families, still preserving precedence and exclusiveness. The new house represented the patronage of the new rich, the Vanderbilts and their like. A later chronicler of the city was to see in the Metropolitan Opera 'the passing of social power into new hands, the final defeat of the city's aristocracy by the great capitalists who were masters of banks, railroads, vast industries'.[1] Six months before that opening, the Vanderbilts' costume ball, eclipsing all other events of recent seasons, was thought to have cost its givers and their extravagantly attired guests more than a quarter of a million dollars.

Sullivan had arrived in New York while the Metropolitan Opera was between seasons, but other theatrical life was busy. In operetta the current success was *Nanon*, which he saw at Niblo's Garden Theatre on 1 July: given in English, it was a German operetta with music by Richard Genée and libretto by 'F. Zell' (Camillo Walzel) – the pair who had been joint librettists for Johann Strauss's *A night in Venice* (1883).

Sullivan had learned in London how to 'use' the press. An interview printed in the *New York Herald* (1 July 1885) – which he considered 'admirably done' – bore the heading 'Tuneful knight asks the American public for fair play'. It forcefully made Sullivan's (and his partners') case against James C. Duff's proposed New York production of *The Mikado*. Duff, in London, had offered Carte $750 a week which had been turned down, and Carte had contracted instead with another New York manager, John Stetson, to present the work in authentic form with members of the London company. 'In defiance of our rights', as Sullivan put it, Duff proposed nevertheless to mount his own production – paying nothing to its British proprietors and relying (since he had no access to the unpublished full orchestral score) on someone else's orchestration of the published vocal score.

Sullivan declared himself confident that the US courts would step in to prevent such an infringement of his 'rights', but he was wrong. He and Carte had contrived that the piano arrangement in the vocal score of *The Mikado* should be the work of an American, George Lowell Tracy, who might claim that *his* rights (which he assigned to Carte) were usurped by an unauthorized production. The cunning was to no avail. The act of publication would be held as making the opera freely available. As early as 2 July the *Chicago News* correctly anticipated the legal interpretation:

Sir Arthur Sullivan, who is now in this country and who is represented by the New York press as being a puffy little Englishman not more than four feet high, announces that he intends to prosecute to the full extent of the law every manager who presumes to produce the comic opera of *The Mikado* without Mr John Stetson's permission. We are curious to see how Sir Arthur's racket will pan out in the American courts. It occurs to us that he should have begun his great and glorious work of reform at home. Mr John Stetson paid $5,000 for the right to produce the opera in America. This money was paid to Mr D'Oyle [*sic*] Carte, who is Gilbert and Sullivan's broker. As soon as he got the money Mr D'Oyle Carte made unseemly haste to publish and issue in printed form the libretto and music of the opera – thereby giving to every person in America or elsewhere the legal right to produce the opera when and how he pleased.

The opening of the Carte/Stetson production was scheduled for about 24 August, by which time the composer proposed to have returned to New York from California. As yet, however, nothing required his action, and he evidently felt no pressure to hasten to Charlotte's bereaved family. Passing the time agreeably, he visited Boston (renewing, no doubt, his acquaintance of 1879), and the fashionable summer resort of Newport, Rhode Island. Then, returning to New York, he deferred his transcontinental journey on learning that Geraldine Ulmar was coming to New York to sing for him. This talented American soprano was already under consideration by Sullivan and Carte as a possible Yum-Yum for their New York *Mikado*, and on 11 July he was delighted to find her a good singer and 'a pretty and very intelligent girl' (*diary*). He cabled his satisfaction to Carte.

He had meanwhile heard from Gilbert who, as ever, was the one who propelled the partnership to embark on new work.

I think that something might be done with a story founded on Frankenstein and the monster. Grossmith (as Frankenstein) constructing a monster (Barrington) which he (Grossmith) has to serve, and which entails every possible inconvenience upon him, might make a good plot. What do you think?

It was an idea which, unfortunately perhaps, never blossomed in that form, though the idea of a human being compelled to obey a supernatural power did, in fact, emerge in their next work. Gilbert also gave voice to that suspicion of Carte which was eventually to break forth so disastrously:

I confess I don't feel very keen about Carte. When he thought you would side with him on the management question, he snapped his fingers at me (figuratively) and referred me to our agreement. . . . He owes every penny he possesses to us – and if he has lost, it is because he has been d–d fool enough to send three companies into the provinces, when one would have been ample. . . . It was the same with the *Pirates*, in the States. He sent four companies on the road, when two would have been ample. . . . When *we* manage the theatre for him he succeeds splendidly. When he manages for himself, he fails. Moreover, when he succeeds, he shows a disposition to kick away the ladder by which he has risen.

That 'ladder'! It was a metaphor on which Gilbert's feelings dwelt dangerously. Sullivan never saw Carte's position in such a way.

Sullivan's 3,540–mile journey by train began on 12 July. The scenery, the stops, the food were all subject to much comment in his diary. From New York to San Francisco took 9 days with changes of train at Chicago, Denver and Salt Lake City – at each of which his arrival was publicly awaited. *HMS Pinafore*, particularly, had secured his celebrity. He had a private drawing-room (which provided sleeping accommodation) aboard the 'Chicago Limited' which brought him to Chicago in 25 hours. Arriving at 9 a.m. he took a hotel room in order to change, and was able to drive out, buy a belt and some silk pyjamas and by 12.30 be away on the Chicago, Burlington and Quincy Railroad for the two-day journey to Denver, Colorado. 'At 8.30 [p.m., 13 July] entered Iowa. No liquors allowed to be sold in this state. Shall not dine in Iowa.'

That evening he began on the train a letter to Fanny Ronalds 'Monday 13 July, 7 p.m., just left Galesburg [Illinois]'. Written at first in a shaky hand as the train moved on, it is the sole letter between the two to survive. Near the close is the instruction, 'Give this letter to Smythe', sufficient reason for the lack of intimate expression; then 'God bless you all' [i.e. her parents and Fanette, Reggie being in America], 'Your loving A'. There is no 'Dear . . .', the letter running as follows:

It isn't very easy to write in the train but I will make an effort, and give you an account of myself since I last wrote on Saturday. I shan't write again after I have posted this, as you may have started for this blessed country. I didn't do much on Saturday, and it was very hot and there wasn't much [illegible] and so I kept quiet – dined with Suydam, and came back to bed.

I got your telegram 'all well' which was a great relief to me, as it was so long since I had heard from you. It seems *ages*. I got my tickets changed, and started off Sunday morning at 9 by the Pennsylvania line to Chicago. The Chicago Limited is the best train in America – a very fine road – magnificent scenery through the Alleghenies, and most luxurious in all the arrangements for sleeping, dining, etc. I fraternized on the road with a man I knew, Howard Dickinson, and we get on very well together as he is a very pleasant fellow. His wife is Mrs Fred Post's first cousin.

[Tuesday 14 July]

I found it impossible to write yesterday as the train jolted so awfully – today I shall write a little bit each time the train stops. We got to Chicago yesterday morning at 9 a.m. Then I went up to the Grand Pacific Hotel – large and magnificent – got a bath, had my hair cut, changed my clothes and was of course interviewed by two reporters whilst I was dressing. I drove about the town a little and saw that it was new, handsome, and bustling, and from my point of view utterly uninteresting, then I started again at 12.30 (in my drawing-room, again secured to Denver) and began my journey westward. It was a lovely day, not too hot, and no dust at all. Dickinson and I played écarté, and I tried to write, but in vain, I had a bad headache, and turned in at 10.

The dining car on this line is not so good as on the Pennsylvania Road, and the hours for meals barbaric – Breakfast at 7, dinner from 11.30 to 12.30! and supper 5 to 7. Oh Cadogan Place! Oh Queen's Mansions! what would ye say to this? We have now got beyond the limit of dining cars and have begun to have meals at the eating stations. We have just had what they call a meal at Lincoln, the capital of Nebraska. 'Dinner for one' was my order, and immediately a rather pretty, sharp young girl brought me eight small saucers each containing a mess enough for a baby. Four different vegetables (each smothered in beastly melted butter), two infinitesimal scraps of meat, some cranberry tart, and a sort of chocolate pudding. Before I had settled where I should begin, she brought me three more plates, raspberries, ice cream, and cheese. Out of the 11 dishes I picked about four mouthfuls, and then was on the point of asking for something toothsome to wash it down with, when my little maiden brought me a glass of iced tea! At least she called it tea, but it must have been made from prairie grass. We were in a temperance zone again!

However, Dickinson and I bought a bottle of old Scotch Whisky yesterday at Chicago (fortunate precaution) and a few bottles of Apollinaris. This, with ice which Sam our black attendant gets us, keeps up our spirits and reminds us of our happy, happy homes. It is blazing hot, and we are passing over plains covered with corn but with only a tree here and there to be seen. It is not the prairies proper, but it is very close to them. I suppose we shall come to a bit of real prairie soon. I wish I could see a buffalo. Denver, I am told is beautiful – so I shall stop a day there for rest (we are due at 7 tomorrow morning) and present the letter Lord Cork gave me to a Mr Duff. I think I shall also stop a day at Colorado Springs (close to Denver) in order to see Manitou, the Garden of the Gods [a spectacular beauty spot and spa]. How far away I am from you all! I wish I knew what you were doing. Here is a station – Dorchester, 83 miles beyond Plattsmouth in the middle of a burning hot plain – no shade anywhere – 5000 miles from you, I am going 2000 miles further and then to think that I have got to get all the way back again to see you. No short cuts, all over the same ground again. I am quite homesick already, and long to [be] back in my comfy little study again. We are stopping at every little shanty kind of station that we go by. We take 42 hours to go from Chicago to Denver and we might do it in 26 or 30 easily if they would run expresses. But I suppose it wouldn't pay. It is as bad as travelling in Germany. If I can post this today, it will get to New York in time for Saturday's steamer, I think, so I will finish now. Mind you cable me the date of your departure from England get Smythe to cable to 'Pinafore New York' – it will be delivered to Suydam who will *retelegraph* it on to me wherever I am. This saves time and money. Give this letter to Smythe. God bless you all . . .

At Denver, Colorado, high in the mountains, he spent a day and night but did not, in fact, stop at Colorado Springs. He visited both Denver's opera house and its cathedral, where he played the organ for an hour 'to a small and select audience' (*diary*). 'Some damned brute' at the hotel smashed his beloved travelling-desk to pieces. 'It is destroyed for ever – I am mad!' he confided to his diary (16 July) as the journey continued by the narrow-gauge Denver and Rio Grande Railroad in intense heat. The admonition to 'drink iced tea' (the last two words double-underlined) was scrawled, apparently as a reminder, on one of the interleaved blotting-pages of the diary.

At Salt Lake City he bought a replacement for his travelling-desk and played on the organ ('a really very good instrument') at the Mormon Tabernacle – where Bicknell Young, who had met him by arrangement and become his host for the day, sang *The Lost Chord*.[2] They took a local train to bathe in the salt lake ('too buoyant to swim in comfortably') and Sullivan went 'dead tired' to bed at the Continental Hotel. He had time next day (Sunday 19 July) to attend the 2 p.m. service at the Mormon Tabernacle, since it was not until 5.30 that the train for San Francisco left via Reno, Nevada. A whole day was spent crossing Nevada, with early breakfast on Tuesday 21 July at Sacramento in northern California before arrival at San Francisco at 11.10. Here he put up at Baldwin's Hotel. An interview in the *San Francisco Chronicle* next day, although published in rotund prose which indicates a literary rewriting on the reporter's part, is revealing of Sullivan's reputation and ambitions. After claiming that he and Gilbert had been surprised that so English a piece as *HMS Pinafore* should have won such success in America, he commented:

If [such works] are entitled to any claim as compositions, I rely entirely on the underlying vein of seriousness which runs through all my operas. In the composition of the scores I adhered to the principles of art which I had learned in the production of more solid works, and no musician who analyses the score of those light operas will fail to find the evidence of seriousness and solidity pointed out.

It is true, then, that you place more dependence on your oratorios, symphonies and hymns as musical works than on your light operas?

It is. My sacred music is that on which I base my reputation as a composer. These works are the offspring of my liveliest fancy, the children of my greatest strength, the products of my most earnest thought and most incessant toil.

To what fact do you attribute the decadence of the Italian school of opera?

The Italian school is dead from its own inherent defects. The works of Verdi, Bellini, Rossini and Mercadante are never sung as is necessary to bring forth what merit is in the composition. The great fault of these great composers was that they wrote for extraordinary voices. As these voices no longer exist, the works cannot be represented as they should. The silver tones of Mario, the godlike strains of Sontag [Henriette Sontag (1806–54), a soprano he had never heard], the divine tones of Grisi, live only as memories. The success of the Italian operas depended upon the wonderful voices of those who sang them. Besides, in analysing the Italian grand opera, you will find that in a great many cases the most widely divergent emotions and the most opposite sentiment were expressed in the same manner, and depended entirely on the singer and his dramatic ability to express the true passion.

What do I think of the Wagnerian episode? I will tell you. Wagner's success was greatly due to his personal influence, his iron will and his untiring industry. His chief merit lies in having shown to the musical world the possibilities of operatic music. He has shown us the combination of the drama and the opera, but deviated from his theory or was at fault in practice in concentrating all dramatic effects in the orchestral portions of his work, and subordinating the stage and its action to the orchestra. He has shown us a picture that can be painted, but has not painted it himself.

What, then, is the opera of the future?

Oh, your question suggests possibilities of which all true musicians dream, and reveals a vision which seems near and enchanting, but which is far off. The opera of the future is a compromise. I have thought and worked and toiled and dreamt of it. Not the French school, with gaudy and tinsel tunes, its lambent lights and shades, its theatrical effects and clap-trap, not the Wagnerian school, with its sombreness and heavy ear-splitting airs, with its mysticism and unreal sentiment; not the Italian school, with its fantastic airs and *fioriture* and far-fetched effects. It is a compromise between these three – a sort of eclectic school, a selection of the merits of each one. I myself will make an attempt to produce a grand opera of this new school.

Yes, it will be an historical work, and it is the dream of my life. I do not believe in operas based on gods and myths. That is the fault of the German school. It is metaphysical music – it is philosophy. What we want are plots that give rise to characters of flesh and blood, with human emotions and human passions. Music should speak to the heart, and not to the head. Such a work as I contemplate will take some time.

He did not immediately hurry from San Francisco (a larger, more developed city in those days than Los Angeles). He took a night trip to Chinatown

with a detective, Devitt, a great character. Saw the [Chinese] theatre and went into all the vilest dens – got home at 1.30.

The theatrical producer Augustin Daly (1838–99) had a company performing in San Francisco in his own recent play *Dollars and Sense* and next day Daly's celebrated leading lady, Ada Rehan (1860–1916), joined Sullivan and others in a visit to the city's military area – including Alcatraz Island, not yet a civil prison. On Friday 24 July the overnight train from San Francisco took him 482 miles south to Los Angeles, where his niece Florry (as the diary calls her) and William Lacy met him at the station. A letter from Fanny Ronalds awaited him, as well as one from Smythe, and he 'wired to Cadogan Place for news' (*diary*). Two days earlier the *Los Angeles Times* had prefigured his arrival with what was evidently already recognizable as a quotation.

Sir Arthur Sullivan, composer of *Pinafore* and *Patience*, arrived in San Francisco yesterday and expects to visit Los Angeles in a few days. He will find us sober men and true, and attentive to our duty.

Florence was now 19 years old, Amy just turned 22, and the youngest surviving daughter, Maude ('Cissie'), 15. Sullivan's younger nephews, Frederic Richard, George and William, are curiously not mentioned at this point in the diary. Because Cissie had a slight attack of scarlatina it was judged better for Sullivan to stay at William Lacy's at first. He moved on 1 August to 'the children's house on the hill', as he called it in his diary. (It was on Old Mission Road, at the back of the County Hospital.) The children were evidently in good shape but their stepfather Hutchinson 'does nothing – never goes out, and looks miserable'. Hutchinson's name appeared in the current city directory as 'Captain, retired' but without occupation; Lacy was listed as cashier of the First National Bank and a partner in the Lacy and Viereck Hardware Co. where the eldest of his six children, also called William, worked as a salesman.

A visit was dutifully paid to Charlotte's grave, but otherwise there was much pleasant social intercourse with the Lacys and with other citizens (including the mayor) who made themselves agreeable. 'Went to a Mexican breakfast, 12 noon. Extraordinary food – all flavourless', runs a diary entry on 22 August. The *Los Angeles Times* reported that the famous composer had 'dropped in for a little chat' but instead of an interview the editor contented himself with reprinting the San Francisco article (see above). Sullivan noted the intense heat, rising on 3 August to 102°F (nearly 40°C), though there was a refreshing overnight visit to a Mr Griffiths' house at 'nice cool Santa Monica', nearby.

A much more strenuous trip lasting nine days was the highlight of his reunion with the family. In the company of Amy and Florence, and also of William Lacy and his eldest daughter Sophy, Sullivan set out on Tuesday 4 August 1885 for the Yosemite Valley in northern California. That spectacular mountain region, containing America's highest waterfall and the famous giant trees exceeding 80 feet in circumference, had already become a state park and since 1874 had been accessible in the relative comfort of a stage-coach from the rail-head. The normal point of origin for the journey was (and is) San Francisco but Sullivan's party set themselves the more distant and arduous route from Los Angeles. They began with a 14-hour rail journey to Madera, then at 5.20 a.m. after a sleepless night they started off in their six-horse stage coach. The composer's diary bears the record: 'Over the broiling plains and up the hills to the Sierra Nevada – miserable journey. At Fresno Flat we go into the woods, and it became cooler and more enjoyable.' After a further whole-day drive they arrived, at 7.30 p.m., at Clark's

Station, a staging stop where this and two other routes converged, at a point now known as Wawona.[3] A description of the scene published in 1888 must have applied:

The very instant the bridge is crossed, on the way to the hotel, the whole place seems bristling with business, and business energy. Conveyances of all kinds, from a sulky to whole rows of passenger coaches, capable of carrying from one to eighteen or twenty persons each, at a load, come into sight. From some the horses are just being taken out, while others are being hitched up. Hay and grain wagons; freight teams coming and going; horses with or without harness; stables for a hundred animals; blacksmiths' shops, carriage and paint shops, laundries and other buildings, look at us from as many different stand-points. That cozy-looking structure on our left is Mr Thos. Hill's studio; but that which now most claims our attention, and invites our sympathies, is the commodious and cheery, yet stately edifice in front known as the Wawona Hotel . . .

After dinner the first place generally visited is Hill's Studio. Here will be found quite a number of beautiful gems of art, the merits of which are assured from the fact that Mr Thos. Hill took the first medal for landscape-painting at the Centennial Exposition of 1876, and also the Temple Medal of the Academy of Fine Arts, of Philadelphia, for 1884, with numerous others . . .

Sullivan, as his diary records, was thankful

to find such a nice, clean, comfortable hotel. Mr Washburn, proprietor, showed us great attention. We went to bed early, and slept soundly. Thirty hours travelling from Los Angeles without sleep or rest, in broiling heat and smothering dust!

Next day was fine and not too hot: pottered about, and paddled our feet in the stream. After lunch, drove out to Mariposa to see the Big Trees. They are wonderful. Saw a magnificent one by the roadside and begged Mr [Walter E.] Dennison, the guardian, to name it after me. Left at 2.30. Home again at 6. The drive (all through forest) was most beautiful. After dinner we all went into Mr Hill the artist's studio, looked at the pictures, and then danced! In the quadrilles a driver (Stevens) 'called' the figures and a local fiddler (Wright) was the orchestra. All very primitive and enjoyable. Saw a forest fire on top of the mountain. Caught cold in the night.

Though plagued by toothache, Sullivan did not let it impair his enjoyment. In a little chapel at a memorial service for President U. S. Grant (the Civil War hero had died on 23 July) he played the harmonium and endured 'an hour's prosy twaddle' from the officiating minister. Sullivan was charmed by two 'chipmonks' (as he spelt them at first) which were caught for him at a cost of $5 and which he determined to take home to England. One at least he succeeded at getting as far as Los Angeles, where it was killed by a cat. Having returned there on 13 August he found that professional demands were pressing in: indeed even at Madera, on the way back from Yosemite, a telegram from Carte awaited him.

Events in New York had moved. John Stetson, the American manager who was to present Carte's company in New York, now wished to advance the opening night of *The Mikado* from 24 August (by which date Sullivan had undertaken to be available) to 20th. Sullivan had to wire Carte that he could not be present in time. When Carte himself arrived in New York (on 17 August) the day was put still further forward to Wednesday 19 August – obviously because Duff's 'pirate' production seemed likely to open on the 20th. The law would not prohibit it. A US circuit court had declared: 'It must be held that by publication of the whole opera, except the instrumental parts, the authors abandoned the entire dramatic property in their work to the public.' Another manager, Sydney Rosenfeld, had already produced the piece in Chicago on 6 July at the Grand Opera House (and there had been a preceding production, apparently quite inadequate, at the Museum Theatre in the same city on 30 June).

So Carte's *Mikado* – that is, the version carrying the sanction of composer and librettist – was heard in New York (at the Fifth Avenue Theatre) on 19 August while Sullivan and Gilbert were respectively in Los Angeles and London, each some 3,000 miles away in contrary directions.

This time (in an arrangement unlike that of 1879) Carte presented not just a few principal singers but a complete company with chorus. They had travelled on the steamship *Aurania* under assumed names (Carte was 'Mr Chapman') so that Duff should not be forewarned by cable that the troupe was on its way. Alfred Cellier, who had travelled with them, conducted *The Mikado* on its opening night. Geraldine Ulmar – who must have learnt her music in advance and been quickly coached in the action – was 'a most graceful and winning Yum-Yum', according to the *New York Herald*. Despite 'some poor singing and some rather feeble clowning' (Grossmith had not come with the company!) the *Herald* critic considered the piece and its execution a complete success: 'This was the *Mikado* of the renowned *Pinafore* dynasty, and the commencement of his glorious reign was hailed with every token of enthusiasm.'

Duff's production, prudently deferred until five days later, was generally considered inferior in what it did as well as in what it lacked – Sullivan's orchestration and Gilbert's stage direction. Financially, Carte and his collaborators had been frustrated in their more ambitious aims. Hindsight suggests, however, that (as in the case of *HMS Pinafore*) Carte's failure to monopolize the stage in America actually benefited his enterprise in the long run because the rival productions served to heighten public interest in the opera itself. The publicity engendered by the legal wrangles must itself have prodigiously served to excite interest in the piece, even when the reports were accompanied by derogatory remarks about the claims of 'this fa-la-la dude' as the *Chicago News* characterized Sullivan on 22 September 1885.

Just too late for Carte's opening, Fanny Ronalds arrived in New York on 22 August, having crossed the Atlantic in the *Etruria*. An exchange of telegrams took place between her and Sullivan, still in California. It was not until a week later that he set off via San Francisco for New York, satisfied that the affairs of his brother's family were in good order. A Mrs Onstott had been prevailed to go and live with them as a companion-housekeeper. As for the wretched Hutchinson, he had been persuaded to go back to his relatives in England with his and Charlotte's baby (who died a few weeks later).

As the composer's diary noted, 'Amy, Flo and Cissie' came, with the Lacys, to see their uncle off at the station. He had a drawing-room for the overnight journey to San Francisco. He stayed at the Occidental Hotel there for three days, renewed old acquaintances, and auditioned a 19-year-old local soprano – 'thin, metallic but brilliant voice; great facility, but not much education'. This was Sybil Sanderson, who was to inspire both Massenet and Saint-Saëns to write operas for her. She became much more a favourite in France than in America. In San Francisco he paid out $281.50 for his rail fare to New York (including a drawing-room as far as Ogden, Utah) and $53 for his hotel bill, then entrained for a route which in comparison with his outward journey was more northerly and quicker (6 instead of 9 days, without overnight stops).

After Ogden, the railway led to Green River, Wyoming where Sullivan was shocked at the sight of soldiers out in force after a massacre of Chinese construction labourers by resentful whites. 'The Christians burnt the Chinese encampment as well,' drily noted the composer of *Onward Christian Soldiers*. Then his journey took him through the Rockies to Laramie and Cheyenne (Wyoming), North Platte and Omaha (Nebraska), and through Burlington (Iowa) to Chicago. Here, on 8 September, there was once again the welcome luxury of a bath at the Grand Pacific Hotel, followed by a ride in the luxurious 'Chicago Limited' train, bringing him to New York on the evening of 9 September. D'Oyly Carte had journeyed out from New York to meet Sullivan's train at Jersey City and give him companionship on the last section of the trip – by ferry across the Hudson River.

Three weeks before, on 17 August, the *New York Herald* had mentioned Gilbert's name in humorously editorializing on the marriage of Lord Coleridge, England's Lord Chief Justice, to a girl who had been placed under his 'protection': his conduct had been like that of 'the presiding officer in Mr Gilbert's operetta, *Trial by Jury*'. Sullivan had indeed returned to a city where his and Gilbert's names were household words, and *The Mikado* the toast of the town. Having escorted Sullivan to the Brunswick Hotel, Carte whisked him off to see at least part of *The Mikado* and to note the full audience. The two then joined Suydam Grant for supper at Delmonico's. Next evening the composer 'sat through the whole of the opera', as his diary noted. He was in harness again.

Fanny Ronalds had not remained in New York: she was in Chicopee, Mass., presumably visiting friends or members of her family. But she and Arthur Sullivan kept in touch by telegram and on 17 September they greeted each other in New York after their long separation. Carte – with Helen Lenoir, now acting as manager of his New York office – meanwhile prepared to make profitable use of the composer's presence. On Thursday 24 September Sullivan would conduct a special performance of *The Mikado* – at increased seat-prices. He had two long rehearsals with an orchestra augmented to 40 players.

Called at 78 [78 Irving Place, where Fanny Ronalds was living]. Conducted gala performance of *The Mikado* at the theatre. House crammed with a fashionable audience. Bouquets given to all the ladies. Very bright and spirited performance – great enthusiasm, and I had to make a speech. Big supper at Del's afterwards given by Suydam.

The speech, however, was not spontaneous – nor was it to the liking of the reporter for the *New York Times*:

Sir Arthur has grown a trifle stouter since his last visit to the United States, and his somewhat woolly hair has grown a little thinner, but his general appearance has undergone no great change, and his air betokens prosperity and contentment, with an occasional tendency to petulance. His magnetism and authority as a conductor were not shown on the occasion under notice, but it will be conceded that they had a slender chance of asserting themselves when the well drilled condition of the band and singers is taken into account . . .

The effect of Sir Arthur's remarks would have been happier had he confined himself to returning thanks for the public's reception on the work just performed, and to expressing his gratification that the 'authorized version' of *The Mikado* had met with the success it merited. The first part of the address – which was evidently a studied effort, for once, when the speaker's memory failed him, he glanced at a card upon which the heads of his discourse must have been written – was in the right vein, and was as graceful in form as it was becoming in spirit. Its second half was less felicitous, and its tone, which recalled the cry of the proverbial fowl on its proverbial platform, and its setting, in which the hope was uttered that art works should have the same protection as newly invented 'beer taps', together with an assumed indignation at the proceedings of other persons, the indignation finding relief in hasty substitutions of civil words for intended vigorous terms, wrought a rather unpleasant impression. Mr W. S. Gilbert no doubt harbours the same opinion as his co-labourer, but his literary judgement would have counselled him to defer their publication until a more suitable opportunity, and, above all, to avoid the inelegant comparisons resorted to by Sir Arthur. Perhaps, however, if Mr Gilbert were let loose in the orchestra he would play greater havoc than Sir Arthur Sullivan on the rostrum.

On 14 September he went to Wallach's Theatre in New York to see Johann Strauss's *Die Fledermaus*. On 6 October he was in Philadelphia where a touring company under Carte's management had already opened, and saw its performance of *The Mikado*. On 6 October the diary entry 'Went to 78' is followed by the tick of gratification. Carte himself, as always, was looking ahead to whatever should be the collaborators' next work. He and Helen Lenoir called on Sullivan to read over the new plot which Gilbert had sent: it was the piece which was eventually to be christened *Ruddygore* (and later re-spelt). On 14 October Sullivan and Carte embarked for home on the north German Lloyd liner *Eros*. Benjamin Hutchinson from Los Angeles was also aboard – but, one may surmise, not much in Sullivan's company. A more congenial fellow-passenger must have been Josephine Findlay, a young singer who was to be chosen to play the role of Zorah (chief bridesmaid) in the new opera.

They landed on 22 October not at Liverpool but at Southampton. Sullivan's servant Louis Jaeger, who had been with him throughout his journey, was of immediate use. 'Left Louis to look after luggage, went and had a *fried sole* and a bottle of pop [champagne] at the RY [Royal York] Hotel with D'Oyly and Miss Findlay.' And so to London: 'Oh, the delight of getting home again. The house looked lovely, so clean and bright.[4] Dined with the two old people [Fanny Ronalds's parents, Mr and Mrs Carter] at Cadogan Place.'

Fanny Ronalds herself did not sail from New York until 24 October. On 1 November Sullivan met her from the ship *Emma* at Liverpool, and eight days later made a reference in his diary to his previous entries concerning that far-off

Californian trip: 'Had large tooth (see Yosemite Valley) extracted by Longhurst with laughing gas.'

Shortly after his return from America Sullivan found the opportunity to spend a few days in Paris, travelling on 20 November in the company of Mrs Beach Grant and her daughter Adèle. (They were returning from a visit to London.) Three days later, Dicey joined him there. The trip seems to have had no professional reason behind it, but it gave Sullivan the opportunity to engage two new servants. The chef arrived in London a few weeks later but did not last long: 'Chef (Léon) drunk last night. Glad he is going' (*diary*, 1 January 1886). On 15 December 'Clotilde Racquet entered my service as kitchen-maid'. Belgian by origin, she was to stay in his service until he died – as was Louis Jaeger. Despite the stormy temper which was often to be chronicled in the diary, Clotilde established a rare *rapport* with Arthur Sullivan, becoming not only his house-keeper, but his adviser and confidante.

His reunion with his kin in California and his talks with Lacy had not, unfortunately, eventuated in a final untangling of Charlotte's estate. Early in the new year, on receipt of a cable from Lacy, he sent $5,000 to pay the debts on the estate by buying the children's house and received a grateful letter from Lacy written on 20 February 1886:

I cannot tell you how much I appreciate your great goodness and kindness of heart and I do look forward to some day and I hope not far distant when I shall again see you and clasp your dear hand again. You speak of my *home* troubles. They are as bad as ever and I am sorry to say will never be better as long as that woman lives [his wife, presumably!], but I have always done my duty and so long as life lasts shall continue to do so. But it takes all the sunshine out of my life . . .

Business is going to the devil – I have been trying all I can to keep things together, but it does not pay of course. I don't mean to say we are going to lose all our money but we will have to lose some. But you know the old saying 'a silver lining to every cloud' and I can see a bright ray of sunshine ahead. It is *Oil* – yes, I think we have no doubt now one of the best properties in California. . . . Our last well is two feet deep and will yield an average of 25 barrels per day. We are well under way with another which by all present indications will be much better. We have contracted with the Pacific Coast Oil Company to take all our oil at the railroad station and now are engaged in putting up tanks and laying pipes to convey the oil and I think before three months are over we shall be producing 75 or 100 barrels per day which will do very well at the dollar and a half per barrel . . .

I have paid the taxes and you will own the house and land in fee simple and all the furnishings, etc. And I want you to let them [the children] know it. It will do them good to let them thoroughly understand that they are *entirely* dependent upon you for all and perhaps deter some of those miserable fortune-hunters from seeking to marry them on account of their supposed fortune . . .

Sullivan's generosity to 'his' American family – to be measured in thousands of pounds – was remarkable in its degree of selflessness. It could give him little sense of visible satisfaction, nor was it probably known to any of his London circle except Herbert. His nephews and nieces seem to have accepted his subvention as a matter of course, and Lacy's gratitude was perhaps more than he received from all the rest. The responsibilities he was shouldering were not primarily those of his long-dead brother but those of Charlotte's feckless second husband, Benjamin Hutchinson. His indignation on being further pressed on Hutchinson's behalf by the latter's father, the Rev. B. Hutchinson, was understandable. The importunate clergyman was reminded in return that he (Sullivan) had been sending Charlotte $500 yearly: 'Your son has never since [the marriage] contributed one penny towards his, his wife's or her children's support . . .'

Later the elder Hutchinson was warned that unless the importunities ceased, solicitors would be instructed 'to recover from your son the large sum which he legally owes me'.

Arthur Sullivan would never again see any of his 'Californian' nephews and nieces. Florence was to predecease him.

23 Triple Assignment

WHILE Sullivan had been in California, his partner had kept a sharp eye – as always – on the Savoy box office. *The Mikado* was maintaining its popularity, and on his return Sullivan found a letter from Gilbert awaiting him. The new libretto was making progress.

I understood from Carte that you would not return until November, unless the business dropped seriously, which of course it hasn't done. So I thought I should be safe in running over to Cairo till the middle of November. If I had known that you were returning so soon I should not have gone – at all events until later.

I am very anxious to know what you think of the plot. It seems to me to fulfil all requirements – and provides good parts for everyone. I enclose four numbers that I have written.

Don't you think it would be wise to revive *Pinafore* at the end of *Mikado*? You see, it is most important that it should be revived with the original cast as far as possible – and I think it is not unlikely that if we postpone its revival for another year, we may have lost Grossmith or Temple or Barrington, or Bond – or all of them. They would remain to play it now, I think, knowing that it would be followed by an original piece – but if they thought that it was to be the first of a series of revivals, they might look out for something better. Moreover, they might be induced to remain for a revival of *Patience* or *Iolanthe*, if an original opera came after *Pinafore*.

My address will be Poste Restante, Cairo, until 8 November – so any letter posted in October will reach me. I fancy I shall be home about four weeks after you.

I enclose four numbers of the new piece. I like them all except Brandram's ballad which might be more effective in longer lines, and sung as a kind of chant – to which its present form is, of course, unsuited. It ought to be grim and dramatic, I think – and ought to end more effectively than it does in its present form. However, I send it to you for what it is worth.

I hope you've had a pleasant voyage.

'Brandram's ballad' was the song which Rosina Brandram was to sing in the character of Dame Hannah, introducing the legend of supernatural events in a Cornish fishing village which was the foundation of the new plot. Misled, perhaps, by Gilbert's flight into Egypt, *Truth* informed its readers that Egypt would be the setting for the next Savoy work – 'a skit upon English commercial enterprise and humbug, as exemplified by the pretended British horror of annexing new territory'.[1] A happy idea, but there is no evidence that Gilbert ever had it.

For Sullivan, operetta was only one of three tasks ahead. There was conducting, with a second Philharmonic season to follow his first. Whatever had been the criticism of individual events by individual reviewers, the committee of the Society had evidently been well satisfied, and the *Musical Times* in August 1885 had concluded its review of the whole series:

It remains only to congratulate the Society upon the engagement of Sir Arthur Sullivan as conductor for the season, the delicacy and precision of the orchestra under his direction having very materially aided the attraction of the concerts.

Then there was the work of the 'serious' composer. He had accepted a commission not only to conduct at the coming Leeds Festival (October 1886) for the sum of 300 guineas (£315) but to provide a major cantata for it. In the summer after his return from America he wrote to Otto Goldschmidt (18 June 1886) that he had been 'slaving away at my *Golden Legend*, which is going on very slowly, but I think satisfactorily'.

Longfellow's dramatic poem of that name (1851) was the source: its story of the saintly peasant girl who offers from pure love to sacrifice herself to redeem a dissolute prince (with Lucifer himself as tempter) offered a theme of strong dramatic appeal in religious guise (the very essence of the Victorian 'sacred' choral work). By 'slaving away' the composer alluded not to composition, which he had not yet begun, but to his striving to reduce the poem to a shape suitable for musical setting – with Joseph Bennett's co-operation.

The composer with whom Sullivan would be matched as a rival in choral music was Gounod, whose reputation was undiminished. At the Three Choirs Festival in Hereford in September 1885 it was reported that the attendance for a performance of *The Redemption* was larger than any other for many years. Sullivan maintained his coolness towards Gounod's music – and his affection for Gounod's Paris. He went there again on 20 November 1885, travelling with Mrs Beach Grant (who still lived in Paris and had evidently been visiting London) and her daughter Adèle. On 22 January he noted in his diary

Letters from Carte, Smythe and Dicey [who was to join him in Paris next day]. Carte enclosed one from Gilbert to him – very offensive and unnecessary. I wrote myself to Gilbert and to Carte (both copied) also to Smythe, L. W., Dresden [i.e. his friend Ernest Dresden] enclosing £73.

Gilbert had in fact returned from Egypt – 'and his re-advent is being celebrated with a "row" as usual', wrote Carte to Sullivan.[2] Carte had decided to precede the nightly performance of *The Mikado* with Alfred Cellier's *The Carp*, to words by F. Desprez. Gilbert reacted in a 'bullying tone', according to a letter which the offended Carte sent to Sullivan:

. . . and it is most ungrateful considering what I have just done for his piece in America. And is your 'vote', as he would call it, given to me in favour of doing the piece, is your wish – your expression of opinion – to go for nothing? Is he to say because he objects that, unless he has an assurance that the project of which you approve is withdrawn, all friendly relations between him and me are at an end, the reason that he objects being not that he thinks it undesirable but simply that he has not been consulted in proper form? *I* don't mean to stand it. I have referred to my agreement and I find that I am expressly permitted by it to produce any one else's pieces besides yours so that they are not the principal piece of the evening.

This letter of 21 November 1885 significantly prefigures the tension – not between Sullivan and Gilbert but between Carte and Gilbert – which set off the later 'Carpet Quarrel'.

The year 1886, as recorded in the diary and letters, and in the comment of newspapers and magazines, gives a fully-rounded picture – professional and domestic – of Arthur Sullivan at the height of his fame. The mayor of a provincial city waited on his arrival; the more frivolous organs of the press speculated on whether he might yet get married. A royal request for a work to grace a state occasion could not be refused. The Commercial Cable Company granted him the privilege of cabling free to 'his' family in Los Angeles on Sundays and on 20 May he asked whether a similar facility for return messages could be given to Amy. The copies which his secretary Smythe made of letters sent (by a duplicating device called a 'letter-press') add to the quantity of material surviving in Sullivan's name from now on. A 'cash account' in the diary for January, noting wins and losses in amounts up to £112, makes it clear that he gambled on at least 18 days of the month. He may well have maintained that for every month he was in London.

[Diary, 4 January 1886]: Went to C.P. [Cadogan Place] to say goodbye – Mrs R. left for Strathfield Saye. Wrote to Spark [secretary of Leeds Festival] and Leeds committee declining to agree to their condition [unknown]. Called at Clarence House and saw the Duke of Edinburgh . . .

[Diary, 6 January]: Mr Belshaw, engineer of the Swan & Edison Co., came and took particulars of the house for electric light; Arthur Grove [son of Sir George, working as an engineer] also.

[Diary, 12 January]: Dined at home [followed by tick: presumably Fanny Ronalds had returned].

[Diary, 17 January]: Very much annoyed to find a par. [paragraph] in the *Referee* raking up the old rumour about me and Miss U. [Geraldine Ulmar]

[Diary, 19 January]: Gilbert's party . . . performance of *Cox and Box* by Grossmith, [Arthur] Cecil and Barrington.

[Diary, 21 January]: Called Uncle John [i.e., Uncle John, his father's brother, called on him].

He had been pressed to go to Birmingham to preside at the Clef Club dinner there:

[Diary, 22 January]: Dinner at Masonic Hall (about 252); on my right was the Mayor (Mr Martineau). I made a capital speech . . . great success.

[Diary, 28 January]: J[oseph] Bennett dined with me. Discussed the *Golden Legend* with him and he took it home to see if he could arrange it for Leeds. Portland [for gambling].

[Diary, 1 February]: Wimbledon with Carte. Saw and carefully examined his electric light installation.

[Diary, 2 February]: Rehearsed with Amateur Society [i.e. as guest conductor of the Royal Amateur Orchestral Society] 'Overtura di Ballo' [again the preferred spelling]

[Diary, 8 February]: Received letter from Adèle Grant announcing her engagement to Lord Cairns.

Diary, 4 March]: 1st concert Phil[harmonic]. Magnificent performance of Scotch Symphony.

Antoinette Trebelli (daughter of the more famous singer of that surname) was the soprano soloist in that programme, with Fanny Frickenhaus as pianist and Tivadar Nachez as violinist.

Symphony no. 3 in A minor ('Scotch')	Mendelssohn
Recitative and aria, 'Deh vieni' (*Le nozze di Figaro*)	Mozart
Piano Concerto	Schumann
Scene, 'The Forest of Arden'	Henry Gadsby
Violin Concerto in C	Moszkowski
Aria, 'Je veux briser'(*Les Diamants de la couronne*)	Auber
Overture, 'Les deux journées'	Cherubini

Sullivan's diary did not mention his fellow-composer Henry Gadsby (see page 92), who conducted his own work.

Preparations had to be made for the Leeds Festival in the following October. The Committee retained an official responsibility for the programme and, as usual, diplomatic correspondence was necessary before the conductor could get his expert advice accepted. Apart from his own new composition, Sullivan's major contribution to the programme was to be the first performance at the festival of Bach's Mass in B minor – a project inspired by the London celebrations of the bicentenary of Bach's birth. On 21 March 1885 Goldschmidt had repeated his Bach Choir presentation of the Mass – this time more closely following the original instrumentation, though with a choral and orchestral body of modern large size (exceeding 600).

Sullivan would follow that approach. The pressure for an 'authentic' performance of old music, while nothing like as rigorous as that of the mid-twentieth century, was making itself felt. History would single out the pioneering of Arnold Dolmetsch in performance on 'old instruments' from about 1890, but it was not *quite* new. On 14 November 1885 the *Illustrated London News* reported that 'Herr Bonawitz' (Johann Heinrich Bonawitz [1839–1917], a German pianist-composer resident in London)

has begun a series of three historical recitals of piano music at Prince's Hall. His first programme comprised an interesting selection of ancient and modern music by composers of English, Italian, German and other nationalities. In some of the older pieces Herr Bonawitz makes use of a harpsichord.

Replying to a letter of 27 February from the festival committee, Sullivan made his own preference clear. Unusually for the time (though it would become a common attitude after his death) he evidently thought Mozart's works ill-suited to the full-sized symphony orchestra. In dissociating himself from the general Victorian enthusiasm for Beethoven's cantata, *Christ at The Mount of Olives*, he again anticipates a later view. It was this work which had been proposed to follow

The Golden Legend at the Saturday morning concert. His letter shows that he remained enthusiastic for Schumann as symphonist but not for Brahms – a view which his recent experience in conducting Brahms's Symphony no. 3 for the Philharmonic had not caused him to modify.

In my opinion, and it is only my personal feeling, the instrumental selections are not well chosen. The Brahms' symphony [no 2. had been proposed] I should omit. The *Midsummer Night's Dream* music might well give place to something less hackneyed. If we did the Scotch Symphony of Mendelssohn, and a suite [!] or overture of Brahms, the programme will be better balanced. Then again, though I yield to no one in my admiration of the Jupiter Symphony, it is hardly of the character to suit an orchestra of such grandeur as that of the Leeds Festival. Would it not be desirable to have the French composers represented? – say by a suite of Massenet or Bizet. So much for the instrumental portion.

With regard to the choral works, I think there is one point to which the earnest attention of the committee ought to be called, and that is, the want of brightness in Saturday morning's programme. I am delighted indeed that they have decided to do Bach's Mass [at another concert], and I am sure it will be a splendid feature. But, for the audience, and for the chorus and artists, something of a lighter and a more brilliant character than the *Mount of Olives* should be given [on the Saturday morning]. Whatever may be our opinion of the merits of the *Mount of Olives*, it cannot be said to be inspiriting. I cannot at this moment think of anything to suggest in its stead, but I will give it my attention.

The multiplicity of his professional and personal concerns is clear from diary entrance and correspondence. His punctiliousness in respect of his late teachers, Helmore (of the Chapel Royal) and Goss (of the Royal Academy) is characteristic.

[Letter, 5 March]: Dearest Katie [Helmore, daughter of his old teacher, offering condolences on her mother's death]. When is the funeral and may I come to it?

[Diary, 11 March]: Meeting of [Royal] College of Music Council at 30 Spring Gardens [the offices of Sir Henry Thring, the Parliamentary Counsel]. Long discussion. It is evident that a crisis is coming soon. The friction between the professional and lay element is getting too violent. Either Sir H. Thring and his staff of lay visitors must give way or the professors will resign in a body. I wish I could explain all this to the Prince [of Wales]. . .

Engine and temporary dynamo [for electric light at his home] started for first time.

[Diary, 12 March]: Engine and temporary dynamo at work – no noise or vibration. But care must be taken about the [illegible], too great a force dangerous. Went to F[ranklin] Taylor's at 5.30, then to [John] Goss Memorial Committee, 7 to 8.45. Met [George] Mount by appointment at Holborn Restaurant to dine and settle [orchestral] deputies for Thursday's concert, Queen's Private Band being engaged for that evening. [The Philharmonic Concert fell due on 18 March, but on that day an engagement to play at Buckingham Palace would take away some of the regular musicians.] Home early [tick].

[Diary, 13 March]: Wrote at [*sic*] finale, first act [*Ruddygore*]

[Diary, 18 March]: Writing – finished frame of finale, 1st act [*Ruddygore*] except end.

On that day he was to have conducted a Philharmonic concert but, evidently unwilling to interrupt the process of composition, got Mount to deputize for him. The public was told he had an 'indisposition' – a word which *Truth* left in sarcastic quotation marks.[3]

[Diary, 19 March]: Called at [?] Notorp's to see Mrs R's bust . . . dined at C.P. [Cadogan Place].

[Letter, 20 March: to Spark, Leeds Festival Secretary]. With regard to the programme, I think it is most admirably drawn up, and only wants lightening. Instead of the 'Jupiter' Symphony, would it not be advisable to give a selection from one of Mozart's operas, either *Idomeneo*, or *Così fan tutte*? It would have somewhat of the character of a novelty, and will bring in the chorus and many of the principal artists. On Friday evening I would do a glee of Bishop's for band and chorus. This will be very interesting, and bring a representative English name into the programme. At present, I do not see my way to making an effective selection from *Die Walküre*. When taken away from the stage, it must lose half its interest. I presume the committee have not lost sight of the fact that the performance of any part of *Die Walküre* will entail an additional cost of about 100 guineas for extra instruments. [Fees for additional players on such occasions ranged from about £3 to about 12 guineas for a principal.]

After a good deal of reflection, I have come to the opinion that the best work we can do on Saturday morning, after my new work, is the first part of *St Paul*. It is bright, dramatic, and full of beautiful and interesting music. It seems very hard that because we cannot do the whole, we should never do a part of the work without being abused. But if the committee are with me, I am quite prepared to take my share of the abuse which we may receive from some quarters; although, from what I hear, we shall receive powerful support from a portion of the press.

[Diary, 21 March]: Sketched [for *Ruddygore*] – no result.

[Diary, 23 March]: Gilbert and Carte [called] – long pow-pow – adjourned for a week to see the result [at the box office] of a week's more performances of *Mikado*. Dined at home [*two ticks follow.*]

[Diary, 25 March]: [Performance of *The Martyr of Antioch* at Nottingham, with a single rehearsal the same afternoon.] Met at Nottingham Station by mayor (Lambert) . . . Concert at 7.30. Crowded and enthusiastic audience. Very good performance of the *Martyr* (Griswold, Patey, Kearton instead of Lloyd, ill, Tufnail[4] and local bass); second part, Shakespearean music, very successful. Home to [his host] at 11. Dead beat.

Carte, worried at the prospect that *The Mikado* might not retain its appeal, urged Sullivan 'to get the new opera finished *now* before you begin the Leeds work'. He was prepared to have a revival of *HMS Pinafore* in the interim, but only a short revival: 'The *Sorcerer* revival' (he noted in a letter of 23 March 1886 to the composer)

was practically thrown away. It began to splendid business but soon went down, the new opera not being ready. The result was that we did not divide anything like what we ought to have done. (You will remember that we share in case of revivals on the whole run, not every three months.) If *Pinafore* be produced now the same thing will I am very sure happen again. We cannot as I believe calculate on more than four months' good business, possibly three, out of *Pinafore*. Then the new opera will not be ready, down will go the receipts, and the *Pinafore* revival will be wasted.[5]

Sullivan did not accede: he completed the Leeds cantata first. But happily *The Mikado* outlasted Carte's expectations and no stop-gap revival was needed.

April brought Liszt to London. He stayed as the guest of Alfred Littleton, managing director of Novello's, the publishers, at the magnificent villa which Littleton had erected at Sydenham. Long retired from his career as concert pianist, Liszt was now acclaimed as composer and general musical celebrity. Aged 74, he was to die some three months later. A 'festival fortnight' (as it was described by Constance Bache, sister of Liszt's pupil Walter Bache) loaded him with formal and informal tributes. The Queen received him at Windsor Castle. He was Irving's guest for a performance of *Faust* (not Goethe's play, but W. G. Wills's version) and for supper at the Lyceum afterwards. Browning was one of those who attended Bache's reception to Liszt held at the Grosvenor Gallery, and the composer lent his presence to two performances of the oratorio *St Elisabeth* (at St James's Hall and the Crystal Palace). Unlike Dvořák, unlike Saint-Saëns, who appeared at the Philharmonic in May, the patriarchal Liszt was in no sense a rival to Sullivan, who accordingly joined in honouring him. To Saint-Saëns in May, however, he was again cool.

[Diary, 1 April]: Called: Sir P. Owen from the Prince of Wales (with his Ode by Tennyson) requesting me to write music for the opening of the Colonial and Military Exhibition. After much hesitation, consented to do it. How am I to get through this year's work?
    Phil. concert at night. [No comment.]

[Diary, 3 April]: Gilbert and Carte [called] at 3. Gilbert attacked me about delay in new piece. Gave it him back. Finally arranged to defer production of new opera till September or October. . . . Drove down to Littleton's at Sydenham – reception to Liszt who arrived at 8 from Paris. Home at 12.

[Diary, 5 April]: Went to St James's Hall (rehearsal *St Elisabeth*) to see Alfred Littleton about Liszt coming to next Phil. and to get tickets for concert [on 6 April]. . . . Dined at home. L.W. [followed by two ticks].

But Liszt declined the invitation to the Philharmonic concert (at which Sullivan would have changed the programme to include one of Liszt's works) because his recommendation of Bache as soloist had been ignored by the Society. The two April programmes, conducted by Sullivan, each opened with a very long symphony (Schubert's 'Great C major', Beethoven's 'Eroica'), plus an aria, plus a concerto, all before the interval!

Third Concert, 1 April 1886

Rose Hersee, soprano; Clotilde Kleeberg, piano;
Franz [František] Ondříček, violin

Symphony [no. 9] in C	Schubert
Aria, 'Pur dicesti'	Lotti
Violin Concerto	Dvořák
Pastoral Introduction and Overture to Part II (*The Light of the World*)	Sullivan
Piano Concerto no. 2 in G minor	Mendelssohn
Cavatina, 'Nobil signor' (*Les Huguenots*)	Meyerbeer
Overture, 'Namensfeier'	Beethoven

Fourth Concert, 15 April 1886

Gertrude Griswold, soprano; Fanny Davies, piano; Joseph Joachim, violin

Symphony in E flat ('Eroica')	Beethoven
Air, 'Il est doux' (*Hérodiade*)	Massenet
Piano Concerto in C minor	Sterndale Bennett
Violin Concerto in E minor	Mendelssohn
Songs, 'Wind in the trees' and 'A lake and a fairy boat'	Arthur Goring Thomas
Overture, 'Jessonda'	Spohr

[Diary, 6 April]: First day Epsom spring [race] meeting. Fine but cold. Went down, and enjoyed the privilege of membership of the New Club stand.

[Letter, 7 April: to Sir Philip Cuncliffe Owen] I am much obliged by your letter and am already in communication with Lord Tennyson. Besides sending me the words of the Ode he has sent me suggestions for the music! This is extremely good since he doesn't know one note from another.

[Diary, 8 April]: Went to Bache's reception to Liszt at the Grosvenor Gallery. Great crowd.

How characteristic is the laconic entry for an occasion which raised the highest excitement among others lucky enough to be present – when, after a short musical performance by others, Liszt himself consented to go to the piano! He played the Hungarian Rhapsody in A minor and Schubert's *Divertissement à l'hongroise.*

[Diary, 9 April]: . . . To smoking concert [i.e. informal concert where smoking was permitted.] Went over to St James's Hall [another concert in Liszt's honour] to fetch Liszt – brought him to the smoker.

At this 'smoking concert', with the Prince of Wales present, the performers were the Royal Amateur Orchestral Society, 'such distinguished [players] that to my knowledge there is not a comparable amateur orchestra in Europe', as Liszt reported to Princess Wittgenstein.

[Diary, 18 April]:. . . went up to a musical party at [Joseph] Bennett's, 109 Finchley Rd [Hampstead]: Joachim, Albani, etc. Accompanied latter in *Lost Chord.*

Emma Albani was to remain one of Sullivan's staunchest and best interpreters. Almost inevitably it was she who was the vocal soloist in the Tennyson-Sullivan *Ode* for chorus and orchestra commissioned for the opening of the Colonial and Indian Exhibition in Hyde Park. Sullivan was 'in uniform' (that of his knighthood) when, in Queen Victoria's presence, he conducted the *Ode* at the opening ceremony on 4 May 1886. 'It was noticeable,' said *The Times*, 'that after each verse Her Majesty smiled her thanks to the singer and clapped her hands.' The work began 'Welcome, welcome with one voice', with the refrain 'Britons, hold your own'. Bearing no title save *An Ode, Written for the Opening of the Colonial and Indian Exhibition*, 1886, it doubtless did its duty for that day.

Sullivan now moved for quietness' sake to York Town in the garrison area of Camberley (Surrey) which he had known as a child. Free from the callers at his

London residence – and from some, at least, of his other distractions – he would find the concentration necessary for the composition of *The Golden Legend*. The new operetta would have to wait its turn. When an important occasion such as a Philharmonic concert called him, he would take the train (an hour or so) from Farnborough to London and, if necessary, sleep at Queen's Mansions before returning to seclusion.

[Diary, 23 April]: Very nice lodgings at 4 Albany Place [York Town] kept by Harris, old bandsman under Father.

[Diary, 24 April]: Began composition of *Golden Legend*: got on very well for first day.

[Letter, 14 May]: Dear Sir Edward [Malet, British ambassador in Berlin] We are trying the experiment of performing the *Mikado* at the Wallner Theatre in Berlin, to begin on 2 or 3 June. It may succeed and it may fail utterly, but your powerful support would go far towards preventing the latter issue . . .

[Diary, 18 May]: Philharmonic rehearsal at 10. Saint-Saëns rehearsed his new symphony.

[Diary, 19 May]: Philharmonic rehearsal and concert. Prince and Princess of Wales present.

Typically, Sullivan made no comment on the exceptional occasion of that Philharmonic concert, when Saint-Saëns not only directed his remarkable new Symphony no. 3 (with organ solo and piano duet) but played a Beethoven concerto. The soloist in a Mozart aria was the distinguished American contralto, Antoinette Sterling (see p. 216).[6]

Fifth Concert, 19 May 1886

Antoinette Sterling, contralto; Agnes Larkcom, soprano; Camille Saint-Saëns, piano

Symphony [no. 103] in E flat	Haydn
Recitative and aria, 'A questo seno . . . Quando miro' [K.374]	Mozart
Piano Concerto no. 4	Beethoven
Symphony [no. 3] in C	Saint-Saëns
Couplets, 'Charmant oiseau' (*Le perle du Brésil*)	Félicien David
Overture, 'Die Meistersinger'	Wagner

[Diary, 22 May]: At work [in York Town]. Drove on to Farnborough to meet Smythe [who must have brought mail, etc.]. Took a long walk [7 miles] and got to York Town at 7.45. Dined and sent Smythe back to Town [London].

[Diary, 26 May]: [back in London] Went in Royal train [to Epsom] to the Derby with Dicey, Carte and Smythe. Duke of Westminister's Ormonde (Archer up) won.

On 13 May 1886 – his birthday – Sullivan's symphony was revived, at St James's Hall, with the composer conducting, at an orchestral concert presented by a leading British violinist, J. T. Carrodus.[7] The unnamed reviewer in the *Athenaeum* (22 May) felt compelled to summon up the occasion of the première in 1866, so enthusiastically received.

At a distance of 20 years the symphony can be criticized with cooler judgement, and it is impossible to look upon it as a masterpiece. The first and second movements contain much that is admirable, but the third and fourth are very weak. The second symphony, which was announced in the Crystal Palace programme for 1868–9, has not yet been given to the world, probably because the composer has discovered that his gifts are better employed in other directions.

The planned performances of *The Mikado* were to be the start of a Continental tour by one of Carte's companies – the company which, in fact, had been playing *The Mikado* in the United States. A German business manager, Dr C. Carlotta, seems both to have managed the tour on Carte's behalf and to have undertaken to look after Sullivan's own professional interests in Germany and neighbouring countries. Chained to his work at home, Sullivan could not go to Germany.

A Philharmonic concert was due on 2 June, the very day on which the performance at the Wallner Theatre would be graced by the German Crown Prince and his English princess. Sullivan had written a separate letter of invitation to their son, Prince William, whom he had met when on the Duke of Edinburgh's cruise five years before. A charming reply, in English, came from the imperial residence at Potsdam:

Dear Sir,

Many thanks for your kind letter which I have just received, and for the interesting news it contains.

For the moment I am unhappily unable to fulfil your wish because I am just recovering from a very serious and rather dangerous attack of earache, which compels me to stay at home and be quiet. But as soon as I shall be able to stir to go to Reichenhall, I shall visit *The Mikado*. Today the first performance will be viewed by my parents and all my sisters, whom I envy immensely their good fortune to see this charming piece of which I have heard and read so much in the English press.

I hope that for the arrival of the Crown Prince they will have 'polished up the handle of the big front door,' for he might have been a Roossian, etc., but he is a Proossian!

I often think of our nice evenings at Kiel, and the charming musik on the yacht, which gave me the lucky opportunity of making your acquaintance.

Yours truly,
William Prince of Prussia

The Philharmonic concert on 2 June was the last of the season. Moszkowski, again favoured, conducted his own new work.

Sixth Concert, 2 June 1886

Franz [František] Ondříček, violin; Christine Nilsson, soprano

Symphony [no. 40] in G minor	Mozart
Aria, 'Ah! perfido'	Beethoven
Violin Concerto	Beethoven
Suite for orchestra	Moszkowski
Song, 'Der Erlkönig'	Schubert
Overture, 'Le Carnaval romain'	Berlioz

For half-a-dozen years the Philharmonic had been up against the annual competition of Richter's much-admired orchestral series, and from 1886 another annual series called the London Symphony Concerts was established under the direction of Georg Henschel, who would be knighted as 'Sir George' in 1914. Richter had become London's pre-eminent conductor, against whom others would be judged. Not often did Sullivan receive such a compliment as came from the *Musical Times*, which considered that Beethoven's *Eroica* had been given at the Philharmonic 'with a perfection rarely heard' and that Sullivan displayed 'the thorough command over his unequalled orchestra which has done so much to raise the fame of the Society in the estimation of all true music-lovers'.

After Epsom and Newmarket, the racing at Ascot drew him on 8 and 9 June but on 10 June his diary includes the sentence 'Didn't go to Ascot': he was at work composing. The Philharmonic rehearsal and concert on 3 June (the last concert of the season) and the rehearsal the previous day are both noted without comment in the diary. The italics of the entry for 6 June denote an important stage reached in the composition of *The Golden Legend*, i.e. the making of the musical ideas into definite numbers or sections. 'Scoring' indicates orchestration: it will be noted that he embarked on this work piecemeal, not leaving it until after completing the whole of the actual composition, as generally with the operettas.

[Diary, 6 June]: *Began framing.*

[Diary, 7 June]: Finished frame of the Prologue (except the 'Nocte surgente').

[Diary, 10 June]: *Began scoring* the Prologue. Awful work. Dined at home. Worked again in the evening till 2.30 a.m.

[Diary, 12 June]: Scoring: awfully tedious and slow work. . . Telegram from Carlotta to say Grand Military Band had performed selection from *Mikado* at Berlin previous evening, rapturous applause.

On 18 June he gave up his York Town lodgings 'with great regret' and returned to London.

[Diary, 23 June]: Alfred Littleton came – agreed to give him the *Golden Legend* on a royalty [i.e. to let Novello's publish the work with payments for performances and sales, not on an outright payment] – he to sign my agreement. Tours [Berthold Tours, music editor for Novello's] to do the P.F. [pianoforte] arrangement. Chappell's name to be on the title-page and special arrangements made with them [as Sullivan's regular publishers]. First performance in London to be at Albert Hall, next at Novello's [the concerts promoted by that firm at St James's Hall], third at Crystal Palace – I to conduct all three. Dined at the Lister-Kayes [Sir John Pepys Lister-Kaye, Bt, and his wife Natica] – Vanderbilts, Mrs Yznaga etc. [American visitors] there. Went to the State Concert afterwards (first time), then to Portland.

A 'state concert' at Buckingham Palace was a gorgeously dressed occasion but, according to Klein (who once smuggled himself in as a chorister), 'one of the slowest and most dispiriting functions that it was ever my lot to witness'.[8] Applause was forbidden by court etiquette, and the Queen herself never attended such a concert (or a state ball) after the Prince Consort's death in 1861. No doubt the social pace was livelier when Sullivan proceeded to Newmarket for the races, staying with his old friends the Clay Ker Seymers at Godolphin House, Newmarket. Sullivan's wealth now enabled him to buy horses as well as bet on them.

Special bells for *The Golden Legend* were being made by the firm of Lund and Blockley, clock-makers, of 42 Pall Mall, London. By now Sullivan was as usual travelling to Leeds for the weekly choral rehearsals. The preparation of the Bach Mass gave special problems. His hope of using the edition pioneeringly prepared by Goldschmidt for the London Bach Choir was frustrated when he discovered that, without consulting him, the festival management had ordered vocal scores for the chorus in a German edition and it was too late to change. He wrote to Goldschmidt that he could not even use the 'excellent organ part' which Goldschmidt had prepared because he was 'in a great difficulty about the *organist*' – the pugnacious Dr William Spark, brother of F. R. Spark, the festival committee's secretary. His decision to use the male altos as a roving reinforcement between the voices led to a letter (dated 14 July, but perhaps written a few days earlier) to F. R. Spark: 'I have arranged a special male alto voice part for the Mass. How many male altos have you? And can I get a vocal score for each, to have the new arrangement inserted so as to bring them down with me for Friday's rehearsal?'

On 19 July he wrote to Goldschmidt:

I have now resolved to do the Mass in its *natural shape* with the three trumpets and extra oboes and flutes and *no cuts*. I thus avoid all share of criticism so far as my share of the work is concerned. The only thing I shall do is to put in a few *p*'s and *f*'s according to the character of the words . . . You would be delighted with the Leeds choir . . . they sing it with the precision of keyed instruments and the body of tone is superb.

Sullivan nowhere stated his reasons for wanting so many woodwind. In the event, he had six oboes and six flutes playing in the Mass, two of the oboists undertaking the *oboe d'amore* parts – now played on proper instruments belonging to (and probably made specially for) the Bach Choir. Each of the trumpet parts was given to a so-called Bach trumpet, a specially constructed straight trumpet with two valves, mistakenly supposed to be similar to the instrument of Bach's day in pitch and tone-quality. A note from Sullivan's secretary had instructed Messrs Silvani and Smith, its makers, to send one over to Stagenhoe for his inspection.

He had moved to Stagenhoe on 23 July. He was still there on 2 August, with Fanny Ronalds as one of his guests, when he noted in his diary that he had finished the second scene of *The Golden Legend* (it was divided into six 'scenes' with prologue and epilogue). The rest of the month found him steadily at work.

[Diary, 11 August]: Began fourth scene (composition).

[Diary, 13 August]: Gave Baird [copyist] scores of Prologue and 1st, 2nd and 3rd scenes to get on with.

[Diary, 14 August]: Finished frame of fourth scene.

[Diary, 15 August]: Framed choral epilogue.

[Diary, 16 August]: Mrs Ronalds and Wyllys [her friend Wyllys Betts] went off to Paris. Scoring Epilogue.

[Diary, 19 August]: Framing hard. Finished composition of 6th scene. Recomposed and scored fifth scene. Worked ten hours.

[Diary, 23 August]: At work scoring sixth scene. Only short solo in second scene (Ursula) to do now.

[Diary, 25 August]: Last day of work! At it all day for the Introduction and Solo in second scene: Got it at 5 p.m. Scored it and finished at 7.45! Thank God.

The planning of the actual performance now demanded his attention. Elsie, the heroine's role, was to be sung by Albani, negotiations being conducted through her husband and manager Ernest Gye. The leading tenor role of Prince Henry was entrusted to Edward Lloyd, a favourite with Sullivan as with the public, the supporting contralto role of Ursula to Patey, and the bass role of Lucifer to Frederic King. Expectancy for Sullivan's new work was at its highest. Meanwhile, the willingness of Metzler's to issue his *Henry VIII* in full score, and of Novello's to do the same for the *Festival Te Deum* (both had previously appeared only with piano accompaniment) was a sure sign of his high standing as a composer.

[Diary, 26 August]: Took up [to London] the score of sixth scene and 'Slowly' [Ursula's solo] at Novello's. Found everything behind-hand at the printers. [Berthold] Tours gone away. Went over to H[Hamilton] Clarke's and got him to arrange second and fourth scenes for the printer. Gave the rest to Baird [probably to make orchestral parts from full score]. Pushed things forward a bit. Went to Lund's in Pall Mall to meet Stainer about the bells for work. Gave full instruction. Then home [i.e. Queen's Mansions] to meet Smythe, wrote some more letters and filled up the band engagements [orchestra for Leeds]. Called at Herries [bank], paid in £758 . . . [Called also at] Metzler [publishers] and back [to Stagenhoe] by 5 [o'clock] train. Wired Gye about music . . .

[Diary, 27 August]: Rested, wrote letters, corrected proofs of full score of *Te Deum* and full score and parts of *Henry VIII*.

[Diary, 28 August]:. . . Worked with [Frederic] Cliffe [arranger of piano accompaniment], getting Albani's part ready. Sent it to her registered, complete. Cliffe returned to town.

[Diary, 30 August]: More letters. Dispatched 19 altogether, amongst others to Mme Rabl [in Berlin], Mme Gautier, Lord, Manns,. . . Spark [at Leeds].

It is tempting to identify 'Mme Gautier' with Judith Gautier (1846–1917), wife of the French poet Catulle Mendès and one of Wagner's mistresses, but Sullivan's business with her is not disclosed.

At Stagenhoe his other guests included Tom Chappell, still Sullivan's closest friend in the publishing world. The next diary entry alludes to the fact that British pitch was still not standard, and the firm making the bells for *The Golden Legend* had to be specifically informed of the high pitch set by the Town Hall organ for the Leeds Festival performances.

[Diary, 1 September]: T. Chappell and Fanny [daughter?] went to Town [London]. Drove into Hitchin [where they would catch the train] with them. Had my hair cut. Bought a straw hat. Boy from Novello's brought PF [piano reduction] of the Epilogue. Blazing hot. Sent tuning-fork for Leeds to Lund and Blockley for bells.

[Diary, 4 September]: I went down to Gloucester to rehearse with Albani [who was appearing at the Three Choirs Festival there]. Left home at 9.40. Arrived Gloucester 4. Left again at 8, home at 2 a.m.

[Diary, 6 September]: Went to Savoy. Long pow-wow with Gilbert and Carte about new opera. Proposed to produce it end of November.

On 10 September he went to Leeds for the choir's first rehearsal of *The Golden Legend*, returning after another rehearsal by the 5.30 express from Leeds to London 'which stopped at Hitchin to set me down'.

The press had for months referred, in anticipation, to *The Golden Legend*. Privately, Sullivan had always used that title for the work; but, like Gilbert, he deprecated any advance speculation on a work until the actual announcement of its performance, and publicly maintained that the title was as yet not fixed. It did not, after all, have to be the same as Longfellow's. Not until 24 August did he write to Bennett: 'Shall we call it *The Golden Legend*? I suppose there is no better title. It has the merit of being known. Will you write a few lines of "Argument" to precede the libretto?'

A week later he felt the necessity of explaining to Bennett why he himself had made changes in the text. At first, before calling in Bennett, he had been unable to arrive at an initially workable text; but once in the grip of sustained composition he felt confident to cut and amend. He would not have allowed himself such independence in a stage work – but here, after all, his material was itself an adaptation, not an original libretto. The words of the cantata were due to appear on their own (along with Bennett's 'Argument' or synopsis) in the pages of the vocal score preceding the music itself, and now Sullivan was sending back to Bennett a 'revise' (revised proof) of the words only:

Here is a final revise according to the latest touchings-up of the score. For the few changes I have made from its original shape here are my reasons:
> Scene II
>> (a): I could not put any chorus into [Ursula's] 'Slowly, slowly' for the simple reason that it was too late.[9] The parts were engraved. It was the very last thing I wrote of the work.
>> (b): I added the 3rd verse of [Longfellow's] Evening hymn, as I was short of words.
> Scene III
>> (a): I have adopted your suggestion of giving Lucifer a mocking solo, accompanied the seond time by the pilgrims singing their hymn.
>> (b): I had to rewrite 'It is the sea' because I found that the chorus entirely robbed the next movement of its effect. The chorus I had written was really, I think, a fine piece of descriptive music – but it had to be sacrificed, as the following number is what I rely upon to bring about a broad and impressive effect. So I cut out the chorus and gave it as a sort of melancholy reverie to Prince Henry.
> Scene IV: I have already explained this to you. There are a few lines cut out, in order to bring the action closer and make it more dramatic, and three lines of chorus added.
> Scenes V and VI: Unaltered.
> Will you send back your proof to Novello's with preface and any remarks you may have to make? . . .

Berlioz had called *The Damnation of Faust* an *opéra de concert*; Sullivan might have done the same for *The Golden Legend*. The work is, though in concert form, a drama of named personages with a chorus used more or less like an operatic crowd. To help the drama forward there are stage directions ('struggles at the door, but cannot open it') which the audience is intended to read as the performance proceeds.

The story hinges on Prince Henry's mysterious, unnamed illness, which can be cured only if

> . . . some maiden of her own accord
> Offers her life for that of her lord.

Elsie, a poor villager, makes that offer and falls within the power of Lucifer, in disguise as a doctor. No less prominent than these three principal roles – tenor, soprano, baritone – is the chorus, whether as pilgrims, followers of Lucifer, or commentators.

The end of the Stagenhoe tenancy on 30 September 1886 did not pass without a disagreeable incident. A stiff letter was dispatched by Smythe to the owner's representative:

I am directed by Sir Arthur Sullivan to enquire by what authority you prevented the removal of the accumulation of dung from the stable yard at Stagenhoe?

It is Sir Arthur's property and he considers it a piece of gratuitous insolence on your part to have prevented the removal of the manure.

Sir Arthur insists upon, and has given peremptory orders for its immediate sale, and the money paid to him . . .

On 29 September, the day before he left Stagenhoe, Sullivan 'worked at Mass and *Israel* till 2.30 a.m.' – presumably in study of the music preparatory to conducting it. Three days of orchestral rehearsal in London (4–6 October) had to cover the new choral works of Sullivan, Dvořák (*St Ludmila*), Mackenzie (*The Story of Sayid*), and Stanford (*The Revenge*), together with an overture by a young Leeds composer, F. K. Hattersley – and the Bach Mass itself. It appears that such substantial scores as Handel's *Israel in Egypt*, Beethoven's Fifth Symphony, Mendelssohn's *Elijah*, and Part I of the same composer's *St Paul* were reckoned so familiar as to need no orchestral rehearsal time except with the chorus at Leeds.

[Diary, 8 October]: Left home with Louis, Alfred, Ellen, and Clotilde [servants] for Leeds, 1.30 train. Arrived and drove to Judges' Lodgings lent me for the festival by the mayor. Had some tea and a steak and rehearsed *Israel* at the Town Hall. Afterwards altered and rearranged position of bells [for *The Golden Legend*].

[Diary, 9 October]: Choral rehearsal *Golden Legend* and [sic] at Town Hall, 2.30. At 7 Dvořák rehearsed *Ludmila* and [was] well received by the chorus. Cigars in the Mayor's room afterwards.

Noticeable once again is Sullivan's coolness to Dvořák (whose *St Ludmila*, commissioned by the festival, was a dramatic cantata on a 'sacred' subject and thus in some sense a rival to *The Golden Legend* itself). The orchestra arrived on 10 October and was plunged next day into morning, afternoon and evening rehearsals. For Sullivan, a mere two rehearsals, as next day, made a light day's schedule at Leeds. Among his house-guests arriving from London would be George Grove, ever his counsellor.

[Diary, 12 October]: Rehearsed 10 a.m. *Advent Hymn* [Schumann's *Adventlied* for soprano, chorus and orchestra] then the *Golden Legend* till 1 (interval one hour). 2 p.m., Bach's Mass, portions of *St Paul*, songs Lloyd and King, overture *Fliegende Holländer*. No evening rehearsal. My guests arrived: Lord and Lady Lathom and Lady Bertha Wilbraham, Lady Feodora Sturt,[10] Tosti, Mrs Ronalds (Grove next day). Albani and Gye [her husband] dined with me also.

Next day the Leeds Musical Festival of 1886 began. In taste and scope, in the tightly-packed concert schedule and in the profusion of items, it stands as typical of the major choral festival of its day; or rather, it was a particularly distinguished example of its kind. Not only Sullivan and Dvořák but the younger Mackenzie and Stanford conducted first performances of their music. *The Revenge*, to Tennyson's patriotic narrative poem, became Stanford's best-known work; Mackenzie's *The Story of Sayid*, soon forgotten, had the deadweight of a text by Bennett. If Mendelssohn maintained his traditional sway with *Elijah*, part I of *St Paul* and *The First Walpurgis Night*, Wagner demanded inclusion not only with the *Fliegende Holländer* overture but with the Prize Song from *Die Meistersinger*, which Edward Lloyd had made his own. Sullivan, as noted above, had rejected a concert version of part of *Die Walküre* but it would not be many years before the Leeds Festival embarked on *Die Meistersinger* itself.

The selection from Mozart's *Idomeneo*, given on Sullivan's own suggestion, represented a rare opportunity to hear music from an opera never performed in the theatre at that period. Bach's *Mass in B minor* was not merely new to the Leeds audience: in Sullivan's full-length version it was, according to the *Musical Times*,

the most complete interpretation of Bach's sacred masterpiece ever heard in this country or, for that matter, any other. Those who favour additional accompaniments and the modernizing of ancient works may suppose that the result of Sir Arthur Sullivan's 'purism' was baldness and poverty. Nothing of the sort. We were conscious of naught wanting to completeness. Bach knew how to obtain results perfect in their way with the means at his disposal, and hence, besides truth of interpretation, we had, at Leeds, a finished thing in the style of a past day it is true, but satisfactory even now.

'Magnificent performance of the Mass' was Sullivan's laconic note in his diary for 14 October. The *Musical Times* had reservations on the solo singing but found that

the [choral] ensemble in such numbers as 'Et resurrexit' and the 'Sanctus' attained the sublime – there is no other word by which to describe it – so grandly were the passages sustained. It seemed that the choir became, for the time, an immense organ, *plus* all that raises the human voice among the noblest of instruments. Naturally, this made an impression upon the audience, even upon those to whom Bach is ordinarily a Dryasdust, and it was interesting to note the sustained attention which the long work received down to the very last chord.

On the morning of the last day of the festival – Saturday 16 October 1886 – Sullivan's new work was given, prompting in the diary no more remark than '*The Golden Legend*. See newspapers.' It was enough. Rarely can a new English work and its performance have won such acclaim.

How can we describe the scene which followed the last note of the cantata! Let the reader imagine an audience rising to its multitudinous feet in thundering approval; a chorus either cheering with heart and soul or raining down flowers upon the lucky composer; and an orchestra coming out of their habitual calm to wax fervid in demonstration. Never was a more heartfelt ovation. Ovation! nay, it was a greater triumph, one such as acclaimed the successful soldiers of Rome.

Such was the report of the *Leeds Mercury* to which Hermann Klein's memoirs of nearly 20 years later added a footnote. Sullivan was modest in acknowledging the applause and almost refused to return to the platform a second time: 'He complained that the girls of the choir had pelted him with too many nosegays the first time'. Less disposed to effusion than the local press, the London reviewers were hardly behind in their praise. The critic of the *Daily Telegraph* (presumably Bennett, not considering his authorship of the libretto a disqualification) declared that 'a greater, more legitimate and more undoubted triumph than that of the new cantata has not been achieved within my experience'.

More remarkably, Stanford in the *National Review* (that is, a prominent musician who did not normally trouble to write criticism, and a magazine which did not review music as a matter of course) declared that *The Golden Legend* would enjoy a place 'even on the shelves of the classics'.

Borne on the wave of such acclamation, Sullivan could no doubt stomach (he would certainly have noticed) the characteristic stings in the praise which *The Times*, presumably in the person of Hueffer, condescended to bestow.

Sir Arthur Sullivan has had the good sense to make no attempt at being what he is not; he has simply put on paper what he felt and how he felt it; hence his success. Popularity, in the true meaning of the word, which is a very different thing from vulgarity and by no means incompatible with refinement of form, is this composer's birthright. Sir Arthur Sullivan is a consummate master of his craft; his instrumentation, if occasionally a little colourless, is, on the other hand, never loud; and, in listening to his music, one has the pleasant feeling of confidence which is inspired by the consciousness that the composer produces exactly the effects which he desires to produce, and never tries to fly an inch higher than his wings will safely carry him . . . The Leeds Festival may boast of having given life to a work which, if not one of genius in the strict sense of the word, is at least likely to survive till our long-expected English Beethoven appears on the scene.

To the composer, *The Golden Legend* meant above all a musical release. He saw it as music of autonomous self-expression – from which, he believed, he was barred in setting Gilbert's texts. As compared with the operettas, the cantata is much less four-square in vocal line and more 'advanced' (that is, chromatic) in harmony. The musical form of the separate numbers is not dominated by the need to identify repeated stanza-patterns in the verse. It is, in a word, freer music; even the interpolated hymn 'O gladsome light' takes an irregular grouping of bars beginning 5, 8, 5, 8, 5, 3. But was the result better, or did the constraints of the Gilbertian texts actually serve to sharpen Sullivan's music rather than to tether it?

The latter must be the verdict of posterity, confirmed indeed by the later experience of *Ivanhoe*. Bennett's text was dramatically weak. At the moment when Elsie is about to sacrifice herself by taking poison, Henry and his minions burst in. What happens then – what, indeed? In the next scene we learn only that 'the prince's nobler self prevailed'; we then see him cured (when? how?) and peaceably married to Elsie. It seems as though an intermediate scene vital to the story has been omitted, a scene which is badly needed if sympathy were to be aroused for Bennett's pallid hero and heroine. Lucifer, sardonic and mischievous, comes off much more successfully.

The Golden Legend arouses chief interest by lyrical scene-painting – the agitation of Lucifer and his minions trying to tear down the cross from the spire of Strasbourg cathedral (prologue); the calm of the slow duet and chorus, 'It is the sea in all its vague immensity'. The amiable grotesqueness given to Lucifer carries a hint of Berlioz's *Damnation of Faust* – the work from which (it was suggested earlier in these pages) Sullivan's beloved 'counterpoint of characters' chiefly derives. Thoroughly Berlioz-like (we may recall not only *The Damnation of Faust* but also a similar effect in the opera *Benvenuto Cellini*) is Sullivan's processional counterpoint as the slow notes of the pilgrims' hymn are heard against Lucifer's quick, jesting 12/8. Lucifer also has his fair share of leading-motive, a device which Sullivan used intermittently in Gounod's fashion rather than pervasively as in Wagner's.

No work more cruelly illustrates the posthumous decline in Sullivan's reputation as a 'serious' composer. As many as 17 performances of the cantata were given in Britain during the season of its première (1886–7) but from 1950 to 1980 not one major British choral series accommodated it. Perhaps Hueffer's 'long-expected English Beethoven' indeed arrived in the person of Elgar (or Britten?), and the gold of *The Golden Legend* was exposed as baser metal.

Even in Sullivan's own time, one younger composer did not fall victim to its allure:

One day he presented me with a copy of the full score of *The Golden Legend*, adding 'I think this is the best thing I've done, don't you?' and when truth compelled me to say that I think *The Mikado* is his masterpiece, he cried out 'O, you wretch!' But though he laughed I could see he was disappointed.

So wrote Ethel Smyth (1858–1944) who was to meet Arthur Sullivan a few years later and to be charmed by the unfeigned cordiality which he extended so readily to younger British musicians.

1 'The Lost Chord' — poster for a film, 1933

William Sterndale Bennett

Ignaz Moscheles

Therese Titiens

Edward Lloyd

2 Teachers and interpreters

1

O GOD THOU ART WORTHY TO BE PRAISED,

Anthem,

COMPOSED BY

ARTHUR S. SULLIVAN.

Ent. Sta. Hall.

Reduced Price 1/6
Separate Vocal Parts

LONDON, NOVELLO, EWER & Cº 1, BERNERS STREET, W. AND 35, POULTRY, E.C.

This Anthem is suitable for the Marriage Service.   4575

3 An anthem by the young Sullivan

4 *The Mikado* in German guise

5 Mary Frances Ronalds

6 'Cox and Box' with Fred Sullivan (left)

7 Places of fame: *top* Leeds Town Hall;
bottom Savoy Theatre, London

8 W.S. Gilbert

24 In Others' Eyes

IF Sterndale Bennett was a slack and unenergetic conductor, Sir Arthur Sullivan, his successor, is altogether a drowsy fellow. That large close-cropped head on a firm neck, that dark face with its black eyes, give one an impression of a passionate man whose anger might explode suddenly like a cannon. Instead of this we have unequalled phlegm. The G minor symphony of Mozart is performed. Sullivan conducts it without lifting his eyes from the full score – just as though he saw it for the first time. The heavenly piece is played badly, without feeling or elegance. It ends, and the public applaud enthusiastically and continuously, but Sullivan does not think of turning round to the audience. He remains unmoved in his armchair, and awaits the second piece – Beethoven's Violin Concerto, played by Ondriček. Sullivan conducts it with his usual phlegm, and all the time looks at the score. Then he again remains in his beloved armchair, until Christine Nilsson appears to sing 'Ah, perfido!'. The Philharmonic seemed to me to deserve no more praise today under his command than it did 24 years ago.

The writer was no less distinguished a critic than Eduard Hanslick – champion of Brahms, scourge of Wagner – who had paid an unannounced visit to England. His remarks in the *Neue Freie Presse* of Vienna were selectively reproduced with indignant comment in the *Musical Times* for September 1886. Hanslick's comments were said to betray 'a deplorable flippancy utterly foreign to our previous conception of his character', while the repeated disparagement of native English musicians in comparison with such Continental visitors as Richter showed Hanslick 'wearing the impenetrable mail of German self-conceit'.

The writer of this anonymous editorial comment was apparently Bennett, to whom Sullivan wrote on 6 September: 'I read your slashing attack on Hanslick with delight. What a fool he seems to have made of himself.' In a few weeks' time, Sullivan would have reason for a different sentiment towards the Viennese critic. In another article reporting his London visit, Hanslick had written enthusiastically of *The Mikado* – praising both its musical quality and the nimbleness of its production. These remarks were excerpted in the *Monthly Musical Record* of 1 November 1886.

Moreover, Sullivan's merits as a composer of operetta were yet again extolled by Hanslick when Carte's continental tour reached Vienna. The remarkable feature of his review in the *Neue Freie Presse* is that, writing within a Viennese operetta milieu adorned by Suppé, Johann Strauss, and Millöcker (*The Beggar Student*, 1882), he used Sullivan's accomplishment as a reprimand to those nearer home.

The Mikado makes no pretensions of being anything other than comical, and this it is in high degree, thanks not so much to the very simple plot as to the droll, wonderfully animated performance. The dialogue sparkles with inventive wit and satirical jibes, particularly in the conversations of the two ministers in the first act and in the negotiations with the Mikado at the close of the second. . . .

Sir Arthur Sullivan's music is not notable for its originality or for any traces of genius, but it has valuable attributes. It complements the words and the situation naturally and easily, is always melodious and lively, and – most important – is stylistically consistent. The more frequently we have occasion, from year to year, to complain of the vulgarization and false enlargement of operetta music – with unnatural borrowings of tragic pathos, Wagnerian instrumentation, heldentenors and prima donnas – the more do we treasure the modest virtues of a musical comedy such as *The Mikado*, including the merely negative ones. . . . Most of the composers now writing for our operetta theatres seem consumed by a desire to show that they can write big operas – and prove only that they know nothing about writing operettas. With a bow to Berlioz, I would compare them with troubadours who wander about the country with trombones strapped to their backs instead of guitars.

Sullivan has been accused of imitating Offenbach. I can only reply that to learn from Offenbach shows better judgement than to slander him . . . It is not expected that the English should attain the effervescent vivacity and the piquant charm of the Frenchman – but Sullivan, in his multiple-voiced pieces, shows himself the more thoroughly schooled musician. The practice which all English composers have in the madrigal is reflected in this musical comedy. Also to Sullivan's advantage is the fact that he is a cultivated singer. The vocal parts in *The Mikado* are so easily encompassed, and restricted to such a modest range, that big lungs and technical virtuosity are no more prerequisites for their performance than they were for the musical comedies of Adam, [J.A.] Hiller, Monsigny, and Grétry. The orchestra subordinates itself modestly to the song, without renouncing the employment of livelier colours or illustrative devices at the right time and place.

Another thing we are thankful for is Sullivan's avoidance of the temptation to write 'Japanese music'. He uses but one original Japanese melody in the chorus of greeting for the entrance of the Mikado, but otherwise is content to write pleasant European music. Contrary examples come to mind – Viennese operas and ballets on Indian, Persian or Arabian subjects, whose composers tirelessly fill the evening with whining oriental melodies and dissonances as an ethnographical education and a pain to the ears . . .

The unparalleled success of *The Mikado* is due neither to libretto nor the music alone, and not merely to the two together: there is also the wholly original stage performance, unique of its kind, by Mr D'Oyly Carte's artists. The Vienna performance is pleasing in the highest degree, indeed conveying an extraordinary delight, and has rightly won general acclaim. The whole strikes us like a fairy-tale, completely novel and yet attractive in its own right, riveting the eye and ear with its exotic allurement.

The Vienna performance of *The Mikado* took place at the Carlstheater on 1 September 1886. (A German translation by Sullivan's agent, Carlotta, was printed line-by-line with the English original.) On 14 September the company added *Trial by Jury* as a curtain-raiser, advertised under the title *Im Schwurgericht* ('In the assize court') – an event which seems to have escaped the notice both of writers on Sullivan and of Loewenberg's almost omniscient *Annals of Opera*.

The Mikado was to maintain its repute abroad – and, fortunately both for Carte and the dilatory Sullivan, kept its magnetism at the Savoy. After *The Golden Legend* Sullivan returned for a few days to Newmarket (staying this time with 'Russie', i.e. Russell D. Walker, a friend frequently mentioned henceforth)

before embarking concentratedly on *Ruddygore*. On 5 November 1886 Sullivan
went to dine with Gilbert, who 'read the piece complete'. It was in the usual two-
act form. In composing the music, Sullivan did not follow the written order of
numbers, probably urged by the desire to have a substantial amount of choral
material ready for rehearsal as soon as possible. By the middle of the month his
copyist had received the opening chorus, no. 2 (Dame Hannah's ballad), and the
finale of the first act; by the end of the month Sullivan had already begun to
rehearse the chorus in their music. Such material must have set out the vocal
parts in full, with a skeleton orchestral part which Sullivan or Cellier could
interpret on the piano at rehearsal and which was yet to be fully orchestrated. His
work progressed well enough for the first stage rehearsal (i.e. with action as well
as music) to take place at the Savoy on 15 December: 'first act – very good'.
Further rehearsals took place during the next few days.

London, meanwhile, was enjoying the scandal of a prolonged, 18-day divorce
case in the highest ranks of society. Lady Colin Campbell petitioned for divorce
on the ground of her husband's adultery with one woman; her husband, son of
the Duke of Argyll, petitioned on the ground of his wife's adultery with four co-
respondents. The jury disbelieved both sides and dismissed both petitions. It was
one of the few matters not of merely private interest which Sullivan allowed from
time to time to intrude into his diary. Among the friends mentioned, Sir Charles
Russell was one of the most eminent lawyers of the day and had conducted
Carte's case against the Comedy Opera Company (p.154). The two men shared a
liking for bezique (which Sullivan still spelt 'besique').

[Diary, 20 December 1886]: Stage rehearsal, first act, 11.30. Home at 4. Wrote till 10.
Finished all the music (except two songs for Grossmith) and sent to Baird [copyist]. Dined
(10.30) at the Beefsteak Club. Tom Bird came in and told me the result of the Colin
Campbell case. Went to Portland. Played besique with Sir C. Russell (6 a.m.!) and won
£102.

[Diary, 22 December]: Musical rehearsal of second act at Lyceum – very satisfactory.
[The Savoy was presumably occupied by continuing *stage* preparations for the first act.]
Dined at the Marlborough [Club] with [Alexander] Mackenzie, Prince of Wales, Duke of
Cambridge, etc., then smoking concert afterwards.

[Diary, 23 December]: First stage rehearsal of second act, very good.

Next day (when there were no rehearsals) Sullivan's nephew Bertie, who had
now found employment with the engineering firm of John Fowler in Leeds,
arrived to join Sullivan's domestic establishment for Christmas. 'Dined at home –
ourselves, plus 4 Chappells – 11 in all' runs the diary entry for Christmas Day
1886, the party comprising Sullivan and his nephew, Fanny Ronalds and her
parents, and two others – perhaps 'Uncle John' and his daughter Jane. Among
other callers that day was 'Findon', presumably Benjamin William Findon, who
was married to Sullivan's cousin Elizabeth Agatha ('Lizzie') and who would
become one of the composer's first biographers. The diary also notes 'presents to
everyone' including his staff of servants and his secretary:

Louis	–	desk and £2
Clotilde	–	gold brooch and £2
Louisa	–	work-bag and £1
Matilde	–	purse and £1
Smythe	–	£30, silver pencil and notebook, and turkey
Ulrick	–	10s
Sarah	–	red bag and £1
Emily	–	work-basket and £1
Janette	–	purse and £2

He also gave a turkey to Cellier, a turkey to his Uncle John (and money for him and his family at 40 Halsey St) and did not omit to call that day on his mother's old friend Mrs Dremel with a present of a 'tower clock and calendar'.

Income tax was a recurrent vexation to those of his comfortable financial circumstances: it had risen to eightpence in the pound. His accounts had awakened the persistent attention of the tax authorities – if we may judge by the letter of 6 November written by Smythe to the 'Surveyor of Taxes': 'Sir Arthur . . . has determined to see the Chancellor of the Exchequer [Lord Randolph Churchill] and the Chairman of Inland Revenue, both of whom he knows personally, to see if he cannot be spared this constant annoyance . . .' Whether this threatening posture had any effect is not divulged.

He had meanwhile conducted *The Golden Legend* at its first London performance – with the Royal Albert Hall Choral Society at that hall on 15 November – and then at St James's Hall on 23 November and at the Crystal Palace on 4 December, both with the Novello Oratorio Choir. Of the latter performance the *Athenaeum* remarked: 'As might have been expected, there was an enormous audience, and the popular acceptance of the work is now placed beyond the shadow of a doubt.' A week later he was at the Crystal Palace again, this time deputizing for August Manns (who was in Glasgow) with a programme which included his incidental music to *The Merry Wives of Windsor* and the overture to *The Sapphire Necklace*. The latter 'belongs to an opera which has not yet been produced, portions only having been given in concert performance': this comment in the *Illustrated London News* confirms the previous indications that a complete or near-complete work had been composed.

With the New Year, the composer's self-imposed schedule for *Ruddygore* became more intense, with his usual stretches of work through the night. 'Grossmith's songs' refer to Robin Oakapple's 'My boy, you may take it from me' (Act 1) and 'For thirty-five years I've been sober and wary' (Act 2).

[Diary, 3 January, 1887]: Scoring, Ghost scene, 2nd act.

[Diary, 4 January]: Scoring. Finished Ghost scene. Scored no. 1 [first act], composed no. 7 (first act) and 7, second act (Grossmith's songs) and finale, second act.

[Diary, 5 January]: Scored nos. 2 and 3 [first act].

[Diary, 6 January]: Scoring 5 and 6 (and hornpipe).

[Diary, 7 January]: Scored Grossmith's first song (no. 7).

[Diary, 8 January]: Began score of finale, first act. Dined at 10.45, went to no. 7 [Cadogan Place] for an hour or two (Chappell, French, Martin, etc.); back again to write till 5 a.m. (finished 6/8 E♭ movement).

[Diary, 9 January]: Scoring at finale, first act. Finished it at 5.10 a.m. (Monday)!

[Diary, 10 January]: Wrote and scored finale second act; ditto Introduction and no. 1, second act [duet for Robin and Adam].

[Diary, 11 January]: [scored] 8 and 9 (first act) [duet for Rose and Richard; chorus of bridesmaids]. Gilbert called in afternoon to suggest new no. 6 in second act. Brought me new words at 9.30. Finished no. 9 at 1 a.m., then wrote and scored new no. 6, second act [the ancestors' 'He yields!']. Bed 6.10 a.m.

[Diary, 12 January]: Scoring 10, 11, 12, first act. Bed 7 a.m.

[Diary, 13 January]: Writing all day. Called: Gilbert, Chappell, Cellier, and C [Carte?]; in the evening Roy [?] Richardson. Scored no. 13 (first act) and 2, 3, 4, 8, 9, 10, second act. Finished whole score at 4 a.m.!

Rehearsals, whether of the music alone or on the stage, demanded his daily attendance from 14 January until the production opened at the Savoy on 22 January 1887. Three nights before that opening, when *The Mikado* had the last performance of its run, *The Golden Legend* was given at the Albert Hall under Barnby's baton[1] (on the same programme as Stanford's *The Revenge*, conducted by the composer).

Ruddygore, or the *Witch's Curse* was billed as a 'supernatural opera'. One of the weaker of Gilbert's librettos, it was seen (especially after the freshness of invention in *The Mikado*) to be rather obviously relying on brushed-up ideas. The central device, a gallery of ancestral portraits who come to life, derives from *Ages Ago*, which Gilbert had written (ages ago, indeed!) with Frederic Clay's music in 1869; the courtly old couple Sir Roderic and Dame Hannah follow their model in *The Sorcerer*; the parody of naval behaviour and language is smarter and funnier in the person of Richard Dauntless than in the frolics of *HMS Pinafore*, but the sense of recall is unavoidable. The plot is supposedly a burlesque of what was called 'transpontine' melodrama – a term still used (cf. p.4) to indicate the unfashionable theatres south of the Thames. But that brand of melodrama was itself hardly alive enough to be made fun of. As the *Weekly Dispatch* put it: 'If stage work of the kind caricatured in *Ruddygore* or *The Witch's Curse* is not extinct, it is relegated to regions unfrequented by the patrons of Mr D'Oyly Carte's theatre'.

The one strikingly original figure of the libretto is Mad Margaret, usually said to be a parody of Shakespeare's Ophelia but equally suggestive of the 'mad' scenes of various operatic heroines – those of *Lucia di Lammermoor* and *I Puritani*, for instance. By a typical 'operatic' extravagance (reminiscent of what happens to the hero of *Martha*), Mad Margaret – when eventually reformed in the image of a school-teacher – can be fortified against any lapse by the word 'Basingstoke'.[2] Mad Margaret was played with great success by Jessie Bond, with Rutland Barrington as Sir Despard and Grossmith as Robin Oakapple – the two characters who strive *not* to succeed to the baronetcy of *Ruddygore* with its burdensome duty of committing a crime a day.

As the piece was originally presented, the portraits were brought to life twice – once to terrify Robin, and a second time to provide partners for the female chorus, a crudity which apparently raised some boos on the first night:

[Diary, 22 January]: Production of *Ruddigore* [sic] at Savoy. Very enthusiastic up to the last 20 minutes, then the audience showed dissatisfaction. Revivification of ghosts, etc., very weak. Enthusiastic reception. Supper at Portland afterwards.

However the libretto might be judged, Sullivan had written a highly accomplished score. The finale of the first act incorporates a quasi-madrigal ('When the buds are blossoming') no less happy than that in *The Mikado*, and a sprightly song and dance in 9/8 time ('Oh, happy the lily') which is unique among the Savoy scores. The persistently recurring refrain, 'Hail the bridegroom, hail the bride', may have been intended by both Gilbert and Sullivan as a parody of the similarly-recurring bridesmaids' chorus in *Der Freischütz*. Most remarkable, musically, is the Ghost Scene of the second act, its unusual harmonies and rhythms almost suggesting a spill-over from the more agitated parts of *The Golden Legend*. The strongly coloured orchestration, with its off-beat piccolo shriek for the ghosts' kiss, admirably serves the sombre grotesqueness on which Sullivan fixed his fancy. Yet it could be maintained – and Gilbert *did* maintain – that the music of this scene is actually over-written. The opening lines, on paper, must surely suggest a regular, tripping meter, probably in 6/8 time:

> 'When the *night* wind *howls* in the *chim*-ney *cowls*
> And the *bat* in the *moon*-light *flies*

But Sullivan imposes quite a different scheme and, in doing so, recklessly accents the unimportant 'When' and 'in' – and similarly throughout. In contrast, the duet for Richard and Sir Despard, 'You understand?' (Act 1, no. 15), is a pre-eminent specimen of how Sullivan's musical genius could flower when very closely following not only Gilbert's metre but the wit of his close-knit rhyme-scheme (''Twere almost a pity, the pretty committee').

The adverse reaction on the first night prompted an immediate response:

[Diary, 23 January 1887]: Gilbert and Carte came. Pow-wow. Several changes and cuts decided on.

[Diary, 24 January]: Alterations made in finale [of 2nd act]: ghosts not brought back to life.

[Diary, 25 January]: Long rehearsal for cuts and changes (without band).

[Diary, 30 January]: Wrote and scored new song (second act) for Grossmith. Took letter to *Figaro*, to Charing Cross – no. 7. [Russie] Walker, Loftus and [Edward] Dicey dined with me.

[Diary, 31 January]: Busy all day. Went to American consulate to sign agreement for American *Ruddygore*. Finished score of new finale. Dined at no. 7. Portland + Ross 22.

'No. 7' in both entries indicates, as usual, a call at Fanny Ronalds's house, 7 Cadogan Place: the 'plus' after 'Portland' presumably indicates a win at cards [over an opponent named Ross?], in this case of £22.

The writing of the 'new song' was prompted by a letter from Gilbert of 25 January:

I can't help thinking that the second act would be greatly improved if the recitation [i.e. recitative] before Grossmith's song were omitted and the song re-set to an air that would admit of his singing it *desperately* – almost in a passion, the torrent of which would take him off the stage at the end. After a long and solemn ghost scene, I fancy a lachrymose song is quite out of place – particularly as it is followed by another slow number, the duet between Jessie [Bond] and Barrington ['I once was a very abandoned person'].

The upshot was not that 'the song' was re-set, implying a change of music only; a new lyric beginning 'Henceforth all the crimes that I find in *The Times*' (instead of 'For thirty-five years I've been sober and wary') was written by Gilbert, set to music by Sullivan, and sung at the third performance (2 February 1887) and thereafter. The introductory recitative ('Away, Remorse!') was *not* removed; it was retained to introduce the new song, and both duly appeared in the first printing of the vocal score. Grossmith did not immediately have to re-learn his part: he was ill and was replaced (from the performance of 31 January) by a successor who was to become no less famous, Henry Lytton.

From 2 February, likewise, the title was re-spelt *Ruddigore* in order to soothe some supposedly outraged susceptibilities – 'ruddy' being too recognizable a synonym for the swear-word 'bloody'. With an irony which has been lost on his official biographers, the well-named Dark and Grey, Gilbert later remarked that he wanted to change the title to *Kensington Gore or, Robin and Richard were Two Pretty Men* – 'but Sullivan wouldn't consent'. (Kensington Gore is a London street.) The vocal score was yet to be published, and all British editions that would appear carried the new spelling '*Ruddigore*'; the form 'Ruddygore' appears on the very earliest librettos and theatre programmes. The original song for Robin, 'For thirty-five years', was never printed but survives in the autograph score. The D'Oyly Carte revival of the work in 1920–21 and later (see p. 408), and the vocal score associated with it, would include no musical number at this point.

Ruddigore reached New York on 21 February 1887 – at the Fifth Avenue Theatre under Stetson's management, but it did not do well. Much more successfully, *The Mikado* took off in translated form. A German version had been prepared by Richard Genée and 'F. Zell' (Walzel), which Sullivan considered 'much the best in all the lyrical portions'; but Dr Carlotta (see p. 250) had made another translation which had some good points in dialogue, and Sullivan hoped that the two versions could be combined. A new German agent, B. Bernstein, was now to look after Sullivan's continental interests. 'If Mr Fritzsche [German impresario] agrees to all the foregoing', wrote Smythe to Bernstein, 'Sir Arthur will be pleased to appoint you his agent upon the terms you mention, namely 10 per cent on all Sir Arthur's receipts accruing from this transaction.'

Sullivan's share was to be 10 per cent of the gross takings at the box office, out of which he made his own payment to Gilbert. It seems to have been always Sullivan and not Gilbert who took decisions about the translated versions of their joint works and about the financial arrangements for their performances. In July 1885 Sullivan had assigned to the Leipzig publishers Bote & Bock the copyright of *The Mikado* for the whole of Germany. They had the composer's instruction to take legal action, if necessary, to prevent the sale within Germany of any 'piratical copies' of the music. But between Britain and Austria-Hungary no copyright agreement existed. So there was no means of preventing an unauthorized production of *The Mikado* in Budapest on 10 December 1886 – in Hungarian, doubtless with the use of a 'home-made' orchestration from the vocal score. From such a performance the composer could not draw a penny of income.

Letters written by Smythe give a glimpse of the range of Sullivan's other professional concerns. A correspondent's inquiry about the tempo of *Onward Christian Soldiers* had drawn this reply in the previous September: 'I am directed by Sir Arthur Sullivan to inform you in reply that the military bands are *all wrong* in taking it is a *slow* march. The real time is $\downarrow$ = 100, and this should be used in church.'

On 28 January 1887 Smythe wrote to a provincial promoter in anticipation of a coming performance:

Always leave out the prefix 'Sir' when Sir Arthur is announced as composer. But the prefix may be used when he conducts a concert.

I am also to call your attention to the fact that *The Golden Legend* will take quite two hours to perform if there are only a couple of encores. If none, all the better, and it will take one hour 45 minutes.

The instruction in the first of these two paragraphs represented Sullivan's fixed wish and was to be often repeated.[3]

At the beginning of February 1887 (not at the end of February, as Flower has it) Sullivan headed for his beloved Riviera. The trip, extended, would keep him from England until mid-April, in consequence of which he failed to fulfil engagements to conduct the Philharmonic in its first two concerts on 10 and 24 March 1887. (The season began unusually late.) He arrived in Monte Carlo on 11 February. On 22 February he sat up late composing a song referred to in the diary as *For Ever* but eventually published under the title *Ever*. A friend referred to as 'Julius' is perhaps Julius Reiss, to be particularized later.

To bed at 2.20 [a.m., 23 Feb]. Hadn't been very long asleep when at 6 a.m. [was] awake[ned] by a tremendous shaking of the house, increasing in intensity – realized at once it was an earthquake. Ten minutes afterwards, another shock – short. Everyone terror-stricken, women rushing about and into the open-air in their night-dresses. At 8.30 another short shock. The first was the worst – it made me feel quite sick. The earthquake extended from Leghorn to Paris. At Savona many lives lost. The damage done to Mentone is considerable. Drove out there in the afternoon with Julius. At night there was a regular panic as another earthquake was expected. No one would sleep indoors. The place was alive with people all night – English Church crammed with people sleeping – all carriages hired also to sleep in. About 2 a.m. (24th) a slight shock occurred. I went downstairs, but soon returned to my sitting-room to sleep on the sofa, having given up my bedroom to Marthe [? servant]. A few vibrations only during the night. Wrote L.W. and sent song [to] Smythe. Wired L. at 11 a.m.

Both of these initial-symbols denoted Fanny Ronalds, to whom as usual he wrote or telegraphed frequently. On 27 February he 'wired L. to say should leave for Naples tomorrow'. It was evidently a sudden decision, perhaps a search for more sun, since the Riviera weather had been dull and rainy. In the event it was not till 1 March that he left Monte Carlo, taking the train via Rome to Naples, arriving on 3 March. At Rome a telegram reached him from Dr Carlotta (who seems to have continued as a personal representative, even while Bernstein managed Sullivan's foreign publication rights). Could he come and conduct *The Golden Legend* in Berlin if it were performed on 26 March by 'royal command' of the Emperor? Albani, for whose participation he had hoped, would not be available on that date, but it was an opportunity not to be missed. In Naples his pain struck again, keeping him in bed for two days, but on 7 March he was 'much better'. He had the companionship of 'Mrs C. and Julius' at his hotel in Naples and decided to travel back with them to the Riviera *en route* for Paris and Berlin. The diary entries in Paris include several references to calling at 'no. 9', in one case particularized as 'no. 9 rue Tilsit',[4] and a visit is also recorded to 'no. 4'. As previously (cf. p. 176), the anonymity of such references raises the suspicion that the addresses are of brothels.

Carte meanwhile pursued the composer by correspondence. He was thinking of engaging a young soprano called Marie Tempest – what was Sullivan's opinion of her?[5] Gilbert (after seeing her in *Dorothy*) had reported that she 'screeched'. Whether Sullivan gave an opinion or not, the proposal was dropped. The future Dame Marie Tempest never worked for Carte and in 1899 forsook music for straight acting: her long and distinguished career would embrace such comedies as Noël Coward's *Hay Fever*.

Berlin was celebrating the 90th birthday of the German Emperor (William I). That the work of a living foreign composer should be included in the celebrations was remarkable, and surely due to Sullivan's personal friendship with the Crown Princess Victoria and her sons, Prince William and Prince Henry. Princess Victoria, their 20-year-old sister, posed as Yum-Yum (while Sullivan played the piano) on two occasions at a private show of *tableaux vivants* at Count Radolinsky's. Sullivan's Berlin diary noted the presence of 'heaps of crowned heads and princes' among whom the Prince of Wales was Queen Victoria's own representative at the imperial celebrations.

[Diary, 21 March 1887]: I accompanied Princess Victoria in her 'Yum-Yum' postures – played the song 'The Moon and I'. She did it beautifully.

Sullivan found her 'fascinating'. In his diary thereafter she was 'Princess Yum-Yum'.

The Berlin performance of *The Golden Legend* (in German, translated by Carlotta) would have been a major step forward in Sullivan's reputation, had it been successful. It was a disaster. The soloists had not been engaged by Sullivan: the tenor and baritone were the reliable Nikolaus Rothmühl and Franz Krolop of the Court Opera, but the soprano was one Pattini, whose mediocrity of talent is doubtless reflected in her absence from all standard musical reference works. She was apparently of Italian birth and sang German badly. Her unreadiness for the role of Elsie had been evident at the final rehearsal on Friday, 25 March, as recorded in the composer's diary:

Went to Opera House to look after arrangements and rehearsed for two hours with Pattini, who was very uncertain in her entries, and very shaky in her time. Called at Friedebergs and ordered some jewellery for the principal artists. Dined quietly at home. Went at 7 to the Opera; at ¼ past was ready – Pattini wasn't. She kept me ten minutes, then appeared without her gloves. I went on, and was cordially (not the English warmth) received by a crowded and brilliant audience. *All* the Royalties there. The performance itself is now a matter of history, alas! Everyone worked well and everyone sympathized with me – it was the most agonizing evening I have ever spent. The audience was *very* patient, and very kind to me. The last chorus created a great effect, and I was recalled enthusiastically three times.

The review in the *Allgemeine Musik-Zeitung* found Pattini 'so inadequate in respect of voice and musicianship that on many occasions the performance was put in peril by her'. Sullivan sent his own account of the performance to his friend Louis Engel, music critic of the *World*, knowing that he would make sympathetic use of it without divulging the source. So indeed he did (6 April 1887) in a way that must have gratified the composer:

He had many disadvantages to contend against. The original bells had been lent to a musical society in Dublin, which, in spite of the urgent entreaties of Sir Arthur Sullivan, and in spite of the guarantee of his publishers to provide efficient substitutes, refused to return them before a certain date. The courtesy and goodwill shown by the secretary and committee of this society will probably not be forgotten by Sir Arthur Sullivan. Deep-toned Chinese gongs were therefore employed; but they failed to give the desired effect. Add to these drawbacks the circumstance that the principal soprano was very uncertain in her part, and you will understand the feelings of the composer when he took his place at the conductor's desk in the presence of one of the most brilliant audiences ever assembled in Berlin. The first scene, sung by Herr Rothmühl (Prince Henry) and Herr Grolop [sic] (Lucifer), went excellently, and was warmly applauded. The solo for Ursula (Lammert) and the unaccompanied Evening Hymn might have been repeated, so rapturous was the applause.

Then came one of the most extraordinary episodes ever experienced in musical history. The soprano rose, and began to sing. Composition, composer, and all the other executants were unheeded, and every one was filled with wonderment at the extraordinary exhibition. Forcing her voice, and singing chronically nearly a quarter of a tone sharp, the young lady disdained the notes the composer had written, but sang with a reckless disregard of time, rhythm, and accent, perfectly astounding. Elsie having continually to sing with Prince Henry, with Ursula, and with the chorus, you will readily understand how, if Elsie's music is spoilt, the whole composition must suffer. Chorus and orchestra looked with consternation to Sir Arthur, who, pale as death, kept steadily to his task, although many people expected he would stop the performance altogether. When the last duet was finished, he looked to the chorus and orchestra, who responded by a splendid performance of the last chorus, which went straight home to the audience, and roused them to enthusiasm. The composer was recalled and cheered heartily many times. The public were kind and patient, and it seemed as if they wished to comfort him for what he (and they) had suffered.

After such a reversal, it says much for Sullivan's determination – and for the flexibility of concert arrangements in those days – that he was able to retrieve his reputation. Emma Albani was, he knew, in Antwerp. In reply to a telegram she consented to appear at a performance a week later.

In the interim he was not without social diversion:

[Diary, 30 March]: Went to the Kronp. Pal. [Kronprinzen-Palais, the Crown Prince's residence on the Unter den Linden] at 4 to 6 and played duets with Princess Christian. 'Yum-Yum' gave me a little bracelet ('It's all I've got'). Dined at Pr[ince] George Radziwill's [son of a personal aide-de-camp to the Emperor].

'Princess Christian' was Queen Victoria's third daughter, Helena, who had married Prince Christian of Schleswig-Holstein. She is probably the 'Princess' referred to in the diary entry of 2 April:

Music with Princess in the afternoon. 7.30, 2nd performance of *The Golden Legend* in the Opera House. Full house. Royal family all there. Very good performance. Albani superb. Duet encored ['Onward and onward the highway runs', with Prince Henry]. Great enthusiasm and ovation at the end. Supped with Gye [Albani's husband] and Albani afterwards. Gave her a bracelet.

In next day's diary the additional note is found: 'Gave her a kiss and a diamond bracelet.' Sullivan's own self-respect was saved, but the critic of the *Allgemeine Musik-Zeitung* – who objected to Albani's singing in English, when the rest of the performance was in German – formed no higher opinion of the work. Even the encored duet was

a movement of disquieting triviality. Nothing that follows is on a higher plane than a reasonable level of craftsmanship. The performance was not much better, and Mr Sullivan's conducting was uninspiring. What was good came only from the ability of choir and orchestra.

He had intended leaving Germany but a telegram from Carte urged him to stay: in a few days the D'Oyly Carte company was arriving from England to play *The Mikado* in Berlin again, and *Patience* too. It was a lengthy tour also embracing Vienna, Munich, Leipzig, Dresden and Breslau (now Wrocław, Poland). Before the company's arrival, the composer himself took the train to Leipzig (on the afternoon of Thursday 7 April) in order to spend Good Friday in his old haunts. 'How changed it is! hardly recognizable – all the dear old-fashioned houses are gone.' By the evening of the Friday he was back in Berlin and met Carte on his arrival. Helen Lenoir was with him.

The company itself, travelling separately, had encountered a bad crossing and were late. Soloists and chorus arrived, in fact, only at 7.30 a.m. next day (9 April). The singers were too tired to be rehearsed for their performance that night, but Sullivan gave the orchestra 'a good drilling' (as he noted in his diary). Great enthusiasm greeted the performance – though it was very much a subsidiary company of Carte's, with none of the leading London performers.

Sullivan did not conduct; indeed 'no one I knew was there'. At the performance on 11 April he was conspicuously present – sitting in the royal box with the Crown Prince and Princess and others. On its homeward journey, the company gave Denmark its first taste of Gilbert and Sullivan, playing *The Mikado* (with Josephine Findlay as Yum-Yum) at the Kasino Theatre in Copenhagen from 17 September to 1 October 1887. It was immediately and flatteringly followed by a 'potted' Danish version and then by a full Danish version which ran for more than 100 performances. The Prince of Wales and his Danish wife, visiting her royal parents on the occasion of the Danish Queen's 70th birthday, were part of a large party which patronized Carte's *Mikado* on 19 September.

Six Philharmonic concerts remained to be conducted by Sullivan. The presence of symphonies by Goetz (see p. 209) and Spohr exemplify the taste of the time, along with the continued obligatory vocal numbers – often from French or German operas but translated into Italian. The *Faust* that was represented was Spohr's, not Gounod's! Among pianists, the 11-year-old 'Master Josef Hofmann' (1876–1957) was beginning a long and distinguished career. Another soloist performed, exceptionally, on the pedal-piano (equipped with an organ-like pedal keyboard) – for which Gounod had written a 'Suite Concertante', billed here as a concerto. The works by Frederic Corder (1852–1932) and Alberto Randegger were conducted by their composers.

Third Concert, 21 April

Marie de Lido, soprano; Barton McGuckin, tenor; Lucie Palicot, pedal-piano

Prelude, 'Die Loreley'	Bruch
Duet, 'Hark! her step' (*The Canterbury Pilgrims*)	Stanford
Concerto for pedal-piano	Gounod
Symphony no. 6 ('Pastoral')	Beethoven
Scena, 'Ah! perfido'	Beethoven
Scena, 'When sets the sun' (*The Story of Sayid*)	Mackenzie
Solo for pedal piano, Toccata in F [BWV 540?]	Bach
Overture, 'Fingal's Cave'	Mendelssohn

Fourth Concert, 5 May

Mme [Janet] Patey, contralto; Benno Schönberger, piano

Overture, 'Husitská'	Dvořák
Aria, 'Che farò' (*Orfeo ed Euridice*)	Gluck
Concerto [No. 3] in C minor	Beethoven
Symphony in F	Goetz
Arietta, 'Lungi dal caro bene'	Sarti
Ride of the Valkyries (*Die Walküre*)	Wagner

Fifth Concert, 19 May

Charles Santley, baritone; Giovanni Bottesini, double-bass

Symphony [no. 41] in C ('Jupiter')	Mozart
Aria with double-bass obbligato, 'Per questa bella mano' [K. 612]	Mozart
Piano Concerto [no. 5] in E flat	Beethoven
Roumanian Suite	Corder
Song, 'Let the dreadful engines' (*Don Quixote*)	Purcell
Concertino for double-bass in F sharp minor	Bottesini
Overture, 'Die Meistersinger'	Wagner

Sixth Concert, 9 June

Ella Russell, soprano; Edward Lloyd, tenor;
Marianne Eissler, violin; Fanny Davies, piano

Symphony no. 3 in C minor	Spohr
Aria, 'Ombra leggiera' (*Dinorah*)	Meyerbeer
Caprice for piano in E	Sterndale Bennett
Scena for tenor, 'Prayer of Nature'	Randegger
Overture, 'Leonora', no. 3	Beethoven
Violin solo, 'Fantasia appassionata'	Vieuxtemps
Duet, 'Angiol che vesti' (*Roméo et Juliette*)	Gounod
Piano solos: Song without words, Book 6, no. 1	Mendelssohn
Novellette in D	Schumann
Overture, 'Euryanthe'	Weber

Seventh Concert, 15 June

Lillian Nordica, soprano; Camille Saint-Saëns, piano;
Nettie Carpenter, violin

Symphony [no. 97] in C	Haydn
Aria, 'Questi affetti' (*Faust*)	Spohr
Piano Concerto in E flat [which?]	Mozart
Overture, 'Kenilworth'	Macfarren
Overture, scherzo and finale	Schumann
Recitative and aria, 'Deh vieni' (*Le Nozze di Figaro*)	Mozart
Introduction and Rondo for violin	Vieuxtemps
Overture, 'Oberon'	Weber

Eighth Concert, 25 June

Mme [Emma] Albani, soprano; Emma Nevada, soprano;
Edward Lloyd, tenor; Josef Hofmann, piano

Overture, 'Jubilee'	Weber
Recitative and air, 'Rachel, quand du Seigneur'	Halévy

Couplets, 'Charmant oiseau' (*La Perle du Brésil*) [Nevada]	Félicien David
Piano Concerto [no. 1] in C major	Beethoven
Symphony no. 4 in A ('Italian')	Mendelssohn
Scena, 'Piano, piano' (*Der Freischütz*) [Albani]	Weber
Piano solos: Waltz [which?]	Chopin
Toccata	Rubinstein
'Overtura di Ballo'	Sullivan

Another affair of state claimed him. Having consented to spare time to set Tennyson's 1886 'Ode for the opening of the Colonial and Indian Exhibition', he could hardly decline a similar commission for the Jubilee year. The passing of fifty years since Victoria's accession was variously celebrated, the Queen herself laying the foundation of the Imperial Institute, a building in South Kensington dedicated to the exhibition and celebration of Britain's imperial influence. (Part of the building survives in Imperial College today, and the institution survives in new premises and with altered emphasis as the Commonwealth Institute.) An ode for the ceremony called forth a setting for chorus and orchestra to a text by Lewis Morris (1833–1907). It was begun by Sullivan in June 1887 and duly conducted by him in the Queen's presence on 4 July.

Previously he laboured to oblige his old friend John Stainer with a setting of the Anglican *Magnificat* for the Festival of the Sons of the Clergy, held on 11 May in St Paul's Cathedral where Stainer was organist. His letter of 4 May apologizing for failure is interesting, since it was apparently the text he found intractable:

It is a shame and humiliation to confess it, but I *cannot* [twice underlined] set the *Magnificat*. I tried it before, years ago when I wrote my little Service in D [the *Te Deum*, *Jubilate and Kyrie*, 1866], but I broke down and only set the Morning Service. I have covered pages with sketches but I hate them all. If I could have got anything satisfactory I would have had it ready for you as I am, as you know, very quick in scoring and writing-out. But my endeavours are fruitless. Pray forgive me. I can't help it.

The *In Memoriam* overture, conducted by Stainer, represented Sullivan at the service instead.

On 17 May 1887 he went to the Bach Choir's concert at St James's Hall at which Stanford conducted Berlioz's *Te Deum* and the first performance of Parry's *Blest Pair of Sirens*. The decisive praise which the latter inspired in the diary ('a very fine, clear and melodious work – pleased me greatly') makes a marked contrast with Sullivan's abstention from comment on many other musical occasions.

But in general it was a summer of relaxation. He went to the races at Ascot, staying at the house (Meadowbank, Winkfield, Windsor) which his friend Julius Reiss had rented. On 9 June he saw Bird of Freedom win the Gold Cup there, went back to London to conduct the Philharmonic that night, and next day went back to Ascot. On 17 July with Fanny Ronalds and others he was on a Sunday afternoon boating party on the upper Thames, afterwards dining at Skindle's Hotel, Maidenhead. From 20 to 29 July he was again in France – at first in the

Normandy holiday resort of Trouville, then in Paris, where he witnessed a violinists' competition at the Conservatoire and renewed his acquaintance with Ambroise Thomas. On Saturday 6 August he

went by 3.14 from Waterloo to Hampton Court with Mrs Ronalds, Carte, H.L. [Helen Lenoir] and Whistler – took steam launch there – to Carte's island at Weybridge – tea there – then on to Chertsey – returned and dined at Oatlands Park Hotel – home at 11. The hottest day I have ever had, I think.

On 9–10 August a visit to Portsmouth and Cowes in the yachting season brought another meeting with the German Crown Prince, his wife and their daughter Princess Victoria, and lunch with Lady Randolph Churchill, Emily Yznaga and Consuelo Yznaga (Duchess of Manchester) – three prominent American ladies of London society together! There can be little doubt that a fourth, Fanny Ronalds, was Sullivan's companion on this occasion too.

Tuesday 23 August is noted in the diary as 'L.W. birthday – all dined here' (i.e. at Queen's Mansions), while next day, after noting his purchase of £4,000 worth of shares and his taking a Turkish bath, Sullivan wrote: 'Dined at Café Royal with G^{d}Ma + Mrs R. Then home.'

'Grandma' is his reference to Mrs Carter, Fanny Ronalds's mother. A grandmother of course she was, but the touching thing is to find Arthur Sullivan embracing the term as though Mrs Ronalds's family was his.

25 'I am not Strong'

The Golden Legend soon crossed the Atlantic. Chicago claimed the first performance, conducted by William Tomlins (11 March 1887); then 'this much discussed work', as the *Boston Herald* called it the next day, was performed by the Boston Oratorio Society at the city's Music Hall on 8 May 1887. Frederic Archer was the conductor. In Britain's choral centres large and small, performances proliferated. Charles Hallé brought it to his Manchester concerts on 10 March 1887: 'Nothing that Sir Arthur Sullivan has previously done reaches quite so high a level', declared the *Manchester Guardian*. Manns followed at the Crystal Palace on 7 May with an advertised total of 3,500 performers. Sullivan himself was the conductor five days later when the work was brought back to Leeds for the jubilee concert of the Leeds Philharmonic Society, and also conducted the Norwich Festival performance on 13 October. Hallé conducted the work again on 7 November in Liverpool in the presence of the composer ('a very fine performance' according to his diary) and brought it once again into his own Manchester series on 2 February of the following year.

Beyond the purchase of vocal scores and the renting of the orchestral parts from the publishers, no fee was apparently charged by the composer for performance.[1] But he kept strict control of the standard of performances: the Berlin experience must have been a potent memory! Inquiring promoters received a reply from Smythe asking what strength of chorus and of orchestra were proposed, whether the orchestra would be London-based or local, and sometimes whether the building had an organ (and if not, what substitute would be used). Approved applicants were required to hire the set of tuned bells which had been specially made, or a set of tubular bells in lieu. Sullivan's publishers, Novello, held both the 'bells' and the 'tubes' at his disposal. From January 1889 he normally made a charge of five guineas [£5.25] (plus carriage) for the 'bells' and three guineas for the 'tubes', but in 1890 his old friend Barnby appealed to him to contribute the bells *gratis* to a performance which was intended to 'rescue' a choral society in danger of collapse.

Sullivan's reply alludes to the engagement of Watkin Mills to sing the role of Lucifer:

I burst into tears this morning when I read your letter; it appealed to my nobler nature. You *shall* have the bells and the tubes also if you like, carriage free, delivered (by our own carts) to your door.

Is there anything else I can do? If Mills should be ill don't let it put you out as I keep a box of 'Lucifers' ready for emergencies or 'Els'ee' might be missed. Having now beaten Burnand on his own ground I will conclude. Blaas you.

'Blaas' for 'bless' was no doubt an imitation of exaggerated diction, whether from the stage or from the pulpit. The 'unbuttoned' style of writing remained typical of his correspondence with close friends – but never with Gilbert. A similar easy manner continued to make him an agreeable companion at house-parties, at the club or at the races. But all such social activity, like his professional work, was circumscribed by the bouts of illness which hit him through the autumn of 1887 and into the new year, as his diary and letters show. For most of this time (from 8 September to 8 December) he had taken a lease of Brome Hall, Scole, Norfolk – convenient for his promised appearance at the Norwich Festival. He paid £500 to its owner, Lady Bateman, and received permission from her 'to set up large drawing-room as billiard-room'.

Brome Hall was a two-mile carriage-ride from Diss, which was reached from London by a 3-hour train journey. On 10 December, he 'drove to Diss to meet no. 7 (3)' – i.e. three people from 7 Cadogan Place who were to be his guests, presumably Mrs Ronalds herself and her parents, the Carters. Her daughter and son-in-law ('Fanette' and Tom Ritchie) joined them next day.

On 15 September the 'irritation' which he had previously noted was 'now pronounced a nasty ulcer'. On 21 September when his guests were taking part in the 'final partridge drive' of the shooting season, he was 'too ill to get up'. On October the diary noted: 'Legs worse, greatly swollen; could neither stand nor walk'. As his promised Norwich Festival appearance drew near he 'hobbled on to platform and got through rehearsal pretty well' (10 October); at the performance, three days later, he was 'very seedy but managed to get through it all right'.

Illness was a principal reason, but not the only one, given by Sullivan when he wrote to 'Dearest G' [Grove] from Brome on 12 October 1887:

It was a great effort to me to give up the Philharmonic for I loved my orchestra, and was proud of our performances. It was also the one great musical interest left to me but I was obliged to let it go. In the first place it tied me down too much – to be compelled to be in London for four or five consecutive months in the year doesn't at all suit my restless nature. Secondly although I look tough enough, *I am not strong* and I used to worry and fret about things – either a passage wouldn't come out as I thought it ought to or if it did after much pains and labour the beastly press would swear at or ignore all one had done. I found it was a hopeless, up-hill fight with the press. They were determined that the Philharmonic should not be a rival to their god Richter, and they damned everything with faint praise.[2] So as I am getting too old to stand up as a target for the Hueffers, Engels, Prouts, Frosts and other similar marksmen of the press, I thought I would let some one else have a try . . .

yr loving A

It was an abandonment of a prized position, and Sullivan's declared reasons do not seem quite strong enough. Had there been criticisms voiced also by his fellow-musicians on the Philharmonic committee? It was no doubt easier to identify 'the marksmen of the press' as his attackers. Henry Frederick Frost

(1848–1901) was a London organist and an occasional critic; Ebenezer Prout, more celebrated as a musical theorist, wrote for the *Athenaeum* from 1879 to 1889. They are here grouped with Francis Hueffer of *The Times* and Louis Engel of the *World* – whose services Sullivan had been glad enough to use over the fiasco of *The Golden Legend* in Berlin! Engel was soon to depart: as a teacher of singing he seduced a female pupil, was ordered to pay £2,000 in damages, and fled the country without doing so. The publishers of his forthcoming book *From Handel to Hallé* announced they would pay the profits to the young woman instead.

'I'm very sorry you have been so ill – I heard of it from Carte,' wrote Gilbert to Sullivan on 26 October. On the following day he was to begin the stage rehearsals for the revival of *HMS Pinafore* and had evidently received a proposal from the composer that one of Josephine's songs should be replaced – almost certainly the earlier one ('Sorry her lot') which is in a 'ballad' manner that Sullivan had since discarded. But there was force in Gilbert's counter-argument – which indeed prevailed:

I feel *most strongly* that we ought to play the piece exactly as we played it originally. The piece is not on its probation – it is a conspicuous success – and any alteration will be a confession of weakness. Moreover Miss Ulmar sang the song at rehearsal in a manner which solicited a burst of applause from the company – it is needless to say that she burst into tears. Everybody was charmed with her method of singing it, and lastly I must confess to a sneaking kindness for the only bit of literature in the piece! The song is so well known that a substituted song will be detected at once – and then the question will come – why was it altered?

The *Pinafore* revival was a stop-gap when declining houses had compelled the withdrawal of *Ruddigore*. What was needed was a new piece, but that prospect seemed likely to founder on Sullivan's dissatisfaction with the genre – particularly when Gilbert once again presented him with what he regarded as a mechanical plot. As far back as 4 September the composer's worry was evident in his diary entry:

At night Gilbert read me a scenario for proposed new piece. Clear, but I think very weak dramatically; there seems no 'go' in it. The 1st act promises to lead to something but that something doesn't appear in the second act which is the old story over again of whimsical fancies and subtle argument – but it is a 'puppet-show' and not human. It is impossible to feel sympathy with a single person. I don't see my way to setting it in its present form.

Sullivan's illness would in any case have prevented immediate developments, but on 31 October (when the two met at a rehearsal at the Savoy) Sullivan learned that Gilbert

had *given up* the subject over which there had been so much difficulty and dispute (charm and clockwork) and had found another about the Tower of London, an entirely new departure. *Much relieved.*

Joseph Bennett had been at the Savoy for the *Pinafore* revival, and was to receive a letter (marked 'Private') from Brome Hall a few days later. It concerned an invitation to deliver a presidential address to the Birmingham and Midland Institute, which had developed a strong School of Music:

I wish you had come round on Saturday night between the acts; we might have had a little chat. I have been very ill for over two months – bad urinary troubles (of course) and tiresome results, such as a complete refusal on the part of my legs to allow me either to walk or stand. I am nearly well now, thank God, but very weak. Now about Birmingham. I think it a very high honour to be asked to become one of their brilliant roll of presidents, and if I were strong and robust, I would accept the invitation without an instant's delay. But, honestly, I dread the ordeal of the Town Hall, and the address. The latter (if I were allowed to read it) I might perhaps get through with the help of a learned and discreet counsellor like yourself, but the Town Hall and the committee, and the reception – all these frighten me. Then again, I am refusing to pledge myself to any public engagements for some time to come, for I have an idea of sauntering about the world for a little time – either south, east or west – for the sake of rest and quiet. If I had the thought of the Town Hall and the address haunting me, my rest and peace would depart. It is very difficult to decline such an honour, but it would be well nigh impossible to accept it, and to this effect I must write to Mr Johnstone. Is there a chance of getting you down here for two or three days quietly before I leave?

Next week, I am full; with grave and earnest sportsmen, whose talk is of partridges and cartridges and who will endeavour to knock out my pheasants for me. From the 26th I am prepared to receive you at even a moment's notice. Try and come.

On Bennett's urging, Sullivan overcame his objections and did indeed deliver the address – almost a year later (see p. 281).

While acting the landed squire in Norfolk Sullivan 'sent birds' (he does not say he shot them himself!) to Gilbert and to his Uncle John on 2 November. The entry for that day in the diary continues: 'Madame Goldschmidt died at Malvern'. That laconic remark does no justice to Sullivan's reverence and affection for 'Madame Jenny', as he had addressed her since his youth. His feelings and memories poured out in the letter of condolence he wrote on 7 November to her husband, Otto Goldschmidt:

My memory carries me back 31 years ago when as a boy in the Chapel Royal I received the greatest and most lasting impression of my life; when, singing at your concerts, I heard *her* for the first time, and was taken notice of and praised by her. She it was who made me think that Music was divine. Then, as Mendelssohn scholar, her kindly interest in me – my return to England and close intercourse in your family life – my reverence for her as a woman and as an artist. . . . Indeed I mourn for her and I look back with something akin to amazement and even awe to that wonderful creation of God, that extraordinary combination of genius, force, strong will, and tenderness . . .
[P.S.] Please don't answer this.

He recovered enough to go shooting and on 3 November to take part in an informal dance in which the servants joined the guests: 'I danced with every maid in the house. We were 35.' But on the following days such notes as 'discharge increased', 'discharge decreased', 'flow began again in the night' denote a recurrence of his kidney trouble. Two days after a 'violent discharge in the night' (15 November), he was put on a course of injections ('began permanganate') but this, while stemming the flow, caused 'great irritation of the bladder'. On the 18th he 'stopped the injections and wrote to Dr Barnes [unidentified]. Irritation and flow greatly increased.'

He went back to London (Mrs Ronalds had already returned) to conduct the revival of *HMS Pinafore* on 12 November. The new scenery was particularly elaborate, with lifelike rigging for the ship of which the yards could be manned. The diary for that day begins with a medical reference.

Flowing freely. Moquet [barber] came to cut my hair. Went to see A. Cooper [doctor]. Then to Portland. Dined at Carte's 6.45. Mrs Ronalds, Mrs Ritchie, H. L. [Helen Lenoir] and Gunn [Michael Gunn, Carte's assistant] there. Curtain rose at 8.30 on the most splendid set ever seen on the stage. The stage was a real ship – great enthusiasm. Very fine performance all round without a hitch. Gilbert and self called at the end. Oyster supper (Gilberts, Cartes, etc.) at Carte's. Then to Portland.

Two visits to the gambling-club on such a day!

In December he was 'very unwell' on the 12th, and 'very ill and in great pain' two days later, when he sent for Dr Cooper. 'I have cold in the bladder and swollen testicle and must keep in bed. Very restless and bad night. Cooper [came] *twice.*' On the 15th he noted a pulse of 105, and on that day and the following he had morphia injections. On the 19th he was 'strapped up for the first time'; on the next day he was again strapped up but 'strapping came off during the night'. On Christmas Day, in bed, he received Gilbert and Carte: Gilbert had brought the complete scenario of the proposed new piece. (That is, of course, the piece in story form, not 'the complete libretto' as Flower states: the lyrics would be worked out later.) At 6.30 p.m. he got out of bed to have dinner with the 'old people and Mrs R.' (Mrs Ronalds and her parents) and went to bed again at 10.45.

Sullivan found the new plot a 'pretty story – no topsy-turvydom, very human and funny also', as he noted in his diary. According to the foreword which W. S. Gilbert wrote for an illustrated edition of four of his Savoy librettos in 1909, the genesis of what became *The Yeomen of the Guard* occurred when, having missed a train at his local Uxbridge station, he happened to see 'a placard advertisement of the Tower Furnishing Company, in which a beefeater was a conspicuous figure'.

On 31 December Sullivan's diary reported his continuing illness:

Pain less but depressed and low. Cold water [treatment]. Have been up in the study every evening since the 24th, can lie down and sit, but cannot stand without pain. Many callers. Dined at 8.30. Mr and Mrs C. [Carter], Mrs R. dined with me and saw New Year in. Trevvy [T. Martin] came in after dinner. All left at 12.15.

His severe pain returned, with Dr Cooper calling on each of the first five days of the New Year. He was asleep when Gilbert called on 2 January (presumably with the first four lyrics; on 8 January he came with three more – 'seven in all'). Sullivan's diary now begins to show an increasing concern with his Belgian maid, Clotilde Raquet, sometimes referred to just as 'C.' At Brome she had already been given a somewhat confidential position in the household. On New Year's Day he was 'very angry with C.' and two days later:

C. came to cry and ask forgiveness 'pour son méchant temper'. Told her if it occurred again I should send her away at once.

The success of the 1886 Leeds Festival, not least with *The Golden Legend*, gave Sullivan good reason to suppose that the conductorship of the coming 1889

Festival would likewise be offered to him, especially as the organizers hoped to persuade him to write a symphony for it. On 18 January 1888 he wrote to the Festival secretary, F. R. Spark:

At last I am well enough to write myself, and with pen and ink [i.e., in his own hand, not through a secretary]. We seem to be arguing in a circle. I hold to the principle that one of the very first steps to be taken in the organization of the Leeds or any other Festival should be the appointment of a conductor – but you and the provisional committee think differently. I cannot undertake to write a new work for a Festival until I know who is to be the responsible authority for its proper production – you will not appoint such an authority until you have selected the new composition. So we are at a standstill. I still am of the opinion (as I have often expressed to you personally) that it is a grave mistake to delay the appointment of a conductor until the musical matters are more than half arranged. There are many cases in which his advice might be sought, and his influence needed with advantage. It is also possible that errors may have been committed, which a little discussion with a responsible musical adviser would have avoided. I wish you and the committee could be induced to come round to my way of thinking.

What say you to it?

Another letter of that date, in Smythe's hand, went to Alfred Broughton, the festival chorus-master, in respect of a performance Broughton was shortly to give of the *Overtura di Ballo*. The letter reveals that only at this stage were the double-bassoon and tuba finally driving out the old lowest-pitched instruments of the woodwind and brass respectively.

I have mentioned your letter to Sir Arthur and he has asked me to say he is delighted to know you will have a good orchestra on February 1 and hopes you will have a successful performance.

Knight, Sir Arthur says, is the best *contra fagotto* you can get. The *contra fagotto* can play for the *serpent*, and the *tuba* (most important) for the *ophicleide*. I send you the metronomic marks of the different movements, viz.

Andante moderato   = 72
Allegro (Valse)   = 80 (QUICK Waltz)
Allegretto vivace   = 160

I am happy to tell you Sir Arthur has been out twice for a carriage airing and is progressing most satisfactorily. He has asked me to thank you and Mrs Broughton for your kind sympathies; also please give his love to his 'little sweetheart' and say he thinks it very kind of her to think of him.

To Sullivan's inquiry about the appointment of a conductor Spark's reply was diplomatic. The committee, he explained, as yet possessed no power to act: constitutionally, the choice of conductor had to wait until festival guarantors had been found and a new executive formed. In June 1888 Sullivan wrote (via Smythe) that his 'inclination' was to write a symphony for Leeds but that he could not commit himself. In October he declined the commission. The hoped-for 'Leeds Symphony' was never written, nor was Sullivan to put his name to any other major choral work for the concert-platform. But he did nevertheless receive, and accepted, an invitation to conduct the 1889 festival.

He went off to stay at the Hôtel de Paris, Monte Carlo, receiving there an astonishing plan from Carte. With a true entrepreneur's restlessness he proposed ceasing productions at the Savoy and taking, or even building, a grander theatre Carte had taken alarm at the long-running success of Alfred Cellier's *Dorothy* (libretto by B. C. Stephenson) at the Gaiety Theatre:[3] described as 'a comedy opera', it had opened on 25 September 1886 and was on its way to a record-breaking 931 performances, far outstripping those of the *The Mikado* on its first run.

If you wish the scheme to go through you will not delay writing to Gilbert at once and putting your views with that decisive clearness which is always at your command. If I do not speedily let the Savoy to a good tenant, or sell it, our scheme cannot I fear go through at all. Gilbert is not fully reconciled to the plan, but he is I think in that frame of mind in which your letter would probably decide him in favour of it. . . . With reference to a point I made that we should not let other *people get ahead*, and my speaking of not letting other people get ahead of us, and of a certain other theatre, and a certain other opera, and company, this was evidently distasteful to Gilbert, as indeed it must be to us, yet I cannot but think that it does good. We have to take unpleasant medicine sometimes.[4]

On receiving that letter of Carte's, written on 13 February 1888, Sullivan must have indeed been stirred (just as Carte hoped) into an immediate letter to Gilbert Himself replying on 19 February, Gilbert alluded to the terms on which Carte as proprietor of the Savoy rented that theatre out to the joint management of himself (as impresario), Gilbert, and Sullivan – 'us'.

I can't, for the life of me, understand the reasons that urge you to abandon a theatre and a company that have worked so well for us, and for whom we have worked so well. Carte has his own interests. He lets the Savoy to us for £4,000 a year and now we have made it what it is, he can let it for £6,000. That I take to be the root of his argument and that consideration can't affect you and me.

We have the best theatre, the best company, the best composer, and (though I say it) the best librettist in England working together – we are world-known, and as much an institution as Westminster Abbey – and to scatter this splendid organization because *Dorothy* has run 500 nights is, to my way of thinking, to give up a gold-mine. What is *Dorothy's* success to us? It is not even the same class of piece as ours. Is no piece but ours to run 500 or 600 nights? Did other companies dissolve because *The Mikado* ran 650 nights?

Gilbert's point was taken. The company was kept in being and it was the Savoy that would house the new opera. But Carte's ambition was not halted. He would indeed build his larger theatre – and would offer Sullivan the chance to realize *his* ambitions there, without Gilbert. The consequences were to be disastrous.

While on the Riviera Sullivan engaged himself in composition a little – working at the finale of Act 1 on 28 and 29 February, but breaking off at 2.30 a.m. next day with the diary comment 'No good'. The pleasures of sociability and travel were his first concern. On 3 March he went across the Italian border to San Remo (by train to Ventimiglia, then by carriage) to call on the German Crown Prince, Princess and daughters. Less than a week later, while he was still at San Remo, the Crown Prince learnt by telegram of the death of his father, William I. As Emperor Frederick III he hastened back to Berlin. Enfeebled by a throat disease (cancer was suspected) he would reign barely three months and Sullivan's admirer, Prince William, would succeed as William II.

Familiar as he was with the Riviera, Sullivan now fancied a change. On 6 March he took ship from Marseilles to Algiers and stayed there for a fortnight. The French-ruled North African city with its European upper society was already 'on the map' for the well-to-do tourist. As an addition to John Murray's well-known series of guide-books, a *Handbook for Travellers in Algeria and Tunis* had appeared in 1887, with a recommendation to visit between the beginning of November and the end of May. Sullivan's visit stirred him to no such excitement as Egypt had evoked in 1881–2, but there were pleasant diversions – Algiers offered a 'battle of flowers' similar to the famous one at Nice – and unpleasant weather. By letter and telegram he kept in touch, as ever, with Fanny Ronalds; the diary reference is again to her residence, 'no. 7'.

Diary, 15 March]: Sirocco still on. Went to 'Bataille des fleurs' (mi-carême) [mid-Lent] on the Boulevard de la République. Nothing very distinguished in flowers or decorations, but very gay and picturesque. Home to dine and remain. Wired no. 7 to write again.

Diary, 16 March]: Sirocco still going. Drove out to see Mr Macleay at his Arab home. Very beautiful and picturesque – garden very fine. . . . Dined at the Mackenzies. Prince and Princess Windisch-Grätz, Countess Auersperg (her mother), Mr and Honble Mrs Prideaux Brune [?],Lady Dorothy Murray and self. Very cheery. After dinner a number of people came and danced . . .

From Monte Carlo on 4 March he had written to 'du lieber, alter Kauz' (a German colloquialism for 'old chap' – probably one of his English colleagues of Leipzig student days) about an invitation to take a directorship in 'the Symphonion Co. Ltd'.

What is a symphonion? It sounds like something between a euphonium and a symposium. Once bit, twice shy, as the old Patagonian proverb runs.

He declined, in fact, to become a director of the company. The symphonion was a large improved musical-box invented in Germany in 1885. Usually in the form of an upright cabinet, it was the first musical 'slot machine' and enjoyed considerable popularity in its day. Another new invention, of more genuinely musical interest, was the 'clavi–harp' – one of several nineteenth-century attempts to sound a harp's strings by the action of a piano-like keyboard. Sullivan's curiosity was roused, but he found himself too tired and unwell to go to a London demonstration of it on 25 April.

He had arrived home from the continent on 1 April, and dined that evening with Fanny Ronalds at no. 7. Before the holiday, he had begun to sit for his portrait by Millais, and now resumed the sittings. But on 8 April the diary indicated: 'Show Sunday – did not go to Millais'. The rowdy pre-Derby parade of the horses at Epsom ('Show Sunday'), with accompanying fairground events, was soon to be abolished as offensive to Victorian observance of the Lord's Day, but Sullivan was keen on the whole atmosphere of the great race-meetings. He was at Epsom again on 11 April to see the City and Suburban won by Sir George Chetwyn's horse, Fullerton. On the same day 'Carte came to tell me of his marriage next day'. It can hardly have been unexpected. It had been three years since the death of his first wife (née Blanche Prowse), and Helen Lenoir had long been his confidential adviser. Sullivan acted as his friend's best man at the Savoy Chapel, and later (as his diary chose to put it) 'saw the young couple off at Charing Cross': Carte was nearly 43, Sullivan himself nearly 46. The bride, who signed the register under her real name of Black, was 34.

On 28 April 'my portrait (not quite finished) [was] exhibited at the Private View, Grosvenor Gallery. Hadn't the courage to go and see it.' Next day he went for the last time to sit for Millais and judged the finished work 'a remarkable likeness'. Now in the National Portrait Gallery, London, the portrait indeed boasts a photographic clarity, but was not to be ranked then or now among the artist's best works.[5]

After Epsom, Newmarket: the racing calendar summoned Sullivan out of London again (1–4 May) and there was then his birthday to celebrate. On 14 May itself three of his cousins (Uncle John Sullivan's children) called on him: Jane 'Rosy' and 'Lizzie' (with her husband Benjamin William Findon). Another caller, according to the diary, was 'Mrs Holmes' – presumably Amy Holmes, a cousin on his mother's side.

The Golden Legend continued to be in demand but there was one occasion which conferred a special recognition – and perhaps compensated for the royal favour shown earlier to Gounod's *Mors et Vita*:

[Diary, 8 May 1888]: Grand performance of *The Golden Legend* at the Albert Hall by command of the Queen, who was present. Very good performance. Afterwards the Queen sent for me and expressed her pleasure at having heard the work. Her first words were: 'At last I have heard *The Golden Legend*, Sir Arthur.' Later on she said: 'You ought to write a grand opera – you would do it so well!' Her Majesty was very gracious and kind.

Though not completely recovered in health, he was able to mount a celebratory dinner on 20 May much bigger than he had essayed for a long time. Ella Russell, the young American soprano whom he heard in *La traviata* at Covent Garden three days before, was among those who entertained the company:

Dinner party here. Present 16. Prince of Wales, Duke and Duchess Paul of Mecklenburg-Schwerin, Caroline Duchess of Montrose, Count and Countess de Fitzjames, Mr and Mrs Leo Rothschild, Hon. Mrs Pereira, Mrs Ronalds, Captain and Mrs W. Calley, Reuben Sassoon, The Mackenzie of Kintail, and Charles Wyndham. After dinner about 41 guests came. Artists: Miss Ella Russell, Miss Phillips, Miss Marjorie Hall, Barton McGuckin, Herr Wessely, Mrs Shaw (the Whistler), Jessie Bond, Barrington and Eric Lewis. At 11.30 when everyone was in the drawing-room the electric light went out! Arthur Grove had just gone, the engineer could not do anything, – so we had to get all the candles we could in the house and light up. The reception rooms' 'cut-out' had fused (we afterwards found out) and no one knew where another was to be found. Everyone was very good natured about it and we managed to get on. Supper at 1.15. The Prince and the Duke and Duchess went at 3.

Arthur Grove, son of Sir George, was on the staff of the firm which had installed the lights. 'Mrs [Alice] Shaw' was a genuine concert celebrity, billed at public appearances as 'Mrs Shaw, the American lady whistler'. The presence of an 'engineer' seems surprising, but was apparently a necessity – with a cost which

Sullivan objected to paying. He later wrote to the electrical company protesting against their charges:

That your man should be here week after week all the year round to run an engine for an average of 65 or 70 hours a week seems to me absurd, as I seldom use more than a few lamps any day except Sunday, and I can only conclude that there is something radically wrong with the installation to render such long hours necessary.

On 8 June, at 11 in the morning as Sullivan's diary noted, Gilbert called with 'new libretto complete, i.e. in the rough. Stayed till 2' – to be followed by Ben Davies, who came to rehearse Prince Henry's role for the performance of *The Golden Legend* scheduled for the following week in Cambridge. (At 30, Davies was a rising star, succeeding Sims Reeves and Edward Lloyd as the favourite tenor of British audiences.) The Cambridge performance on 12 June was presented by the Cambridge University Musical Society of which Stanford had become permanent conductor – at the age of 20! – fifteen years before. Sullivan conducted, staying at Stanford's house, finding it 'very comfortable and jolly'. Hubert Parry had been his train-companion from London to Cambridge on the previous day.

Next day he went to join a house-party for the races at Ascot – staying with 'Russie' [Walker] and greeting his old friends Ernest Dresden and Edward Dicey. On the 15th the news of the death of the German Emperor, Frederick III, reached the racecourse by telegraph: there was 'universal sorrow' (said Sullivan's diary), but it was not such sorrow as to halt the race-meeting. Seeking isolation from London again in order to concentrate on the new opera, Sullivan entered on 18 June into a six-week tenancy of a country house – this time Booth Lodge at Fleet in Hampshire – and on the 19th 'began to work'. Fleet was only about five miles from Farnborough, where the empress Eugénie, widow of Napoleon III, had made her home, with Sullivan's friend Mme Conneau in attendance. Sullivan accepted an invitation to tea on Saturday 23 June, 'rehearsed some music . . . [and] had a long walk with the Empress'.

In continuing his practice of moving in summer to a country retreat, Sullivan's aim was to avoid the distraction of casual callers such as would have interrupted his day in London. But, as always, he had guests and enjoyed the company of friends in the neighbourhood. On 6 July 'Bertie' came to stay (apparently for an indefinite period) and on the 15th Fanny Ronalds arrived with her mother for a fortnight. On 22 July 'after lunch, Russie, Bertie and I rowed up to Odiham and rowed back – capital exercise'. Indeed it was, even if they divided between them the doubled eight-mile stretch of the Basingstoke Canal. On 27 July he went to the races at Sandown (near Esher, Surrey), and next day later travelled north to Chester to conduct *The Golden Legend*, noting 'an excellent performance': the distinguished American operatic soprano Lillian Nordica (1857–1914) sang as Elsie, partnered by Edward Lloyd and (as Lucifer) Robert Grice, the last-named possessing 'a superb voice . . . I predict a future for him'. (A mistaken prophecy!) Before the performance his valet Louis 'didn't return from his walk, so I had to dress myself'. The reference is, of course, to putting on evening dress for the concert – a process in which a valet's assistance was similar to that of a theatrical 'dresser'.

On 1 September *The Golden Legend* was due to be performed at the Birmingham Festival with Hans Richter conducting. Sullivan smarted not only because his formal permission for the performance had not been asked, but because he had read the announcement that under Richter's direction the work 'would be executed, probably for the first time, in all its grandeur and beauty'. That was the phrase he quoted in a protesting letter to the festival committee on 8 August – upon which the committee apologized and said that it was only 'for the first time in Birmingham' that such glory was promised. The correspondence, published in *The Times* on the day the festival opened (28 August), can have done nothing to unfreeze Sullivan's hostility to Richter as the intrusive, over-praised foreigner. Despite the experienced participation of Albani and Lloyd (with the Irish baritone A. J. Foley, known as Signor Foli) Richter's performance was strongly criticized in the *Musical Times* as deficient in understanding of the composer's style. Sullivan, who did not attend, must have been gratified – not least when the reviewer called it 'that most popular of modern works'.

The new operetta was, as usual, formally unnamed. Gilbert's initial liking had been for 'The Tower of London'; later he favoured 'The Tower Warders'. (Not, of course, 'wardens', as given in the Flower biography – a mistake arising from a misreading of Gilbert's handwriting, coupled with ignorance on the biographers' part about what the guardians of the Tower are called.) The title was still 'The Tower Warders' on 2 July when Sullivan recorded in his diary that he had 'finished sketch of no. 3'. This indicated the double chorus, 'Tower warders, under orders . . .'– no. 3 of the present score, 'When our gallant Norman foes', which Sullivan elsewhere refers to as 'No. 4 (Tower Legend)'.

The musical setting of the piece had progressed sufficiently for rehearsals to begin at the Savoy on 10 August, three days before Sullivan ended his stay at Fleet and returned to London. The young Henry J. Wood, not yet 20, had been engaged as a musical assistant. For Grossmith, Gilbert had written the role of the tragic jester, Jack Point; such other stalwarts as Richard Temple (Sergeant Meryll) and Rosina Brandram (Dame Carruthers) had roles also tailor-made for them, as did the mischievous Jessie Bond (Phoebe). Geraldine Ulmar, who had proved herself in New York with Yum-Yum, was Jack Point's companion, Elsie. She soon became 'Dolly' to Sullivan, just as Bond was 'Jessie': hence the diary entry 'Rehearsed with Dolly'. The male singers are referred to by their surnames! Courtice Pounds, plucked from the chorus and seasoned by touring as a soloist, was to prove a valuable solo tenor and to create the role of Fairfax.

When Sullivan in the course of composition found that the flow of musical thought demanded alterations in the words, Gilbert was ready to oblige. He wrote on 10 August:

I sent you the tripping refrain for 'How say you maiden' some weeks ago, together with the altered 2nd verse of 'To thy fraternal care'. However, I [now] send another draft of the refrain in question. I am not quite clear what alteration is wanted in the duet between

Wilfred and Phoebe in 1st scene – but as you say this can wait until we meet, so let it be. I remember you wanted something, but I am sorry to say I can't remember what it was.

I could not write the 8 lines at end of finale because I couldn't remember what led up to them. Now that I have the manuscript of course I can do it easily. But you say you don't want them. If you would like to have them, let me know.

Certainly the two erased lines in 3rd verse of 'I have a song to sing O' can stand if you wish it.

I shall be at Queens Hotel, Manchester, all next week.

Very truly yours
W. S. Gilbert

P.S. 'Down he *dived* into the river' will be better than 'jumped'.

But now Sullivan asked for something more, a changed construction in the second act. Gilbert's first response was evidently to decline, and Sullivan hit back, as his diary noted on 16 August: 'I wrote him back a snorter and asked whether the rehearsals were to be continued, as I wouldn't set the piece as it was.'

Gilbert's own form of 'snorter' was the inevitable reply:

I give you Act 2 on the 8th June, having settled with you the musical construction of that act months before. I read that Act to you on 8th June and you express yourself delighted with it. Subsequently you decide that the piece shall be produced on or about 15th September. On 10th August the music is put into rehearsal. On 17th August, after the piece has been in rehearsal a week you write to ask me to practically re-write and re-construct Act 2 as you can do nothing with it, although you have written five numbers of it before making this discovery! I quite agree with you that your expression of approval should not debar you from requiring me to make alterations when you come to tackle the piece in detail, but when these alterations amount to practical reconstruction, and I am asked to do this while the piece is actually in rehearsal, I think I am justified in saying – as I did say – that it is rather rough on me. To this mild and I think, reasonable, not to say humble, protest you reply in a tone which you describe as a tone of enthusiasm, *I* describe it as a tone which you might fitly and properly display to an obstinate clerk, but one to which I am quite unaccustomed, and scarcely know how to digest.

How the clash was resolved is not revealed in detail, but the 'cuts and changes in second act' (see the diary entries below) suggest that Sullivan must have got some of his own way. At first he refused to be hurried. On 22 August, taking the boat-train from Euston to Stranraer, he went with Fanny Ronalds, her son 'Regie' and 'Grandma' (Mrs Carter) on a trip to Belfast where her daughter Fanette and son-in-law Tom lived. Mrs Ronalds remained there when Sullivan left, London-bound, on the 27th. Later references to 'no news' and 'all right' from Belfast suggest that Fanette was expecting a baby.

The opening of the new work was deferred till early October, but still Sullivan underwent his usual hectic routine of the last few weeks before a production – with rehearsals and composition (often well into the night) proceeding simultaneously, and other work demanding his time too: he had undertaken to conduct *The Golden Legend* for the Three Choirs Festival at Hereford – and did so without rehearsal! He charged neither fee nor expenses on this occasion, and probably on similar occasions also.[6] Successive diary entries narrate the accumulation. The 'C.' on 13 September is unexplained: in other entries the initial certainly stands for his maid Clotilde, whose fits of temper and subsequent apologies continued to be noted.

[Diary, 3 September 1888]: Rehearsal, Savoy, 12–5.30. Worked all night. Finished finale, 1st act, at 5 a.m.

[Diary, 4 September]: Rehearsal, Savoy, 12–5.30.

[Diary, 5 September]: Began scoring opera: nos 1 and 3.

[Diary, 6 September]: Rehearsal (1st act) at Savoy on stage.

[Diary, 7 September]: Long music rehearsal [i.e. without action] at theatre. Rehearsed no. 1 and finale, act 2.

[Diary, 8 September]: Scoring no. 4 (Tower Legend).

[Diary, 9 September]: Savoy principals (except Grossmith and Temple) here at 5.30 to rehearse. [They had probably been at the theatre till then.] All stayed to dinner afterwards (10). A little scoring afterwards.

[Diary, 10 September]: Long rehearsal 1st act at Savoy. Scored at night.

[Diary, 11 September]: Left Paddington [Station] 12 . . . arrived Hereford 5.31 . . . Eight o'clock, conducted performance of *Golden Legend* in Shire Hall – crammed house. Very good performance – only band *rough*, a lot of fossils amongst them.

[Diary, 12 September]: Left Hereford 9.45 arrived home 3. Grove came and talked over the Birmingham address [see below, p. 281]. Dined at Guards Club (for Marlborough). [His own club, the Marlborough, presumably enjoyed the other club's hospitality during a period of closure.] Home to write. Scored nos. 8 and 9 (1st act) – chorus and 'I have a song'.

[Diary, 13 September]: Rehearsal, Savoy 2nd act – goes well. Home to work. Scored Trio (10) and Song (11), 1st Act. Dined at home. C. . .

[Diary, 14 September]: No rehearsal at theatre. Worked at cuts and changes in finale of 2nd act – also finished vocal score ditto. Very tired. Dined at home. Went for an hour to say goodbye to Nordica and her mother, who sail for America tomorrow, 15th. Portland [Club]. [Saw] George Lewis. Wrote to Belfast.

On 15 September Gilbert wrote to Sullivan using a new title for the work, 'The Beefeaters'. Only later was the final change made to *The Yeomen of the Guard*. Gilbert must have liked its rhythm and sonority, though he knew that it was technically wrong: the yeomen warders at the Tower are in fact quite distinct from the Yeomen of the Guard, a corps attached to the Sovereign.

A series of sensational and grisly London murders gripped the attention of the newspapers and the nation that autumn. The assailant, known as Jack the Ripper, was never found. Amid Sullivan's usual chronicling of his process of composition of rehearsals, a reference to those murders (in Whitechapel, in London's East End) stands out at the end of September.

[Diary, 15 September]: Fine day. Got up at 12 [noon]. Began 2. Scored no. 13 (first act). Dined at home. Went up to Portland at 9.45. No one there. Returned at 11. Worked till 4[a.m.]. Wrote recit, and scored that and Song (no. 11). Wrote to Belfast. From ditto. No news yet.

[Diary, 16 September]: Scored 2, 5 (1st act). 1 (2nd act).

[Diary, 17 September]: Scored no. 6 (patter), 2nd act.

Diary, 18 September]: At home all day. Began scoring finale 2nd act, *finished at* 5 a.m.

Diary, 19 September]: At home all day. Scored 2, 3, 4, and 7 (2nd act). Went to Portland Club) at 11. Home again 11.45.

Diary, 20 September]: Went to rehearsal 1.30 (1st act). Settled to cut No. 2. Tried new bell – all right. Home at 5. Scored no. 8 (quartet 2nd Act). Went to theatre; rehearsed with Dolly. Home to score; finished no. 9 and consequently all the opera at 5 a.m.!

Diary, 22 September]: Correcting proofs – thinking about overture – telegram from Belfast 'All right'! Thank God . . . [*Later Sullivan added*: Mrs R. and Regie left Belfast. Detained all night in the [Irish] Channel by fog.]

Diary, 23 September]: Began sketching Overture.

Diary, 24 September]: Began scoring Overture.

Diary, 25 September]: First band rehearsal of new opera. 11.30 St Andrew's Hall. Very heavy work – could not get through it all. *All* scored and copied except Overture. Went on with score of Overture – finished it at 3.30 a.m. Frank Cellier slept here, having been to *Dorothy* anniversary supper. He came in about 3.

Diary, 28 September]: Full rehearsal, band and voices (music only) at the theatre (St Andrews Hall under repair). Had a regular flare-up with Gilbert between the parts. He worried everyone and irritated me beyond bearing – in one of his worst moods. I can't stand it any longer and get as angry and irritable as he is. Eventually we made it up. Rehearsed the overture.

Diary, 29 September]: Wrote new song 'Is life a boon?' Scored it, and took it to the theatre to Baird. Last night of the *Mikado*. Great excitement, and tremendous enthusiasm for Barrington. Speeches before and behind the curtain. Left at 12. Very wet night. Portland.

Diary, 30 September]: Pounds came at 3 and rehearsed the new setting of 'Is life a boon?' I went to the theatre at 4.30 to arrange seats in orchestra. Four stalls taken off. Heard at the theatre of the double murder at Whitechapel the previous night.

[Diary, 1 October]: Rehearsal with band, scenery – and lights – at 11.30. Pounds sang the new song ('Is life a boon?') to everyone's amazement and delight! All went well and smoothly. Had to take off two more stalls (six in all) for the orchestra.

A song allotted to Richard Temple, in the role of Sergeant Meryll, caused disagreement. Beginning 'A laughing boy but yesterday', it served as an expression of Meryll's fatherly pride, but did not in itself advance the plot.

[Diary, 2 October]: Full dress rehearsal at 4. Over at 10. Everything went smoothly. Another irritable passage with Gilbert à propos of Temple's song. Am anxious myself to cut it but object to being 'hectored' in the matter. All supped at Carte's afterwards.

On the very morning of the opening night, 3 October, Sullivan received from Gilbert a letter sent by messenger:

I desire before the production of our piece to place upon record the conviction that I have so frequently expressed to you in the course of rehearsal, that unless Meryll's introduced and wholly irrelevant song is withdrawn, the success of the first act will be most seriously imperilled.
Let me recapitulate:
The act commences with Phoebe's song – *tearful in character*. This is followed by entrance of warders – *serious and martial in character*. This is followed by Meryll's song –

sentimental in character. This is followed by the trio for Meryll, Phoebe and Leonard - *sentimental in character.*

Thus it is that a professedly comic opera commences.

I wish moreover to accentuate the hint I gave you on Friday that the Warders' couplets in the finale are too long, and should be reduced by one half. This, you will observe is not 'cutting out your music,' but cutting out a *repeat* of your music. And I may remind you that I am proposing to cut, not only your music, but my words. Also that I write not as an author but as an expert in stage management.

Only just before the curtain rose on *The Yeomen of the Guard, or the Merryman and his Maid* was a compromise arranged – as the diary tells:

Tired and nervous. Drove to the theatre at 8 to meet Gilbert and settle one or two points - arr. to cut down 2nd verse of couplet in Finale; to leave in Temple's song for the first night. Crammed house – usual enthusiastic reception. I was awfully nervous and continued so until the duet 'Heighdy' which settled the fate of the opera. Its success was tremendous; 3 times encored! After that everything went on wheels, and I think its success is even greater than the *Mikado*. 9 encores.

'Temple's song' thus survived – for one night only. It was deleted from later performances and does not appear in any printed score. The much-encored 'Heighdy' duet, as Sullivan calls it, was 'I have a song to sing, O'. Its cumulative verse-form evidently had Sullivan in some difficulties until Gilbert himself recalled to the composer a sea-shanty of similar pattern. It was the only time Sullivan acknowledged his collaborator's *musical* help.

Publication of the vocal score (by Chappell, as usual) followed swiftly and profitably. 'It is said', reported the *Era* on 24 November 1888, 'that

nearly a thousand parcels, weighing several tons, of the music of the opera *The Yeomen of the Guard* were dispatched by the various lines of railway throughout the United Kingdom on Friday 16th inst., the day of publication. The employees of the publishers worked day and night to supply the enormous demand for this latest joint production of W. S. Gilbert and Sir Arthur Sullivan.

26 The Furthest Point

WHEN Bunthorne had been left without a bride at the end of *Patience*, or Ko-Ko had found himself landed with the unwanted charms of Katisha, the only possible theatrical reaction was laughter. Not so when Jack Point, the 'merryman' of *The Yeomen of the Guard* (another Grossmith role), lost his bride and fell 'insensible' amid the rejoicing at curtain-fall. It was to be the sole moment of real pathos in the entire Gilbert and Sullivan canon – and whether 'insensible' meant just 'overcome with grief' or (in Henry Lytton's later interpretation) 'dead' mattered only in degree. For librettist and composer, *The Yeomen of the Guard* was a reaching-out, and from Gilbert's point of view a halt. It marked the furthest point that he permitted himself to go towards 'serious' opera.

Sullivan relished the musical opportunities it provided. 'Its composition yielded him more genuine pleasure than he had found in any opera of the topsy-turvy type,' according to Cellier, who also remarked that *The Yeomen* 'remained Sullivan's favourite of all his offsprings given to the stage'. That this work was indeed innovatory was recognized by the critic of the *Era* (6 October 1888):

It remains to be seen whether the former admirers of Gilbert and Sullivan's 'topsy-turvy' operas will accept with the same enthusiasm the new departure they have made, exchanging the grotesque fancies and wild extravagances of the past, the oddities of expression and whimsicalities of character for an altogether soberer style of opera, approaching more closely than they have done before the old school of English opera.

In the context of an action set in the sixteenth century, the 'old English' musical manner re-emerged with direct allusiveness as in *Ruddigore*, not in exotic parody as in *The Mikado*. The quartet 'Strange adventure', though not this time marked 'madrigal', and having no *fa-la* refrain, none the less distils an antique flavour; likewise 'I have a song to sing, O' with its drone accompaniment and (in the last verse) modal scale. Gilbert himself essayed the tricky classical metre of 'elegiacs' (so acknowledged in the libretto) in the finale to Act 2:

Comes the pretty young bride, a-blushing, timidly shrinking . . .

– to which the composer's response in a free 9/8 was particularly apt. For once, the curtain rose not on a generalized chorus but on a single character – Phoebe,

279

seated on Tower Green, the musical accompaniment reflecting (on a model which had been established by Schubert and Wagner) the turning of her spinning wheel. It was a break from Savoy convention, but Gilbert's own farcical play *Engaged* (1877) had similarly opened with a young woman spinning and soliloquizing.

The recurrent musical theme chosen by Sullivan to represent the Tower of London itself is not more prominent than the little tag which had characterized the Lord Chancellor in *Iolanthe*. Even on Sullivan's own terms it is curious to find it *not* recurring in the final dramatic resolution of the plot. It nevertheless forms an imposing 'principal subject' of the overture and makes a sharp effect in what Sullivan referred to as the 'Tower legend' (Dame Carruthers' 'When our gallant Norman foes') and in Sergeant Meryll's welcome of his supposed son to the company of the Yeomen. The composer's affectionate portrait of the iron-disciplined Dame Carruthers is rounded off in the often omitted duet with Sergeant Meryll. Never was Sullivan's orchestration more deftly appropriate than in the introduction of the lugubrious bassoon when *her* 'Rapture, rapture' is replaced by *his* 'Doleful, doleful'.

Indeed the score never falls below the best level of Sullivan's music – from the nimble swagger of Jack Point's duet with Shadbolt (the 'head jailer and assistant tormentor') to the subtle chromatic changes with which Phoebe wheedles Shadbolt in 'Were I thy bride'. The finale to Act I occupies its usual place of climax in the structure of the whole, but a quite special effect is the climax *within* it – the sudden change of key and mood brought by the 'funeral march'. The bell at the moment when the doomed prisoner's arrival is expected is a highly effective addition by an early 20th-century D'Oyly Carte conductor, Harry Norris.

At this point the prisoner does *not* arrive – to the alarm of all and to the special alarm of Elsie, who has for reasons of convenience gone through a form of marriage with him without knowing his identity. This component of the plot was far from original. As if echoing one another, the London reviewers recalled the same dramatic device in Wallace's opera *Maritana* (1845), to a libretto by Edward Fitzball – still a popular work in 1888. *Punch* indulgently hypothesized 'an original opera, *The Beefeater's Bride, or the Merryman and his Maritana*' by an unknown team of 'Sulbert and Gillivan' and imagined how it would have been received:

The stern critics would promptly have pointed out that in good old Fitzball-and-Wallace, *Maritana*, Don César is in prison and condemned to die, and so is Colonel Fairfax in *The Beefeater's Bride*; that the Don is married in prison to a veiled gypsy dancer, Maritana, and the Colonel is married in prison to a veiled gypsy dancer, Elsie Maynard; 'Maynard,' the critics would have bitterly exclaimed, 'is but a poor English rendering of *Maritana*!' With scathing irony they would have shown how in the old opera, Don César escapes being shot, and returns 'all alive-O'; while in the new and original work Colonel Fairfax escapes being decapitated, and also reappears on the scene. Don César enters disguised as a monk; Colonel Fairfax comes in as a Beefeater. Don César and Maritana subsequently fall in love with each other; so do Colonel Fairfax and Elsie Maynard. Don César is pardoned by the

King for a very good reason; the Colonel is reprieved for no reason at all, except to finish the opera, 'a reason' the satirical critic would have added, 'sufficiently satisfactory to the audience'.

In view of the later recognition of *The Yeomen* as among Sullivan's best scores (and one of Gilbert's best creations, too) the carping or at best cautious tone of some of the reviews strikes an odd note. The approval of *The Times* went no further than in declaring that 'Sir Arthur Sullivan's score is fully equal to previous achievements'. The eventual long run of 423 performances was not prognosticated by the first six months at the box office. (In New York, under licence from Carte but with an American cast, it ran at the Casino Theatre for only 100 performances from 17 October 1888.) On 12 March 1889 Sullivan wrote to his collaborator: 'I confess that the indifference of the public to *The Yeomen of the Guard* has disappointed me greatly'.

After the London première of *The Yeomen* a different duty awaited the composer as the date drew near of his promised Birmingham address, 8 October 1888. With only four days to go, not having begun to draft his speech, Sullivan telegraphed the Birmingham and Midland Institute that he would be unable to be present. The event was postponed until 19 October: he began writing his text four days before. In Birmingham Town Hall before 3,000 people he 'distributed the prizes, then delivered address slowly and clearly – everyone delighted'. (The tone of the diary entry is almost one of surprise.) Perhaps there was a special satisfaction in being a guest of honour in the city which had rejected him as festival conductor and favoured Richter instead. Printed in advance, and entitled simply 'About Music' it was nationally reported. With some stretching of history ('In 866 King Alfred instituted a professorship of music at Oxford'), Sullivan reminded his audience of England's past musical greatness.

I would now only urge you to use all your efforts to restore her to that proud position. The means lie in education. We must be educated to appreciate, and appreciation must come before production. Give us intelligent and educated listeners and we should produce composers and performers of corresponding worth. . . We want [i.e. we need] good listeners rather than indifferent performers . . .

As a plea for the musical education of *listeners* it is rather exceptional for the time – especially Sullivan's use of 'appreciation' almost as a technical, instructional term, such as it was to become in the twentieth century.[1]

Such a speech was a rarity for him: he never showed much inclination to be drawn into matters of public policy. But in the previous January he had become a vice-president of the 'Sunday Society' and in July one of the patrons of the Peckham Rye Musical Sunday Evenings for the People. His name was a valued reinforcement in the cause of Sunday concerts, against a Sabbatarian opposition that was still powerful, though lessening. A conventional Anglican though he remained, Arthur Sullivan no longer held the views which had kept the young student away from Sunday concerts at the Leipzig Gewandhaus. His reasoning was ethical:

My own opinion, based upon experience in England and in foreign countries, is that half the drunkenness, and consequently half the crime, are the result of enforced idleness both of mind and body which the lamentable lack of rational and elevating recreation on Sundays produces. As a musician I hold strongly to the opinion that no influence is higher or more ennobling than that of good music, and [that] every effort that is made to bring all classes within the effect of its power, more especially on the Day of Rest, ought to be encouraged and supported. I shall of course continue my subscription to your society.

Those were to be his words in writing again to the Peckham Committee in May 1889.

He had meanwhile returned to music for Shakespeare, fulfilling with much success a commission to collaborate in Henry Irving's production of *Macbeth*. Irving's company, with Ellen Terry as his leading lady, had been established at the Lyceum Theatre for a decade; his prestige was immense and the lavishness of his productions a byword. For his *Faust* he had employed an orchestra of about 35 which supplied not only the entr'actes (they included two operatic overtures, Spohr's *Faust* and Marschner's *Der Vampyr*) but also the 'melodramatic music' (played as a background to the action). For this the 'Dance of the Will-o'-the wisps' from Berlioz's *The Damnation of Faust* was used, as well as specially written music by Hamilton Clarke and Meredith Ball. Sullivan had been present at the opening of that production (19 December 1885) and had doubtless noted the subsequent comment of the *Musical Times* praising Irving's enterprise in the face of 'the entire absolute indifference of an English theatrical audience as to what music is played' and pleading that 'one of our foremost composers' should be asked to provide the score for a Lyceum production.

As if in delayed fulfilment of that plea, Bram Stoker waited on Sullivan on 2 June 1888 with Irving's proposal for a collaboration on Shakespeare's *Macbeth*. (Stoker, who was to become famous in 1897 as the author of *Dracula*, was at this time Irving's company manager.) The composer gave a provisional assent on the spot and on 13 July fixed the remuneration at five guineas a night. The sum was extremely modest, but Sullivan no doubt reckoned on the ability of such music to furnish a suite for orchestral concert programmes. Hermann Klein claimed credit for persuading Irving that not only music for the play itself should be commissioned, but also an overture – despite Irving's feeling that 'overtures to tragedies' had become obsolete.

An undated note from Irving to Sullivan shows the great actor-manager prescribing the kind of military signals required in the play – or rather confirming what had evidently been already under discussion:

Trumpets and drums are the King's [Duncan's] *behind scenes.*

Entrance of Macbeth, *only drum.* ('A drum, a drum, Macbeth doth come.')

Distant march would be good for Macbeth's exit in 3rd scene – or drum and trumpets as you suggest.

In the last act there will be several flourishes of trumpets. ('Make all our trumpets speak,' etc.) and roll of drum sometimes.

Really anything you can give of a stirring sort can be easily brought in.

As you say, you can dot these down at rehearsals – but one player would be good to tootle-tootle, so that we could get the exact time.[2]

Apart from such strictly utilitarian music, and apart from the overture, Sullivan provided preludes to Acts 2, 3, 5 and 6 (Irving had divided the usual fifth act into two) and incidental passages in Acts 1, 3, 4 and 6 – including 'melodrama', i.e. music as background for speech. In the witches' cavern (Act 4) there were choral settings for female voices of 'Black spirits and white' and 'Come away, come away'– non-Shakespearean interpolations customary in the play.

Christmas intervened before the production opened. Sullivan's guests on 25 December included 'No. 7 (5)' – five members of Fanny Ronalds's establishment, individually identified in Sullivan's list of presents. Old Mr Carter received 'two boxes Villar Rothschilds' [cigars], his wife 'silver scissors and button-hook', Fanny herself 'eight pair — ' (the dash is Sullivan's) and her son Regie a cigar-case. Against the name of 'Mrs Ritchie' (her daughter Fanette), are the words '20 pair gloves', the '20' being presumably a slip of the pen for '2'. The servants' gifts were also noted, Louis receiving 'gold [cuff]-links and cigar-case', Clotilde 'gold chain and dressing-gown', Eliza a boa (a fur or feather collar) and Mary a dress. On New Year's Eve, amid 'the blackest fog I have seen for years', it would be Sullivan's turn to go (with Bertie) for celebrations at Fanny Ronalds's home, 7 Cadogan Place.

The opening of *Macbeth* on 29 December was a crammed, excited occasion as an Irving first night was bound to be. Two days before, Sullivan had written to his old comrade Arthur Cecil (he had played Bouncer in the first public performance in *Cox and Box*) in a way that interestingly hints at how the Savoy's own stalls and boxes were packed on first nights with known 'followers':

I have not dared to write to you about *Macbeth* on Saturday for I have tried fruitlessly to get you stalls. Irving of course has his own clientèle for first nights as we do at the Savoy, and all stalls were promised. The only thing he has been able to do is to give me a box – it is not on the Grand Tier but just above it and it is an excellent one. I accepted it at once and if I were you I would take it and come to the first performance. I have obtained a promise from Bram Stoker that if four stalls should be returned *I* am to have them, instead of the box. Let me know whether you will accept the box (a Christmas box from me).

My love to all. I received the choric 'Song of the Soap' from the children and was much pleased at their remembrance of their poor old, over-worked and decrepit friend.

His nephew was with him when Sullivan drove to the Lyceum – where he himself was to conduct on the opening night, having superintended rehearsals of orchestra and chorus. The diary entry runs:

> . . . We left at 7.15 for
> The *production* of *Macbeth* at the *Lyceum Theatre*
>   Words by Shakespeare.
>   Music by Sullivan.
>   Produced by Irving.
>   Great Success!
> Author, composer and stage-manager called enthusiastically.
> Only the two latter responded.

The long review of the music in the *Daily Telegraph* of 3 January 1889 (reprinted in the stage journal, the *Era*, on 26 January) deplored the audience's talking through the overture and other parts of the music. Bennett, who may be presumed the reviewer, praised the 'appropriate charm' of the score and its 'quaint, old-world flavour' at certain suitable points.

Speaking generally, we must say of Sir Arthur Sullivan's *Macbeth* music that it ranks with the best of his previous efforts in the same line.

Since the last such 'effort' had been *Henry VIII* (produced in 1877 – further back than *Pinafore*!), this was not the most rapturous acclaim. Some of the music from *Henry VIII* was in fact played between Acts 1 and 2 of *Macbeth*.[3] Performing opposite Irving, Ellen Terry showed (according to a heavily ironical notice in the *Standard*) that 'Lady Macbeth can be metamorphosed into a model of womanly sweetness and charm'.

It was expected that the whole of the *Macbeth* music would be published in piano score, but for some reason it was not. The overture alone was printed five years later in orchestral score and appeared likewise in a military band arrangement. Though the opening of the overture suggests a tragic tone, with its hammer-like succession of three identical minor chords, Sullivan chose not to anticipate in his overture the outcome of the play: the piece ends in a major key with the recurrence of a theme of festive pomp. The original presentation of this theme strongly recalls the appearance of the 'Tower' theme in the overture to *The Yeomen*. The overture to the play is more 'motivic' (that is, using short thematic cells rather than whole tunes) and in harmonic respects may also be considered the more advanced, but of the two it is significantly the *Yeomen* overture that remains memorable.

A younger actor-manager, Herbert Beerbohm Tree (1853–1917) also recognized Sullivan's theatrical flair. Manager of the Haymarket Theatre since 1887, he treated London on 2 January 1889 to a rare matinée-revival of *The Merry Wives of Windsor*, using the music which Sullivan had written for the last London showing of the play in 1874. *The Times* praised not merely the general spirit of the production, and Tree's own impersonation of Falstaff (Tree was thin, which made his feat more remarkable) but also Sullivan's music, which 'lends an infinite charm to the fairy dances'. The production was judged successful enough to join Tree's general repertory.

The Mikado continued its travels abroad. The Berlin production at the Friedrich Wilhelmstädtisches Theater on 6 December 1888 made use of the translation by Zell and Genée which had already proved its worth in Vienna. This was a particularly successful production, reaching its 200th performance on 30 December 1891. But the German-language vocal scores of *The Mikado* aroused Sullivan's fury: in a letter of 7 January 1889 he castigated Bernstein for allowing their publication with alterations in his work: 'I find both the finales altered in a most outrageous and unmusicianly manner. The second finale especially is an insult to my musicianly feelings.'

Equally offensive was a production at the Carlstheater, Vienna (2 February 1889) of *The Yeomen of the Guard* in the guise of *Capitän Wilson*, orchestrated from the vocal score by Julius Stern, with Gilbert's text adapted by the partnership of Victor Leon (the future librettist of Lehár's *The Merry Widow!*) and Carl Lindau, and published by the Viennese firm of Weinberger. According to the letter of protest which Sullivan sent to the city's *Neue Freie Presse*, this version had five additional numbers falsely claimed to be from the composer's pen.

Sullivan's protest was reported in the *Era*. On purely legal grounds Sullivan had no case (as with the Budapest production reported in the previous chapter): Austria–Hungary had not yet signed the recently formulated Berne Convention on international copyright. Taking advantage in the reverse direction, British managements had been able to produce Johann Strauss's operettas without copyright fee. The absence of international agreement now enabled the Carlstheater in Vienna to mount *The Pirates of Penzance* (1 March 1889) without Sullivan's authority, and similarly using someone else's orchestration of the published vocal score. Zell and Genée themselves set their hands to translating this unauthorized *Pirates*, a decidedly unsporting gesture in Sullivan's eyes.

The Yeomen (or 'The Yeoman', as Sullivan more than once negligently wrote the title) was not the only work whose integrity had to be watched over, nor was it only abroad that transgressions occurred. He sanctioned and profited by the dance-arrangements which continued to be made from the operettas. He often complimented the military bands' performances of his music. But when he learned that *The Lost Chord* was to be tricked up in dance-rhythm by one of the Guards' bands he sent a peremptory warning by messenger at 7 p.m. on the day itself (4 February 1889):

The Lost Chord travestied as a hornpipe *must not be performed this evening* or at any other performance at the Guards' barracks. Otherwise I shall be forced into the unpleasant position of having to take legal proceedings and applying for very heavy damages and penalties.

There were domestic problems: 'Gave it to Clotilde hot and told her she must go. She accepted her notice but I don't think *she* thinks I mean it!' She was right: she was never to leave his service, for all the recurrent exasperation in his diary. More serious was a further bout of his kidney trouble. 'Very weak and depressed' on 17 January, he was none the less given permission by Dr Cooper next day to make a promised visit to the house-party given by the Prince of Wales at the royal residence of Sandringham in Norfolk. It would give him the pleasure of a reunion with Queen Victoria's daughter, the Empress Frederick of Germany: in widowhood she preserved that title. Her visit to England had been only reluctantly permitted by her own son, William II, politically suspicious of his mother's English connections.[4] Her trusted adviser, Count Seckendorff, accompanied her.

[Diary, 18 January 1889]:. . . Louis [servant] went with luggage to Sandringham by 12.2 [train from Liverpool St Station]. I followed by 2.35 train. Travelled with Col. Gouraud and phonograph (with Mr Hamilton). Arr. at Wolferton [railway station] 6. Arr[iving] at Sandringham I was most cordially welcomed by the Prince and Princess and all the family.

All the five children were there, also the Empress of Germany and her three daughters. It was the first time I had seen Her Majesty since the Emperor's death. She looked so sad, and I was quite touched by her affectionate greeting of me. I really couldn't speak. Before dinner the Prince came up to my room, to see if I was comfortable! After dinner we had the phonograph. Lord and Lady Salisbury, Lord and Lady Downe, Lord Calthorpe, Archdeacon Farrar, Seckendorff, Sir S. P. Fane were also staying there. Pool finished up the evening.

Salisbury was in his second term as Prime Minister; Archdeacon Farrar was the author of the pious and popular *Eric, or Little by Little*, written forty years before. ('Pool' was the billiard-table game.) Gouraud was Thomas Alva Edison's representative: private musical recordings using Edison's invention were just beginning, and it may be that the whistling accomplishments of Mrs Shaw – which were certainly committed to Edison's cylinders at this time – were among those that greeted the royal ears. The phonograph indeed became a newly fashionable: Sullivan 'went to A. Rothschild's phonograph party' on 8 February and had recorded his own brief message for Edison on 5 October 1888.

The extended Continental holiday which was Sullivan's regular indulgence – a recuperation which he 'earned' with each new operetta – could now be taken at last. It was a trip which led him for the first time to Venice, but before that to the familiar environs of Paris and the Riviera. He had the company of the Prince of Wales at the start, and of Reuben Sassoon both on the journey and in Paris.[5] (They stayed at the Grand Hôtel.) As in the case of 'Leo' (Rothschild), the name 'Reuben' without surname in the diary betokens the easy intimacy which Sullivan struck up with this member of the wealthy, philanthropic Jewish family whose operations in Baghdad and Bombay had given them the sobriquet of 'the Rothschilds of the East'.

[Diary, 12 February 1889]: Tremendously busy all day – saw no one – wrote many letters. L.W. at 5 till 7. Said goodbye to everyone [i.e. servants] and started for Ch[aring] Cross [Station] with Smythe – went by Prince of Wales' 'special' with H.R.H., [Gen. Sir Stanley] Clarke and R. Sassoon in the Saloon. Very cold. Special boat ('Empress') brought us over to Calais (*very* smooth passage) in an hour and seven minutes. Supped with H.R.H. at Calais – excellent supper, private room, left by morning mail [train] for Paris. Reuben and I in a coupé salon . . .

While in Paris, in what seems a fit of scholarly curiosity unusual for him, Sullivan had determined to inspect the manuscript of Beethoven's *Appassionata* Sonata – donated to the Paris Conservatoire only a month before. In search of it on 18 February, he presented himself mistakenly at the Bibliothèque Nationale and had to be directed to the library of the Conservatoire. There he met the librarian of the Conservatoire, the composer Jean-Baptiste-Théodore Weckerlin (1821–1910) and carried out his inspection, noting the event in his diary. Three days later, travelling by train via Marseilles, he reached the warmth and welcome of Monte Carlo.

Sociable diversions included a visit from the Prince of Wales, who was staying at Cannes, on 21 February. He wrote letters to 'L.W.' and – on what level of discourse? – to Clotilde Raquet, now his housekeeper. Of course, he gambled.

[Diary, 19 February 1889]: Lost 3,000 [francs, approximately £300] in afternoon. Drew £300 of Smith [bank] . . . Played again before dinner, won back 11,000, am now 8,000 to the good again. Won 1,600 from S. B. [unidentified] at besique.

Alfred Cellier and his wife were among other English visitors to the Riviera, and so were Richard D'Oyly Carte and his new wife. Carte and Sullivan can hardly have avoided discussion of the negotiations – already thorny – that were proceeding between Sullivan and Gilbert about their next collaboration. The root cause of their mutual unease was Sullivan's wish to write a more serious, more autonomously musical kind of opera. Before leaving London Sullivan had put the point frankly to Gilbert. 'I explained' (says the diary, 9 January 1889)

that I wanted to do some dramatic work on a larger musical scale, and that of course I should like to do it with him if he would, but that the music must occupy a more important position than in our other pieces – that I wished to get rid of the *strongly marked rhythm*, and *rhymed* couplets, and have words that would give a chance of developing *musical effects*. Also that I wanted a voice in the *musical construction* of the libretto. He seemed quite to assent to all this.

Sullivan's ambition had been reinforced by Carte's progress on his new theatre. Its foundation stone had already been laid in the previous December at a ceremony in the presence of both Sullivan and Gilbert. It was at this theatre, eventually named the Royal English Opera House, that Sullivan and Carte without Gilbert were to launch the kind of work on which the composer had set his heart.

On his first day in Paris, Sullivan wrote to Gilbert 'a long, reflective letter' (*diary*) which does not survive. Gilbert's reply to 'Dear S.' (20 February 1889) was mild. (Each time, incidentally, it was the 'Yeoman' in the singular.)

I have thought carefully over your letter, and while I quite understand and sympathize with your desire to write what, for want of a better term, I suppose we must call 'grand opera,' I cannot believe that it would succeed either at the Savoy or at Carte's new theatre unless a much more powerful singing and acting company were got together than the company we now control. Moreover, to speak from my own selfish point of view, such an opera would afford me no chance of doing what I best do – the librettist of a grand opera is always swamped in the composer. Anybody – Hersee, Farnie, Reece – can write a good libretto for such a purpose; personally, I should be lost in it. Again, the success of the *Yeoman* – which is a step in the direction of serious opera – has not been so convincing as to warrant us in assuming that the public want something more earnest still. There is no doubt about it that the more reckless and irresponsible the libretto has been, the better the piece has succeeded – the pieces that have succeeded the least have been those in which a consistent story has been more or less consistently followed out. Personally, I prefer a consistent subject – such a subject as the *Yeoman* is far more congenial to my taste than the burlesque of *Iolanthe* or the *Mikado* – but I think we should be risking everything in writing more seriously still. We have a name, jointly, for humorous work, tempered with occasional glimpses of earnest drama. I think we should do unwisely if we left, altogether, the path which we have trodden together so long and so successfully. I can quite understand your desire to write a big work, well, why not write one? But why abandon the Savoy business? Cannot the two things be done concurrently? If you can write an oratorio like *The Martyr of Antioch* while you are occupied with pieces like *Patience* and *Iolanthe*, can't you write a grand opera without giving up pieces like *The Yeoman of the Guard*? Are the two things irreconcilable?

As to leaving the Savoy – I can only say that I should do so with the profoundest reluctance and regret. I don't believe in Carte's new theatre – the site is not popular, and cannot become popular for some years to come. Our names are known all over the world in connection with the Savoy, and I feel convinced that it would be madness to sever the connections with that theatre. If you don't care to write any more pieces of the *Yeoman* order, well and good. But before launching a grand opera remember how difficult we have found it to get effective singers and actors for the pieces we have already done. Where, in God's name, is your grand opera soprano (who can act) to be found? From me, the press and the public will take nothing but what is, in essence, humorous. The best serious librettist of the day is Julian Sturgis. Why not write a grand opera with him? *My* work in that direction would be, deservedly or otherwise, generally pooh-poohed.

Julian Russell Sturgis (1848–1904), the future librettist of Sullivan's *Ivanhoe*, had been born in the United States but had lived in Britain since early childhood. His sole operatic libretto had been for Arthur Goring Thomas's *Nadeshda* (1885), but the virtues of that were apparently sufficient for Gilbert's commendation. Thus Gilbert, with a grace which was rare for him, cleared the field for Sullivan's ambitions in his new direction, pleading merely that he should continue to plough the Savoy furrow as well.

Other visitors included Alfred Cellier. If either he or Richard D'Oyly Carte sought to persuade the composer to return to the lighter style of partnership with Gilbert, they failed. Sullivan's line now hardened. Even at the Savoy he would insist on a reform. Only a draft survives (12 March) of his next letter to Gilbert, but the letter itself is unlikely to have differed much. Admitting that the 'seriousness' of *The Yeomen* had not been an attraction to the Savoy public, Sullivan continued:

If the result means a return to our former style of piece, I must say at once, and with deep regret, that I cannot do it. I have lost the liking for writing comic opera, and entertain very grave doubts as to my power of doing it. You yourself have reproached me directly and indirectly with the seriousness of my music, fitted more for the cathedral than the comic opera stage, and I cannot but feel that in very many cases the reproach is just. I have lost the necessary nerve for it, and it is not too much to say that it is distasteful to me. The types used over and over again (unavoidable in such a company as ours), the Grossmith part, the middle-aged woman with fading charms, cannot again be clothed with music by me. Nor can I again write to any wildly improbable plot in which there is not some human interest.

(And here I differ from your opinion that the most successful of our works have been those where the plot has been wild and irresponsible. *Pinafore* (bar the changing of Capt. Corcoran and Rackstraw at the end, which is an episode of no dramatic importance to the piece), *Patience* and *Mikado* – these have been plots with a consistent story and mildly humorous, but worked out by human beings. This by the way.)

You say that in a serious opera, *you* must more or less sacrifice yourself. I say that this is just what I have been doing in all our joint pieces, and, what is more, must continue to do in comic opera to make it successful. Business and syllabic setting assume an importance which, however much they fetter me, cannot be overlooked. I am bound, in the interests of the piece, to give way. Hence the reason of my wishing to do a work where the music is to be the first consideration – where words are to suggest music, not govern it, and where music will intensify and emphasize the emotional effect of the words.

Now, is there any *modus vivendi* by which my requirements can be met, and which you can enter into willingly and without any detriment to your hearty interest in the piece? And will it not facilitate matters if you bear in mind that in September there will be very little of the old Savoy company left? Grossmith goes; Barrington has gone. Temple wants to go, and Miss Ulmar *must* go: we can't keep her on. [That is, she was certain to accept attractive offers from other managements.] Consequently there will remain Jessie [Bond], Brandram, Pounds and Denny, two of them admirable for comic opera [presumably Bond and W. H. Denny, who had sung as Shadbolt in *The Yeomen*], the other two stronger vocally than histrionically. To complete the cast musically we must have a good bass and a good soprano, and unless they have good singing parts assigned to them it is of course no use by attempting to do the music.

Gilbert's reply was written on 19 March:

Your letter has filled me with amazement and regret.

If you are really under the astounding impression that you have been effacing yourself during the last twelve years – and if you are in earnest when you say that you wish to write an opera with me in which 'the music shall be the first consideration' (by which I understand an opera in which the libretto, and consequently the librettist, must occupy a subordinate place) there is most certainly no 'modus vivendi' to be found that shall be satisfactory to both of us.

You are an adept in your profession, and I am an adept in mine. If we meet, it must be as master and master – not as master and servant.

By this time Sullivan was in Italy. He had travelled to Genoa (20 March) and then to Verona, where he

visited amphitheatre (very fine), cathedral (gaudy) and *museo*. Left Verona [by train] at 4.50 a.m., arr. at Venice 7.35 Gondola to Danieli's [one of the leading hotels] – splendid suite of apartments – Council Chamber (!) and two bedrooms *au midi* [facing south], (nos. 9 and 10). Supped and strolled about.

His companion (if there was one) in the two-bedroomed suite the diary does not identify. It may have been Reuben Sassoon and was certainly not Fanny Ronalds, with whom he was in correspondence by letters and telegrams to London.

Faced in Venice with the necessity of a decision about the Savoy – and mindful of what was the financial risk in abandoning it – Sullivan now seems to have had cold feet. Before replying to Gilbert he wrote on 26 March to Carte, making an effort to put Gilbert in the wrong by raising an issue about rehearsals which had not so far figured in the discussions. His complaint was that rehearsals were conducted to his disadvantage:

Day after day everyone is called, and the *chorus and others hang about for a couple of hours* doing nothing whilst two people are rehearsing a long scene of dialogue. When the chorus begin they are tired, and then over and *over again goes the music in order to get an exit or a bit of business right* until the music gets sung so badly and so carelessly that it is impossible to put it right again. Gilbert *of course* has the right to call what rehearsals he likes – and anyone he likes and at any hour. This I am not questioning; my objection is that *I* am the sufferer by this kind of rehearsal, that my music gets cruelly murdered.[6]

While in Venice, he went (29 March) 'to the Rossini Theatre to hear [Bellini's] *Norma*. Norma and Adalgisa both about 40, with worn-out voices. Tenor like a butcher. Oroveso [the principal bass role] excellent. Band rough, chorus coarse.'
Sullivan to Gilbert, 27 March 1889:

I was so annoyed at your abrupt letter to me [i.e. that of 19 March, above] that I thought it wiser not to answer it without a few days' delay. I wrote to Carte yesterday to mention some of the points on which I thought I had just grounds for dissatisfaction. As he will probably repeat them to you, I need not enter into particulars again. I write therefore only to say that it seems to me a silly and unnecessary thing for you and I to quarrel over a matter that can really be so easily arranged, and that I really don't think my requests are unreasonable.

All I ask is that in the future, (1) my judgment and opinion should have some weight with you in the laying out of the *musical situation*, even to making important alterations after the work has been framed, because it is impossible sometimes to form a right judgment until one begins to work at the number or situation itself.

(2) That I should have a more important share in arranging the attitudes and business in all the musical portions, and, (3) that the rehearsals should be arranged in such a way as not to weary the voices, and cause everyone to sing carelessly and without regard for tune, time or accent.

In no way do I trench upon your ground, or demand anything but what has to do directly with the music and its efficient representation.

It is to these matters (and more specially the first – that of the musical construction of the book) that I attach the greatest importance, and I cannot but feel that you will admit they are rational.

If you will accept all this in the same spirit in which I write, we can go on smoothly as if nothing had happened, and I hope successfully. If not, I shall regret it deeply, but, in any case, you will hear no more recrimination on my part.

Gilbert to Sullivan, 31 March 1889:

The requirements contained in your letter of the 27th are just and reasonable in every way. They are requirements with which I have always unhesitatingly complied, and indeed I have always felt, and fully appreciated, the value of your suggestions whenever you have thought it advisable to make any. You ask (1) that your judgment and opinion should have some weight with me in the laying-out of the musical situation, even to making important alterations to the work after it has been framed. This is a right I have never attempted to question. . . . You ask (2) that you should have a more important share in arranging the attitudes and [stage] business in all the musical portions. [But] you are probably not present at more than one in six [rehearsals] during the first fortnight when business has to be arranged . . .

If that letter stood alone there would be nothing to prevent our embarking at once, in a cheerful and friendly spirit, upon the work which (subject to your approval) I have been constructing during the last 10 days. But unhappily the letter does not stand alone. It was preceded by a letter to Carte (avowedly written that its contents might be communicated to me) which teems with unreasonable demands and utterly groundless accusations – the very least of which, if it had the smallest basis of truth, would suffice to disqualify me absolutely from collaboration with you. In that most cruelly unjust and ungenerous letter you say 'except during the vocal rehearsals and the two orchestral rehearsals, I am a cipher in the theatre'. Have you no recollection of 'business' arranged and re-arranged to meet your reasonable objections? Have you [a] recollection of any expressed wish of yours that was not acted upon, without expostulation, argument or demur, upon the spot? . . .

You say that our operas are Gilbert's pieces with music added by you, and that Carte can hardly wonder that 12 years of this has a little tired you. I say that when you deliberately assert that for 12 years you, incomparably the greatest English musician of the age – a man whose genius is a proverb wherever the English tongue is spoken – a man who can deal *en prince* with operatic managers, singers, music publishers and musical societies – when you, who hold this unparalleled position, deliberately state that you have submitted silently and uncomplainingly for 12 years to be extinguished, ignored, set aside, rebuffed, and generally effaced by your librettist, you grievously reflect, not upon him, but upon yourself and the noble art of which you are so eminent a professor.

The rhetoric of such a tribute raises the suspicion that Gilbert was writing for posterity, but there is no reason to doubt that this was genuinely how he saw the position.

Among those who gave company to Sullivan while in Venice was a well-known figure of London musical circles, the Belgian-born Theo Marzials, who was music librarian at the British Museum and a prominent writer of words for music. But two weeks in Venice were evidently enough. With all Europe to command and no pressing engagement at home, Sullivan took it into his head to visit the Hungarian capital. Although the old towns of Buda and Pest (on opposite banks of the Danube) had been united since 1873, Sullivan's diary refers simply to 'Pesth' (the German spelling). But, having decided apparently on the spur of the moment to go there, he changed his mind with equal suddenness.

[Diary, 6 April 1889]: Decided to go to Pesth. Wrote L.W. (right), received [letters] from L.W., Smythe, Gilbert, [John] Hare, Clo. [Clotilde]. After dinner Marzials came and took me to Mrs Branson's, an American lady who 'receives' here. Very nice and well-bred. Young Browning [presumably the poet's son] and two or three other people there.

[Diary, 6 April]: Wired Carte, going to Pesth. . . . Left Venice at 2.40 [p.m.] In the train, found I should have to change in the middle of the night for Pesth, and no sleeping-car or salons. Suddenly changed my mind and took a sleeping-car for Vienna. Wired to Hotel Imperial [at Vienna] and L.W. Rained hard all day and night. Bribed the conductor and got a little compartment to myself.

He had not been in Vienna since the time of his and Grove's Schubert discoveries, 22 years before. He was now a celebrity, with *The Pirates of Penzance*, *The Mikado*, and *The Yeomen of the Guard* still ringing in Viennese ears. Of these *The Mikado* was to remain the most popular, as Sullivan found on his first day in the city, when he took a cab to the Prater (Vienna's park), strolled there and heard the bands playing:

Left letters and cards at Sir A. Paget's and Lavino (correspondent, *Daily Telegraph*). Wired Carte and L.W. Called at Madame de Serrès – she was in Paris. Bought a box for the opera (fl. 25). Strolled about, found town much changed and improved since I was here in '67. Drove out to the Prater and had coffee. *Mikado* selection on four different programmes. Came on to rain. Dined at home and went to see *Lohengrin*. Very well done. Little Lola Beeth as Elsa, [Ernest] van Dyck as Lohengrin.[7] Lavino joined me and came home with me afterwards for a chat.

[Diary, 10 April 1889]: Still Vienna. Worried by newspaper interviewers; one waylaid me at door. Spoke about two minutes to him, and saw most ridiculous account in the *Tageblatt* next day. Drew £40 from Rothschilds.

Among those who called on him at his Vienna hotel was his translator, Camille Walzel, whose theatrical pseudonym was 'F. Zell'. Sullivan understandably nursed a resentment over Walzel's involvement in the unauthorized production of *The Pirates* (p. 285). Hence the diary's brief comment on 12 April:

Called: Walzel (Zell). Gave it him hot.

27 'Monarchs of all they Savoy'

WHILE in Venice Sullivan had received, on 2 April 1889, a set of Italian verses from Gianandrea Mazzucato – a son of the eminent musician who had welcomed him at the Milan Conservatory 24 years before.[1] This was to be the text of a song he had promised to write for *The Profligate*, a new play by Pinero which was to be produced in London. Sullivan sent ten guineas to Mazzucato and straightway began working on the song – 'E tu nol sai', a light love-song in barcarolle rhythm which would also be published under an English title, with words by B. C. Stephenson ('You sleep'). Two of the play's four acts were set in an Italian villa, and in Arthur Pinero's evolution the play was an important one – the acknowledged master of farce (*The Magistrate*, 1885) was developing into the caustic moralist of *The Second Mrs Tanqueray* (1893).

Homeward bound from Vienna, Sullivan chose as usual to stop on the way in Paris. The American soprano Emma Eames, destined to become one of the most celebrated of opera singers, had just made her Paris debut in Gounod's *Roméo et Juliette*. Sullivan attended one of her subsequent performances:

[Diary, 7 April 1889]: Paris. Shopping, etc. Carte with [his] two boys and Bertie [Herbert Sullivan] arrived in evening. I went to hear *Romeo and Juliet* at the Grand Opera. Miss Eames, Juliet, very pretty, tall and graceful, pupil of [Matilde] Marchesi. Bright, clear voice, sings well but very cold and no personal magnetism.

'Cold' singers he did not like. Both for the Savoy and for his eventual 'grand opera' he sought – in addition to a voice – that element of personal charm which distinguished such a singer as his first idol, Jenny Lind.

Back at home on 20 April, he threw himself immediately into professional and social routine. On his first night in London he went to the Lyric Theatre for Cellier's new operetta, *Doris* – which would never come near matching the success of Cellier's *Dorothy*. Four nights later came the opening of the Pinero play – the opening, too, of a new theatre, the Garrick, built and owned by Gilbert and occupied by a company under the direction of Sullivan's old friend John Hare. (Johnston Forbes Robertson, Kate Rorke and Lewis Waller played the leading roles.) In the theatre itself an attempt was made to take comfort even further than at the Savoy: 'The stalls, of which there are 170, are provided with a silk pocket for programmes and with a box large enough to contain a tall hat and an overcoat'. So *The Times* reported after the first night – not mentioning Sullivan's song, however.

The composer must have thought the song ineffective with its original guitar accompaniment, for next day he 'went to Chappell's to arrange a substitute instrument for the guitar to accompany my song in *The Profligate*. Fixed up a *pianino* [small upright piano] with paper [against the strings].'

In the diary he went on to record that he himself sat in the wings that night and played the accompaniment.

On the day of *The Profligate* he wrote again to Gilbert. The draft indicates that he now accepted the latter's proposal that he should essay both his 'serious' opera and another in the Savoy series:

You admit that my requirements are just and reasonable, although holding to opinions [that] they have always been met. Be this as it may, there should now be no difficulty in working harmoniously together in another piece, as we both thoroughly understand the position, and I am quite prepared to set to work at once upon a light or comic opera with you (provided of course that we are thoroughly agreed upon the subject) and to think no more of our rather sharp discussion.

I am enabled to do this all the more willingly since I have now settled to write an opera on a large scale ('grand opera' is an offensive term) to be produced next spring. I have my subject of my own choice, and my *collaborateur*; also an agreement with Carte to keep the new theatre for me for this purpose, and not to let it to anyone else before then. In this manner I can realize the great desire of my life, and at the same time continue a collaboration which I regard with a stronger sentiment than that of pecuniary advance. All this involves an immediate setting to work with the Savoy piece so as to get it finished by August or September. How will this fit in with your arrangements?

In another letter (a draft only survives, dated 8 May) Sullivan continued his mild tone.

If [some previous comments] gave you pain I very much regret having brought them forward. Carte tells me that you again proposed [for a libretto] the subject of a theatrical company: I hope you will not press it, as it has already been the means of nearly breaking up our collaboration. . . . I understood from Carte some time ago that you had some subject connected with Venice and Venetian life, and this seemed to me to hold out great chances of bright colour and taking music. Can you not develop this with something we can both go into with warmth and enthusiasm and thus give me a subject in which (like the *Mikado* or *Patience*) we can both be interested, which will relieve all necessity for argument and discussion?

This, presumably, helped Gilbert to decide on *The Gondoliers*. The happy result was described in the composer's diary next day: 'Long and frank explanation with Gilbert, free and outspoken on both sides.[2] Shook hands and buried the hatchet.' The hatchet was not to stay buried, nor did Gilbert for ever abandon the idea of an opera libretto revolving round a theatrical company: it surfaced in *The Grand Duke*. But for the present the way was clear. Sullivan would write his serious opera with Julian Sturgis as librettist, and before that he would deliver the next work for the Savoy.

Next month the diary recorded 'my "buffday" – 47!' At his celebratory dinner that day (13 May 1889), as if in token of the reconciliation, were Gilbert and his wife. So were Sullivan's friend and legal adviser George Lewis and his publisher Tom Chappell, their wives, and a few others including 'Mrs R.' and 'Regy' (so noted in the diary, in place of the usual spelling), and 'Bertie'. There is a further and surprising note: 'William Lacy asked but did not turn up'. It would seem that Charlotte's brother or (more likely) his son of the same name was in London and must have brought tidings of Sullivan's 'family' in California. News of a son born to Florence had reached him on the French Riviera during March.

On his other 'family' (that is, Fanny Ronalds and her relations in London) he continued to lavish a close affection. The diary entry of 19 May, 'Governor in great pain all the time', refers to Joseph Carter, Fanny Ronalds's father, who was approaching his end. Sullivan was in the room along with Fanny at the moment of death, which he recorded as '18 minutes to 2' in the night of 21/22 May. 'Fanette' and 'Regy' were there too: 'I tried to calm their grief a little'. Sullivan later added a postscript to a previous diary entry (22 April) referring to a dinner in his own flat: 'This was the last time the poor old Governor dined here'. On 25 May, 'in the sunshine and under a large plane tree, we consigned poor old Grandpa to his last rest'.

'Grandpa': the term is seemingly quite unselfconscious. Sullivan had no doubt adopted it along with 'Grandma' on hearing Fanny use it to her children. It was also convenient, and perhaps not surprising, that in addressing his own nephew Bertie he referred to Fanny Ronalds as 'Auntie'. What is more striking is his use of 'Auntie' as a simple identification of Fanny in his own diary from this year on. 'Bertie, Auntie and I went to the Surrey Theatre', he had written on 12 January 1889. Thus his relationship with the woman who had for so long been his mistress (now past her 50th birthday) took on a new colouring of family companionship embracing *her* parents, *her* children, and his own nephew who now lived as his son.

No longer are the established sexual symbols found in the diary against her name, but they are occasionally found elsewhere: a prominent tick follows the entry 7 June 1889) 'Drove down to Richmond to drive with ABC'. She is unidentified but there is another reference to a drive with her – this time to Greenwich – on 9 July.

June brought, as usual, visits to the races at Epsom – he twice went by the 'Royal Special' train, presumably as the Prince of Wales's guest – and at Ascot. His choice of a country house that summer was Grove House (later called Bridge House), Weybridge, in the Thames Valley, some 19 miles from London. He paid a visit of inspection on 5 July with Fanny Ronalds, returning to attend Queen Victoria's State Concert given in honour of the visiting Shah of Persia at the Albert Hall. Here (where the Shah, if he remembered it, had heard *The Light of the World* in 1874) the visitor was now regaled with 'Come, Margarita, come' and 'Io Paean' from *The Martyr of Antioch* as part of a mixed orchestral, band and choral programme ending with the Coronation March from Meyerbeer's *Le*

Prophète. Sullivan's prominence on such state occasions (he and Millais were also among the guests at the Prince of Wales's garden party for the Shah) left no doubt of his standing in the country's 'establishment'.

An invitation sent from Grove House on 12 July to Alexander Mackenzie, who had recently become principal of the Royal Academy of Music, shows Sullivan's *camaraderie* as well as his working regime.

My dear Mackenzie,
    For 'Evans' sake drop the 'Sir Arthur' when you write to me and treat me as a friend. I am here in retreat hard at work, for London is impossible: my time is at anyone's disposal except my own. I wish I could induce you to come and work here whenever you want to do anything uninterruptedly – a bedroom and study (to say nothing of food and wine) are at your disposal always from 24 hours to a week. It is astonishing what a lot of scoring one can get through between 10.30 and 5.30 without a break. I am delighted that we are to have your new violin work at Leeds, and it is a great comfort to me that you will come and conduct it yourself.

Mackenzie's work for violin and orchestra, entitled *Pibroch*, was to be launched at the Leeds Festival by no less an artist than Sarasate, but before that there was a summer if not 'of roses and wine', then of riverside pleasures as a counterpoint to musical work. Carte's country residence, Eyot Lodge, was also at Weybridge.

[Diary, 22 July]: Went out on river and walked a bit.

[Diary, 17 August]: Bertie came at 4 – canoed with him down to Carte's island, back before dinner.

With Fanny Ronalds, away at this time in Belfast, Sullivan kept in touch by correspondence. His diary for 23 August noted 'Mrs Castlerock's birthday – wired her'. The nickname is unexplained.

The comfortable bank balances which he recorded in his diary that summer must have reminded him of the extent to which he depended on the Savoy. 'Carte's royalties to 25 June' (quarterly), amounted to £1,409.3.2, with a cheque from Bernstein (from German takings) of £87.16.9. By the end of the month his balance was £6,816.16.6 – not including, of course, the valuation of his stocks and shares. As compared with that, the coming Leeds Festival would net him a sum of minor magnitude: the total of fees eventually paid to conductor *and all* *soloists* was £1,725.4s.10d., of which his share was probably £315, as before.

But Leeds was of immense importance to him. Here England saluted him as serious composer and masterful conductor. Though he had declined the invitation to write a new work, there was to be a repetition of *The Golden Legend* and a concert performance of the *Macbeth* music. Among the major standard works which he would be required to conduct were Brahms' *Requiem*, the third act of Wagner's *Tannhäuser*, Schubert's Mass in E flat and Berlioz's *Faust*: the word 'Damnation' was tactfully avoided in this and many other Victorian performances.

As usual, Leeds made a big event of the Festival conductor's first appearance in the schedule of chorus rehearsals (held, up to that point, under the direction of the chorus-master). Sullivan was introduced by the mayor, John Ward, and was called on to speak both at the beginning and end of proceedings, both speeches being reported in the *Leeds Mercury* and elsewhere. He took the train to Leeds for his first rehearsal on 1 July, returning home at 4 a.m. the next day. On 26 July he again went to rehearse the Leeds Festival Chorus, this time in Berlioz and Schubert. After spending the night privately (perhaps at the mayor's home which was just outside the city), he took on a Saturday schedule which might have exhausted a fitter man:

Studied Schubert's Mass before lunch. Drove into Leeds at 2. Rehearsed rest of *Faust* and Schubert's Mass in afternoon. Left by 5.30 [train to London]. Arr. at no. 1 [Queens Mansions], 9.45 Clotilde awaiting me. Dressed quickly and went to Savoy Hotel. Supper given to the 'beau monde' by the directors (in Mr and Mrs Hwfa Williams' name) as a house-warming.[3] 210 guests, very good supper, beautifully decorated room, and a great success. Went home about 2.30 dead tired.

The Savoy Hotel was built by Carte from the profits of his theatrical enterprise. Overlooking the Embankment (its extension to the Strand was a later addition), it was as distinctly innovative as Carte's Savoy Theatre had been. Originally with terraced balconies on every floor, it was the first great hotel in London to provide a private bathroom to each bedroom. Sullivan was a director of the Savoy Hotel Company, Hwfa Williams was a fellow-director and Carte was Chairman. Sullivan also became a member of the Committee of Taste, a confidential body set up later to advise the management on recipes, wines, menus and the like, and various allusions to these occur in later letters to Carte.[4] Sullivan evidently placed a very large proportion of his investments there: in December 1895 his holdings of debentures and of preference and ordinary shares were valued in the Savoy Hotel accounts at £17,810.[5]

Sullivan's enjoyment of sociable occasions was not confined to that milieu. In the previous month, after Ascot, he

returned to Windsor – lodging at Roberts the grocer's. Dined at Grenadiers' mess (Colonels Maitland, Easton and Oliphant). After dinner, full band (under Godfrey) played on the lawn by lamplight, *Henry VIII*, *Yeomen*, and *Lost Chord* – played till nearly 12. Delightful evening.

This was the celebrated Dan Godfrey senior, bandmaster of the Grenadier Guards from 1856 to 1896.

Gilbert's new libretto surely summoned up for the composer his own remembered Italian pleasures. The author had begun to deliver it, in instalments, on 1 July.

I am getting on well with Act 1 [he had written to Sullivan on 21 June]. . . . The first nine pages of Ms are *all music*, and no dialogue. I think it might be convenient for you to have this long number to begin with.

Thus it was the librettist, not the composer, who originated the operatic scheme of the opening of the work, unprecedented in their collaboration. *The Gondoliers* (as it was to be named) begins with a long ensemble with solo interpolations – more like the traditional finale, and encompassing the whole scene of the bride-choosing without the interruption of a single spoken word in more than 15 minutes of music. Not until a fortnight later did Sullivan begin to set it to music, accomplishing the opening sections ('List and learn' and 'For the merriest fellows are we') in a single day, 15 July. He did not continue the composition in strict dramatic order. The diary on 22 July noted that he had composed the 'entrance of the Duke of Valladolid' (as the Duke of Plaza-Toro was evidently first, and less comically, named).

The Duke's song and the Grand Inquisitor's song were written on 24 July, the previous day having been partly taken up with a visit from Edward Lloyd, who was to repeat his principal role in *The Golden Legend* at Leeds. He 'left at 2 o'clock, I having previously rewritten the end of *Sometimes* [a song of 1877] which he wants to take up again'. On 31 July there was a long visit from Julian Sturgis: '[We] settled down with scenario of *Ivanhoe*, very satisfactory.'

What had held him up in composing that long opening number was perhaps a feeling that an extra verse was needed. That is the implication of a letter from Gilbert (8 August) to 'Dear S.', which interestingly shows the libretto under construction:

I enclose
(1) another verse to 'Thank you, gallant gondolieri' (one for each girl, now)
(2) expostulatory song for either of the girls, when Grand Inquisitor informs them that they must be separated from their husbands [eventually Gianetta's 'Kind sir, you cannot have the heart']
(3) Farewell duet, addressed by Tessa and Gianetta to their husbands ['Now Marco dear, my wishes hear'] – before the final chorus.
I have not written the final chorus because you said you thought it had better wait until you had decided on a rhythm.
    I hope you will like the numbers . . .

On 15 August Sullivan 'finished framing of no. 1 (very long)'. As compared with his descriptions of how his earlier works were accomplished, stage by stage, we may note here the terminology of 'composing' and 'framing', instead of 'sketching' and 'framing'. When he says that he 'sketched' or 'composed' (or occasionally just 'wrote') a number it seems to have meant the same thing – the creative act itself by which the melodies and harmonies took shape in his mind; 'framing' implied the drawing-up of a skeleton score of the music for voices, leaving only the task of orchestration ('scoring'). The making of a voice-and-piano version, for rehearsal and publication, came later as a reduction of the orchestration. Neither at this nor at any time did he compose his orchestral part as a piano part first of all.

Work on the 'serious' and the 'comic' opera, and on preparation for Leeds, was now interrupted by the Three Choirs Festival at Gloucester. He had been engaged to conduct not only *The Golden Legend* but also his 20-year-old oratorio, *The Prodigal Son*, and the *In Memoriam* overture. After a rehearsal there on 2 September a 'special train' (i.e. a train chartered and run for his convenience) returned him from Gloucester to the main-line station, Swindon. On Thursday 5 September the actual performances followed the familiar all-day festival pattern.

He conducted *The Prodigal Son* and *In Memoriam* in the morning, Part II of Spohr's *The Last Judgement* in the afternoon (all in the cathedral) and *The Golden Legend* at the Shire Hall that evening – 'excellent performance – great enthusiasm' (*diary*). A three-and-a-half-hour train journey from Gloucester brought him to London at 2.25 a.m., after which he was 'soon in bed' at Queen's Mansions.

Next day, before going 'home' (as he put it) to Weybridge, he busied himself in London.

Up at 9.30. Called at Kilgour's[?] office and signed for syndicate of Victoria [South African] diamond mines. Went to Savoy Theatre to hear Mme Raunkilde sing. Brilliant high soprano voice, inflexible. No charm and attraction in the quality of voice, no meaning in what she sings. Good fireworks, won't do for Savoy. Visited [Geraldine] Ulmar who was ill in bed. Into restaurant [of Savoy Hotel] to discuss kitchen affairs with François and Charpentier. Home at 4. Bertie arrived at 6. Went over to Walton[-on-Thames], played besique with Mrs [?George] Lewis.

Next day he went to the nearby racecourse at Sandown and won £65.

By 19 September, when he left Weybridge to resume residence in London, he had progressed well with *The Gondoliers*. In the second act he first completed what his diary calls the 'trio' (Don Alhambra's 'There lived a king', in which Marco and Giuseppe join) and the quartet 'In a contemplative fashion'; then he passed to 'the entrance of the girls, with quartet and duet to follow' (no 'quartet' now survives at that point). He sent a consignment of this material, from both acts, to his copyist, Baird. But his setting of 'In a contemplative fashion' evidently did not satisfy him, and led him to ask his collaborator to change the words. On 22 September Gilbert wrote to him and enclosed a rewritten version:

I have altered the 'In a contemplative fashion' as you suggested. The only question is whether the two last verses, which the girls sing at each other – and with which the two men have nothing to do – wouldn't be better in the original flowing metre, as lending itself better to the volubility of two angry girls. I don't care a pin, myself, which it is, but I thought you might find the original dactylic metre better for that purpose. Just as you like – here it is, in both forms . . .

P.S. It has just occurred to me that a good effect might be produced by continuing the 'Let us grasp the situation (*pp*) through the second half of the number . . .

This was Gilbert at his most co-operative, and musically perceptive as well. Sullivan *did*, as his partner suggested, use the dactyls – 'Ańd if I caťch her I'll pińch her and scratch her,' etc. – and did take the hint of Gilbert's postscript.

On 21 September Sullivan was again at Leeds for an afternoon rehearsal. With officers of the festival, he settled the eventual disposition of the orchestra on the platform – 'very great improvement', he noted in the diary. But the rehearsal at this stage was of the chorus only – for Beethoven's 'Choral' Symphony and Sullivan's own *Golden Legend* and *Macbeth*. Orchestral rehearsals would begin in London (since, as usual, London players were used) two days later.

The intervening day was a Sunday (22 September) but he barely relaxed from work except to receive a morning call from Uncle John. In the afternoon he rehearsed the two 'bridal couples' from the new opera (Geraldine Ulmar and Courtice Pounds, Jessie Bond and Rutland Barrington) in the music he had written for them, and in the evening he went back to composing. On the following Saturday evening, 28 September, he went to the Lyceum to see Irving's presentation of *The Dead Heart* (a play about the French Revolution, altered by W. H. Pollock from a play of 1859 by Watts Phillips). Sunday brought a mixture of work and relaxation: 'Called at Miss MacIntyre's – rehearsed Boito's aria with her [for Leeds] – took her and her mother with Bertie to dine at the Savoy. Home at 10.30 to work.'

The India-born soprano Margaret MacIntyre had made a brilliant stage debut as Micaela in *Carmen* at Covent Garden in May of the previous year – a debut attracting more praise than Melba's in the same month.

Gilbert, meanwhile, continued to re-fashion the libretto in order to accommodate Sullivan's needs. He wrote on 28 September 1889:

You will see that I have altered the Nurse's ballad in finale, act 2, to a dramatic recitative, to avoid reminding the audience of Buttercup's song at the end of *Pinafore*. . . . The nurse is now a Spanish bandit's wife – a picturesque, fierce, melodramatic old woman. [If the words do not attract you] I can rewrite them in five minutes. Perhaps a short but very dramatic scena – fierce, tigress-like – would be better. Just as you like.

The composer's diary chronicled not only his work but the recurrent tantrums of Clotilde – sometimes in cryptic entries like 'Storm' (23 September) or 'C. cloudy' or 'Breezes began'. On 29 September the isolated word in quotation marks, 'Splained', refers to the Belgian accent with which she *explained* herself. But she evidently made herself indispensable. She was among the four servants (Louis, Josephine and Emily were the others) with whom Sullivan travelled by train to Leeds on 4 October. The city had again put the Judges' Lodgings at the disposal of the man who was his country's most celebrated living musician.

Those quarters, with their resident housekeeper, now became 'home' in his diary entries. On Saturday 5 October he was 'putting things to rights at home, writing letters, etc' before beginning a choral rehearsal which, with an hour's break for tea, went on from 3 p.m. till 8.30. More arduous yet was the orchestra's first rehearsal next day: actual performances on Sunday might still be frowned on, but on that day musicians were at work from 10 a.m. till 5 p.m. (with a short lunch-break, presumably) and then from 7 p.m. till 10.15. Sullivan shared the baton with two of the composers who were to conduct their own new choral works – Stanford with *The Voyage of Maeldune* and Frederic Corder with *Argantyr*, two secular dramatic works (the former to a poem by Tennyson). Members of the festival chorus were evidently expected to take leave from their regular occupations on the Monday and Tuesday, for a 12-hour (!) choral rehearsal on the Monday was noted by *The Times* as contributing to a sense of fatigue shown when the festival itself began on Wednesday 9 October.

For Sullivan the week brought the established round of concerts and social engagements. 'Dinner party at 6' ran the diary entry for Wednesday, when Grove arrived as guest; and 'dinner party as usual' featured in the next three days. As usual there was, on each day until the Saturday, a morning concert at 11.30 (lasting, with an interval, till 2.30 or even 3 p.m.) and an evening concert at 7.30. Apart from new items conducted by their composers, and short choral items by Wilbye and C. H. Lloyd entrusted to the festival chorus-master, Alfred Broughton, Sullivan was entirely responsible. As a sample of festival fare of its period, as well as evidence of the load of a festival conductor, the complete programmes deserve to be set down. Square brackets indicate items *not* conducted by Sullivan. The solo violinist on both Thursday evening and Friday morning was Sarasate.

Wednesday morning
　Berlioz, *The Damnation of Faust*
Wednesday evening
　[F. Corder, *The Sword of Argantyr*]
　Wagner, *Tannhäuser*, Act 3

Thursday morning
　Bach, *God's time is the best* (Cantata no. 106)
　Schubert, Mass in E flat
　Handel, *Acis and Galatea*
Thursday evening
　[W. Creser, *The Sacrifice of Freia*]
　[C. H. Lloyd, *The Rosy Dawn*]
　Boito, 'L'altra notte' from *Mefistofele*
　[Mackenzie, *Pibroch* for violin and orchestra]
　Wagner, Trial Songs from *Die Meistersinger*
　[Raff, Aria and Moto Perpetuo from suite for solo violin]
　Gounod, overture, *Mireille*

Friday morning
　[Parry, *Ode on St Cecilia's Day*]
　Mendelssohn, Violin Concerto
　Beethoven, Symphony no.9
Friday evening
　[Stanford, *The Voyage of Maeldune*]
　Beethoven, overture, *Leonora* no. 3
　Weber, 'Leise, leise' from *Der Freischütz*
　Mendelssohn, music to *A Midsummer Night's Dream*

Saturday morning
　Brahms, *Requiem*
　Mendelssohn, *Hymn of Praise*
Saturday evening
　Sullivan, music to *Macbeth*
　Sullivan, *The Golden Legend*

The Golden Legend received a notable welcome after a very successful performance,

the finest I have ever heard. Afterwards the enthusiasm was indescribable – cheering and waving their handkerchiefs at me for five minutes. All over at last. Saw the band off by the 'special' [train to London], then home [still in Leeds] to supper and quiet.

Albani sang her original role of Elsie and Lloyd his as Prince Henry, supported by 'Miss Damian' (contralto), Watkin Mills (baritone) and W. H. Brereton (bass). As usual these were part of a 'resident' team of singers throughout the festival, of which another was Margaret MacIntyre. The festival chorus, 317 strong, ran into unexpected criticism (right from *The Damnation of Faust*, which was unfamiliar to them) both during and after the festival, to which Sullivan felt constrained to make a public reply in a letter of 24 October to the festival secretary, F. R. Spark. It had the spirit of a general rallying his troops, though the campaign was over and the territory lost:

I have read the correspondence and remarks in the Leeds newspapers about the late festival with amazement and deep regret.

I am amazed to find so much importance attached to those few criticisms which were not so lavish in the expression of their praise as most others; and I deeply regret to see that these criticisms should have had so great an effect as to create, in some members of the chorus, a feeling of depression and of mistrust, both in themselves and in those who worked so loyally with them.

Is there any legitimate reason for this? Is there any foundation for such a superstructure of discontent? I, with all the weight and authority that many years of hard work and experience in my profession may be supposed to give me, and with the recollection of three previous festivals, unhesitatingly say, 'No!' and, in spite of all that has been said and written, I assert that the chorus of 1889 was as fine, on the whole, as any that have preceded it . . .

Many of the criticisms, written by men whose knowledge and experience give their opinions great weight and value, were conceived in a spirit of justice and kindness combined. From these we may learn much. Others we can afford to treat with silent contempt, especially those written by amateurs, who discover mistakes that were never made, or who gratuitously offer their counsel as to how the chorus should sing, the orchestra accompany, and the conductor beat time.

Who were these 'amateurs'? In a private letter to Joseph Bennett (25 October 1889) thanking him for *his* notices in the *Daily Telegraph*, Sullivan had disparaged Fuller Maitland (of *The Times*) and Sedley Taylor (an occasional critic) as 'priggish amateurs'. His own letter to Spark had not divulged the comments which he himself had confided to his own diary: the chorus had sounded 'a bit tired' in Berlioz and had begun Brahms' *Requiem* 'very badly'. His own conducting drew varied reviews: the *Birmingham Daily Post* (whose critic presumably had the Birmingham Festival and Richter's performances to compare) praised 'the superb orchestra, which Sir Arthur Sullivan appears to be able to do anything with' while others found his temperament sluggish.

There is no electric spark to the [Berlioz] Hungarian March taken at the tempo adopted by Sir Arthur Sullivan.

Sir Arthur Sullivan's reading of the [*Tannhäuser*] score was quite in keeping with the spirit of the vocalists. It was correct but tame throughout, and under his baton the Venusberg music attained a decency and decorum truly irreproachable.

These reviewers (in the first example from the *Glasgow Herald*, in the second from the London weekly, the *Guardian*) might almost have been echoing Hanslick's adverse comments on Sullivan of three years before. But the new works themselves won the weighty approval of a German critic. The comments of Otto Lessmann, who wrote at length of the festival in the Berlin *Allgemeine Musik-Zeitung*, were proudly reproduced in the *Musical Times* (November 1889) and in summary elsewhere. He hailed not only the enthusiasm of the audience but the achievements of British music, as such. His unpatronizing welcome to the new works of Stanford, Mackenzie, and Parry (whose *St Cecilia* 'would be an appropriate ornament to any German concert-room') might be said to mark the beginning of that German recognition of Britain's music which is usually said to originate with the welcome to Elgar a decade later.

But when Lessmann came to review the all-Sullivan concert which ended the festival his enthusiasm was checked. In such a committed and capable performance, he conceded, *The Golden Legend* achieved a distinctly higher status than had been suggested by the unfortunate first hearing in Berlin, and even by the second (see p. 259). Yet he still allowed the work only a 'powerful effect in parts', while the *Macbeth* music

can be properly understood only in connection with performance of Shakespeare's tragedy. The small and, in part, very delicately treated subjects are too evanescent to make an effect taken out of their connection. The overture is an orchestral work of the utmost brilliancy, which one can hardly characterize by any deeper title.

In concert terms the *Macbeth* music was indeed insubstantial and probably seemed monotonous in key as well – the prelude to the third act in G being followed by the prelude to the fifth act in G minor and to the sixth in G, then by two female choruses in D minor and D major, both in common time. Sullivan had taken no opportunity to 'fatten' the suite from its original theatrical dimensions, and the result was that his final Shakespearean work (as this turned out to be) raised none of the excitement which the youthful *Tempest* had won nearly 30 years before. If he was to re-establish himself as a 'serious' composer it would have to be with *Ivanhoe*; and meanwhile *The Gondoliers* was at the complex point of gestation when some parts were in rehearsal while others were still being written.

He was back in his London home on 14 October; the next day 'all no.7' (Fanny Ronalds and presumably others of her family) returned to London from Belfast. On the 17th an important stage was reached – the 'reading' of the new opera. On this occasion it was not at the Savoy Theatre but at the Savoy Hotel that Gilbert read the piece aloud to his principals (only six were present, Sullivan noted) and to others concerned. Afterwards Sullivan rehearsed the singers in a few of the numbers in a private room at the hotel. The formal music rehearsals began at the Savoy Theatre, François Cellier again in general supervision. Sullivan sometimes attended but sometimes felt compelled to stay at home composing the remainder of the work. The old habits held: he not uncommonly stayed at his desk until well after midnight.

[Diary, 1 November 1889]: Went to rehearsal at Savoy. Walked home with G. afterwards. V. tired. Dined at Alfred Rothschild's. Home at 11.45 [p.m.]. Didn't do much writing.

[2 November] Mother's birthday. At home all day. Sent Clotilde and [?] down to put a cross of flowers on Mother's grave. Wrote 'Here is a fix' and finale to 2nd act. Dined at 9.30, then called at no. 7. Finished up with Russie [Walker] and Trevvy [Martin] at the Portland.

[3 November] [Louis] Engel came and stayed two hours. Mr and Mrs T. Chappell [came] – couldn't do any work. [Dinner party at home, including 'no. 7'.] After dinner, besique – all left at 12.30 [a.m., 4 November]. Then I wrote out frame of 'Here is a fix' and finale 2nd act. Finished at 4 a.m.

[4 November] Too tired to go to rehearsal. G. had a preliminary sort of stage rehearsal of half of 1st Act; came here afterwards. Later no. 7 came, afterwards Bernstein: we drew up contract for Paris and sent it to Renard [a Paris manager planning a production of *The Mikado*. Dinner at 9. Began work about 11, wrote *four* numbers: 'Thy cold disdain', 'O, bury, bury', 'Rising early' (rewritten) and Brandram's song in 2nd Act.

'Thy cold disdain', changed in later entries to 'Thy wintry frown', refers to a solo for Luiz sung at the opening performances but soon replaced by the recitative and duet for Luiz and Casilda which are now familiar. Before Giuseppe's 'Rising early in the morning' there was apparently a recitative, later dropped, 'Ruthless my heart'. 'Brandram's song' indicates the Duchess's formidable account of matrimonial combat, 'On the day when I was wedded'.

[Diary, 5 November 1889]: G. called for me. Long music rehearsal at the Savoy. Wrote duet for Duke and Duchess.

[6 November] First stage rehearsal 11.30 to 4.30. Home to work. Framed 'Thy wintry frown', 'O, bury, bury', – Recit. 'Ruthless my heart', and 'Rising early'.

[7 November] Framed 'Small titles and orders', 'On the day that I was wedded', and end of 2nd Act finale.

[8 November] Rehearsal at 11.30 to 3 . . . Home at 5.15. Rewrote 'Thy cold disdain', and 'O, bury, bury'. Wrote 'There lived a king', and 'Take a pair of sparkling eyes', also completed no. 1. (1st act.) Finished at 5 a.m. with 'Take a pair'.

[9 November] Began scoring. 23 pages.

[10 November] Began at 11.30 to score. . . . Scored down to end of 'Buon giorno' – 18 pages. (2.30 a.m.)

[11 November] Scoring all day. Finished down to beginning of 'Thank you gay and gallant'. 36 pages. 4.30 a.m.

[12 November] Rehearsed all 2nd Act music at Savoy 12.15 to 4.30. Long consultations with Carte. Home at 6, dined 6.45. Scored down to end of no. 1. (13 pages.)

[13 November] Scoring all day. Rewrote and scored 'Thy wintry frown', and scored nos. 2, 3, 4 and 5. (24 pages.)

[14 November] Long music rehearsal 11.30 to 4. Rewrote and scored duet (no. 6) and scored 7 8, and 9. (23 pages.)

[15 November] Very seedy all day. Scored no. 10. Dined at Savoy Hotel. Farewell dinner to Dicey [who had just resigned his editorship of the *Observer*].

[16 November] Scoring all day. No. 11 and finale down to beginning of salterella [sic] ('For everyone who feels inclined'), 31 pages, 3 a.m.

[17 November] Scored salterella [*sic*] and recit. following. 16 pages. G. Lewis, Dresden, Martin, French, Mrs Huyshe, and no. 7 [Fanny Ronalds] dined here.

[18 November] Scoring. Finished finale 1st act. 10.15 p.m. (14 pages) Then 7 pages of no. 1 (2nd act) 21 pages.

[19 November] Rehearsed 2nd act (stage) 11.30 to 4.30 . . . Home, slept 1½ hours. Finished no. 1. Went up to T. Chappell's at 11 p.m.

[20 November] Scoring all day, nos. 2, 4 and 5 (4 pages). Framed no. 3 (35 pages). Bed at 4. G. and Cellier came to talk about two quintets in second act. C. [Clotilde] cloudy.

[21 November] Scoring all day. No. 5 (Cachucha) and 6 (29 pages). Also the strings and references of [sic] end of finale. Storm [evidently Clotilde's!].

At 3 a.m. on November 26 he completed the scoring of the finale of Act 2. 'All the opera (introduction and few pages excepted) finished', his diary noted. After a stage rehearsal and dinner at home he 'went to the Haymarket Theatre to see [Robert Buchanan's play] A Man's Shadow – I am out of prison at last!' Just in time: he had undertaken to conduct a Manchester performance of The Golden Legend with Hallé's orchestra and choir on Thursday 28 November. He left London by the 5.40 p.m. train on the previous evening, rehearsed in Manchester at noon, and after the evening performance at the Free Trade Hall was able to note in his diary 'a first-rate performance – chorus good, band excellent'. The invaluable Edward Lloyd was Prince Henry, this time with Margaret MacIntyre as Elsie; Hope Glenn, a personal friend of Sullivan's, was the contralto and Watkin Mills again the baritone. There was 'Stormy applause for me at the end'. Taking a 10.55 p.m. train from Manchester, he was not home till 4 a.m.

A melancholy duty awaited him that day (29 November) – the funeral at Brompton Cemetery (where his own parents and brother lay buried) of his old friend Frederic Clay, who had died four days before.

Only on 2 December, five days before the opening night of the operetta, did the first orchestral rehearsal take place. The composer heard his work and was pleased:

Beautiful effect. Home to dine. After dinner wrote – arranged and scored the overture, finishing at 3 a.m. Gilbert came down [to Sullivan's flat in Queens Mansions] after rehearsal at the Savoy at 11.15 [3 December]. Finally settled title The Gondoliers, or The King of Barataria. Good title, I think. Also settled to cut out dangerous dialogue [apparently likely to offend patrons by its remarks on matrimony] at the end of the piece.

One of the most animated and clever ensemble numbers had been dropped during rehearsals but was now put back – in a different position.

[Diary, 5 December 1889]: Settled . . . to substitute second quintet ('Here is a fix') previously cut, for first one ('Till time shall choose'), much to everyone's delight.

On 7 December the composer

went to the theatre at 8 with no. 7 [Fanny Ronalds and family]. Began at 8.35. Of course, crammed house. Everything went splendidly with immense 'go' and spirit, right up to the end. Gilbert and I got a tremendous ovation – we have never had such an enthusiastic house and never such a brilliant first night. It looks as if the opera were going to have a long run and be a great success. Portland [Club] afterwards.

Sullivan's friends were prominent in the auditorium. One box was taken by Reuben Sassoon, another by Alfred de Rothschild. In a third, assuredly by

Sullivan's personal invitation, sat Frederick Lehmann with his daughter (Sullivan's 'Little Ni', now Lady [Guy] Campbell). Facing each other in opposite stage boxes, as the *Daily News* noted, were Fanny Ronalds and another American famed for beauty and social position, Mrs John Mackay, each with a party of friends. In another box Lady Randolph Churchill provided yet another assertion of the American conquest of London 'society'. Augustus Harris, most famous of Covent Garden managers, was there; likewise John Hollingshead, the former manager of the Gaiety, where *Thespis* had first coupled Gilbert's and Sullivan's names.

Not till 18 December 1889 did Sullivan's old friend Francis Burnand (the librettist of *Cox and Box* and the editor of *Punch*) write his comment:

My dear Arturo Sullivano – Magnificento! Just seen *Gondoliers*. I delighted in the Italian recitatives. 'In a contemplative fashion' is a triumph. How did you arrive at it? Whence came the suggestion of the musical treatment?

The orchestra throughout is *in several volumes* [a private joke, evidently]. Not so *eccentric* as *The Mikado*, because of its subject. . . . Place some of it, costumes and all, on the stage *as an extract without saying from what*, and they'd say 'grand opera'.

I envy you and W.S.G. being able to place a piece like this on the stage in so complete a fashion. . . . Look out for Mr Punch . . .

Mr Punch indeed delivered himself in the next issue: the new work 'deserved to rank immediately after *The Mikado* and *Pinafore* bracketed . . .'. In its issue of 4 January 1890 Punch cartooned the composer and librettist in the roles of the two gondoliers on their joint throne. The caption, 'Monarchs of all they Savoy', was pure Burnand.

28 Transitions, translations

BURNAND'S generosity of acclaim for his old friend Sullivan – and his old rival, Gilbert – was representative of a general chorus. Readers of the *Sunday Times* were told of *The Gondoliers* as 'this brightest of operas', while the *Globe* (a London evening paper) declared it 'one of the best, if not the best, of the Gilbert-Sullivan operas'. The comment of the *Illustrated London News* was: 'Mr Gilbert has returned to the Gilbert of the past, and everyone is delighted. He is himself again.' These words have been misinterpreted as a preference for *The Gondoliers* (more comic, less serious) over *The Yeomen of the Guard*, but the context makes it clear that both works were recognized as representing Gilbert's happiest style, while the more dubious enterprise from which he had 'returned' was that of the serious spoken drama. *Brantinghame Hall* (St James's Theatre, 29 November 1888) had been his most recent stumble in that field.

The plot and its setting had allowed the composer *two* sets of local colour. In the first act, Venice was painted in swaying barcarolle-like measure, an additional exotic touch coming from the note A flat in the key of G at the words 'Two there are for whom in beauty ev'ry maid in Venice sighs'; the placing of the second act in the quasi-Spanish location of Barataria (the name is from Cervantes' *Don Quixote*) stimulated Sullivan's composition of the *cachucha*. The *Sunday Times* declared:

The theme, which recalls the real Spanish *cachucha*, is inspiriting beyond measure; the dance, in itself a treat to witness, is executed with a precision and elan that a troupe of terpsichorean professionals might envy. Nothing in its way to equal this has ever been done at the Savoy. We predict that all London will want to see the *cachucha* danced by Geraldine Ulmar [Gianetta], Jessie Bond [Tessa], Courtice Pounds [Marco], Rutland Barrington [Giuseppe] and the incomparable Savoy chorus . . .

No remembrance of the bolero which Sullivan had long ago written in *The Contrabandista* stirred the reviewers as they vied in enthusiasm for the new dance. In this scene the chorus 'wore comparatively short skirts for the first time' showing to the writer in the *Topical Times* that they were 'a very well-legged lot'.

In its rhythmic and melodic appeal the *cachucha* might indeed be ranked, as a miniature, with the very best non-Spanish imitation of the Spanish style – Chabrier's *España* and Rimsky-Korsakov's *Spanish Caprice* included (they, too, were works of the 1880s). The repeated 'percussive' rhythm of a solo cornet is a detail which makes an immediate and brilliant effect; less obvious is the almost 'classical' form of the piece, in which the 'second subject' (to the words 'Old Xeres we'll drink . . .') is first heard in the dominant, later in the home key.

Familiar Gilbert-and-Sullivan finger-prints were present too. The Duke of Plaza-Toro (a typical 'Grossmith part', though in Grossmith's absence it fell to a newcomer, Frank Wyatt) still had his patter-song, with a drum on stage effectively backing its refrain, 'If ever, ever, ever I get back to Spain'. He also had his dominating Duchess (the old Ko-Ko/Katisha relationship) in Rosina Brandram. Marco's 'Take a pair of sparkling eyes' was in form and function a typical ballad like Ralph's in *Pinafore*, borne aloft on Sullivan's melody despite the dreadful Gilbertianism of 'dainty fingerettes'. The Mediterranean setting did not exclude an old English dance (the gavotte, matched to 'I am a courtier grave and serious'), while the quasi-madrigals and quasi-glees of *The Mikado* and its fellows were matched in the quintet 'Try we lifelong'.

Economical as ever, Gilbert re-worked the comic baby-swapping motive of *Pinafore*. Of the two jolly gondoliers, who manage quickly to adjust their republican principles when they are placed on their joint throne, neither turns out in fact to be the true king; it is the Duke's drummer, Luiz, who gets the crown and the Duke's daughter, Casilda. (Decima Moore, a newcomer, made a hit in the latter part.) The journalist who called Gilbert 'the Swift of the suburbs'[1] had the exact measure of the author's satire: the middle-class virtues of industriousness and common sense go unchallenged, but the impoverished, hypocritical nobility is mocked, and likewise the lower-class notion of 'republican equality'. As the very Gilbertian Grand Inquisitor (W. H. Denny) put it, 'When everyone is somebody, then no one's anybody'.

As with *The Yeomen of the Guard*, changes in the text of *The Gondoliers* were made *after* the first night – a great many by Gilbert, a few by Sullivan. Chief among the musical substitutions was the new duet 'O rapture, when alone together' (Luiz and Casilda), replacing Luiz's 'Thy wintry frown' (see p. 304). But there were also changes in 'Jessie's song' (i.e. Tessa's 'When a merry maiden marries') and 'one or two other little things' as Sullivan's diary put it. On 12 December he went again to see *The Dead Heart*, an unusual repetition for him. Perhaps the attraction of the drama lay chiefly in the acting of Irving, of Ellen Terry, of the veteran Squire Bancroft, and of Ellen Terry's son, E. Gordon Craig, making his debut . . . or had Sullivan an operatic adaptation in mind? A newer play which he saw with approval at the Shaftesbury Theatre two nights later was *The Middleman* by Henry Arthur Jones ('capital piece and very well acted').

House–party pleasures beckoned too. At 4.20 on 16 December he took the train at St Pancras to attend a large weekend party given at Luton Hoo by the former Mrs Gerard Leigh (she was now Mme de Falke, wife of the Danish Minister to the British court) with the Prince of Wales as guest of honour. Three days later he was off again – this time on the longer, 90-mile journey from Liverpool St Station to Saxmundham in Suffolk. Some seven miles from there stood Great Glemham House, with its 70-acre park, belonging to his friend Edward Crabb, who had invited him for a few days' pheasant-shooting.

He was back in London by Christmas Day, but that day was hardly a holiday. A *Gondoliers* company had been assembled by Carte to perform in the United States: it was not a whole cast but a group to provide reinforcement of the American performers who had been engaged. They held a rehearsal at 10.45 a.m. on 25 December which Sullivan attended, before returning home – 'working all the afternoon'. (Gilbert had left for a holiday in India.) On that evening there was a festive dinner with the folk of 'no. 7' and other guests. Probably it was in the company of Fanny Ronalds and members of her family that Sullivan went – as he liked to do – to the pantomimes and other special seasonal shows to be seen at London theatres. He saw *Cinderella* at her Majesty's on 27 December[2] and a mixed ballet-and-variety bill at the Alhambra on 31 December (Marie Lloyd was advertised among the performers), having previously dined at the Savoy with his old friend Ernest Dresden. On that morning, the last of the old year he had attended Robert Browning's funeral at Westminster Abbey, the poet having died in Venice on 16 December and the coffin having been brought to London.

On 25 December, with the sanction of the composer but not in his presence, *The Yeomen of the Guard* became the latest of his works to be staged in Germany and in German. The place was Berlin and the title *Der Königsgardist* ('The Royal Guardsman' – note the singular!). Zell and Genée were once more the translators of the production at the Kroll Theatre (where Carte's company had given the original versions of *The Mikado* and *Patience* two years before). The German score of *The Yeomen*, published by Bosworth in Leipzig, discloses many changes from the original – 'when our gallant Norman foes', for instance, transferred from Dame Carruthers to Sergeant Meryll, and the patter-trio from *Ruddigore* incorporated into the second act! One insertion at least had the composer's authority – though, since the instruction to Bernstein was posted as late as 23 December 1889, it will have been too late for the opening night: 'I have sent the song off by this afternoon's post. Please get a pianoforte arrangement made for the vocal score; and get the song copied into the full score and band parts.' This was possibly the Act 1 song for Sergeant Meryll, removed from the original production.

In the project for a French version of *The Mikado* Sullivan showed himself ready for a still greater freedom of adaptation. But the negotiations, involving both French and Belgian theatrical managements, proved complex – and finally disastrous. The Paris manager concerned was Renard, who planned to use a translation by Armand Silvestre and was first to secure Sullivan's assent; but the Brussels manager, Victor Silvestre (apparently unrelated to Armand) got more quickly to the point of an actual production. To Victor Silvestre's translator and adaptor, Maurice Kufferath, Sullivan wrote on 4 December (signing the letter himself, though it is in Smythe's hand):

I think you are somewhat unjust in your opinion of my agent, Mr B. Bernstein. I am convinced that his sole object and desire is to obtain a first-rate reproduction of *The Mikado* in Brussels, and that he certainly has not wish to throw obstacles in your way; because you must remember that if the piece is not performed in a manner completely satisfactory to myself, I should exercise my right to withdraw my permission for its performance and Mr Bernstein is naturally anxious that such a *contretemps* should not arise. I do not at all like the idea of the part of Nanki-Poo being performed by a woman, however gifted and attractive she may be. I have never permitted either a man to play a woman's part, nor a woman to play a man's part, in any pieces I have written for the stage. Artistically it is wrong, and I dislike it very much. Please do not think any more of the idea.

With regard to Paris. I am too far pledged to M. Renard to withdraw now the permission which I gave him to play the *Mikado* in Paris, and the only thing to do is, to endeavour to obtain a good representation.

According to the agreement between M. Victor Silvestre and Mr Bernstein, your translation becomes my absolute property for all countries after the first performance in Brussels. As you know, M. Renard was at that time anxious to produce the *Mikado* in Paris quickly, and entrusted M. Armand Silvestre to make another French version for Paris. I need not go into this matter now further than to say that I have insisted upon your name being coupled with M. Armand Silvestre as joint adaptor of the piece. M. Renard now wishes to have your translation immediately so that it can be arranged with that of M. Armand Silvestre's, and the rehearsals (which have been stopped for some time) pressed forward with vigour.

Will you send it to me, or, will you send it direct to M. Renard? Please let me know. It will not be played in Paris until after its production in Brussels. Forgive my writing in English but I can only dictate my letters as I am so occupied, day and night, preparing my new opera [*The Gondoliers*] which is to come out next Saturday.

Kufferath had evidently persuaded the composer that an insertion of ballet would improve the appeal of *The Mikado* in Brussels. On 27 December 1889 (the day when, in fact, the Brussels production took place) Smythe wrote to Kufferath:

I am directed by Sir Arthur Sullivan to send you the ballet music for this, book-post, and to say that Sir Arthur does not think it very characteristic. He thinks it might have been very much better. However, he supposes it must do.

Sullivan can hardly have composed *new* ballet music in that time: doubtless he 'borrowed' some material from *L'Ile enchantée* or another early score of his own. Whether or no this supplementary music ever reached the Brussels stage, the production was a failure. Smythe wrote to Kufferath that Sullivan was not surprised at the news 'as he never thought the opera suitable for adaptation into French'.

Soon afterwards the negotiations for a Paris production of the work came to an ignominious halt. The failure of the Brussels *Mikado* frightened the Paris translator, Armand Silvestre, who declined to let his work go forward. The Paris manager, Renard, then proposed to use the translation which Kufferath had written for Brussels. But this, in Sullivan's view, would be to court a repetition of the disaster. In a telegram dated 11 January (1890 and signed 'Pinafore' (which he still used as his telegraphic address) he told Renard that he should defer the production till autumn, when the Brussels failure would no longer be in everyone's memory: '. . . Folie donner adaptation Kufferath. Remettez représentation automne. Bruxelles sera oublié. Faites tout possible d'avoir Silvestre. Viendrai immédiatement si nécessaire.'

A letter (also in French) of the same date, amplifying the telegram, made Sullivan's point that not a translation was wanted but 'a good adaptation', and emphasized that if Silvestre were to suggest changes – 'whether cuts or newly composed numbers' – Sullivan was ready to make them.

I have more than once told you that *The Mikado* as it stands is not to French taste; that it must be adapted, not translated; that the humour of the libretto lies in the wit of the language, and that even the music needs to be lightened [*allegée*] a little.

But Renard's financial backers were pressing him. He could not wait, and said so in a letter which Sullivan forwarded to Bernstein on 11 January. With it, Sullivan sent a covering letter of his own:

Now you will see in his answer that he says firstly that it is not possible for him to put off the performance of the *Mikado* as his situation is grave and critical, and that he cannot continue playing intermediate pieces as he has done since the first days of October – the date at which I gave him authority to play the piece, an authority which should have been followed immediately by my sending him the music. He also says that he has gone to considerable expense in preparing the piece, part of which has been paid, and the rest having to be paid within a very short time, etc, etc.

You will observe, however, that in the latter part of his letter he suggests a means of escaping from the difficulty, and even of getting rid of the contract altogether. He says: 'I am persuaded that with a small indemnity we could compensate the *entrepreneurs* and stop the works in progress'. Now it seems to me that it will be very easy for you now to get me out of the whole business, because in M. Renard's contract, which I enclose for your guidance, the whole matter is treated as a settled thing that M. Armand Silvestre's adaptation should be used in Paris. Kufferath's is only mentioned incidentally – namely, that should any portion of his adaptation be used by M. Armand Silvestre then I should pay for it, and that it should cost M. Renard nothing.

I should, therefore, say to M. Renard: 'You are bound by your contract to Sir Arthur Sullivan to use the adaptation of M. Armand Silvestre. If Mr Silvestre has backed out of it, we must back out of it too. To use Kufferath's translation after its deadly failure in Brussels would be folly of a criminal nature.' You can explain to him that I am in no way responsible for any cost he has been put to in the preparation, as nothing should have been commenced until all arrangements had been agreed upon and the contract properly signed.

With regard to an indemnity, I leave it entirely to your discretion what to arrange. If you see that by paying a small sum of money (not to exceed 5,000 francs [just over £500]) we could get out of the whole thing, I think you had better close the matter on these terms. But if he wants a larger sum than this, I should refuse it and insist upon his fulfilling the terms of his contract with reference to M. Armand Silvestre.

Please do not forget that he has the full score and band parts, and therefore if the contract is dissolved these must be given up to you.

And so Sullivan, none too gracefully, was able to back away from the project. There was no Paris *Mikado* – and indeed the city of Offenbach's triumphs seems never to have witnessed a single professional production of any of Sullivan's theatrical works.

In the same letter, Sullivan informed Bernstein that 'all my plans have changed suddenly as I have to go to America next Thursday' [i.e. 16 January]. But was that true, or an excuse for his abandoning his previous readiness to go to Paris to negotiate with Renard? Certainly he had been thinking of going to

America in order to conduct Carte's company in *The Gondoliers*, but on that very day of the letter Sullivan's diary entry makes it clear that he had decided against it: 'Mr and Mrs Carte called. Urged me to go to America with them. Declined.

On 19 January Sullivan *did* go to Paris – not to negotiate with Renard however, but to call on Mrs Grant's daughters Adèle and Edith (now 'grown a big girl') at the Hôtel Vendôme, and then to proceed to his beloved Riviera. He stayed at the Hôtel Métropole in Monte Carlo: 'Tables very hostile – am now minus 10,000 [francs – just over £1,000]'! He sent a box of fruit one day and flowers on another to 'no. 7'. On 26 January he

dined in the hotel with the Maples' party. Very good dinner – Hungarian band. After dinner the 'monde' came in [i.e. a general crowd] – Blanche de la Barre, Garner[?], Hélène Arnaud, Countess d'Esscher, Marie Beckmann, and some men. Danced till 12.30. Did not go to casino. Had my hair cut. Jean [masseur, came].

An amorous relationship is implied by the diary record of two letters received (11, 14 January) from an unidentified 'R', and another by the record of a meeting on a trip to Brussels (22 March): 'Saw E.W. Long conversation. A little bit "touched". Arranged for future.'

While at Brussels he saw, on 24 March at the Théâtre de la Monnaie, the new opera *Salammbô*, composed by Ernest Reyer on a story derived from Flaubert's novel of that name. 'To me a complete blank – feeble imitation of Wagner, no melody, rhythm, style or distinction. No invention.' It was a damning verdict, which history has substantially endorsed.

Yet another foreign trip followed in the spring of 1890. Sullivan returned to Monte Carlo, and this time (staying at the Hôtel de Paris) was accompanied not only by Fanny Ronalds but by her mother ('Grandma') as well:

[Diary, 5 April 1890]: Took Grandma to the [gaming] rooms – she is fully persuaded the croupiers cheat!

Before returning home he extended his journey as far as Milan and Basle. He was probably still in the company of Fanny and her mother, since the diary records that in Paris on 17 April on their way home 'I went to Grand Hotel, the others to Continental'. He returned to London, on his own, next day.

Carte had meanwhile been supervising *The Gondoliers* in New York. It had opened – under his joint management, but before his arrival – at the New Park Theatre on 7 January 1890. Gianetta was sung by Esther Palliser, who was talented enough to be chosen presently for the heroine's role in *Ivanhoe*, but the cast was in general inadequate and 'the opera nearly died of the affliction'. (The verdict is that of George C. D. Odell, the modern annalist of the New York stage.) The reinforcements arrived from London, and a move was made to another theatre (Palmer's) but a run lasting no longer than 19 April could be reckoned only a moderate success.

On his return to London, Carte received a note in which Sullivan – on his habitually amicable terms with royalty – reported a conversation with the Prince of Wales, who seemed a little annoyed about the fact of his visits to the Savoy being publicly enumerated in the newspapers. On the last two occasions he visited the theatre, it was stated in the newspapers that he went for the *third* and *fourth* time respectively. The same remark was made about H.R.H. the Princess of Wales on her *third* visit. I am not at all surprised at His Royal Highness's annoyance, as, of course, he does not like to be made the medium of a gratuitous advertisement for *The Gondoliers* or any other piece.

Was the Savoy management (Sullivan asked) responsible for deliberately planting the reports? Carte, smart showman that he was, might well have evaded a direct answer.

On 24 April, in reply to a renewed invitation from the Leeds Festival to contribute a new work, Sullivan wrote from London to F. R. Spark:

On the one hand it is my great desire to write again for the Leeds Festival, a task which has hitherto been as delightful to me in every way as successful. On the other hand are the grave doubts I entertain as to whether I can really accomplish the undertaking. I have already entered into formidable engagements which will spread over two years, and after that I am not sure that I shall have the strength to sit down and work hard again at a composition of so much importance as a festival production. [Thus?] I shrink from entering into an engagement which may become a source of enmity and trouble to me, as the time approaches for me to fulfil it. If therefore I am called upon to give an absolute decision now, one way or the other, I shall have no alternative but to decline. Two years and a half is too distant a period for a man of my age to pledge his creative power, more especially when, as in my case, he has so much on hand already . . .

Would it be possible for the committee to go on with their other arrangements, and give me to the end of this year before receiving a definite answer? I shall by that time have completed the important work I am now engaged upon, and I shall know much better how I stand with regard to the future.

The 'important work' was, of course, *Ivanhoe*. In it he foresaw the liberation of his theatrical music from the supposed clamps of Gilbert. Might it not indeed establish for him, in middle age, that Continental reputation in 'serious' music which had seemed within his grasp a quarter of a century before and which *The Golden Legend* had failed to achieve? Walter Scott, the source of *Kenilworth* and *Marmion* in Sullivan's young years, was again his literary quarry. *Ivanhoe* would furnish that basis of national pageantry and historical 'atmosphere' which had been lately invoked by Massenet in *Manon* (1884), by Verdi in *Otello* (1887), and also by Wagner in *Die Meistersinger*, which had reached London as lately as 1882. Besides, *Ivanhoe* would be sure of an appeal to Sullivan's immediate audience. As Hesketh Pearson put it in his dual biography of Gilbert and Sullivan, the subject was 'healthy, romantic, popular, moral and clean'.

There had been more than one operatic version of *Ivanhoe*, the most celebrated being Heinrich Marschner's, produced in Leipzig in 1829, entitled *Der Templer und die Jüdin* ('The Templar and the Jewess'). In Schumann's *Symphonic Studies* for piano (1834) occurs a quotation from that opera with reference to the words 'Proud England' – in tribute to Sterndale Bennett, to whom Schumann's piece was dedicated. Marschner's score must have been known to Bennett's Leipzig-educated pupil, Arthur Sullivan. Indeed he may have passed directly to Sturgis some suggestions, derived from W. A. Wohlbrück's libretto for

Marschner's score, for the construction of his own work – which is, likewise, in three acts.

Not the hero's beloved Rowena but the Jewish maiden, Rebecca, is the true heroine in both operas, and in both cases the song which chiefly characterizes her is a prayer for the steadfastness of her faith. Both composers seized on the comic episode in the novel in which the disguised King Richard finds himself in the forest as guest of that genial rascal, Friar Tuck. (Here Marschner took more literally Scott's own verses, 'The barefooted friar', and added an ironic refrain of 'Ora pro nobis' and the direction 'mock-holy' – both of which would have been too shocking for Sullivan's audiences.) Most conspicuously, it is in the final ensemble of the opera that Sullivan's libretto follows Marschner's in the 'telescoping' of events from the novel. Thus Ivanhoe's defeat of Bois-Guilbert in combat, King Richard's expulsion of the Templars' order from English soil, the reunion of Ivanhoe and his beloved Rowena, and the isolation of Rebecca are all encompassed within a single musical structure.

The new opera was not only to open Carte's new London theatre: it was to do so on a novel principle. The opera would not be part of a repertory season but would run continuously, night after night, like a 'Savoy' work but with alternate casting of principal roles. The italics in the diary entry of 10 May were Sullivan's own: 'Ben Davies came – arranged with him to sing *four times* a week in the new opera (£70 a week).'

Mindful of the necessity that other works should be available for the English repertory he hoped to build up, Carte wrote to Frederic Cowen asking for 'a grand opera or comedy piece . . . I mean a serious and important work'. But with nothing else actually in hand, Carte was to be accused later of imprudence in attempting to establish English opera in a new theatre with only a single work. Yet if there was any composer who promised the necessary artistic strength to undertake such a work, it was the man who had *The Golden Legend* as well as *The Mikado* and *The Yeomen of the Guard* to his name. Carte would tempt the theatrical public by expensive, spectacular staging – just as Irving did. Like Irving, he hoped to recoup the heavy initial outlay by many repetitions – assuming, as he did, a public for 'serious' English opera comparable to that which Sullivan had won for his collaborations with Gilbert. That assumption, perhaps the greatest act of faith that any commercial impresario has ever placed in opera, was to be tested.

On 14 May 1890 Sullivan again moved to Grove House, Weybridge, to find comparative seclusion for the creative work ahead. On the previous day he had noted in his diary 'My 48th birthday, hélas!' and on the 17th he 'took up the first act of new opera, *Ivanhoe*, and began it. Didn't do much.'

But his seclusion did not shield him from two enemies to concentration. One was illness; the other was Gilbert. Back from India, Gilbert scrutinized the Savoy Theatre accounts, drawn up by Carte, which regulated the sums paid out quarterly in equal amounts to Gilbert, Sullivan and Carte himself. By the agreement in force since 1883, this partnership rented the Savoy from its owner

(Carte himself) at £4,000 per annum. Before arriving at the figure of profit to be distributed, Carte was entitled to deduct those costs which were 'incidental to the performances'. Gilbert was convinced not only that Carte spent too freely but that he was improperly deducting costs not really 'incidental' at all. It was unfortunately typical of Gilbert's impetuous character that he had gone in person to make a strong protest to Carte, whose wife was also present.

The upshot was a quarrel which was to split Gilbert from Sullivan and to range them on opposite sides in a court of law. It was a quarrel which brought latent animosities into open and hurtful confrontation. Just as the creative partnership of composer and librettist had been longer, more profitable, and more squarely in the public eye than any other of its kind in the history of the British theatre, so now did their dispute run to excess in length and bitterness. *Ivanhoe* would be composed and produced before the dispute was finished, but something else was also finished. Though Gilbert and Sullivan *were* to collaborate again, their sun was never to blaze as it had, 'in ever-living glory'.

29 On the Carpet

On 22 April 1890 Sullivan went as the Prince of Wales's guest to the races at Epsom, travelling there and back from London in the royal train. On that day the letter arrived from Gilbert which began the Carpet Quarrel, as it later became known.

I have had a difficulty with Carte. I was appalled to learn from him that the preliminary expenses of the *Gondoliers* amounted to the stupendous sum of £4,500!!! This seemed so utterly unaccountable that I asked to see the details and last night I received a resumé of them. This includes such trifles as £75 for Miss Moore's second dress – £50 for her first dress – £100 for Miss Brandram's second dress (this costly garment has now, for some occult reason, been sent on tour); £450 for the wages of the carpenters during the time they were engaged on the scenery: £460 for the gondola, the sailing boat, the two columns and the two chairs and fountain for Act 2; £112 for timber, £120 for ironmongery, £95 for canvas – and so forth. But the most surprising item was £500 for new carpets *for the front of the house!*

In Gilbert's face-to-face interview with Carte, the dialogue of charge and counter-charge had risen to a dangerous level of offence. To Gilbert, Carte was the man who had ascended the ladder of success on the backs of the librettist and composer; to Carte, Gilbert was totally unappreciative of the way in which the maintenance and conduct of the theatre had helped to build, and keep, the audiences for Gilbert's and Sullivan's work. Gilbert gave what was in effect an ultimatum. Unless Carte would reconsider the recent financial calculation, he (Gilbert) would write nothing further for the Savoy until a new contractual agreement was drawn up to replace the present one.

Sullivan's immediate reply (23 April) to 'My dear Gilbert' was an attempt to cool the latter's temper and to set any present difficulty against the profitable experience of the past.

I can scarcely tell you how much I regret that any heated personalities should have entered into the discussion about the accounts, and I hope that all unpleasantness will soon be removed. With reference to the charge for renewals and repairs I am not prepared, without further examination, to give a decided opinion, and I shall go into the matter at once, comparing accounts with the agreement, and bearing in mind what our custom has been.

I certainly agree with you that the stage 'preliminaries' are appallingly high, but with this I cannot well or with good grace take exception, as you yourself control these expenses, ordering dresses, scenery, properties, etc., which I have always (with one notable exception) acquiesced in as a matter of course. You are an expert on these matters, and I naturally leave everything in your hands.

I think we are charged abnormally high for our stuffs, silks, lace, etc., but it seems impossible to get a price or an estimate beforehand: and when things are in train, the production near, and time of the greatest importance, we are, to use your own phrase, entirely in these people's hands; and I really don't see how it is to be otherwise if our pieces continue to be put upon the stage with the same perfection of detail that has characterized all our joint works. Let us talk the matter over.

To Gilbert it must have been clear that Sullivan was not going to side with him on the simple basis of ranging the joint creative talent against the managerial interest. Moreover Gilbert knew that Sullivan and Carte were already committed to each other over *Ivanhoe* and that Sullivan could hardly risk falling out with Carte. Nevertheless, convinced that he had justice on his side and that Sullivan could not fail to respond to that appeal, Gilbert called on Sullivan on Saturday 26 April and again the following morning. What happened is recalled in Sullivan's own words – in a separate memorandum to which the composer no doubt intended to refer if he himself should have to approach Carte. The text of the memorandum, given in the Flower biography with crucial omissions, is actually as follows:

[26 April 1890]: Long interview between Gilbert and myself. He gave me an account of the interview between Carte and himself showing that he had been treated very unceremoniously, arrogantly and insolently by Carte. I could not agree with him on some of the disputed points about which the quarrel arose, such as the question of the renewal of worn-out carpets, and the responsibility of the preliminary stage expenses but undertook to point out to Carte the impropriety of using the words ascribed to him by Gilbert. As a discussion of the accounts seemed advisable, and very much desired by Gilbert, I undertook to arrange a meeting at my house between Gilbert, Carte and myself for calm consideration of them, Gilbert himself stipulating that we should meet and discuss them on the condition that no reference whatever should be made on either side to the heated conversation which had taken place between himself and Carte.

I undertook to arrange this, and proposed that it should stand over for a week as I was anxious to go out of town [to Newmarket for the races], and the delay would tend to smooth matters.

[27 April 1890]: Gilbert came to see me in the morning, and brought with him a paper containing the heads of a new agreement to be made between us three. These he read to me, and left the paper with me for consideration. He also brought Carte's letter to him of the [blank]. I asked him to leave this letter with me, so that I might if necessary refer to it in my discussion with Carte. I again proposed to delay taking any active steps for a week as I was compelled to point out to Gilbert that I had noticed considerable irritability on Carte's part and that I had rather keep away from him for a few days so that we could all meet in a more 'tranquil frame of mind'. Gilbert agreed with me in this quoting from *The Gondoliers*, and giving me the impression that the breach should not [be] widened, but, on the contrary, that our mutual relations should be placed on our former amicable footing.[1]

Back from Newmarket, where he had stayed with his old friend 'Russie' Walker, he wrote – again in soothing vein – to Gilbert on 3 May (Saturday), posting the letter next day. Noting in his diary that he had not retained a copy, he summarized its points as follows:

I cordially agreed with him that it would be better to have a new agreement which should be so drawn up to obviate the possibility of any dispute as to the construction to be put upon it. But I thought it might be better to let that stand over until the necessity o desirability of writing a new piece for the Savoy Theatre should arrive – that i consequence of the great success of *The Gondoliers* this contingency [would not be likely to happen for some months. I pointed out that even if we had a new agreement it could no act retrospectively and therefore it was in every way desirable to settle the disputed point in the old agreement first. I also added that I had so much anxious work on hand at presen that I was not in the position to give the time and thought to the discussion and preparatio of a new agreement.

Sullivan showed himself unwilling to discuss a new agreement for the present Gilbert was unwilling that the existing agreement (under which he considere Carte had cheated) should continue. Thus it was that he wrote to the composer i a letter of 5 May that 'the time for putting an end to our collaboration has at las arrived'. The 'at last' sounds like a cry of relief but it is possible to read it a meaning simply 'after so long'. The letter continued:

I am writing a letter to Carte (of which I enclose a copy) giving him notice that he is not t produce or perform any of my libretti after Christmas 1890. In point of fact after th withdrawal of *The Gondoliers*, our united work will be heard in public no more.

Another long letter from Gilbert (written on 8 May) with strong references t Carte's insolent behaviour failed to change the composer's attitude. But Gilbert' threat to withdraw his works at Christmas 1890 was empty – as Carte was no slow to remind him. The agreement currently in force 'was made for two year expiring at Christmas 1891, [and] is binding upon all parties until after that date' Sullivan, plagued additionally by a recurrence of his old kidney trouble, foun Gilbert's attitude unbearable.

[Diary, 6 May 1890]: Felt ill all day. Received letter from Gilbert breaking off finally ou collaboration. *Nothing* would induce me to write again with him. How I have stood him s long I can't understand.

Sullivan wrote back to Gilbert (presumably on 6 May; a copy of the letter, i Smythe's hand, is undated) in phrases which exposed the wounds caused b Gilbert's knife. The whole long letter must be quoted:

The tone of your letter fills me with surprise and indignation, and leaves me no alternativ but to acquiesce in the decision you have come to, to put an end to our collaboration and t carry out which you have already taken formal steps. It is clearly impossible for you t work any more with one who, as you state, displays towards you 'marked discourtesy' - 'consistent hostility, veiled or otherwise' – 'contemptuous indifference' and 'placidity i tolerating insults inflicted on you'.

The only reason I can find for this series of baseless and uncalled-for charges, is that do not in every case act in accordance with the impulse which seizes you – in fact that occasionally allow myself to be guided by my own opinion and judgement. With referenc to the marked discourtesy in refusing to meet you to discuss matters, I most emphatically protest against such a construction being put upon my action. You have twice asked me t meet you to discuss a proposed new agreement. I certainly declined – not to meet you – bu to consider a new agreement whilst the present one was still under dispute.

The moment was most inopportune and matters would have become more complicate and more difficult to arrange. Such at least was my opinion, an opinion clearly expressed t you in writing. But in adhering to my own resolution, and in opposing your wish, it seem

have incurred your grave displeasure. The other charges – viz – 'hostility, veiled or
otherwise' (an ungenerous insinuation) and 'contemptuous indifference' are so hopelessly
absurd that I cannot seriously consider them; but I must allude to the other accusation,
viz. that I tolerated with placidity the insults inflicted upon you. I spoke very seriously to
Carte on the subject of the words which you say he used and frankly told him that it was an
intolerable insult and that nothing could justify him in addressing you in such a manner.
But both Carte and Mrs Carte (who was present at the interview) utterly and emphatically
denied his having used such words, and they adhere to the statement as to the words used
made in his letter to you.

As I had of course perfect faith in the integrity of all concerned in this lamentable affair
I did all I could to try and discover a misunderstanding, or an error of memory
somewhere, so that I might reconcile and explain these conflicting statements. But before
I could get very far in my efforts to heal the breach, a task you will remember you
entrusted to me, you unfortunately interfered. You would not allow me to act in my own
way – you insisted on at once entering into a discussion as to the future. And, your
imperious will receiving a check by my firm determination to settle one question before
entering upon another, you have now taken a step which has caused me the deepest pain,
but which under the existing circumstances I do not feel justified in attempting to induce
you to reconsider.

In such a way the mutual antipathy and resentment spilled out, even though
the nominal dispute did not lie between Gilbert and Sullivan at all, but between
Gilbert and Carte. Gilbert's case against Carte was weak. In renting the theatre,
the trio were responsible for maintaining the building in the state in which they
found it. Thus, as Carte put it in a letter to Gilbert: 'I cannot conceive how it
could be argued that the restoring of carpets worn out, upholstery, and painting,
etc., where necessary, should not come under the heading of "wear and tear" just
as much as the renewals of electric lamps as they wear out.'

Moreover, according to Carte, Gilbert had got the cost wildly wrong:

I pass by the observation in your letter that the cost of restoring the carpets is £500, which
sum I see you have reduced to £330 in your second letter, the actual amount being £140,
merely remarking that this is a fair sample of the general inaccuracy of your letters, due no
doubt to your not having properly examined the accounts.

Into this already embittered situation Carte's wife stepped with firmness and
delicacy. That Helen Carte could write personally to Gilbert, correctly presuming that even Gilbert would recognize hers as an independent, conciliatory voice,
says much for this remarkable woman's character. Her letter went back to the
initial heated interview between Gilbert and her husband:

I know, of course, that both of you believe absolutely in what you say you said. But you
must remember that you were very excited indeed on that occasion – you burst out so
suddenly and addressed Mr Carte in a way that you would not have used to an offending
menial. All I was able to say myself was 'I'm sure you are not thinking about what you are
saying, Mr Gilbert'. I really felt you did not think fully what you were saying. When you
first burst out you said we were robbed right and left and that Mr Carte did not even check
his carpenter's accounts, and that you had made him what he was. All this you said in a
very violent and insulting way, although no one had said or done anything to provoke it.
You then went on to the carpet matter and finally said there must be a new agreement. Mr
Carte had by that time not unnaturally got annoyed and said 'Very well, he would put the
rent at £5,000 instead of £4,000'. Then *you* said 'If so, he must get another author for the

Savoy'. The first words as to not writing any more for the Savoy came from you. Mr Carte did not then or at any time say 'Then you write no more for the Savoy' or anything to tha effect. On this point I'm perfectly clear. I was quite calm myself and very grieved that th conversation should be taking such an unpleasant tone.

Further conversation followed and you asked Mr Carte very heatedly what *he* did fo the share he got and he said he must decline to discuss that. He asked if you wer dissatisfied with the existing state of things and wished to break it off. You said you were and he then said you'd better go and see Sir Arthur Sullivan and talk to *him*. You then lef the room with the remark about the ladder.

You seemed so different from your usual self and it all came so suddenly and was reall so entirely unprovoked. You have always been so courteous to me personally that I do no like writing anything that may annoy you but it seemed to me to be quite as much due t you as to Mr Carte that I should say what occurred at the interview. The fact that yo *believe* Mr Carte said the words you impute to him must have been, and has evidentl been, an annoyance to you, as you believe yourself to have been deliberately insulted. It i right therefore *to you* as well as to Mr Carte that your mind should be disabused of thi mistake so that you may be able to look at the business matters before you in a calm way Anything in the conversation that might be considered insulting was certainly in some o the things you said to Mr Carte, not in anything he said to you, although as I have stated he was of course more or less excited towards you because of the conversation.

Regrettably, the date of this letter was not specified when it was published b Leslie Baily in his *Gilbert and Sullivan Book* (1952) and remains unavailable. Bu Gilbert was not to be moved. He was now aggrieved not only with Carte but wit Sullivan's failure to give comradely support. To the reproaches of Sullivan' letter of 7 May he hit back next day:

You accuse me of having groundlessly charged you with marked discourtesy towards me Allow me to explain myself.

On Saturday last [3 May] I wrote to you, earnestly begging you to make a appointment to discuss (a) the question of the fresh agreement which, in your letter of th 3rd inst. [see p. 317] you declare to be essential before we could begin upon a new piece and (b) a means whereby my present relations with Carte should be placed upon such footing as to preclude a repetition of the insult which, as you know, he has recently place upon me. I reminded you that it was necessary, if a new piece were to be done, that should set to work upon it at once, as you insist – and very reasonably insist – that th whole work shall be constructed in every detail and the first act completely written befor you will consent to write a note of the music.

I also told you that I had allotted the next six months to this matter, leaving you a liberty to compose the music when it suited your convenience to do so, or for that matter not to compose it at all. In your reply you pass by, without notice, my remarks as to m present relations with Carte and confine yourself to declining to meet me on the ground (a) that many months must elapse before it can be necessary even to think of a new piec and (b) that you cannot give up any time or thought to future Savoy matters as you wish t give yourself up entirely to the work you have in hand – you further imply that you, an not I, are to decide as to when it would best suit me to commence my libretto and that it i my duty to wait until it occurs to you to give the word to begin. If all this does not amoun to 'marked discourtesy' towards a man with whom you have been in intimate professiona relationship for 14 years, then I do not know the meaning of the words.

With reference to the conflicting accounts of my interview with Carte, you are, o course, at liberty to believe him and his wife, on the one hand, or me on the other, at you pleasure. But the letter that he addressed to me after the interview has been for some day in your possession [see p. 317] and cannot possibly be misunderstood. You agreed with m hat nothing could justify such a letter, coming as it did from a man whom we, by our exertions, had raised from poverty to affluence – that in it, he addressed me as if I were a refractory chorister – and you accounted for its insolent tone by stating that Carte's irritability had, of late, developed in so unaccountable a fashion that you had taken care to avoid him lest he should insult you. I hold that that letter should have convinced you, if you had any respect for my position as a collaborator of 14 years' standing, that I was justified in my demand to be protected at once from a repetition of the outrages therein contained. It was mainly to settle these terms that I urged you to meet me and to name your own day and hour for the appointment.

With regard to the 'imperial will' with which you are pleased to credit me:- in a matter in which my self-respect is involved, I must claim the right to be arbitrary. If the insult had been inflicted upon us jointly, it might have been for us jointly to decide as to the steps that we should jointly take to protect ourselves from further outrage. But in the case in question it was I, and not you, who had been insulted by Carte and it was consequently for me, and not for you, to say upon what terms I would continue in association with him. Those terms you have declined to consider on the grounds of the many more important matters that are at present occupying your attention.

As I have said, this is a matter in which I claim the right to be arbitrary. That you are not of the opinion that it is my custom to assume an imperious or dictatorial air towards you I gather from the following extract from a letter which I received from you on the Monday that followed the production of *The Gondoliers*.

'Don't talk of reflected light. In such a perfect book as *The Gondoliers* you shine with an individual brilliancy which no other writer can hope to attain. If any thanks are due anywhere, they should be from me to you for the patience, willingness and unfailing good nature with which you have received my suggestions and your readiness to help me by acceding to them.'

It was (once again) the kind of letter which Gilbert might contemplate with literary self-satisfaction, but a phrase like 'if you had any respect for my position as a collaborator of 14 years' standing' could only add to Sullivan's resentment. What is more, Gilbert quickly found after posting the letter that he had misquoted Sullivan – necessitating a further letter the same day.

I find that the exact words you used are 'imperious will' – not 'imperial will'.

As I have pen in hand I may state that you are mistaken in supposing that I entrusted to you the task of 'healing the breach' between Carte and myself. You volunteered to see Carte and point out to him the enormity of the letter he had written to me, and you further asked me to leave the letter with you that you might be able to quote from it with exactitude. It never entered my mind that the breach could, by any possibility, be healed.

Back and forth went the letters without a day's loss. On 9 May Sullivan wrote again, this time indicating his unwillingness 'to continue a correspondence which, with arguments and counter-arguments, can do no practical good'. But the path of silence was not left open to him. Journalists had got wind of the separation and Gilbert proposed to issue a press statement in the name of both of them. Sullivan's reply, sent to Gilbert on 16 May, was indignant:

I have steadily refused to be interviewed or to furnish any information with reference to our break-up, intended for publication. Men can have differences without taking the public into their confidence, and the ways of modern journalism are to me detestable. I should therefore strongly advise you to tell Mr Salaman and others that our collaboration had ceased for reasons into which it was not necessary to enter. For I must protest against your proposed note to him, which implies that *I* broke up our collaboration. As you well know, and as your letters show, this is not the case, nor had I the faintest idea that such a thing could possibly occur, after the pleasant manner in which our last brilliant success had been carried through. Over and over again I have said laughingly but earnestly: 'I will write twenty more operas with Gilbert, if he will always be as nice and ungrudging in his concessions, and as ready to help me as he has been from beginning to end in this piece' And such was my full intention and desire. You will therefore understand my amazement and indignation when I found myself unceremoniously chucked aside, and in a manner which left no doubt as to the firmness of your intention. You have been unjust and ungenerous to me.

Because I hesitated as an *ex parte* statement (I use the phrase in its literal sense – not in a way that might be considered offensive) to fly at Carte and call him to account for his alleged behaviour to you – because also I refused to make my own will absolutely subservient to yours – you write me a letter in which you revel in reproaches, bring accusations against me which are baseless and unjustifiable, and, on the strength of imaginary injuries, withdraw from all further collaboration with me. And now you wish it given out to the world – or rather wish it generally inferred – that it is in consequence of my writing an opera of a different character that the collaboration has ceased. I decline to be a party to letting this statement go forth. I much prefer no reason at all being given by either of us, but if you choose to give any explanation on your own responsibility, you must not throw the onus of the break upon me.

On that same day at Weybridge (he had moved there two days previously) Sullivan received two notes from Carte by special messenger. Gilbert, it appeared, was trying to get members of the Savoy company to 'secede'. He had 'already succeeded with Ulmar and was trying with Decima Moore'. If Gilbert was really inducing singers to leave the Savoy, it must have meant that he was already planning the production of his *non*-Sullivan operetta, *The Mountebanks* The text had, it seems, already been written and the ailing Arthur Goring Thomas had been approached as composer. The text was eventually set by Alfred Cellier, but the work was not produced till 4 January 1892, when the cast included Geraldine Ulmar but not Decima Moore.

With the Gilbert affair so constantly and so heavily occupying him, it is not surprising that Sullivan hardly touched *Ivanhoe* that month (May 1890). His ideas on what *Ivanhoe* should be like, however, emerge in his response to an inquiry from across the Atlantic. News of his break with Gilbert had travelled fast, and the inquiry came from the veteran dramatist Dion Boucicault, now in New York. Boucicault's thoughts were apparently still running on the lines of 'his' *Lily of Killarney* (see p. 50) of nearly 30 years before:

Hearing that you are at liberty and divorced from an association with Gilbert, I venture to lay before you a scheme I have nursed for some years past and which I believe that you could realize: ballad opera.

The subject: comic-idyllic but *not* burlesque.

If the suggestion carries with it any satisfaction to your mind, I would be glad to co operate with any dramatist you might select – I providing the plot, characters and movement – subject to your views – and such scenes of dialogue as belong to the dramatic part, while my collaborator at your elbow executes the lyric part.

I think Gilbert's material – always delicate and original – lacked dramatic situation and afforded you little opportunity for pathetic display and power, which appeared to me your forte.

Sullivan's reply (6 June) indicated that his ideas had travelled in a different direction:

I think the whole tendency of stage music now is to get rid as much as possible of songs, duets and other *set pieces* and to become as *dramatic* as possible. In all the series with Gilbert, I found a dainty, pretty song was generally a drag and stopped the interest of the public in the action of the piece.

It is on these lines that I am doing a serious opera now – a work I cannot hope to complete before the end of the year, so that I cannot hope to turn my attention to anything else yet. I hope to come to America next year for business out West, and in passing through New York will discuss the matter further.

By describing it negatively Sullivan showed what he hoped *Ivanhoe* would be – its songs would not seem like 'set pieces' (i.e. detachable and rounded-off); instead of 'stopping the interest' of the audience in the development of the story, they would advance the plot. By inference he was here unfair to his past achievement: in Gilbert's pieces he had contrived many a 'dainty, pretty song' that *did* advance the plot. An outstanding example is Phoebe's 'Were I thy bride' in *The Yeomen of the Guard*, during which the temporarily stolen keys are surreptitiously replaced on the doting jailer's girdle. But the aim was plainly a more continuous musical texture, the very opposite of a work divided as Boucicault suggested between 'lyric' and 'dramatic' elements, the latter including 'scenes of dialogue'. *Ivanhoe* would be all sung – in the terminology of the time, 'grand opera' and not Boucicault's 'ballad opera'.

Time was pressing: Sullivan's contract with Carte stipulated that *Ivanhoe* was to be ready for a production not later than 10 January 1891. Yet in the previous June, when he began in earnest on the composition, work still proceeded fitfully. Energy, it seemed, was lacking. He evidently found it difficult to concentrate on the completion of one act at a time. As early as 11 June he had (according to his diary) 'practically finished sketch of first act'. But 'sketch' here only meant the melodic outlines, and the next day he 'put away first act for revision', and began the duet in the second act for Rebecca and the Templar. On the following day he continued with the 'finale duet' of that act for the same characters. Then there was a two-week gap covering the almost obligatory seasonal trip to the races at Ascot (Sullivan rented a house nearby, Brook Lodge) and it was 29 June before he resumed work with King Richard's song, also in the second act. He then went back to the first act, 'framing' what he had sketched. But by the end of July he had finished the 'frame' of the act only up to the end of the first scene, with two more scenes to go.

He allowed himself to be distracted from composition – partly by social pleasures, partly by professional concerns. The diary of 8 July 1890 alludes to the new location of the Royal College of Music in Prince Consort Road, South Kensington, very close to the older building, which Sullivan also called at. The first reference to 'home' is of course to 1 Queen's Mansions, though he was still renting the Weybridge house.

Went to town [London] for the ceremony of laying the foundation stone of the Royal College of Music by the Prince of Wales. Arr. there at 12.15 (called to see Grandma on the way). Ceremony very successful. Saw Miss [Margaret] MacIntyre who said she would like to sing in *Ivanhoe*. Called at the College on my way, then to Julian Sturgis [he lived at Hans Road, Knightsbridge] – out. Then to no. 7 – then to Portland, back to Sturgis, and home to dress for dinner. Found Clotilde there [though she was supposed to be at Weybridge] – no time to speak – told her to be back at 11. Dined at the French Ambassador's (Edinburghs, etc. etc. there) – left at 11 – called for Clotilde at the Mansions ('splanation', tears and apology) and home to Weybridge by last train.

'The Edinburghs' were the Duke and the Duchess. Under pressure of official duties, the Duke was now not on such informal terms with Sullivan as in his younger bachelor days, and in three years would leave London for Germany in his transformed role as the Duke of Saxe-Coburg-Gotha.

The tension between Gilbert and Carte (with Sullivan inevitably now ranged on the latter's side) grew yet worse. On 4 July another quarterly distribution of the Savoy profits was due. Carte withheld them on the excuse that the objection raised by Gilbert to the two previous distributions ought first to be resolved. The matter then became one for the courts. The public was soon regaled not only with the present quarrel but with the revelation that over the past 11 years Gilbert and Sullivan had each earned £90,000 under Carte's management – £70,000 from London performances and £20,000 from provincial and North American ones. And the point at issue was a carpet worth £140!

On 30 July Gilbert served a writ on Carte for an account of the preceding quarter and a payment of his share. Carte sent Gilbert £2,000 but Gilbert claimed that it should be at least £3,000. In the High Court he moved for a receiver to handle (in place of Carte) the takings from *The Gondoliers*. Sullivan was opposed to Gilbert's application for a receiver and told him so in a letter of 15 August. Thus Sullivan became a co-defendant with Carte in Gilbert's action. After two adjournments, the case came up before Mr Justice Lawrence, sitting as a Vacation Judge, on 3 September. The hearing took less than a day: an arrangement was reached whereby Carte undertook to send Gilbert £1,000 next day, with a full account to follow within three weeks. But no receiver was appointed and Carte carried on his business as before. Apart from the lawyers, no one had gained.

Nor was the situation changed, save in one pitiful respect. The partnership of W.S. Gilbert and Arthur Sullivan lay shattered – and it had been shattered not by the court but by the barrages of words before that, with Gilbert undoubtedly to blame and Sullivan caught in an animosity between Gilbert and Carte. As the *Musical Standard* put it: 'The eminent and genial composer of *The Gondaliers* found himself in a warm place just because he happened to be seated near a fire.'

30 'English Grand Opera'

LIKE Sullivan, Ethel Smyth had studied at the Leipzig Conservatory and would not be confined, as a number of Victorian women composers had been, to songs and domestic piano pieces.[1] Like Sullivan, she was launched on a wider career by the Crystal Palace Saturday concerts, still conducted by August Manns after 35 seasons. Hers was the pen that left this affectionate description of the sojourner at Weybridge:

Among the pleasant things that befell early in that year [1890], was making the acquaintance of Sir Arthur Sullivan, who came up to me in the house we met in, introduced himself as 'colleague' so delightfully, with such a blend of chaff and seriousness (the exact perfection of cadence there is in his work) that my one idea ever after was to see him whenever I could.

Living at Frimley, Surrey, in the house of her father, Major General J. H. Smyth, she received this letter from Weybridge dated 14 June:

Me voilà, in the same house I occupied last year, not very far from you, only two stations. When you want some tea come and have it with me: I generally strike work about 5. Had I not been ill and in pain on that eventful Saturday [26 April, when her *Serenade* had been given at the Crystal Palace] I should have been a gratified witness of your success. I had made all arrangements to go but I had a combined attack that day, by my old physical trouble and . . . Gilbert! Nevertheless, I was really pleased to read such nice things about the work of the *gracieuse jeune fille*, and I hope that you are beginning a brilliant and dignified musical career.

Arthur Sullivan had enjoyed such a 'brilliant and dignified' career for more than a quarter of a century. Despite his unfeigned geniality towards the 32-year-old Ethel Smyth, there was a curious 'psychological' age-gap. He was only 16 years her senior, yet in 1895 he would even describe himself as 'old enough to be your father'. In some ways he was already behaving like an old man. The appellation of 'Auntie' for Fanny Ronalds was hardly a social necessity now that 'Bertie' was a grown man, yet it occurs with increasing frequency in the diary: 'Wonderful little woman is Auntie' (5 September), 'Went up to town in the afternoon to meet Auntie' (22 September); 'Went to Westgate at 5.15 with Bertie and Auntie' (27 September). This from a man of 48 about his mistress, or former mistress! At this time no sexual activity seems to be indicated in the diary, though a cryptic sentence such as 'Registered letter with £5 note to E.W.' (6 August) presumably refers to the amorous adventure of the past noted in the previous chapter.

August and September marked better progress on *Ivanhoe*. On 6 August he 'framed' the chorus 'Plantagenesta' in the first act – the chorus which leads to the first combat of Ivanhoe with the Templar, Bois-Guilbert. By 29 August he had almost finished framing the second act. But, self-critical, he went back and 'began to change first act, just to change the words'. Then, as if a lack of inspiration prevented him from proceeding to compose the third act, he made an attempt to orchestrate what he had already written. But that did not work either. He was still in the first scene of that act when he gave up: 'How awfully slowly it goes!' was the comment in the diary on 6 September. Next day, he 'stopped scoring and began to sketch third act'.

By the end of September he had composed *most* of the opera. He could now begin to score it more or less consecutively – pausing, however, to compose or re-compose where a section had been omitted or no longer satisfied him. (Sturgis, in that case, might be required to rewrite the words.) By this time he had left Weybridge, spent a few days with 'Russie' Walker at Newmarket, and returned to his London home. A telegram from Vienna had reported the successful launching of *The Gondoliers* (Theater an der Wien, 20 September 1890), with Zell and Genée again the translators. It did not hold the taste of the Viennese, however; of English operettas only *The Mikado* and, in 1897, Sidney Jones's *The Geisha* did that.[2]

Illness again weakened him, slowing down his schedule until Carte's hoped-for production date (10 January 1891 at the latest) receded into impossibility. The symptoms described in his diary entry for 10 October indicate something other than his old kidney disease – more like influenza. The first sentence appears, by the placing on the page, to have been inserted later.

Felt il[l] all day long. Interrupted all day long: Burgon, F. Cellier, Cartes [Mr and Mrs], Bertie, Auntie. Only did 9 pages. About 7.30 [p.m.] [began] to feel pains and shivers – tried to eat some dinner – didn't like it, and got so bad afterwards that I had to go to bed. I shook the *room* with my shivering and clattering. Had fire lit, piles of blankets, eiderdown, etc. on me, took strong dose of spirits of nitre (Clotilde insisted upon my taking a glass of brandy and a devilish good thing it was) and I perspired all the night – sheets were wet through – didn't sleep much [*The preceding must have been written next day, and then the following is added*:] but at 8.30 felt better and rang for my coffee – up at 9.30 – after breakfast fell ill again and had to sleep till 1.

'Bertie', now a qualified engineer, was leaving for an overseas assignment. He and his uncle took their farewell on 15 October when Sullivan was about to conduct a Norwich Festival performance of *The Martyr of Antioch*.

Drove with Bertie to Liverpool St [Station] to leave at 5 for Norwich. I said goodbye to him at station. He starts tomorrow in the [ship] Westmeath on Seaton's staff to lay a cable between Hayti and Brazil.

Two days before, Sullivan had finished scoring the first act. Working hard, and on 20 October working through the night till 4 a.m., he still chafed at what he considered slow progress in orchestration and rewriting.

Diary, 20 October]: Worked hard and finished 1st Scene of Act II, including re-writing Templar's solo 'Her southern splendour', 4 a.m. Only 52 pages in 5 days!

Diary, 21 October]: Began forest scene. 16 pages.

Diary, 22 October]: At Work. Contd. forest scene – 12 pages score; then stuck at night, and had to recompose a good deal before King's song. Wrote long letter to J. Sturgis.

Diary, 23 October]: At work.

Diary, 24 October]: At work all day up to 3 a.m.

Diary, 25 October]: At work all day. Finished score to end of [King] Richard's song.

Diary, 26 October]: At work all day. Forest scene. Wrote and scored Friar's song ['Ho, jolly Jenkin']. Very good. I think. 14 pages.

Diary, 27 October]: Wrote till 3.15 a.m. Finished forest scene; much of it re-written. 16 pages.

The relationship with Gilbert was not to be left in limbo. It was Gilbert who made efforts to restore it to normality – at first with a letter to Helen Carte (6 September) and a copy to Sullivan, 'offering reconciliation and to let bygones be bygones!' The exclamation mark is Sullivan's, who added in his diary: 'He is extraordinary'. On 16 September 'Mrs Carte came to report her interview with G. She seems to have put everything straight before him, and not minced matters. He ought to feel thoroughly ashamed of himself but I don't suppose he does.'

Sullivan had himself replied to Gilbert that, if there were to be a reconciliation,

let it be a thorough one with confidence restored all round, not merely a patched-up truce.

But confidence cannot be restored whilst you still contend that no other course was open to you but to take the action which was an injury and humiliation to me. And you are doing yourself and your nature a gross injustice in pleading thus. I would much rather believe, as I now solemnly believe, that you plunged without forethought into these disastrous proceedings in a fit of uncontrolled anger greatly influenced by the bad health you were suffering from . . .

Don't think me exaggerating when I tell you that I am physically and mentally ill over this wretched business. I have not yet got over the shock of seeing our names coupled, not in brilliant collaboration over a work destined for world-wide celebrity, but in hostile antagonism over a few miserable pounds. I am tempted to make a suggestion which, whether you accept it or not, you will I am sure receive in good part, and that is that you withdraw the action at law against Carte, and let the disputed matter be settled by a friendly arbitration (not a legal one of course) and not by ourselves . . .

But after a further meeting with both D'Oyly and Helen Carte, Gilbert withdrew his action unconditionally and without any provision for arbitration. It seemed as though the position was exactly as it had been at the origin of the dispute and those concerned had undergone 'all the worry, anxiety and expense for *absolutely nothing*', as Sullivan put it in his diary. But there was one important change. The agreement between Carte and his creative pair was no longer in operation: Carte could not, as before, compel them to fashion a new piece at six months' notice. Even when the partnership resumed it did not do so on the promise of an unbroken chain of works.

The diary continued to chronicle the progress on the composition and orchestration of *Ivanhoe*. Ernest Ford had been engaged as arranger of the piano part from the vocal score, and Alfred (not François) Cellier as chorus-master though François would eventually take over the conducting from Sullivan. Domestic concerns intruded too, including the illness of a favourite dog:

[12 November 1890]: Re-composing 1st scene (3rd act); wrote Ivanhoe's song ['Happy with wingéd feet'] and many little details . . .

[13 November 1890]: Didn't go out. Called: Ford with P.F. [pianoforte arrangement] of 2nd scene (2nd act); gave him 3rd scene (2nd act). Cellier called to say he had had chorus for new opera together for first time – enthusiastic about it. Wrote to Sturgis to suggest substitution of new song for Rowena instead of Ivanhoe in 1st act [presumably Rowena's 'O moon, art thou clad in silver mail?']; also to Auntie, and Nordica. Rewrote Rebecca's song ['Lord of our chosen race'] and finished frame of 1st scene, 3rd act. Shut up at 2 a.m.

[14 November, 1890]: Framing 2nd scene, 3rd act. Servants went to the theatre. Clotilde wishes to leave at Xmas!

[15 November, 1890]: At work all day. Finished frame of 2nd scene, 3rd act. Clotilde repents of her hasty decision [to leave]! Smoothed her down. I think the poor girl is really ill, and worried about her family affairs. Went to Portland at night and played [cards] with Russie [Walker] and Trevvy. Obliged to send Tommy to Sewell's [veterinary surgeon] fear he has an abscess.

[17 November, 1890]: Didn't go out. Cellier came after (1st) rehearsal of finale chorus Auntie to tea. Got up at 6.15 a.m. and began to work. Wrote till 10, then dressed and breakfasted – began again at 12. Clotilde's cough so bad, was obliged to go and see what was the matter. Got her some medicine, which relieved the pain and soon sent her to sleep Wrote till 5 a.m. 10 pages [of score].

A 23-hour day!

Sometime the creative process jammed: on 18 November, writing till 2.45 a.m., his total for the day was only 9 pages. On 30 November, however, he worked a normal day, entertained guests to dinner, sat down again at his desk at 1.45 a.m., wrote till after 5 a.m., and had 76 more pages to show. On 6 December after a night without sleep, he was visited by Sturgis: they 'settled end of opera. Took out present sombre ending and arranged to put in a brighter one. The opera was now to end with a general ensemble and choral praise of love, with Rowena's and Rebecca's voices rising to a top B.

[Diary, 13 December 1890]: Put the last note to score at 6 p.m. *Absolutely finished*, thank God. Seven months' hard labour, 715 pages of score.

[Diary, 31 December]: Poor old Tommy died during the night. He came to me in November 1882 from Edward Hall from whom I claimed him as 'assets' for the £7,000 lost through Cooper, Hall and Co. Never will be seen such a dear, loving, intelligent dog again.

Sullivan later gave orders to have the dog stuffed and displayed in a glass case.

Intensive rehearsals of the cast began on 29 December 1890 and orchestra rehearsals on 13 January. Having delivered the complete score too late to meet Carte's hoped-for production date, the composer had in consequence to pay Carte £3,000 by way of penalty for keeping the theatre empty and involving Carte in contractual payments to performers and others. On 29 January a full-dress rehearsal was held from 11 a.m. to 6 p.m. and then 'all through the opera again from 8 to 12 [midnight]. Dead beat. Between rehearsals I gave the band dinner at the Duke of Argyll. About 70 sat down. Very good and very pleasant.'

An orchestral strength of 63 had been engaged for *Ivanhoe* (almost twice the normal Savoy contingent) and a chorus of 72, paralleling the pictorial lavishness accorded to the nine scenes. The theatre accommodated 2,300 persons, as compared with just under 1,300 at the Savoy. Sited at Cambridge Circus, not far north of Gilbert's Garrick Theatre, it was 'an ornament of the district not long ago notorious for the filth and wretchedness of its dens'. So it was described by the musical journal *The Lute*.[3] The district was indeed that of Seven Dials, whose 'lowly air' had been picked out in *Iolanthe*.

At 8 p.m. on Saturday, 31 January 1891, the Royal English Opera House was to open. (The Savoy carried on as usual, with *The Gondoliers*; at the Court Theatre, Pinero's *The Cabinet Minister* had achieved over 180 performances, and Henry Arthur Jones' plays *The Silver King* and *The Dancing Girl* were respectively at the Court Theatre and the Haymarket.) Via the press, D'Oyly Carte addressed the public directly that morning:

Ladies and Gentlemen, – I am endeavouring to establish English Grand Opera at the new theatre which I have built. To inaugurate such an enterprise nothing seems more suitable than an opera written by the foremost English composer, Sir Arthur Sullivan. This opera, with a libretto written by Mr Julian Sturgis, to a subject of national interest, will be produced tonight. I have engaged a strong company of artists, a company sufficiently numerous to give six performances a week, which I purpose doing. It is a remarkable circumstance that in the capital of England, the most populous city in the world, where there is such an enormous population interested in music and the drama, where there are at this moment so many English composers and singers of exceptional talent, there is no theatre devoted to the production and performance of English Grand Opera.

I am not aware that any similar enterprise, that is, an endeavour to play Grand Opera all the year round, or for the greater portion of the year, has ever been attempted in any other country except with the convenient, if sometimes repressive, assistance of a subsidy from the State, which, it is unnecessary to say, this theatre does not enjoy. I purpose, however, trying the experiment. Whether it will succeed or not depends on whether there is a sufficient number of persons interested in music and the drama who will come forward and fill the theatre. I believe there is: but this remains to be proved. I may add that I have made arrangements with other distinguished composers and authors to write operas to follow Ivanhoe, which operas will be produced if the enterprise is a pecuniary success. The intention is to run each opera, that is to say play them, six times a week, at any rate at first. This is the only way in which the expenditure necessary to secure a proper representation in the matter of scenery and costumes can be recouped, a result which is impossible with a limited number of isolated performances of any one piece alternated with others.

I have the gratification of being authorized to state that His Royal Highness the Prince of Wales and Her Royal Highness the Princess of Wales, and also their Royal Highnesses the Duke and Duchess of Edinburgh, will honour the performance tonight with their presence; and I have only in conclusion to express a hope that all who are interested in the highest form of development of lyric art will give this undertaking their frank and hearty support. The theatre will be opened tonight with a representative piece. I trust that the performance and the surroundings will be found worthy of the work of the composer of whom the English nation is rightly proud. If so, the enterprise is in the hands of the public, and it rests with them whether a national opera house at all be established on a permanent basis or not.

Though over-pressed with applications for tickets from friends and colleagues, Sullivan had saved two places for Gilbert and warmly invited him to come as his guest. On the very day of the first performance Gilbert replied in a single curt phrase: 'I decline your stalls.'

Sullivan's diary alludes to that note as well as to the incident at the first performances when the denizens of the 'pit', notoriously inclined to vocal activity, put in their contribution to the opening night.

Lovely day. 3 letters from Gilbert, 2 answered, his last a rough and insolent refusal to come to the performance of *Ivanhoe*. Busy all day with tickets, etc. Went to the theatre (R.E.O.) at 7.40. Tremendous crowd outside. At 8 Prince and Princess of Wales with Princesses Victoria and Maud and Duke and Duchess of Edinburgh entered their box. 'God save the Queen' played by orchestra, Cellier conducting. At 8.5 I entered. Tremendous reception by a brilliant and packed house. The night was really superb. Began *Ivanhoe*, but the 1st 60 or 80 bars quite inaudible owing to the noise made by the pit on account of standers in the gangway – then they were removed and the opera went on and went splendidly, without a hitch from beginning to end. All sang well [cast named]. Went up after the 1st act to the Prince's room; he and the Duke came and smoked cigarettes in my room afterwards. Great enthusiasm at the end; everyone called. I went on with Sturgis. Gave all the stage hands five shillings each afterwards. Supped at the Orleans [Club]. Large party given by E. Dresden and G. Foâ. Then to Portland. Home at 4.

In the course of a letter received by Sullivan three days after the first performance, Princess Louise wrote:

The Queen wishes me to write and tell you with what pleasure she sees in the papers of today that your opera met with such a great success on Saturday. It is a particular satisfaction to her, as she believes it is partly owing to her own instigation that you undertook this great work . . .

Sullivan, by permission, dedicated the opera to his Sovereign. She never went to see it.

Ivanhoe received three 'inaugural performances' (as listed, subsequently, in the printed libretto) all conducted by the composer. Alternative singers were provided for the chief roles – not as separate 'first' and 'second' casts, but in different mixtures. Thus on both Saturday 31 January and Monday 2 February Ben Davies as Ivanhoe confronted Eugène Oudin as Bois-Guilbert, the Templar; Rowena was sung by Esther Palliser at the first performance, by Lucille Hill at the second; and Rebecca was sung by Margaret MacIntyre at the first and by Charlotte Thudicum at the second. Friar Tuck was sung at all three performances by a Canadian bass with the appropriate name of Avon Saxon. Oudin, Palliser and Marie Groebl, who sang the lesser role of Ulrica, were all American.

After Sullivan's performances, Cellier took over *Ivanhoe*, with Ernest Ford as deputy conductor. There then ensued an unparalleled and paradoxical event in British operatic history. Put to the test of being enacted on successive evenings,

Ivanhoe achieved 160 performances – far more than had been allotted within a single season to any previous British 'grand opera'. (Even the hundred performances of *The Bohemian Girl* had been spaced over more than a year to 7 December 1844.) Yet *Ivanhoe* 'failed': falling attendances compelled Carte to discontinue it before it had recouped its costs. Hermann Klein in his reminiscences, *Thirty Years of Musical Life in London*, blamed Carte for faulty management in running the work to death – a plausible view, no doubt shared by many.

But there are no grounds for supposing it would have sustained longer life had it been first presented in a normal opera season. It is an uneven and defective work. Ernest Ford, having been associated with *Ivanhoe* both in preparing the vocal score and in conducting, later wrote in his *Short History of Music in England* that the second scene of Act 2

should have been entirely eliminated. It was unworthy of the work and the composer. It was forced, theatrical, and destitute of spontaneity or inspiration.

That a man of such acumen [as Sullivan] could fail to recognize it is impossible. As a matter of fact, he once told me that this scene spoilt the act, which, it may be said, with this exception contained the most splendid music of the opera. It is inconceivable that, had he found the opportunity, he would not have composed an entirely new one.

Not all its hearers would have wished to sacrifice that scene entirely: it contains the attractive baritone aria 'Woo thou thy snowflake' which had won favourable comment. Ford wrote that it was the 'continuous' performances that prevented Sullivan from making modifications after the first night, since 'even a temporary withdrawal would have involved the closing of the newly-built opera house'. The excuse does not ring entirely true, since such modifications *were* incorporated during initial (uninterrupted) runs at the Savoy.

Not merely the unevenness of the work, but its discrepancies in musical style, were acutely pointed out in *The Times* by J. A. Fuller Maitland, who had occupied the chief critic's chair since Hueffer had died in January 1889. Like other critics he was allowed to lavish space on such an important event as the opening of Carte's new house: his initial notice occupied about 50 column-inches of small print dealing only with the new piece and its theatrical setting, the performers being the subject of a later notice. He welcomed – as he could hardly fail to do – Carte's bold enterprise and the handsomeness of its initial presentation. But at the crucial point of judgement he showed himself unconvinced by the work:

Two questions will inevitably be asked, and will receive, no doubt, different answers from different authorities; will *Ivanhoe* enhance the composer's reputation and that of English art, and will the work take a place among the classics of dramatic music and attain a real immortality? To the first an unqualified affirmative may surely be given, for even if it be held to lack the poetic charm and distinction of *The Golden Legend*, its best portions rise so far above anything else that Sir Arthur Sullivan has given to the world, and have such force and dignity, that it is not difficult to forget the drawbacks which may be found in the want of interest of much of the choral writing, and the brevity of the concerted solo parts.

On the second question an opinion can only be formed with difficulty and offered with diffidence. The general structure of the work is a curious example of transition between two opposing systems, each of which in its own day has produced masterpieces of undoubted supremacy. The finest scenes, as, for instance, that in which the great duet occurs, suggest by their continuous and sustained treatment that the composer has adopted the modern methods, and that each scene, if not each act, is regarded as a complete entity; the interest given to his recitatives, and the unmistakable influence of Berlioz and, in lesser degree, Wagner, upon the orchestration and treatment of the themes, encourage this view. On the other hand, in many of the scenes, we meet a series of numbers, which only require slightly more conventional development to rank with the set pieces of old-fashioned opera, and this impression is confirmed by the perpetual full closes, most of which are preceded by a pause on an effective note for the voice, and, of course, followed by a break in the continuity of the action.

It is curious, too, that no two of the scenes are joined together by music; in one case there is no connexion, even of key, between two adjacent sections of the same act. If, as at present seems most probable, the modern theories of dramatic music should obtain universal acceptance, *Ivanhoe* will have a struggle for permanent existence, and will stand on the merits of its second act, the portion which unites grace and strength with continuity of design; of course, if a strong reaction should set in against these theories, the work, as a whole, will be generally considered as a masterpiece of design, as well as a collocation of individual beauties.

Objections to the work were also raised by Bernard Shaw, appointed music critic of *The World* in the previous year on the ignominious flight of Louis Engel (p. 266). But even Shaw temporized, or pretended to do so. He informed his readers that he had written a notice *before* attending the first night (having attended rehearsals), and then changed his mind. With malicious wit he then proceeded to tell the readers what he had changed his mind *from*:

On second thoughts I have resolved to suppress my notice of *Ivanhoe*. I was upon my high horse last week when I wrote it; and when I went on Saturday, and saw how pleasantly everything went off, and how the place was full of lovely and distinguished persons, and how everybody applauded like mad at the end, and, above all, how here at last was an English opera-house superbly equipped for its purpose, I felt what a brute I had been to grumble – and that, too, after having been indulged with peeps at the proofs of the score, admission to rehearsals, and every courtesy that could pass betwixt myself and the management, without loss of dignity on either side. Just as a sort of penance, and to show what I am capable of I give a couple of paragraphs from the discarded notice. Here they are:

'Proceeding then at once to the faults of *Ivanhoe*, I maintain that it is disqualified as a serious dramatic work by the composer's failure to reproduce in music the vivid characterization of Scott, which alone classes the novel among the masterpieces of fiction. . . . Take for example Scott's Bois Guilbert, the fierce Templar, the original "bold, bad man", tanned nearly black, disfigured with sword-cuts, strong, ambitious, going on for fifty, a subject for Verdi or Velasquez. Is it possible to sit patiently and hear the music of the drawing room, sensuous and passionate without virility or intelligence, put into the mouth of such a figure? Not with all the brass and drum sauce in the world.'

And so on at length, with considerable criticism of Sturgis' re-writing of Scott. After which:

But enough of this unsociable document. The truth is that the theatre is very pretty; and so is the opera. . . . I do not say that the ceiling is equal to that of Henry VII's chapel in Westminster, or that the score is in any essential point an advance upon that of

Macfarren's *Robin Hood*, which had a long run at Her Majesty's thirty years ago; but who ever said they were? My business is to praise them for what they are, not to disparage them for what they are not. *Ivanhoe*, then, has plenty of charming songs in it; and the crash-bang and the top notes in the exciting situations are as stirring as heart could wish. The score is as neat as a new pin. The instrumentation, from the big drum upwards, is effective, practised, and stylish, with all the fullness given by the latest improvements; the tone-colors, though rich, are eminently gentlemanly; there is no Bohemian effervescence, no puerile attempts at brilliancy or grandiosity; all is smooth, orderly, and within the bounds of good breeding.

'Plenty of charming songs,' yes; but that hardly fulfilled Sullivan's promise, in the letter to Boucicault quoted earlier, that the music would constantly push the drama forward. Too often the effect was static, tableau-like. As Maitland had noted, each of its nine different scenes came to a full close, without an orchestral link to the next. The songs were sometimes strophic, the music being literally repeated for a second verse; and even when not strophic they were liable to end on a prolonged cadence calculated to focus the audience's attention on the singer's voice and to bring about a round of applause. And yet the 'Wagnerian' or pseudo-Wagnerian touches[4] – the recurrence of themes associated with particular characters – were sufficiently obtrusive elsewhere to repel listeners who disliked the technique.

Such an unhappy and long-winded compromise between the old 'ballad' style and the newer 'Wagnerian' allusiveness made *Ivanhoe* strangely old-fashioned for its period. From Italy, in the columns of the *Musical Times*, came news of success won by a new opera of precisely contrary direction – an opera which compressed its passionate modern drama into one act, divided in two by an intermezzo played with the curtain up. Mascagni's *Cavalleria Rusticana* would gain no less success in London when it arrived later in 1891.

Sullivan knew, according to Ford, that 'Ho, jolly Jenkin' would be much liked in general but disparaged by the loftier critics as 'redolent of the Savoy'. Next to it in popularity, and incomparably more distinctive in vocal line and the refined orchestration with its throbbing viola part, was Rebecca's prayer in the final scene of Act 2. Klein wrote later:

I was particularly struck by the Oriental character of the harmonies and intervals in Rebecca's song, 'Lord of our chosen race,' and I told Sullivan that I thought nothing could be more distinctively Eastern or even Hebraic in type.
'That may well be so,' he rejoined. 'The phrase on the words "Guard me" you especially refer to is not strictly mine. Let me tell you where I heard it. When I was the Mendelssohn Scholar and living at Leipzig, I went once or twice to the old Jewish synagogue, and among the many eastern melodies chanted by the minister, this quaint progression in the minor occurred so frequently that I have never forgotten it.'

Sullivan may have learnt from Verdi (the High Priestess's chant in *Aida*) how effectively a single 'outlandish' turn of melody or harmony can evoke an exotic rite.

During the early weeks of the opera, apparently untroubled by criticism, the composer indulged his familiar pleasures. On 6–9 February he was at Sandringham for the Prince of Wales's house-party (with male guests only). Three days later, he was off with 'Bertie' – who had returned from his cable-laying – to Paris and thence to Monte Carlo. A new casual sexual liaison developed at Monte Carlo, to judge by the repeated 'tick' signs in the diary, and there is a correspondence with an unidentified 'O.' – as well as the expected letters to and from 'Auntie' and Smythe. He drove over to Nice and saw Verdi's *Otello* on 25 February, making no written comment. Another occupation during this visit was in prospecting for a villa to rent for the longer stay which he planned for the following winter. While he was away, Queen Victoria on 6 March saw *The Gondoliers* in a 'command performance' by Carte's company at Windsor Castle, afterwards commenting on 'the music which I knew and am very fond of'. The sequel six months later was a command performance of *The Mikado* at Balmoral.

The 100th performance of *Ivanhoe* on 25 May brought Sullivan back to the rostrum at the Royal English Opera. The diary is complacent: 'Crowded and enthusiastic house. I conducted and received ovation. Portland [Club] . . .'

He declined an invitation to conduct his *Macbeth* overture at the Philharmonic (Cowen did so, on 5 June 1891) because he was kept busy correcting the proofs for the full score of the opera which Chappell's were to publish. But the opera was declining in its public appeal. While Sullivan's diary was concerned with an 'awful row downstairs' – Clotilde again announcing her intention to leave – Carte withdrew *Ivanhoe* and his new theatre stood dark. His experiment, his re-floating of 'English grand opera', had failed as a financial undertaking.

Not until the following November did Carte reopen the Royal English Opera, and then with a French work which mocked the theatre's name. The years of Gilbert and Sullivan's success had not entirely eclipsed French operetta on the English stage. Among would-be inheritors of Offenbach's mantle was Edmond Audran, an almost exact contemporary of Sullivan's (1840–1901); he was the composer of *La Cigale*, produced by a rival management at the Lyric Theatre in London in July 1890 with Geraldine Ulmar as one of its stars. Carte chose a French composer who was to leave a more distinguished reputation: André Messager (1853–1929), composer of the ballet *The Two Pigeons* and later of the operetta *Véronique*.

His latest work (introduced at the Opéra-Comique, Paris, in the previous April) was *La Basoche*: the title referred to a Parisian student guild of medieval times and the plot hinged on a confusion between the 'king' of the students and King Louis XII. The English version which Carte commissioned was the joint work of Sir Augustus Harris (Covent Garden's impresario) and Eugène Oudin, the American baritone who had sung the role of Sullivan's Templar with such success. Given that no work by an English composer was ready, it appeared to be no bad choice. Tuneful in style, colourful in staging, it was hailed by the *Era* with much more enthusiasm than that journal had summoned for *Ivanhoe*:

The Basoche is more than a success: it is a triumph . . . It is not only the most artistic and beautiful comic opera the modern stage has witnessed for years [so much for the Savoy!] but is equally remarkable for the acting and the singing.

Shaw in the *World* was equally enthusiastic. By this time he was no longer inclined to be polite about *Ivanhoe*: it was 'a good novel which has been turned into the very silliest sort of sham "grand opera" '. But he praised *La Basoche* for a cool and witty dramatic treatment and a score of 'charming liveliness' without 'the licentious stupidity and insincerity of opéra bouffe'. It was *this* work, admirably staged and performed, that Shaw hailed as a fulfilment of Carte's dream:

I think it must be admitted that, incredible as it may sound, we have at last got an opera-house where musical works are treated as seriously and handsomely as dramatic works are at [Irving's] Lyceum.

The cast, conducted by François Cellier, was indeed a strong one, with Ben Davies, David Bispham, Esther Palliser and Lucile Hill. *Ivanhoe* was revived and played in alternation with it. Carte was next planning to produce the *Elaine* of Herman Bemberg (1859–1931), who was French, despite his name. But the public failed to second Shaw's enthusiasm for *The Basoche*. Dwindling box-office receipts forced Carte's hand yet again, and the Royal English Opera closed its doors on 26 January 1892. Carte's losses were reported as £36,000. *Elaine* was heard (in French, with Melba) at Covent Garden in the following July: it was a failure, and the English translation made in vain by Oudin was uselessly published two years later. Carte sold the theatre to Sir Augustus Harris, who at the time controlled not only Covent Garden but also Drury Lane, Her Majesty's and the Olympic. It was reopened as the Palace Theatre of Varieties in December 1892.

Carte was not ruined, for the Savoy still flourished. When *The Gondoliers* closed (after a respectable run of 18 months) in June, a successor was waiting: Edward Solomon's *The Nautch Girl* was put on stage only ten days after the former piece closed. Moreover, Carte still had his companies on tour, answering the provincial demand for Gilbert and Sullivan. Advertisements for the first week of November 1891 informed the public that Mr D'Oyly Carte's 'B' company was at Bury, his 'C' company at Hull, his 'D' company at Sheffield, and his 'E' company giving three performances each at Tunbridge Wells and Ealing.

The Nautch Girl was billed as 'the new Savoy opera': only posthumously were Gilbert and Sullivan to have an exclusive claim to that label. The new work, with the subtitle 'or, the Rajah of Chutneypore' took an imaginary province of India in the same spirit as Gilbert had taken Japan – that is, for some jokes about the real India (particularly the barriers of caste) but also jokes on nepotism and other home-grown failings. Disparaging comparisons with *The Mikado* were inevitable, particularly when Solomon's score turned out to be an inexpert essay in the sub-Sullivan manner. According to Shaw, Rutland Barrington's appearance as the Rajah 'changed the fortunes of the evening and, in fact, saved the opera'. For the new work the 'book' was written by George Dance (later one of the most powerful theatrical managers) with the lyrics by himself and Frank Desprez.

This split between 'book' and 'lyrics' and the bringing-in of several different collaborators (literary and musical) was to become characteristic of the English light musical theatre – 'musical comedy', as it soon was known. The unified command of a Gilbert (which extended to the stage direction as well) was hardly to be repeated until the very different reign of Noël Coward.

Sullivan bore the enterprise no ill-will. Rutland Barrington and Jessie Bond (who had leading roles) were, after all, performers who had brought his own work to triumph. On 16 June he 'went to Savoy at 2.30, attended rehearsal of Solomon's opera – much cheered by company!'

'Emperor of Germany arrived in England', the diary noted on 4 July 1891. Sullivan went on that day (a Saturday) to a large house-party given at the Duke of Marlborough's residence near Oxford, Blenheim Palace. The musical arrangements were presumably in the hands of Sullivan's ex-pupil Francis Cunningham Woods, private organist to the Duke. Sullivan's diary records that at the musical performance on the Sunday evening the artists were 'Nordica, Lloyd, Hollman, Woods, Mrs Ronalds and self'. No doubt *The Lost Chord* was one of the items demanded when Fanny Ronalds sang to the composer's accompaniment. She had sufficient status of her own at Blenheim as a close friend of 'Jennie', Lady Randolph Churchill, the Duke's sister-in-law.

His old illness recurred, with what he later described as the 'usual' pain – presumably in the kidneys.

[Diary, 7 July 1891]: Attended at [Dr] Robson Roose's. Thoroughly examined, all right except what I suspected – great uric acid formation and consequently trouble ahead.

[Diary, 9 July 1891]: Garden party [for the German Emperor, given by the Prince of Wales] at Marlborough House. Kept well in the background, and didn't stay long. Had a chop at home. Went to the Albert Hall at 10, arrived just before the Imperial party – *Golden Legend* performed (omitting scenes 1, 4 and 5). [Barnby was the conductor.] I came away before it was over. Portland. . .

[Diary, 10 July 1891]: Consultation at Robson Roose's with self and Reginald Harrison. Examined me and said I must go to Contrexéville [Spa] as soon as possible. Walking back, I saw the Imperial procession returning from the City. Dined at no. 7. Portland. *Squall.*

The 'squall' was Clotilde's. But he was able to write 'domestic reconciliation complete!' before leaving London on 19 July (taking Louis with him) for the French spa which his doctors had recommended. Characteristically he not only spent two days in Paris *en route* but paid a visit to the races at nearby Vincennes. On 21 July he arrived at Contrexéville in the Vosges mountain region of east-central France. On 22 July the 'cure' began at the early hour which Sullivan now knew to expect: 'Dr Debout came to see me at 6.30 [a.m.], ordered me bath at 7 and *three* glasses [of spa water] between 8 and 9, breakfast at 10. Read papers, wrote to L.W., Smythe, Cl[otilde] . . .'

Clotilde had gone away to Brussels, presumably on a family visit. Her curious relationship with Sullivan is shown by her twice telegraphing him, once just to say she was 'ennuyée' (bored).

At the end of a month the composer was no better: a 'tremendous pain' in his back on 19 August was treated by a chloroform compress. But he could recapture his vein of good humour in correspondence with his young professional admirer:

Etablissement Contrexéville,
10 August, 1891.

Dear Miss Smyth,
    In answer to your questions:
(1) I am not in London, and consequently
(2) You cannot find me any morning.
But if you pack up a small portmanteau at once and jump into the next train leaving for Paris you will be here 21 hours afterwards, and I need not tell you how really delighted I shall be to see you. There is a constant delirious whirl of dullness here, the counterpart of which is only to be found in England at a Young Men's Christian Association Weekly Evening Recreation. I am up at 6 am, *massé'd* and douched, and drink 6 pints of the mineral water, walking all the time until breakfast at 10. Nothing more to eat or drink till 6 when we dine – then to bed at 10, to resume the same existence at 6 next morning. I need scarcely tell you that the two meals are the two great events of the day . . .
    I still want a house in your neighbourhood and am likely to want it, as I shall never get one to satisfy me. I want one unfurnished, so that I may always have it to myself, to live there when I like. What has become of you that you have never given me a sign of life for so long? Absorbed in some great work I suppose. May an old man's blessing rest on you.

Yours sincerely,
ARTHUR SULLIVAN

The last sentence was no doubt intended chaffingly, but it is easy to suspect a note of genuine melancholy beneath. Neither Ethel Smyth's efforts to find a suitable Surrey house, nor Sullivan's own when he returned, met with success.

Fanny Ronalds had also been ill and had sought French spa treatment – further south at Aix-les-Bains. Having undergone the regulation 30 days of his own 'cure', Sullivan went to join her (and her mother) there. 'Has Contrexéville done me good?' he asked himself in his diary.

I can't say yet as I still have the same pains as before. But the doctor thinks I shall get rid of my little calculus now without pain or trouble – [illegible] nervous. Travelled by [local trains to] Dijon, where caught the 2.12 express – Macon – and arr. at Aix at 7.15 – hot, damp, and muzzy. Rooms (109) for me at the [Hôtel] de l'Europe. Dined with Gdma and Auntie, then [illegible] joined us.

The term 'Auntie' again seems to denote the stability of what was now a non-sexual relationship, but indications in the diary (while at Contrexéville) of a correspondence with a 'P.C.' probably denote a new incipient love affair. In the middle of his stay there he had evidently contemplated going to Germany and wrote to the British Embassy in Paris asking for a passport (and one for Louis too) as 'I haven't such a thing about me'. An Englishman travelling about western Europe would not normally need a passport; the Franco-German frontier crossing at Metz or Strasbourg must have been under special scrutiny. But he changed his mind: restlessness gripped him again and he went instead to Switzerland. He spent three days in the mountain resort of Zermatt ('haven't spoken to a soul whilst at Zermatt – know no one and don't want to') and then five days at the Hotel Schweizerhof, Lucerne, during which time 'Auntie' and 'Grandma' were at a different hotel in the town.

They left on 8 September, Sullivan spending four days in Paris on the way home.

In California, 'his' family – that is, Fred's children – had not ceased to be a charge on his responsibilities. William Lacy, their maternal uncle, saw himself as a kind of steward on behalf of 'Dear Arthur', to whom he wrote from Los Angeles on 6 July 1891. The letter-head was that of his new business, the Puente Oil Company (Lacy and Rowland, Proprietors), Producers of and Dealers in Crude Petroleum. The family had suffered a blow. Florence, who had married Charles McClung Stephens in 1887, died in February 1891 at the age of 25.

Dear Arthur,
  Although I have received no answer to my last letters to you I again write about the children here . . . Not hearing from you, I took counsel with Amy on her return from San Diego and she thought it best to go back to the house to endeavour to keep the family together or at least to have a house for them where they could each go to at all times. I also thought this better so she got her old servant Ruth to return and take charge of the place, and her husband who has worked in the town stays there at night. I sent George and Willie [the two youngest] to boarding school in Los Angeles. I arranged for them to stay with Amy each Sunday. They are fairly good boys and I think getting along with their studies and now home for their holidays. Dick was at San Diego but not doing well. I went down there and found on enquiry that he was not likely to succeed there at all and his surrounding influences were not good. I brought him back here, gave him a good lecture and procured him a position with the [Los Angeles] *Times* office, the best daily paper we have in southern California. He promised to do well and has faithfully kept his promise and I cannot praise him too highly. . . . Maude has been staying at my house ever since I wrote to you last, and although I have repeatedly and strongly advised her to go back to Amy and her house, she persistently refuses. . . . She proposes going to England with a school-fellow whom I do not know. I do not think it would be wise to allow her to do this, but I have no authority over her and she will listen to no advice from me. So if you think it would not be well for her to do this, I believe a *cable* from you would prevent it. . . . If you wish Maude to come to you then she should only do with a proper chaperone but if you wish her to stay with Amy I wish you would so tell her by letter to her.

Maude, whether by an admonition from Sullivan or not, seems not to have pursued her plan to come to England. She did so, however, many years later – after Sullivan's death – with a husband, Richard Lacy, the second son of William Lacy. Whatever guidance the two uncles gave to 20-year-old Dick (Frederick Richard) they could hardly have anticipated his eventual career, as an actor in Hollywood's silent movies and later in 'talkies', including the Marx Brothers' *Duck Soup* (1934).[5] On her 30th birthday, 6 July 1893, Amy married Florence's widower, Charles Stephens. The marriage would have been illegal in England – a prohibition particularized by Gilbert in *Iolanthe*: 'He shall prick that annual blister,/Marriage with deceased wife's sister'.

If Sullivan himself was still considering a further visit to California (as his letter to Boucicault had intimated only a year before), the wish was never fulfilled.

31 Return to the Savoy

BETWEEN Sullivan and Gilbert there was an armistice. The move to turn it into a genuine reconciliation came from Gilbert, and the mediator he chose was Tom Chappell, whose firm published the operettas. Sullivan wrote to Gilbert on 4 October 1891:

Tom Chappell tells me that you propose that you and I should submit the matters which have been the cause of our rupture to a third party, and, according to his decision, that one or the other of us should confess himself in the wrong, and thereupon we could renew our old friendly relations.

The matter originally in dispute being really all settled and forgotten, I feel that it would be a great mistake to reopen them now, and a reference to a third party would only produce interminable arguments and counter-arguments without either side being convinced.

I have no desire to rake up old grievances, or to enter into a fresh discussion as to who was right and who wrong. So far as I am concerned the past is no more thought of, and I am quite ready to let bygones be bygones, and to meet you at all times in the most friendly spirit, provided that the disagreeable events of the past eighteen months are never alluded to, or at least never discussed. I say this in good faith, and I hope you will meet me in the same spirit.

Gilbert agreed: there should be no thought of recriminations.

It is perhaps unnecessary to assure you that all feeling of bitterness has long since passed from my mind, but there remains a dull leaden feeling that I have been treated with inexplicable unfairness by an old and valued friend with whom I have been *en rapport* for many years, and with whose distinguished name I had had the good fortune to find my own indissolubly associated in a series of works which are known and valued wherever the English language is spoken. This is the present state of my mind as regards our relations towards each other, and if you can suggest any reasonable means whereby this cloud can be removed, it will give me infinite pleasure to adopt it.

Sullivan replied with immediate impulse, on 6 October 1891: 'Let us meet and shake hands. . . . We can dispel the clouds hanging over us by sending up a counter-irritant in the form of a cloud of smoke.' A meeting was arranged – not without a lengthy last-minute statement of position from Gilbert. In a letter dated 11 October he declared himself 'anxious that our meeting shall be carried on, if possible, without reference to papers which may provoke further discussion – so, in the interests of peace, I shall bring none with me'. The outcome is recorded in Sullivan's diary entry for next day:

Gilbert came (by appointment) at 12 – stayed till 2. Full reconciliation and shook hands.

The intention was, of course, that they should collaborate once more – although each had, in their mutual separation, been pursuing other partnerships. Sullivan was in negotiation with a new librettist, Sydney Grundy, and Gilbert was already committed to separate works with two other composers, Alfred Cellier and George Grossmith; but they were able to look beyond that. From the Jockey Club rooms at Newmarket Sullivan wrote to Gilbert on 14 October:

> As regards the new pieces which we hope to write together, I hope our understanding was clear that, in view of two new pieces of yours coming out shortly, and of my being not pledged but in the middle of negotiations for a book [libretto], the time for writing and producing our new joint work was to be a matter for consideration and discussion. I say this because I am sincerely anxious (as I am sure you are) that nothing should ever arise which should lead to another misunderstanding between us.

Secure in the new understanding, Sullivan now occupied himself with what was perhaps the oddest of all the stage works which he was invited to undertake. The 82-year-old Tennyson had completed, at the behest of the American manager Augustin Daly, a play in verse called *The Foresters*, with the subtitle *Robin Hood and Maid Marian*.[1] Daly's leading lady, Ada Rehan, was to play Marian – and Sullivan, who had met Daly and Rehan in California, was asked to provide the music. He evidently refused to let the embarrassing episode of *The Window* rankle in his memory. In return for writing the musical score (nine short numbers only) Sullivan asked for, and presumably got, an agreement from Daly to pay a royalty of 'five guineas per performance in England and a separate arrangement in America'. Partly through Daly, partly in a direct approach to Tennyson, the composer urged some modifications in the text of a Fairies' Scene: 'These ethereal creatures are always difficult to deal with when embodied in flesh and blood at twenty shillings [£1] a week.' Four days later (1 December) he added: 'You can never get ten chorus girls capable of singing a little solo each.' Indeed, Tennyson's comic fairies might well have baffled even the composer of *Iolanthe*:

TITANIA	Nip her not, but let her snore.
	We must flit for evermore.
1ST FAIRY	Tit, my Queen, must it be so?
	Wherefore, wherefore should we go?
TITANIA	I, Titania, bid you flit,
	And you dare to call me Tit!
1ST FAIRY	Tit, for love and brevity
	Not for love and levity.
TITANIA	Tit for love, thou naughty lob,
	Wouldst thou call my Oberon Ob?

Friar Tuck entered the play too (shades of *Ivanhoe*!) – but he had nothing to sing, and no equivalent of 'Ho, jolly Jenkin' survives to provide even one memorable number from *The Foresters*. It was unveiled at Daly's Theatre, New York on 25 March 1892, but Tennyson's death was to intervene before Daly produced the play in London on 3 October 1893 at the recently opened theatre in Leicester Square which also bore his name.

Early in 1892 Sullivan had returned to the Riviera for a longer stay than any of his previous – avoiding the expense of extended hotel bills by renting the villa selected on his previous visit. The Villa Masse was located near Monte Carlo in the village of Turlie-sur-Mer. 'Bertie' was with him as well as his servants Clotilde and Louis, other servants being engaged locally. From this period his nephew remained by his side as a household companion. Thus the account of Sullivan's last years, as it appears in the Flower biography in which his nephew collaborated, is based from this point on first-hand (if fallible) recollection.

The task which Sullivan hoped to tackle on the Riviera was the composition of *Haddon Hall* – his first non-Gilbert work for the Savoy. Sydney Grundy (1848–1914) was not ill-qualified for the librettist's task. He had won recognition as a playwright, particularly with *A Pair of Spectacles* (1890), and had provided the libretto for Edward Solomon's *The Vicar of Bray*, a light opera of 1882 which Carte now chose to revive as a short-lived successor to Solomon's *The Nautch Girl*. But a recurrence of his kidney complaint, more severe than ever before, not only kept Sullivan from work but broke his daily routine. Confined to bed, restricted in diet to calf's-foot jelly, he was forbidden even to deal with correspondence.[2] His diary has no entries for April 1892. The Flower biography tells of 'days of violent struggle against the recurring onslaughts of pain' when the composer got up and 'dragged himself to his desk'.

Occasionally he would become well enough to drive out, enjoy the sunshine, take dinner at a fashionable hotel in Monte Carlo, and – of course! – visit the tables. But the extremes of pain returned. He was given morphia injections, lay 'as if in a coma', and scarcely recognized the presence of Clotilde and Louis. The Queen telegraphed for news. It looked as if he might be dying, and he himself thought so.

When he spoke, it was to give instructions for what was to take place after his demise. . . . A fresh paroxysm of agony ensued, and those by the bedside believed it must be the last. Then his nephew and the servants carried him from his bed and put him in a hot bath, an action that saved his life.

Two days more, and the patient was well on the road to recovery. Then the bedroom door opened and Squire Bancroft [the well-known actor-manager] came in. In the presence of his old friend life began to clamour in him again. Two days and no morphia! He grew stronger with the passage of hours until, at the end of the month [actually 20–21 April] an attempt was made to take him back to London. At Calais four sailors carried him on board the steamer, and laid him out in a large cabin.

Brought safely back to London, he was still a sick man. On 14 May 1892 the entry in the diary is in his nephew's hand: 'Uncle's birthday – 50 years of age'. Four days later, with Herbert's typically erratic spelling, a solicitous visit by Sullivan's closest royal admirer is recorded: 'Duke of Edinborough called'.

According to a statement which he submitted to the Inland Revenue, Sullivan's income for the financial year ending in the spring of 1892 had declined to about half of the £7,000 of the previous year:

The chief source of my income is derived from my operas when running at the Savoy Theatre but I have not received one penny from that source since the end of 1890. Neither did I derive any income whatever from the Royal English Opera House during the year 1891.

His savings were evidently sufficient for him to accommodate this decline without change in his way of living, but much must have been hoped from his prospective return to the Savoy. Sullivan's contracts for *Haddon Hall*, both with his publisher and with Carte, had been drawn up a year previously. From Chappell's, Sullivan would receive one shilling [5p.] on each copy sold of the vocal score, and half as much on each copy of the piano arrangements, dance music, separate songs, etc. 'with the trade allowance of a 13th copy' (i.e., retailers getting 13 copies for the price of 12). On vocal scores, which eventually were published at 5 shillings [25p.], this represented a royalty rate of 20 per cent. For performances, Carte would pay the composer 'half the net profit earned by him' on the London run, and then for provincial performances £750, £500 and £250 for each of the first three years; terms for an American production and for a later revival were left open. It was added that, 'in calculating profits, the percentage paid to the author of the libretto to be deducted and all usual expenses on the same basis as has been the practice with the operas of Arthur Sullivan and W. S. Gilbert at the Savoy.'

Thus the librettist was to be paid a fixed percentage at the box office but not to be, as Sullivan was (and Gilbert had been), a partner in division of the profit. This did not indicate a lesser *artistic* status for Grundy than Gilbert had enjoyed. Grundy's name occupied a place above Sullivan's, in precisely the same way as Gilbert's, on the eventual vocal score.

Not only *Haddon Hall* was now pressing, but the Leeds Festival was due again in October 1892. He had been urged again to contribute a new work, but took up a tactically reserved position, expressed in a letter to Spark:

I stand in a different position from other composers towards the Leeds Festival, and I will tell you quite frankly why I declined to give a definite answer to the request of the provisional committee that I should write a new work for the next festival. It might be that the new committee would like to make other arrangements with regard to the conductor, the orchestra and other musical elements. They might think it desirable to choose a new man to conduct. They will be perfectly justified in acting upon their own judgement and although I should feel hurt I should have no cause of complaint, and if another were chosen could you or the committee expect me to come and conduct my own work or even send it for performance?

He *was* eventually reappointed to the conductorship. The festival committee proposed to engage Barnby to share some of the events, no doubt reckoning that the latter's more vigorous style with the baton would help the choir regain its glory after the criticisms of 1889. Sullivan absolutely refused: 'On this point there must be no misunderstanding. I allow no one to conduct, except those composers who have written new works for the festival.'

That uncompromising stand, as expressed in November 1891, was impossible for Sullivan to maintain in his weakened state of 1892. Not only was he unable to contribute a new work, he was also unable to fulfil the schedule of going to Leeds for weekly choral rehearsals. Barnby loyally deputized, whereupon bare justice dictated that, as a reward, he should be allowed to conduct one major work (Dvořák's *The Spectre's Bride*) at the festival itself.

While still at Turlie-sur-Mer, Sullivan wrote in March to a Leeds committee-member, W. S. Hannam, about the committee's proposed programme:

Don't you think that in putting in so much instrumental music and cutting out broad choral works like [Handel's] *Alexander's Feast* and [Mendelssohn's] *Lauda Sion* you are doing that which I know you are anxious to avoid, viz, weakening the programme? This next festival is to be a critical one because the *chorus* will be the element by which it will be judged and my anxiety is to put in broad choral works. I am sorry to say I cannot agree with you about Brahm's [*sic*] symphony [no. 3] in F. There are fine points in it (which can be brought out by entirely disregarding the marks of expression in the score) but it is in my opinion entirely lacking in spontaneity and full of clever scholastic padding. I love the little B flat [symphony no. 2] of Schumann but I believe everyone will prefer to listen to the 'Italian' [Mendelssohn's symphony], if it were put to the vote. However, the committee will of course weigh all of these matters and it is for them to decide . . .

The principal events at Leeds were to be a revival of Bach's *Mass in B minor* and a performance of Mozart's *Requiem*, and Wagner was again to be put under tribute with a long selection from *Die Meistersinger*. (Klein reported that he once caught Sullivan at Covent Garden listening to this work with score in front of him: 'You see, I am taking a lesson. Well, why not? This is not only Wagner's masterpiece, but the greatest comic opera ever written.')[3] He himself carried out what he called the 'difficult and ungrateful task' of making cuts in the third act to bring it within the time-limits envisaged.

A new choral work by Cowen, *The Water Lily*, promised to be a considerable attraction of the festival, but the composer withdrew it after the festival committee would not be budged from its allocation of Ben Davies and Plunket Greene to the tenor and baritone solos. (Cowen wanted the more robust tones of Edward Lloyd and Norman Salmond, who were singing at other concerts of the festival.) In its place Sullivan suggested something of Arthur Goring Thomas:

The second act of *Nadeshda* goes admirably in the concert-room, and would be a novelty to 999 out of 1,000. His sad death [on 20 March 1892] has created a great deal of interest in his works and I think a selection from them would gratify everyone.

But the committee declined (they might reasonably have feared an operatic 'overdose', with *Die Meistersinger* also on the programme) and also declined 'a selection from Sir Arthur's successful opera, *Ivanhoe*' as Smythe put it on the composer's behalf. In place of Cowen's cantata they unwisely scheduled a weak work of Schumann's, *The Pilgrimage of the Rose* ('Schumann's fairy failure' was to be the eventual headline in the *Yorkshire Evening Post*). Of Goring Thomas they admitted only a light *suite de ballet*. The only new works scheduled were those commissioned by the Yorkshire committee from Yorkshire composers of undistinguished reputation: Frederick Cliffe would provide a symphony, and Alan Gray a choral setting of Shelley's *Arethusa*. The unusual step was taken, probably with Sullivan's encouragement, of giving a recent but *not* newly commissioned work by Parry, *De Profundis*, performed at Hereford in the Three Choirs Festival in the previous year.

Nine times Barnby deputized for Sullivan at the weekly choral rehearsals. When Sullivan himself was at last able to stand before the Leeds chorus, at the rehearsal on 20 July, the reporter of the *Leeds Mercury* found him 'thin and pale'. The festival committee took alarm, and now proposed to retain Barnby as assistant conductor throughout the festival period, and Spark notified Sullivan accordingly. The answer was masked by Sullivan's habitual courtesy.

The question between us is a very simple one, viz: whether the committee should make arrangements to engage an assistant conductor without consulting me. If I had appointed an assistant (with or without reference to them) I should have acknowledged their right to veto the appointment, as I could not claim to delegate my office to another without their permission. But any desire for 'assistance' should come from me, not from them.

Sir Joseph Barnby, however, denies positively that he made any definite promise to be present at the festival (unless in case of emergency), and only yielded after much pressure to my earnest request that he would conduct one performance as a mark of good will and friendship towards myself.

But as you state that an arrangement for him to be present the whole week was duly made, and approved by the committee (without my knowledge), and as the committee are much concerned at his not coming, and are to meet to consider the subject, I thought the best course to take was to resign and relieve them from all further embarrassment and anxiety.

All the really hard work of the festival I have already done, and very little remains for the conductor, but to conduct. I always consider that when we begin the full rehearsals, the real hard work is over, and the rest is only healthy physical exercise and intellectual pleasure.

Believe me, dear Mr Spark, and convey this to the committee, that I have no feelings of anger or resentment; but I am deeply hurt, and I cannot sever my connection with my greatest musical enjoyment without the most profound regret.

The festival committee, after 'an excessively unpleasant quarter of an hour' (according to a guarded report in the *Sunday Times* on 4 September) extricated itself from the embarrassment and persuaded Sullivan to retract his resignation. His name remained on the announcements, and on the eventual programme, as the festival's titular conductor. As usual his preliminary functions included the selection of the orchestra from London players. Even the form in which the musicians were engaged was a matter with which Sullivan concerned himself. 'May I suggest to you' he wrote to Spark,

that you should speak of the 'orchestra' and not of 'bandsmen' as the latter term is applied to the profession exclusively to military performers and you might hurt the feelings of our more sensitive instrumentalists.

But as a collective term Sullivan still referred to 'the band' – as indeed orchestral musicians still do.

The specification of instruments, which similarly fell to the festival conductor, showed Sullivan's determination to do things properly. The *Meistersinger* extract would require four extra horns and four extra trumpets. (He suggested that they be had from the military band stationed at Leeds.) The score of Mozart's *Requiem* required two basset-horns: it was important that the clarinettists engaged for the festival should be able to play those instruments. Bach's *Mass in B minor*, was, as in 1886, to be given (uncut) with the three specially made high trumpets. Apparently only one such trumpet had actually been made to order in 1886, the others being borrowed from London; but now Sullivan asked for a second one to be made at a cost of 7 guineas (£7.35). He changed his mind, however – perhaps finding that *both* of the other trumpeters possessed such instruments. At any rate, on 2 July 1892 he requested the makers, Silvani and Smith, to cancel the order unless they had begun work already. They *had* begun, so Sullivan offered to pay for the instrument himself.

Here it may be remarked that the technical improvement of instruments kept Sullivan's keen interest. He promised Silvani and Smith that he would try to come and inspect their 'bombardon', an improved form of tuba. Occasionally, as in his approval of a transposing-keyboard piano, his openness and enthusiasm led him up an unprofitable path. He hailed as 'a perfect instrument' the new form of slide-trumpet championed by the distinguished player Walter Morrow, but it lost the field completely to the valve-trumpet. Later he would praise, and even make a financial investment in, James Clinton's 'combination clarionet' (the old spelling was still used); this was an unsuccessful attempt, one of several, to establish an instrument which would rid the player of the necessity of changing from a 'clarinet in B flat' to a 'clarinet in A', and in this case would also permit the selection of either Philharmonic (high) or the lower Continental pitch.

As the date for *Haddon Hall* approached, Sullivan kept his musical journalist friends fed with news. In a letter of 2 September to Hermann Klein he combined his professional tidings with witty congratulations on the birth of the critic's elder son.

My heartiest congratulations and best wishes. May the boy become a great man, *doch immer ein wenig Klein!* [. . . yet still a bit 'klein', i.e. little].

We are struggling for the 17th [September] but between you and me I don't think we can possibly get it out on that day. Carte thinks we can, but Harris (Charles) and I *know* we can't. You may therefore reckon on the 24th [Carte, as for *Ivanhoe*, favoured a Saturday opening], and take your holiday in peace.

Charles Harris, a brother of Sir Augustus Harris, was the 'stage manager' (in modern terms, the director) – since Grundy, unlike Gilbert, did not view such a function as his own.

Duly unveiled on 24 September at the Savoy, *Haddon Hall* was described as 'an original English light opera'. Perhaps the term 'light', which had never been used as a label for Sullivan's works with Gilbert, was now thought necessary to distinguish the new piece from the genre of *Ivanhoe*. But *Haddon Hall* represented no simple reversion to the old Savoy-satirical style. Its plot was historical, or quasi-historical, on the celebrated elopement of the heiress, Dorothy Vernon, from her ancestral Derbyshire home. The period had been advanced by Grundy from 1561 to 1648 in order to place it in the frame of the conflict between Cavaliers and Roundheads. The love-interest was given a conventionally straight, romantic treatment by both Grundy and Sullivan, and the barbs of satire were directed only at the English kill-joy Puritans and their Scottish fellow-hypocrite, The McCrankie.

Sullivan finished scoring the work on 11 September, hardly two weeks before the first night, as usual noting in his resumed diary the day's total pages of orchestral score (34) and the time of finishing (11.40 p.m), and adding: 'The whole opera done. Thank God.' Lucille Hill, who had found favour as Rowena in *Ivanhoe*, was chosen to sing the role of Dorothy, with Savoy 'regulars' in other leading parts – Courtice Pounds as the tenor hero, John Manners; Rutland Barrington as his rival, Rupert; Rosina Brandram as Lady Vernon; and W. H. Denny as The McCrankie, enlivening his part with an attempted bagpipe solo which was not the product of Arthur Sullivan's pen.

Grundy proved himself no Gilbert:

> Oh, heart's desire!
> I see thee once again.
> I seem to hear the heav'nly choir
> Sing 'Life is not in vain'.

His Puritans, so far from being capable of defending themselves by wit or paradox, are merely silly:

> Down with love and down with marriage!
> Down with all who keep a carriage!
> . . .
> Pleasure – we can do without it,
> Down with court and down with king:
> And – just while we are about it –
> Down with ev'ry blessed thing!

But in dramatic layout and in variety of metre, Grundy's work – in three acts – was sufficient to allow a considerable achievement on the composer's part. A vein of intimacy and sentiment rules the opening numbers, among them a quartet in quasi-madrigal style which is not inferior to the cherished examples in Sullivan's earlier works. Later, the music to the comic numbers is in Sullivan's expected nimble vein – with a unison hymn-like strain for the Puritans which is the nearest that Sullivan ever permitted himself to ecclesiastical parody. Its presentation is particularly effective because the Puritans have by this time (the opening of Act 3) come to see the error of their ways and the solemn theme can thus be simultaneously matched with a jolly choral patter in 6/8 time.

Structurally, however, Sullivan's chief innovation was in the very long finale to the second act – the music being continuous even though the scene is changed. Beginning midway through the scene of Dorothy's elopement with her lover, the single musical number extends right through the ballroom scene at which her parents learn of her flight. Thus the latter scene is entirely without speech – following the convention of 'grand opera' rather than 'Savoy opera'. The transition between the two scenes is bridged by 'storm music' of a conventional operatic kind; 'it recalls, in a feeble way, the prologue to *The Golden Legend*' commented the *Athenaeum*. Despite this qualification, this finale as a whole (covering no less than 45 pages of the vocal score, out of 169 for the whole opera) has almost a Meyerbeer-in-miniature feeling in its succession of moods and contrast of textures, and it remarkably ends *pianissimo*. Moreover it manages to incorporate, without losing the dramatic tension, the comic elements in the characterization. Despite some weaknesses of melody in *Haddon Hall* (notably the heroine's own main tune, ending 'To thine own heart be true'), it must be claimed as a better work than *Ivanhoe*.

Bernard Shaw went further than that: 'I contend that Savoy opera is a *genre* in itself; and that *Haddon Hall* is the highest and most consistent expression it has yet attained.'

Shaw's view was that in setting Gilbert's 'aridly fanciful lyrics' Sullivan could be no more than adroit and witty, and that he was not, on the other hand, a genuine dramatic composer. But 'he has over and over again proved that in the sort of descriptive ballad which touches on the dramatic his gift is as genuine as that of Schubert or Loewe'. Hence the 'huge success' which Shaw reported of *Haddon Hall* at its opening performance. There was 'episode after episode of descriptive ballad music, full of unforced feeling, and tenderly handled down to the minutest details of their skilful and finished workmanship'.

The staging won Shaw's general approval too, the ballroom scene being 'a Cartesian triumph'. This must be the only instance of the application of that adjective to D'Oyly Carte rather than to Descartes.

The public accorded Sullivan-without-Gilbert the respectable total of 214 performances in the opening London run of *Haddon Hall*, and Carte added it to his touring repertory. Gilbert-without-Sullivan won less success with *The Mountebanks*, with music by Alfred Cellier, produced at the Lyric Theatre on 4 January 1892. The composer, a close associate of Sullivan's since he had been 'second boy' and Sullivan 'first boy' at the Chapel Royal, had died scarcely a week before the opening of the production. He was only 47.

Sullivan, in the spring of 1892, was nearly 50. His next theatrical work would be awaited with keen expectation, for the best-known creative pair in Britain's theatrical life were known to be once more coupled in harness. Gilbert's response to the challenge of the Nineties was to revert to open political satire for the first time since *Iolanthe* a decade before.

32 Satire

RECONCILED with Gilbert, the composer was not yet ready to begin work with him. Weak as he was from his illness, Sullivan had first to face again in October 1892 the strain of the Leeds Festival conductorship. As usual, there was initially a three-day concentration of orchestral rehearsals in London – open to the press and serving to warm public interest. At the first rehearsal on Monday 26 September the *Leeds Mercury* found him visibly stronger:

Despite the exertions in connexion with the prolonged rehearsals for his new opera, *Haddon Hall*, at the Savoy Theatre, produced on Saturday evening last, and his brief journey to Cardiff to conduct *The Golden Legend* [21 September],[1] Sir Arthur looked in very fair health, and seemed prepared for the heavy strain of the preparation of the festival programme in London this week, and again at Leeds next week.

After lunch on that day Barnby should have taken over to rehearse *The Spectre's Bride*, but he was excusably delayed at the Guildhall School of Music: it was his first day in the office of principal. Sullivan, to avoid the loss of time, tirelessly went on rehearsing. At Leeds itself he would benefit from one day's relaxation, at least. The festival was scheduled to begin on a Wednesday, as usual, but for the first time the preceding day was to be a rest day, with rehearsals suspended. Sensitive to the charge that the choir had in the past come to the public performances already over-exerted, the committee was at pains to see that the troops of 1892 were fresh for battle and ready to expunge the censures of 1889. Full rehearsals with choir and orchestra therefore began not on the Monday but on the Saturday (Sunday also being an exempt day for the choral singers), even though this incurred the additional costs of bringing the orchestral players from London two days earlier.

There was another change at this festival, likewise designed to improve the choral quality. Members of choral societies based in Bradford, Huddersfield, Halifax, Dewsbury, and Batley were enlisted, as well as those of Leeds, the 'strangers' totalling about two thirds of the entire festival chorus. There were still 17 male altos – quite sufficient (even against 69 contraltos) to make a distinct contribution of vocal colour.

Spark was as usual waiting for Sullivan when he arrived at the Great Northern Station at 5.30 p.m. on Friday 30 September. A house had been taken for him in Virginia Terrace. That same evening he plunged into a rehearsal with the choir alone; when rehearsals with orchestra began, he excited comment by rehearsing *Elijah* instead of taking such a familiar work for granted. Beginning at

11.30 a.m. on Wednesday 5 October, *Elijah* was the opening work of the festival; when it came to a close at 2.45 p.m. several of the audience forgot the etiquette attaching to 'sacred' music and burst into applause.

Sullivan remained very much in command throughout the festival. Having yielded to Barnby only the Saturday morning concert containing *The Spectre's Bride*, he conducted as usual everything but those 'novelties' or other works which were directed by their own composers. On this occasion such works were few and comparatively short. Mackenzie was represented by his *La Belle Dame sans merci* (not a choral setting of Keats, but an orchestral 'ballad') and the young Edward German by his overture, *Richard III*. Cliffe's symphony and Gray's *Arethusa* met only polite acceptance, Parry's *De Profundis* winning a heartier welcome. 'Weak in new works', as the *Yorkshire Evening Post* put it, the festival justified itself by re-establishing its choral standards. Once again Sullivan triumphed in his conducting of Bach's *Mass in B minor*, uncut; it could not be the sensation it had been in 1886, but some thought it was actually better performed. Equal success attended the *Meistersinger* extract – in English, and uncertainly announced by the *Yorkshire Post* one month before as *The Meistersingers of Wurtemburg*. No less an opera critic than Hermann Klein of the *Sunday Times* found something in it which he could not find in London:

The concluding chorus was sung as it has never been sung before; for there is no opera chorus in the world that could approach the calibre of these Leeds singers, much less furnish 70-odd sopranos capable of finishing up on a clear, bell-like high C.

Albani and Edward Lloyd sang the parts of Eva and Walther, with Plunket Greene as Sachs. Beckmesser's part was omitted.

The first half of the final Saturday evening concert was taken up by that peculiarly Victorian concoction, a 'selection' of items by Handel in which the cheerful pagan revelry of *L'Allegro* and *Alexander's Feast* was mixed with godly exhortations from *Samson* and *Messiah*. Then, mirroring the opening of the festival by the National Anthem and Mendelssohn, the close was provided by Mendelssohn (the *Hymn of Praise*) and the National Anthem. The four days represented a double triumph – an assertion by Sullivan of his physical powers and a vindication of the Yorkshire choir. Noting that this was the fifth festival at which he had 'occupied the conductor's chair' (again, the sitting position!), the *Yorkshire Post* on 10 October found him not only recovered from his severe illness, but displaying 'an energy which has not always characterized his wielding of the baton'.

Nor had the festival failed to represent him as a composer – in one case unexpectedly. The death of Tennyson in the early hours of Thursday 6 October was marked in next day's concert when the scheduled performance of the *Mass in B minor* was preceded by the *In Memoriam* overture – some of the audience respectfully rising to their feet and finding with dismay that they were standing for 15 minutes. Novello's must have been swift in placing the orchestral parts on a train to Leeds. In other programmes Sullivan conducted an orchestral suite from his youthful *Tempest*, the popular 'Come, Margarita, come' from *The Martyr of Antioch* (sung by Edward Lloyd), and 'The night is calm' (with Albani and the festival chorus) from *The Golden Legend*.

His well-wishers still hoped that he might turn again to orchestral composition. In October 1892 came an invitation to write a new work for the Philharmonic Society. Rebecca's prayer-scene from *Ivanhoe* had been included in the seventh and final concert of its 1892 season on 15 June under Cowen's conductorship. Acknowledging the invitation, Sullivan wrote only that he would consider it. Meanwhile the public was not allowed to regard *Ivanhoe* as dead. A paragraph which had appeared in the *Daily News* on 30 September 1892 bears every evidence of having been prompted by the composer himself. Here, it seemed was a response to the line of criticism taken (p. 331) by the first regular conductor of the opera, Ernest Ford. The newspaper's readers learned that

Sir Arthur Sullivan has wisely resolved to thoroughly revise his opera *Ivanhoe*, and the production of the work in German at the Imperial Opera House, Berlin, has accordingly been postponed until next year. Certain rumours, which have even found their way into print, to the effect that the composer is taking but scant interest in the Berlin performances are, we have the best reason to believe, quite inaccurate. On the contrary, after he has closed the Leeds Festival, and has enjoyed a very brief holiday, Sir Arthur proposes practically to rewrite the second act of the opera; while throughout the work the tenor hero will have far greater opportunities, and will be much more in evidence than heretofore. Later, in 1893, *Ivanhoe* in its new and improved form will, we understand, be reintroduced to London.

But 1893 and indeed 1894 would pass without a sign of any such production. In London, at least, it would take a bold impresario to risk Carte's experience of having his fingers burnt.

Sullivan went back to the Riviera, once again taking a house of his own. It was a villa called Diodato at Cabbé-Roquebrune, not far from his previous abode at Turlie-sur-Mer, but on the French side of the border with Monaco. His friend Sir Charles Russell was also wintering in the region. A Christmas Day disappointment was lightly dealt with in Sullivan's letter of 26 December to Lady Russell:

Hot fomentations etc have restored my cook to good health and this morning she is *désolée* at yesterday's mishap. I had a dinner alone consisting of two cutlets and some cheese, and the turkey and plum pudding are awaiting your arrival. Will you come tonight or tomorrow, whichever is most convenient? And will Sir Charles come and play his besique beforehand?[2]

Grove arrived to stay with him in January 1893, and soon afterwards came Gilbert, whom Sullivan assured warmly in advance:

Don't misunderstand my silence. . . . [It is simply] so that I should not, by any word or phrase accidentally used, prejudice the understanding we are striving to arrive at. . . . You will of course come *here* and make this your home. . . . There is not a single question to be discussed between us except how we shall make a brilliant opera.

During his three-day visit Gilbert read to the composer a sketch-plot of their proposed new work. Afterwards he wrote to Sullivan from his new home at

Harrow – a mansion called Grim's Dyke, built by the celebrated Norman Shaw and surrounded by 110 acres of grounds:

I arrived here, all right, last night, after a beastly passage and three tiresome days in Paris. I send you Cook on Billiards – the study of that work *has made me what I am in billiards*, and if you devote six to eight hours a day to it regularly, you may hope to play up to my form when you return.

But the composer did not hurry back, nor press ahead with the composition. He sent back to François Cellier, who was conducting *Haddon Hall*, a new song for the role of Dorothy.[3] At Mentone (then on the Italian side of the border) he arranged – perhaps through his old friend Juliette Conneau – to conduct two Sunday concerts with a 74-strong orchestra, one of his own music on 5 March and one by several British composers two weeks later. His selection for the second concert took a typically generous view, including four works by composers younger than himself: Parry's overture to *The Frogs* of Aristophanes; Mackenzie's 'Benedictus' and 'Courante' from the incidental music to the play *Ravenswood*; the scherzo from Stanford's *Irish Symphony*; and Cowen's suite, *The Language of Flowers*.

Back in London in April, he had another royal duty to fulfil. The Imperial Institute, the laying of whose foundation-stone had called forth his setting of the Lewis Morris *Ode*, was now ready for opening. He quickly wrote an *Imperial March* – an orchestral work which Elgar may well have heard and rightly decided that he could do better in the same style. On 10 May, three days before Sullivan's 51st birthday, he noted in his diary (which he was now compiling with something of his old assiduity): 'Opening of Imperial Institute by the Queen. Duchess of Marlborough called for me and Bertie at 10.15, then to pick up Mrs Ronalds – arr. at Institute 10.45. Very fine sight. I directed (in levée dress) orchestra of 98.' The march was repeated at the Philharmonic (Mackenzie now being the Society's conductor in Cowen's place) on 15 May. On 18 May he 'dined with Bertie at no. 7' and next day 'went to see Auntie'.

On the birthday itself (13 May) it had 'rained telegrams' – but, as he wrote ever-lovingly to Nina Lehmann,

somehow yours had a little charm of its own. The glamour of the past was on it, and to me the romance of my life is in the past – the present is all hard, prosaic facts, although 20 years hence today will probably be in the realm of romance also. But, dearest Ni, what a good time we had, didn't we? Two children devouring picture books were not so happy as we were, and upon my word I think we were as innocent! I took it into my head the other day to go to the New Gallery private view [of the new seasonal exhibition], and there the first person I saw was little Nina [the daughter of his correspondent]. To her I attached myself at once and never left her, for I wanted to see neither picture nor person so long as I could be with her. She is just the same as ever, utterly unchanged and unspoilt. Shall I ever see you, I wonder? In your little excursions between Portobello [near Edinburgh], the Scilly Islands and other proximate places, do you never pass through London? I want a long – a very long talk with you.

Now goodbye, dear heart. Keep always a little wee corner for me in your warm heart.

There were not many to inspire such tender nostalgia in Sullivan. But he must have felt something similar in the same month when he subscribed to a fund in commemoration of Jenny Lind. A medallion bearing a relief of her profile and the inscription 'I know that my Redeemer liveth' was duly unveiled in Westminster Abbey in the following year.

His birthday was marked by a visit to the races at Kempton Park and to the opening night of a new light opera at the Savoy. *Jane Annie*, with music by Ernest Ford, and a libretto by no less illustrious a pair than J. M. Barrie and Arthur Conan Doyle, was Carte's hope for bridging the gap until Gilbert's and Sullivan's own new work should be ready. 'Dialogue dull – music *very* pretty' wrote Sullivan in his diary. On 23 May the diary records, with an enthusiasm quite unusual for Sullivan, his visit to Leoncavallo's new opera: 'Went to Covent Garden to hear *Pagliacci*. Liked it immensely. Dramatic and brilliant. Portland [Club, afterwards].' Four days later he went for a three-day visit to Gilbert:

5.20 train to Harrow with Bertie. Gilbert met me at station with wagonette, looked far from well, gout very bad, drove to his house 'Grim's Dyke' – lovely place, no one but ourselves there, very quiet and pleasant.

Again forsaking London, he took a house (Dorney House) at Weybridge in order to concentrate on the opera – a task which the failure of *Jane Annie* made all the more urgent in Carte's plans. Gilbert visited him:

I will come on Thursday as you suggest by the train arriving 12.23 – returning from Weybridge by the 5.47. I assume you are not averse to standing a bit of bread and cheese and a drop of beer to a pore working man wot's been out of work for some years . . .

The composition of what was to become *Utopia (Limited)* got under way at last on 19 June 1893. Despite the diary entry for that day, 'Began new opera: slow work', Sullivan seems to have slipped easily into the work, completing the first of Gilbert's two acts within a month and receiving the librettist's compliments on the ending of that act as the best finale he had ever composed.

'Utopia' was a South Sea Island whose king, hearing of the perfection of England, has sent his daughter Zara to complete her education there. When she returns she is accompanied not only by the handsome young Captain Fitz-battleaxe, commanding her escort of British Household Cavalry, but by five other 'flowers of progress' – officials who will remodel the country on English lines. One is 'Mr Goldbury, a company promoter', who takes advantage of 'the Joint Stock Companies Act of Parliament, '62' (a phrase which Sullivan set to music) to transform the kingdom itself into a limited company. Eventually the islanders revolt under the pressure of too much perfection – but it only takes one English attribute which had been temporarily forgotten, namely 'Government by Party' to assure everyone that chaos will happily come again.

Along with her political advisers the princess has brought home her elderly English governess. The character of Lady Sophy was the rock on which, for reasons that could have been anticipated, the partnership of composer and librettist nearly foundered again. Sullivan wanted no more to do with grotesque amorous spinsters in the line of Lady Jane, Katisha, and Dame Carruthers, and pleaded that the second act should show genuine pathos in Lady Sophy's part. In a long and sweetly reasonable letter from Grim's Dyke dated 3 July, Gilbert put it that the part was merely humorous, not grotesque: 'She is in love with the king (as a lady of 45 may well be with a man of 50) but her frenzy is not of a gross or animal type as you seem to imagine.' Gilbert won his point. Human vitality, with no sentimental traits, are enough to establish Lady Sophy in her own distinctive mould.

For the role of Princess Zara, Sullivan was persuaded to accept Gilbert's American 'discovery', Nancy McIntosh. Gilbert furnished a description: 'rather tall, extremely fair – very nice-looking without being beautiful – good expressive face – no appreciable American twang – something like a good and ladylike version of [Blanche] Roosevelt'. Nancy McIntosh remained a protégeé of Gilbert's: she became virtually an adopted daughter to him and his wife, with whom she went to live at Grim's Dyke.

Gilbert had recently returned from the German spa of Homburg, where he had gone in search of relief for his gout. In correspondence he kept up his suggestions, seasoned by social banter:

Cut no. 14 certainly. Don't you think that a nigger prelude with bones, tambourine, banjo etc. would introduce the king's song very well?
. . . P.S. Mrs Breeze (Marie Parsons) is here. She has lost all her husband and most of her good looks.

'No. 14' was the king's solo beginning 'Society has quite forsaken': Gilbert was consenting to 'cut' (abbreviate), not to omit it. In the suggestion of a 'nigger prelude' is the germ of the most audacious musical stroke in the opera, itself part of the most brazen scene of satire in the whole Gilbert and Sullivan canon. Lord Dramaleigh (the English Lord Chamberlain) instructs King Paramount how he is to hold his Council with his team of English advisers:

King. Like this?

Dramaleigh. Like this.

King. We take your word for it that this is all right. You are not making fun of us? This is in accordance with the practice at the court of St James's?

Dramaleigh. Well, it is in accordance with the practice at the court of St James's Hall.

The scene-direction preceding these lines is 'They range their chairs across the stage like Christy Minstrels' – the blacked-up entertainers who frequently occupied the lower part (beneath the concert auditorium) of St James's Hall. The effect was, on stage at the Savoy, to demean court behaviour to the level of 'low' entertainment, with bones, banjo and the rest. Not only did Sullivan simulate the general musical style of that entertainment; he borrowed the tune *The Keel Row* which was associated with the minstrels in the guise of 'Johnny get your gun'. There was gentler mockery in 'A tenor, all singers above' – Captain Fitz-battleaxe's song, in which a tenor's ability to show off his voice is penalized by his being in love. Sullivan may not have realized that singers will never sing this song badly enough, at least by intention.

Even then, not all had been settled. Sullivan found it impossible to set Gilbert's words to the finale of the second act, beginning 'There's a little group of isles beyond the wave'. At such a late stage Gilbert could only suggest, for the only time in their collaboration, that the music should be composed first and he would fit words to it. Sullivan went ahead, and Gilbert fitted some words (beginning, 'There's an isle beyond the wave, held by a blameless race') which he himself described as 'mere doggerel – but words written to an existing tune are nearly sure to be that'.

This in turn was considered unsatisfactory. According to the reporter of the *Westminster Gazette* who covered the public dress rehearsal on 6 October 1893, the cast was told that the finale would not be rehearsed; a new one was being written which would not be rehearsed until a few hours before the opening. So the first-night audience heard a lyric that began:

> When monarch of barbaric land
> For self-improvement burning . . .

And even *this*, as we shall note, was discarded after the run of the production was under way.

It was a hot summer. At Weybridge the composer found recreation in rowing, and in a new diversion, tricycling. The diary on 17 August recorded the visits by Gilbert and by François ['Frank'] Cellier, who was again to be the musical director.

Terrible heat, 90° [about 32°C]. Impossible to work owing to regatta and fair being held. Two large musical steam roundabouts outside my house, so gave myself up to the regatta and sports. Frank Cellier arrived 5.30. Worked at opera with him at night.

One week later Sullivan 'finished up alterations, etc.; framed duet "Words of love", rewrote many little bits. Lettered everything [i.e., placed the letters which show musical repetitions] for copyist.' On 4 September the cast began rehearsals – for which, as usual, printed copies of the libretto (though not yet in the corrected form in which it would reach the public) were on hand.

But Sullivan's work was not finished; there were more 'little alterations' noted as late as 12 September, and he was still orchestrating, as well as attending rehearsals when he could. On 29 September – or rather at 2.30 a.m. next day – the score was complete. Gilbert – gout notwithstanding – took his usual role as stage director; and, for the first time in the series, broke his habitual secrecy and admitted the press to the dress rehearsal on 6 October.

Next evening *Utopia (Limited), or, The Flowers of Progress*, 'an original comic opera', had its opening performance. (The parentheses in the title were later omitted.) Those who queued for the unreserved part of the theatre beguiled their waiting hours by singing 'hits' from previous, well-remembered works by Gilbert and Sullivan. Were the 'wonder-working days of old' about to return? An unprecedented £7,200 had been spent on scenery, properties, and costumes for the work that would give the answer. 'Went into the orchestra at 8.15 sharp. My ovation lasted 65 seconds! Piece went wonderfully well – not a hitch of any kind, and afterwards G. and I had a *double call.*' So Sullivan reported the first performance in his diary, noting that he had been 'shockingly nervous as usual – more than usual'. Nancy McIntosh sang the heroine's role without the assurance of style which came from Rutland Barrington (King Paramount the First, the ruler of Utopia), W. H. Denny (Scaphio, one of the two intriguers at court) and Rosina Brandram (the English governess, Lady Sophy). Another kind of continuity was clear when the representative of Britain's navy – Captain Corcoran, who else? – introduced himself.

> Though we're no longer hearts of oak
> Yet we can steer and we can stoke,
> And thanks to coal, and thanks to coke
> We never run a ship ashore!
> ALL What, never?
> CAPTAIN No, never!
> ALL What, *never?*
> CAPTAIN Hardly ever!

There was a more original cleverness, uniting the art of composer and librettist, in the duo in Act 1 where Scaphio and Phantis are supposed to *dance* their meanings, and in the trio in Act 2 (with Tarara, the Public Exploder) where their conspiratorial thoughts are not sung at all but whispered while the orchestra continues:

> SCA. Suppose we all – (*whispers*).
> PHAN.   Now *there* I think you're right.
>   Then we might all – (*whispers*).
> TAR.   That's true – we certainly might.
> PHAN. I'll tell you what – (*whispers*).
> SCA.   We will if we possibly can.
>   Then on the spot – (*whispers*).
> PHAN. and TAR.   Bravo! a capital plan!
> SCA. That's exceedingly neat and new!
> PHAN.   Exceedingly new and neat!
> TAR. I fancy that that will do.
> SCA.   It's certainly very complete.
> PHAN. Well done, you sly old sap!
> TAR.   Bravo, you cunning old mole!
> SCA. You very ingenious chap!
> PHAN.   You intellectual soul! (*all shaking hands*).

Here the musical device of the 'wordless orator' in *The Zoo* (pp. 95–6) is paralleled, if not recalled.

Perhaps it was Gilbert's newly sharp social satire that moved Bernard Shaw to deliver such a favourable verdict:

I enjoyed the score of *Utopia* more than that of any of the previous Savoy operas. . . . The orchestral work is charmingly humorous; and as I happen to mean by this only what I say, perhaps I had better warn my readers not to infer that *Utopia* is full of buffooneries with the bassoon and piccolo, or of patter and tum-tum. Whoever can listen to such caressing wind parts – zephyr parts, in fact – as those in the trio for the King and the two Judges in the first act, without being coaxed to feel pleased and amused, is not fit even for treasons, stratagems, and spoils; whilst anyone whose ears are capable of taking in more than one thing at a time must be tickled by the sudden busyness of the orchestra as the city man takes up the parable. I also confidently recommend those who go into solemn academic raptures over themes 'in diminution' to go and hear how prettily the chorus of the Christy Minstrel song (borrowed from the plantation dance, 'Johnnie, get a gun' [sic]) is used very much in diminution, to make an exquisite mock-banjo accompaniment. In these examples we are on the plane, not of the bones and tambourine, but of Mozart's accompaniments to 'Soave sia il vento' in *Così fan tutte* and the entry of the gardener in *Le nozze di Figaro*.

But other reviewers were less enthusiastic. Even the *Musical Times* qualified its favourable view by a nostalgic backward glance:

It is only in comparison with such masterpieces of humour and musical and dramatic satire as *Patience*, *The Mikado*, *The Yeomen of the Guard* and *The Gondoliers* that the libretto of *Utopia (Limited)* seems a trifle dull, particularly in the first act, and the music for the most part reminiscent rather than fresh.

In the same issue (November 1893) the magazine praised the grace and simplicity of Sullivan's settings for Tennyson's *The Foresters*, just produced (see p. 340).

The *Pall Mall Gazette* more severely called *Utopia*

a mirthless travesty of the work with which [Gilbert's] name is most generally associated. . . . The earlier works indeed were inspired by a common spirit, constructed according to the same formula, but the spirit did not flag, the formula did not seem to be mechanical, the result did not seem to be monotonous. With *Utopia (Limited)* it is different. The philosophy of inversion, of veiled cynicism, of sugared suggestion which had served his turn through a dozen operas suddenly fails him with the ominous number. The quips, whims, jests, the theory of topsy-turvy, the principle of paradox, the law of the unlikely, seem to have grown old in a single night. . . . Mr Gilbert has failed to make the old seem new.

Certainly the impression of 'the mixture as before' (but weaker) was understandable. In *Iolanthe*, the *tan-tan-ta-ra* of the Peers' Chorus was funny because the swagger and the trumpet-calls served ironically to underline the Peers' impending defeat; in the new piece, the *tantantarara-rara-rara* (lamely rhyming with 'Princess Zara') was mere military-operatic posturing.

Within a week of its opening the second-act finale had been found unsatisfactory and altered yet again. This time, Sullivan wondrously found himself able to set Gilbert's *original* words ('There's a little group of isles beyond the wave' – see p. 354). A song for Zara in Act 1, 'Youth is a boon avowed', was removed at the same time. Shortly afterwards there was a change made in the staging. In the meticulous dressing-up of the mock-drawing-room scene, the king had worn a British field-marshal's uniform with the Order of the Garter. It was intimated from on high that the Prince of Wales objected, being himself the only person entitled to that particular combination of honours, and the offending Order was removed.

A run of 245 performances might well have gratified the management of other and less expensive productions. To Carte it meant almost a public rejection. He turned again to Messager: but *Mirette* (3 July 1894) won even less success, although *The Times* thought the French composer 'has set himself or has been required, to assimilate his music as far as may be to that of Sir Arthur Sullivan'.

According to John Wolfson's book, *Final Curtain* (1976), a proposed revival of *The Mikado* was abandoned because Gilbert insisted on Nancy McIntosh's playing Yum-Yum and Sullivan refused. Once again the two men's paths diverged. Gilbert took his next libretto to a younger composer, Frank Osmond Carr (1858–1919) and another management, while Sullivan rejoined his old partner, Francis Burnand, in the desperate gesture of revising their operetta of 26 years ago, *The Contrabandista*.

On 14 May 1894, for once not at his home but at the Garrick Club, Sullivan held his customary birthday party. The 52-year-old composer's guests included the Prince of Wales, Sir Augustus Harris, Henry Irving, Beerbohm Tree and Carte – but not Gilbert. The French *diseuse*, Yvette Guilbert, was among the entertainers who kept the guests amused until 4.45 a.m. In the same month Sullivan also met Paderewski (at a dinner given by Hermann Klein), enjoyed the racing at Newmarket, Lingfield, and Kempton, and saw Verdi's new opera, *Falstaff*, at Covent Garden – typically recording the event with no comment whatever on the music or the performance.

For Sydney Grundy's play *An Old Jew*, which had opened at the Garrick Theatre on the previous 6 January, Sullivan had obliged his former collaborator with a single song, 'Bid me at least goodbye'. It won him a windfall: the American *Ladies' Home Journal* gave him £100 for the right to print it. A more substantial theatrical opportunity came with an invitation to compose a ballet score for the Empire Theatre. He demanded a very high fee: 5 per cent of the gross box-office takings with a guaranteed minimum of 100 performances, or £2,000 if it should run for less. If these terms were accepted (he wrote), 'I will go to Vienna at once and carry out the arrangements I propose making'. Was Sullivan already in touch with Ignaz Schnitzer (1839–1921), the Austrian librettist of Johann Strauss's *The Gipsy Baron*? Nothing came of the idea, but this seems the only mention of Vienna that could have prompted Schnitzer himself many years later to speak of a planned collaboration with Sullivan which was prevented by the composer's death.

He had now become slack again in compiling his diary: there are no entries at all for November and December 1894, the very period when *The Chieftain* (as *The Contrabandista* was now renamed) was being prepared and put on the stage. The audience at the Savoy on 12 December 1894 was presented with a substantially rewritten work of considerable ingenuity in words and music. The original first act had been largely retained, but with a new and better finale: the second act was quite new, bringing Dolly Grigg to Spain on the trail of her husband, the tourist now installed willy-nilly as a chieftain of Spanish brigands.

Early in that second act occurred what *The Times* considered the best number in the whole opera, a love-duet in French and English 'in which the mannerisms of French light opera are as clearly parodied in the music as the tricks of its singers are by Miss Florence St John'. A newcomer to the company, she sang the role of Rita, while continuity with the old Savoy tradition was assured by the presence of Courtice Pounds (Vasquez), Richard Temple (Sancho) and Rosina Brandram (Inez). Walter Passmore was Grigg, winning an encore for 'From rock to rock' – which *The Times* critic, evidently with a long memory, called 'a famous song'. This was the song (held over from *The Contrabandista*) in which the hapless hero narrated his adventures and misadventures.

A song in the new second act, sung by one of the Spaniards disguised as a Polish travel courier, shows that Burnand had lost none of his mania for puns. In the space of three lines he referred not only to England's leading travel agency and to a well-known publisher's guide-books, but to a literary celebrity as well:

> They travel through France with a trustworthy Cook,
> And ev'ryone says from their much-Murray'd look
> 'Mark! Innocents Twain all abroad!'

But in song, and on the stage, such ingenuity was less telling than when read in the pages of *Punch*. Leaving soon afterwards for the Riviera, Sullivan received news that *The Chieftain* was playing to thinning houses at the Savoy, taking £1,400 in the first week but only £1,300 in the second and third and £1,200 in the fourth. From the Hôtel de Paris at Monte Carlo Sullivan sent back new songs and new dance music in order to strengthen and – as he hoped – save the show.[4] A letter of 29 January 1895 to Burnand, discussing a replacement of Inez's song in Act I, 'Let others seek the peaceful plain' shows Sullivan wishing to give a sharper character to the music. In *The Contrabandista* of 1867 the song had been a fairly anonymous specimen of contralto ballad style. (Even then – see p. 86 – Sullivan had recognized its weakness.) Now it was to take on local colour:

Now about Brandram's song. I have tried hard [with Burnand's new words] but cannot get it into shape. The metre is against my setting it in a Spanish, dancing rhythm, and it is disjointed in form, which wouldn't matter except that in this particular place I want a strongly marked, *catchy*, rythmical [*sic*] number, like the quintet in 2nd act [musical opening quoted]. Here are nonsense words and music which give an idea of a characteristic Spanish rythm [*sic*]. Two or three verses of this, with words which will admit of a 'la la la' in the chorus, and I could make a bright, lively opening number.

Sullivan set down a nonsensical 'specimen' of words which would permit the musical changes:

> I was walking alone on a Saturday,
> On the latter day,
> Which was platter-day . . .

The changes duly appeared in a second edition of the vocal score, with Inez's song marked 'Allegro molto alla habanera'. The *habanera* (or tango) accompaniment was set against just the kind of 6/8 melody which Sullivan had proposed. But it is obvious by the clumsy scansion ('My parents were *of* great gentility') that Burnand had not grasped the musical point very well.

Nor did the 'improvements' suffice to rally the public, and *The Chieftain* was taken off after only 96 performances. Failure also attended *His Excellency* – a good libretto of Gilbert's (about a practical-joking governor of a Danish town) set to Carr's inferior musical score and produced at the Lyric Theatre on 27 December 1894 with Grossmith, Barrington, and, inevitably, Nancy McIntosh in the cast. '*His Excellency* started out well', Gilbert was to write later to Helen Carte (quoted by Wolfson), 'and if it had had the benefit of your expensive friend Sullivan's music, it would have been a second *Mikado*.'

Once more (it was to be his last time) Sullivan's gifts were to be harnessed to the 'legitimate' theatre. Irving wanted to put the Arthurian legends on the stage. Just as, with Faust, he had commissioned G. W. Wills rather than attempt Goethe, so now he declined to dramatize Tennyson and commissioned a *King Arthur* from J. R. Comyns Carr, a dramatist (and art critic) of some experience, soon to be 'Joe Carr' in Sullivan's diary. The subject of King Arthur's court had intermittently engaged Sullivan since those far-off days when Rachel Scott Russell had exhorted his fledgeling muse to soar; it had also fascinated Edward Burne-Jones, from whom Irving commissioned the scenery, costumes, and armour. In the announcements of the play (as Bernard Shaw pointed out to his readers in the *Saturday Review*) Sullivan dropped the 'Sir' while Burne-Jones, lately created a baronet, paraded his.

The score – both vocal music on stage and orchestral interludes – was substantial enough to induce Sullivan to conduct the opening night at the Lyceum on 12 January 1895. The notice in the *Illustrated London News* by the distinguished drama critic, Clement Scott, must have pleased the composer immensely. The production in its varied detail was 'the best specimen of the stage art of our time' and

the assistance of Sir Arthur has been of inestimable value. The music is exactly what was wanted – ever subordinate to dramatic effect, and yet always assisting it. The chant of the water-nymphs in the mystical prologue, the song of the knights preparing for departure in search of the Holy Grail, and the exquisite dirge that announces the funeral procession of Elaine will long haunt the memory.

To Bernard Shaw, however, the whole was a monument of sham grandeur. His readers were informed that Carr was 'no more a poet than I am'; Burne-Jones was a trivializer, while Sullivan 'sweetens the sentiment of the scenes here and there by penn'orths of orchestral sugar-stick, for which the dramatic critics, in their soft-eared innocence, compare him to Wagner'.

For introductions and entractes, Sullivan re-used some of his existing music. An abbreviated version of the early *Marmion* overture served as a prelude to the Prologue of the play (Shaw wrongly identified it as among the 'pretty specimens of his best late work'). The *Imperial March* was performed before Act 1, movements from *The Tempest* before Acts 2 and 4 and part of his Symphony to introduce Act 3. There were 38 musical numbers in all.[5]

Of the incidental music proper, a suite of five vocal movements was published after his death. Two were from the prologue (beginning with the chorus of Spirits of the Lake from which rises the sword Excalibur); the others were 'The Chaunt of the Grail' from Act 1, when Sir Percival is about to leave on his Quest, 'The May Song' (Act 2, Scene 1) and the 'Funeral March and Final Chorus' (Act 2, Scene 2). All this amounted to hardly more than a limb of what an opera by Sullivan entitled 'King Arthur', or perhaps 'Guinevere', might have been. He went so far as to ask Carr to write a libretto, but of that projected collaboration nothing survives. *Requiescat* not only Arthur but Rachel!

33 The End of the Partnership

FOURTEEN years had lapsed since the poses of the young Oscar Wilde had helped *Patience* to a topical fame in 1881. Now, in one of the rare references in his diary to public events, Sullivan on 6 April 1895 entered the bald statement 'Oscar Wilde arrested and brought up at Bow St' [magistrates' court]. Thus began one of the most celebrated criminal processes of the age. Accused of homosexual offences, Wilde underwent two trials (at the first, the jury disagreed) and was sentenced to two years' imprisonment with hard labour.

A few weeks before, on 14 February, the London theatre had been enriched by *The Importance of Being Earnest*, 'which is the awkward name of the new play by Mr Oscar Wilde' as *The Observer* put it (17 February). That newspaper's critic considered that 'the only two persons in the play who bear any relationship to comedy as distinct from Gilbertian extravaganza are the cynical dowager, Lady Bracknell and the cynical manservant Lane . . .'.

As others were to note, Wilde had actually borrowed several incidents from Gilbert's farcical comedy *Engaged* (1877). Perhaps the critic also implied by the adjective 'Gilbertian' that the two young men and two young women of Wilde's play were merely manipulated puppets, mouthpieces for their author's wit and likely to be jerked this way or that in the cause of epigram or paradox. At any rate the newly coined adjective as a description of such a technique was immediately comprehensible. On that 17 February, *The Observer* did not report, but the *Sunday Times* did, the production of *Ivanhoe* by the Carl Rosa company at the Court Theatre, Liverpool, three days before. It was a brief notice, pointing out that this was a revised version of the score, which 'was pronounced a decided improvement upon the original'. Neither there nor in the *Liverpool Review* (23 March) were details given of the revision, with which the company then went on tour; nor did the *Era* of 16 February say more than that the work had been 'judiciously "cut", this operation having been carried out with discretion and striking effect'.

Barton McGuckin brought the authority of the 1891 performances to the title-role. The other performers were less well known, and the company's regular conductor, Claude Jacquinot, was in charge. Presumably because they expected the production would come to London (it did not), and perhaps also because Sullivan was not quite the composer he was formerly esteemed to be, the leading London critics seem not to have attended. To the absent Sullivan (he was at Monte Carlo) the revision had a more important goal: he was anxious that the long-delayed production in Germany should present his work in its best and most cogent form.

The dour Walter Smythe, for so long his secretary, had now retired from his service. To help deal with his correspondence and such matters, Sullivan now had a different type of helper. Wilfred Bendall, being a composer, could assist in musical as well as commercial concerns. (He arranged the piano part for several of Sullivan's published vocal scores including the posthumously issued *King Arthur*.) The association seems to have begun late in 1894 or early in 1895. On 9 February, presumably enclosing a cheque, Sullivan wrote from Monte Carlo to express

gratitude for all the valuable help you gave me at a critical moment, . . . [not] as in any way representing my indebtedness to you but to cover the loss of time which you might have devoted to something more lucrative than to my affairs.

Sullivan's delicacy here is surely admirable. He was to treat Bendall to much more informal confidentiality than he had Smythe.

Preparations were now afoot for the 1895 Leeds Festival, arranged as usual for early October. Appointed once more as conductor, Sullivan duly met the united chorus for the first time on 16 March when he took a rehearsal in Leeds. (They had previously rehearsed in their component units in different Yorkshire towns.) On the London scene he was now rarely to be seen as a conductor, but when Manns was indisposed he took charge of a Crystal Palace Saturday concert on 30 March at which his old friend Joachim was the soloist. The great violinist was now 63 but his performance of Beethoven's Violin Concerto remained, according to the *Musical Times*, 'an unrivalled interpretation of the greatest work of its class'. With no comment to make on the composer's conducting of his own *Macbeth* overture, the reviewer noted that Schumann's Symphony no. 4 in D minor 'was played carefully rather than impressively under Sir Arthur Sullivan's direction'.

He soon left England again: it was from Paris that he wrote to Manns on 12 April congratulating him on recovery from that indisposition and recalling that on that same day 33 years ago Manns had given *The Tempest* its second performance, a week after its first. 'How much do I not owe to you, my dear old friend, for the helping hand you gave me to mount the *first* step of the ladder! I shall always think of you with gratitude and affection.'[1]

Sullivan was again to acknowledge that debt by accepting a directorship in the Crystal Palace Company in October 1898.[2] It was recognized as a strengthening of its management at a time of financial difficulties.

During the summer of 1895, Sullivan had his London flat redecorated and partly refurnished, leaving his nephew in charge (and Clotilde in residence) while he himself took a country house: it was Meadowbank at Winkfield, near Windsor, where he had stayed with Julius Reiss in 1887. A letter to 'Dear Bertie', dated 18 June 1895, begins quite in the humorous vein of his younger years, and goes on to give a rare glimpse of his domestic and working arrangements. The reference to a typed scenario probably looks ahead to *The Grand Duke*; the 'responsibility' in the opening sentence probably refers to Fanny Ronalds. Walter Pallant, later referred to, was a City stockjobber whose literary or theatrical views were evidently valued.

I hope you and your responsibility got home safely and in good time. We got on very well until we got into the middle of Winkfield parish and there we lost our way. Not a soul to be seen nor a house visible.

But arriving at a dismal-looking lodge which looked uninhabited, we shouted and made a row until a woman's head appeared. Evidently we had aroused her out of bed. The fair creature (about 65) gave us sufficient information to put us on our right way and we got here about 9.30. The party were all at their after-dinner coffee. After a successful turn at besique, we all went to bed about a quarter to 12. The 'party' is (or are) Russie [Walker], A. Wagg, Ernest Dresden, Gaston Foâ, Paul Hardy and your long-suffering and affectionate uncle.

No sign of rain today – we shall have bad fields, I fear [i.e., not many entries for the races at Ascot], as few people like to run their horses on such hard ground.

1. Will you send or take the two typewritten acts of the scenario to Walter Pallant – they are on the table or in a basket. Tell him I will discuss them with him on Friday night. Look at Inglis' card (on the mantleshelf) and let me know what our dinner is on Friday – I don't know whether it is 8 or 8.15 or 8.30.
2. As soon as the corridor is re-papered (the side bit, I mean) get a bookshelf moved there and arrange the books etc. That will be one job for our hands. The cigar cupboard fixed will be two jobs ('for our hands' understood, as the Latin grammar hath it).
3. Get as much paper and envelopes as you can into the Chippendale stationery case and wrap up the large folio letter-paper, so that it doesn't get dirty. If you can dispose of the contents of another basket somewhere, so as to let me have another one for letters etc, I shall be glad. They are useful and keep the writing-table clear.
4. Go to one of your big City stationers and see what is to be had in the way of a stationery case for my table. I want a *large* one, with not too many silly divisions in it (they make the divisions either just too large or just too small for the paper generally) and which has a cover of some sort – either shutters or a flap to keep the dust out. It needn't have a lock and key, but it must be large and commodious, holding (as you know) letter paper, notepaper, two or three sizes of envelopes (*my* envelopes and paper of course) and also the long envelopes I use. Perhaps it may also take in foolscap. I don't lay any stress upon dainty extras in the way of drawers, trays, stamp boxes etc – they are unnecessary – but try and find me a good large *useful* one, such as you know I should like. I don't mind whether it is in oak or mahogany or what the wood is.
5. Look after the 'expédition' [sending away] of the garden produce. Fruit, vegetables and flowers (send the roses, never mind how big) to *Grandma* (it pleases the old lady to have them addressed to *her*)
Uncle John, 100 Edith Grove,
Mrs Dremel [his mother's old friend], and
Smythe [former secretary]
Did you write to Findon for me? You might also send his wife a small hamper if the things can be spared. I love to give away to my friends – half the enjoyment of a garden consists in that. And I know Clotilde thinks as I do, about not *wasting* things.
6. If you hear of any dead certainties, wire to me, 'The Iron Stand, Ascot Racecourse', between 1 and 5. But I should not rely too implicitly upon Adler's or Beira's racing tips!

7. I hope Clotilde did not sleep in her own room last night. I told her to sleep in one of the downstairs rooms until hers was quite ready again. I will write to her tomorrow to give her instructions about two or three things.

Now I will dress. I am writing this early in the morning, as there is no chance of writing during any other part of the day, with this rowdy lot about me!

Did you think Clotilde's idea of a boat-stand with a cover to it, placed lengthwards, and a gate is feasible? I must think it out. Good morning.

Later in that summer Sullivan moved to another rented property in the half-rural Thames Valley area – River House, Walton-on-Thames. From there on 8 August 1895 he wrote apologetically to the composer and conductor Eduard Strauss (the youngest brother of Johann) who was visiting London. The letter was originally in German:

To my horror, I have found under a pile of papers some unopened letters, one of yours among them! What can you think of me, and what a dreadful opinion you must have of my politeness!

I do hope, however, my dear Herr Strauss, that you will not believe I would *wilfully* be guilty of such rudeness, or fail to reciprocate your friendliness. I can only ask your forgiveness, and assure you that I am truly sorry about this unfortunate incident. I have indeed many times thought of coming to London to make your acquaintance, but my work keeps me tied here, and every time that I have to go to the city it disturbs those few ideas I have left.

I did have the opportunity when we were both at Alfred Rothschild's, but during the performance (after dinner) I felt unwell and had to lie down; then, when I came down again, you had already gone. So, as far as you are concerned, I've been really unlucky! How much longer are you staying in England? I would so like to see you at some time and have a chat about music, and Vienna, and Wiener Schnitzel, etc.

Could you, perhaps, if you're not doing anything else, come for a couple of hours next Sunday [11 August]? I'm not very far from London.

Take the train at 2 o'clock from *Waterloo Station* (main line) to *Walton*, which arrives at a *quarter to three*. I'll meet you there. Stay for dinner at 8 o'clock, and I'll take you back to London at *10 o'clock*. No evening dress or white tie – just 'habille de campagne' [*sic*].

I don't know if your wife is with you, but if she is, I hope she will give me the pleasure and come with you, *sans cérémonie*. Write me a short note, and answer 'yes', not 'no'.[3]

Whether the two actually did meet is not, apparently, recorded. Evidently the company at Alfred Rothschild's musical soirées was so numerous, and the hospitality so informal, that two celebrated musicians could be present without being introduced to each other.

Carte, whatever his disappointment over *Utopia Limited*, evidently hankered to put Gilbert and Sullivan back in double harness. After some diplomatic manoeuvring he succeeded in getting Gilbert to offer Sullivan the plot on which he was working, one in which three different elements of comedy would coalesce. There was the involvement of a dramatic company in a situation where its members would be required (as in *Thespis*!) to play 'real-life' roles; there was the poking of fun at foreign names and the pretensions of little German principalities; and there was the fanciful invention of a 'statutory duel' – the resolution of a quarrel by the drawing of cards, the winner taking the loser's position and the loser becoming (as a later age would put it) a non-person.

The Grand Duke, or The Statutory Duel, as the piece was eventually to be titled, had a large cast and a particularly complicated plot. Carte's company was still under long-term contract: it included two useful but not particularly distinguished sopranos, Florence Perry and Emmie Owen, who had acquitted themselves well in *Utopia*. Also, for the first time, a star soprano had been engaged whose native tongue was not English. Ilka von Palmay was a Hungarian who had won success at Drury Lane in the Saxe-Coburg company's production of Zeller's operetta, *Der Vogelhändler* ('The Bird-Seller').[4] She had already played Gilbert and Sullivan's parts in German – indeed, appearing in *The Mikado* variously as Yum-Yum *and* as Nanki-Poo until Sullivan forced the management to cancel the *travesti* casting. The new piece would eventually take positive and paradoxical advantage of her foreign accent: she would play the part of an *English* comedienne in a German theatrical troupe.

But originally, as shown by a letter written by Sullivan to Gilbert on 10 August 1895, the role of the English comedienne was unthought-of. Of two sopranos playing the roles of principal young (German) actresses in the troupe, Palmay was to be the sprightly soubrette, Elsa. The other (yet to be chosen) would play the demure *ingénue*, Lisa, who would carry the serious love-interest. An older woman's part (the Countess von Krakenfeldt) would be given, as usual, to Rosina Brandram, the contralto. A fourth principal female part, that of the young Princess of Monaco, would appear in the second act only. But this casting was now subjected, in the hands of composer and librettist themselves, to a bewilderingly complex process of switching and juggling. The draft of a letter from Sullivan (the finished copy does not survive) gives musical reasons for his initial dissatisfaction.

I have made out a rough music plot of your sketch, as I always do, by which you will see that, as it stands at present, there is scarcely anything for Elsa to do. It is however an advantage, as it gives you a *tabula rasa* to work upon, according to the special qualifications of the actress and singer who is to play the part.

I am going to make a startling suggestion with regard to the cast, which although you may not see your way to accept it, I am sure you will not reject without considering it, as it is for a purely musical reason I make it. It will turn very difficult musical situations into very easy ones for me.

How would it be to make *Lisa* the principal soprano part (Palmay) and make Brandram, Elsa? She might be the leading tragedy lady of Ludwig's company, or the contralto of the troupe, not necessarily old, but staid and earnest, a suitable wife for the manager, and from whose mouth the theatrically high-flown sentiments of romantic plays would come very forcibly. Then see what an advantage this is to me.

In all the concerted music [involving these two] we should have a soprano and a contralto, instead of two sopranos, and in all concerted pieces where Countess Krakenfeldt is the only female we get a soprano [the singer originally allotted to the *ingénue* part] instead of a contralto. This would make the thing run as easy as possible for me, for I assure you that I am at my wit's end sometimes to deal with concerted pieces that have no middle part – i.e. no tenor or contralto . . .

In this letter Sullivan's politeness – even over-politeness – was obviously intended to avoid provocation at all costs. The same circumspection is shown in the letter which Gilbert sent next day:

Of course I quite understand that it would greatly simplify matters for you if Lisa were a soprano and Elsa a contralto – but can't this advantage be secured without such a mortal disruption as your suggestion would involve? To make the ingenue part a (more or less) comic old woman, and to turn the (more or less) comic old woman into a young girl – taking, moreover, the leading characteristics of Lisa and giving them to Elsa and leaving Lisa a colourless soprano and nothing else, would, I am afraid, involve a total reconstruction and consequently great loss of time – to the manifest detriment of the story. Certainly let Lisa be the leading soprano and Elsa the contralto, but (I suggest) not an elderly and plain contralto but a young, pretty and sympathetic girl. Such a girl (perhaps a mezzo would do?) would not be difficult to find. Then Brandram could play the Countess (who ought certainly to be middle-aged and plain – though not ugly) and Perry the Princess of Monaco.

So Palmay would now play Lisa; a mezzo-soprano yet to be engaged would play Elsa; and Brandram would have her usual 'heavy' characterization as the Countess. On Monday morning, 12 August, Sullivan called on D'Oyly and Helen Carte, secured their assent to the change, and apparently wrote to Gilbert to inform him so.

But then, back at his temporary home in Walton-on-Thames, Sullivan immediately took it into his head to propose a *further* change – to let Brandram play neither the Countess nor Elsa, but Lisa, whose love-interest would have to be transferred elsewhere. Though the full documentation of correspondence is missing at this point, it appears that Sullivan telegraphed Gilbert with the new proposal, received a reply which he took for an assent, and only *then* proceeded to tell the Cartes – first by telegram, then by a letter which enclosed a letter from Gilbert. No wonder the Cartes, having supposed on Monday that arrangements were watertight, were aghast to find them undone on Wednesday! Helen Carte, telegraphing back to Sullivan, evidently thought that Sullivan and Gilbert had not really understood each other's intentions:

LETTER RECEIVED BUT FEAR IT MAKES MATTERS WORSE AND MUCH REGRET YOU TELE-GRAPHED GILBERT WITHOUT COMMUNICATING FIRST WITH US AS PROMISED. THE PROPOSED ARRANGEMENT UPSETS EVERYTHING INCLUDING PALMAY ENGAGEMENT ALTOGETHER. PALMAY WOULD BE IMPOSSIBLE AS THE SYMPATHETIC INGENUE ELSA AND GILBERT CLEARLY CONVEYS THAT THE COUNTESS WOULD NOT FIT PERRY WHOM HE OBVIOUSLY INTENDS FOR ELSA. THIS MEANS THAT EITHER YOU MUST BE CONTENT WITH PERRY AS YOUR SOPRANO OR ELSE THAT SHE PLAYS THE SMALL PART IN SECOND ACT AND OWEN IS SHELVED ENTIRELY AS GILBERT DOES NOT CONSIDER OWEN SUITED TO ELSA AND IN EITHER CASE WE LEAVE OUT PALMAY. MOREOVER GILBERT EVIDENTLY INTENDS MAKING BRANDRAM MORE GROTESQUE AND LAUGHED-AT IN [THE PART OF] ELSA THAN SHE WOULD HAVE BEEN IN THE COUNTESS. TELEGRAPH ME IMMEDIATELY EXPLAINING WHAT YOU REALLY MEAN ABOUT THE CAST AS IT IS QUITE IMPOSSIBLE WE CAN CONFIRM UNLESS EVERYTHING IS CLEAR ABOUT THE PROPER EMPLOYMENT OF THESE ARTISTS. MONDAY ALL WAS SATISFACTORY NOW ALL IS CONFUSED. PLEASE WIRE GILBERT IMMEDIATELY SAYING THAT ON CONSIDERATION YOU PREFER REVERTING TO THE FORMER ARRANGEMENT.

She followed it on the same day with a letter making the same point with greater detail of explanation and a marked degree of reproach:

You will remember that on Monday morning I begged you never again *until all questions were settled* to send off important letters or telegrams to Mr Gilbert without giving us a chance of consulting with you first. You remember that D'Oyly and I (I especially) have had over *six months* of arduous and most anxious correspondence and interviews to bring about what has now happened – and what I knew you wished – and now that in consequence things are in train for a real settlement surely it is not asking much that you should not send off important communications to Mr Gilbert involving us without giving us a chance of expressing our opinions – especially when they are diametrically opposite to what we have clearly arranged with you at our last meeting. It would seem to me that simply because Mr Gilbert agreed to a suggestion of yours as to Brandram playing Lisa (a suggestion which you will recall you made *without* consulting us at all) you thought no more of what was to be done with the rest of the cast but instantly expressed yourself delighted.

It is indeed hard to resist the conclusion that Sullivan had bungled matters – and at this point the Cartes' managerial persuasiveness was strong enough to reassert the basic original casting. Brandram would revert to her 'heavy' role as the Countess, and Palmay would earn her star's pay with a brilliant soubrette part – but neither as Lisa nor as Elsa; the newly invented part of Julia Jellicoe solved the difficulty. The parts of Lisa and Elsa were telescoped into one: the character was actually named Elsa in the first printing of the libretto (made by Gilbert for the eventual rehearsals), but she became Lisa when Florence Perry played the part in the production itself – in which, confusingly, a different 'Elsa' appeared as a purely subsidiary role.

The composer's diary has few entries for this period, either about the composition of *The Grand Duke* or about anything else. The preparations and performances of the 1895 Leeds Festival intervened before the new opera was ready. The dating of the festival gave Sullivan and his committee a commemorative opportunity. The 200th anniversary of Purcell's death (21 November 1695) was widely marked. At the Royal College of Music, *Dido and Aeneas* was staged in a performance under Stanford's baton that marked the beginning of its modern revival. At the Philharmonic Society, Mackenzie conducted an all-Purcell programme in which the so-called 'Golden Sonata', originally for two violins and continuo, was incredibly performed in an arrangement for two pianos and orchestra. Leeds botched the opportunity. A new ode by Parry to words by Robert Bridges, *Invocation to Music*, was vaguely linked to the tercentenary, but Purcell himself was represented only by a choral snatch from his *King Arthur* ('Come if you dare', with Hirwan Jones as tenor soloist).

The choice of Handel's *Messiah* to open the festival on 2 October occasioned some surprise: as an entire work it had been absent from festival programmes for 21 years, doubtless on the ground that it was sufficiently to be heard on other occasions. Greater still was the surprise when Sullivan insisted that such a well-known work should be properly rehearsed by orchestra and soloists.[5] But if that insistence arose from artistic scruple, such scruple seemed to be absent in Sullivan's 'lopping off' the orchestral *ritornelli* at the end of some of the arias and choruses, including 'For unto us a child is born' and 'Behold the lamb of God'. It is true that in solo numbers such orchestral endings were liable in those days to be interrupted by applause for the singers, but their curtailment was 'a feature as objectionable as it was unusual' in the eyes of the *Monthly Musical Record* and others. The critics were less ready to comment on the apparent absurdity of imposing cuts on *The Flying Dutchman* (in English) in order that it could be preceded, in the same concert, by Mendelssohn's 'Italian' Symphony!

Much gratified fuss was made over the presence at the festival of the Prince of Wales and of his sister Princess Louise. The latter, together with her husband the Marquis of Lorne, were house-guests of Sullivan in the Judges' Lodgings, which the city corporation had again placed at his disposal. Of his own works not only *The Golden Legend* was given (with Emma Albani, Edward Lloyd and Watkin Mills participating in what was acknowledged an outstandingly good perform-ance) but also the confrontation scene for Rebecca and the Templar from *Ivanhoe* (with two American soloists, Medora Henson and David Bispham). Beethoven's *Mass in D* was revived. From the pen of Massenet, whom Sullivan had commended to the festival some years before, came a newly commissioned symphonic poem called *Visions* which was unanimously condemned as mere sweepings from the composer's studio floor. If what the festival committee had hoped for was praise for the chorus, then they were rewarded – but not for much else.

Certainly the festival gave no enhancement to Sullivan's reputation as a conductor. Just as the choirs had once warmed to the vigour of Barnby, now they responded to the geniality of Parry (who conducted his own *Invocation to Music*). Sullivan's style of conducting was now widely recognized as old-fashioned. It did not project a personality. Even the *Athenaeum*, intending a compliment in its review of the 1895 festival, would write only that Sullivan 'conducted throughout with calmness and judgement'. The critic of *The World* drew an openly unfavourable comparison – mentioning Hermann Levi and Felix Mottl, two conductors who (like Richter) came wearing the mantle of the Bayreuth Festival:

We are so spoilt with our Richters and Levis and Mottls and Nikisches that Sir Arthur Sullivan sitting at his desk no longer impresses. . . . Bands are now more used to more guidance than his undernourished beat can give, and the conductor whose eye is so much on his score is at a disadvantage.

In sitting to conduct, Sullivan was only transferring to the concert-hall what was (and is) accepted in the opera-house. It may be, though it was never claimed, that it was a necessary consequence of his physical weakness. Singled out by Hanslick in his dismissive notice of Sullivan a decade since, the seated posture was hardly to be found among other leading conductors on the English scene. In marked contrast was the vigorous image presented by the young Henry Wood, who in this very summer (August 1895) had begun his conductorship of the

Promenade Concerts in the recently opened Queen's Hall and who even modelled his bearded appearance on that of Arthur Nikisch.

The festival hired its orchestral players, as usual, from London. But in Leeds's neighbouring city the Bradford Permanent Orchestra (probably with a substantial amateur component) detained Sullivan with the compliment of a programme consisting entirely of his own music, which he conducted on 12 October – afterwards receiving the tribute of two pieces of plate.[6] The slow movement from the youthful Symphony in E was on the programme: that he should have allowed the work to be quarried in this manner argues that his own faith in the complete symphony had diminished. In the event, apparently through non-arrival of parts, it was not played. *In Memoriam*, the *Ballo* overture, the *Imperial March* and extracts from *The Light of the World*, *The Martyr of Antioch*, *The Golden Legend*, and the music to *Henry VIII* were heard. The Bradford Festival Choral Society participated along with William Thornton and the young Clara Butt: she also sang (and was encored in) *The Lost Chord*.

To help span the gap while *The Grand Duke* was being prepared, Carte revived *The Mikado* on 6 November 1895 – a highly successful revival, not least because Rutland Barrington as Pooh-Bah, Jessie Bond as Pitti-Sing, and Rosina Brandram as Katisha were on hand to play their original roles.[7] Florence Perry (and not Gilbert's protégée, Nancy McIntosh) played Yum-Yum, with Walter Passmore as Ko-ko, Scott Fishe as the Mikado, and Charles Kenningham as Nanki-Poo. The audience was additionally gratified by seeing Sullivan conduct the first night.

Almost immediately after that reopening, Sullivan was off to Berlin: at last the Berlin Court Opera was to give *Ivanhoe*.[8] A translation had been made by Dr Carlotta, and the work was fortunate enough to be placed in the hands of such a fine conductor as Karl Muck (First *Kapellmeister* of the theatre since 1892). But the other portents were not good. To Bendall, Sullivan wrote from the Hotel Bristol, Berlin, on 16 November, thanking him for forwarding the most recent accounts (relating to *The Mikado*):

The first week's Savoy returns are very satisfactory. I do hope they will keep up, for everyone's sake. We have not been at all lucky at the theatre for some years and it is time luck turned.

Bad luck still pursues *Ivanhoe* here. [*Note in the margin*: Two nice active heroines – Rebecca a sprained knee and Rowena acute lumbago!] I am not sanguine about the success at all. . . . None of them except King Richard have two-pennyworth of voice, nor can they sing. The chorus is awful. . . . They tell me they have spent 70,000 marks [£3,500] on the production but I told Pierson [the administrative director] today, I don't see more than 20,000 at present. The most satisfactory part is the orchestra and the excellent little conductor, Dr Muck. . . . I don't go out of an evening here, and employ my time at the second act of the new opera [*The Grand Duke*, evidently still being composed or revised].

In his diary he noted that *The Chieftain* had been successfully produced (as *Der Häuptling*) at the Burgtheater, Munich, on 12 November. To 'Bertie' in a letter of 16 November he wrote that the projected opening of *Ivanhoe* had been postponed

for a week. Despite the desire for his presence in London he would have to stay in
Berlin, for the Emperor was to attend the dress rehearsal, and the public

like the excitement of seeing the composer at the first performance and of throwing him
bouquets or rotten eggs. . . . I want to make my little friend Dr Muck (pronounce *Mouck*
please!), the conductor who has set up my work here, a present . . .

On Tuesday 26 November *Ivanhoe* had its first – and last – German
production. The revision to which the score had been subjected was to no avail,
and the work failed with both the public and the critics.[9] In the authoritative
Allgemeine Musik-Zeitung a severe judgment was pronounced by Otto Lessmann
– the very critic whose favourable view of English music, in opposition to
Hanslick's, had been paraded in England.

To this deplorable concoction [the libretto], the talented composer of *The Mikado* has
written music that is so negative and dreary in invention, so conventional in its make-up,
so destitute of any sort of originality, that it can worthily stand beside the libretto. A great
deal of industry, a great deal of care and attention, and – above all – a great deal of money
vanished in the performance; but, in spite of the marvellous staging (and the useless
dedication of the conductor) the opera was irredeemable. . . . The splendid sets could,
perhaps, be used in *Marschner's Der Templer und die Jüdin*, where the same subject is
treated. That would be no bad exchange.

No less sharp was the edge of Eugen von Pirani's review in the (Leipzig) *Neue
Zeitschrift für Musik*. In the issue of 1 January 1896 he noted the 'cool, icy
reception' by the audience, called the story 'a chaos' and made few exceptions in
censuring the individual numbers. King Richard's 'I ask not wealth nor
courtier's praise' was 'no drinking-song but an oratorio aria'; Friar Tuck's 'Ho
jolly Jenkin' was as a 'chansonette' from the domain of operetta and an indication
of where the composer's true talent lay. No blame was laid on the performers: of
them the critic had 'only good things to say', and praised Muck's skill in bringing
off effectively 'even the weakest numbers of the opera'.

In his diary Sullivan left no note of his reaction – whether of anger or of
disappointment – to Berlin's reception of *Ivanhoe*. One person who did not lose
faith in Sullivan was, evidently, the royal official in charge of the opera house,
Count Bolko von Hochberg. In the last year of Sullivan's life *The Mikado* would
be presented there as a royal command performance (10 June 1900), a quite
exceptional excursion into operetta in a theatre devoted to 'serious' opera. The
prompting may have come from higher still: William II retained his boyhood
admiration for the English composer (p. 165). Was the invitation an astute
diplomatic gesture amid the growing hostility between the two countries, fanned
by German support for the Boers in the Transvaal?

On 28 January 1896 the death of Joseph Barnby robbed Sullivan of his oldest
and closest friend in the musical profession. The playing of the *In Memoriam*
overture was the tribute of the Philharmonic Society at its first concert of the year
on 21 February, conducted by Mackenzie. From that same season, at last, the
Philharmonic was persuaded to adopt the low 'Continental' pitch to which

Barnby had nailed his colours 27 years before. The Queen's Hall concerts also adopted it, the Leeds Festival under the complacent Sullivan remaining an outpost of the older and (for singers) cruel high pitch.

As the date neared for the opening of *The Grand Duke*, Anglo-German hostility was rising. On the defeat of the 'Jameson raid', an irregular British foray into Boer territory, the German emperor compounded the British humiliation by telegraphing his congratulations to Kruger, the Boer president. It would hardly have been surprising if Gilbert had added some anti-German political acid to the libretto of *The Grand Duke* by the date of its emergence at the Savoy on 7 March. But in fact he diluted the acid that was already there. A first printing of the text, used for rehearsal, had named the Grand-Duke as Wilhelm and described him as 'of German royalty a sprig': in the final version he was Rudolph, the reference to 'German royalty' disappeared, and in the next line he became 'a miserable prig' instead of 'a miserable pig'.

John Wolfson (*Final Curtain*) sees such changes as deliberately prompted: 'There must have been someone whom Gilbert was trying not to offend'. Perhaps it was Sullivan himself who suggested that such references might be taken as a decidedly discourteous response on *his* part to the patronage of 'German royalty' (in the person of a Wilhelm!) at Berlin. Wolfson's hypothesis of an intentionally malicious resemblance between the speech of Ilka von Palmay's Julia Jellicoe and that of Queen Victoria falls to the ground because the Queen did *not*, as he supposes, speak 'heavily accented English'.[10]

In its name, the grand duchy of Pfennig-Halbpfennig ('penny-ha'penny') exemplified the petty meanness of its ruler. His life threatened by political conspiracy, the Grand Duke contrives to be the loser in a 'statutory duel' – the winner being Ludwig, leader of the theatrical troupe, who takes over the royal duties and is confronted by unexpected matrimonial complications. (The Princess of Monaco had been betrothed to the Grand Duke in infancy – a rather obvious borrowing from *Princess Ida*.) Matters are restored when it is discovered that the duel has been wrongly conducted, an ace having been reckoned as the highest instead of the lowest card.

It was the most heartless and mechanical of all Gilbert's works for Sullivan. Such extravagances as the love-potion in *The Sorcerer* or the gallery of ghosts in *Ruddigore* still left room for the play of genuine tenderness and the arousal – even through laughter – of genuine sympathy; but in *The Grand Duke* contrivance is all, and the pairing of male and female characters at the end is like tidying the board after a game. Even the contrivance itself is not water-tight, since the conspiracy to dethrone the Grand Duke, a vital motive to the plot at first, is forgotten by the end. (So is the comic signal of eating a sausage roll.) A weakening of artistic resolve must have caused Sullivan to accept a plot and a treatment which in earlier years he would have rejected as lacking in those genuine human feelings to which his music responded so happily.

Instead, Sullivan's best contributions had to be of other kinds. There was the clever pomposity of the march (in 3/4 time!) as the theatrical company paraded in their new role as the grand-ducal retinue, in their pseudo-Greek costumes from *Troilus and Cressida*; there were the catchy 6/8 tunes to which the Baroness celebrated the joys of feasting at someone else's expense ('Come bumpers, aye ever so many') and the Herald announced the arrival of the Princess of Monte Carlo and her father. For the Notary's song, revealing the procedure of the Statutory Duel, Sullivan hit upon a particularly fetching, though straightforward, solo-and-refrain tune in which the refrain incorporated a delightful descant.

'Success great and genuine, I think', wrote Sullivan in a diary entry for 7 March which ended 'Thank God opera is finished and out'. A decided asset to the cast, as usual, was Rutland Barrington, looking grotesque and immense as Ludwig: mocking the incongruities of the theatre, Gilbert had specified a huge Louis Quatorze wig with classical Greek garb below. Ilka von Palmay was a success, too: she had 'a pleasing voice of rare freshness' (according to the *Musical Standard*) 'and her acting quite lifted the piece when she was on the stage'. Walter Passmore as the Grand Duke did well in what was obviously the 'Grossmith' part of the Grand Duke (alias, one might say, King Gama). But it was not enough. The liberal encores demanded on the first night and the favourable judgment of most reviewers belied the wider public's reaction. *The Grand Duke* ran for only 123 performances, almost exactly half the total for *Utopia*; it was more significant in 1896 that Stanford's *Shamus O'Brien* (a 'straight' comic opera, not an operetta) achieved no less than 100 performances in a continuous run.

The Grand Duke was the last joint work of W. S. Gilbert and Arthur Sullivan. After conducting the first performance, the composer hastened yet again to Monte Carlo. From there on 12 March, five days after the première, he wrote to his old friend Burnand: 'Why reproach me? I didn't write the book! . . . I arrived here yesterday dead beat, and feel better already. Another week's rehearsal with W.S.G. and I should have gone raving mad. I had already ordered some straw for my hair.'

Carte, in whose management his wife pursued her active role, was not taken unprepared by the failure. Without missing a single night at the Savoy he brought back *The Mikado*. Unflagging popularity carried it to its 1,000th London performance. Sullivan had once again gone abroad – this time he was in Switzerland – so the appropriate celebration was deferred until the 1,037th performance at the Savoy. There, on 31 October 1896, the composer conducted his score and afterwards appeared on stage with Gilbert to acknowledge the applause. (Carte, it was announced, was too ill to appear.) A 'Gilbert and Sullivan Birthday Book' was presented to every member of the audience, and the theatre was festooned with British, American and Japanese decorations.

He had left Walton-on-Thames on 22 July for his Swiss holiday, travelling to Basle in the company of David Seligman and his wife and Adolph Hirsch. The recent extension of the Swiss railway system enabled him to travel all the way by train to his favoured resort, Thusis. Later, at St Moritz, he 'made a mess' (as he put it in a letter home to his nephew) of Mrs Ronalds's birthday in August. '

thought it was the 29th and it is the 23rd'. On the correct day she sent him a poem headed 'In remembrance' and signed 'L.W.'. It ended:

> If I have ever made you glad,
> Have ever made one single hour
> Pass brightlier than else it had,
> Have planted in your life one flower –
> If I have ever had such power,
> I cannot now be wholly sad.

There is a gracefulness in these words of resignation which transcends Sullivan's 'made a mess'. Mary Frances Ronalds was not, in a formal sense, separated from Arthur Sullivan – since, in a formal sense, she was never united with him. Nor did he ever cease to maintain a solicitous responsibility for her. But the close companionship was over, and since it was she who had basked in *his* sun it must have been she that felt the cold.

34 Jubilee

LONDON 'society' had bestowed its favour on St Moritz as a summer resort, and the Duke and Duchess of York (the future King George V and Queen Mary) were among the congenial company which Sullivan found there. 'The great majority of tourists,' as the Baedeker of that pre-skiing era pointed out, 'visit Switzerland between the middle of July and the end of September.' The attractions of St Moritz, the highest village in the Engadine (6,000 feet) were not confined to its bracing atmosphere and picturesque situation. There were also the famous mineral baths, a short walk's distance from the village, with luxury hotel nearby. But medical treatment is not indicated in the letter written from St Moritz to 'Bertie' on 22 August 1896, which shows that Clotilde had been a previous recipient of the composer's confidential correspondence. The two were now living at River House, Walton-on-Thames, which Sullivan had rented for a second summer.

Acting on your admirable suggestion, I haven't written much to you, as I knew Clotilde would share my news with you. There has not been much news to share, for here 'one day resembleth another' except in the matter of weather, and there is a delirious dullness in the life generally. I get up in the morning (before I go out even), breakfast, read *The Times* and *Telegraph*, and then stroll about till lunchtime, if it doesn't pour. Out again from lunch to dinner-time, if it doesn't pour – then the regular Swiss hotel evening, sitting in the large hall, smoking, talking, and passing the time until we come up into my sitting room, for an hour's chat before going to bed. When it rains, it does so conscientiously – never ceasing, even for meals. The first three days (Sunday, Monday, Tuesday) of this week were divine. The sun shone brilliantly and gave warmth, whilst there was a crystal sort of coldness in the air which made one feel 21 again, and ready to walk up to the top of the Alter Spitz before breakfast . . .

I am now all alone. Adolph Hirsch left last Monday for England (business, he *says*, but I think for private matters from what he hinted to me). This morning Mr and Mrs Seligman departed. I am very sorry, for they are such dear nice people and I shall miss them dreadfully. I stay on here on account of the air, for although it is miserable when wet yet one day of sunshine and crisp air makes amends. I have a few *hotel acquaintances* whom I don't cultivate much, and I know the Royalties and suite, Leo Rothschild and his wife. I dined with the L.R.'s last night at this hotel and had a most delightful evening, sat between the Duchess of Teck [the Duchess of York's mother] and Lady Ampthill. We all went downstairs to the hotel ball afterwards. Also the Labouchères, Ch[arles] Wyndham and Mary Moore, Mrs Parkinson Shape and others are here, but I don't run after them, and our own little set here was much pleasanter.

'I shall perhaps go on to Maloja on Monday for a day or two, as the Bancrofts and Pineros are there, but if the rainy weather lasts I shall go back to Lucerne, and stay at Bürgenstock or the Rigi. I don't want to come back to England yet; and shall not go back

Walton[-on-Thames] in any case. And this brings me to a matter upon which, my dear
boy, I must talk to you seriously. River House is lovely, and the place suits me admirably,
but I have not had the enjoyment out of it that I looked forward to. One of the great
pleasures of a place like that is to ask one's friends to stay a day or two, or even to dine and
sleep only. But I have observed that although I let you stay the whole summer or autumn
with me, and use the house as if it were your own, you have degrees of courtesy and
welcome for my friends. If you like them, well and good. If not, you show it in too marked
manner to please me. I need not indicate in more detailed manner what or whom I mean,
because your intelligence renders it unnecessary. But I have noticed it ever since I took the
house and *I don't like it.* And the same thing I am sorry to say applies to others in the house.
Their likes and dislikes are shown too plainly in the manner my guests are treated and
served. I am not speaking so much of the past three months because the circumstances
were exceptional, but it has always been so. Consequently you will not be surprised that I
wish so much to get rid of River House, and that I don't mean to return to it.

I learn from Clotilde's letter that Mr Bendall was very rudely treated by her and by you
too: he certainly did not complain, as you will see by the cutting from his letter I enclose.
But *I* resent it. I gave him a pressing invitation to go down when he liked, and he has never
yet gone down without proposing himself beforehand. When you received his letter (I
learn all this from Clotilde) and told Clotilde, which you probably forgot to do, she should
have wired saying that it was not convenient for various domestic reasons and asking him
to change the day of his visit. If he was *not* put off, he should have been made welcome. I
have long noticed that you appear anything but friendly to Bendall. I suppose it is because
he attends to all my business with the greatest devotion and regularity, and you can't when
entrust anything to you. When I left, Adolph [Hirsch] authorized you to get any calls
that might be made in my absence paid at his office. You got *one* paid (Claridge's) and
wired the fact to me, and that seems to have exhausted your energy, for the next one that
came (Riverside Orange Co: Deb[entures]) you returned to Bendall after keeping it a
week, without a word, and so he has sent it on to me. Have you paid the other smaller ones
that I left on the table at River House, and did you get the transfer made of 50 Menzies
Crusoe to Louis? I know you would not willingly neglect anything which I asked you
to do, but, my dear boy, forgetfulness and thoughtlessness are not cardinal virtues, are
they? . . .

I read in the papers here that a most striking looking, professional beauty had been seen
bathing at Blankenbergh and all that was known of her was that her clothes (which
someone peeped at in the bathing-machine) were marked C.R.

Now goodbye, my love to Clotilde and to all the 'family'.

The gossip about the bather on the Belgian coast at Blankenbergh[e] was most
unusual for Sullivan. The 'professional beauties', so called, were 'an elite group
of England's most beautiful women, whose photographs were sold in shops all
over the country' (see Ralph G. Martin, *Jennie*, 1969), of whom Lady Randolph
Churchill was one. Among other personages named by Sullivan, Charles
Wyndham was an eminent actor-manager (after whom Wyndham's Theatre is
named) and Mary Moore, the sister of the Savoy's Decima Moore, was his
leading lady; he was to marry her in 1916 after his first wife died. That Sullivan's
circle should extend to other rich and cultivated Jewish families besides the
Rothschilds and Sassoons is not surprising; David Seligman was a London
merchant banker, and his wife Sybil an amateur singer, pupil of Sullivan's friend
Tosti. She was to become the intimate of Puccini in the years after 1900.

Leaving St Moritz: on 1 September, Sullivan did proceed (as his letter had predicted) to Lucerne, but stayed at the Hotel National. In those peaceful lakeside surroundings he formed an affectionate relationship with a young Englishwoman:

Dear Miss Violet,
What do you and yours propose doing? Shall we sit under the trees, or lie on the grass, or saunter on the Promenade? Or shall we write a joint letter to your sister? What time do you wish to see me today? I will of course obey any order you may give.

Yours sincerely
A.S.

According to Leslie Baily (who published this letter for the first time in 1952 'Miss Violet' was just 20 and Sullivan proposed marriage to her. Baily did not disclose the identity of 'Miss Violet', from whom he got the story in 1947, nor did he specify any actual evidence, beyond the fragment of another letter from Sullivan: 'I am off in half an hour. It *was* painful last night. I couldn't stand it any longer, so I left. Yesterday was the most miserable day I ever spent.' According to Baily's informant the composer offered her 'a secret marriage' at a register office and told her he thought he had only two years to live: she would be the inheritor of all he possessed.

'Miss Violet' can now be identified as Violet Beddington, one of whose sisters ('your sister' in the letter quoted) was Sybil Seligman.[2] Violet later married the novelist Stephen Hudson (real name Sydney Schiff) – one of whose works, *Myrtle* (1925), has a chapter reproducing the relationship of a famous musical knight with an older woman ('Leonora' = Fanny Ronalds) and a younger one who, in Switzerland, refuses his proposal of marriage. The later friendship of the Schiffs with Katherine Mansfield, Proust and Stravinsky gives Sullivan a curious, if tenuous, link with an artistic world remote from his own.

After Switzerland Sullivan not only revisited Munich and Vienna but accepted an invitation to stay with the 'Empress Frederick' – the title by which Queen Victoria's eldest daughter was still known, though it was a decade since her husband had died. Two of her daughters were with her at this time, so Sullivan had the pleasure of a reunion at Kronberg Castle (in the Taunus mountain region) with his former 'Princess Yum-Yum' (Princess Victoria, now Princess Adolf of Schaumburg-Lippe) as well as Princess Sophie (Princess Louis of Hesse). 'Sat down ten to dinner. After dinner I sat at the piano and played all sorts of scraps to please Her Majesty.' Next day (24 September) he took the train from Frankfurt to Paris on his way home.

With Victoria of England he was not on such informal terms, but the approaching Diamond Jubilee would bring him into closer contact. It was taken for granted that as England's leading composer he would have a place in these celebrations, which were to reach their formal peak with services on Sunday 20 June 1897. He wrote a hymn-tune for that day, to words commissioned (at his suggestion) from William Walsham How, Bishop of Wakefield, beginning 'O king of kings, whose reign of old'. Now known as Bishopgarth, it was a weak tune, weakly harmonized: the repeated notes of 'Onward Christian Soldiers' were heard again, feebly. Sullivan rejected words submitted to him by the new Poet Laureate, Alfred Austin, for a national song.

His more substantial contribution to the jubilations was to be, surprisingly, a ballet score. Rather than remain in fog-laden London to compose it, he went with Clotilde in December 1896 to find a villa once again on his beloved French Riviera. (On 19 November 1896 at the Albert Hall he had conducted *The Golden Legend* for the last time.) He had again been ill and wanted 'to get out of the cold, as my poor kidneys won't stand much of the latter'. The Villa Mathilde at Beaulieu was chosen to be his rented home from late December right through the following spring: higher up the hill was the much grander house which Lord Salisbury had built as his own property. Louis proved handy to help prepare music-paper and Clotilde as Sullivan's partner in games of cards.

From there on 30 December he wrote to his nephew urging him to be kind to 'Auntie'.

I am so glad you have been a good deal to no. 7 and that you are in constant rapport by telephone and otherwise. You see, my dear Bertie, it is a very trying period of life for her. . . . In spite of misfortune, imprudence and jealousy, she kept [her social] influence for many years. Now, the years will tell, although her mind and spirits remain young, and this is a terrible time for any woman to go through. And so all of us who are really fond of her must be gentle and considerate.

The writing of a ballet score – it was to be called *Victoria and Merrie England* – was not merely in its musical nature different from his habitual operatic tasks. (He had written no independent ballet score since *L'Ile enchantée* in 1864.) It also took him into a less elevated theatrical world. The commission came from the Alhambra Theatre in Leicester Square, which for more than a decade had made a speciality of ballet and was now under the management of Alfred Moul. It had a resident choreographer, Carlo Coppi, and a resident musical director known as 'Monsieur' Georges Jacobi (he was of German birth but had developed his career in Paris). Not 'classical' ballets with music by Delibes or Tchaikovsky provided the Alhambra's fare, but a succession of newly choreographed works, for over 100 of which Jacobi composed or arranged the music himself. Invariably, the ballet was part of a long 'bill' otherwise made up of popular music-hall turns. Its genre has been summed up by Selwyn Tillett:

Always in a single act, the ballets were really mime-dramas, containing a large number of individual scenes and 'speciality' dances, with several grand tableaux (fights, shipwrecks and other visually startling dramatic effects). The rapid pace of the action did not allow time for the expansion of the more lyrical moments, so that although the ballets were not devoid of choreographic merit they contained little in the way of the romantic *pas-de-deux* or long solo passages.

Of the two nightly productions, one was normally an expressly comic adventure yarn, while the other had less plot but a good deal of patriotic sentiment and music; it also provided an excuse for the girls of the *corps de ballet* to parade *en travesti* in the bare essentials of military dress while revealing a substantial acreage of leg.[3]

To this specification Sullivan's work would conform, with a 'military' element which would indeed be female. In the penultimate scene a tableau-vivant would represent an actual painting of Victoria's coronation and in the final scene 'the four emblematic pedestal groups, representing EUROPE, ASIA, AFRICA AND AMERICA' would be 'exact reproductions of the sculptures on the base of the Albert Memorial, Hyde Park'.

His labours on this task in the clement climate of the Riviera left Sullivan with leisure for regular visits to the tables at Monte Carlo. His old friend Ernest Dresden and his newer friend Adolph Hirsch were in the area too. At a lunch party in Lord Salisbury's villa 'the Prince of Wales, Sir Edward Monson, and others were asked to have the honour of meeting me' (the jocular tone comes in a letter to 'Bertie'). On Easter Sunday came an opportunity to serve the Queen in person. She was at Cimiez, just outside Nice, in a hotel consequently renamed the Regina (and now an apartment block). Morning service was in a hotel room designated as a chapel, Sullivan playing a harmonium in place of an organ.

Letters sent back to Bendall in London show Sullivan's intention to quote national airs in the new ballet and also to re-use music from some of his own long-discarded scores. He had evidently been uncertain of the traditional tune of 'A fine old English gentleman', which was to be incorporated in a scene of Christmas cheer (Scene 6). The letter is dated 21 January 1897:

In business jargon – your favours to hand. I enclose a cheque for £200 for my L. & C. Bank account – please be *very* economical, not to say mean, in your payments, as I am as short as ever I was – I mean the 'ready'. Don't pay out a halfpenny more than you are compelled. The 'fine old English gentleman' was embodied into the ballet before your letter came, as I recollected it. Thanks all the same. I have received a wire from Moul asking me to stay my hand in Mistletoe Dance of Sixth Scene until I hear from him. I hope he is not going to alter much, as the whole scene is done, & is *very* good. He again appeals about the 3rd scene, but I think it is a mistake. I shan't bother about it yet in any case. I am going to M.C. [Monte Carlo] this afternoon to try and find a copyist. I hardly like trusting my only copy of the Sixth Scene to the post. If I can't find one, I must risk it & register it.

Music paper. Don't think of this any more. I bought all I want at Nice on Monday, and Louis rules the bars for me. I can also do without the bit from *The Sapphire Necklace* as I have a page or two of the score here – enough to show me the cast of the scoring. I want however the full score of [music quotation, see p. 418]: it was on my study table shortly before I left London. It is on *upright* paper and *not* in my handwriting. It was amongst all that music I brought upstairs, and is perhaps in the spare room. Send it registered. It has struck me that something – either score or band parts of the *Ile enchantée* – was saved from the Crystal Palace fire. Now I want you to set to work at once about it and find out.

You must get Manns to have a search made by West in the Crystal Palace Library, and at the same time tell Middleditch to ransack the library at Covent Garden, and if necessary you must see the mortgagee – Mr Faber I think it is. I am pretty well *certain* there is a set of band parts existing somewhere, and I believe they are in Covent Garden library. Tell Middleditch that I will make him a handsome present if he will search *thoroughly*. If they are found, wire me at once.

I have had a letter from old Adèle [his former maid], asking me if I had received her good wishes! That means she wants a hundred francs. *I* will send it from here. Get my royalty accounts in as soon as you possibly can. Hurry up Vert. They won't be much this half year, but it is always *something*. Weather frightfully bad still. The sun came out on

Monday, and so Clotilde and I trotted off to Nice for shopping. When we arrived we were received by a *hailstorm* & it has rained ever since until this morning which begins well.

(After lunch) Just begun to rain again, and the stor-my winds do blo-o-o-o-o-ow!
Yrs sincerely,
A.S.

We play nothing but Deratschky [?][4] now – never nap. The cards Clotilde holds are *fiendish*, it costs me about 6 francs every night.

'Hurry up Vert' referred to Nathaniel Vert, a concert agent whose office was in the same building as Chappell's publishing house. Sullivan had for some years used his services in arranging for concert appearances, and now was apparently using him also in collecting his royalties as a composer.

To Sullivan's relief, the search for the material of *L'Ile enchantée* was successful: Bendall managed to recover at least the string parts, and was next instructed to get Sullivan's copyist, Baird, to reconstruct a score from those parts, 'leaving me to fill in the wind [instruments]'. Moul and Coppi came to stay at the Villa Mathilde for a consultation, and shortly afterwards he was able to send back to Bendall 'more than 100 pages of score'. Bendall was to make the piano reduction before passing the newly composed score to Baird, who would copy the parts. The orchestral practices of the Alhambra had to be adhered to: Tell Baird to copy 6,4,2,4 strings [i.e., first violins, second violins, violas, and cellos and double-basses together]. Ask Jacobi whether the cellos play with the basses or separately, so as to be copied separately . . .' [2 March]

But concert performances were hoped for, and required larger scoring:

I am writing for *4 horns* in view of concert performances. It is easier to reduce them to 2 [for the theatre] than to increase 2 to 4. This scene [Scene 3, with a sequence of country dances] has given me great trouble and labour to score. I have been up till 5 a.m. three nights running and I am a bit tired [6 March].

In the grand finale, separate tunes were not only to represent England, Scotland, Wales and Ireland but to be combined one against the other. Alas, it could not be done and Sullivan sent the last instalment back to England with more modest counterpoint. On 27 March he wrote to Bendall, having presumably sent some form of skeleton score to Coppi already:

The last scene was a beastly one to score – so many notes to fill in. When it came to the triple subjects – the Union – I stopped dead, and couldn't get on. Something stood in the way, and I didn't know what. At last, daylight came to me. It was the 'Men of Harlech' who resolutely barred my passage. So I swept them clean away – gallant little Wales has been sacrificed and I am triumphant. Don't attempt, in your P.F. [pianoforte] arrangement, to unite the three tunes. Take one only, or four bars of one and four of the other, and *in small extra lines*, show what is going on at the same time, without trying to make it playable. I return you the new arr[angement] of Scenes 5 and 6 with a few alterations – most of them tending towards simplifying the thing. To tell you the truth, I was terrified at your arrangement of the movement in 6/8, A♭, in Scene III. It was absolutely unplayable. . . . The whole movement wants *adapting*, not arranging, and I would suggest your leaving out the L.H. figure altogether (it is purely orchestral colour) and giving the following shape and accent to it [music quotation].

. . . Now that the work is finished I am attacking my pile of letters. Tomorrow I shall devote the whole day to them. I will begin with yours, and see what wants attending to in them. The only thing that I recollect is the haunting theme of 'a cheque' which I enclose

Telephone to No 7 [Fanny Ronalds], and tell I am well and delighted to get her little note about 'Utah' mine [shares]. Tell her also that if I can't manage a letter to her tomorrow, I will on Monday, so that she may rely upon hearing from me on Wednesday. . have written one of *16 pages* to Mrs Carte. Weather dull and muggy here, and the wind is getting up.

The letter to Helen Carte was concerned, in all probability, with the problems of casting the forthcoming revival of *The Yeomen of the Guard*. Then in mid-April, announcing that he would be returning to England at last, he wrote to Bertie that 'we' (he, Louis and Clotilde) would journey together as far as Paris, where Clotilde would proceed to London and he would stay for a few days 'as Auntie is coming for a holiday. It will do her much good.'[5] The plumbing at the Villa Mathilde had evidently not been reliable: 'Clotilde was blown up *twice*. I told her "third time lucky" always, and so have forbidden the gas in the bath to be lighted any more'. ('*In* the bath' is probably not an error. Among the types of gas heating marketed at the time was one which was incorporated in the fixture, under the bath-tub.)

Before he left, however, a further letter to Bendall showed Sullivan worrying about the *sense* of the opening scene, in which a figure representing 'England's Genius' (i.e. her guardian spirit) was supposed to bestow an awakening kiss on Britannia.

Will you see Moul, and ask him what we are to do about the name of 'England's Genius'. You can't have 'Britannia' and 'England's Genius' both. It struck me as I was correcting the proof that it is anomalous to have England's Genius prophesying that Britannia will be great. How would the 'Spirit of History' do, or some such name as that?

A commonsense suggestion, but it was not adopted. It was as 'Britain's Genius' that Pierina Legnani, the *prima ballerina*, appeared in the opening scene. She was a dancer of genuine historic distinction, who had introduced the famous 32 *fouettés* into Act 3 of *Swan Lake*. Sullivan's and Coppi's ballet was unveiled before a distinguished audience on 25 May 1897. The performance lasted (as the *Daily News* noted) from 9.55 to 11.35, with long waits for scene-changes. The music was generally admired in the press for its apt and sometimes humorous characterization; besides the contrapuntal entrance of the English, Scottish and Irish troops, the score included a sort of comic fugue (a dance for four feudal retainers in Scene 6) and a movement in unusual 5/4 time – as a dance for the attendants of Herne the hunter (Scene 4).

The ballet ran for six months during which the Prince and Princess of Wales and other members of the royal family were said to have attended no less than 19 times. To Sullivan it brought a very handsome reward – £2,000 in advance and a share in the takings – at a time when his need for 'the ready' (see p. 378) was pressing. It was one of the few theatrical works of his last decade which did not fail. The manuscript full score is lost. But Bendall's piano reduction, published at the time, survives to show that Sullivan's lighter style was not – that is, not quite always – dependent for success on Gilbert and Gilbertianisms. There was, at later performances of the ballet, an item in the accompanying variety bill which was historic: a 'cinématographe' which showed, on film, the Diamond Jubilee procession itself.

At the Savoy, after the failure of Mackenzie's *His Majesty* (20 February 1897, with libretto by Burnand and R. C. Lehmann), the successful revival of *The Yeomen of the Guard* on 5 May also served to buoy Sullivan's reputation: he did not conduct, but both he and Gilbert took curtain-calls. Carte had, in Sullivan's view, been unwise in renewing Ilka von Palmay's contract: the sentence 'Palmay very unfitted for Elsie' in the composer's diary is curiously crossed through with a thick pencil line. Whether she would have been any better as Phoebe (Sullivan's own suggested change!) was open to question.

While on the Riviera he had written to Bertie of his intention to go to Nice and visit 'the poor old Duke of Saxe-Coburg, who is very lonely'. This was his valued and intimate patron of younger days, the former Duke of Edinburgh. In London he received a rather pathetic appeal from the 78-year-old Sims Reeves, now fallen on hard times (and just remarried). 'I have sung through 57 years of the Queen's reign, God bless her': would Sullivan place himself at the head of a fund-raising appeal? It was a cry to which the composer's memories must surely have driven him to respond. Reeves' death in October 1900 would precede Sullivan's by only two months.

The Queen's subjects had heard the Jubilee hymn – printed officially, 'to be used in all churches and chapels in England and Wales, and the town of Berwick-upon-Tweed . . . as part of the service to be used on that day' (20 June 1897). Its publication and sales over three months actually netted a profit of £200 for the composer, which he handed over to the Prince of Wales's Hospital Fund.[6] Sullivan himself, perhaps surprisingly, seems from his nephew's biography not to have been involved in any of the major celebrations. He was, however, invited for an audience at Windsor Castle on 5 July.

Went about 6. Nice little room. Dined at 8.30 with the Household. After dinner was received by the Queen in the Long Corridor. Had 20 minutes' conversation with Her Majesty who was most kind and gracious. After I retired, she sent me the Jubilee Medal by Miss Phipps. Played billiards and smoked with the Household until bedtime.

It was recognition of a sort, though Victoria saw no necessity to confer further formal dignity on her reign's most eminent composer. It was left to George V to bestow a baronetcy on Elgar and Elizabeth II to raise Britten to the peerage.

A letter in *The Times* on Tuesday 20 July 1897 found Sullivan protesting as he was ready all his life to do – against the slighting of British music on its home ground. He attacked 'our military musical authorities' for their Jubilee selections, citing the recent 'Review of Colonial Troops' by the Prince of Wales, when the music played by the band of the Grenadier Guards was by Offenbach, Hérold, J. F. Wagner (*Under the double eagle*) and the Austro-Hungarian bandmaster, Joseph Gungl.

On great national occasions it is not unreasonable to expect that the public should be reminded that British tunes do exist. I know of nothing more inspiring than 'I'm Ninety-four', 'The Girl I Left Behind Me', 'Hearts of Oak', 'The British Grenadiers', and our whole rich collection of Scotch, Irish and Welsh national airs. It is inconceivable that at a national *fête* in Berlin the German military bands would confine themselves to performing French and Italian tunes.

No doubt to avoid the implication of personal animosity he signed his letter 'A British Musician'. The protest was genuine and disinterested: it was not that *his* music was neglected by the bands. On the previous Saturday, the Queen held a dinner party at Windsor at which the Band of the Royal Horse Guards under Charles Godfrey concluded the evening's selection with Sullivan's *Imperial March*.

In the following month Sullivan succumbed to Richard Wagner's spell – or at least joined the pilgrimage to the Bayreuth Festival, with Bendall as companion. It was no novelty for a British composer to do so. Parry had been to the first festival in 1876 and made another visit in 1882. Stanford attended in 1876 and 1883; Delius, Elgar, and Granville Bantock had followed. So had Ethel Smyth, who came again in 1897. ('All the world is Wagnerian now, and Bayreuth is a world's fair', she commented in a letter.) Sullivan's first musical encounter was with *Parsifal*, conducted on 11 August by Anton Seidl, with the distinguished Belgian tenor, Ernest van Dyck, in the title-role.

Put on light clothes and went to the performance of *Parsifal*. Although many points open to severe criticism, the work and performance impressed me immensely. Theatre, which holds over 1,600, quite full. Saw many English friends, Prince and Princess of Wales, Lady de Grey, Arthur Balfour [the future Prime Minister], Charles Worthy and his wife, Mr Wagg and Elsie, etc.

Three days later he began the four evenings of *The Ring* in which the greatest Wotan of his time, Anton van Rooy, took part; the English mezzo-soprano Marie Brema sang as Fricka, and the composer's son conducted.

Beginning of *Ring* performance, *Rheingold*, commenced at 5, and went on without break till 7.30. Then home to dinner. Much disappointed in the performers; all of them. Orchestra rough and ragged, conducted by Siegfried Wagner. Vocalists (except Brema, van Rooy who has a beautiful voice, [and] [Alois] Burgstaller who has also a voice but not yet 'placed') beneath contempt. Sometimes stage management is good, but much is conventional and childish. It is difficult to know how Wagner could have got up any enthusiasm or interest in such a lying, thieving, blackguardly set of low creatures as all the characters in his opera prove themselves to be.

Next day:

Performance of *Walküre*. (House party, Lady de Grey, Emily Yznaga, A. J. Balfour, etc., Prince and Princess of Wales.) Very pleasant party – good lunch. Back at 3.15. Unfortunately fell asleep and didn't wake till 5 and so missed first act. Much that is beautiful in the opera – less dreary padding than in the others.

The remaining operas evoked remarks in similar vein:

Performance of *Siefried*. I think it intolerably dull and heavy, and so undramatic – nothing but 'conversations', and I am weary of *leitmotiven*. Burgstaller (tenor) is young and good-looking and has a very pretty voice, but he will kill it if he sings Siegfried and similar roles much more. He was dead beat at the end of the opera. What a curious mixture of sublimity and absolute puerile drivel are all these Wagner operas. Sometimes the story and action would disgrace even a Surrey pantomime . . .

Last *Ring* performance: *Götterdämmerung*. First act 4 to 6. Dull and dreary. Second act 6.30 to 8. Just as dull and dreary. Third act 8.45 to 10. Very fine and impressive. The *leitmotiven* seemed all natural and not dragged in, and the whole act is much more dramatic and musically finer than any of the others. Spoke to Ethel Smythe [sic].

After these two last performances (16 and 17 August) he went again to hear *Parsifal* on 19 August, with Wilhelm Grüning in the title-role.

Last performance [of the festival] – 100th of *Parsifal*. Not so good as the previous one. Kundry sung by [Sullivan left a space which he did not fill in: the singer was Anna von Mildenburg], not nearly so good as Brema, and Grüning a long way behind van Dyck as Parsifal. The orchestra (again under Seidl) rather slovenly. Altogether this performance not so impressive as the first one I heard. Home to supper and bed.

On 12 August Sullivan had left his card at the home of Wagner's widow, Cosima, but did not apparently meet her. In his diary he noted a 'row going on between Mad. Wagner and Brema' on the day of his second visit to *Parsifal*.

'I have got to hate a *leitmotif*!' he wrote home to his nephew on the evening after that performance: 'Each opera has about a dozen phrases, which are repeated over and over again in different rythms [sic] and shapes until one wearies of them. *Parsifal* is by far the best and most attractive and impressive.'

Sullivan's denigration of the voices and the stagecraft did not represent mere individual petulance. Such criticism from British visitors was not uncommon. Shaw's advocacy of an English equivalent to Bayreuth was based not only on the wish to make Wagner's works accessible but on an assurance that the performances would be actually better: 'What has been said lately about the inferiority of the staging to that of the Lyceum is quite true. Admirable as the [Bayreuth] orchestra is, we can beat it in London as certainly as we can build the theatre the moment we are wise enough to see that it is well worth our while' [1889].

Three days later Sullivan had exchanged the artistic stimulus of Bayreuth for the invigoration of the Alps. Fanny Ronalds was with him. From Splügen in Switzerland he sent birthday wishes to his feckless nephew, who had found an occupation as a stockbroker in the City of London: 'Dear Bertie, . . . You are 30, half-way through the average of a man's life; and so, my dear boy, cease being a boy (as you are in many respects) and assume all the qualities and attributes and responsibilities of manhood . . .'

Having shown Fanny Ronalds the Alpine scenery in visits to Splügen, Thusis, and Disentis, Sullivan was back at Walton-on-Thames on 5 September: 'Glad to be home. Sat up till 12.15 recounting my experiences to Clotilde.'

Queen Victoria allowed him to keep warm the contact they had made at Cimiez. He wrote to Carte: 'I have spent most of my time lately at Windsor, and have had *three* long and pleasant chats with the Queen (bless her, she is so kind and gracious). We are beginning to be talked about!'

A letter to 'Dearest old Arturo' came in December from 'ever your affectionate old friend, G. Grove'. Only in 1894 had Grove given up the directorship of the Royal College of Music (Parry succeeded him); he was now 77 and, to judge by his wording, Sullivan had lately failed to keep in touch with him.

Do send me a good word or two by way of 'Christmas wishes'. To me there's not much that's 'happy', or anything but trying, about the 'season' – but one has to keep up the form! I am groaning under the bequest of my old brother's estate in Buckinghamshire, which produced nothing to speak of, and has been spoiled by his absurd [generosity] to the tenants, to whom he gave whatever they asked to such a degree that he has kept up every charity, schools, church, organist, etc, etc, etc. Easy for him who had a big income behind him, but impossible for me who have only £700 a year!

I should like to see your handwriting once more. I came on an old note of yours the other day and found the old *smart* come into my eyes at once.

Good-bye and God bless, dear old chap.

Despite the disappointments of *Utopia Limited* and *The Grand Duke*, Carte retained faith in Sullivan. Not only friendship prompted him, but prudent calculation. No other composer had brought success to the Savoy after the six-month revival of *The Yeomen of the Guard*. Carte surprised his public by giving them Offenbach: but *The Grand Duchess* ran for only 99 performances, and *The Gondoliers* was brought back on 22 March 1898, to run until a new piece which Sullivan was composing (without Gilbert) should be ready.

The libretto was being jointly written by Arthur Pinero and the dramatist of *King Arthur*, J. Comyns Carr. *The Beauty Stone* was romantic, not at all satirical and not Gilbertian: the libretto was set in Flanders amid medieval magic and chivalry. As in *The Golden Legend*, the Devil was present in disguise as a friar. There were three acts (seven scenes), with no less than 21 solo parts. The beauty stone is a charm by which Laine, an ugly and crippled peasant girl, is able to transform herself and captivate a noble lover. When she loses that magical power she finds she no longer needs it, for the Lord of Mirlemont has been blinded in battle and loves her for her own sake. The vocal character of Laine was contrasted with that of the hero's Moorish mistress, Saida, and of the roguish village girl, Jacqueline.

In December 1897 and later, Sullivan complained in his diary that both Pinero and Carr ('gifted and brilliant men, with *no* experience in writing for music') were unhelpful and inflexible when he wanted alterations in order to improve the musical construction. He also complained in a strictly private letter to Helen Carte ('My dear child') that he thought his two collaborators had been over-sharp in securing terms from the Cartes. He returned to the Riviera to compose, once again renting the Villa Mathilde at Beaulieu, but the upshot was far less successful than with the previous year's labour on *Victoria and Merrie England*. Produced at the Savoy on 28 May 1898, *The Beauty Stone* lasted a mere seven weeks. The critics who found the story ridiculous, the fake-medieval language unwelcome, and the characters unsympathetic also justly found Sullivan's musical inspiration wavering between the 'romantic' style and what the critic of the *Musical Standard* called (and every reader would understand the term) the 'old Sullivanesque':

The effect is as if the composer were laughing at his own initial seriousness. And the worst of it is the music that is not old Sullivanesque is characterless and might have been written by any composer of the day. The most successful numbers are the opening chorus of the second scene in the first act in which we are transplanted to the Savoy comic-opera, 'When the rose-leaf lies on the dew' [chorus with tenor solo], an example of the sentimental and melodious Sullivan of the old days, and Jacqueline's 'It is the lute that sings, not I! not I!' But I do not feel inclined seriously to discuss the music, which practically only illustrates the lighter side of the 'romantic drama' with any measure of success; to say that is equal to saying that Sir Arthur's share is somewhat of a failure, and I am afraid that must be the verdict.

The critic, who wrote regularly in the magazine under the doubly punning name of 'R. Peggio' (peggio being Italian for 'worse') liked best among the performers Pauline Joran who played Saida.[7] The heroine, Laine, was played by Ruth Vincent, the Lord of Mirlemont by George Devoll and the Devil by Walter Passmore – it was, after all, the principal comic role! Sullivan as usual conducted the first night. In Pinero's output the work is unremembered; in Sullivan's declining days it was a sad milestone.[8] But *The Golden Legend* still maintained its attraction; not until Elgar's rise was Sullivan's star to be dimmed. The page of the *Musical Standard* on which 'R. Peggio' concluded his notice also carried the announcement of a Saturday afternoon concert at the Crystal Palace on 25 June 1898 'in honour of the 60th anniversary of the Queen's coronation' (evidently a clever way of prolonging Diamond Jubilee fervour). Patti would return to the Palace after a gap of 17 years, and 3,000 voices of the Handel Festival Choir and 500 instrumentalists would perform such favourites as the 'Hailstones' chorus from Handel's *Israel in Egypt*, a selection from Mendelssohn's *Elijah* – and the finale to *The Golden Legend*.

On 15 February 1898 the Carl Rosa Opera Company had surprisingly given a full operatic staging (at the Lyceum Theatre, Edinburgh) of Sullivan's Leeds Festival piece of 1880, *The Martyr of Antioch*.[9] ('I didn't anticipate *that*', was Sullivan's comment, quoting *Patience*.) For the Leeds Festival of autumn 1898 (it was to be his last) Sullivan had actually undertaken to write a new choral work, as desired for so long by the festival committee. But he had not the energy, or not the confidence, to go through with it. A letter from the Grand Hôtel, Paris on 21 April 1898 to Bendall identifies the librettist as the music critic Paul England – and shows that the enterprise was already faltering:

It is exactly the question of England's libretto that troubles me. If I tell him to stop, it will leak out at Leeds at once, and the committee will know that I don't mean to do a cantata. And yet I feel he ought not to go on working, as I am sure I shan't write a work for the festival, nor could I set his words as they stand. They are too long, and each subject is developed too much.

Of course I must pay him for what he has done already, and I think you had better write and ask him *not* to do any more until I return. You can indicate that it is probable I shall not write for the festival. It will be best to prepare him in this way. I fear I can't retain the conductorship of the festival if I don't write a work. My position will not be a pleasant one, as I shall be attacked right and left for what they call disappointing them. I shall wait until I return to London, and then will take the necessary steps. There will be no difficulty about a conductor, as Stanford is ready – aye, and willing! What else did he accept the Leeds Phil. Soc. for?

The suggestion that Stanford was, in fact, jockeying to ease himself into Sullivan's position is strengthened in Elgar's posthumously published correspondence. Sullivan was in Paris with Mrs Ronalds, whose health had been poor and who had been upset by the recent death of her mother. 'Mrs R. is much better', Sullivan added as a postscript to the above letter, 'and now and then has a bit of colour in her cheek.'

A setting of Kipling's *Recessional* was another musical work in view. Only three days after the poem had originally appeared in *The Times* (on 17 July 1897, striking a note of warning amid the Jubilee festivities) it was reported that, with the poet's agreement, it would be set to music by Sullivan. Almost a year later, with the task still unfulfilled, the composer was still in communication with the poet. Kipling's own attitude was almost deferential. His letter of 14 May 1898 was in reply to one which does not survive:

Dear Sir Arthur Sullivan,

Many thanks for your note. If a layman may speak in the presence of a master I quite recognize the difficulty you find about *Recessional*. The thing is a hymn in spirit and method and it seems to me should be dealt with on hymn lines. I wrote it to a well worn choral in *Ancient and Modern*; and barring an American attempt (I have no authority over musical rights across the water) by one [Reginald] De Koven who purposes to be a musician, nothing has been done to the verses.

I generally find that as soon as I have formally given up the notion of a story or rhyme, the idea I have been hunting arrives. It may be – and I shall be lucky if this is so – that some day you will see your way to the one, inevitable setting that must be floating about somewhere. It is far better that it should go unset than be badly done and I have seen nothing in the scores of vamps sent to me 'for approval and immediate authorization' that makes me change my mind. Please accept the thing as yours if you care to use it, and when you care to use it. There will be no other setting authorized by me.

Sullivan was never to complete that setting.

He had begun to dread the onset of a new bout of kidney trouble, especially under the inevitable stresses which the Leeds Festival would bring. A general muscular trouble had already set in, which he attacked with baths and massage during a three-week stay (July and August 1898) at Badgastein, Austria. At one point he had hot potato poultices on both thighs. There was good company, however, in the person of Lord Rosebery, lately Prime Minister: 'We have taken our walks together. He is a most interesting man and brilliantly clever.'

A letter to Helen Carte, undated but evidently before the opening of *The Beauty Stone*, had begged for the loan of £1,700 as he was 'staggered by receiving two accounts which I am unable to pay' (gambling debts, perhaps).[10] Recalling Pooh-Bah's use of 'insult' for an acceptable bribe, he added: 'The insult is, as you understand, a cash transaction, as Pooh-Bah would say, [re-]payable in three weeks, maybe less.'

Financial pressure was clearly behind his response on 1 July to 'My dear Davis', on being invited to take up a new theatrical collaboration. James Davis was the librettist of Sidney Jones' *The Geisha*, which had been such a success two years before (Daly's Theatre, 25 April 1896). For that work he had adopted the pseudonym of 'Owen Hall' ('owing all', i.e. in debt!).

With regard to your proposal, I am quite willing to entertain the idea of doing a piece with you, although a short time ago I had nearly made up my mind to give up comic or comedy opera writing, but as I want to devote the next three or four years to making money and nothing else, and as there are very few other ways open to a composer, I might as well go on. And this brings me to the question of conditions. I will have nothing more to do with profit-sharing – I want a certainty with the speculative element in it; i.e. a percentage on the gross receipts.

And here I think the sliding scale is the fairest. I needn't at this stage of the discussion fix definitely what the proportion would be, but it would be about, say,

over £260: 12½ per cent
over £200 and under £260: 10 per cent
over £170 and under £200: 8 per cent
and so on, until when the receipts were below £100 I would take nothing. That would be one condition. Then –

2. No artist to be engaged without the consent of the author and composer.

3. The orchestra to be not less than 33 in number.

4. Both stage manager and musical director to be subordinate to the author and composer who are to be the supreme authorities. Then the other conditions of less importance but which are necessary in agreements of this character, and which are always inserted, such as no changes of dialogue or music allowed without consent etc. etc.

Finally – and this I am sure you won't be hurt at, and will see the justice of, *I must like the book*. I don't mean *approve* of it; it would be impertinence on my part to suggest that your work should be submitted for my approval, but I mean it must be a subject I like, and treated in a manner that I like, otherwise I couldn't set it. A libretto or a poem may be the finest in the world, and I may admit it to be so – admire it even enormously; but for all that I may not be able to set it, and then it is of no use my trying.

The Geisha, with its Japanese tea-house setting and its catchy, short-phrased tunes (among them 'The Amorous Goldfish' with its 'glit-glit-glitter' refrain) would have been enough to establish Davis's credentials in Sullivan's eyes, though he had been responsible only for the 'book', i.e. the story and dialogue, not the lyrics. The proposed collaboration with Sullivan was likewise intended for Daly's Theatre, but it came to nothing – and 'Owen Hall' next went on to write the book of another famous musical comedy, Leslie Stuart's *Florodora* (1899). Was this the plot that he had in mind for Sullivan?

Leaving Badgastein, Sullivan stayed among Alpine scenery – going west to Innsbruck, then revisiting his favoured Swiss resort of Thusis. Lionel Monckton, the future composer of *The Quaker Girl* and (with Howard Talbot) *The Arcadians*, was there: 'Very nice fellow, and a real gift for music' (Diary, 11 August 1898). Returning to England, Sullivan was not long before going to take the waters again – this time at Spa in Belgium. From the Hôtel d'Orange he wrote on 16 September to Bendall that 'the Leeds committee are getting worse and worse. Fancy cutting three movements out of the Mass [Bach's *Mass in B minor*] without saying one word to me about it. I have written a *stinger* to Hannam about it.'

This was weaker than the old Sullivan, who would have launched in the committee's direction a politely phrased but steel-backed ultimatum telling them he would either do the work as he saw fit or not at all. As it was, he would inevitably have to bear the public responsibility for whatever was performed, and he must have known what hostility this act of truncation would arouse from the newspaper critics.

The responsibility for engaging the Leeds orchestra was also his once more. The closing scene of *Die Walküre* was to be given, and also the 'Prelude and Liebestod' from *Tristan and Isolde* – Wagner being as big a draw as ever. In a letter of mid-September to Bendall Sullivan referred to the two leading London trumpeters of the day, Walter Morrow (who was to play first trumpet) and John Solomon. Sullivan's process of 'thinking aloud' in his letters to Bendall is nowhere more clearly shown.

Please write at once to *Morrow* (not tomorrow or today!) and ask him if he knows of a *bass trumpet* [player], or whether Solomon can play the part (in the *Walküre*) on an ordinary valve trumpet. Perhaps it would be best to write direct to Solomon – it will save time. Tell him to get Middleditch [Covent Garden orchestral librarian] to show him the part and to bear in mind that it is to sound an *octave lower* than the ordinary trumpet (in D). I must have another trombone also for the Wagner selection night. I should like to engage Collier. . . . I shall want him for rehearsal in London on Monday (26th [September]) and (if there are four trombones in the *Tristan* Introduction and Liebestod, of which I am not sure, but you can see from the score) Wednesday also.

In the same letter, having read newspaper reports of a hurricane in Barbados in which about 50,000 were said to be homeless, he added: 'I am in great anxiety about my poor old cousins [the Philipps] in Barbados. . . . I fear telegraphing is no good, but you might write a line or two at once to ask if there is anything they want. . . . It is dreadful to think that they are probably homeless.'[11]

Evidently he could not summon the extra effort of writing such a letter himself, nor trust the indolent Herbert to do so. What was important to him was that the gesture should be (albeit rather impersonally) made. His continuing regard for that branch of his maternal family was to be made clear also in his will.

At the beginning of October, 1898 the *Musical Times* reported Sullivan as 'unable to fulfil his promise of a choral composition' for Leeds. Cowen, with a rather hastily composed setting of Collins' *Ode on the Passions*, had been summoned to the rescue. It was the final stage of Sullivan's inability to follow the success of *The Golden Legend* and all that he had previously contributed before it to the choral festival tradition.

35 Valedictions

Two of his letters from Austria, in that summer of 1898, carried an admonishment to 'Dear Bertie' after his nephew had suffered a medical upset:

Don't grow up into a livery, jaundiced, probably querulous old man [10 August] . . . Do try to live regularly – as plainly as you like, but not a feast one day and a fast the next. I only wish I had attended more to my eating and drinking when I was young – what trouble, pain and worry I should have avoided! [12 August]

Sullivan's own health was obviously causing concern, and not to him alone. According to his nephew's biography, both Stanford and Cowen were kept standing by during the Leeds Festival that October in case its stresses proved too much for him. The final leave-taking took place in an emotional fashion, as his diary recorded on 8 October. The final concert ended with Mendelssohn's *Hymn of Praise*, with Albani, Medora Henson, and Ben Davies as soloists.

Last day of Festival. After last performance, the chorus cheered me so tremendously, that I suddenly broke down, and ran off the orchestra crying like a child. When I came out of my room again, all the chorus was waiting for me, and I shook hands with all! Then went and had a light supper at Albani's, and at 11.10 saw the band off in their special [train]. Red and blue fire, and cheering as usual. When at supper was surprised by a serenade (by about 30 of the male chorus). I invited them in, gave them champagne and cigars, and they sang half a dozen pieces, retiring at 1 a.m. Went to bed tired – rather a trying day.

On the whole, the best performances we have had. The chorus better balanced than ever and of beautiful tone. Orchestra superb, and playing with more delicacy and subdued tone than usual.

It is hard not to read such an account as a valediction, though this was not announced as Sullivan's last festival. The programmes had included some unusual features. For the first time at a Leeds Festival, Palestrina's music was heard: Sullivan conducted the *Stabat Mater*, using the edition which Wagner had prepared for Dresden but preferring an uninterrupted choral flow (a Chapel Royal tradition?) to Wagner's suggestion of a double quartet of soloists. In Bach's *Mass in B minor*, the omission of the 'Agnus Dei' and 'Dona nobis pacem' roused the fury of *The Times*: it was a 'vulgar desecration' and 'a barbarity that would be entirely impossible at Birmingham' – i.e., at the Birmingham Festival, where Richter still conducted. Next month, however, the *Musical Times* would take a cooler view:

Though one cannot but sympathize with those who resented being deprived of a single note of Bach's music, it was surely going too far to denounce the omission as an act of vandalism. It is only necessary to point out that a Mass is different from an oratorio, never being meant to be heard continuously; that this particular Mass is in its origin practically a compilation from various sources; and that it is hardly consistent to protest against omissions in Bach and to accept the omissions, and worse than omissions, to which Handel's music is always subjected in performance.

The same (anonymous) 'special correspondent' praised Sullivan's reading of Beethoven's Ninth Symphony: though 'not so broad or impressive in its general outlines as that of Richter, for example' it was 'thoroughly sympathetic and artistic' and 'marked by a close attention to details'.

Cowen came to conduct his new cantata, Parry his familiar *Blest Pair of Sirens*, Stanford his new *Te Deum*, and Elgar his new *Caractacus*. It was Elgar's first appearance on a Leeds Festival programme and a highly successful one.[1] 'There is, indeed, in *Caractacus* sufficient material to set up half-a-dozen average composers for life' declared the *Musical Times*: with such judgements the critics recognized the hand which was to produce *The Dream of Gerontius* two years later. For the effective rehearsing of a new piece like *Caractacus* much depended on the efficiency and courtesy of the chief conductor of the festival, Sullivan himself. A grateful acknowledgement (written from the Junior Conservative Club in London) was to follow. Elgar's awareness of being a self-taught provincial is evident:

Dear Sir Arthur Sullivan,
   Forgive my troubling you with a note when you are very much occupied but I could not let the last day of the rehearsals go by without sending my thanks to you for making my 'chance' possible and pleasant – this is of course only what one knows *you* would do but it contrasts very much with what some people do to a person unconnected with the schools – friendless and alone, and I am always

Yours very gratefully,
Edward Elgar

On 30 December, from Elgar's home in Malvern, came a further allusion to the Leeds encounter:

Here is the end of the year and with it inevitable reflections: but my sins, musical or otherwise, are not interesting and my virtues x – so I think of the happier things of '98 – the chief and most pleasant of which was meeting you.
   So I am moved to send a little note to wish you all good things in the New Year which we (my wife joins me in this) trust may be most happy and prosperous.

Sullivan's recognition of the gifts of Smyth, German, Elgar and also Samuel Coleridge-Taylor was prompt and, where his favour was needed, ever helpful. *Hiawatha's Wedding Feast* received its first performance under Stanford's baton at the Royal College of Music on 11 November 1898 and immediately marked out the 23-year-old Coleridge-Taylor for distinction.

Much impressed by the lad's genius. He is a *composer* not a music-maker. The music is fresh and original – he has melody and harmony in abundance, and his scoring is brilliant and full of colour – at times luscious, rich and sensual. The work was very well done.

In similarly generous terms he recognized the exceptional qualities of the young Henry Wood as conductor. Sullivan had considered conducting a

Tchaikovsky symphony at Leeds and asked Wood – already known for his affinity with Russian music – to recommend one and to include it in a Promenade programme at Queen's Hall where Sullivan could hear it. After the performance of no. 5 on 31 August 1898 Sullivan wrote to 'Dear Mr Wood':

I have a fairly long experience of orchestral playing and orchestral conducting, and I say quite sincerely that I have never heard a finer performance in England than that of the Tchaikovsky symphony under your direction last Wednesday.

It was a perfect delight to listen to such accent, phrasing, delicacy and force, and I congratulate both the gifted conductor and the splendid orchestra. And what a lovely work it is! I could see that you and the band too revelled in bringing out its beauties.

Forgive me this little outburst of honest admiration.[2]

But the symphony was not in Sullivan's programme at Leeds. He was presumably insufficiently confident of mastering an idiom new to him, and might justifiably have wondered how the critics would compare his own performance with that of a conductor 27 years his junior.

At the Savoy he had his own opportunity for a retrospective view. On 17 November 1898 Carte celebrated the 21st anniversary of *The Sorcerer* with a special performance of the work at the Savoy. Sullivan went along to conduct and was called on stage to take his bow afterwards. So was Gilbert. They did not speak to each other, and the two former partners went separately from the theatre.

Yet, although the energy to compose a festival cantata had gone for ever, Sullivan never doubted his continuing ability to write for the stage. The idea of going outside Britain for a librettist recurred to him: on 21 October 1898 he was in Paris, where he had already met two writers and was about to be introduced by his old friend Juliette Conneau to a third. (The identity of these writers is unknown.) He was also renewing in Paris the friendship which had arisen with Yvette Guilbert during her London visits. Now at the height of her fame as a singer of topical, passionate songs, she was 33 and had recently married. 'A rumour has already arisen *here* about me and Yvette', he wrote to Bendall. But if a theatrical collaboration was mooted, it never became reality.

In March 1899 he was busy promoting a singular invention of his own, the 'Sullivan safety shaft' to minimize the likelihood of injury and damage from a runaway horse. The usual jovial tone of his correspondence with Bendall is once again evident in a letter from Biarritz, the fashionable resort in the south-western extremity of France which he had for once favoured over his Riviera haunts:

Now, in your spare time, I wish you would write a nice, interesting and graphic account of *my* invention for fallen and runaway horses, so that when the time comes, I can send it round to *all* the newspapers (it shall be printed of course) for them to deal with as they like. What they want and prefer is a statement of fact with a *technical* description of the patent, so that they can make up their own article, quoting from mine. I don't think it necessary to put it into the form of a romance, and try to beat H. Wells, or Kipling, or even Rider Haggard on their own ground. But a beginning something in this style – 'Musicians are generally supposed to be so absorbed in their Art, that' etc. etc. or 'As Isaac Newton discovered the theory of gravity from the simple action of an apple falling, so Sir A.S. from

seeing a horse run away from which a terrible result ensued conceived the idea that', etc
etc., or 'Is it really possible that at last the loss of life arising from carriage accidents can be
avoided? It would seem so', etc. etc.

Of course great stress must be laid upon its utility for horses that have fallen; and also
people must be reassured as to the abuse of it. It would only be resorted to when the
coachman (even the best and most experienced) felt without doubt that the horses were
out of his control, and if the coachman fell or was thrown, the occupant of the carriage
could get through the front window to the handle. I think if you would consult Barry and
Holmes – the latter for all the technical terms such as 'Futchel' (?) etc. – you could make a
real good job of it.

With equal vigour he wrote to Bendall about a new piece for the Savoy (it was
to be *The Rose of Persia*) and the tricky matter of negotiation with the Cartes.

Enclosed is a pretty good long letter, and it has taken me a *very long* time to consider,
construct, and write. I want you please to copy it, and then send it to Mrs Carte, PRIVATE.
Read it carefully and give me your opinion of it. I have had to weigh and choose *every word*
with the greatest care, because they are both so sensitive – especially do they dislike any
reference at all to myself or Gilbert having contributed to their rise and fortune. The only
thing was to tell the truth, and acknowledge that there is the contract and that I signed it.
But I cut out of my sketch letter, that if I signed it without reading it carefully, it was
because I had signed almost hundreds of documents they had put before me in *blind
confidence*, without even reading them at all. [James] Davis's letters about preparing
agreements etc. were all *kidding*. I have silenced him, and we shall hear no more about
Daly's piece [i.e., a collaboration for Daly's Theatre] until after the Savoy piece is rit [*sic*].
If the Cartes don't assent to my proposal, it will be disastrous, as I once said to you 'you
can take a composer to the water, but you can't make him write'. If they contact you or you
have an opportunity of talking to them do urge it. I must shut up. I have a lot of things to
say – answers to your queries, cheques etc, but it is too late. I will write tomorrow.

The new piece for the Savoy was to have a new librettist: Basil Hood (1864–
1917) who had retired in 1898 from his career as an army officer and had already
won some theatrical success. Sullivan was anxious not only to get the most
advantageous terms from the Cartes for the new work but also, if possible, to re-
negotiate the existing agreements for his older works. He took legal advice on
whether the older agreement was really watertight.

[Diary, 3 May 1899]: Called: Wilkinson – held opinion that agreement with Carte could
not be sustained. T. Chappell – told him I *had* given permission to Bosworth [German
publisher] to publish 'marches' from operas in England. Drove up to Portland [Club].
Auntie called there. Dined at Brooks' [Club] with Arthur Collins.[3] Portland – disastrous;
rubiconed every game but one – minus [£]51.

To 'rubicon' (at bezique or piquet) was to lose a game with a loser's score so small
that it was added to the winner's. Next day his diary reported a visit in the
company of 'Auntie' (Mrs Ronalds) to the Alhambra Theatre, where *Victoria and
Merrie England* was still being performed. These are the only entries for that
month in the diary, which never again became the repository for more than very
occasional comment.

A letter of 24 May to 'Dear Helen' survives in Bendall's hand, as a fair copy.

Before we meet tomorrow to discuss theatre business I should like you to read this little
exposition of my ideas, so that we may both be prepared upon the points to be considered.

I will make it as short as I can . . . It seems to me that your action is based upon an erroneous idea, viz. that I am eager and anxious to write for the Savoy Theatre. Now I have endeavoured by all possible means to show you that the contrary is the case; but separate please the two things – writing for the Savoy and writing for *Carte* – I refer only to the theatre. I have urged you to give up the theatre and even give up management. The first on financial grounds, the second for health's sake. I have urged it because I feel instinctively – superstitiously if you like – that the luck has gone from the theatre for a time at least. It was built for a special purpose and its raison d'être is now over; every kind of combination has been tried and failed. Do you think it encouraging to devote months again to work which I feel, however good it may be, will have no other result than the works which have preceded it since 1890, and how long is it to go on? I say nothing of your losing thousands every year, for you will say that doesn't concern me. No more it does, but I have nevertheless no passionate longing to see you lose money. Then your health. Is it worth while to wear yourself out prematurely for nothing at all? You ought to think of that.

Now about the agreement. The more you consider it, the more your own sense of justice will I am sure cause you to see how one-sided and impracticable it is. It is morally suicidal on my part. According to your view I am bound to supply you with one opera a year (time not stated) – to write for no one else, and on indefinite terms. On your part you pay me nothing for this; you don't even undertake to produce the opera.

So that (a *reductio ad absurdum*) if you, by a stroke of luck, got a very great success, a piece that ran 600 nights, you could compel me to deliver two operas during that period, and you need not produce either of them. I am of course taking the strict letter of the agreement. Now to avoid a long controversy, and perhaps unpleasant discussion, will you agree to the following proposition? Let the present agreement hold good until the production of the new piece, and *no* longer . . .

After all if the new piece by a rare stroke of fortune turns out a great success, it will require no agreement to induce me to write a successor. If it is *not* a success – well, I don't think you will want another; therefore my proposition seems one you can very well accept.

Helen Carte's tone in reply – in typewriting with handwritten inserts on Savoy Theatre stationery – was one of sweet reasonableness.

Frankly I am not excited about doing any more comic operas; I am anxious simply to do what is RIGHT by everybody, and I see that Captain Hood is going to be dreadfully disappointed if the piece is not done, and he is such a very good fellow, and I see that *you* would like to do it; and that is *all there is about it*. I naturally do not want to make any foolish arrangement, and I am quite sure you do not want me to. About expenses, these have unfortunately very considerably gone up. The theatre used to be put down at £4,000 for the accounts, or £5,000 to include the rates, taxes and insurance. The rent we are now paying for it to the company [i.e. the Cartes' payment as licensees to their company which owned the theatre] is £6,000 *without rates, taxes or insurance*. This is not a mere nominal payment *but a real one* and has to be actually paid of course, as the debenture interest and reserve fund have to be put aside from it.

She assured Sullivan that the scale of his proposed reward – a percentage of the box-office takings, not a division of the profits as in the palmy days with Gilbert – would on all likely expectations be the best he could wish for:

Altogether, *whichever way* you take it I think you will find that the balance is always in favour of yourself. There is no way in which such a scale could bring you less than a third of the profits unless by some such extraordinary success as the *Mikado* in the old days by which it ran for *months and months to enormous receipts*. I think we agree that none of us expect anything of THAT kind, and obviously in trying to arrive at terms that will throw the whole of the risk upon US and insure your getting something *worth getting* there must be a element of chance left for the persons who stand the racket to get SOME good if by som extraordinary fate a big success is achieved.

Thus Helen Carte explicitly stated her managerial view that the days of very lon runs for Sullivan's type of comic opera were over. Her use of the phrase 'stand th racket' suggests a reflection of her American experience.

A revival of his symphony at the Crystal Palace (29 April 1899) brough Sullivan back there as conductor. But at Leeds the festival committee wa anxious to get rid of him. Though technically the conductor was newly appointe for each festival, it would have been unthinkably brutal for the committee simpl to have announced a different appointment for 1901. Sullivan was desired t 'resign', and to do so on the ground of ill-health. Indeed his health did constitut a risk. But the committee's desire for change for artistic reasons must b understood. Sullivan's failure to compose a new work, while not a failure a conductor, was a symptom of waning powers. (While on holiday at Disentis i Switzerland in August 1899 he was 'working very hard' – but doubtless on th opera with Hood.)[4] On the rostrum, seated as was his custom, he was not th most inspiring figure. To galvanize the 350-strong chorus, newly recruited an newly assembled on each triennial occasion, a different personality was no unreasonably preferred.

Sullivan declined the excuse of ill-health, and even after formally signing tha he would give up the appointment he wrote to Spark insisting on the point. A draft of the letter (undated, but presumably some time in 1899) survives, witl many crossings-out and some alternatives, but a fairly definite form can b extracted:

There is a slight error in your letter which it is as well to correct. I have not taken quite th course you recommended, viz. to withdraw from the festival on the plea of ill health. Thi I cannot do. But to save public unpleasantness, I have intimated to you my resolve not t accept the conductorship, without giving any reason.

Because thank God, I am well, and without going into medical details, it is almos impossible humanly speaking that I should have a recurrence of my illness. Even th slightest indication of hesitation on the part of the committee would be quite sufficient fo me to take this step. So I suppose the committee judged and acted upon report only, whic rarely errs on the side of moderation or even accuracy. You will see from what I have no told you that I cannot stultify myself by pleading ill-health as a reason for severing m connection with the festival. I am quite willing that the committee should give out that w are not of the same opinion as to the work and duties required of the conductor, and tha therefore we agree to part.

I see no other truthful and at the same time perfectly reasonable cause for separation and I ask you as a friend to bring your influence to bear upon the committee to this end And that is why I say I am bewildered by the attitude of the committee because I feel tha they have judged and acted [unfairly]. The question is one entirely between the committe and myself, and they are quite justified in making such conditions as they think ar beneficial for the festival, and choosing the man whom they think will best carry them out I am not aware that there was anything in my conduct to prejudice the success of th festival and consequently there is no reason or necessity to give an explanation of thi nature to the committee. Now you will see that I cannot stultify myself by giving ill-healt.

as a reason for declining to conduct again if the offer were made to me. I might adduce other reasons, but certainly not that one at this moment 'pour cause', and so I don't see what I can do in the matter.

I am sorry for one reason for since I have picked up my health again, I had formed a project which with regard to the next festival which now that there is no probability of my being connected with it I don't mind telling you. In 1901, I shall have been 40 years before the public (as I date my career from the time I returned from Leipzig in 1861) and I intended making the festival an occasion of publicly retiring from the active pursuit of my profession, and to do this with éclat I meant to produce a work (which I am engaged upon now) which would be I hope a worthy successor to *The Golden Legend* and form a dignified close to my personal public appearances. The words are from one of the (in my humble opinion) finest poems in the English language, and it has taken a strong hold upon me. This was my project, and I confess to feeling some disappointment that it is not to be carried through. I could not however produce it [at] Leeds, unless I were in supreme control of the festival as heretofore.

This suggestion of a composition yet to come may have stirred only scepticism when Spark read out the letter to his Leeds committee. Sullivan's resignation from the festival conductorship was announced – with no reference to his health – in the *Musical Times* of December 1899. The manner of the severance was abrupt; the festival committee sent no thanks to Sullivan for his long service, and some suspicion of improper procedures (never voiced by Sullivan, however) continued to hang over the event.[5]

By this time 'the Transvaal crisis' (as the newspapers had called it) had become the Boer War. Cheering crowds attended the embarkation of soldiers and nurses from England, patriotic songs swelled in the music-halls, and the high-minded few who resisted the imperialist urge were reviled as 'pro-Boers'. Swinburne, the former aesthete now turned jingo, poured on them 'loathing more intense than speaks disgust' in a poem published in the *Illustrated London News*. Sullivan's sympathies were not in doubt: he would set Kipling's newly written and immediately popular war poem about the soldier far from home, *The Absent-Minded Beggar*.

> When you've shouted *Rule, Britannia* – when you've sung *God Save the Queen*,
> When you've finished killing Kruger with your mouth –
> Will you kindly drop a shilling in my little tambourine
> For a gentleman in khaki ordered South?
>
> He's an absent-minded beggar and his weaknesses are great –
> But we and Paul [Kruger] must take him as we find him –
> He is out on active service, wiping something off a slate –
> And he's left a lot o' little things behind him.
>
> (*refrain*) Duke's son – cook's son – son of a hundred kings
> (Fifty thousand horse and foot, going to Table Bay)
> Each of 'em doing his country's work, and who's to look after their things?
> So pass the hat for your credit's sake, and pay – pay – pay!

Sullivan told Cunningham Bridgeman that it was a difficult poem to set: 'I puzzled me to compose Gilbert's "I have a song to sing, O", but that was child' play compared to the setting of Kipling's lines.[6] If it wasn't for charity's sake could never have undertaken the task.'

But charity won, and the song swept the nation after its first performance o: 13 November 1899 at the Alhambra Theatre. A note on the song-cover read:

The whole of the proceeds received from the sale of this edition of 75,000 copies, or fo singing rights, go without deduction to the wives and children of soldiers and sailors of a arms and grades now on active service. The entire cost of engraving, printing, an publishing this edition has been contributed to the cause by Messrs. Enoch and Sons, ι and 14a, Great Marlborough Street, London W.

Not surprisingly, such critics as Fuller Maitland of *The Times* took an attitud of lofty disapproval to *The Absent-Minded Beggar* and two days later Sulliva: thanked 'my dear Ben' (probably Ben Davies, the tenor) for his sympatheti remarks which had 'acted as a salve to Fuller Maitland's sneer. Did the idio expect the words to be set in cantata form, or as a developed composition wit symphonic introduction, contrapuntal treatment, etc.? Look out for the 29th the first night of the new opera, and look out for the *dervish* music in it.'

To bring on stage the dancing dervishes who had fascinated him almost 2 years before (pp. 170–1) must indeed have been a pleasurable task for Sullivan ii composing *The Rose of Persia*, or *The Story-Teller and the Slave*. In order to fine seclusion for its composition, he had taken yet another country home Ashridgewood near Wokingham in Berkshire, during the previous summer. A further pleasure was the realization that the whole piece *worked*, in a way that ha: eluded him for a decade. So too thought the public, who gave *The Rose of Persi.* the span of 200 performances. It was not a particularly long run (the popula American musical comedy, *The Belle of New York*, with music by Gustav Kerker, ran in London for more than three times as long). But it reversed th decline in totals at the Savoy and allowed Sullivan to bask again in theatrica success. On the first night, 29 November 1899, he recorded in his diary:

First performance of *Rose of Persia* at Savoy Theatre. I conducted as usual. Hideous nervous as usual – great reception as usual – great house as usual – excellent performanc as usual – everything as usual – except that the piece is really a great success I think, whic is unusual lately.

The ovation was, in the words of the *Daily Telegraph*, 'quite after the pattern tha became familiar in the Savoy's palmiest days'.

Alone of Sullivan's later librettists, Hood had dared to write in Gilbertia: style, with ingenious word-play in a plot of mixed identities derived from th *Arabian Nights*. Hassan, a philanthropist, relieves the boredom of the compan of his 25 wives by nightly entertaining a crowd of beggars at his house, but i compromised by the visit of the Sultana (in disguise as a dancing-girl). He husband the Sultan, who visits in the disguise of a dervish, then has the whim c taking the drugged Hassan to his palace and parading him as the Sultan himself

He whom you call Hassan
    (Prepare for great surprise)
Is quite another man –
    The Sultan, in disguise!

Endeavour, if you can,
    This fact to realize:
The Sultan is Hassan
    And vice-versa-wise!

Each is another man –
    That is, *id est*, or *viz.*,
The Sultan is Hassan,
    Hassan the Sultan is!

With an oriental location which stimulated orientalisms in the score, with a sentence of death turned away by a verbal quip, with a court executioner (and even a rhyme for him, as 'the royal retributioner'), the parallels between *The Rose of Persia* and *The Mikado* were not hard to find. There was even a madrigal – with a touch of chromatic harmony absent from the earlier example. But the new score itself was of a quality that enabled the *Daily Telegraph* to declare: 'The musician is once again absolutely himself'. Or, as the *Musical Times* put it:

Speaking broadly, Sir Arthur Sullivan's music is less distinctive in regard to tune than that of his early operas; but in matters of detail and general treatment it is more elaborate and on a higher artistic plane, the consummate knowledge of effect displayed being a very striking feature of the work. It is music that to hear once is to want to hear again and again.

Walter Passmore (Hassan) and Henry Lytton (the Sultan), together with Rosina Brandram as the first of Hassan's 25 wives gave the new piece a strong link with the Savoy tradition. The casting of an American soprano, Ellen Beach Yaw, as the Sultana added the unusual savour of a very high soprano whose range embraced the top F associated with the Queen of the Night in *The Magic Flute*.[7] A cadenza written for her in *The Rose of Persia* survives in Sullivan's hand.

The success of Basil Hood in creating the verbal springboard for Sullivan's newly animated music was recognized. He embarked on another work for Sullivan, *The Emerald Isle*: the composer would not live to finish it, and *The Rose of Persia* was his last complete work for the stage. Its successful opening was followed in December 1899 by two more London performances of *The Golden Legend* (by the Royal Choral Society under James Coward), which testified to the continuing popularity of that work. It had been heard also at the Three Choirs Festival at Gloucester in the preceding September.

On 26 December he acknowledged a child's gift of flowers with a charming letter from his London home to 'Dear little maiden':

It was kind and dear of you to send me the lovely flowers, and although they were rather tired and exhausted after their long journey (you see they are not accustomed to travelling like you and me), yet after I had given them some light refreshment, especially something to drink, they brightened up wonderfully, and have been entertaining some friends in the drawing room this evening most cheerfully. As they only arrived this afternoon, it is very much to their credit, isn't it? Thank you very much for your kind thought of me. If you should happen to see your father soon, will you please give him my kind remembrances and wish him a Happy New Year from me, and also keep some love and good wishe yourself.

A postscript, apologizing for having forgotten her Christian name, wa accompanied by the words 'Onward, Christian [*or rather, in Sullivan'* *abbreviation*, Xtian] Soldiers' and a quotation from that favourite hymn.

Early in 1900 two patriotic occasions in aid of war charities claimed him as conductor. On 20 January at the Albert Hall he directed massed brass bands in the National Anthem and a march founded on 'The Absent-Minded Beggar'; or 18 February at Her Majesty's Theatre he conducted massed military bands in 'patriotic picture' of Britain and her dependencies – selected, presumably, from *Victoria and Merrie England*.

On Christmas Day there had been dinner at 'Mrs Ritchie's' (evidently Mrs Ronalds' daughter was in town) and on 29 December he 'dined at Auntie's'. The domestic and social circle would continue to surround him in his final year. The Portland and Garrick clubs were convivial as ever, 'Bertie' was affectionately tolerated, and Clotilde gave faithful but sometimes excitable service: 'Cl subdued at first – before going to bed, storm broke – everything wrong! Sa calmly, said very little. Dull, damp, cold. Walked up to Portland in afternoon played a little.'

So Sullivan confided to his diary on 10 April 1900, the day on which he returned to London after yet another trip to Monte Carlo and Paris.[8] Three day later he dined with 'Auntie, Fanette and Bertie' at home. He was working on patriotic song with lyrics by Basil Hood, but abandoned the task on finding the verse-rhythm intractable. A birthday celebration on 13 May was recorded in hi diary with a formal guest-list which shows his respect for the superstitiou avoidance of 13 at table:

Arthur Sullivan born 13 May 1842!
At home all day. Had a little birthday party at the Savoy of waifs and strays. Mr Ronalds, Lady K. Coke, Mrs Crutchley, Mr and Mrs Carte, Mr H. Sullivan, Vincen [unidentified] (Emma not well enough to come), W. Pallant (picked up at last moment to make 14th), Alfred Oakley, Mr Herring, Bendall, [Lionel] Monckton, [gap] and self. M and Mrs Blow came in after dinner – played poker (2 tables) till 12.30, then home.

Four days later 'home' would indicate Shepperton, where Sullivan had once again taken a house for the summer. He presided at the 'Anniversary Festival (dinner and music) of the 160-year-old Madrigal Society, held in London at the Holborn Restaurant – the same society which had once utilized his voice as a boy treble. His own *Love and Beauty* (from that youthful, 'buried' opera *The Sapphire Necklace*) was among the madrigals performed. Then he took a train home at the unusually late hour of 11.38 p.m. 'Had ordered a cab to meet me in Shepperton but alas! no cab there. Luckily found a friendly policeman who walked home with me, and carried my bag!'

By now the British military success under Field-Marshal (later Lord) Robert had turned the tide of the Boer War and placed victory in sight: on 26 May

Sullivan accepted an invitation to compose a Te Deum for a service at St Paul's Cathedral to celebrate the coming peace. Meanwhile, however, the Boer cause continued to attract the support of Germany and Sullivan found himself in embarrassment when – being in Berlin to conduct the production of *The Mikado* at the Royal Opera – he was injudicious enough to reveal to a British journalist a conversation with the Kaiser. In suggesting that the Kaiser, were he to revisit England, would receive 'a grander reception than ever your Majesty has had before', Sullivan certainly pushed flattery too far.[9]

Brooding all day long [17 June] over unfortunate interview.[10] Curse the press and all their correspondents. I cannot get over the fact that after all these years of care and avoidance of disclosing anything – even the most ordinary incidents – about the Royal Family, I should have let my enthusiasm run away with my discretion . . .

On 27 May he had noted in his diary, as usual, the anniversary of his mother's death – 18 years before – and two days later went to place flowers on her grave. More exceptionally, on 7 June, he noted the occurrence of 'Father's birthday – 1805'. It was a summer not only of remembrance but of new losses. George Grove ('poor old G.', as Sullivan's diary put it) was buried on 31 May: Sullivan found it 'impossible' to attend the funeral. On 31 July he 'received terrible news of the Duke of Saxe-Coburg [the former Duke of Edinburgh] last night – upset me dreadfully – another of my oldest and best friends gone.' Ten days later Lord Russell of Killowen – the Lord Chief Justice, formerly Sir Charles Russell – died in London. 'Another friend gone! They go with cruel rapidity.' Sullivan cannot but have been mindful of his own bouts of ill-health and what they might portend. A diary entry while he was at Monte Carlo in the previous March recorded: 'Very seedy all day. Passed two pieces of calculus. Took nitre and pills at night. Profuse perspiration.' But when he was well he was energetic. While at his summer home at Shepperton he occasionally went sculling on the Thames.[11] Tricycling gave him diversion: on 12 July he and Bertie

triked down to Laleham [2 miles] where the servants (4) were having a little picnic in a boat.

On Saturday 21 July he was at his old haunt, the Crystal Palace, as guest of honour at the first National Brass Band Festival.[12] He had actively supported its planning, and the directors of the Crystal Palace (of whom he was now one) presented the principal trophy, valued at a thousand guineas. It was, in the history of the bands, an early mark of recognition by an important composer, and it was the last public appearance of Sullivan's life.

Blazing hot. Came up to town [i.e. to London from Shepperton] – lunched at No. 7. Went down to C.P. Competitions of brass bands going on all day. First prize Grand Challenge Trophy won by Denton Originals – 2nd by Black Dyke. At the concert of combined bands, when the winners were announced, some of the bands left the orchestra [stage], disappointed at not having won! Furious at this 'un-English' behaviour, I ran round and planted policemen at every exit, but I was too late to do much good. The best performance was a selection from *Tannhäuser* by the Black Dykes – really splendid, with brilliant fire and go; at the end of the concert I delivered the prizes, conducted the 'Ab. M. B.' [*Absent-*

Minded Beggar] March, and then went to dine with Bertie, Bendall etc. and enjoy the fireworks at the same time – home at Shepperton at 12.45!

Energetically too – almost as if it were a warding off of a newer and more serious attack – he went travelling again. His diary from Switzerland, with Louis accompanying him as usual, contains descriptive passages in a style recapturing that of almost 20 years before, complete with a jocular quotation from Longfellow's *Excelsior* – so familiar in Victorian drawing-rooms in Balfe's musical setting. Sullivan had evidently arranged a reunion at Pontresina with his old friend Albert Visetti. The train would take him, as usual, as far as Chur and Thusis, but thereafter he made a hazardous choice of a mountain pass road. The Albula pass, with a hospice near its highest point (2,315 feet), would drop him into the Inn Valley at a hamlet called Ponte, now known by its Romansch name of La Punt. Once there, the 10-mile concluding stage of his journey would be easy.

Left by 9.55 train arr. Thusis 10.50. Carriage ordered before, awaiting me. After light refreshment, started at 11.15 in confident belief of arriving at Ponte about 8. Mistakes caused delays en route. Mistake 1st: stopped for lunch at Tiefenkastell at 1 o'clock, starting again at 2.30. Horses did not require rest so early. Mistake 2nd: as I chose the Albula Pass, which is much longer than the [Julier Pass, the alternative route], ought to have slept at Bergün. . . . Tried for a 3rd horse, couldn't get one – many delays before I got one at last at Bergün. Began to rain hard at Bergün. Poured in torrents the rest of the way. arr. at the Hospice at *8.30* [p.m.], pitch dark, pouring, and a thick fog arisen. 'Try not the Pass, the old man (at the Hospice) said', literally, to my coachman. But he spoke in Romansch, and I only learnt afterwards that he had said it was very dangerous. However, I went on. The coachman couldn't see the horses' heads. Louis sat outside to support and help the driver. He was never so deadly terrified in his life – the road greasy and slippery, and moreover the Albula is the narrowest of all the Pass roads. If a horse had stumbled and fallen, I think nothing could have saved us. But thank God we got down safely, and when we pulled up at Ponte for a few minutes' breathing, I felt as if I had just passed thro' the most critical hour of my life. On we went, the poor brave little horses tired to death, but bringing us safely to the Hotel Roseg [at Pontresina] at 11 [p.m.]. Everyone astounded at our recklessness! Visetti came down to see me whilst I ate a mouthful, and 'so to bed'.

He returned to make Thusis his main point of stay. Pleasant memories of previous visits years before had persuaded him that it would be a good place to work on *The Emerald Isle*. 'I find I have *done* it (as far as Hood has given me) and it turns out rattling good – dramatic and bright.' So he wrote from the Hotel Viamala to Bendall on 30 August. This referred to his first stage of composition ('sketching') for when he turned to 'framing' three days later he found Bendall had let him down. The diary entry is good-tempered: 'Began *framing*. Commenced with Finale [of Act 1?]. Wired home for scoring paper. Bendall is a genius – thinks others like himself – packed me up about 20 sheets of paper to write the opera on.' On the same day (3 September) 'Auntie wired at 4.50. Transvaal annexed. War collapsed.'

A letter of 11 September describes it as 'a *very great* blow' to him that Basil Hood did not come and join him: 'I can't frame until he has made alternatives'.

In a letter headed 'Sunday' (evidently 9 September, though it refers to 5 September as 'three days ago') he wrote to Helen Carte from Thusis with apparent confidence in *The Emerald Isle* but with details of the illness which was, in fact, to be his last.

My dear Helen,

I have been here over a fortnight working hard and fairly successfully. The first act is done (barring a few details which I must settle with Hood before giving to Baird) and I should have had it all framed and dispatched to England before now if I hadn't been stopped these last few days by something which I think you especially can sympathize with, and that is violent neuralgia.

I have never had it before, and wish I had not had it at all. It takes the form of violent headache with deadening pain all down the side of my face, and renders me incapable of even writing a letter when it comes on, which happens five or six times a day. It has almost entirely stopped my work for five days, for it invariably comes on when I begin to write.

However, I am now struggling on the best way I can, and in spite of the pain, hope to send off a good packet to Baird this week. The 2nd act I received from Hood on the 5th – that is three days ago. So you see pretty well how the matter stands. Of course it is a great disadvantage being so far away from Hood – there are so many little points that require *personal* discussion. It is impossible to explain everything by correspondence, and besides it means that a whole day might be devoted to explaining a few simple points in a letter – writing out phrases, suggested alterations, etc. Then, when I came here, I was quite sure that Hood was coming out to me, as he did last year at Disentis, and I counted upon it. But, unfortunately, he is not able to come, and the only thing for me to do is to get back home as soon as I can. I believe Clotilde is hurrying things up – she always has a 'spring cleaning' this time of the year – and I hope to be allowed to enter my own house again about the 15th or 16th. I should think you might fairly count upon beginning the vocal rehearsals about the 23rd – I propose that date because by then there will be *plenty* of music ready for them, with a constant supply to follow.

In the middle of September, still in Thusis, he caught a chill, followed by bronchitis. He left for Paris and home. He had ten weeks to live. For a revival of *Patience* at the Savoy on 17 November Helen Carte had hoped that Gilbert, Sullivan and her husband would all take a curtain-call. All three were ill: 'I suggested to D'Oyly that he should have an original effect of three bath-chairs discovered – or a procession of bath-chairs. Or, *you* [Sullivan] standing and the two in a bath-chair each at the sides.' Sullivan's reply was headed 'In bed' (undated):

It is not a question of taking a chill if I come out but of ever getting out at all again. I am regularly bowled over – kidneys and throat. Pray tell Gilbert how very much I feel the disappointment. Good luck to you all. Three invalid chairs would have looked *very well* from the front.
Ever yours, A.S.

Carte and Gilbert alone took that curtain-call. Cunningham Bridgeman recalled them as 'supported by stout walking-sticks, reminding us of Chelsea pensioners'.

To revive *Patience* was considered quite daring: the 'aesthetic' movement which had been so topical an object of ridicule in 1881 had long since passed away. Nevertheless the Savoy audience was warmly responsive. The Berlin production of *The Mikado* at the Opera House in June 1900 was also a success and continued in repertory till 18 September 1901 – a surprising total of 66 performances. As Berlin's musical historian, Adolf Weissmann, was to put it:

'Just as, earlier, *Die Fledermaus* had breached the rule that operetta should not mingle with grand opera, so now Arthur Sullivan's burlesque, *The Mikado*, was given a place of honour and aroused a strong resonance of applause.'[13]

Two major revivals (one of them in German) in two capital cities: the double event must have gratified the composer, and he may have known also of the two-week season of *The Mikado* at the Metropolitan Opera, New York, in November 1900. (It was capped by an extra performance of *Cavalleria Rusticana* and *HMS Pinafore* – surely a unique coupling.) Such news may even have re-animated his hope of surviving this bout of illness as he had survived others. It was not to be so.

He arrived home on 19 September but at the end of the month removed himself to the Wellington Hotel, Tunbridge Wells, apparently for the special medical care which the Kentish spa town could provide. 'Have been here just a fortnight, and what have I done?' he wrote in his diary on 14 October.

Little more than nothing, first from illness and physical incapability, secondly from *brooding*, and nervous terror about myself. Dr Manser examined me *very* carefully this morning – chest, heart, lungs, etc – says I am sound enough, but my throat still in a bad state. But practically I have done nothing *for a month*. Have now finished and framed first act, and they are rehearsing it.

François Cellier came to stay at Tunbridge Wells in order to help Sullivan prepare a working vocal score of *The Emerald Isle*. The day that Cellier returned to London was the day of Sullivan's last entry in his diary, 15 October 1900. The shaky handwriting has been deciphered by others as follows: '*Lovely day*. Fr. Cellier left at 11.10. I am sorry to leave such a lovely day.'

But as there is a small dot after 'leave', and the 's' of the following 'such' may be a capital letter, it is possible that (less sentimentally) he was 'sorry to leave [Tunbridge Wells]'. He was in London the next day and wrote to Helen Carte. 'Forgive me dictating this letter, as I want to save my hand for music. . . . Luckily my general health is now much better and I seem to have got into the swing of work again . . .'

On 21 November his condition worsened. His throat ailment prevented his speaking in more than a whisper. There was no crisis, but as a precaution it was arranged that Sir Thomas Barlow, a royal physician, should call the following morning. He became drowsy and was left alone for the night.

About six o'clock the next morning his bell was heard ringing violently, and when his housekeeper, Clotilde Raquet, and his valet, Louis Jaeger, hurried into his room, dissolution had begun.

'My heart!' he exclaimed. 'My heart!'

He lay quietly, breathing intermittently and with difficulty. His life appeared to slip away as his nephew held him in his arms. Presently his breathing ceased.

So his nephew's biography tells the story. It adds that a message was got to Fanny Ronalds (presumably by telephone) within the last hour of his life, and that she waited frantically and in vain for a cab. She arrived at 1 Queen's Mansions too late. Arthur Sullivan died in the early morning of Thursday 22 November 1900, aged 58.

According to the same source, Sir Thomas Barlow arrived at the same time. It was, however, Buckston Browne, Sullivan's doctor, who signed the death certificate, specifying the cause of death as 'bronchitis, 21 days; cardiac failure'. It was not, apparently, necessary to mention the kidney trouble which had plagued him for more than 20 years.

A not quite identical account of Sullivan's death prefaced the immensely long and detailed obituary in the *Daily Telegraph* next day. According to this account, the composer died in the arms of Clotilde and Louis only; Herbert Sullivan, though residing in the house, reached the bedside too late. No mention is made of Barlow.

In 1882, Sullivan had drawn up a document 'to be opened immediately after my death'. In it were brief instructions for his funeral including a wish to be buried 'in the same grave with my father, mother and brother in Brompton Cemetery'. That grave had already been opened to receive his body when burial in St Paul's Cathedral (among so many of the nation's great men) was offered; and the Queen authorized another service immediately beforehand in the Chapel Royal, St James's Palace, where on 27 November the uniformed boy choristers saluted their predecessor. The chief mourners, along with Herbert Sullivan, were the composer's surviving uncle, John Sullivan, and his daughter Jane. Sir Walter Parratt, master of the Queen's music since 1893, was the Sovereign's representative at St Paul's.

The musical arrangements at the cathedral were undertaken by the composer's old friend Hermann Klein. After the coffin had been lowered into the crypt of St Paul's, and the Dean had pronounced the Benediction, a wish of Sullivan's was fulfilled with the singing of 'Brother, thou hast gone before us' from *The Martyr of Antioch*, performed by 'the ladies and gentlemen of the Savoy Theatre'. François Cellier conducted them – 'voices tremulous with deep emotion', as the *Musical Times* was to report in its first issue of the new century, January 1901. The pall-bearers were Stainer, Sir George Martin (who had succeeded Stainer as organist of St Paul's), Col. Arthur Collins, and François Cellier himself.

Telegrams and letters of condolence flowed in to Fanny Ronalds from those who no longer needed to conceal their knowledge of her relationship with the composer. They included 'Jennie' (Lady Randolph Churchill), Leopold de Rothschild and, from Paris, 'Beckie [Mrs Beach] Grant', as well as Tosti, George Grossmith and other colleagues. Princess Louise had telegraphed to Fanny Ronalds for news during Sullivan's last days, and a copy survives of a letter which (after his death) she wrote to 'Dear Princess': 'In the communion of friendship he was so gentle, so tender, so thoughtful that the sweetness of his disposition endeared him to all.'

36 Legacy

THE failure in his last decade to maintain his previous record of financial success was clear when Arthur Sullivan's estate was valued on 15 January 1901 at the gross figure of £54,527 10s. 8d. (personal estate £32,193 10s. 5d.) – the possessions of a man 'comfortably off' rather than rich. The gross figure was resworn in December 1902 at £56,536 13s. 10d. He had not modified his habits of gambling or his well-to-do way of life; the mania for continental travel was unabated even at a time when (as in 1896) he was paying rent on a summer home in England in addition to maintaining his London flat. Carte was more prudent: although he had undergone his own share of financial reversals, he would leave £240,000 Gilbert would leave £120,000.

Sullivan had made his will in London on 4 March 1899, before the visit to Biarritz. The executors were named as Edward Dicey, Richard D'Oyly Carte, and Charles William Matthews, a barrister friend. A codicil dated the same day was presumably an afterthought once he had arrived in his solicitors' office: it increased his money bequests to his servants Clotilde Raquet and Louis Jaeger to £1,000 each, an extraordinarily generous sum which might represent twelve years' wages. Previously the amounts had been £500 and £400, the distinction being made in Clotilde's favour 'only because she cannot work in the world with the same strength as a man'. They also received various objects of value. There was likewise a bequest of £1,000 to Herbert and each of the other five surviving children of Fred and Charlotte (Amy, Maude, Frederic Richard, George, and William), and lesser sums to other relatives.

There were gifts to D'Oyly Carte, to Helen Carte, to Mrs Beach Grant, and to Gilbert – prefixed in the draft only as 'W.S.', as if Sullivan could not call to mind the full forenames which would normally have been set out in a will. (They never went beyond the formality of surnames when addressing one another.) Gifts of objects and of money to François Cellier and Wilfred Bendall recognized their loyal professional assistance. Herbert Sullivan was the residuary legatee, receiving not only the bulk of domestic property but also those musical scores not otherwise disposed of, and the composer's diaries and other papers. To 'my old and dear friend Mary Frances Ronalds', the deceased Arthur Sullivan left no money (the *Boston Post* had speculated that she would get a quarter of a million dollars) but a valuable dinner service and dessert service and other objects, and also 'the original manuscript of *The Lost Chord* and any other autograph score she may like to have; also any other musical and vocal scores she may care to have'.

Nowhere could the composer be so suitably commemorated as at the Crystal Palace, where August Manns had introduced *The Tempest* 38 years before. Now an incredibly vigorous 75, Manns was still in charge of the Crystal Palace concerts. On 8 December 1900 he conducted part of *The Tempest* and the *In Memoriam* Overture, together with selections from the *Festival Te Deum*, *The Martyr of Antioch*, *The Golden Legend* and *The Merchant of Venice*.

By the time the Philharmonic season opened, another death had supervened – that of Queen Victoria (22 January 1901), who had been the society's patron throughout the 63 years of her reign. The work chosen as tribute to her on 27 February was not the *In Memoriam* Overture, nor any other British composition, but an orchestration of Chopin's 'Funeral March' from the Piano Sonata in B flat minor! The protests which Sullivan had so often voiced on behalf of his country's music would need to be restated for another generation. Sullivan was himself represented in this concert by the suite from *Macbeth*. It was repeated at the opening concert of 1906, but no other note of his music was heard at the Philharmonic in the decade following his death. Sullivan's music was actively cherished, however, by Sir Henry Wood, both at the Queens Hall Promenade Concerts and elsewhere.

Richard D'Oyly Carte, so long a sick man, died on 3 April 1901 and never saw Sullivan's last, partially completed work for the Savoy, *The Emerald Isle, or The Caves of Carrig-Cleena* (finished by Edward German), produced on 27 April. At least one of German's numbers pointed smartly towards his *Merrie England* – which, also with a libretto by Hood, was produced in 1902 under Helen Carte's management at the Savoy. The music Sullivan had written was mostly in familiar vein, except for some musical 'Irishism' which had been anticipated by Stanford in the cantata *Phaudrig Crohoore* and the opera *Shamus O'Brien*. His wit at least showed in the entrance music for the Lord Lieutenant: this representative of English officialdom on Irish soil had 'God Save the Queen' as a half-hidden bass line. Sullivan's other substantial posthumous work was the *Te Deum* with which he had anticipated the Boer War victory. It was heard at St Paul's Cathedral on 8 June 1902, published in full score, and forgotten.

François Cellier, who had been musical director for *The Emerald Isle*, retired from the Savoy in 1913 and died on 5 January 1914. Helen Carte continued her late husband's enterprise at the Savoy. Having remarried, she died as Mrs Stanley Boulter on 5 May 1913. Fanny Ronalds's death, by an extraordinary mischance, was falsely reported in the New York and Boston papers as having occurred in Paris on 3 June 1910; in fact she continued to live at 7 Cadogan Place, dying there on 28 July 1916.

A memorial plaque in Sullivan's honour, sculpted by Sir W. Goscombe John, stands in St Paul's Cathedral. Another memorial was raised to Sullivan in the Embankment Gardens, between the Savoy Theatre and the Thames as it flowed along towards the composer's native Lambeth. It bore a quatrain chosen by Gilbert from *The Yeomen of the Guard*:

Is life a boon?
If so, it must befal
That death, whene'er he call,
Must call too soon.

Gilbert himself, granted a knighthood at last in 1907 by Edward VII, died on 29 May 1911, collapsing after going to the assistance of a young woman who had got into difficulties when swimming in his private lake at Grim's Dyke.

The virtual coincidence of Sullivan's death with that of Queen Victoria and with the end of the old century lent a sharpness to some of the immediate posthumous assessments of his work. He incarnated a chapter that had closed. But among his British colleagues it was generally recognized that he had given a new weight to English music – both in the way in which his broad output had captured his countrymen's ears, and in his acceptance abroad as a representative composer. Such an assessment was that of Sir Alexander Mackenzie, who in May 1901 was given the quite unusual honour (itself a tribute to Sullivan) of delivering three illustrated lectures to general audiences at the Royal Institution on the subject of his old friend's life and work. He found a fundamental Englishness in Sullivan's music itself, lending new vigour to older traditions. Thus a great part of *HMS Pinafore*, with its debt to glee and hornpipe, 'will likely pass into our English folk-music, if it has not already done so'. The paper presented by Charles Maclean to the scholarly audience of the Musical Association in March 1902 made the point in its title: 'Sullivan as national style-builder'. Rather rashly it suggested that on return from study in Leipzig Sullivan *deliberately* substituted his own English style of instrumental music for the German style he had learnt, and next (from 1871 to 1875) 'wrested light opera from Italian and French influence, and reduced that also by the force of his genius to a national shape. At the same time he felt his way towards de-Germanizing the sacred or semi-sacred oratorio . . .' – a task to be fulfilled in *The Golden Legend*, which would appear very beautiful 'to a mind not over-warped in favour of German art'.

Both speakers (their talks were later printed) treated Sullivan as a composer of considerable stature and one who fulfilled himself in a variety of genres. 'Humanly speaking', Mackenzie concluded, 'he ought to have been as happily content with the result of his life's labour as is the nation in the possession of his works.'

But the less flattering view of the same phenomenon was also taken. Had Sullivan achieved his following by trivializing his art? Were not such 'vulgar' productions as *The Lost Chord* and *The Absent-Minded Beggar* a profanation of 'gifts greater, perhaps, than fell to any English musician since Purcell'?

Such was the condemnatory tone of Fuller Maitland's obituary article in the *Cornhill* magazine (March 1901). Maitland recognized the musical skill of the operettas, but a critic who could disparagingly speak of operetta composers as 'the Offenbachs' (as if that talent was not unique!) could not consider *The Mikado* as a fulfilment for a man who had essayed *The Golden Legend*.

. . . The Offenbachs and Lecocqs, the Clays and Celliers, did not degrade their genius, for they were incapable of higher things than they accomplished; by temperament and inclination they were fitted for the lightest kinds of music, and failure for them lay in the attempt to produce works of greater pretension. The lovely *Contes d'Hoffmann* of Offenbach, and the serious ballads of Clay, which are still too well known to need detailed mention, are the inevitable exceptions to the general rule. . . . If the author of *The Golden Legend*, the music to *The Tempest, Henry VIII*, and *Macbeth*, cannot be classed with these, how can the composer of *Onward, Christian Soldiers* and *The Absent-Minded Beggar* claim a place in the hierarchy of music among the men who would face death rather than switch their singing-robes for the sake of a fleeting popularity?

Ernest Walker, in the first edition (1907) of his *History of Music in England*, would take the point further, accusing Sullivan not merely of writing pot-boilers but of failing even in his supposedly 'serious' music – either by a deliberate, superficial popularizing or by inherent artistic infirmity.

His best pages are nearly all comparatively early, but even then he turned out a great deal of very inferior music, and in later years the success of the operas seems to have blunted his capacity for really vitalized work on independent lines. We can never recollect without shame that the composer who stood for contemporary English music in the eyes of the world could put his name to disgraceful rubbish like *The Lost Chord* or *The Sailor's Grave* or, in what purported to be serious artistic work, sink to the abysmally cheap sentimentality of the opening tune of the *In Memoriam* overture . . . [one of the tunes which Maclean held up for admiration as English rather than German!]
  The later orchestral pieces, such as the *Macbeth* overture, come to singularly little, and *Ivanhoe*, the one 'serious' opera, is a purely elementary work all through, with a few fairly dramatic pages, but as a rule mere commonplace. . . . For the best-known English composer in the very prime of life, and putting forth his full powers, *The Golden Legend* is, as a whole, a melancholy production. . . . Sullivan is, after all, merely the idle singer of an empty evening.

A heavy charge of moral disapproval rests in those last words – an emphasis lacking in William Morris's original self-deprecatory phrase, 'the idle singer of an empty day'. Yet curiously, and in not quite the way he meant, Walker's view may be called prophetic. The view of Sullivan as an all-round composer, the view of Mackenzie's lectures, became with the change of public taste quite unsustainable. The *Ballo* overture might survive in the concert repertory, *Orpheus with his Lute* might claim new life in Janet Baker's recording, but these were a few tiny elements floating up from the huge sunken cargo of Sullivan's 'serious' music. *The Golden Legend*, retaining popularity up to World War I – Henry J. Wood conducted the third Norwich Festival performance in 1911 – lost its following thereafter. *Ivanhoe* was unsuccessfully revived in Sir Thomas Beecham's season at Covent Garden in spring 1910 (Percy Pitt conducting) and has, understandably, never been professionally staged since. What never sank, and what indeed commands the admiration of both the public and the expert, is the body of comic operas, signed by Sullivan's wit and melodic lightness.
  Yet to assert the primacy of these works is paradoxical – an inversion of the composer's own attitude. He was sure that the fullness of his gifts could only be realized by him, and appreciated by others, outside the realm of the operettas.

Often enough he had complained of being subjected in them to an undesirable constraint: 'They are Gilbert's pieces, with music added by me' (letter to Carte, 26 March 1889). But the truth was that where he slipped Gilbert's leash, Sullivan nearly always went astray. The frame formed by Gilbert's lines and Gilbert's plots was precisely that in which his own gifts – so limited in kind, but so sharp in execution – could flourish.

That Gilbert and Sullivan's stage works did not fade away in the course of changing fashions in the light musical theatre, but were kept in being by a family management, was itself remarkable. On Helen Carte's death, the business passed to Rupert D'Oyly Carte (1876–1948), Richard's younger son by his first marriage. Not merely in keeping companies on tour but in mounting London seasons at the Princes Theatre, 1919–26, and in reopening a rebuilt Savoy Theatre in 1929, Rupert found the public still faithful. *Utopia* and *The Grand Duke* were not revived, but *Ruddigore* re-emerged in 1920 (Glasgow) and 1921 (London) in an altered version with musical revisions by the company's musical director, Geoffrey Toye, but apparently stemming also from his predecessor, Harry Norris.[1] A vocal score printed a few years later corresponds to the new performing version. An abbreviated version of *Cox and Box* was admitted as the only non-Gilbert work in the 'canon'. Under Rupert's daughter Bridget D'Oyly Carte (1908–85) the company maintained a considerable British and American following, but it was not enough: the enterprise went into suspense in 1982, a byword of traditionalism to the last.

The determination *not* to modernize the lyrics or dialogue (a very few phrases excepted) and to preserve most of Gilbert's stage directions and the original dance-style had the effect of re-defining the works not as topical but as classical. The up-to-the-minute police of 1879 (in *The Pirates of Penzance*) became funny, old-fashioned police, much as the very word 'Victorian' became synonymous with the ridiculously old-fashioned. Amateurs, performing the works under licence, had to observe the tradition. Thus not only the words and the music but the manner of performance bound the public as amateurs to the public as audience. The sense of tradition was strengthened by continuity in casting. Rutland Barrington, the Corcoran in the original production of *HMS Pinafore*, was still playing that part 30 years later in 1908, and Henry Lytton sang in principal roles from 1887 to 1934. His knighthood (1930) specifically recognized his achievement in 'Gilbert and Sullivan' – that uniquely fused entity which became an entrenched possession in Britain and, to a greater or lesser extent, in the other English-speaking countries.

In 1923, when Herbert Sullivan came to make his will, Clotilde Raquet was in his service as housekeeper. He died on 26 December 1928, leaving his uncle's papers to trustees for his wife, Elena Margarita; on her death (she had remarried and been a second time widowed, as Mrs P. F. R. Bashford) the papers passed to trustees for Ruth, her daughter by the second marriage. In 1966 a sale by those trustees broke up what had been Herbert Sullivan's share of the literary estate, the composer's diaries being eventually acquired by Yale University (Beinecke

Library). The 'Bashford' sale had taken further a dispersal of the autograph scores which had been initiated by Sullivan's own bequests. None of the operetta scores had been left to Fanny Ronalds, but to François Cellier he had left his scores of *The Pirates of Penzance* and *Patience*; to Richard D'Oyly Carte that of *Iolanthe*; to the Royal Academy of Music *The Mikado* (and *The Martyr of Antioch*); to the Royal College of Music *The Yeomen of the Guard* (and *The Golden Legend*). The sixth edition (1980) of *Grove's Dictionary of Music* would find it necessary to specify the whereabouts of the various manuscript full scores of the stage works.[2]

Other companies, among them Sadler's Wells Opera (later named the English National Opera) and the New York City Opera occasionally included one of the Gilbert and Sullivan pieces in their general repertory. To a newer generation it was plausible to present Offenbach, Sullivan and Johann Strauss as operetta composers of equal and classic stature. In such productions a genuine 'operatic' sound, unmicrophoned, was preserved as well as the original scoring. When the New York Shakespeare Festival's highly successful *Pirates of Penzance* arrived at Drury Lane in 1982, what was remarkable was that, beneath the percussive reorchestration of the score and through the microphoned sound-system, Sullivan's harmonies had been conscientiously preserved and were as telling and fresh as ever.[3] The prolongation of the piece by interpolations from *HMS Pinafore* and *Ruddigore*, however, represented just the kind of meddling for which Sullivan castigated Continental publishers and theatrical managements.

More radical treatments had been essayed: *The Hot Mikado* and *The Swing Mikado* were offered to New York in 1939, and postwar London saw *The Black Mikado*. With the evaluation of such productions these pages are not concerned, save to note that true works of art survive any amount of dressing-up, parody, inversion and playful extension. It is not generally known that Gilbert as well as Tom Stoppard wrote a *Rosencrantz and Guildenstern*, yet *Hamlet* itself continues to do pretty well.

A remarkable appreciation of Gilbert and Sullivan purporting to come from the 84-year-old Stravinsky appeared in the *New York Times* on 27 October 1968 in the form of an interview, 'tape-recorded at his home in Beverly Hills'. Demonstrably based on a confusion of recollected D'Oyly Carte and other performances, it was later revealed as an over-enthusiastic concoction by one of Stravinsky's associates, Lillian Libman. The interview was innocently accepted by Percy Young in his 1971 biography. It is a pity that such a tribute must now be discounted along with the supposed remarks of Debussy about Sullivan (and others) which appeared in the *Musical Times* in 1924 and are now regarded as a fabrication by the author of the articles, Andrew de Ternant. Perhaps the most interesting of genuine tributes is a wordless one – the quotation of 'I have a song to sing, O!' in Michael Tippett's *Divertimento on 'Sellinger's Round'* (1954). The union of the original folk-tune (the 'Round') with Sullivan's familiar strain and Tippett's original invention makes an effect of its own.

His personality was of particular charm and affability:

I do not remember ever hearing a harsh word from Sir Arthur Sullivan. His wonderful tact steered him through all the shoals of dispute and controversy, which with most men would have provoked enmity. His every suggestion came with such grace and courtesy as to still all idle argument.

François Cellier's tribute was echoed by many others. To Hermann Klein, one of the newspaper critics with whom the composer maintained a relationship finely poised between detachment and confidentiality, Arthur Sullivan was 'one of the most lovable men I have ever met; also one of the most diplomatic and discreet'.[4] Klein added that 'for a spoilt child of Royalty and *la haute société* he was remarkably modest'.

One might add that, as the modern biographer of Tennyson[5] said of his subject, he

remained curiously classless, and though it would be grossly unfair to say he was a snob, in time he found as much pleasure in meeting other artists and intellectuals in the great houses of the aristocracy as he had taken in a chop or a pint of indifferent port . . . when he was a young man –

except that in Sullivan's case his taste for elevated circles was granted fulfilment while he was still young.

Few names, apart from those of Prime Ministers, generals, and a few poets and novelists, were better known and more positively identified by his countrymen. His circle was wide and indeed cosmopolitan, but his intellectual curiosity very limited. Outside music, Sullivan's mind seems rarely to have turned to abstractions, to literature beyond such fashionable novelists as Anthony Hope and Stanley Weyman, or to politics except as news of the day. His religion hardly went beyond a superficial conformity to the Church of England: neither on the threshold of death nor earlier in his mature years is there evidence of 'spiritual' guidance sought or offered. A strong family piety together with a deep commitment to friendship and to his art – these purely human values were, perhaps, enough.

Even in his own art his outlook was conservative and he was given neither to experiment nor speculation. Exceptionally one 'speculative' passage survives in a letter of 1889 to his teacher of more than 30 years before, Thomas Helmore:

It sounds paradoxical, but there are times to me when the music would be more beautiful and more complete without notes. I suppose it is that the diatonic and chromatic scales are so limited. How often have I longed to be free of fixed intervals! More especially in the prologue to *The Golden Legend*, I felt myself hampered by having to express all I wanted to say by voices and instruments of limited means, and definite, unchangeable quality . . .

But in general he accepted and grasped what was to hand. Even in operetta he and Gilbert were hardly inventors; but, by a consistency of aim and an adherence to certain formulas recognizable despite their variety of application, they standardized operetta in its English form. The fact that, a century later, amateur bodies by the dozen would still function under the very name of 'Gilbert and Sullivan societies' is a significant tribute.

It was not only his musical accomplishment but his charm of manner that gave him a passport – as it had given one to Mendelssohn – to the highest circles in the land. Both in aristocratic company and among his fellow-artists he was welcomed for sociability rather than stimulus. But his charm of manner was by no means a parade of graces. It sprang from an unusual capacity for sympathy and understanding, both in and out of professional life.

His diary (at last on public access) is a revelation, but it is also an enigma. Those countless mentions of new works heard without a single word of comment! The curious absence of remark on the impact of meeting such celebrities as Liszt, Dvořák, or Saint-Saëns! The vivid jottings from Egypt, America, the Swiss mountain passes (both in the diary and in letters, especially to his mother, 'Bertie' and Bendall), side-by-side with laconic notes recording a haircut or a mere listing of dinner-guests, at best an aid to future recollection! For whom, indeed, was the diary written? Such a question might require a psychologist to answer. The sexual references are perhaps there because they had to be somewhere and there was nowhere else; the complicated cover-up, by means of multiple initials for (apparently) the same person, seems like a measure of extreme secrecy to balance the extreme frankness involved in the record of many a 'heavenly night' – a phrase characteristically cloaked in German.

In earlier years the entries in his diary had included occasional passages of self-examination. In later years such passages are absent. Nor do letters or friends' reminiscences divulge how he finally saw the perspective of his life. Were there regrets and disappointment? There must have been. His career as conductor ended prematurely in London; in Leeds, for all the acknowledged achievement of his festival conductorship, he was finally forced out against his will. His sole grand opera failed. His first symphony had lost its appeal; his second had been announced but never produced; his cello concerto he had seemingly disowned. Of his cantatas and oratorios, the latest (whatever it was) always earned a respectable hearing, and *The Golden Legend* rather more than that. But they did not build up cumulatively, as Elgar's were to do, into a standard component of the choral repertory. The immortality he did achieve – that of the operettas – would hardly have been sufficient for him, trapped as he was by the equation of 'serious' (not comic) with 'serious' (important).

Among Sullivan's contemporaries, perhaps only Bernard Shaw escaped the trap. In order to make his point explicit in 1890 he had to challenge Victorian assumptions of value in musical art. He chastised the first edition of Grove's Dictionary for allotting 'one shame-faced column' to Offenbach as against nine columns to Sterndale Bennett, and for failing to recognize that *The Grand Duchess of Gerolstein* was 'an original and complete work of art [which] places its composer heavens-high above the superfine academician'. He continued:

Sir Arthur Sullivan was a Mendelssohn Scholar. He was an organist. He wrote a symphony. He composed overtures, cantatas, oratorios. His masters were Goss and Sterndale Bennett himself. Of Magnificats he is guiltless; but two Te Deums and about a dozen anthems are among the fruits of his efforts to avoid the achievement of an effect. He has shown his reverence for the classics in the usual way by writing 'additional accompaniments' to Handel's *Jephtha*; and now he has five columns in Grove and is a knight. What more could a serious musician desire? Alas! the same question might have been put to Tannhäuser at the singing-bee in the Wartburg, before he broke out with his unholy longing for Venus. Offenbach was Sullivan's Venus as Mendelssohn was his St Elizabeth. He furtively set *Cox and Box* to music in 1869 [actually 1866], and then, overcome with remorse, produced *Onward, Christian Soldiers* and over three dozen hymns besides. As the remorse mellowed, he composed a group of songs – 'Let me Dream Again', 'Thou'rt Passing Hence', 'Sweethearts', and 'My Dearest Heart' – all of the very best in their *genre*, such as it is. And yet in the very thick of them he perpetrated *Trial by Jury* in which he outdid Offenbach in wickedness, and that too without any prompting from the celebrated cynic, Mr W. S. Gilbert.

Sullivan's 'wickedness' in *Trial by Jury* was to have submitted the tender sentiment of Bellini's 'D'un pensiero' to the burlesque of 'A nice dilemma'. Mockingly, Shaw pictured Sullivan attempting to redeem himself by an eloquent setting of certain words: 'I have sought, but I seek it vainly,/That one lost chord divine'.

But no retreat was possible after 'A Nice Dilemma': not even a visit from the ghost of Sterndale Bennett could have waved him back from the Venusberg then. *The Sorcerer* belongs to 1877 as well as *The Lost Chord*; and everybody knows *Pinafore* and *The Gondoliers* and all that between them is; so that now the first of the Mendelssohn Scholars stands convicted of ten mockeries of everything sacred to Goss and Bennett. They trained him to make Europe yawn; and he took advantage of their teaching to make London and New York laugh and whistle.

Those who read the article in the *Musical Standard* learnt that it had originally appeared in the *Scots Observer*. In neither place was it signed, but to modern eyes its authorship is patent. Ten years later there was no need for Shaw to obituarize Arthur Sullivan: he had already done the task to perfection.

37 1842–1992

In the season which was to embrace the 150th anniversary of Arthur Sullivan's birth, 13 May 1992, the English National Opera played its non-Japanese *Mikado*, first staged in 1986. Jonathan Miller as director and Stefanos Lazaridis as stage designer had set the action in an all-white London hotel foyer in the 1920s, where guests and staff apparently enacted – as a joyous, self-contained celebration – the operetta itself. The dance-steps were those of the Charleston, and no more than token mock-Japanese comic gestures, such as an indication of narrow-slit eyes, were occasionally made.

It could be seen as simply one of many examples of a current vogue in operatic production, the jolting of an opera out of its period, such as Miller himself had done a few years previously in his 'New York Mafia' version of Verdi's *Rigoletto*. But surely it was more. It worked on an evident presumption that 'everybody' already knows what Gilbert and Sullivan's *The Mikado* is about, and that the narrative and the jokes – which depended originally on recognizing British foibles in Japanese disguise – are not obscured but reinforced by the turning of the disguise inside-out.

Nothing could demonstrate more clearly the place retained in British public culture by 'G & S' (the abbreviation has remained familiar). Only a continuing familiarity, likewise, could make possible such highly successful parodies as *The Ratepayers' Iolanthe* and *The Metropolitan Mikado*, political satires staged in London in 1984 and 1985 with Margaret Thatcher's Conservative government as their target. Similarly, the conversational and musical references to Gilbert and Sullivan's work in David Puttnam's film, *Chariots of Fire* (1981) had passed without the necessity of being explained.

The present chapter, an addition to the previous edition of the book, begins with some account of recent developments in 'G & S', followed by a consideration of the awakened interest in Sullivan's work without Gilbert. Finally, a new look is taken at some salient, and newly revealed, aspects of the composer's musical style.

The dead *do* rise again: such must have been the incredulous reaction to the news that the D'Oyly Carte Opera Company, whose demise in 1982 had seemed final (even the costumes were sold off), was to rejoin the living theatre six years later. Bold indeed were the plans for the New D'Oyly Carte Opera Company, which called on substantial commercial sponsorship (chiefly from British Midland Airways) to back a generous bequest from Dame Bridget D'Oyly Carte. A nationwide tour began in the medium-sized, economically depressed north-east town of Sunderland in advance of a London presentation of *Iolanthe* and *The Yeomen of the Guard*.

The approach was deliberately new. A young and vigorous musical director, Bramwell Tovey, announced a fresh regard for Sullivan's 'true' scores, purged of accretions, and reinstated the composer's cornets in place of the trumpets which in conformity with twentieth-century norms had been substituted for them. The soloists were mostly of operatic calibre, the stage productions were untraditional. But the initial enlistment of a semi-permanent ensemble, with its own chorus and orchestra, did not last. The length of seasons dwindled, Tovey left, and there was no fulfilment of the grandiose plans for a trans-North American tour in 1990 and even a visit to Moscow (where Stanislavsky's pre-1890 production of *The Mikado* might have been recalled). In 1991, the booing in Birmingham of a clownish *Gondoliers* on its opening night indicated an unsteady artistic direction. But deeper than this, perhaps changes in public taste and economic conditions had clouded the prospects of a G & S *company* (as distinct from the revival of a single piece), much as the previous decade had seen the collapse of New Sadler's Wells Opera's attempt to combine G & S with Viennese operetta in short seasons.

Similarly, in the United States, while *HMS Pinafore, The Pirates of Penzance,* or *The Mikado* might occasionally appear in an opera company's repertory with no offence to the presence of Mozart or Verdi, the concept of a self-sufficient professional operetta company had long ceased to be viable. The sole exception – and here the professionals were mainly young singers just out of college, providing chorus as well as solo parts – was to be found in the small town of Wooster, Ohio. Newly assembled each summer, the Ohio Light Opera managed in the course of several seasons to perform *every one* of the Gilbert and Sullivan scores from *Trial by Jury* to *The Grand Duke*, with other national strands of operetta represented by such composers as Offenbach, Johann Strauss, and Victor Herbert.

Sound-recordings, which had helped to universalize the operettas for each new generation of listeners since the early 1900s, did not cease to do so. Indeed some issues of the 1980s did most of all to clarify the new notions of the 'purified' score, sometimes reviving original musical thoughts which the composer had later rejected – or others had rejected on his behalf. An additional stimulus towards the performance of 'rejected' material came with the publication at this time of Ian Bradley's new edition of the Gilbert texts, exposing the librettist's early thoughts as preserved in the versions submitted to the Lord Chamberlain's office for the legally required theatrical censorship.

Thus the New Sadler's Wells Opera recording of *Ruddigore* displayed Sullivan's 1886 score (not the D'Oyly Carte company's revision of the 1920s), and with some music which composer and librettist had cut even before the vocal score of *that* edition had been printed. The same company's recording of *HMS*

Pinafore gave a few sung solo lines to the minor character of Hebe – which Gilbert and Sullivan themselves had cut after the first few original performances. Were the creators of artistic works, one wondered, no longer able to claim respect for their second thoughts? The same recording even presented the listener with a choice of three different endings, all at one time or other having borne the composer's sanction – though one of them, switching to *Rule, Britannia* (in a different key from the score's final number!) was surely intended for a once-only, properly-to-be-forgotten occasion.

Here – as also in some recordings by the New D'Oyly Carte Opera – the scholarly impetus and practical advice came from David Russell Hulme, whose doctoral dissertation had involved the textual examination of the composer's autograph scores, with divergences noted from the 'tradition' established by successive D'Oyly Carte musical directors. Another scholar active in textual rectification of Sullivan, David Mackie, was the adviser for a remarkable *complete* series of Gilbert and Sullivan's works heard in the winter of 1989–90 on the BBC's 'light music' station, Radio 2. The performances, pre-recorded in the studio under Sir Charles Mackerras and others, failed to achieve issue afterwards as commercially available recordings – a deplorable missed opportunity.

Meanwhile, the explosion of opera on video cassette did not leave G & S behind. In 1992, Jonathan Miller's *Mikado* from the English National Opera found itself facing the rivalry of a more traditional version from the Australian Opera. Such video productions could be expected to reproduce stagings in the theatre, but a remarkable British video series in the early 1980s was studio-made, mostly under the experienced musical direction of Alexander Faris. It included rare offerings of *The Sorcerer* and *Princess Ida*. In the latter, the director Terry Gilbert – reverting to W. S. Gilbert's source, Tennyson's *The Princess* – set the action as a play within a Victorian house party, a pretty notion in every sense.

In printed musical form, the unavailability of full scores (that is, reproducing the orchestral parts, not reducing them to a piano accompaniment) had long irked researchers and others. A New York publisher had announced in the early 1980s the publication (in instalments) of all the Gilbert and Sullivan operettas in newly prepared critical editions – that is, with a scholarly examination of all variants. But the project was still unhatched ten years later, and the first such scholarly full score came from Britain with David Lloyd-Jones's edition of *The Gondoliers* (Eulenburg miniature scores, 1984).

If in the compound entity of Gilbert and Sullivan the last decade has been one of keeping-up and adjustment, the case of Sullivan's other work has been very different. Here the positive term 'renewal' can be – cautiously – used. Sullivan as an all-round composer (which was his own conception of himself) is an image far more sharply focused in 1992 than a dozen years before, when material for the first edition of this book was being gathered in Britain and the United States. The new focus derives not only from the claims of Sullivan's music itself, but from the rehabilitation of British mid- and late-19th century music in general. Whereas a few years ago none of the five piano concertos by Sullivan's teacher, Sterndale

Bennett, was available on record, now all five are. Likewise two symphonies by that more obscure figure, Cipriani Potter (pp. 12, 36), have been recorded and given public performance in London. Parry as symphonist has re-emerged, and Elgar's early (Victorian rather than Edwardian) works such as *Caractacus* (see p. 390) have been re-studied.

An appropriate 'contextual' exposure of Sullivan was offered by a series of BBC broadcasts from Belfast in 1989 when selections from Sullivan's works were coupled with those of Hermann Goetz (see p. 209), the whole being linked by a narrator in the character of Bernard Shaw. The (authentic) Shavian tendency to belittle Sullivan's non-operetta works lent an edge to the programme which offended some zealots of the Sir Arthur Sullivan Society. Yet not only was the dual context stimulating; the performances were also. A long sequence from *Ivanhoe* not only confirmed the inner pathos of Rebecca's 'Lord of our chosen race' but showed Sullivan's skill in assigning it to its musical place within the gathering tension of the plot.

The Sir Arthur Sullivan Society may be excused its sensitivity. Since its foundation in 1977 it has carried the composer's flag in performances, recordings, research, publication and conferences. Harnessing amateur performers, it has sponsored recordings and occasional performances of such works as *The Light of the World* and *The Martyr of Antioch*. Its most ambitious venture, the complete recording of *Ivanhoe*, suffered artistically and technically from low budgeting, but at least the work became widely accessible. Such accessibility was denied to *The Golden Legend*: its centenary (1886) was marked by a first-class professional revival at Leeds Town Hall under Sir Charles Mackerras, which went unrecorded because not enough money could be raised to persuade a commercial company to undertake it. Poor attendance at the concert itself signalled that Sullivan had not won readmittance to the choral 'canon'. Perhaps the best intermediate step with *The Golden Legend* would be to programme the epilogue alone, as Sir Henry Wood sometimes did.

The research carried out by members of the Society complemented rather than duplicated the professional archival care which has continued to be devoted to both Gilbert and Sullivan at the Pierpont Morgan Library in New York. An exhibition there in 1989 placed more of Sullivan's manuscript work on view than ever before. Much smaller, but none the less constituting a unique repository within Britain, an Arthur Sullivan Archive was inaugurated at the Royal Academy of Music in 1987, founded on the donation of research material used for this book. A different specialization led the Victorian Studies Department of the University of Leicester to hold a conference (1986) on *Shakespeare and the Victorian Stage*, resulting in a book of that name including a chapter on *Sullivan and Shakespeare* by the present writer. Two years later, a University of Leicester conference on *Gilbert, Sullivan and their Circles* brought about a performance of Macfarren's *Jessy Lea* (see pp. 50–51) and Clay's *Ages Ago* and broke new socio-economic ground in Tracy C. Davis's paper on 'The Savoy Chorus' (the people, not the musical component).[1]

The birth of the Royal Academy's archive was saluted by a rare performance of the *In Memoriam* overture by the student orchestra. Rare too was any professional programming of the orchestral works apart from the *Overtura di Ballo*, though the *Macbeth* overture won an isolated place in a Royal Philharmonic Orchestra concert at the Festival Hall, under Vernon Handley, in 1989. An optimistic publisher (R. Clyde) made both the *In Memoriam* and the *Ballo* overtures newly available in full score, as well as *The Golden Legend*. Other notable new publications have included several albums of songs and one of Sullivan's complete piano music, including the *Allegro risoluto* which had remained in manuscript, its harmonic asperities no doubt hard nuts for mid-Victorian taste to crack.

An event of particular curiosity, perhaps a 'resurrection' as unexpected as that of the D'Oyly Carte company, was the performance and recording (in 1986) of the supposedly vanished Cello Concerto. Commissioned by the cellist Julian Lloyd Webber, the re-created version was the work of Charles Mackerras and David Mackie. In the absence of an orchestral score or a piano reduction of the orchestral part, their source-material consisted of two surviving copies of the soloist's part, one bearing indications of an orchestral bass-line. The number of bars and the proportion of *solo* to *tutti* passages was therefore known, with only an orchestral texture of appropriate themes remaining to be constructed.

Proportion, indeed, is what torpedoes the work, the three movements being laid out in 75, 147 and 547 bars. The first movement promises the usual concerto form but cuts itself off where a lyrical second subject is expected, the slow second movement then following without a break. The long third movement is not without vigour and tunefulness, but the intrinsic interest of the themes throughout cannot be said to compensate for the disproportion. The unveiling of the re-created version revealed all too well why Sullivan and his original soloist (see p.43) seem to have abandoned the original.

Among other commercial recordings of 'Sullivan without Gilbert', the new standard was set by the fine 1968 recording of Sullivan's symphony, coupled with the *Overtura di Ballo*, under the conductorship of Sir Charles Groves. The *In Memoriam*, overture and a selection from *The Tempest* were among works that followed, both eventually achieving transfer to the new medium of CD. The 'old' D'Oyly Carte Opera Company, in its final years, had already admitted such works as the *Macbeth* overture as 'fillers' on its operetta recordings, and the new company was set to pursue the same path. Particularly bold, and quite unexpected (especially as originating from the United States), was the issue of a CD/tape of fifteen Sullivan songs – ranging from early Shakespeare settings to *The Lost Chord* and *The Absent-minded Beggar* – admirably sung by Jeanne Ommerle and Sanford Sylvan.

The Cello Concerto was, however, not the only 'vanished' work to await restoration. Was the early opera *The Sapphire Necklace* (p.35) ever completed? We may never know, since it was never performed. But *Thespis*, the first joint work with Gilbert, was indeed performed (1871). With the disappearance of the scores, was posterity obliged to be content with no more than the single ballad re-set to altered words, and one fragment re-used in *The Pirates of Penzance* (p.136)? So indeed it seemed. But recently, in the most brilliant piece of detective work in all the research into Sullivan's music, a substantial and surprising recovery was made. Not only for its own interest, but for the light it sheds on the relation (or non-relation) between Sullivan's instrumental music and his other music, the story bears telling in some detail.

That a composer, in writing a new piece, should re-use some of his previous work (either varying the earlier work, or lifting it more or less wholesale) is a common occurrence. Bach's many 'self-borrowings', Handel's transfer from an amorous Italian cantata to 'For unto us a child is born' (*Messiah*) are well known. In Sullivan's case, the ballet music and the dance-like movements of incidental music to plays provide a regular network of borrowing, beginning with Sullivan's earliest stage score, *L'Ile enchantée* (1864). Despite the loss of the composer's original full score, the music for this ballet sufficiently survives in a set of orchestral parts and some other material. No fewer than eight out of 16 sections were called up for use more than thirty years later in *Victoria and Merrie England* (1897). Other material went into incidental music to *The Merchant of Venice* (1871), *The Merry Wives of Windsor* (1874), *Macbeth* (1888) – and into a piano piece, no. 4 of *Day Dreams* (1867).

But one part of *Victoria and Merrie England* that is known to have been of prior origin ('I want the full score of . . .', p. 378) is not to be found in *L'Ile enchantée* (nor indeed in any other earlier 'completed' work). Yet this piece, in a copyist's manuscript, is located in the Pierpont Morgan Library among the *L'Ile enchantée* papers, along with another piece, a waltz which bears the give-away heading 'Act 2. Ballet no. 3'. By an examination of copyists' handwriting, paper-numberings, and a contemporary cartoon which with seeming improbability shows a harp in the orchestra pit for *Thespis*, Roderick Spencer and Selwyn Tillett[2] showed in 1990 that these two pieces formed part of the ballet music for *Thespis* in 1871, added to three which Sullivan re-used from *L'Ile enchantée*. Thus from Gilbert and Sullivan's earliest ('lost') collaboration a five-movement ballet suite, at least, has become accessible – and has been recorded.

Sullivan's 'light orchestral' style, exemplified in his ballets and in the dance-like numbers of his incidental music to plays, certainly sits happily with the music of the operettas. But in all his orchestral self-borrowing, Sullivan never borrowed an orchestral number to make a vocal one, if we except the pointing of the finale from *The Merchant of Venice* (1871) to 'Never mind the why and wherefore' in *HMS Pinafore*. On the other hand, for all the apparent hand-in-glove closeness between Gilbert's words and Sullivan's music, it is noticeable that Sullivan's operetta music has always made a strong appeal in 'absolute' terms of melody and harmony – in orchestral selections and the overtures as concert pieces. The brilliant re-use of this music by Charles Mackerras in his ballet music, *Pineapple Poll* (1951), itself often heard in concert form, reinforces the point.

Sullivan, it has to be remembered, lived at a time when 'light music' – linked often to the dance, or to national airs – was a respectable and money-making sideline for the most 'serious' composers. Today's loftier taste has banished such works as Liszt's *Hungarian Rhapsodies* or Massenet's *Scènes Pittoresques* from the standard orchestral concert, along with the ballet music from Rossini's *William Tell* and Gounod's *Faust*. It might be argued that Sullivan's light music as a whole, embracing not only the operettas but the orchestral suites from *The Tempest* onward, stand up better against their European counterparts than do the 'serious' works such as the Symphony. Indeed the exceptional success of the *Overtura di Ballo* points to its unique harnessing of dance-like melody and rhythms to a construction of symphonic dimensions.

The discovery that this work rests on a metamorphosis of a single thematic idea through all its movements (see p. 62) hints at a route towards an eventual deeper analysis of Sullivan's style than is possible in a biography of this nature. Indeed, such a deeper, unifying analysis has not yet been attempted. Gervase Hughes' *The Music of Arthur Sullivan* (1960), unprecedented in its day for consideration of the less familiar works, was nevertheless preoccupied with stylistic detail and with resemblances to other composers' idiom. Today's musicological climate has room for a more structural approach. Meanwhile, metamorphosis of themes has since been shown – by the present writer[3] – to underlie the rich diversity of *The Mikado*, where the Japanese-pentatonic figure of 'Miya sama, miya sama' produces, among other things, the introductory melody of 'The sun, whose rays' and the tune of Ko-Ko's and Katisha's 'If that is so, sing derry-down-derry' as the following examples show:

Mi - ya   sa - ma,   mi - ya   sa - ma,   On   n'm - ma   no   ma - yé   ni

Ex. 1a

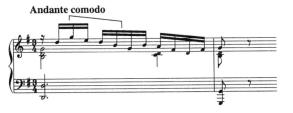

Ex. 1b

Allegretto con brio

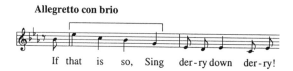

If that is so, Sing der-ry down der-ry!

Ex. 1c

The more overt (though not so extensive) metamorphosis of the Lord Chancellor's theme in *Iolanthe* is well known. But the process may be more profound: one wonders if the 'independent' counter-melody in the overture to *Iolanthe* (see p. 84) will not turn out, after all, to be a major key relation of some of the Lord Chancellor's minor key music with which it shares a 6/8 rhythm. Sullivan embraced the principle of metamorphosis (deriving it, no doubt, from Schumann rather than from Liszt) as early as his music to *The Tempest* (1861), where a theme representing Prospero's magical powers recurs in varied guise. At first a plaintive 'warning' figure on the oboe (example 2a), it changes its rhythm and character as the main tune of the Banquet Dance (example 2b). The metamorphosis is dramatically appropriate since the ostensibly jolly banquet is in fact a manifestation of Prospero's magic.

Andante con moto

P espress.

Ex. 2a

Allegro grazioso

Ex. 2b

All such investigation and speculation is not, of course, intended to diminish the recognition of Sullivan's pre-eminence simply as a melodist and as a word-setter. In 1990 the latter function was penetratingly analysed by Robert Fink – the first such analysis invoking the modern aesthetic theory of musical expectation, as expounded by Carl Dahlhaus and Leonard B. Meyer. (The appearance of Fink's article in the American scholarly journal *Nineteenth Century Music* testified to the

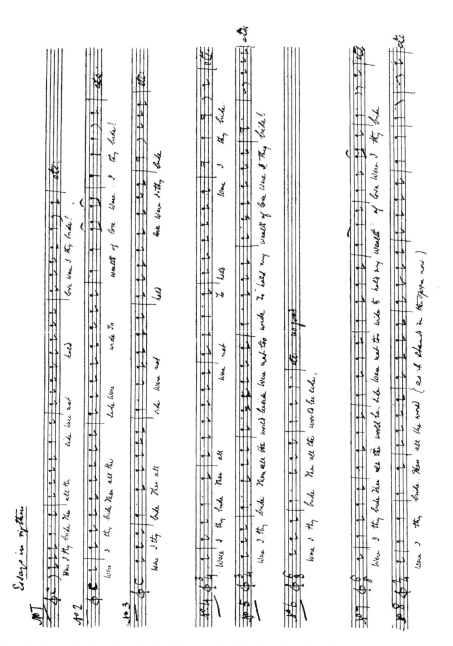

Facsimile reproduction of the "Essays in Rhythm" referred to on page 422.

new 'respectability' accorded to the music of Britain in the pre-Elgar era.) Fink finds a starting-point in Sullivan's own insistence on first getting the rhythm right, as expounded to his early biographer Arthur Lawrence. Taking Phoebe's 'Were I thy bride' from *The Yeomen of the Guard* as his example, the composer set down various settings which had to be rejected before the right one was found. Sullivan's 'Essays in Rhythm' (reproduced in his own handwriting on page 421) led him to the familiar final form of the tune:

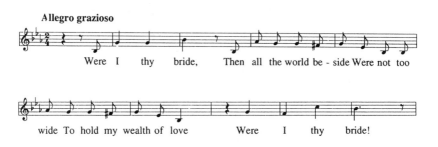

Ex. 3b

One must add that it is not only the rhythm which required a decisive 'primary' approach on Sullivan's part (that is, before detail of melody). A remarkable structure is adopted, complex though transparent, which contrasts with the simplicity of Phoebe's earlier song, 'When maiden loves' (two stanzas set identically, plus coda). Here, confronted by Gilbert with no less than eight five-line stanzas of identical pattern, each but the last ending with the conditional 'Were I thy bride', Sullivan takes a master's path to avoid monotony and to make room for greater manoeuvre. To each stanza he gives the same metrical setting, line-by-line, but he groups the stanzas formally in pairs. By the end of the first pair, a modulation from E flat to the dominant key of B flat has been established; the second pair starts as the first but ends in the home key; the next pair continues the melody through more remote keys; the final pair (stanzas 7 and 8) gives a sense of rounding-off in repeating (nearly!) stanzas 3 and 4. Throughout, the words 'Were I thy bride' never lose their even, four-note utterance, nor does the lightly pattering accompaniment cease – an insistence within diversity.

But Sullivan's resourcefulness is not finished yet. Shadbolt, having been wheedled by Phoebe's false assurances, at last gets the truth: 'I'm not thy bride!'. A change of chord (as compared with the parallel place at the end of stanza 4) cues the surprise, and the vocal declamation is appropriately altered too. Nothing could be more dismissive than that *staccato* articulation of the downward final notes: see example 4.

Fink's own analysis, concentrating on *The Mikado*, shows how radically Sullivan's musical patterns may diverge from Gilbert's verbal ones, so that after

Ex. 4

being out of step a sudden coming together gives an exciting emphasis. He points out that the opening line of the quartet (Yum-Yum, Pitti-Sing, Peep-Bo, Pooh-Bah) in Act 1, 'So please you, sir, we much regret', scans *naturally* – that is, verbally – as a plain sequence of iambic feet, just as one says 'As I was walking down the street'. Each two syllables might be expected to take the space of two musical beats, making eight beats. Instead, Sullivan's bouncy rhythm squeezes syllables 2–5 and temporarily loses the verbal beat, only to regain it with the coincidence of verbal and musical stress on '(re)gret' – the very point of impudence[4] which is at the core of the whole number:

Ex. 5

Yet Sullivan's harmony as well as his rhythm and melody can be significant as text-setting. In the seventh bar of Yum-Yum's melody, 'The sun, whose rays' occurs an unexpected chord of D minor within the key of G major. Not only harmonically audacious and piquant, it is also marvellously apt in mirroring the verbal switch from positive statements ('are all ablaze', 'he scorns') to the negative of 'He don't exclaim, "I blush for shame . . .".' It does not matter, of course, that the next stanza has no such verbal switch; the point has already been musically made.

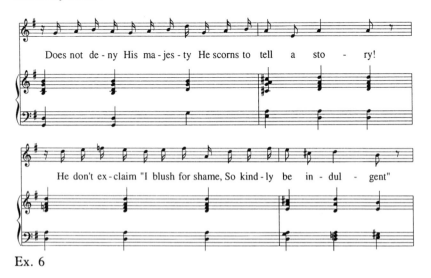

Ex. 6

The first-act finale of *Iolanthe* provides a far-reaching harmonic shift of similar verbal felicity:

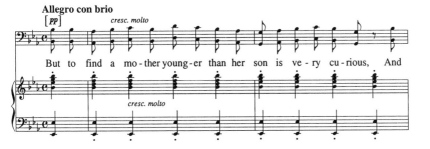

Ex. 7

The composer presents the resolution of the chord-sequence at the same moment as the resolution of the doubt ('spurious!'). Moreover, he accentuates the point with a squeeze of harmonic rhythm: compare the number of chord-changes in successive bars. The same chord sequence has, in fact, been already heard in the preceding stanzas, but in those stanzas the main melody at this point of climax has been given to the orchestral accompaniment. That downward vocal diminished fifth – clinching the word 'spurious' – is reserved for this stanza only, a fine example of a composer in absolute command of word-setting.

Such instances leave no doubt that Gilbert's tight rhyme-schemes, plus the expectation of response a composer could get for such text-setting in the theatre, stimulated Sullivan to his peak of boldness and ingenuity. The lack of such qualities in most of his drawing-room songs and hymns is just what penalizes them. The point was vigorously made half a century ago by Erik Routley, then editor of the *Bulletin of the Hymn Society of Great Britain and Ireland*. Castigating Sullivan's hymn-settings for 'trivial and second-rate' melodies and harmonizations, he exempts only the untypical *Hush'd was the evening hymn* (tune-name 'Samuel'), designated by Sullivan as a children's hymn and set for unison voices. Such settings as *For ever with the Lord* and *A few more years shall roll* (tune-names 'Nearer Home' and 'Leominster') are written off by Routley[5] as 'excellent examples, with their sticky harmonies and deadly melodies, of what hymn-tunes should not be.' It is possible to feel, however, that the high-aesthetic dismissal of 'Onward, Christian Soldiers' for its repetitious notes (and for other reasons) somewhat misses the point. Repeated notes *may* be monotonous – but audiences of *The Mikado* are not struck with boredom at 'The threatened cloud has passed away . . .'.

Routley's fault-finding may, perhaps, be applied even more cogently to many of the solo songs. It is as if Sullivan, when writing for the drawing-room just as in writing for the church, had actually convinced himself that the obvious was the desirable. Such a song as 'Sleep, my love, sleep' prompts the genuine question how such a 'schooled' composer as Sullivan could arrive at a setting which might have been rejected for banality by such a self-taught troubadour as Stephen Foster (composer of 'Beautiful Dreamer' as well as 'Old Folks at Home'). It is indeed plausible that he *deliberately* invited a low-level response. The gap between the worst of his ballads and the best of his art-songs (such as the Schubertian *Orpheus with his lute* and the Gounodesque 'Oh, ma charmante') is barely imaginable.

David Eden, whose book *Gilbert and Sullivan: The Creative Conflict* (1986) is one of the few to venture on psychological analysis, goes further:

His [Sullivan's] entry into the Chapel Royal may be regarded as the most grievous blow ever suffered by English music, for it tainted him with the spiritual bankruptcy of Victorian Anglicanism. He would have done better to enter a circus . . . . As all his works show, he blossomed whenever the requirements of his text carried him away from religion and domesticity.

Whether those exquisite 'madrigals' and the like would have ever appeared in the operettas *without* the Chapel Royal experience may be doubted, however, and Eden's generalization is not sufficient to explain either the failure of *Ivanhoe* or, on the other hand, the attractiveness of the 'light orchestral' idiom without words.

Both debate and exploration will continue. Extension of interest outside the

English-speaking world is indicated by the imminent publication (1992) of Meinhard Saremba's German book[6] on the composer, the first in any language other than English. That such a book should come from Germany, where at least part of Sullivan's musical style originated, is appropriate. Saremba concludes that the works of theatrical collaboration with Gilbert are 'not just for the English stage' and indeed have a musical richness greater than the term 'operetta' in its usual Continental sense suggests. Arthur Sullivan now being known in greater breadth and with greater contextual reference than at any time since his death, the prospects for his post-150th-birthday reputation are auspicious.

Notes on the Text

Each note is prefaced by the opening words of the phrase to which it refers. Bibliographical references in small capitals (e.g. HIBBERT/ILN in the first entry) are more fully detailed in the Bibliography, p. 467.

In identifying library collections, BL is used for the British Library, Reference Division and PML for the Gilbert and Sullivan collection in the Pierpont Morgan Library, New York. All *letters* referred to come from the collection in the latter library, unless otherwise identified. BDC indicates one of a number of letters kindly supplied (in a typed transcript, the originals having perished) by Dame Bridget D'Oyly Carte.

Among references to periodicals, GSJ indicates the *Gilbert and Sullivan Journal*, MT the *Musical Times*, SASS the journal of the Sir Arthur Sullivan Society.

Chapter 1

1 *Two hundred men*: for this and the following details, see HIBBERT/ILN, p. 13ff.

2 *The annual output of pianos*: for details see EHRLICH. In the quoted output figures, some pianos of course went for export; but conversely the British consumer bought French and (later) German and American models.

3 *spreading railway network*: see BEST, especially pp. 68–72.

4 *London's population*: that is, for the area of what had become the London County Council. See GOMME p. 127.

5 *'The Lost Chord'*: see EHRLICH p. 96.

6 *singing classes at Exeter Hall*: for the whole of this stage of the sight-singing movement, see RAINBOW/L.

7 *arrangements are being made*: the 'Henschel' and 'Richter' series were concert-promotions centred on (and with the financial interest of) the eminent conductors named; similarly with Pablo de Sarasate (1844–1908), a violinist immensely popular in London as elsewhere. Ambrose Austin was the manager of the St James's Hall and a promoter on his own account. The report cited is from *Truth*, 19 August 1886.

8 *Lambeth*: see the extensive description in WALFORD vol. VI, especially p. 25.

9 *her nickname*: the form 'Clema' was used by her husband, according to ALLEN/S; 'Clemma' occurs in a letter to her written from Barbados on 2 August 1852 by her second cousin Thomas Seymour Philipps.

10 *1805 or 1806*: Thomas Sullivan's army records at the Royal Military College show him first enlisting on 3 September 1820, aged 15 years 0 months. The birth-year of 1805 is thus indicated, though the month does not tally with the birthday which the family observed. The College record of his re-enlisting on 28 April 1845 at '39 years 7 months' is consistent with the age first noted.

11 *various other family traditions*: including an account of how Thomas Sullivan and a comrade narrowly prevented the heart of Napoleon from being carried off by rats! The records of Sullivan's army service are now in charge of the headquarters of the Duke of Edinburgh's Royal Regiment (Berkshire and Wiltshire). Correspondence between the curator of its records, and the late Leslie Weaver, who investigated the matter was kindly shown to me by the latter. It is this investigation which exposes as fanciful the anecdotes told about 'Sergeant' Sullivan in the pages of S/FLOWER. See also SASS 15 (1983).

12 *Duke of York's school*: see the description in WALFORD: 'The affairs of the Royal Military Asylum are regulated by the commissioners appointed by the Government, who have to apply to Parliament for an annual grant for the support of the institution. The commissioners also have the selection of the children whose admission is regulated in accordance with the following rules: "Orphans, or those whose fathers have been killed, or have died on foreign stations. Those who have lost their mothers, and whose fathers are absent on the duty abroad; those whose fathers are ordered on foreign service, or whose parents have other children to maintain." The children are supported, lodged, and educated until they are of suitable age to be disposed of as servants and apprentices. The boys undergo a regular military training and it is a pleasing sight to witness them going through their exercises, with their military band of juvenile performers.' S/FLOWER states that Arthur Sullivan's grandmother (wife of Thomas, senior) was its first matron. This is untrue. Mr Leslie Weaver found, in the minute-books of the school, a note of appreciation of 'Mrs Bold' as the only matron of the school from its inception in 1803 until she retired in 1840. See also WALFORD vol. V p. 77.

13 *music-copying*: this and other details come from FINDON.

14 *returned to the Royal Military College*: information (here and in the next chapter) supplied to Leslie Weaver by the Central Library of the College.

15 *'learned to play every wind instrument'*: the quotation, in the composer's own words (an autobiographical article in the periodical *M.A.P.*, 4 February 1889) refers definitely to the period when the composer's father was at the Royal Military College, where 'the band my father conducted was small but very good'. In YOUNG/S the quotation is wrongly referred to Thomas Sullivan's later period at the Royal Military School of Music where the band was not small and Sullivan did not conduct it.

16 *how funds could have been available*: but by April 1854 'Isabella', apparently a daughter or ward of Plees, was living with the Sullivans at Sandhurst while Arthur was at school in Bayswater – possibly a reciprocal arrangement. At this date Plees was still writing rather formally to Mrs Sullivan, and it seems unlikely that the arrangement had been long in operation or had arisen from long-standing friendship.

17 *later recollection*: article in *M.A.P.* (*supra*).

18 *Sandhurst parish church*: see LAWRENCE p. 237.

19 *uniforms of navy blue*: see RAINBOW/CR p. 77, quoting an unattributed earlier source.

20 *enrolment in the Chapel Royal*: for the early musical career, see the article on him by his friend George Grove in GROVE I.

Chapter 2

1 *W. H. Cummings*: see his article in MT, February 1907, quoted in RAINBOW/CR. To this book, the first to recognize Helmore's decisive role, I owe much in this chapter.

2 *musical changes in Anglican worship*: see TEMPERLEY/EP for a consideration of this whole topic.

3 *a madrigal*: lot 168 in SOTHEBY.

4 *'I shall miss . . .'*: letter from his mother quoted in ALLEN/S.

5 *the reopening of the Crystal Palace*: for Sullivan's participation, see LAWRENCE.

6 *an anthem . . . was given*: source, S/FLOWER only, quoting letter from Sullivan of May 1855.

7 *first boy*: letter to his mother quoted in LAWRENCE.

8 *His father . . . received the news*:see Helmore's daughter's reminiscences in MT, February 1901.

9 *'On Sundays between services . . . '*: ibid.

10 *Earlier that month*: letter dated 3 September 1856, in the possession (1991) of Peter Joslin.

11 *a cartoon of* 1857 by John Leech: reproduced in DE MARÉ (1973), p. 117.

12 *John Goss*: for the 'lineage' and the fugue, see David Mackie, 'Fugue "a tre" after Mozart', in SASS no.8 (June 1980). The false attribution of this fugue to Sullivan persists in *Grove* VI.

13 *Bishop Charles J. Corfe*: see MT, February 1902.

14 *Helmore's own report*: the transcription in S/FLOWER is inaccurate ('diversions' instead of 'divisions', i.e. florid variations). Original at PML.

15 *Grisi and Mario*: Sullivan mentioned Drury Lane Theatre when recalling the incident much later (LAWRENCE), but these artists were not then performing there. He could have heard them at Covent Garden in May–July 1855 in *La favorita, Lucrezia Borgia*, or *Don Pasquale* (all by Donizetti); or in 1856, after the Covent Garden theatre had been destroyed by fire, and before the new one opened in 1857, in performances at Her Majesty's Theatre or at the Lyceum.

16 *a massed parade in Scutari*: for this incident and the bands generally, see FARMER.

17 *Kneller Hall*: Thomas Sullivan was 'chief professor of the clarinet', according to the article on him in *Grove* I (written from personal knowledge by Grove himself); there is a mistaken tradition at Kneller Hall itself that he taught 'the lower brass' (supported by an inscription on a photograph, but the inscription is not contemporary with the photograph). The tradition is supported in a shadowy anonymous source quoted in BINNS, p. 60.

18 *a skilled industrial labourer*: for this and the level of such earnings generally, see BEST, passim.

19 *Pimlico was*: see the chapter on the 'Pimlico riots' in RAINBOW/CR, p. 143.

20 *amateur dramatic society*: see Edward Peacock's first-hand account in MT, March 1901.

21 *Benedict suggested*: letter to Smart, in the possession of Terence Rees.

Chapter 3

1 *'Sullivan's excellent talent'*:the text of Moscheles' letter as given in S/FLOWER is taken from a translation (now in PML) made by Klingemann for Sullivan's benefit. I have slightly improved Klingemann's English.

2 *I can say without hesitation*: Undated letter from Clay to Sullivan (year 1863 authenticated by Christopher Knowles) written from Dresden. Around this time another friend of Sullivan's, Seymour Egerton, Earl of Wilton, was also taking lessons in Leipzig (as an amateur) and had brought his wife with him.

3 *'as they are on Sunday'*: letter quoted in LAWRENCE.

4 *'We, that is to say . . .'* letter in the possession of Peter Joslin.

5 *the composer John Barnett*: ALLEN/S confuses the two John Barnetts and has the father studying alongside his son Domenico and daughters. The student was John F. Barnett (nephew of the elder John): outstripping Sullivan as a pianist, he had the honour of appearing as a soloist with the Gewandhaus Orchestra in March 1860.

6 *played the double-bass part*: see an entry in a diary kept by Sullivan at Leipzig, quoted in BAILY/GSB, p. 21.

7 *'I come in for all the conducting now'*:source S/FLOWER (only), p. 27.

8 *'grand nigger performance'*: for this and other recollections (obviously Sullivan's own) of Leipzig, see LAWRENCE.

9 *conduct an operetta*: letter quoted in LAWRENCE, p. 29.

10 *The season was . . .*: this and the following information come chiefly from the reports in the *Neue Zeitschrift für Musik* (Leipzig, weekly).

11 *Joachim . . . Viardot-Garcia*: it was in Leipzig that Joachim, as a boy, had made his first public appearance in 1843, as a supporting artist to Pauline Viardot-Garcia (1821–90), the celebrated mezzo-soprano for whom Berlioz made the now standard adaptation of Gluck's *Orfeo ed Euridice*. See p. 35.

12 *visited the Leipzig synagogue*: see KLEIN/T., p. 336.

13 *Bache*: his letters home from Leipzig (BACHE, pp. 133–9) have valuable references to Sullivan's student days.

14 *thrice called upon*: letter to his mother, 11 April 1861, quoted in ALLEN/S., p. 8.

15 *from his brother Fred*: letter of 14 January 1860, quoted in ALLEN/S., p. 7.

16 *not of music, but of reading . . .*: according to YOUNG/S, p. 29.

17 *constables*: according to YOUNG/S they were conscripted, as a matter of police duty, into church attendance and into the choir. In the absence of evidence this seems unlikely. This being a wealthy parish, they might well have been paid.

18 *'rubbed up my Hebrew'*: later, in 1868, Grove would find his friend Tennyson 'working hard at Hebrew' (see GRAVES/G). Under the inspiration of theological studies the cultivation of the language in Victorian times was much greater than in non-Jewish circles than today. Grove said he had been taught the Hebrew alphabet at school. J. W. Davison (see DAVISON) seems to have dabbled in Hebrew also.

19 *Admission to the Crystal Palace*: see the *Illustrated Crystal Palace Guide*, 1862. Return tickets by rail from London Bridge, at 1s. 6d. third class, *included* admission to the Palace. Visitors arrived at the Palace's own station and walked under cover the whole way in.

20 *Hermann Klein*: see KLEIN/T. In some later writings he spelt his name 'Herman'.

21 *Frederick Lehmann*: His brother Rudolf (1819–1905) married Amelia Chambers, Nina's sister: that is, the two brothers married two sisters. A daughter of the Rudolf Lehmanns was Liza Lehmann (1862–1918), the composer. But it was a son of

Frederick (not Rudolf) and Nina Lehmann who was named (with English spelling) Rudolph (1856–1929): see p. 34. See LEHMANN/J and LEHMANN/RC.

22 *May Banks*: one of the leading British sopranos of the time, she was curiously not included by Grove (despite his professional contact with her) in the first edition of his *Dictionary of Music and Musicians*. Her dates I have been unable to ascertain.

23 *probably in Davison's pen*: music criticism in the daily press of that day was generally anonymous.

24 *Athenaeum*: 12 April 1862. Coincidentally, the same issue carried a long, enthusiastic review of what is now recognized as one of the most important of Victorian paintings, Frith's *The Railway Station*.

25 *sent to Helmore*: letter, no. 162 of Sotheby's Catalogue, 11 May 1959.

26 *almost 30 years later*: see HANSLICK, pp. 288–295.

Chapter 4

1 *actress . . . prostitute*: See BAKER/RVA, especially his attempt ('The Position of the Actress') to find reasons for the attitude. P. 101: 'If theatrical costume encouraged the view that actresses were women of easy virtue, facial cosmetics took the parallel a stage further. In general, Victorian women used make-up sparingly and with discretion. Prostitutes, on the other hand, were conspicuous for flouting this convention, hence the common description of them as "painted women" . . . Women wearing make-up were readily categorized as actresses in tones of disparagement which reflected the traditional association made with prostitutes.'

2 *a French observer*: see ESQUIROS, quoted in DE MARÉ p. 143.

3 *'orchestra' meaning 'band' and choir together*: the word 'orchestra' was also used on occasion in its classical sense, i.e. an area for performance. In the *Illustrated Crystal Palace Penny Guide* (1862), the 'Great Handel Orchestra' was the name given to such an area.

4 *Charles Dickens was to be heard*: he gave ten readings between 13 March and 27 June. *The Boots at the Holly Tree Inn* was an item adapted from a story, *The Holly Tree*, which Dickens had written for the Christmas issue of *Household Words* in 1855.

5 *in Chorley's company*: Chorley published a further eulogy of the work ('There has been no such first appearance in England in our time') in the *Athenaeum* on 19 April.

6 *'He seized my hand . . .'*: Sullivan's own account, in the magazine *M.A.P*, 4 February 1899.

7 *'Shall I tell you . . .'*: letter reproduced from LEHMANN/RC.

8 *'The German colony'*: quoted, in Hallé's words, in KENNEDY/HT, p. 20.

9 *'I write to wish you'*: quoted in LEHMANN/RC.

10 *The complete work*: 'An opera, *The False Heiress*' was sold for £275 to Metzler, the publisher, on 16 July 1868; Sullivan bought back the score and 'all the rights of publication and performance' on 24 May 1880, but granted to the firm 'the right of publishing and performing the song *Over the Roof* from the said opera'. See REES/SRC, supplemented by a letter from Dr Rees to the author, 21 October 1981.

11 *certain revisions*: these had been made for a performance of some items by the Musical Society (letter from Sullivan to its secretary, Charles K. Salaman, 3 May 1862). It took place on 20 September 1862. Sullivan asked Salaman for a loan of the altered parts for a performance of the symphony in Liverpool.

12 *a note of his visit*: source, S/FLOWER, who gives 'Rosa', not 'Rose' – but Carl Rose (see p. 23) had not yet adopted the other form. 'Courtenay', evidently a singer, is unidentified.

13 *Dickens himself*: Chorley, but not Sullivan, is mentioned in the near-contemporary biography of Dickens by John FORSTER and in Edgar JOHNSON'S authoritative modern biography. PML holds a letter from Dickens to Frederick Lehmann, 4 November 1863, referring to 'your bright boy': 'I send my love to him and to his mother'. Though ALLEN/S assumes this to refer to Sullivan, it is much more likely to refer to Lehmann's own wife and son.

14 *sombre tone*: the Guards bands had not played at Windsor itself between the Prince Consort's death and the royal marriage. *Illustrated London News*, 14 March 1863.

15 *'all the military bands'*: letter of Sullivan to Charles K. Salaman, 6 February 1863, quoted in ALLEN/S. The *Princess of Wales's March* was later republished (also for piano solo) as a *Marche danoise* with a statement that it had been composed 'on Danish airs'. YOUNG/S wrongly lists a *March danois* (sic) as a different work. The *Procession March*, however, *is* different: see following note. An advertisement by the publishers Cramer, Beale in the *Illustrated London News*, 14 March 1863, lists both.

16 *in St George's Chapel*: ALLEN/S supposes Sullivan's march was played there, but it is not included in the music as named in the report on the ceremony in the *Illustrated London News* of a few days later. It is of some interest, since the church use of Mendelssohn's *Wedding March* is often said to stem from royal example, that this was not performed either. The 'War March of the Priests' (very popular at the time) from Mendelssohn's *Athalie* was performed. For the chaotic organization of the ceremony see LONGFORD/ V: 'Lord Palmerston [Prime Minister] and Lady Westminster had to travel back [from Windsor to London] third class on the special train, the latter loaded with half a million pounds' worth of diamonds. Disraeli sat on his wife's lap.'

17 *'presented'*: see *Musical Standard*, 13 March 1869.

18 *A. J. Hipkins*: letter in BL Additional Manuscripts 41636/32. A letter [in PML] to Sullivan from one Robert Tennent written from Ireland on 10 May 1866 and presuming a considerable intimacy, may have a connection. Perhaps 'Aramis', youngest of the Three Musketeers, was his sister, with Sullivan the other one of the trio.

19 *'Whilst I was playing the organ solo'*: the source of this story is Sullivan's own 12 pages of memoranda prepared for Charles WILLEBY to incorporate into his book of 1893. Compiled so long after some of the events they purportedly describe, these memoranda may not be wholly or literally reliable. In this instance the incident has been identified (see TILLETT/VME) with a dance for Salvioni herself, not for the second *danseuse*.

20 *William Allingham*: see his *Diary*, 17 July 1863.

21 *L'Ile enchantée*: not first given on 14 or 28 May as variously stated, but on 16 May. The announcement in *The Times* on that day specified 'first time' – to follow *La sonnambula* with Patti (a fairly short opera without ballet). It could not have been given on 14 May, when the opera was Meyerbeer's *Robert le diable*, which includes its own ballet and which was advertised without after-piece.

22 *wrote directly to Costa*: letter quoted in MT, June 1901.

23 *an unusual five-bar phrasing*: music example in HUGHES.

24 *at the Prince's Theatre, Manchester*: The omission of this stage performance of *The Tempest* from the record of Sullivan's earlier years in the first edition of Grove's

Dictionary of Music and Musicians.(1879–89) is curious – particularly because Grove himself, a personal friend, wrote the entry on Sullivan. The omission was corrected by a letter-writer in the *Era*, Beddoes Peacock, on 14 June 1889. According to the theatre announcement, the music was 'with the exception of Purcell's and Dr Arne's songs, by Mr A. S. Sullivan'. The correspondent commented: 'Notwithstanding that Lancashire was at the period going through the throes of the cotton famine, the production was a success in the fullest acceptance of the term, being visited during the 31 representations allotted to it by 62,000 persons, and was reproduced the following Easter, when it was played 14 times.'

25 *Lodge of Harmony*: I am indebted for information to Leslie Wilson, J.P., the secretary (1981) of the Lodge. See also KLEIN/T p. 54.

Chapter 5

1 *Bernard Shaw*: see his *Music in London* (collected ed. 1927) vol. 3 p. 68.

2 *Liverpool Philharmonic Society*: see LIVPHIL 10 July 1865, 13 and 15 April 1867.

3 *Col P. Paget*: see Sullivan's letter to him, 31 July 1865: copy in the possession of Peter Joslin.

4 *The second song was encored*: report in *The Times*, 15 April 1867.

5 *to the Liverpool Philharmonic Society*: letter addressed to G. Kurtz, 7 February 1867, in BL Additional Manuscripts 33965/92.

6 *appeared in English*: translated by E. Wilberforce, 1866: it was for A. D. Coleridge's translation of 1869 that Grove compiled an appendix.

7 *Fred Sullivan was with them*: these and other details are from Arthur Sullivan's notebook about the trip, now in PML.

8 *'When we wrote our names'*: letter to his mother, 9 October 1867.

9 *claimed to have been at his christening*: note in Sullivan's hand in his notebook at PML (see above).

10 *wrote Grove*: The sources are his letters to a Sydenham friend, Olga von Glehn, and the appendix to Coleridge's translation of the Schubert biography (see previous footnote). Both are quoted in GRAVES/G.

11 *'Using as intermediaries . . . Moscheles'*: a personal letter from Sullivan (Sotheby's sale catalogue 11 May 1959, item 75) sends 'My kindest love and remembrances to Dear Mrs Moscheles, and tell her that I have kept my promise to her and have turned 25 years without marrying, am I not good?' (24 September 1867).

12 *great success*: letter quoted in S/FLOWER (p. 57)

13 *'Rienzi'*: quoted in S/FLOWER (p. 57) from an entry by Sullivan in a 'note-book' (now lost?).

Chapter 6

1 *avid reader of the Press*: 'Dearest Mum . . . Did you see Friday's *Pall Mall Gazette*? There was an article on English opera, mentioning me' (letter undated, presumably 1866). There are many similar indications of Sullivan's keenness in spotting such references, both at this period and later. Membership of gentlemen's clubs gave access to newspapers and magazines.

2 *Musical Times*: see pp. 263, 288, 350, 425 in 1866. The criticism of the symphony alluded to the St James's Hall performance. The *Manchester Guardian* notice is reproduced in KENNEDY/HT, p. 41.

3 *Pyne-Harrison company*: led by the singers Louisa Pyne and Walter Harrison. See WHITE and ROSENTHAL.

4 *Verdi had been interested*: Sullivan learnt that from the newly published *Reminiscences* (1864) of the impresario Benjamin Lumley.

5 *not yet translated*: its first public performance in English was in London in 1871. The Moray Minstrels' performance was probably in French, since those concerned with it always referred to it by the French title and no mention survives of a translator. See LAWRENCE for Sullivan's own account.

6 *given the Moray Minstrels*: that this was the first performance seems established by the weight of evidence: see the exhaustive article in GSJ, January 1968. Later, Burnand claimed (letter to the *Illustrated Sporting and Dramatic News*, 22 November 1879) that an earlier performance had been given at *his* house: this seems in fact to have been a rehearsal.

7 *first public performance*: the advertisement in *The Times* on 11 May definitely indicates that this was the performance in question. There was a repetition at the Royal Gallery of Illustration on 18 May (presumably without orchestra, which could not be accommodated there). YOUNG/S cites a Manchester performance before this (17 December 1866) with a 'Mrs Bouncer': but this must have been the play, not the operetta.

8 *Twiss . . . Blunt*: Not 'Twist' as in YOUNG/S. Arthur Blunt, an amateur actor, later turned professional under the name of Arthur Cecil.

9 *Du Maurier's diary*: quoted in ORMOND.

10 *in Paris*: date and place from description of the MS in SOTHEBY.

11 *complete an overture*: Mary Carr, née Hamilton, told MT (February 1901) that she 'saved his life' by helping Sullivan to copy out the violin parts 'on the morning of its first band rehearsal' after he had worked all night scoring.

12 *John Scott Russell*: see EMMERSON/R and EMMERSON/A. Mr Emmerson tells me (private communication) that John Russell added 'Scott' (his mother's surname) to his own name. 'Scott Russell' is not therefore a double-barrelled surname, though it serves to distinguish him from other famous Russells of the day.

13 *'This is the first 13th of May'*: in Rachel Scott Russell's letter, 'Dr Pole' is doubtless William Pole (1814–1900) – like Grove, a civil engineer and a musical scholar; 'the Byngs' probably refers to the family of the clergyman at whose church Sullivan was organist (p. 79); 'Hiller' is the composer Ferdinand Hiller (see p. 67).

Chapter 7

1 *Baroness Burdett-Coutts*: at that time she was the only woman raised in her own right to the peerage (in recognition of her public service, 1871). She died in 1906, aged 92, and is buried in Westminster Abbey.

2 *three songs*: see REES/SRC. On the contract the songs are named as 'In the Summer Long Ago', 'The Moon in Silent Brightness', and (unidentifiable in any published form!) 'We Gathered the Roses'.

3 *an agreement with Boosey*: according to YOUNG/S, p. 60.

4   *Millais . . . Dickens*: see MILLAIS, 1/75.

5   *'and, finally . . .'*: letter to 'My dear Gruneisen', Monday [13 December 1869].
Charles Gruneisen was a critic (and also a distinguished war correspondent) who had
adversely commented on *Kenilworth*. Characteristically, that did not prevent Sullivan
from cultivating him.

6   *legal action*: Reeves won his case, in which Sullivan gave evidence in his support, but
emerged the worse off because of costs, adverse publicity, and the fact that he was
never again asked to sing with the Edinburgh Choral Union. See WADDELL.

7   *John Goss*: His letter quoted in ALLEN/S, p. 22.

8   *'overtura'*: Beethoven (in the *Grosse Fuge* for string quartet) also presumed such an
Italian word, but the Italians render 'overture' as 'sinfonia'.

9   *Josiah Pittman* (1816–86): he held the post still described by the archaic title of
maestro al cembalo (presumably accompanying recitatives at the piano) at Her
Majesty's Theatre till 1868, and thereafter until 1880 at Covent Garden.

10   *'If people like . . .'*: letter from Sullivan, presumably to his mother, quoted in S/
FLOWER, p. 61.

11   *Unregistered brothels*: see ZELDIN p. 307.

12   *Madame Conneau*: for her role in Nice, see SARRY.

13   *Miss Romanes*: presumably a sister of the eminent scientist and theologian George
John Romanes (1848–94), who would have been known to Grove and thus to
Sullivan.

14   *'I was extremely sorry'*: Gounod's letter (in French) is addressed from 9 Park Place,
Regents Park, W., and is dated 'Thursday 15th' – which must refer to December
1870.

15   *'Ages Ago'*: Jane W. Stedman's book on Gilbert's career before his collaboration with
Sullivan (see STEDMAN/GB) reproduces the complete musical score of *Ages Ago*, as well
as the libretto.

16   *Leslie Baily*: see BAILY/GSB, p. 11.

17   *said to have netted £40,000*: obituary of Gilbert in *Daily Telegraph*, 30 May 1911.

18   *Gilbert is doing . . .*: quoted (no date) in S/FLOWER, p. 68. The piece was probably *Our
Island Home*, for which Reed himself eventually composed a score. See REES/T, p. 5.

Chapter 8

1   *the French low-standard pitch*: according to MT January 1869 (quoted in SCHOLES p. 406)
the variety of pitch in British use was such that Broadwood's were obliged to stock
pianos at three different pitches. The Society of Arts was not able to exert decisive
pressure. The Leeds Festival, under Sullivan's conductorship from 1880, did not
conform to low pitch (requiring a re-tuning of the organ) until 1898.

2   *'Bloody Week'*: see COBBAN.

3   *an official French medal*: bequeathed by Sullivan to the Royal Academy of Music.

4   *Mrs Helmore*: see letter from the Helmores' daughter, Kate, MT, Feb. 1901.

5   *Christine Nilsson* (1843–1921); *Ilona de [or di] Murska* (1836–74): leading operatic
sopranos of the time. Sullivan's draft mis-spells the name as Nillson. He was later to
know Christine Nilsson and her husband really well.

6 *Gaiety*: 'A Gaiety Girl' was not merely a recognized type of sophisticated charmer. It was to be the actual name of a musical comedy (1893) by Sidney Jones, better known as composer of *The Geisha*.

7 *Toole . . . £100 a week*: see *Dictionary of National Biography*.

8 *Thespis*: see REES/T for an exceptionally thorough historical investigation.

9 *'Onward, Christian Soldiers'*: see also MATTHEWS.

10 *Brown-Borthwick* (1840-94): a collection of Sullivan's letters to him, from which these extracts are quoted by permission, is in the possession of Dr Chalmers Burns. The wedding anthem was *Rejoice in the Lord*.

11 *at least 45 other hymns*: some were issued as 'sacred part-songs'. To his own edition of *Church Hymns, with Tunes* (Society for Promoting Christian Knowledge, 1874), Sullivan contributed 14 already-existing hymns and 24 new ones.

12 *with whom he often stayed*: A letter of 1901 from Herbert Sullivan to F. G. Edwards, quoted in YOUNG/S, states that the composer was actually staying there when he composed it. Gertrude Clay Ker Seymer herself was not so sure (letter in MT, July 1902) but she did claim that the hymn was dedicated to her. It would have been against convention, in the case of a hymn, for such a dedication to be printed.

13 *a biography*: see VAN DER KISTE.

Chapter 9

1 *School of Art [etc] at the Crystal Palace*: see the advertisements (e.g. 4 and 25 October 1873) in the Saturday concert programmes at the Palace. Education for women (hence the 'Ladies' Division') was a cherished intellectual cause. Benedict, Prout and Stainer were also (part-time) teachers at the school.

2 *The Orchestra*: issue of 3 May 1872, reproducing *The Times*.

3 *Joseph Bennett*: see the tribute to him in MT, December 1910. He wrote copiously for various music journals as well as for the *Daily Telegraph* and did not retire from journalism until 1905. Successive editions of *Grove* have been strangely lax in dating his career.

4 *A letter from Swinburne*: see LANG, p. 354. According to Swinburne, Sullivan requested him to send *any* suitable verses. Swinburne realized that these could only come at the beginning of Act III, scene 4, and (since this had been cut from the text of the production) Hollingshead promised to reinstate the missing part if Swinburne would oblige with the verses. In 1893 Sullivan was asked to set a political poem of Swinburne's, *The Union* (on behalf of Irish 'loyalist' sentiment) but he declined.

5 *'larx'*: letter, undated, possibly December 1871.

6 *'Brit. Orch. Soc.'*: The British Orchestral Society, which began operations in December 1872, had George Mount as its conductor and consisted of '75 of our best native instrumentalists' (*Illustrated London News*, 28 December 1872).

7 *Baron Meyer Rothschild*: as far back as 1838, Queen Victoria had granted permission for both brothers, Lionel and Meyer, to be styled in Britain by their Austrian rank of Baron. See COWLES/R.

8 *Mentmore*: through Hannah's marriage it became the Rosebery family home. She had inherited when her mother died in 1877. The selling-off of Mentmore's assets was to be a cultural scandal a century later (1978).

9   *Lady Lindsay*: her father was Henry Fitzroy, MP; her mother was another Hannah
    Rothschild (d. 1864), daughter of Nathan Mayer Rothschild. Lady Lindsay was born
    after 1842 (date uncertain) and died in 1912 – six days after which event, at the age of
    88, Lindsay remarried. See *Burke's Peerage*, under 'Crawford', to which earldom the
    Lindsays were kin.

10 *kidney trouble*: 'My malady began in 1872' (Sullivan's autobiographical notes, now in
    PML, compiled apparently for WILLEBY).

11 *Unhappily shortened*: 'The work has been somewhat shortened, we can hardly say
    condensed. Indeed, we think that most of the excisions are to be regretted.' (*The
    Orchestra*, October 1874, p. 104.)

12 *Lewin*: see FOSTER/AO p. 843.

13 *'sang "Orpheus" charmingly'*: Sullivan's letter to his mother of 5 May 1873 refers to
    'Miss Liddell', a usage which (without forename) indicated an elder daughter where
    there was more than one.

14 *unsolicited tributes*: the Manchester donation is mentioned in the entry on Sullivan in
    the *Dictionary of National Biography* (Supplement 1901).

15 *The Concert Society*: document in PML. An alternative scheme with some 'extra'
    rehearsals is also sketched.

Chapter 10

1   *'Her face was'*: the description is from MOORE/GE.

2   *A gift for the reins*: see LESLIE/J.

3   *'I paid for it'*: this is the anecdote as told in the privately printed *Afterthoughts* by
    Frank Griswold, a chronicler of fashionable New York, quoted in MARTIN/LRC.

4   *separated about* 1867: the (false) obituary notices of Fanny Carter Ronalds in the
    Boston Evening Transcript and *New York Times*, 4 June 1910, and that of her husband
    Pierre (or Peter) Lorillard Ronalds in the *New York Times*, 24 October 1905, give this
    date of 1867 for their mutual separation. Her obituaries added that shortly before
    this, Napoleon III 'helped to rescue her from one of the artificial lakes in the Tuileries
    [Gardens, Paris] into which she had fallen'. Apparently both husband and wife had
    journeyed to Paris but the husband returned to America alone. The marriage-date of
    6 November 1859 is also confirmed by these false obituaries.

5   *perhaps receiving a pension*: the pension is mentioned (without the 'perhaps') in the
    Boston Evening Transcript 'obituary', just cited.

6   *Consuelo Yznaga*: see ELLIOTT.

7   *23 years*: letter of Fanny Ronalds replying to condolences sent by Princess Louise.

8   the *'diplomate étranger'*: the pseudonymous author of *La société de Londres*: see ESCOTT.

9   *'Queen Anne is . . .'*: the quotation, and those following, are from OLSEN, p. 150 ff.

10 *'Marmion'. . . revived*: the newer version was said (in a programme note by Grove) to
    have been 'revised by the composer to such an extent as to be virtually a new work'
    when it was given at the Crystal Palace on 26 October 1874.

11 *Hanslick*: see PLEASANTS.

12 *'East Lynne'*: the fact that the author of the novel was never paid a penny for any of the
    profitable stage adaptations of her work was a major cause of concern about laxity in
    the law of copyright (see DNB, article 'Wood, Ellen').

3 *At the Gaiety*: for a résumé of such entertainments, see *The Orchestra*, October 1874, p. 84; also November 1874, p. 147.

4 *both star and proprietor*: for Selina Dolaro's enterprise see *The Orchestra*, March 1875, pp. 249–50.

5 *Henry Irving*: for an account of the combination of business and artistic functions, see DONALDSON.

6 *not a 'double barrel'*: see DNB, article 'Carte'. HARTNOLL and many other usually dependable sources wrongly treat 'D'Oyly Carte' as a combined surname.

7 *in association with Cramer's*: see *The Orchestra*, September 1874. The librettist was the prolific H. B. Farnie.

8 *'He read it through'*: quoted in ALLEN/FN (who has 'The *words* were written', obviously an error).

9 *'The reviewer in Fun'*: issue of 10 April 1875, quoted in ALLEN/FN.

20 *'The greatest hit'*: *Daily Telegraph*, undated, quoted in ALLEN/FN, p. 31.

21 *two different editions*: both were made from the manuscript full score, which survives. Cramer's (1975) is the fuller and much superior, and was further improved in its 1991 revision.

22 *asked Alan Cole*: letter of 22 November 1877. For the 1879 changes see David Russell Hulme's articles in the *Savoyard*, May & September 1978.

Chapter 11

1 *counter-marshalling*: see ROWELL/L p. 82 and, for Gilbert as a stage director, STEDMAN/GS and BOYER.

2 *'He would not go again . . .'*: the anecdote is in LAWRENCE, p. 106.

3 *over the Splügen pass*: letter undated [August 1875].

4 *'it seems that I must'*: letter to his mother, 28. September 1875.

5 *Musical Times*: January 1876, quoted in SCHOLES p. 210.

6 *Brighton Aquarium*: these and other figures for holiday crowds were given in *The Orchestra*, May 1876.

7 *' very fishy indeed'*: see SHERSON p. 73.

8 *the Royal Academy of Music*: MT February 1875 refers to his 'professorship' there and in a letter to his mother (1877, exact date unknown) he writes of 'teaching today (school and R.A.M.)'.

9 *John Ella*: his is apparently the credit for the first use in Britain of analytical programme-notes, of which Grove and later Tovey became the great exponents. Ella's remarks are from a speech reported in *The Orchestra*, February 1876.

10 *Society of Arts*: for the involvement of the Society in the enterprise, see SKIDMORE.

11 *Mass in B Minor*: for the Bach Choir and this London performance see KLEIN/T (Jenny Lind-Goldschmidt 'sat beside the Princess Christian in the front row of this aristocratic choir').

12 *Levy . . . Wieniawski*: Isaac Levy (dates unknown) was one of two or three great cornet virtuosos of his time; the more 'classical' Henryk Wieniawski (1835–80) had

first appeared in London in 1859 and had recently (1872–4) completed a 215-concert world tour with the pianist Anton Rubinstein.

Chapter 12

1   *Götterdämmerung*: the opera had been first performed at Bayreuth only four months before, but the Funeral March had been conducted by Wagner himself in Vienna as a separate piece in March 1875, and it had been similarly given at a Covent Garden promenade concert (conducted by Arditi) on 4 October 1876.

2   *Dear old Fred*: letter to 'Maggie' [unidentified], 19 January 1877.

3   *'Tomorrow Grove and I'*: this letter ('Wednesday') may be conjecturally dated 1877; it also mentions Sullivan's plan to go to Carlsbad to take the waters for his illness (see below, p. 182). But he abandoned the idea: 'I couldn't muster up enough courage to go alone'.

4   *Contradictory 'information'*: see S/FLOWER pp. 82–3, the former account being quoted from FITZGERALD.

5   *Temperley*: see TEMPERLEY/R.

6   *Caruso's writing-out*: quoted in ALLEN/S.

7   *J. Comyns Carr* (1849–1916): qualified as a barrister, he became a leading art critic, a founder-director (with Lindsay) of the Grosvenor Gallery, and an adviser to Beerbohm Tree in his management of the Haymarket Theatre. See his memoirs: CARR/CB.

8   *by Hamilton Clarke*: not (according to HULME/SOR) by A. Cellier.

9   *the 'Figaro'*: quoted in ALLEN/FN p. 49.

Chapter 13

1   *fifty years later*: see KLEIN/MM.

2   *Mrs Cripps/Little Buttercup*: she was called Little Buttercup on the first-night programme, though in successive editions of the vocal score she bears her formal name of Mrs Cripps in the musical pages, remaining Little Buttercup in the list of *dramatis personae*.

3   *Grossmith as a star*: see BAILY/GSB p. 129 and BOND p. 132. By the time of *The Gondoliers* (1889) Jessie Bond had pushed her salary up to £30 weekly and Gilbert would cry out: 'Make way for the high-salaried artiste!'

4   *Shepherd*: presumably the orchestral manager already referred to (p. 101) in connection with Sullivan's Scottish seasons.

5   *'Miss Anna'*: she does not recur in any later correspondence I have seen. She may or may not be the 'A' of another mystery of this time – the letters 'A.M.W.' or 'per A. & M.W.' below Sullivan's signature on two letters, one dated 31 August 1878 and sent to Henry Dyke Acland (Bodleian Library, Oxford, Acland MS.d.54 fol. 299), the other in a letter to D'Oyly Carte quoted in YOUNG/S.

6   *My dear Carte*: quoted (no date) in YOUNG/S, p. 113.

7   *much later*: Sullivan's own article in *M.A.P.*, 1899.

8   *greeted then as a novelty*: *Illustrated Sporting and Dramatic News*, 31 August 1878. It was played on 29 and 31 August, 4, 23, 27 September at least (information from Peter Joslin).

9   *Poor old Scott Russell*: I am indebted for this information to George S. Emmerson.

10 *a single (anonymous) musical review*: see LAMB, also MT 1 February 1905.

11 *for a fortnight*: letter (BDC) to Carte, 4 October 1879, in which Sullivan remarked: 'The America scheme did not originally emanate from you, it came from *me*, in consequence of offers I had from America to go over and conduct the *Pinafore* while the rage was on.'

12 *'Princess Toto'*: the heroine has the remarkable facility of forgetting everything immediately it has occurred – a typical Gilbert artificiality.

Chapter 14

1   *They like 'emotional' singing . . .*: quoted (no source given) in YOUNG/S.

2   *'very successful' operation*: letter (BDC) to Gunn, 30 July 1879.

3   *He relied*: this account is based on Carte's letter (BDC) to Sullivan, 26 August 1879.

5   *'The Prodigal Son'*: Carte, having returned to London, confirmed the arrangement in a letter (BDC) to Sullivan, 26 August 1879. Carte also hoped for 'a great Sullivan festival' in Philadelphia, which did not happen.

6   *Blanche Tucker Roosevelt*: originally surnamed Tucker, she claimed a connection with the distinguished Roosevelt family. See MATZ for her remarkable career.

7   *the Dremels*: later references are to Mrs Dremel alone (presumably widowed). She was a close friend of the composer's mother and he kept loyally in touch with her after his mother's death.

8   *sketches of the first act at home*: S/FLOWER carelessly and nonsensically transcribes 'Ist' as 'last'.

9   *'Thespis' manuscript*: see *The Savoyard*, xx, 1/2 (1981). An attempt to show that this insertion was *not* a late expedient is unconvincing.

10 *a long list of code-words*: copy in PML.

Chapter 15

1   *remains a mystery*: see FULD, p. 261.

2   *in order to deter*: see Gilbert's article in *Scribner's Monthly*, 11 June 1879, quoted in ALLEN/FN. Indeed the eventual publication was deferred for almost a year. In both the [British] first-published score and first-published libretto there is an advertisement for the music of Sullivan's *The Martyr of Antioch*, first performed on 15 October 1880; publication of this work can hardly antedate its first performance. From this, ALLEN/FN correctly argues that the *Pirates* publication must also have been *not earlier* than October 1880. But (not noted in ALLEN/FN) a letter of Sullivan's in the possession of Peter Joslin to 'My dear Adams' (29 October 1880) makes it probable that the date of publication was *still a month or more ahead*, since the composer was able only to 'hope it will be in print very soon'. 'Adams' has been identified by Peter Joslin as Sir Francis Ottiwell Adams.

3   *a souvenir album*: For drawing my attention to this and other valuable American sources I am much indebted to Thomas O. Jones of Rockville, Maryland.

4   *'We must produce the "Pirates" '*: letter to his mother, 6 February 1880.

5   *on 3 April*: YOUNG/S copies S/FLOWER (p. 107) and wrongly gives the 8th.

6   *partial and provisional*: the text of *The Pirates of Penzance* as presented at Paignton on
30 December 1879 ended (see ALLEN/FN) with a satirical account of the perfection of the
House of Lords – a song which (with separate verses for the Major-General, the
Sergeant, Ruth and Mabel) not only anticipated the thrust of 'When Britain really
ruled the waves' from *Iolanthe* but almost shared its metre. The text survives because
Gilbert's libretto was deposited at the Lord Chamberlain's office for licensing; it
cannot be presumed that this song was actually set by Sullivan, and actually
performed.

7   *The Times*: quoted in ALLEN/FN p. 109.

8   *Leeds Festival commission*: see SPARK p. 147.

9   *Mme Albani: see* SPARK p. 144.

10   *a local columnist*: SPARK p. 172 (no precise source quoted).

Chapter 16

1   *A force of 306 choral singers*: details of the festival are in SPARK. Press notices collected
by the organization of the Leeds Musical Festival (for this and other festival years) are
at the City of Leeds Central Library.

2   *the right note of flattery*: source not particularized, quoted in SPARK.

3   *Aline Osgood*: named simply as 'Mrs Osgood' in the programme, she was a Bostonian,
according to a biographical note in a popular song-album of the time. Sullivan
dedicated his song 'My dearest heart' to her.

4   *aesthetic*: see DE MARÉ.

5   *Miss de la Motte*: presumably a relative of W. A. de la Motte (1775–1863), a drawing-
master at the Royal Military College. The families would therefore have been
acquainted in Sandhurst days.

6   *'Patience' became pressing*: Sullivan's delay also meant that Carte could not fulfil the
date of production which he had promised his American manager in what Helen
Carte would afterwards call 'the disastrous [American] season of 1880–81': see her
letter (BDC) of 15 April 1886 to Sullivan. *Patience*, when it arrived in New York, did
well (27 weeks) but the delay almost landed Carte in a lawsuit.

7   *musical handwriting*: information from Dr. David Russell Hulme.

8   *New piece ('Patience')*: the baton with which Sullivan conducted this opening
performance, and six other batons, all but two with inscriptions denoting the
occasions on which they were used, were bequeathed by the composer to the Royal
Academy of Music. They are 'each fitted with a wrist-cord, and thick and heavy by
modern standards' (see SASS no. 8, June 1980).

9   *Ignatius Pollaky*: his business was sometimes international, as shown by the
advertisement inserted (with the address simply as 'Pollaky, no. 13 Paddington
Green') in *The Times* of 29 April 1876: 'To Townsman of Cottingham, Visitor to
Neuchatel, Switzerland, etc. I, the undersigned, am prepared to pay you £1,000 (in
sovereigns) for documentary evidence proving contents of your letters (severally
written and posted from London, November 8, 1872 . . . [and others]) on condition
however that said evidence is placed in my hands within one month . . . '

Chapter 17

1   *Marlborough Club*: he had joined the Club (facing the gates of Marlborough House
and Clarence House on Pall Mall) in January 1881.

2 *Sir Henry Thompson*: Zachary Cope's biography of him (1951) is properly entitled 'Versatile Victorian'. See COPE.

3 *Marquis d'Aoust*: see the *Dictionnaire de Biographie français* (1933): his date of birth is given as 'about 1825', his date of death unknown.

4 *lit entirely by electricity*: only the auditorium was lit by electricity on the opening night – it reached the stage on 28 December 1881.

5 *Rachel Scott Russell*: she died in India in 1882.

6 *Osman Pasha*: possibly the Turkish general, Osman Nuri Pasha (c. 1837–1900), Minister of war in the Turkish government (which held nominal sway over Egypt) from 1878 to 1885.

7 *'fatuous prig'*: in the Summary Diary for 1881 (Yale, Beinecke Library).

8 *Primrose League*: the anecdote is in LONGFORD/B.

Chapter 18

1 *'an Austrian swashbuckler'*: the Summary Diary (Yale) here amplifies Sullivan's main diary for 1881/2.

2 *a lot of parsons*: the *table d'hôte* indicates the shared, general table and fixed-price meal.

3 *new scenery*: see the comments of ALLEN/FN and the reports quoted there.

4 *A. C.* Dr. Alfred Cooper was not only Sullivan's medical adviser but on evidently friendly terms with him – see p. 162, 12 May 1881.

5 *Sullivan's terms*: see LAWRENCE, pp. 228–9. The information is supplemented by David Russell Hulme's investigations.

6 *In New York*: The company which was to give *Iolanthe* was actually called the D'Oyly Carte Opera Company, apparently the first use of this form.

7 *Dolaro*: according to SHERSON (p. 266), when she fell ill in an impoverished condition in New York a benefit performance 'was arranged for her to defray the expenses of a stay in Florida, but Dolaro said "Better to die in New York than to live in Florida" and die she did, soon afterwards.'

Chapter 19

1 *'The Era'*: quoted in ALLEN/FN, p. 175.

2 *'Perola'*: the mystification was finally banished by the booklet on *Iolanthe* issued (1982) by the Sir Arthur Sullivan Society.

3 *W. Beatty-Kingston*: quoted in the SASS booklet on *Iolanthe* (1982).

4 *a satirical representation of Gladstone*: see BAKER/COP.

5 *the pantomime*: Sullivan's diary refers just to 'the Surrey pantomime', without naming it. Theatres on the south bank (the 'Surrey side'), though not fashionable, held their own with pantomime (at Christmas) and melodrama.

6 *programmes with Sullivan's name*: the deceptive distribution is particularized in ALLEN/FN, p. 205.

7 *Lillian Russell*: the only book devoted to her, Parker Morell's *Lillian Russell: the Era of Plush*, is unreliable, with evident factual errors: the date of *The Pirates of Penzance*

is wrong; Gilbert and Sullivan are said to be at odds in a lawsuit over *Princess Ida*. Lillian Russell's death on 6 June 1922 (not 1921, as in several reference books) prompted an obituary in *The Times* next day which did not mention the quarrel with Gilbert and the legal action resulting.

8   *'Come down to my room'*: the allegation is echoed by Morell (see preceding note) and by John Burke's *Duet in Diamonds*, 'the flamboyant saga of Lillian Russell and Diamond Jim Brady in America's gilded age' (Putnam, New York, 1972). The reminiscences in *Cosmopolitan* say she sued Gilbert and Carte for £5,000; they do not mention a settlement.

9   *Hermann Klein, Edmund Yates*: quoted in ALLEN/FN, pp. 207–8.

Chapter 20

1   *letter 1 April 1884*: dated 2 April in S/FLOWER, but Sullivan's diary for 1 April confirms that it was written that day, though a fair copy for post was made on the 2nd.

2   *Sunday afternoon chats*: see KLEIN/T p. 192.

3   *the fee offered*: see minutes of directors' meetings in RPHIL.

Chapter 21

1   *Helen Lenoir*: with considerable ingenuity, but convincingly, Paul Seeley has identified her as Susan Couper Black, born 12 May 1852. See SEELEY. She 'became Helen Lenoir when she joined the acting profession' and had registered as 'Helen Susan Black' at the University of London in 1871–4. Later she persistently subtracted five years from her age.

2   *the copyright of 'Sweethearts'*: see SASS no. 9 (October 1980).

Chapter 22

1   *a later chronicler*: see MORRIS.

2   *Bicknell Young*: apparently an ex-student of Sullivan's from the National Training School for Music (*Salt Lake City Sunday Tribune*, 19 July 1885).

3   *Wawona*: this description and the general background to Yosemite are from HUTCHINGS.

4   *and so to London*: presumably it was Sullivan's friend Labouchère, editor of *Truth*, who spoke through the columns of that paper on 1 April 1886: 'I learn that while he was in America, Sir Arthur Sullivan made inquiries whether it was possible for himself or Mr Gilbert to become a citizen of the United States, and thus secure a legal *locus standi* against transatlantic piracies. Mr Boucicault has already taken that step. But according to American law, a lengthened residence in the States is an indispensable preliminary, and I do not suppose that either Sir Arthur or his partner would care to expatriate himself for the period necessary'.

Chapter 23

1   *'Truth' informed its readers*: issue of 1 April 1886.

2   *and his re-advent*:letter (BDC), Carte to Sullivan, 21 November 1885.

3   *an 'indisposition'*: see *Truth*, 28 March 1886. 'Sir Arthur Sullivan did not put in an appearance at the second Philharmonic concert. As he would, at any rate, have had so

little to do [Ebenezer Prout and Giovanni Bottesini conducted works of their own], his "indisposition" need not alarm his friends.' The Society's official historian (see FOSTER/PS) wrongly gives Sullivan as conductor.

4   *Tufnail*: the baritone Musgrove Tufnail.

5   *letter of 23 March 1886*: BDC.

6   *a Mozart aria*: the aria *Quando miro* (K.374) was apparently given with a recitative taken from another aria.

7   *Sullivan's symphony . . . revived*: *Truth* made the same comparison with 1866: 'So promising an effort by a young gentleman who was then only four-and-twenty may possibly be of some interest to the composer, but the public recognize that the symphony can in no sense of the term be considered a mature work, and they are quite willing to forget it. Sir Arthur once began a second symphony which, with rare sagacity, he has left unfinished . . .' Sullivan himself did not venture to give it at the Philharmonic during his conductorship.

8   *State concert*: see KLEIN/T p. 118 ff.

9   *'Slowly, slowly'*: intended by Bennett as a choral number, it was changed by Sullivan into a solo, but Bennett still wished for *some* choral participation. See JONES/GL.

10   *Lady Feodora Sturt*: still known to Sullivan as such, she had in fact become Lady Alington in 1883 by her husband's succession to his father's peerage. She was to be a noted Edwardian hostess and lived until 1934.

Chapter 24

1   *under Barnby's baton*: not, as stated in S/FLOWER, under the composer's – though he was present.

2   *reformed in the image of a school-teacher*: the whimsical dance given to the 'reformed' Margaret and Despard was the work of John D'Auban (see the *Savoyard*, Vol. 20 no. 1, 1981) who choreographed all the Gilbert and Sullivan pieces from *The Sorcerer* on, except for *The Gondoliers*. The characters originally sang of themselves as teachers in 'a Sunday school': the appropriate demeanour and the black, Quaker-ish garb of the soloists were retained even when Gilbert substituted 'a National school', presumably to placate religious susceptibilities.

3   *often repeated*: as in the instruction to his new secretary, Bendall, in a letter of 7 September 1896: '. . . But please say the usual thing, viz., that they must put Arthur Sullivan not Sir A. Sullivan. Always please make this condition, and always cut out the "Sir".' (In this case it was to grant permission for the use of one of his hymn-tunes, 'Pilgrimage'.)

4   *rue Tilsit*: The correct street-name is *rue de Tilsitt*.

5   *Marie Tempest*: see letter (BDC) from Carte to Sullivan, 15 March 1887.

Chapter 25

1   *no fee was apparently charged*: see the letter from Sullivan's secretary, Smythe, in reply to an inquiry from a society in Glossop, Derbyshire.

2   *their god Richter*: Richter's authority was founded first on his supreme technical command of the conductor's art (sometimes he had no score before him), second on his audiences' knowledge of his intimacy with the composers themselves – especially

Wagner, whose popularity in the concert-hall never wavered. A characteristic notice was that of the *Athenaeum*, 12 June 1889, reviewing a concert of five days before: 'One of the most crowded audiences of the season attended the sixth Richter concert given on Monday evening at St James's Hall, when the programme consisted of two important selections from Wagner's works – the entire third act of *Tristan und Isolde* and the final scene of the third act of *Siegfried*. It is abundantly clear that for the concert-going public Wagner is still a name to conjure with, for even standing-room was hardly to be found.'

3 *'Dorothy'. . . at the Gaiety Theatre*: When it was still somewhat short of 900 performances the *Era* commented on 29 November 1888 that the average receipts were 'about £160 per performance . . . [which is], we believe, quite unprecedented'. It was the first show at the Gaiety under the new management of George Edwardes (1852–1915), who had at one time been in Carte's employ.

4 *'If you wish . . .'*: letter (BDC) 13 February 1888.

5 *not . . . among the artist's best works*: 'Before dealing with the rest of the portraits, we may notice Sir J. Millais's portrait of Sir A. Sullivan, which is on an easel here, and exhibits the painter's rare insight into character, avoiding caricature, and his energetic perception of the pictorial qualities he desires to secure. Here our praise must end. Haste has prevented the thorough execution of the flesh, dress, and background; the features deserve more modelling and variety of colour, and the whole is rather thin.' (*Athenaeum*, 5 May 1888.)

5 *neither fee nor expenses*: 'The Hereford Festival Committee are nothing in my debt. I was only too delighted to be present and render some little help' – letter to the committee chairman, reproduced in the *Era*, 13 October 1888.

Chapter 26

1 *'appreciation'*: the work which more than any other standardized the term in its musical sense, Stewart Macpherson's *Music and its Appreciation*, did not appear till 1910.

2 *'get the exact time'*: not, of course, the absurd 'get the exact tune'(S/FLOWER).

3 *Macbeth . . . in piano score*: the expectation that the whole score would be published is clear from a letter of Ellen Terry's (17 March 1889) to Sullivan.

4 *politically suspicious*: see SINCLAIR, pp. 228–9.

5 *Reuben Sassoon*: it was of a piece with his munificence that at the Shah of Persia's visit to London in July 1889 (see p. 295) he should provide the entire cost of an evening of ballet and other entertainment at the Empire Theatre, Leicester Square. Sassoon was one of the London Jews who formally petitioned the Shah on behalf of the Jews in Persia.

6 *Day after day*: letter (BDC).

7 *little Lola Beeth*: a Polish soprano who had yet to make her Covent Garden debut (1896); she had been a pupil of Pauline Viardot, through whom Sullivan might have got to know her – hence the affectionate diminutive! The Belgian tenor Ernest van Dyck (1861–1923) was among the great opera singers of his day, Lohengrin being one of his most celebrated roles.

Chapter 27

1 *Gianandrea Mazzucato*: he was a translator of operas into Italian – including *Die-Meistersinger* for its first London performance in 1882.

2 *free and outspoken*: not, of course, 'unspoken' (S/FLOWER).

3 *the 'beau monde'*: a very good indication of this is in the extensive guest list published by the *World* next day (27 July). Some, of course, must have been personally invited by Sullivan. It is interesting to note 'Col. P. Paget' (the dedicatee of his early *Idyll* for cello). Three Rothschilds (Alfred, Leopold, Baron Alphonse) and two Sassoons (Arthur and Reuben) were there, and the usual contingent of American women included Lady Randolph Churchill, her sister Mrs Moreton Frewen, and the Duchess of Manchester.

4 *committee of taste*: Savoy Hotel archives DF/BDC/I.

5 *Savoy Hotel accounts*: in Savoy Hotel archives.

Chapter 28

1 *'the Swift of the suburbs'*: *Illustrated London News*, 14 December 1889.

2 *'Cinderella'*: 'the insect ballet and the Shakespearean tableaux have no more to do with the fairy story of *Cinderella* than with a Sanskrit legend', complained the *Illustrated London News* on 4 January 1890.

Chapter 29

1 *The memorandum* [26 April 1890]: S/FLOWER wrongly ascribes this text to the composer's diary, and reproduces it with crucial omissions.

Chapter 30

1 *Ethel Smyth*: for the quotations, see SMYTH.

2 *the taste of the Viennese*: for the reception given to various works, see HADAMOWSKY.

3 *The Lute*: issue of 1 March 1891.

4 *pseudo-Wagnerian touches*: see the thorough analysis in YATES.

5 *Richard Sullivan*: he died on 24 July 1937 at Los Angeles; his last film was *All the King's Horses* (1935).

Chapter 31

1 *The Foresters*: before the official London opening, a private performance was given at the Lyceum on 17 March 1892.

2 *confined to bed*: there is a description in the Associated Press dispatch from Monte Carlo, printed in the *New York Times*, 8 April 1892. The quoted description ('When he spoke . . .') is from S/FLOWER.

3 *Klein reported*: see KLEIN/T, p. 196.

Chapter 32

1 *to Cardiff*: on the second day of the first Cardiff Triennial Festival (20–23 September 1892) he conducted *In Memoriam* at the morning concert as well as *The Golden Legend* in the evening.

2 *letter . . . to Lady Russell*: kindly supplied by Mr A. R. Davis.

3   *a new song for the role of Dorothy*: recitative and song (2/4, 6/8, then Coda): details in a letter (BDC) to 'Dear Frank' [Cellier] 11 February 1893.

4   *new dance music*: an undated letter (BDC) to François Cellier, conducting, gave instructions on its musical and stage performance, e.g. 'Observe the delicate touches of the G.C., *piatti* [*gran cassa, piatti* – bass drum, cymbals]. See that they come in at the right place . . . The introduction must not be *danced* through. Comic business, preparation, etc., but the dance proper must not begin until the place marked for it.' He remarked that he had written 'Miss St John's new song' [i.e. Rita's], 'two or three times'.

5   *38 musical numbers*: for an examination of the autograph score, see TILLETT.

Chapter 33

1   *wrote to Manns*: letter quoted in SASS no. 12 (Summer 1982), p. 14.

2   *the Crystal Palace Company*: already in 1898 he had addressed the shareholders of the company recalling what the concerts had meant to him. The report in the *Norwood Review* is quoted in SASS no. 12 (Summer 1982), pp. 14–15.

3   *Eduard Strauss*: Sullivan's letter kindly supplied by Dr Ernst Hilmar, Vienna City Libraries.

4   *Ilka von Palmay*: so named in programmes, etc. But in an interview in the *Sketch*, 15 April 1896, she said the form 'Ilka Palmay' was correct.

5   *Greater still was the surprise*: 'Rehearsed, with such a work? Certainly, Sir or Madam. It is time to pay attention to an oratorio which has been for generations condemned to suffer from heedless assumptions that the music can, in some supernatural fashion, look after itself.' Joseph Bennett in MT, November 1895.

6   *Bradford Permanent Orchestra*: for full review of this occasion see the *Bradford Observer*, 14 October 1895.

7   *Carte revived 'The Mikado'*: There had been a back-stage upset at rehearsals when Emmie Owen (Peep-Bo) and Florence Perry challenged Gilbert's authority in the way they wanted to perform their parts. Sullivan in a letter of 7 November 1895 to Helen Carte called them 'a couple of little fools, harried into such conduct by Jessie [Bond]. . . . The taps with the fans were *never done* [in the original performance], neither by Braham nor Ulmar, and both Gilbert and myself dislike it'. A lapse of memory? In the original 1885 production Sybil Grey, not Geraldine Ulmar, had been the other 'little maid' with Leonora Braham and Jessie Bond.

8   *Ivanhoe*: a German libretto printed for the occasion indicates that Sullivan made several substantial cuts from the original. But, though the last two scenes were now labelled 'Act 4', there was no structural remodelling.

9   *revision*: for the Berlin libretto see MEARS/B.

10 *not . . . heavily accented English*: the remarks of her granddaughter Princess Alice in the BBC television programme *Victorian Memory* 1978, supply evidence.

Chapter 34

1   *the future . . . Queen Mary*: she and the Duchess of Teck, meeting Sullivan, sang songs from the operettas 'by heart' to his piano accompaniment. See BROWNING, pp. 39–40.

2 *Violet Beddington*: see the article by Wyn and Barbara Wade in GSJ, Autumn 1977, p. 276. The chapter from *Myrtle* is reprinted in SASS 19, Winter 1984.

3 *Its genre*: see TILLETT, p. 7.

4 *'Deratschky'*: writing not clear, game not identified.

5 *wrote to 'Bertie'*: inscribed 'Saturday night', it is deduced to have been written on 3 or 10 April 1897.

6 *A profit of £200*: see *Daily Telegraph*, obituary, 23 November 1900.

7 *Pauline Joran*: Cunningham Bridgeman, an experienced judge, called her 'unquestionably the finest *prima donna* ever seen on the Savoy stage' – see CELLIER, p. 349.

8 *unremembered*: with perhaps one exception – see ROWELL/PIN.

9 *The Martyr of Antioch*: the Carl Rosa performance of 25 January 1898 was announced in the *Scotsman* (15 January) as 'the first performance on any stage'. The pairing with Mascagni's *Cavalleria rusticana* was 'unfortunate', said the *Scotsman* on the 26th. The company then toured the work, the Brighton performance being reviewed in MT April 1898.

10 *letter to Helen Carte*: from the Villa Mathilde, Beaulieu, 3 February 1898 (BDC).

11 *hurricane in Barbados*: see *The Times*, 17 September 1898, with a cable from the Governor.

Chapter 35

1 *Elgar's first appearance*: see the letter in YOUNG/E.

2 *'Dear Mr Wood'*: quoted in POUND p. 68.

3 *Arthur Collins*: Col. Collins, one of the royal equerries, was to be a pall-bearer at Sullivan's funeral.

4 *At Disentis*: letter to W. H. Cummings, 6 August 1898.

5 *some suspicion*: see STANYON.

6 *Cunningham Bridgeman*: see CELLIER. Bridgeman was the author of the latter part of this book.

7 *Ellen Beach Yaw*: exceptionally, CELLIER (p. 353) is mistaken in listing the first-night cast of *The Rose of Persia*. Ellen Beach Yaw sang the part of the Sultana Zubeydeh, and the listing reproduced, with Isabel Jay allotted to this part, comes presumably from the programme of a later performance.

8 *trip to Monte Carlo*: other indications of illness that month (March 1900) include '–5' and 'Usual pain –3': they perhaps mean that he could sleep only up to those hours in the early morning.

9 *pushed flattery too far*: for this and other quotations from the interview see PEARSON.

10 *'Brooding all day . . .'*: text of diary entry from S/FLOWER.

11 *sculling*: e.g. 12 August 1900 'Sculled up to backwater before dinner'.

12 *National Brass Band festival*: see LISLE (Summer 1983).

13 *Berlin's musical historian*: see WEISSMANN.

Chapter 36

1   *an altered version*: see HULME/RUD.

2   *the whereabouts*: updated in SASS 22 and 23 (1986).

3   *New York Shakespeare Festival . . . 'Pirates'*: see the *Savoyard*, xx/i, 1981, p. 18, for the musical aspects of the original production.

4   *to Hermann Klein*: see KLEIN/MM p. 204ff.

5   *the modern biographer of Tennyson*: see MARTIN/T p. 402.

Chapter 37

1   *Tracy C. Davis*: see *Theatre Notebook*, 44/1, 1990.

2   *Roderick Spencer and Selwyn Tillett showed*: see TILLETT/VIE.

3   *by the present writer*: see *Opera*, August 1986.

4   *the very point of impudence*: according to the autograph full score, however, the word which occupies this point of emphasis is not the sarcastic 'regret' but 'recollect' ('So please you, Sir, to recollect'). But this must have been Sullivan's error in copying Gilbert's words from his sketches into his full score. Gilbert would never have had 'recollect' as a (false) rhyme to 'etiquette', as would happen here. Sullivan has mis-remembered 'recollect' by confusion with a later stanza, which has the rhyme 'recollect/respect'. For a similar copying error on Sullivan's part, see p. 211.

5   *Erik Routley*: see Bibliography.

6   *Saremba*: see Bibliography.

Appendix 1
Arthur Sullivan's Family Tree

The genealogy on Sullivan's mother's side rests largely on a compilation of her own, now in the Gilbert and Sullivan Collection, Pierpont Morgan Library, New York. The chart overleaf owes much to the painstaking genealogical research of the late Leslie Weaver.

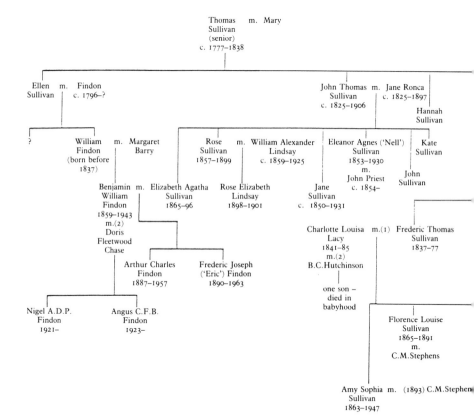

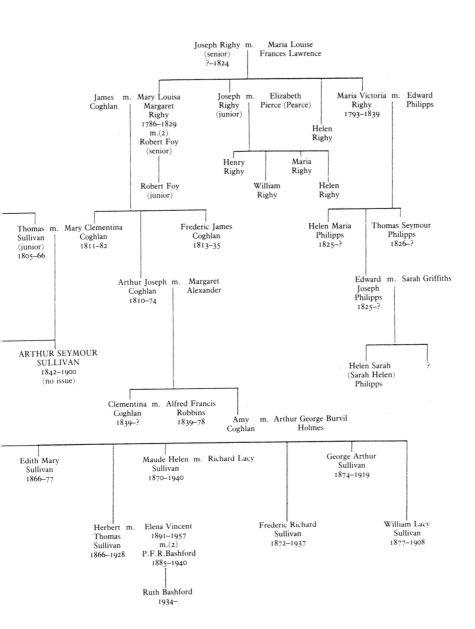

Appendix 2
The Supposed Jewish Connection

'THE only man in England who is permitted to write in a style which is in the main of home growth is the Irish Jew, Sir Arthur Sullivan.' So wrote Samuel Butler (1835–1902), in his posthumously published *Notebooks*. Like a certain major-general, the celebrated author of *The Way of all Flesh* had a pretty taste for paradox. The assertion that Sullivan was Jewish is to be found in a number of other references during or just after his lifetime. Early issues of the *Jewish Year Book*, which began publication in 1897, listed Sullivan among 'Jewish Celebrities of the Nineteenth Century', where he is placed among 'persons who had but one Jewish parent'. (The birth-date is wrongly given, 1844 instead of 1842.) The list is stated to have been derived, with additions, from a list originally compiled in 1885 'for the comparative estimate of Jewish ability (*Journal of the Anthropological Society*, 1887)'.

No evidence is, however, adduced. Nor is it provided by Percy M. Young, who revived the fancy in his biography of the composer (1971). As noted in Chapter 1 of the present volume, Sullivan's mother's maiden name, Coghlan, is as Irish as his father's; *her* mother was of Italian descent (née Righy, probably Righi in its original form). It is true that a sister of his grandmother married a Philipps, a name which *could be* Jewish; but that would not, of course, be an ancestor. In a paper read to the Musical Association in 1902, Charles H. Maclean erroneously supposed that Phillips [*sic*] was the name of the composer's maternal grandmother, commenting that 'the Phillips may not unlikely be Jewish', and adding feebly: 'Sullivan's appearance was very Jewish when he was a young man'.

By infant baptism and religious upbringing Sullivan was a member of the Church of England. His mother seems originally to have been Roman Catholic. In default of any references to a Jewish background in any known document of the Sullivan family itself, the onus of proof rests on those who assert such Jewishness. The argument from physical appearance is notoriously unreliable. (Indeed Young quotes another account in which Sullivan's swarthiness is 'explained' by his being partly Black!) In the age of Mendelssohn, Meyerbeer, and Offenbach, it seems likely that the notion of Jewishness was out of pure romantic imagination pasted on to the image of a composer who was dark, of short stature, and commercially successful. In Sullivan's case it may even have been fed by his friendship with the Rothschilds.

A curious parallel arises in the case of Johann Strauss. Paying tribute to him in November 1894, the *Musical Times* wrote: 'In face of the achievements of such a common benefactor of humanity, whose race is writ large in his name and physiognomy, we can imagine that even the most rabid anti-semite must feel a temporary abatement of his ignoble and un-Christian animosity'. In other words, because he bore a name which *some* Jews have, and looked as if he *might* be Jewish, he had to be Jewish! Similarly the *Jewish Year Book* in 1896–7 listed Johann Strauss as a (converted) Jew. But he was not, though one of his eight great-grandparents was.

Immediately after Sullivan's death the matter came up again, a correspondent writing to the *Jewish Chronicle* (30 November 1900) that Sullivan was of Jewish descent, and claiming to have heard it 'about 25 years ago' from the composer's brother Fred. The story this time was that 'an ancestor', on enlisting in the army, had changed his name from Solomon to Sullivan! In the following issue a witty counter-comment was made by the Rev. A. A. Green. The references are to the Boer War casualty lists, as supposedly perused by a Jewish reader:

> Oh, he scans the grim death columns in the *D. T.* and the *Times*,
> And the notes of death-knell solemn are to him the sweetest chimes,
> For he cannot rest contented with obituary news
> Without writing to the papers that the great men, all, are Jews.

Why, even the commander-in-chief, Lord Roberts ('Bobs'), might be claimed as Jewish:

> The sacred temple treasury of doubt the matter robs,
> For what are shekels but the ancient Hebrew name for bobs?

Bobs = shillings = coinage. To name Arthur Sullivan as Jewish is to stand by almost as slender an association.

Appendix 3
Arthur Sullivan: List of works

MUSICAL works are listed in the following order of categories, broadly following Grove's *Dictionary of Music and Musicians*, 6th edition, 1980 (significant differences, however, will be noted): 1. *Theatre*; 2. *Choral with orchestra*; 3. *Orchestral and band*; 4. *Solo instrumental and chamber works*; 5. *Services, anthems, etc.*; 6. *Hymns*; 7. *Part-songs, carols, etc.*; 8. *Solo songs, vocal duets and trios, including those contributed to plays*; 9. *Miscellaneous*. Where place of performance is not mentioned, 'London' is to be understood unless otherwise indicated.

There follows (not in *Grove*) a list of operatic vocal scores and other works of which Sullivan was sole or joint editor, and a mention of prose writings.

The Miller and his Man, to which Sullivan contributed two songs with text by Burnand (see 8), was described as 'a drawing-room extravaganza for Christmas' and was not publicly staged in his lifetime. What is thought to be the first public staged performance was given by the Boston Chamber Soloists at Cambridge, Massachusetts, on 15 December 1984. It was first printed in the *Illustrated London News*, 24 December 1876.

Opus numbers were attached by Sullivan only to a few early works, and those misleadingly. Sullivan's secretary and musical associate, Wilfred Bendall, when compiling the list of works for Lawrence (see Bibliography) sensibly dropped the opus numbers. So does the present listing.

1. Theatre

Title and genre (opera/operetta unless otherwise stated)	Text	First production
The Tempest, incidental music.	Shakespeare	Leipzig, Gewandhaus, 6 Apr 1861; rev. version, Crystal Palace, 5 Apr 1862; staged, Manchester, Prince's Theatre, 15 Oct 1864
*The Sapphire Necklace (later The False Heiress)	H. F. Chorley	comp. 1863–4; not produced, orig. score lost; overture and 2 excerpts, Crystal Palace, 13 Apr 1867
L'Ile enchantée, ballet	H. Desplaces [choreography]	Covent Garden Theatre, 14 May 1864
Cox and Box, or The Long-lost Brothers	F. C. Burnand, after J. M. Morton: 'Box and Cox'	private perf. (with piano), 26 May 1866; Adelphi Theatre, 11 May 1867 (orch. version)
The Contrabandista, or The Law of the Ladrones	Burnand	St George's Hall, 18 Dec 1867

456

The Merchant of Venice, incidental music	Shakespeare	Manchester, Prince's Theatre, 19 Sep 1871
*Thespis, or The Gods Grown Old	W. S. Gilbert	Gaiety Theatre, 26 Dec 1871
The Merry Wives of Windsor, incidental music	Shakespeare	Gaiety Theatre, 19 Dec 1874
Trial by Jury	Gilbert	Royalty Theatre, 25 Mar 1875
The Zoo	B. Rowe [pseud. of B. C. Stephenson]	St James's Theatre, 5 Jun 1875
Henry VIII, incidental music	Shakespeare	Manchester, Theatre Royal, 29 Aug 1877
The Sorcerer	Gilbert	Opera Comique, 17 Nov 1877; rev. version, Savoy Theatre, 11 Oct 1884
HMS Pinafore, or The Lass that Loved a Sailor	Gilbert	Paignton, Royal Bijou Theatre, 30 Dec 1879; New York, Fifth Avenue Theatre, 31 Dec 1879
Patience, or Bunthorne's Bride	Gilbert	Opera Comique, 23 Apr 1881
Iolanthe, or The Peer and the Peri	Gilbert	Savoy Theatre, 25 Nov 1882
Princess Ida, or Castle Adamant	Gilbert, after Tennyson: 'The Princess'	Savoy Theatre, 5 Jan 1884
The Mikado, or The Town of Titipu	Gilbert	Savoy Theatre, 14 Mar 1885
*Ruddygore, or The Witch's Curse	Gilbert	Savoy Theatre, 22 Jan 1887
The Yeomen of the Guard, or The Merryman and his Maid	Gilbert	Savoy Theatre, 3 Oct 1888
Macbeth, incidental music	Shakespeare	Lyceum Theatre, 29 Dec 1888
The Gondoliers, or The King of Barataria	Gilbert	Savoy Theatre, 7 Dec 1889
Ivanhoe ('a romantic opera')	J. Sturgis, after Scott	Royal English Opera House, 31 Jan 1891; rev. version, Liverpool, Court Theatre, 14 Feb 1895
The Foresters, incidental music	Tennyson	New York, Daly's Theatre, 17 Mar 1892
Haddon Hall	Sydney Grundy	Savoy Theatre, 24 Sep 1892
*Utopia (Limited), or The Flowers of Progress	Gilbert	Savoy Theatre, 7 Oct 1893
The Chieftain [revision of The Contrabandista]	Burnand	Savoy Theatre, 12 Dec 1894
King Arthur, incidental music	J. Comyns Carr	Lyceum Theatre, 12 Jan 1895
The Grand Duke, or The Statutory Duel	Gilbert	Savoy Theatre, 7 May 1896
Victoria and Merrie England, ballet	C. Coppi [choreography]	Alhambra Theatre, 25 May 1897

The Beauty Stone	A. W. Pinero, Carr	Savoy Theatre, 28 May 1898
The Rose of Persia, or The Story-teller and the Slave	B. Hood	Savoy Theatre, 29 Nov 1899
The Emerald Isle, or The Caves of Carig-Cleena [completed by Edward German]	Hood	Savoy Theatre, 27 Apr 1901

*Items which formed part of *The Sapphire Necklace* and *Thespis* and which achieved independent publication or performance are listed in the appropriate categories (7 and 8) below; see also pp. 72–3.

The spelling of *Ruddygore* was changed, after the opening, to *Ruddigore*, and the parentheses were dropped from *Utopia (Limited)*.

Individual songs used in the plays *Olivia* (1878), *The Profligate* (1889) and *An Old Jew* (1894) are listed in Section 8, p. 461.

2. Choral with orchestra

Published only in vocal score except where 'full score' is indicated. The *Te deum* of 1872 has accompaniment for military band in addition to orchestra, the posthumous *Te deum* (1902) has accompaniment for strings, brass, percussion and organ. Otherwise, a normal orchestra is used.

Kenilworth (words: H. F. Chorley), masque, pub. Chappell, 1865; Birmingham Festival, 8 Sep 1864
The Prodigal Son (words: composer, from Bible), oratorio, pub. Boosey, 1869; Three Choirs (Worcester) Festival, 8 Sep 1869
On Shore and Sea (words: T. Taylor), dramatic cantata, pub. Boosey, 1871; Royal Albert Hall, 1 May 1871
'Te deum laudamus', 'Domine salvam fac reginam' (words: liturgical), pub. Novello, 1872 (full score 1887); Crystal Palace, 1 May 1872
The Light of the World (words: composer, from Bible), oratorio, pub. Cramer, 1873; Birmingham Festival, 27 Aug 1873
The Martyr of Antioch (words: H. H. Milman [adapted by W. S. Gilbert]), sacred musical drama, pub. Chappell, 1880 (full score 1899), Leeds Festival, 15 Oct 1880
Ode for the opening of the Colonial and Indian Exhibition (words: Tennyson), pub. Chappell, 1886; Royal Albert Hall, 4 May 1886
The Golden Legend (words: Longfellow, adapted by Joseph Bennett), pub. Novello, 1886 (full score, 1886); Leeds Festival, 16 Oct 1886
Ode written and composed for the occasion of laying the foundation stone of the Imperial Institute (words: Lewis Morris), pub. Chappell, 1887; Imperial Institute, 4 July 1887
'Te deum laudamus': a thanksgiving for victory (words: liturgical), pub. Novello, full score 1902; St Paul's Cathedral, 8 June 1902

3. Orchestral and band

Published in full score unless otherwise noted; date of first performance added.

Overture in D minor [lost], Royal Academy of Music, 13 July 1858
Overture, 'The Feast of Roses', after Moore's 'Lalla Rookh' [lost], Leipzig, Gewandhaus, 25 May 1860
Procession March [arr. piano solo and piano duet, pub. Cramer, 1863], Crystal Palace, 10 Mar 1863, and various band performances on that day
Princess of Wales's March (also called Marche danoise) [arr. piano, pub. Cramer, 1863], military band performances, Mar 1863
Symphony in E [pub. as 'the Irish', Novello, 1915], Crystal Palace, 10 Mar 1866

Overture in C, 'In Memoriam' [pub. Novello, 1885], Norwich Festival, 30 Oct 1866
Overture, 'Marmion', after Scott's narrative poem [unpub.], St James's Hall, 3 June 1867
Concerto for cello and orchestra in D [lost, except for solo part; but see pp. 43 and 417], Crystal Palace, 24 Nov 1866
'Overtura [*sic*] di ballo' [pub. as 'Overture di ballo', Novello, 1889], Birmingham Festival, 31 Aug 1870
Imperial March, arr. piano, pub. Chappell, 1893, Imperial Institute, 10 May 1893
'Absent-minded Beggar' March [unpublished; it is not just an arrangement of the song but contains original material]; brass band version, Crystal Palace, 21 July 1900

An earlier overture in C minor on *Timon of Athens* and various other pre-1858 works in manuscript (including a piano sonata) were listed in Mackenzie's obituary tribute in its German publication (see MACKENZIE, bibliography). But such works, unacknowledged by Sullivan and unperformed, can have but a doubtful claim to existence. The choice of such an obscure Shakespearean play seems improbable.

4. Solo instrumental and chamber works

Date of composition is given where not immediately followed by publication.

Scherzo ('Capriccio no. 1'), piano solo, 1857, MS.
Capriccio no. 2, piano solo (unfinished), 1857, MS.
String quartet in D minor, [lost], performed at Leipzig, May 1859
Romance in G minor, string quartet, 1859; pub. 1964
Thoughts, piano, pub. Cramer, 1862
    (no. 1 later pub. as 'Reverie' for violin and piano
    no. 2 as 'Melody' for violin and piano)
An Idyll, cello and piano, 1865; pub. in bazaar souvenir, 1899*
Allegro risoluto, piano, 1866; pub. 1976
Day Dreams (six pieces), piano; pub. Boosey, 1867
Duo concertante, cello and piano, pub. Lamborn, Cock 1868
Twilight, piano, pub. Chappell, 1868

    *In the Souvenir of the Charing Cross Hospital Bazaar (Royal Albert Hall, 21–22 June 1899), with contributions from 39 authors and 9 composers, Sullivan's *Idyll* appears (pp. 181–5) with a facsimile of the composer's signature.

5. Services, anthems, etc.

Date of composition is given where not immediately followed by publication.

  i. Te Deum, Jubilate, Kyrie (in D major), 1866 (pub. 1866 and 1872)
 ii. Anthems (see also 9):
    By the waters of Babylon, c. 1850 (unpub.)
    Sing unto the Lord, 1855 (unpub.)
    Psalm 103, 1856 (unpub.)
    We have heard with our ears, c. 1860, pub. 1865
    O love the Lord, pub. 1864
    O God, thou art worthy, 1867, pub. 1871
    O taste and see, pub. 1867
    I will lay me down in peace, 1868, pub. 1910
    Rejoice in the Lord, pub. 1868
    Sing, O heavens, pub. 1869
    I will worship, pub. 1871
    Thou, O Lord, art our father, 1874

I will mention thy loving-kindness, pub. 1875
I will sing of thy power, pub. 1877
Hearken unto me, pub. 1877
Turn thy face, pub. 1878
Who is like unto thee?, pub. 1883
iii. Adaptations of Russian church music:
Turn thee again, pub. 1874
Mercy and truth, pub. 1874
iv. Anglican chant for Psalm 150 (MS, no date)

6. Hymns

This list attempts to identify each Sullivan hymn-tune against the text to which it was first assigned. The three hymn-texts given with the 'Old 137th' were all allotted to that tune in *Church Hymns with Tunes*, the collection published in 1874 under Sullivan's editorship. (An alphabetical list of hymn-tune names is found in the entry on Sullivan in *Grove*, 6th edition, 1980.)

First line	Words by	Name of Tune	Date
A few more years shall roll (arrangement from G.W. Martin)	Horatius Bonar	'Leominster'	1902
Angel voices, ever singing	Francis Pitts	'Dulce sonans'	1874
Art thou weary, art thou languid	Trans. J.M. Neale	'Rest'	1872
At Thine altar, Lord, we gather	Mary Bradford Whiting	'Dulce sonans'	1874
Be Thou with us every day	T.B. Pollock	'Litany, No. 3'	
Brightly gleams our banner	T.J. Potter	'St Theresa'	1874
Christ is risen!	A.T. Gurney	'Resurrexit'	1874
Come, Holy Ghost, our souls inspire	Trans. Bishop J. Cosin	'Veni, Creator'	1874
Come, ye faithful, raise the strain	J.M. Neale	'St Kevin'	1872
Courage, brother! do not stumble	Norman Macleod	'Courage, brother'	1872
Crown Him with many crowns	Matthew Bridges	'Coronae'	1874
Draw nigh, and take the body of the Lord	Trans. J.M. Neale	'Coena Domini'	1874
Father, before Thy throne of light	F.W. Farrar	'Old 137th'	1874
Father of heaven, Who hast created all	Trans. Catherine Winkworth	'St Francis'	1874
For all Thy love and goodness (arrangement from Aldrich)	Frances Jane Douglas & Bishop W. Walsham How	'Springtime'	1874
For ever with the Lord (arrangement from J. Woodbury)	James Montgomery	'Nearer Home'	1874
From Egypt's bondage come	T. Kelly	'Pilgrimage'	1874
God bless our wide Dominion	Marquess of Lorne	'Dominion Hymn'	1880
God moves in a mysterious way	William Cowper	'St Nathaniel'	1867
God the all-terrible! King who ordainest	Henry Fothergill Chorley & John Ellerton	'Ultor omnipotens'	1874
Hark! a thrilling voice is sounding	Trans. Edward Caswall	'Lux eoi'	1874
He is gone – a cloud of light	A.P. Stanley	'St Patrick'	1874
Holy Spirit, come in might (arrangement from S. Webbe's collection)	Trans. Edward Caswall	'Light'	1902
Hushed was the evening hymn	James D. Burns	'Samuel'	1874
I heard the voice of Jesus say	Horatius Bonar	'Audite audientes me'	1874
In the hour of my distress	Robert Herrick	'Evelyn'	1874
It came upon the midnight clear	E.H. Sears	'Noel'	1874
Jesu, in Thy dying woes	T.B. Pollock	'Lebbaeus'	1874

Jesu, life of those who die	T.B. Pollock	'Litany, No. 2'	1875
Jesu, my Saviour, look on me	Charlotte Elliott	'Hanford'	1874
Jesu, we are far away	T.B. Pollock	'Litany, No. 1'	1875
Lead, kindly light	J.H. Newman	'Lux in tenebris'	1874
Let no tears to-day be shed	Trans. R.F. Littledale	'St Millicent'	1874
Let us with a gladsome mind	John Milton	'Ever faithful, ever sure'	1874
Lord, in this, Thy mercy's day	Isaac Williams	'Lacrymae'	1872
Love Divine, all love excelling	Charles Wesley	'Falfield' or 'Formosa'	1867
My God, I thank Thee Who hast made	Adelaide A. Procter	'Carrow'	1875
Nearer, my God, to Thee	Sarah F. Adams	'Proprior Deo'	1872
Of Thy love some gracious token	T. Kelly	'Of Thy love' or 'St Lucian'	1868
O Jesu, Thou art standing	W. Walsham How	'Lux mundi'	1872
O King of Kings	W. Walsham How	'Bishopgarth'	1897
O love that wilt not let me go	George Matheson	'Chapel Royal'	1902
O Paradise!	F.W. Faber	'Paradise'	1874
O Strength and Stay upholding all creation (arrangement of an old tune)	Trans. John Ellerton	'Marlborough'	1874
O where shall rest be found	James Montgomery	'Ecclesia'	1874
Onward, Christian soldiers	Sabine Baring-Gould	'St Gertrude'	1871
Our Blest Redeemer, ere He breathed	Harriet Auber	'Promissio Patris'	1874
Rock of Ages, cleft for me	A.M. Toplady	'Mount Zion'	1867
Safe home, safe home in port	Trans. J.M. Neale	'Safe home'	1872
Saviour, when in dust to Thee	Robert Grant	'St Mary Magdalene'	1872
Show me not only Jesus dying	Josiah Condor	'Christus'	1874
Sing Alleluia forth in duteous praise	Trans. John Ellerton	'Holy City'	1874
Sweet Saviour! bless us ere we go	F.W. Faber	'Valete'	1874
Tender Shepherd, Thou hast still'd	Trans. Catherine Winkworth	'The long home' or 'Gentle shepherd' or 'Tender shepherd'	1872
The homeland, the homeland	H.R. Haweis	'Hymn of the homeland'	1867
The roseate hues of early dawn	Cecil Frances Alexander	'The roseate hues'	1872
The Saints of God, their conflict past	Archbishop Maclagan	'Saints of God'	1874
The Son of God goes forth to war (arrangement from Croft)	Bishop R. Heber	'St Ann'	1869
The strain upraise in joy and praise	Trans J.M. Neale	'The strain upraise'	1868
Thine arm, O Lord, in days of old	E.H. Plumptre	'Old 137th'	1874
Thou God of Love, beneath Thy sheltering wings	Jane Euphemia Browne	'Thou God of Love'	1867
Thou, to Whom the sick and dying	Godfrey Thring	'Bolwell'	1902
To mourn our dead we gather here	Mary Bradford Whiting	'Victoria'	1899
To Thee, O Lord, our hearts we raise	W. Chatterton Dix	'Golden sheaves'	1874
We are but strangers here	T.R. Taylor	'Fatherland' or 'St Edmund' or 'Pilgrimage'	1872
'Welcome, happy morning!' age to age shall say	Trans. John Ellerton	'Welcome, happy morning' or 'Fortunatus'	1872
When through the torn sail	Heber	'Heber'	1869
While shepherds watched their flocks by night (arrangement of an old carol)	Nahum Tate	'Bethlehem'	1874

Who trusts in God, a strong abode	Trans. Benjamin H. Kennedy	'Constance'	1874
Winter reigneth o'er the land (arrangement)	Bishop W. Walsham How	'Clarence'	1874
With the sweet word of peace (arrangement of an old melody)	George Watson	'Parting'	1874

Also four accompaniments to hymns [1858] in Helmore's *The Hymnal Noted*: no. 50 ('When in silence and in shadow'), no. 61 ('Almighty God, who from the flood'), no. 83 ('Now Christ, ascending whence he came'), no. 91 ('The world and all its boasted good'). See also the 'Five Sacred Part-Songs' in Section 7.

7. Part-songs, carols, etc.

Date of composition is given where not immediately followed by publication.

Madrigal ('O lady dear'), 1857, unpub.
It was a lover and his lass (Shakespeare), performed at Royal Academy of Music, 1857, unpub.
Fair daffodils (Herrick), 1857, pub. 1903
Seaside thoughts, 1857, pub. 1904
The last night of the year (H. F. Chorley), pub. 1863
When love and beauty (H. F. Chorley) from *The Sapphire Necklace*, published 1898
O hush thee, my babie (Scott), pub. 1867
The rainy day (Longfellow), pub. 1867
Evening (Houghton, after Goethe); Joy to the victors (Scott), Parting gleams (A. de Vere); Echoes (T. Moore); I sing the birth (B. Jonson); The long day closes (Chorley); The beleaguered (Chorley): as 'Seven Part-Songs', pub. 1868
All this night (trad. carol), pub. 1870
It came upon the midnight clear (E.H. Sears; not the same setting as under 'Hymns'); Lead, kindly light (J. H. Newman; same setting as under 'Hymns'); Through sorrow's path (H. Kirke White); Watchman, what of the night?; The way is long and drear (A. Procter): as 'Five Sacred Part-Songs', pub. 1871
Upon the snow-clad earth (trad. carol), pub. 1876
Hark! what mean those holy voices? (trad. carol), pub. 1883
Wreaths for our graves (L. F. Massey), pub. 1898

8. Solo songs, vocal duets and trios, including those contributed to plays

The listing is alphabetical. All items are solo songs unless otherwise indicated. The author, as identified on the published song, is given in parenthesis; the dedication, if any, follows, then the publisher (London unless otherwise indicated). The date is of publication; for unpublished songs the date of composition and the location of the manuscript is given. For songs in plays the date of first performance is also given. Songs excerpted from larger (theatrical and concert) works are not listed, except for those from *The Sapphire Necklace* and *Thespis*, which were not themselves published.

Absent-minded Beggar, The (Rudyard Kipling): *Daily Mail*/Enoch (1899)
Answer, The (A. Tennyson): see *The Window*
Arabian Love Song (P. B. Shelley), ded. Fred Clay: Chappell (1866)
At the Window (A. Tennyson): see *The Window*
Ay de mi, My Bird (George Eliot): see *The Young Mother*
Bid Me at Least Good-bye (Sydney Grundy), sung in *An Old Jew* (Grundy):1st perf., Garrick Theatre, London, 6 January 1894: Chappell (1894)
Birds in the Night: Boosey (1869) (Lionel Lewin) [New words for 'Hush'd is the bacon' from *Cox and Box*]

Bride of the Isles (Henry French; new words for the following song)

Bride from the North: Cramer (1863)

Care is All Fiddle-de-dee (F. C. Burnand), written for *The Miller and his Man* (Burnand): Cramer (1874)

Chorister, The (F. E. Weatherley): Metzler (1873) [Same music as The First Departure: see *The Young Mother*]

Christmas Bells at Sea (C. L. Kenney): Novello (1875)

Coming Home (R. Reece), duet for s. and m-s [new words for 'The Buttercup dwells' from *Cox and Box*]: Boosey (1873)

County Guy (Walter Scott), ded. Lady Alexina Duff: Ashdown (1867)

Cradle Song ('The Days are Cold') (Dorothy Wordsworth): see *The Young Mother*. See also *Little Darling, Sleep Again*

Distant Shore, The (W. S. Gilbert): Chappell (1874)

Dove Song (W. Brough): Boosey (1869)

Dream, my love, dream (Clarance [sic] Austin; new words for 'Sleep, my love, sleep')

E tu nol sai (G. Mazzucato) [English version, You Sleep (B. C. Stephenson)] sung in *The Profligate* (A. W. Pinero), 1st perf., Garrick Theatre, London, 24 April 1889: Chappell (1889)

Edward Grey (A. Tennyson): Lucas, Weber (1880)

Ever (Mrs Bloomfield Moore): Chappell (1887)

First Departure, The (Rev. E. Monro): see *The Young Mother* [Same music as *The Chorister*]

From East to Western Ind = Rosalind

Give (Adelaide A. Proctor), ded. Mrs. T. Helmore: Boosey (1867)

Golden Days (Lionel H. Lewin), ded. Madam Patey: Boosey (1872)

Gone! (A. Tennyson): see *The Window*

Guinevere (Lionel H. Lewin), ded. Therese Titiens: Cramer (1872)

I Heard the Nightingale (Rev. C. H. Townsend), ded. Capt. C. J. Ottley: Chappell (1863)

I Wish to Tune my Quiv'ring Lyre (Anacreon, trans. Lord Byron): Boosey (1868) [orig. with orch. accomp., according to Grove I]

I Would I Were a King (V. Hugo, trans. A. Cockburn), ded. Prince Leopold: Boosey (1878)

Ich möchte hinaus es jauchzen (A. Corrodi), ded. Rosamund Barnett: in L. Baily, *The Gilbert and Sullivan Book* (1952) see Bibliography (comp. 1859)

If Doughty Deeds (Robert Graham), ded. Mrs Scott Russell: Chappell (1866)

In the Summers Long Ago (anon): Metzler (1867) [Same music as *My Love Beyond the Sea*]

In the Twilight of our Love: Chappell (1881) [Re-texted from 'Silver'd is the Raven hair' from *Patience*]

Let me Dream Again (B. C. Stephenson), ded. Mme C. Nilsson: Boosey (1875)

Letter, The (A. Tennyson): see *The Window*

Lied mit Thränen halbgeschrieben (Eichendorff): MS Pierpont Morgan Library (comp. March 1861)

Life that Lives for You, A (Lionel H. Lewin): Boosey (1870)

Little Darling, Sleep Again: Metzler (1876) [New title for 'Cradle song': see *The Young Mother*]

Little maid of Arcadee (words after Gilbert) from *Thespis*: Cramer (1872)

Living Poems (H. W. Longfellow), ded. Edith Wynne: Boosey (1874)

Longing for Home (Jean Ingelow): Novello (1904)

Looking Back (Louisa Gray), ded. Mme Trebelli: Boosey (1870)

Looking Forward (Louisa Gray): Boosey (1873)

Lost Chord, The (Adelaide A. Procter): Boosey (1877)

Love Laid his Sleepless Head (A. C. Swinburne), ded. Hon. Eliot Yorke, sung in *The Merry Wives of Windsor* (Shakespeare), Gaiety Theatre, London, 19 December 1874: Boosey (1875)

Love that Loves Me Not, The (W. S. Gilbert), ded. Mrs D. B. Grant: Novello (1875)

Maiden's Story, The (Emma Embury), ded. Mrs Quintin Twiss: Chappell (1867)

Marquis de Mincepie, The (F. C. Burnand), written for *The Miller and his Man* (Burnand): Cramer (1874)

Marriage Morning (A. Tennyson): see *The Window*

Mary Morison (Robert Burns): Boosey (1874)

Moon in Silent Brightness, The (Bishop Reginald Heber): Metzler (1868)

Morn, Happy Morn (W. G. Wills), trio, sung in *Olivia* (Wills), 1st perf., Court Theatre, London, 30 March 1878: Metzler (1878)

Mother's Dream, The (Rev. W. Barnes), ded. Edith Wynne: Boosey (1868)

My Child and I (F. E. Weatherley): Boosey (1901)

My Dear and Only Love (Marquis of Montrose): Boosey (1874)

My Dearest Heart, ded. Mrs Osgood: Boosey (1876)

My Heart is Like a Silent Lute (Benjamin Disraeli, from *Henrietta Temple*): Novello (1904)

My Love Beyond the Sea (J. P. Douglas), ded. Hon. Mrs Swinton: Metzler (1877) [Same music as 'In the summers long ago']

Nel ciel seren (Rizzelli): see Venetian Serenade

No Answer ('The mist and the rain') (A. Tennyson): see *The Window*

No Answer ('Winds are loud and you are dumb') (A. Tennyson): see *The Window*

None But I Can Say (Lionel H. Lewin), ded. Mme Cornélie D'Ankara: Boosey (1872)

O Fair Dove, O Fond Dove (Jean Ingelow), ded. Miss Rachel Scott Russell: Ashdown (1868)

O Israel [sacred song], ded. Mrs C. V. Bridgeman: Novello (1855)

O Mistress Mine (Shakespeare), ded. C. Santley: Metzler (1866)

O Swallow, Swallow (A. Tennyson, from *The Princess*): J. Church Co., Cincinnati (1900)

O Sweet and Fair (A.F.C.K.), ded. Mrs Francis Byng: Boosey (1868)

Oh! bella mia (F. Rizelli): Cramer (1873) [Italian version of *Oh! ma Charmante*]

Oh! ma Charmante (V. Hugo), ded. Mme Conneau: Cramer (1872)

Old Love Letters (S. K. Cowan), ded. Mrs Ronalds: Boosey (1879)

On the Hill (A. Tennyson): see *The Window*

Once Again (Lionel H. Lewin), ded. Sims Reeves: Boosey (1872)

Orpheus with his Lute (Shakespeare), ded. Louisa Crampton: Metzler (1866)

Other Days (Harry Graham), published 1943.

Over the Roof (Chorley) from *The Sapphire Necklace*: Cramer (1866)

River, The (anon.): in *The Sunlight of Song*; Routledge/Novello (1875)

Roads Should Blossom, The: (words unattributed) MS Pierpont Morgan Library [comp. 1864 for Mary Anne Harrold's wedding]

Rosalind (Shakespeare), ded. W. H. Cummings: Metzler (1866)

Sad Memories (C. J. Rowe): Metzler (1869)

Sailor's Grave, The (H. F. Lyte), ded. Mrs Bourne (Hilderstone Hall): Cramer (1872)

St Agnes' Eve (A. Tennyson), ded. Mrs Ronalds: Boosey (1879)

Shadow, A (Adelaide A. Procter), ded. Madam Patey: Patey & Willis (1886)

She is not Fair to Outward View (Hartley Coleridge), ded. A. D. Coleridge: Boosey (1866)

Sigh no More, Ladies (Shakespeare), ded. Sims Reeves: Metzler (1866)

Sisters, The (A. Tennyson), duet for female voices: in *Leisure Hour* 1881: Lucas, Weber (1881)

Sleep, My Love (R. Whyte Melville), ded. Madam Patey: Boosey (1874)

Snow Lies White, The (Jean Ingelow): Boosey (1868)
Sometimes (Lady Lindsay of Balcarres): Boosey (1877)
Spring (A. Tennyson): see *The Window*
Sweet Day, So Cool (George Herbert), ded. Mrs Goldschmidt: Metzler (1864)
Sweet Dreamer (H. B. Farnie): Cramer (1874) [English version of 'Oh! ma Charmante']
Sweethearts (W. S. Gilbert), also as duet: Chappell (1875)
Tears, Idle Tears (A. Tennyson, from *The Princess*): J. Church Co., Cincinnati (1900)
Tender and True: Chappell (1874)
There Sits a Bird in Yonder Tree (Rev C. H. Barham, from *Ingoldsby Legends*): Cramer (1873)
Thou Art Lost to Me (anon.), ded. Mrs Charles Freake: Boosey (1865)
Thou Art Weary (Adelaide A. Procter): Chappell (1874)
Thou'rt Passing Hence (Felicia Hemans, from *The Highland Message*): Chappell (1875)
Thou wast all to me, love (Poe); unpublished
To One in Paradise (Edgar Allan Poe): Novello (1904)
Troubadour, The (Walter Scott): Boosey (1869)
Venetian Serenade – Nel ciel seren (F. Rizzelli, English words by W. Rainsom): Cramer (1873)
Village Chimes, The (C. J. Rowe): Boosey (1870)
Weary Lot is Thine, Fair Maid, A (Walter Scott), ded. B. Charles Stephenson: Chappell (1866)
We Gathered The Roses (words by?) [Sold to Metzler 21 September 1867; unpublished, unidentified in any other guise.]
We've Ploughed Our Land (anon.): in *The Sunlight of Song*, Routledge/Novello (1875)
What Does Little Birdie Say? (A. Tennyson): Ashdown (1867)
When? (A. Tennyson): see *The Window* (10)
When Thou Art Near (W.J. Stewart): Boosey (1877)
Where is another sweet as my sweet? (A. Tennyson): see *The Window* (= no. 6)
White Plume, The (J. P. Douglas; new words for 'Bride from the North'): Weippert (1872)
Will He Come? (Adelaide A. Procter), ded. Lady Katherine Coke: Boosey (1865)
Willow Song, The (Shakespeare), ded. Mme Sainton-Dolby: Metzler (1866)
Window, The, or The songs of the wrens (A. Tennyson), eleven songs: (1) On the Hill; (2) At the Window; (3) Gone!; (4) Winter; (5) Spring; (6) The Letter; (7) No Answer ('The Mist and the Rain'); (8) No Answer ('Winds Are Loud and You Are Dumb'); (9) The Answer; (10) When?; (11) Marriage Morning: Strahan (1871)
Winter (A. Tennyson): see *The Window*
You Sleep (B. C. Stephenson) [English version of E tu nol sai]
Young Mother, The, three simple songs, ded. Lady Muriel Talbot: (1) Cradle Song ('The Days are Cold') (anon.); (2) Ay de mi, my bird (George Eliot); (3) The First Departure (Rev. E. Monro): Cramer (1874)

9. Miscellaneous

Cadenza for Mozart's piano concerto in A (K 488), 1859 [lost?]
Arrangement: Additional accompaniments for Handel's *Jephtha*, 1869.
Completion of John Goss's anthem *There is none like unto the God of Jeshurun*, pub. 1882.
Arrangement for orchestra of Russian national anthem, 1874?
Arrangement of *God Save the Queen* [lost]
Three-part canon, *I am at a loss what to write in this book*, entry in Baron Ferdinand de Rothschild's *Livre d'or*, autograph MS, 1886, pub. 1957.

Sullivan was named as sole editor for the following vocal scores in Boosey's Royal Edition from the late 1860s:

Beethoven	Fidelio
Bellini	La sonnambula
Flotow	Martha
Gounod	Faust
Mozart	Don Giovanni
Rossini	Il barbiere di Siviglia
Verdi	Il trovatore

In the same series he was joint editor, with Josiah Pittman, of:

Auber	Les Diamants de la couronne
	Fra Diavolo
	Le Domino noir
	Masaniello
Balfe	The Bohemian Girl
Bellini	Norma
	I Puritani
Donizetti	Don Pasquale
	La favorita
	Lucia di Lammermoor
	Lucrezia Borgia
Gounod	Mireille
	Le Médecin malgré lui
Meyerbeer	Dinorah
	Les Huguenots
	Robert le diable
Mozart	Die Zauberflöte
	Le nozze di Figaro
Rossini	Guillaume Tell
	Semiramide
Verdi	Un ballo in maschera
	Rigoletto
	La traviata
Wagner	Lohengrin
Weber	Der Freischütz

He also edited Mendelssohn's *Songs without words* for Cramer (before 1874)

Prose Works

1. Anonymous review of the opera *Esmeralda* by Fabio Campana (1819–82) in *The Observer*, 19 June 1870.
2. Contributions to *Grove's Dictionary of Music and Musicians*, 1st edition, 1879–89: articles on CLAY, FREDERIC, and PLAIDY, LOUIS, signed 'A.S.S.' (Plaidy was one of Sullivan's principal teachers in Leipzig; see p. 21.)
3. 'About music', text of address delivered at Town Hall, Birmingham, 19 October 1888 (in LAWRENCE, see Bibliography).
4. Article, 'In the days of my youth' (no. 34) in the periodical *M.A.P.* (apparently 'Mainly about people'), 4 February 1899. This article was probably 'ghosted' but was presented as Sullivan's own.

Appendix 4
Bibliography

SOURCES of major musical and biographical reference, plus a number of books yielding important social background, are listed here. This is not, however, an attempt at a complete list of books about Arthur Sullivan and his works: a number of books merely retailing older material, or simply fanciful (e.g. Lillian Bradstock's 'romantic prose versions' of the Gilbert and Sullivan operettas) are omitted. Much information is also to be found in annotations to recordings issued on LP, tape, and CD.

The general alphabetical listing is by author. Where the source is anonymous, then the most convenient title-heading is used within square brackets, e.g. [Leipzig] for publications of the Leipzig Conservatory. BL signifies the British Library (manuscript department), London. The transactions of the [Royal] Musical Association are indicated as 'Proc. Mus. Ass.'; GSJ indicates the Gilbert and Sullivan Journal, MT the Musical Times, SASS the journal or other publications of the Sir Arthur Sullivan Society.

The files of *The Times*, the *Illustrated London News*, the *Musical Times* and the *Orchestra* (intermittently published) were found valuable throughout. The biographies by A. H. Lawrence and by B. W. Findon, published within or shortly after the composer's lifetime and written by people who knew him (Findon was a second cousin on Sullivan's father's side), are obviously of special importance but – in so far as they rely on the memory of the composer in later years for what is supposed to have happened decades before – are not always trustworthy in detail.

Those sources which are mentioned in the text or in the *Notes*, p. 428 are identified at the left of the entry by a special key-word.

All titles listed were published in London unless otherwise stated, except that no place-name has been given for publications of the Sir Arthur Sullivan Society, based in various UK locations.

Abeshouse, B. S. *A Medical History of Sir Arthur Sullivan* (New York, privately printed), 1966

Acland, Henry Dyke. Manuscript collection in Bodleian Library, Oxford (Acland MSS d. 54)

Adburgham, Alison. *A Radical Aristocrat: Sir William Molesworth of Pencarrow*, 1990

Albani, Emma. *Forty Years of Song*, 1911

ALLEN/FN   Allen, Reginald. *The First Night Gilbert and Sullivan* (New York), 1958, revised ed. 1976

—— *Gilbert and Sullivan in America* (New York), 1979

ALLEN/S   —— *Sir Arthur Sullivan: composer and personage* (New York), 1975

Allingham, William. *A Diary*, 1985

Andrews, Allen. *The Splendid Pauper* (Philadelphia), 1968

Anon. *The Green Room Book, or Who's Who on the Stage*, 1907

Anon. *Harmony in the Lodge*, Masonic Square, December 1977

Anon. '*Sir Arthur Sullivan as an Old Friend knew him,*' *Argosy*, lxxiii, 1901, p. 161

Anon. 'Arthur Sullivan,' *University Magazine*, iv, 1879, p. 483

Arditi, Luigi. *My Reminiscences*, 1896

Argent, W. J. *Philharmonic Jubilee* (Liverpool), 1889

BACHE Bache, Constance. *Brother musicians, Reminiscences of Edward and Walter Bache*, 1901

BAILY/W Baily, Leslie. *Gilbert and Sullivan and their World*, 1973

BAILY/GSB Baily, Leslie. *The Gilbert and Sullivan Book* 1952 and later revisions

BAKER/COP Baker, Kenneth. 'In the comic opera of politics' in programme of *Iolanthe*, Salisbury Amateur Operatic Society, May 1981

BAKER/RVA Baker, Michael. *The Rise of the Victorian Actor*, 1978

Baldwin, F. G. C. *The History of the Telephone in the United Kingdom*, 1925

BANCROFT Bancroft, Marie and Squire. *The Bancrofts: Recollections of Sixty Years*, 1909

Barker, Felix, and Peter Jackson. *London: 2000 years of a City and its People*, 1974

Barker, Harley Granville. *Exit Planché, enter Gilbert*, 1932

Barnby, Muriel. 'My Letters from Gilbert and Sullivan', *Strand Magazine*, January 1921

Barnett, John F. *Musical Reminiscences and Impressions*, 1906

Barrington, Rutland. *Rutland Barrington – by Himself*, 1908

—— *More Rutland Barrington – by Himself*, 1911

Batley, Thomas, ed. Sir Charles Hallé's Concerts in Manchester [programmes 1858-95]. (Manchester), 1895

Beatty-Kingston, W. *Music and Manners*, 1887

Beerbohm, Max. *Around Theatres*, 1930

Bennett, Joseph. *Forty Years of Music, 1865–1905*, 1908

Bennett, J. R. S. *Life of William Sterndale Bennett*, 1907

Bentley, J. *Ritualism and Politics in Victorian Britain*, 1978

Berman, Leon E. *Gilbert's First-Night Anxiety*, Psychoanalytic Quarterly (New York), 1976, vol. 45 (1)

BEST Best, Geoffrey. *Mid-Victorian Britain 1851–75*, 1971

Bettany, C. *100 Years of D'Oyly Carte and Gilbert and Sullivan*, 1975

Bevan, Frederick. *The Life and Works of Sir Arthur Sullivan* (Adelaide), 1921

Blackburn, Vernon. 'Arthur Sullivan', *Fortnightly Review*, lxix (1901), p. 81

BINNS Binns, P. I. *A Hundred Years of Military Music*, 1959

BOND Bond, Jessie. *The Life and reminiscences of Jessie Bond*, 1930

Boosey, William. *Fifty Years of Music*, 1931

Booth, Michael R. [and others]. *The 'Revels' History of Drama in English, vol. 6 (1750–1880)*, 1975

—— *Victorian Spectacular Theatre*, 1981

Boston Evening Transcript, obituary [false!] of Fanny Carter Ronalds, 3 June 1910

Bott, Alan and Clephane, Irene. *Our Mothers*, 1932

Bowman, Lynn. *Los Angeles, Epic of a City* (Berkeley, California), 1974

BOYER Boyer, R. D. *The Directorial Practice of W.S. Gilbert* (Ohio State University doctoral dissertation), 1970

Bradley, Ian. *The Annotated Gilbert and Sullivan*, 1982 and 1984

Bratton, J. S. *The Victorian Popular Ballad*, 1978

Bridge, Sir Frederick. *A Westminster Pilgrim*, 1919

Bridgeman, C. V. 'Chapel Royal Days of Arthur Sullivan', *Musical Times*, Mar. 1901

British Medical Journal, 25 Feb. 1956 (p. 472). Sir Arthur Sullivan (answer to query)

Brown, J. D. *Biographical Dictionary of Musicians*, 1896

Brown, L. Parmley. [article on] 'Lillian Russell'. *Dictionary of American Biography* (New York), 1935

Browne, Alexander P. *Sir Arthur Sullivan and Piracy*. North American Review (New York), 1889

Browning, Oscar. *Memories of Later Years*, 1923

Bruyas, Florian. *Histoire de l'opérette en France* (Lyon), 1974

Bunnell, Lafayette Houghton. *Discovery of the Yosemite* (3rd ed., New York & Chicago), 1892

Burke, John. *Duet in Diamonds* (New York), 1972

BURNAND   Burnand, Francis C. *Records and Reminiscences*, 1904

Calder, Jennie. *The Victorian Home*, 1977

Carr, Alice Comyns. *J. Comyns Carr: Stray Memories, by His Wife*, 1920

CARR/CB   Carr, J. Comyns. *Coasting Bohemia*, 1914

—— *Some Eminent Victorians*, 1908

—— 'Arthur Sullivan'. *Fortnightly Review*, lxix (1901), p. 81

Carse, Adam. *The Life of Jullien* (Cambridge) 1951

Carte, Richard D'Oyly. *Monograph of the Royal English Opera*, 1891

CELLIER   Cellier, François Arsène and Bridgeman, Cunningham. *Gilbert, Sullivan and D'Oyly Carte*, 1914 and 1927 [US title: *Gilbert, Sullivan and their Operas*, (Boston) 1914]

Churchill, Allen. *The Upper Crust*, 1970

Churchill, Lady Randolph. *Reminiscences of Lady Randolph Churchill*, 1908

Clarke, Sir Edward. *The Story of My Life*, 1918

COBBAN   Cobban, Alfred. *History of Modern France*, vol. 2, second ed., 1965

Cohen, Morton N. *The letters of Lewis Carroll* (New York), 1979

Colles, H. C. *The Royal College of Music; a Jubilee Record*, 1933

Cooper, Martin. *Opéra Comique*, 1949

—— 'The Fickle Philistine' in *Opera News*, New York, xxxii (April 1968), p. 8

COPE   Cope, Zachary. *The Versatile Victorian . . . Sir Henry Thompson, Bart.*, 1951

Cowles, Virginia. *Edward VII and His Circle*, 1956

COWLES/R   —— *The Rothschilds: a Family Fortune*, 1973

Crewe, Quentin. *The Frontiers of Privilege*, 1961

Cruickshank, R. J. *Dickens and the Early Railway Age*, 1949

[Crystal Palace] Collection of concert programmes, various years [in BL, cat. c. 370]

[Crystal Palace] Illustrated Crystal Palace Penny Guide, 1862

Cummings, William H. 'Music During the Queen's Reign', *Proc. Mus. Ass.* xxii, 1896

Darbyshire, Alfred. *The Art of the Victorian Stage*, 1907

Dark, Sidney and Rowland Grey. *W. S. Gilbert, His Life and Letters*, 1923

Darlington, William Aubrey. *The World of Gilbert and Sullivan* (New York), 1950

Davis, Tracy C. *The Savoy Chorus* in *Theatre Notebook*, 44/1, 1990

DAVISON   Davison, Henry. *From Mendelssohn to Wagner*, 1912
               Deane, Phyllis, and W. A. Cole. *British Economic Growth 1688–1959*, 1962
               Deighton, A. S. *The Impact of Egypt on Britain* in P. M. Holt (ed), *Political and Social change in Modern Egypt*, 1968
               De La Mare, Walter (ed). *The Eighteen-Eighties* (Cambridge), 1930
DE MARÉ   De Maré, Eric. *The London Doré Saw*, 1973
               Dicey, Edward. 'Recollections of Arthur Sullivan', *Fortnightly Review* lxxvii, 1905, p. 74
DNB   *Dictionary of National Biography*, 1885–
               Donakowski, Conrad L. *A Muse for the Masses* (Chicago), 1977
DONALDSON   Donaldson, Frances. *The Actor-Managers*, 1970
               D'Oyly Carte Opera Company. Press cuttings (31 volumes, but not all consecutive) relating to Richard D'Oyly Carte, his family and his operatic enterprises, formerly in the possession of Dame Bridget D'Oyly Carte.
               Dunhill, Thomas Frederick. *Sullivan's Comic Operas*, 1928
               Dunn, George E. *A Gilbert and Sullivan Dictionary*, 1936
               Edel, Leon (ed.). *Henry James Letters* vol. 2, (Cambridge, MA) 1975
               Eden, David. *Gilbert and Sullivan: The Creative Conflict*, 1986
               —— *Sullivan and Brome Hall* in SASS 28 (1989)
               —— [contributions to] SASS booklet *Ivanhoe*, 1990
               Edwardes, George. 'Thirty Years of Musical Comedy' in *Tit-Bits*, 11 July 1914
EHRLICH   Ehrlich, Cyril. *The Piano: a History*, 1976.
               —— *The Musical Profession in Great Britain since the 18th Century*, 1985
               —— *Harmonious Meeting* [The Performing Right Society], 1989
ELLIOT   Elliot, Elizabeth. *They All Married Well*, 1960
               Elkin, Robert. *Royal Philharmonic*, 1947
EMMERSON/R   Emmerson, George S. *John Scott Russell*, 1977
EMMERSON/A   —— *Arthur Darling* [privately printed, London, Ontario] 1980
               Engel, Louis. *From Handel to Hallé*, 1890
               Ensor, R. C. K. *England 1870–1914*, 1936
ESCOTT   Escott, Thomas Hay Sweet (Translator). *La Société de Londres*, 1885
ESQUIROS   Esquiros, Henri-François Alphonse. *L'Angleterre et la vie anglaise* (5 vols), (Paris), 1859–69
FARMER   Farmer, Henry George. *The Rise and Development of Military Music*, 1912
               Farr, Dennis. *English Art, 1870–1940*, 1978
               Fèret, Charles James. *Fulham Old and New*, 1900
               Fétis, F. J. *Biographie des musiciens: Supplément II* (Paris), 1880
               Finck, Hermann. *My Melodious Memories*, 1937
FINDON   Findon, B. W. *Sir Arthur Sullivan: His Life and Music*, 1904; revised as *Sir Arthur Sullivan and His Operas*, 1908
               Fink, Robert. *Rhythm and Text Setting in 'The Mikado'* in *Nineteenth Century Music* (Berkeley, CA), xiv/1, 1990
FITZGERALD   Fitzgerald, Percy Hetherington. *The Savoy Operas and the Savoyards*, 1894 [US title, *The Operas of Gilbert and Sullivan* (Philadelphia), 1894]
               —— *The Garrick Club*, 1904
FORD   Ford, Ernest. *Short History of Music in England*, 1912
FORSTER   Forster, John. *Charles Dickens*, 1872–4
FOSTER/AO   Foster, Joseph. *Alumni Oxonienses*, Oxford 1888

FOSTER/PS   Foster, Myles Birket. *History of the Philharmonic Society*, 1912
Fowler, J. T. *Life and Letters of John Bacchus Dykes*, 1897
Francillon, Robert. *Mid-Victorian Memories*, 1914
Frewen, Moreton. *Melton Mowbray and Other Memories*, 1934
FULD   Fuld, James J. *The Book of World-Famous Music*, 1966
Ganz, Wilhelm *Memories of a Musician*, 1913
Gänzl, Kurt. *The British Musical Theatre* (Basingstoke), 1986
Gilbert, William Schwenck. *Original Plays*, 1902
—— various manuscript papers in BL
—— *New and Original Extravaganzas* by ed. I. Goldberg (Boston), 1961
—— *Topsyturvydom* ed. Charles Plumtre Johnson (Oxford), 1931
Girouard, Mark. *The 'Queen Anne' Movement*, 1977
—— *Life in the English Country House*, 1978
—— *The Victorian Country House*, 1979
Glasstone, Victor. *Victorian and Edwardian Theatres*, 1975
Gloag, John. *Victorian Taste*, 1962
Godwin, A. H. *Gilbert and Sullivan*, 1926
Goldberg, Isaac. *A Handbook on Gilbert and the Gilbert–Sullivan Operas* (Boston), 1913
—— *The Story of Gilbert and Sullivan; or the 'Compleat' Savoyard* (New York), 1928
GOMME   Gomme, G. Lawrence, *London in the reign of Victoria*, 1898
Goodman, Andrew. *Gilbert and Sullivan at Law*, 1983
—— *Gilbert and Sullivan's London* (Tunbridge Wells), 1988
Graves, C. L. *Hubert Parry*, 1926
—— *Leather Armchair: the Book of London Clubs*, 1963
GRAVES/G   —— *The Life and Letters of Sir George Grove, C.B.*, 1903
Green, Martyn. *Here's a How-de-do*, 1952
Greene, Harry Plunket. *Charles Villiers Stanford*, 1935
Griffiths, Major Arthur. *Clubs and Clubmen*, 1907
Grossmith, George. *A Society Clown: Reminiscences* (Bristol), 1888
—— 'Sir Arthur Sullivan: A Personal Reminiscence', *Pall Mall Magazine*, xxiii, 1901, p. 250.
GROVE   Grove, George. *A Dictionary of Music and Musicians*, 1879–89 and subsequent editions [numbered as GROVE VI (= sixth edition, 1980) etc.]
Guedalla, Philip. *The Second Empire* (New York), 1922
Guest, Ivor. *Louis Napoleon in England*, 1952
HADAMOWSKY   Hadamowsky, F. and H. Otte. *Die Wiener Operette*, 1947
Hallé, C. E. and M. *Life and Letters of Sir Charles Hallé*, 1896
Halton, Frederick J. *The Gilbert and Sullivan Operas: A Concordance* (New York), 1935
HANSLICK   Hanslick, Eduard. *Musikalisches Skizzenbuch*, pt. iv, *Moderne Oper* (Berlin), 1888
—— *Aus dem Concert-Saal, 1848–68* (Vienna/Leipzig), 1897
Harris, Charles Townsend. *Memories of Manhattan in the Sixties and Seventies* (New York), 1928
Harris, Frank. *My Life and Loves* (New York), 1963
Hartnoll, Phyllis ed. *Shakespeare in Music*, 1964
HARTNOLL   —— ed. *Oxford Companion to the Theatre*, revised edition 1967
HAUGER   Hauger, George. *Seventy Years of Musical Theatre: a First Hand-list, 1831–1900* (author's MS., 1977)
—— 'English Musical Theatre 1830–1900', *Theatre Notebook* 1982, no. 2.

Havergal, Francis T. *Memorials of Frederick Arthur Gore Ouseley*, 1889

HAWEIS   Haweis, Rev. H. R. *Music and Morals*, 1871

HELMORE   Helmore, F. *Memoir of the Rev. Thomas Helmore*, 1891

Helyar, J. ed. *Gilbert and Sullivan International Conference* [Report] (Kansas City), 1970

Henschel, Sir George. *Musings and Memories of a Musician*, 1918

Hibbert, Christopher. *Gilbert and Sullivan and Their Victorian World*, 1976

HIBBERT/ILN   ——*The Illustrated London News - a survey*. 1975

Hipkins, Alfred James. Manuscript collection, BL MSS 41636

Hobhouse, Hermione. *Lost London*, 1971

Hogarth, George. *The Philharmonic Society of London*, 1862

Hollingshead, John. *Gaiety Chronicles*, 1898

—— *Good Old Gaiety*, 1903

Horn, Pamela. *The Rise and Fall of the Victorian Servant*, 1975

Horne, Alistair. *The Terrible Year*, 1971

Hueffer, Francis. *Half a Century of Musical Life in England*, 1889

Huggett, Frank E. *Life Below Stairs*, 1977

Hughes, Alan. *Henry Irving, Shakespearean*, 1981.

HUGHES   Hughes, Gervase. *The Music of Arthur Sullivan*, 1960

HULME   Hulme, David Russell. '*The Zoo': a study of the autograph full score* in *The Savoyard*, 1978

—— '*Cox and Box' or the long lost music* in *The Savoyard*, 1981

HULME/SOR   [contributions to] SASS booklet '*The Sorcerer' and 'Trial by Jury*', 1984

—— *Sullivan's 'Macbeth' music* in SASS 1819, 1984

—— *The operettas of Sir Arthur Sullivan: a study of available autograph full scores*, PhD thesis, University of Wales, 1986

HULME/RUD   *An investigation of the musical sources* in SASS booklet *Ruddygore* [sic], 1987

HUTCHINGS   Hutchings, J. M. *In the Heart of the Sierras* (Oakland, California), 1890

Hyde, H. Montgomery. *The Trials of Oscar Wilde*, 1974

Jackson, Stanley. *The Savoy*, 1964

Jacob, H. E. *Johann Strauss: a Century of Light Music* (rev. ed.), 1949

Jacobs, Arthur. 'Sullivan, Gilbert, and the Victorians', *Music Review*, May 1951, p. 122

—— *Gilbert and Sullivan*, 1951

—— 'The Secret Diaries of Sir Arthur Sullivan', *High Fidelity* (New York), xvii, 1977

—— *Sullivan and Shakespeare* in R. Foulkes (ed.), *Shakespeare and the Victorian Stage* (Cambridge), 1986

—— *The Mask of the Mikado* in *Opera*, August 1986

—— *A Sullivan Archive*, MT April 1987

James, Robert Rhodes. *Lord Randolph Churchill* (New York), 1960

Jewish Year Book. 1896, etc

Joachim, Joseph, and Andreas Moser. *Briefe von und an Joseph Joachim* (Berlin), 1912

JOHNSON   Johnson, Edgar. *Charles Dickens: His Tragedy and Triumph*, 1952

Johnson, H. Earle. *First Performances in America (to 1900): Works with Orchestra* (Detroit), 1979

JONES/GL   Jones, Brian. '*The Golden Legend': a new letter comes to light* in SASS 17 (1984)

Jones, John Bush. ed. *W. S. Gilbert: a Century of Scholarship and Commentary* (New York), 1970

Joseph, T. 'Towards a G. & S. Bibliography', *Library Review*, 1971

—— *George Grossmith* (Bristol), 1982

Julian, John. *Dictionary of Hymnology*, 1915

Kaubisch, Hermann. *Operette* (Berlin), 1955

Keefer, Lubov. *Baltimore Music* (Baltimore), 1962

KENNEDY/HT   Kennedy, Michael. *The Hallé Tradition* (Manchester), 1960

KENNEDY/CH   —— (ed.) *Autobiography of Sir Charles Hallé*, 1972

Kenney, Charles Lamb. *Memoir of Michael William Balfe*, 1875

King, Alec Hyatt. 'The Wandering Minstrels and their Archive' in H. Leuchtmann and R. Münster, *Ars Jocundissima: Festschrift für Karl Dorfmüller* (Tutzing), 1984

KLEIN/T   Klein, Hermann. *Thirty Years of Musical Life in London: 1870–1900*, 1903

KLEIN/G   —— *The Golden Age of Opera*, 1933

KLEIN/MM   —— *Musicians and Mummers*, 1925

Kneschke, Emil. *Das Conservatorium der Musik in Leipzig* (Leipzig), 1868

Kracauer, S. *Offenbach and the Paris of his Time*, 1937

Kreissle von Hellborn, Heinrich. *The Life of Franz Schubert* translated by A. D. Coleridge, 1869

Kuhe, Wilhelm. *My Musical Recollections*, 1896

Lamb, Andrew. 'Sullivan's Continental Journeys', *GSJ*, May 1967, p. 96

—— ' "Cox and Box" – a Postscript', *GSJ*, Jan 1968, p. 132

—— 'A Tradition and an Anomaly', *GSJ*, Jan 1968, p. 196

LAMB/OC   —— Sullivan as Opera Critic, *GSJ*, May 1970, p. 288

—— The Memoirs of Julia Jellicoe, *GSJ*, May 1972, p. 416

—— Sullivan, Arthur Seymour, in Grove's *Dictionary of Music and Musicians*, 6th ed., 1980

—— 'Gilbert & Sullivan for Dancing', *GSJ*, Summer 1973, p. 32

—— ' "Ivanhoe" Revived – at Last!', *GSJ*, Autumn 1973, p. 53

—— 'G & S and the Gaiety', *MT*, Dec 1971, p. 1162

—— ' "Ivanhoe" and the Royal English Opera', *MT* May 1973, p. 475

—— 'A Note on Sullivan's Instrumental Works', *MT* 1975, p. 234

Landauer, Bella C. *Gilbert and Sullivan Influence on American Trade Cards* (New York), 1936

LANG   Lang, Cecil J. *The Swinburne Letters*, 1959

LAWRENCE   Lawrence, A. H. *Sir Arthur Sullivan*, 1899

—— *Sir Arthur Sullivan's Diaries*, Harper's Magazine (New York) 1902

Lazard, George Somes. *Tennyson and his Pre-Raphaelite Illustrators*, 1894

Legge, Robin H. & W. E. Hansell. *Annals of the Norfolk and Norwich Triennial Music Festivals*, 1896

LEHMANN/J   Lehmann, John. *Ancestors and Friends*, 1962

LEHMANN/RC   Lehmann, R. C. *Memories of Half a Century*, 1908

[Leipzig] *Hochschule für Musik Leipzig, 1843–1968* (Leipzig), 1968

—— *Festschrift zum 75 Jahrigen-Bestehen des königliches Konservatoriums der Musik zu Leipzig* (Leipzig), 1918

LESLIE/J   Leslie, Anita. *Jennie: The Life of Lady Randolph Churchill*, 1969

—— *Mr Frewen of England*, 1966

—— *The Fabulous Leonard Jerome*, 1954

Lewis, Lloyd, and Henry Justin Smith. *Oscar Wilde Discovers America* (New York), 1936

LISLE   Lisle, David. *Sullivan and the Crystal Palace*, a series of articles in SASS,

1981–2

LIVPHIL Liverpool Philharmonic Society. Minutes of General Committee (MS., [Royal] Liverpool Philharmonic Society)

Lockhead, Marion. *Young Victorians*, 1959

LOEWENBERG Loewenberg, Alfred. *Annals of Opera*, revised ed., 1977

LONGFORD/B Longford, Elizabeth. *A Pilgrimage of Passion: the life of Wilfred Scawen Blunt*, 1979

LONGFORD/V —— *Victoria R. I.*, 1954

Los Angeles. *Los Angeles City and County Directory* (Los Angeles), 1885

—— *Guide Book and Street Manual for Los Angeles, California* (Los Angeles), 1882

Los Angeles. *A Guide to the City and its Environs* (New York), 1941

Low, George. See Tillett

Lowerson, John, and John Myerscough. *Time to Spare in Victorian England*, 1977

Lubbock, Mark. *The Complete Book of Light Opera*, 1962

Lumley, Benjamin. *Reminiscences of the Opera*, 1864

Lysons, Daniel, and others. *Origins and Progress of the Meeting of the Three Choirs* (Gloucester), 1895

Lytton, Henry A. *A Wandering Minstrel*, 1933

—— *Secrets of a Savoyard*, 1922

McAllister, Ward. *Society as I have found it*, 1890

Mackenzie, Alexander C. 'The Life and Work of Arthur Sullivan', *Musical News*, 11, 18, 25 May 1901

Mackie. David. *The Songs of Arthur Sullivan* (MA thesis, University of Birmingham, 1974)

Mackinlay, Sterling. *Origin and Development of Light Opera*, 1927

Maclean, Charles. 'Sullivan as National Style Builder', *Proc. Mus. Ass.*, XXXVIII, 1902

MacPhail, Ralph, jun. *Additional Adventures of Messrs Box and Cox* (Bridgewater, Virginia, privately printed), 1974

MacQueen-Pope, W. *Gaiety, Theatre of Enchantment*, 1949

—— *Haymarket, Theatre of Perfection*, 1948

Magnus, Sir Philip. *King Edward VII*, 1964

—— *Gladstone*, 1954

Mair, Carlene, ed. *The Chappell Story, 1861–1961*, 1961

Maitland, J. A. Fuller. *English Music in the Nineteenth Century*, 1902

—— *A Door-keeper of Music*, 1926

—— 'Sir Arthur Sullivan', *Cornhill Magazine*, March 1901

Mallet, Marie. *Life with Queen Victoria*, 1968

Mander, R. and J. Mitchenson. *A Picture History of Gilbert and Sullivan*, 1962

MANDER —— *The Theatres of London*, 1963

—— *The Lost Theatres of London*, 1965

Mapleson, James Henry. *The Mapleson Memoirs*, ed. H. Rosenthal, 1966

Marshall, Florence A. *Arthur Seymour Sullivan* (article in *Famous Composers and their works*, ed. T. K. Paine (Boston), c. 1891

MARTIN/LRC Martin, Ralph G. *Lady Randolph Churchill*, 1969

MARTIN/T Martin, Robert Bernard. *Tennyson: The Unquiet Heart*, 1980

MATTHEWS Matthews, Betty. ' "Onward Christian Soldiers": A Centenary Note', *MT*, December, 1972, p. 1232

MATX Matz, Charles. 'Blanche Roosevelt', *Opera News* (New York), 23 March,

1973, p. 26

Maude, Mrs Raymond. *The Life of Jenny Lind*, 1926

Mayhew, Henry. *London Characters*, 1874

Meares, Stan. *A Century of 'Ivanhoe'* in SASS booklet *Ivanhoe*, 1990

—— *'Ivanhoe': the Berlin Revision* in SASS 31 (1990)

MILLAIS   Millais, J. G. *The Life and Letters of Sir John E. Millais*, 1899

Mikhail, E. H. (ed.). *Oscar Wilde: Interviews and Recollections*, 1979

Mitford, Algernon. *Memories*, 1915

MOORE/EEL   Moore, Jerrold Northrop. *Edward Elgar: Letters of a Lifetime*, 1990

MOORE/ME   Moore, Greville. *Memoirs of an old Etonian*, 1919

Morris, Lloyd. *Postscript to Yesterday*, 1947

MORRIS/NY   —— *Incredible New York*, 1951

Moscheles, Charlotte. *Life of Moscheles, with Selections from his Correspondence*, 1873

Moscheles, Felix. *In Bohemia with Du Maurier*, 1896

Nevill, Ralph. *London Clubs*, 1911

Nevill, Ralph and C. E. Jerningham. *Piccadilly to Pall Mall*, 1908

[New York] *Trow's City Directory of New York* (New York), 1885

—— *New York Social Register* (New York), 1891

—— *Club Men of New York* (New York), 1893

New York Times. *Obituary of Peter Lorillard Ronalds*, 24 Oct 1905

—— *Obituary* [false!] *of Fanny Carter Ronalds*, 4 June 1910

Nicoll, Allardyce. *A History of English Drama* (vol. v, *Late Nineteenth Century Drama, 1850–1900*), 1959

Novello, Ewer & Co. *A Short History of Cheap Music*, 1887

ODELL   Odell, George C. D. *Annals of the New York Stage*, 1927

OLSEN   Olsen, Donald J. *The Growth of Victorian London*, 1976

ORMOND   Ormond, Leonée. *George du Maurier*, 1969

Palmer, Arnold. *Movable Feasts*, 1952

Parrott, Ian. 'Arthur Sullivan (1842–1900)', *Music and Letters*, xxiii, 1942, p. 202

—— 'Sullivan, Arthur Seymour', *Musik der Geschichte und Gegenwart*, xii, 1965, p. 1727

Pearsall, Ronald. *Victorian Popular Music*, 1973

PEARSON   Pearson, Hesketh. *Gilbert and Sullivan*, 1953

—— *Gilbert, His Life and Strife*, 1957

PELLINGHAM   Pellingham, Peter. *Handbook for London*, 1849

Petrie, Sir Charles. *The Victorians*, 1960

PLEASANTS   Pleasants, Henry (ed. and trans), *Edward Hanslick: Vienna's Golden Years of Music* (New York), 1958

Poladian, Sirvart. *Sir Arthur Sullivan: An Index to the Texts of His Vocal Works* (Detroit), 1961

Ponsonby, Arthur. *Henry Ponsonby: His Life from his Letters*, 1942

Pope-Hennessy, James. *Queen Mary*, 1959

POUND   Pound, Reginald. *Sir Henry Wood*, 1969

Pulling, Christopher. *They Were Singing*, 1952

R.A.N. 'Sir Arthur Sullivan and the Scholarship', *Country Gentleman*, December, 1900

RAINBOW/CR   Rainbow, Bernarr. *The Choral Revival in the Anglican Church*, 1970

RAINBOW/L   —— *Land Without Music*, 1967

Raynor, Henry. 'Sullivan Reconsidered', *Monthly Musical Record*, xxxix, 1959, p. 163

REES/T	Rees, Terence. *Thespis: A Gilbert and Sullivan Enigma*, 1964
REES/SRC	—— *Sullivan's Royalty Contracts*, GSJ, Spring, 1973
	—— *A Sullivan Discography*, 1986 [new edition forthcoming]
	—— *A Note on 'Thespis'*, SASS 32 (1991)
	Rogers, Clara Kathleen. *Memories of a Musical Career* (Boston), 1919
	Ronald, Landon. *Variations on a Personal Theme*, 1922
ROLLINS	Rollins, C. and R. J. Witts. *The D'Oyly Carte Opera Company in Gilbert and Sullivan Operas*, 1962
ROSENTHAL	Rosenthal, Harold D. *Two Centuries of Opera at Covent Garden*, 1958
	Rothschild, Mrs James de. *The Rothschilds of Waddesdon Manor*, 1979
	Routley, Erik. *Arthur Seymour Sullivan* in *Bulletin of the Hymn Society of Great Britain and Ireland*, II/7, July 1949
	—— *The Music of Christian Hymnody* [later revised as *The Music of Christian Hymns*], 1957
	Rowell, George. *The Victorian Theatre*, 2nd ed., 1978
ROWELL/I	—— *Theatre in the Age of Irving*, 1981
	—— *Queen Victoria Goes to the Theatre*, 1978
ROWELL/PIN	—— *Sullivan, Pinero and 'The Beauty Stone'* in SASS 21 (1985)
	Russell, Carl Parcher. *A Hundred Years in Yosemite* (Yosemite, California), 1931
RPHIL	[Royal] Philharmonic Society. MSS documents, BL Loan Collection, 40
	Santley, Charles. *Reminiscences of My Life*, 1900
	Saremba, Meinhard. *Arthur Sullivan* [in German], (Wilhelmshaven), 1992
SARRY	Sarry, Léon. *Nice d'antan* (Nice), 1921
	Saxe-Wyndham, H. *Arthur Sullivan*, 1903
	—— *Arthur Seymour Sullivan*, 1926
	—— *August Manns and the Saturday Concerts*, 1909
	Schang, F. C. *Visiting Cards of Celebrities* (Paris), 1971
SCHOLES	Scholes, Percy A. *The Mirror of Music*, 1947
	Searle, Townley. *A Bibliography of Sir William Schwenck Gilbert*, 1931
SEELEY	Seeley, Paul D. *Who was Helen Lenoir?* in *The Savoyard*, February 1983
	Sharp, R. Farquharson. *A Short History of the English Stage*, 1909
	Shaw, George Bernard. *Music in London, 1890–4*, 1932
	—— *London Music in 1888–9 as heard by Corno di Bassetto*, 1937
	—— *Our Theatres in the Nineties*, 1932
	—— *Shaw on Music*, selected by Eric Bentley (New York), 1955
	Sheppard, E. *George, Duke of Cambridge*, 1906
	Shereff, Jesse. *Bibliography of Books on and Gilbert and Sullivan* (New York, privately printed), 1974
	Sherr, Richard. 'Schubert, Sullivan and Grove', *MT*, August 1980, p. 499
SHERSON	Sherson, Erroll. *London's Lost Theatres of the Nineteenth Century*, 1925
	Simcoe, H. Augustine. *Sullivan v. Critic, A Study in Press Phenomena*, 1906
	Simpson, Harold. *A Century of Ballads*, 1910
SINCLAIR	Sinclair, Andrew. *The Other Victoria*, 1981
	Sitwell, Edith. *Victoria of England*, 1936
SKIDMORE	Skidmore, John. *The National Training School for Music* in *Journal of the Royal Society of Arts*, February 1992
	Smalley, George W. *Anglo-American Memories*, 1911

Smart, Sir George. Manuscript collection, BL Add MS.41771 and 4222

Smith, M. van Wyk. *Drummer Hodge: The Poetry of the Anglo-Boer War 1899–1902*, 1978

SMYTH   Smyth, E. *Impressions that Remained*, 1919

SOTHEBY   Sotheby & Co. *Catalogue of Valuable Printed Books*, 'Music . . . which will be sold . . . Monday 13 June 1966 [includes lot 200: 20 vols of diaries and full scores of Sullivan. Diaries: 20 vol. 8vo uniform original black morocco with brass locks (which have been forced)']

Sousa, John Philip. *Marching Along* (New York), 1928

SPARK   Spark, Fred R. and Joseph Bennett. *A Full History of the Leeds Musical Festivals, 1858–89*, 1892

Spencer, Roderick. See Tillett

Stanford, Charles Villiers. *Studies and Memories*, 1908

—— *Pages from an Unwritten Diary*, 1914

—— *Interludes*, 1922

Stanislavsky, Konstantin. *My Life in Art*, 1925

STANYON/LEEDS Stanyon, Anne. *The Great Leeds Conspiracy* in SASS 31 (1990)

STEDMAN/GB   Stedman, Jane W. *Gilbert before Sullivan*, 1967

STEDMAN/GS   —— *Gilbert's Stagecraft* [in Jones, q.v.]

Stevens, Denis, ed. *A History of Song*, 1960

Sullivan, Arthur. *Diaries* [MS. Beinecke Library, Yale University]

—— Manuscript letters in BL 45170, 41639, 41636, 41628, 41771, 33965

—— Manuscripts (various) in Pierpont Morgan Library, New York

S/FLOWER   Sullivan, Herbert and Sir Newman Flower. *Arthur Sullivan, His Life, Letters and Diaries*, 1927, 1950

Sutton, Max Keith. *Gilbert and Sullivan* (New York), 1973

TEMPERLEY/EP Temperley, Nicholas. *Music of the English Parish Church*, 1979

TEMPERLEY/R   —— (ed.) *The Romantic Age 1800–1914* (Athlone History of Music in Britain, vol. 5) 1981

Tennyson, Charles. *Alfred Tennyson*, 1949

Terriss, Ellaline. *Ellaline Terriss by Herself*, 1928

Thompson, F. M. L. *Victorian England: the Horse-drawn Society*, 1970

Thompson, J. M. *Louis Napoleon and the Second Empire*, 1954

Thomson, David. *England in the Nineteenth Century*, 1950

TILLETT/VME   Tillett, Selwyn. '*Victoria and Merrie England*' – a Note, SASS 1981

—— *Iolanthe or Perola?* in SASS booklet *Iolanthe*, 1982

—— '*The Martyr of Antioch*' – a Note, SASS 1983

—— '*On Shore and Sea*' (introduction), SASS 1984

—— [contributions to] SASS booklet *Trial by Jury* and *The Sorcerer*, 1984

—— '*King Arthur*' in SASS 21 (1985)

—— '*Each in his accustomed place*' in SASS booklet *Ruddygore* [sic], 1987

—— '*To horse – to horse – the fugitives pursue.*' in SASS 25 (1987)

—— [with G. Low] *The Ancestors' Ancestry* in SASS 25 (1988)

—— [with R. Spencer] *Victoria and the Enchanted Island* in SASS 30 (1990)

Times, The. *Fifty Years: 1882–1930*, 1932

Trevelyan, G. M. *English Social History*, 1944, etc.

Turnbull, Stephen. '*The Yeomen of the Guard*' *and the Gramophone* in SASS booklet *The Yeomen of the Guard*, 1988

—— '*Ivanhoe*' *and the Gramophone*' in SASS booklet *Ivanhoe*, 1990

Turner, M. R. and A. Miall. *A Parlour Song Book* vol. 2, *Just a Song at Twilight*, 1972, 1975

Turner, Rigbie. *Nineteenth-Century Autography Music Manuscripts in the Pierpont Morgan Library* (New York), 1982

VAN DER KISTE Van der Kiste, John, and B. Jordaan. *Dearest Affie* [the Duke of Edinburgh], 1984

Van Vechten, Carl. *In the garret* (New York), 1920

WADDELL Waddell, James. *A History of the Edinburgh Choral Union* (Edinburgh), 1908

Wainwright, David. *The Piano Makers*, 1975

WALFORD Walford, Edward. *London Old and New*, n.d.

Walker, Ernest. *A History of Music in England* (Oxford), 1907

Walkley, Christina. *The Ghost in the Looking-Glass: The Victorian Seamstress*, 1981

Walters, Michael. [contributions to] SASS booklet *Princess Ida*, 1988

Ward, Mrs E. M. *Memories of Ninety Years*, n.d.

Warwick, Frances, Countess of. *Life's Ebb and Flow* (New York), 1929
—— *Discretions* (New York), 1931
—— *Afterthoughts*, 1931

Wearing, J. P. *The London Stage, 1880–99* (Metuchen, NJ), 1979

WEISSMANN Weissmann, Adolf. *Berlin als Musikstadt* (Berlin), 1911

Weldon, Georgina. *Musical Reform*, 1872
—— *Hints for Pronunciation in Singing*, 1875

Wells, Walter J. *Souvenir of Sir Arthur Sullivan*, 1901

WHITE White, Eric Walter. *The Rise of English Opera*, 1951
WILLEBY Willeby, Charles. *Masters of English Music*, 1893

Williamson, Audrey. 'Sullivan's Ballets', *Dancing Times*, April 1951
—— *Gilbert and Sullivan Opera: A New Assessment* 1953; revised edition 1982

Wilson, Fredric Woodbridge, ed. *A Gilbert and Sullivan Birthday Book* (Dobbs Ferry, NY), 1983
—— *An Introduction to the Gilbert and Sullivan Operas* (New York) 1983
—— *'The Mikado', 1885–1985* [Exhibition catalogue, Pierpont Morgan Library] (New York), 1985
—— *An introduction to the Gilbert and Sullivan Operas from the Collection of the Pierpont Morgan Library* (New York), 1989

WOLFSON Wolfson, John. *Final Curtain: The Last Gilbert and Sullivan Operas*, 1976
WOOD Wood, Henry J. *My Life of Music*, 1938

Wood, Roger. *A D'Oyly Carte Album*, 1953

Woodward, E. L. *The Age of Reform, 1815–1870*, 1938

YATES Yates, Martin. *Sullivan's Settings of Tennyson's 'Princess'* in SASS booklet on *Princess Ida*, 1988
—— *Contrast and Unity in the score of 'Ivanhoe'* in SASS booklet *Ivanhoe*, 1990

Young, G. M. (ed. G. N. Clark). *Early Victorian England: Portrait of an Age*, 1977

YOUNG/E Young, Percy M. *Letters of Edward Elgar and other writings*, 1956
—— *The Concert Tradition*, 1965
—— *A History of British Music*, 1967
YOUNG/S —— *Sir Arthur Sullivan*, 1971
—— *Sir George Grove*, 1980

Zedlitz, M. A. von. 'Sir Arthur Sullivan', *Strand Musical Magazine*, i, 1895, p. 169

ZELDIN Zeldin, Theodore. *France 1848–1945*, 1973

Index

'ABC' 295
Acland, Henry Dyke 440
Adams, Sir Francis Ottiwell 441
Adams, Stephen 144
Adelaide, Queen 3
Adèle (maid) 176, 180, 185, 378
Adler 363
Agnew, J.H. 70
Aidé, Charles Hamilton 156, 201
Albanesi, Carlo 201
Albani, Dame Emma 145, 148, 177–8,
 216, 238, 243, 245, 257, 259,
 261, 274, 302, 349–50, 389
Albert, Charles d' 155, 156
Albert, Eugene d' 155, 156, 167
Albert, Prince Consort 18, 67, 77,
 82
Albrecht, Eugene 23
Alexander II, Tsar of Russia 75,
 163
Alexander III, Tsar of Russia 163
Alexandra, Princess of Wales 36
Alfred (servant) 245
Alice, Princess 448
Allen, Reginald 113, 177, 209
Allingham, William 39, 433
Alma-Tadema, Sir Laurence 32
Ampthill, Lady 374
Anderson, Mary 196
'Anna, Miss' 124, 440
Aoust, Marquis d' 167
'Aramis', See Tennent, Annie
Archer, Frederic 264
Arditi, Luigi 91, 440
Argyll, Duke of 251
Arnaud, Hélène 312
Arnim, Hélène 108
Attwood, Thomas 14
Atzel, Baron d' 174
Auersperg, Countess 271
Austin, Alfred 377
Austin, Ambrose 3, 428

Bach, Johann Sebastian 20
Bache, Constance 237
Bache, Walter 22, 25, 237–8
Bailey, Leslie 65, 320, 376
Baird, George 207, 242–3, 251, 277, 379,
 401
Baker, Dame Janet 407
Baker, Kenneth 185
Balfe, Michael William 84
Balfour, Arthur J. 382
Ball, Meredith 282
Bancroft, Sir Squire 130, 308, 341, 374
Banks, May 28, 33, 432
Bantock, Sir Granville 382
Baring-Gould, Sabine 74
Barker, Richard 131
Barlow, Samuel 135
Barlow, Sir Thomas 402–3
Barnby, Sir Joseph 13, 26, 63–4, 68, 74,
 130, 144, 146, 189, 199, 264,
 336, 342–4, 348–9, 368, 370–1
Barnby, Muriel 202, 253
Barnes, Dr. 267
Barnett, Alice 158, 183
Barnett, Clara 22
Barnett, Domenico 22
Barnett, John (and Mrs) 22, 431
Barnett, John Francis 22–3, 144, 146,
 200, 431
Barnum, Phineas T. 130
Barrie, J.M. 352
Barrington, Rutland 115, 117–19, 143,
 157, 216, 220, 233, 253, 255,
 272, 289, 300, 307, 335–6, 346,
 355, 359, 369, 372, 408
Barry 392
Barry, Sir Charles 10
Bashford, Elena M. 408
Bashford, Ruth 408
Bateman, Lady (Agnes) 265
Battenberg, Prince Louis Alexander of
 209

Beatrice, Princess 186
Beatty-Kingston, W. 184
Beckman, Marie 312
Beddington, Violet 376
Beeth, Lola 291, 446
Belmont, August (and Mrs) 88, 142, 201
Belshaw (engineer) 233
Bendall, Wilfred 4, 361, 369, 375,
    378–80, 385, 387–8, 391–2, 398,
    400, 404, 445
Benedict, Sir Julius 19, 37, 41, 43–4, 50,
    130, 217, 437
Bennett, Charles 52
Bennett, Joseph 2, 78–9, 106, 149, 199,
    204, 232–3, 238, 244, 247, 249,
    266–7, 284, 302, 437, 448
Bennett, Sir William Sterndale 14, 18,
    20, 30, 33, 91, 93, 106, 204,
    313, 411
Bentham, George 115
Beresford, Lady Charles 201
Beringer, Oscar 208
Berlioz, Hector 4
Bernhardt, Sarah 154, 175
Bernstein, B. 255, 257, 284, 296, 304,
    309–11
Betts, Wyllys 136
Biddulph, Sir Thomas 77
Bird, Tom 251
Bispham, David 335, 368
Blagrove, Henry 48
Blomfield, Bishop C.J. 11
Blondin 27
Blow, Mr and Mrs 398
Blum Pasha 201
Blunt, Arthur ('Arthur Cecil') 52, 116,
    130, 216, 233, 283, 435
Blunt, Wilfrid Scawen 171
Bold, Mrs 429
Bonawitz, Johann Heinrich 234
Bond, Jessie 119, 125, 183, 209, 253,
    255, 272, 274, 289, 300, 307,
    336, 369, 440, 448
Booth, Charles 2
Borthwick, Sir Algernon and Lady
    201–2, 215
Bott, Alan and Irene Clephane 118
Bottesini, Giovanni 214, 261, 445
Boucicault, Dion 50, 322–3, 338, 444
Boulter, Mrs Stanley, *See* (Mrs) Carte,
    Richard D'Oyly
Braham, Leonora 157, 192, 209, 448

Brandram, Rosina 208–9, 231, 274, 289,
    308, 316, 346, 355, 358, 365–7,
    369, 397
Branson, Mrs 291
Breeze, Mrs, *See* Parsons, Marie
Brema, Marie 382–3
Brereton, W.H. 302
Bridgeman, Christopher 15
Bridgeman, Cunningham 396, 401, 449
Bridges, Robert 367
Britten, Benjamin 248, 381
Broadfield, Edward John 86
Broadwood, Henry 19
Brooke, Lord and Lady 201
Broughton, Alfred 269, 301
Broughton, James 147
Brown (Brown-Brothwick), Rev. Robert
    74, 437
Browne, Dr Buckston 403
Browne, Lady Margaret 201
Browning, Robert 32, 39, 58, 237, 291,
    309
Brunton, Spencer 159
Buck, Dudley 20
Bülow, Hans von 21
Bunting 101
Burdett-Coutts, Baroness 58, 435
Burgon 326
Burgstaller, Alois 382
Burnand, Sir Francis Cowley 51–4, 86,
    150, 186, 202, 209, 306–7,
    357–9, 381, 435
Burne-Jones, Sir Edward 359
Burns, Chalmers 437
Butcher, Dean 175
Butt, Dame Clara 369
Byng, Rev. the Hon. Francis (later Lord
    Stafford) 79
Byron, H.J. 65–6

C., Miss, *See* 'Charlotte C.'
C., Mrs 257
Cadogan, Earl 90
Cairns, Lord 233
Calley, Capt. W. (and Mrs) 272
Calthorpe, Lord 286
Calvert, Charles 40, 70, 112
Campbell, Sir Colin and Lady 251
Carlotta, Dr C. 240–1, 250, 255, 257,
    369
Carpenter, Nettie 261
Carpi (singer) 216
Carr, F. Osmond 357, 359

Carr, J. Comyns 112, 359, 384
Carr, Mary 435
Carrodus, J.T. 239
Carroll, Lewis 85, 112, 127
Carte, Bridget D'Oyly 408
Carte, Richard D'Oyly 66, 73, 77, 92
    (thereafter, *passim*)
Carte, Rupert D'Oyly 408
Carter, Joseph Ballard (and Mrs) 128,
    135, 161, 166–7, 180, 189, 200,
    228, 263, 265, 268, 275, 283,
    295, 312, 324, 337–8
Carter, Mary Frances, *See* Ronalds,
    Mary Frances
Caruso, Enrico 111
Castlereagh, Lord and Lady 201
Cecil, Arthur, *See* Blunt, Arthur
Cellier, Alfred 13, 115–16, 126, 132,
    136–7, 141–4, 181, 189, 198,
    201, 226, 287–8, 293, 322, 328,
    330, 340, 347
Cellier, François (Frank) 115, 127, 132,
    180, 191, 204, 207, 251–3, 277,
    303, 326, 335, 351, 354, 402–3,
    409–10, 448, 449
Chambers, Amelia 431
Chambers, Robert 27
Chappell, Arthur 47
Chappell, Cecil 131
Chappell, Frank 113, 131, 159
Chappell, Thomas (and family) 132, 159,
    161–2, 181, 207, 241–3, 251,
    253, 295, 304–5, 339, 392
'Charlotte C.' 176, 179
Charpentier (chef) 299
Cherry (conjuror) 201
Chetwyn, Sir George 271
Chichester, Mrs 126
Chopin, Fryderyk 4
Chorley, Henry F. 2, 28, 33, 35–6, 39,
    54, 62, 78, 89, 432–3
Christian IX, King of Denmark 163
Christian, Prince and Princess of
    Schleswig-Holstein 156, 259,
    439
Christy Minstrels 32
Churchill, Lord and Lady Randolph
    88–9, 171, 215, 252, 263, 306,
    336, 403, 447
Churchill, Sir Winston 88
Clarke, Gen. Sir Stanley 286
Clarke, Hamilton 116, 126, 243, 282

Clary, Mlle 72
Clay, Cecil 162
Clay, Ernest, *See* Clay Ker Seymer
Clay, Frederic 21, 34–5, 55, 64, 79, 128,
    132, 136–7, 141, 146, 162–4,
    187, 189, 305, 431
Clay Ker Seymer, Gertrude and Ernest
    75, 187, 241, 437
Clerk 76
Cliffe, Frederic 243, 343
Clinton, George Arthur 345
Clotilde (servant). *See* Racquet
Coburg, Duke of, *See* Ernest II
Cockburn, Sir Alexander 97, 110, 116
Coghlan, Charles 5
Coghlan, Fred 6
Coghlan, James 5
Coke, Lady Katherine 167, 201
Coke, Miss 201, 398
Cole, Alan 68, 96, 99, 104, 116
Cole, Sir Henry 67–70, 104, 111
Coleridge, Arthur D. 87
Coleridge, Lord 227
Coleridge-Taylor, Samuel 390
Collins, Lt.Col. Arthur 392, 403, 449
Colvin, Sir Auckland 169, 172
Connaught, Duke of 161
Conneau, Juliette (and Dr) 63–4, 70, 89,
    120, 273, 351, 391
Cook, R. Furneaux 132
Cooper, Dr Alfred 162, 178, 204, 268,
    285, 443
Coppi, Carlo 377, 379–80
Corder, Frederic 260, 300
Corfe, Bishop C.J. 15
Cork, Earl of 215, 222
Corrêa, Juan Arthur de Souza 201
Costa, Sir Michael 4, 16, 18, 38–9, 145,
    155
Costa, Pasquale 201
Courtenay (singer) 36
Coward, James 397
Coward, Noël 336
Cowen, Frederick Hymen 144, 199,
    204–5, 314, 334, 350–1, 388–90
Crabb, Edward 162, 308
Craig, E. Gordon 308
Craven, Hawes 208
Cross, Henry 148
Cross, Richard Assheton 168
Crutchley, Mr and Mrs 398
Cummings, William H. 10, 42, 449

Cunliffe-Owen, Sir Philip 124, 237–8
Cusins, Sir William G. 91–2, 144, 204, 215

Daines (horse stabler) 180
Daly, Augustin 223, 340–1
Damian, Miss 302
D'Auban, John 445
David, Ferdinand 21, 25
Davies, Ben 273, 314, 330, 335, 343, 389, 396
Davies, Fanny 238, 261
Davis, A.R. 447
Davis, James 387
Davison, James W. 2, 4, 23, 28, 42, 54, 78, 89, 120, 125–7, 150–1, 431
Debout, Dr. 336
Debussy, Claude 409
De Grey, Lady 382
De Koven, Reginald 386
Delacour, John 162
Delahaye (organist) 167
De la Barre, Blanche 312
De le Motte, Miss 155
Deldevez, Edouard 125
Delius, Frederick 382
Della Sala 174
Delle Sedie, Enrico 35–6
Delphine (maid) 188, 200, 217
De Maré, Eric 153
Denbigh, Earl and Countess of 201
Dennison, Walter E. 225
Denny, W.H. 289, 346, 355
Desplaces, H. 39
D'Esscher, Countess 312
De Ternant, Andrew 409
Devitt 223
Devoll, George 385
'D.H.' (identity of) 161–5, 176–80, 203
Dicey, Edward 126, 154, 166, 168–76, 200, 218, 232, 239, 254, 273, 304, 404
Dickens, Charles 32–3, 36, 59, 432–3
Dickens, Miss 35
Dickinson, Howard 221
Disraeli, Benjamin 58, 90, 119, 433
Ditson, Oliver 134
Dockett, Minnie 113, 127
Dolaro, Selina 92, 181, 439, 443
Dolmetsch, Arnold 234
Downe, Lord and Lady 286
Doyle, Sir Arthur Conan 352

Dremel, August (and Mrs) 134, 162, 178, 252, 363, 441
Dresden, Ernest 120, 201, 232, 273, 304, 309, 330, 363, 378
Dreyschock, Raimund 21
Duff 222
Duff, James C. 219, 225–6
Du Maurier, George 26, 51–2, 153, 156
Dungarvon, Lord 174
Dvořák, Antonín 214, 245, 411
Dykes, John Bacchus 74

Eames, Emma 293
Easton, Col. 297
Eden 162
Eden, David 426
Edinburgh, Alfred Duke of (and Duchess) 67, 75–6, 79, 82, 102, 104, 108, 129, 148, 155–6, 160–4, 168, 176–7, 186, 201, 208–9, 216, 233, 324, 329–30, 341, 381, 399
Edison, T.A. 286
Edward VII, *See* Wales, Prince of
Edwardes, George 446
Edwards, F.G. 437
Egerton, Seymour, later Earl Wilton 75, 201, 431
Eissler, Marianne 261
Elgar, Sir Edward (and Lady) 168, 248, 381–2, 385–6, 390
Eliot, George 58
Elizabeth, 'Eliza' (servant) 188, 283
Ella, John 103
Ellen (servant) 245
Elliott, Carlotta 214
Ellis, Col. Arthur 215
Emily (servant) 252, 300
Emma (unidentified) 398
Emmerson, George S. 55, 435, 441
Engel, Louis 258, 265–6, 304, 332
England, Paul 385
Ernst, Gustav 208
Ernst II, Duke of Coburg 82, 127
Esquiros, H.F. 30
Etherington, Maris 214
Eugénie, Empress 64, 89, 273
Everard, Harriet 118–19
E.W. 312, 325

Faber 379
Fane, Sir S.P. 286
Faris, Alexander 415

Farnie, H.B. 439
Farquhar, Harvie 162
Farrar, Very Revd. Frederic William 286
Farren, Ellen ('Nelly') 71–2
Farrer 174
Finch (servant) 168, 170, 173, 175
Findlay, Josephine 228, 260
Findon, Benjamin William, and
      Elizabeth Agatha ('Lizzie'), née
      Sullivan 251, 272, 363
Fink, Robert 420, 422
Fishe, Scott 369
Fitzherbert, Miss 201
Fitzjames, Count and Countess de 272
Fitzroy, Henry 438
Florian, Count and Countess de 201
Flower, Sir Newman 6, 59, 136, 209
Foâ, Gaston 330, 363
Foli, 'Signor' 274
Ford, Ernest 328, 330–1, 350, 352
Forster, John 52, 433
Forster, W.E. 70
François (chef) 299
Franz, Robert 22
Frederick (Friedrich), German Crown
      Prince, later Emperor (*see also*
      Victoria, Princess, daughter of
      Queen Victoria) 259–60, 263,
      270
French 253, 304
Frewen, Moreton (and Mrs) 89, 201, 447
Frickenhaus, Fanny 234
Frith, William Powell 432
Fritzsche (impresario) 255
Frost, Henry Frederick 265–6

Gadsby, Henry 92, 234
Gambetta, Paul 170, 185
Garner 312
Gaskell, Elizabeth Cleghorn 33
Gauntlett, H.J. 74
Gautier, Mme 243
Genée, Richard 255, 285, 309, 325
German, Edward 390, 405
Giesinger, Minna 25
Gilbert, Sir Humphrey 65
Gilbert, Terry 415
Gilbert, William Schwenck (and Mrs)
      64–5, 71 and thereafter *passim*
Gilbert, William (senior) 64–5
Gladstone, William Ewart 58, 160, 168,
      184–5, 202
Glehn, Robert and Olga von 69, 434

Glenn, Hope 305
Goddard, Arabella 4, 31, 124, 213
Godfrey, Charles, jun. 382
Godfrey (coachman) 109–10, 127
Godfrey, Dan, sen. 297
Goldschmidt, Otto 13, 26, 29, 60–1, 79,
      106, 130, 155, 232, 234, 242,
      267
Goldsmidt, Gen. Sir F. 174
Gordon, Gen. Charles 217
Goschen, G.J. (Viscount) 84–5
Goss, Sir John (and Lady) 14, 18, 42,
      62, 235, 411, 430
Gounod, Charles 64, 67, 111
Gouraud, Col. 285
Grant, Adèle 97, 137, 180, 201, 218–19,
      229, 232–3, 312
Grant, David Beach (and Mrs) 82–4,
      97–8, 132–7, 143, 166, 178,
      180, 201, 218, 229, 232, 403
Grant, Douglas Stewart 97–100
Grant, Edith 218–19, 312
Grant, R. Suydam 133, 142, 218–19,
      222, 227
Grant, Ulysses S. 225
Granville, Lord 170
Grau, Maurice 133
Gray, Alan 343
Green, Roger 71
Greene, Plunket 343, 349
Gregory, Sir William (and Lady) 172
Grey, Sybil 448
Grice, Robert 273
Grieg, Edvard 20
Griffiths 224
Grisi, Giulia 16, 130, 223
Griswold, Frank 438
Griswold, Gertrude 201, 236, 238
Groebl, Marie 330
Grossmith, George 115, 117–19, 131,
      143, 157, 183, 192, 201, 209,
      215–16, 220, 226, 233, 251–6,
      274, 276, 288–9, 308, 340, 359,
      403
Grossmith, Weedon 201, 215
Grove, Arthur 233, 245, 272, 276
Grove, Sir George 17, 26–8, 35–6, 44–7,
      55–6, 58–9, 61, 68–9, 89, 100,
      109, 113, 141, 146, 150, 170,
      177, 185, 213, 265, 300, 350,
      384, 399, 430–1, 433–4, 438–9
Groves, Sir Charles 417

Grundy, Sydney 340–2, 345–6, 357
Gruneisen, Charles 436
Grüning, Wilhelm 383
Guilbert, Yvette 357, 391
Gung'l, Joseph 381
Gunn, Michael 130, 162, 192, 217, 268, 441
Gurney, Edmund (and Mrs) 162
Gye, Ernest 145, 243, 245

Haggard, Sir Henry Rider 391
Hall, Charles 162
Hall, Edward A. 154, 162, 166, 178, 180–2, 328
Hall, Marjorie 272
Hallé, Sir Charles 31, 33–4, 40, 49, 58, 91, 145, 155, 264
Hamerik, Asger 141
Hamilton (attendant on phonograph) 285
Handley, Vernon 417
Hannam, William S. 343, 388
Hanslick, Eduard 29, 92, 249, 302, 368, 432
Hardy, Paul 363
Hardy, Thomas 162
Hare, John 121, 156, 291
Harriet (maid) 200
Harris (ex-bandsman) 239
Harris, Sir Augustus 306, 334, 357
Harris, Charles 345
Harrison, Dr Reginald 336
Harrison, Walter 435
Hattersley, F.K. 245
Hauk, Minnie 208
Hauptmann, Moritz 20–1
Haweis, Rev. H.R. 2
Hawes, William 10
Hegar, Friedrich (Frederick) 23
Helen (cousin?) 16
Helena, Princess, *See* Christian (Prince and) Princess
Helmore, Kate 77, 235, 430, 436
Helmore, Rev. Thomas (and Mrs) 8–16, 26, 35, 69, 147, 235, 410, 429
Henderson, Robertina 28
Henry, Prince of Prussia 165, 257
Henschel, Sir George 216, 241, 428
Henson, Medora 368, 389
Herring 398
Hersee, Rose 237
Hewitt, Admiral Sir William 164
Hill, Lucille 330, 335, 346
Hill, Thomas 225

Hiller, Ferdinand 67, 435
Hipkins, Alfred J. 38, 128
Hirsch, Adolph 372, 375, 378
Hochberg, Count Bolko von 370
Hofmann, Joseph (Josef) 260, 261
Hogarth, George 32
Hollingshead, John 66, 71, 73, 78–9, 306, 437
Hollman 336
Holmes 392
Holmes, Alfred 92
Holmes, Amy 272
Holmes, Henry 92
Holmes, William 57
Hood, Capt. Basil 392–4, 396–8, 400–1, 405
Hopetown, Lord 201
Hothfield, Lord and Lady 201, 215
How, Bishop William Walsham 376
Howson, Emma 119
Hueffer, Francis 150–1, 189, 211–12, 247–8, 265–6, 331
Hullah, John 3, 155
Hulme, David Russell 442–3
Hutchinson, Rev. B. 230
Hutchinson, Capt. Benjamin C. 177, 212–13, 224, 226–8, 230
Huxley, T.H. 58
Huyshe, Mrs 304
Hyde, H. Montgomery 153

Ionides 161
Irving, Sir Henry 30, 92, 216, 237, 282–3, 300, 314, 357, 359, 439
'Isabella' 429
Ismail, Khédive 91

Jack (servant) 76, 80, 82, 83, 109, 112
'Jack the Ripper' 276
Jacobi, George 377
Jacquinot, Claude 361
Jaeger, Louis 178, 180, 185, 200, 212, 217, 228, 245, 252, 273, 285, 300, 341, 377–8, 380, 400, 402–4
James, Henry 89
Janette (servant) 252
Jay, Isabel 449
Jean (masseur) 312
Jerome, Clara 88–9
Jerome, Jennie, *See* Churchill, Lord and Lady Randolph
Jerome, Leonard 88–9, 130, 142

Jerome, Leonie 201
Jerrold, Douglas 1
Joachim, Henry 31
Joachim, Joseph 21, 25, 31–2, 35, 92,
    207, 209, 214, 238, 362, 431
John, Sir W. Goscombe 405
Johnson, Edgar 433
Johnstone 267
Jones, Hirwan 367
Jones, Sidney 387
Jones, Thomas O. 441
Jopling, Louise 85
Joran, Pauline 385
Joseph (servant) 132–4
Josephine (servant) 300
Joslin, Peter 430–1, 434, 440–1
Jullien 4, 78

Kay-Shuttleworth, Sir James 3
Kearton (tenor) 236
Kendal, Dame Madge 66
Kenningham, Charles 369
Kilgour 299
King, Agnes 84
King, Frederic 148, 243, 246
Kipling, Rudyard 386, 391, 395–6
Kleeberg, Clotilde 214–15, 237
Klein, Hermann 2, 27, 32–3, 107, 116,
    192, 199, 241, 247, 331, 333,
    343, 345, 349, 357, 403, 410
Klingemann, Carl (and Mrs) 19, 20, 430
Knight (bassoonist) 269
Knight (servant) 127
Knowles, Christopher 431
Krause, Emil 23
Krolop, Franz 258
Kruger, Paul 371, 395
Kufferath, Maurice 309–11
Kurtz, G. 434

Labouchère, Henry 155, 374, 444
Lacource 36
Lacy, Charlotte Louisa, later Sullivan,
    later Hutchinson 22–3, 43, 71,
    84, 109–10, 134, 177, 188,
    212–13, 229–30, 404
Lacy, Sophy 224
Lacy, William, jun. 295
Lacy, William, sen. 188, 212–13, 224,
    229, 295, 338
Lambert (Mayor of Nottingham) 236
Lambton 162
Lammert (contralto) 258

Lang, Andrew 200
Langtry, Lillie 170
Lara, Isidore de 201
Larkcom, Agnes 239
Lathom, Earl of (and Lady) 246
Lavino (journalist) 291
Lawrence, Arthur 35
Lawrence, Mr Justice 324
Lazaridis, Stefanos 413
Lear, Edward 58, 79
Lebano, Felix 201
Leech, John 14
Legnani, Pierina 380
Lehmann, Frederick and Nina (and
    daughter Nina, 'Little Ni')
    27–8, 33–5, 85, 89, 190, 306,
    351, 431–2, 433
Lehmann, Liza 431
Lehmann, Rudolf 27, 431
Lehmann, Rudolph (R.C., 'Rudie') 34,
    44, 381, 432
Leigh, Mrs Gerard (Dudley) 162, 308
Leighton, Lord 32
Lely, Durward 157, 192, 209, 248
Lemmens-Sherrington, Helen 40
Lenoir, Helen 209, 227–8, 259, 263, 268,
    271 (thereafter, as Mrs Richard
    D'Oyly Carte, *passim*)
Léon (chef) 229
Leopold, Prince, Duke of Albany 16,
    112, 124, 128, 156, 176, 200
Leslie, Henry 155
Lessmann, Otto 303, 370
L'Estrange (naval officer) 164
Lethbridge 162
Levi, Hermann 368
Levy, Isaac 107, 439
Lewin, Lionel 54–5, 85, 200
Lewis, Arthur J. (and Mrs) 51–2, 299
Lewis, Eric 272
Lewis, Sir George 131, 162, 177, 201,
    276, 295, 304
Liberty, Arthur Lazonby 204
Libman, Lillian 409
Liddell, Alice 85
Liddell, Dean Henry George 85, 438
Liddell, Lorna Charlotte ('Miss Liddell')
    85
Lido, Marie de 260
Lienau, Robert 23
Lind, Jenny 13, 26, 29, 41–2, 88, 91,
    106, 130, 267, 293, 352, 439

Lindsay, Sir Coutts (and Lady) 81, 82–4, 98, 101, 109–10, 112–13, 132, 153, 166, 438, 440
Lister-Kaye, Sir John (and Lady) 241
Liszt, Franz 4, 236–8, 411
Littleton, Alfred Henry 61, 188, 236–7, 241
Lloyd, Edward 148, 151, 201, 214–15, 236, 243, 246, 261, 273–4, 298, 302, 305, 336, 343, 349, 368
Lloyd-Jones, David 415
Lloyd, Marie 309
Lloyd Webber, Julian 417
Loftus 254
Longhurst (dentist) 229
Lord 243
Lorne, Marquess of (*see also* Louise, Princess) 142–3, 215, 368
Louis (servant), *See* Jaeger, Louis
Louisa (servant) 252
Louise, Princess, later Marchioness of Lorne 110, 142, 156, 162, 204, 209, 215, 217, 330, 368, 403, 438
Lumley, Bejamin 435
Lunn, Henry C 49, 62
'L.W.' or 'L.' 161, 175, 373 (and diary references *passim*)
Lynch, Dr. 191, 212
Lytton, Henry 255, 279, 397, 408

'M.' 203
Macfarren, Sir George 39, 50–1, 92, 185
McGuckin, Barton 260, 272, 361
McIntosh, Nancy 353, 355, 357, 359, 369
MacIntyre, Margaret 300, 302, 305, 324, 330
Mackay, Mrs John 306
Mackenzie, Sir Alexander 251, 296, 351, 367, 370, 406–7
Mackenzie of Kintail, The 272
Mackerras, Sir Charles 415–18
Mackie, David 415, 417, 430
Maclean, Charles 406–7
Macleay 271
McNeill, Sir John Cordell 185–6
Macpherson, Stewart 446
Macready, Mrs 32
Mainzer, Joseph 3
Maitland, Col. 297
Maitland, J.A. Fuller 302, 331, 333, 396, 406

Malet, Sir Edward 169, 239
Malortie, Baron de 174
Manchester, Duchess of, *See* Yznaga, Consuelo
Mandeville, Lady 201
Manns, Sir August 27–8, 33, 42–7, 78, 91–2, 155, 214, 243, 252, 264, 325, 405
Manser, Dr. 402
Mansfield, Katherine 376
Mapleson, J.H. 102, 130
Marchesi, Mathilde 293
Marie Alexandrovna, Grand Duchess 75
Mario, Giovanni 16, 92, 223
Marlborough, Duke and Duchess of 336
Marthe (servant?) 257
Martin 253
Martin, Sir George 403
Martin, J.B. 162
Martin, Ralph G. 375
Martin, 'Trevvy' 268, 304, 328
Martineau (Mayor of Birmingham) 233
Marx Brothers 338
Mary (servant) 283
Mary, Queen 156, 448
Marzials, Theodor 291
Mason, Miss 175
Matilde (servant) 252
Matthews, Charles William 404
Matthison, Arthur 28
Maud, Princess 217, 330
Mazzucato, Alberto 98
Mazzucato, Gianandrea 293, 446
Mecklenburg-Schwerin, Duke and Duchess Paul of 272
Mehlig, Anna 42
Melba, Dame Nellie 300, 335
Mellon, Alfred 37, 43
Mendelssohn-Bartholdy, Felix 2, 4, 20, 411–12
Mendès, Catulle 243
Metzler, George 113, 116–17
Meyerbeer, Giacomo 4
Middleditch, C. 378, 388
Mildenburg, Anna von 383
Millais, Sir John Everett 54, 59, 162–3, 167, 186, 216, 271–2, 295, 446
Millaud, Albert 84
Miller, Johnathan 413, 415
Mills, Watkin 264–5, 302, 305
Mitford, Algernon 203, 215–16

Molesworth, Lady Andalusia 162, 170, 179
Molique, Bernhard 31, 33
Molloy, J.L. 144
Monckton, Lionel 387, 398
Monson, Sir Edward 378
Montrose, Caroline, Duchess of 272
Moore, Decima 308, 316, 322
Moore, Mary 374
Moquet (barber) 268
Morris, Lewis 262
Morris, William 67, 407
Morrow, Walter 345, 388
Morton, John Maddison 51
Moscheles, Felix 26
Moscheles, Ignaz 2, 4, 20–1, 26, 42, 47, 430
Moszkowski, Moritz 215, 240
Mottl, Felix 368
Moul, Alfred 377–80
Mount, George 80, 103, 235, 437
Muck, Karl 369–70
Murray, Lady Dorothy 271
Murray, Mrs 137
Murska, Ilma di 69

Nachez, Tivadar 234
Napoleon I 429
Napoleon III 22
Nevada, Emma 216, 261
Nikisch, Arthur 368–9
Nilsson, Christine 69, 82, 101–2, 106, 179, 216, 240, 249, 436
Noel, Lady Anne 171
Nordica, Lillian 261, 273, 276, 328, 336
Norris, Harry 280, 408
Notorp (?) 236
Nubar Pasha 168

Oakley, Alfred 398
Odell, George C.D. 312
Offenbach, Jacques 51, 92, 409, 411–12
Oliphant 174
Oliphant, Col. 297
Ommerle, Jeanne 417
Ondříček, Franz 237, 240, 249
Onstott, Mrs 226
Oppenheim, W. (and Mrs) 201
Osborne, Lady Emma 76
Osgood, Aline 150, 442
Osman Pasha 169, 443
Oudin, Eugène 330, 334
Ouseley, Sir Frederic Gore 15

Owen, Emmie 365, 448
Owen, Sir Philip Cunliffe, *See* Cunliffe-Owen

Paderewski, Ignacy 357
Paget, Sir A. 291
Paget, Mrs Arthur 202
Paget, Col. Patrick 43, 447
Palicot, Lucie 260
Pallant, Walter 363, 398
Palliser, Esther 312, 330, 335
Palmay, Ilka [von] 365–7, 371–2, 448
Palmerston, Lord 433
Parratt, Sir Walter 403
Parry, Sir Hubert 273, 344, 368, 382, 384, 390
Parsons, Marie 353
Pasdeloup, Jules 63, 106, 125
Passmore, Walter 358, 369, 372, 385, 397
Patey, Janet 102, 148, 151, 236, 243, 260
Patti, Adelina 91, 111, 130, 200, 385, 433
Pattini (soprano) 258
Pauer, Eduard 155
Paul, Isabella (Mrs Howard Paul) 115
Paxton, Joseph 1
'P.C.' 337
Peacock, Beddoes 434
Peacock, Edward 430
Pearson, Hesketh 66, 313
Pereira, Mrs 201, 272
Perren (tenor) 61
Perry, Florence 365–7, 369, 448
Persia, Shah of 295–6, 446
Phelps, Samuel 78
Philipps (family) 6, 187–8, 388, 428
Philips, Miss 272
Phipps, C.J. 167
Phipps, Miss 381
Piatti, Alfredo 32–4, 43, 47, 98
Pierson (Berlin opera manager) 369
Pierson, Henry Hugo 92
Pinero, Arthur W. 293, 374, 384–5
Pirandello, Luigi 210
Pirani, Eugen von 370
Pittman, Josiah 63, 436, 466
Plaidy, Louis 21–2, 146
Plees, William Gordon 7, 429
Pohl, C.F. 46
Pole, William 56, 435
Pollaky, Ignatius Paul 158, 442
Ponsonby, Sir Henry F. 185–6

Post, Mrs Fred 201, 221
Potter, Cipriani 12, 37
Pounds, Courtice 274, 277, 289, 300, 307, 358
Powell, Dr Gordon 179
Power, Sir George 119
Power, Harold 52
Prideaux-Brune (?), Hon. Mrs. 271
Proust, Marcel 376
Prout, Ebenezer 148, 265–6, 437, 445
Prowse, Blanche (Mrs Richard D'Oyly Carte) 271–2
Puccini, Giacomo 375
Pugin, Augustus 10
Puttnam, David 413
Pyne, Louisa 31, 435

'R. Peggio' (critic's pseudonym) 385
Rabl, Mme 243
Radolinsky, Count 257
Randegger, Alberto 102, 110, 156, 199, 260
Raquet, Clotilde 229, 245, 252, 268, 283, 285–6, 291, 297, 300, 304, 305, 326, 328, 334, 336, 341, 362–4, 374–5, 377, 380, 383, 398, 401–3, 404, 408
Raunkilde, Mme 299
Reed, Thomas German (and Mrs Priscilla) 50, 53–4, 64–6
Rees, Terence 72, 430
Reeves, Sims 33–4, 40, 61, 78, 86, 91, 102, 106–7, 381, 436
Rehan, Ada 223, 340
Reinecke, Carl 24, 47
Reiss, Julius 256–7, 262, 362
'Rem' 175–7, 178–9
Renard (Paris impresario) 304, 309–12
Richards, Brindley 43
Richardson, Roy (?) 253
Richter, Ernst Friedrich 20–1
Richter, Hans 145, 167, 199, 214, 240–1, 249, 274, 281, 302, 368, 389–90, 428, 445–6
Ries, Louis 47
Rietz, Julius 20–1, 24
Righy (Righi) family 5–6
Rimbault, E.F. 10
Rimsky-Korsakov, Nikolay 165
Ritchie, Thomas Hay (for wife, *see* Ronalds, 'Fanette') 200–1, 265
Roberts (grocer) 297
Roberts, Lord 398

Robertson, T.W. 97
Romanes, G.J. 436
Romanes, Miss 64, 79–80, 436
Ronalds, 'Fanette' (Fannie Florence) 88–90, 128, 154, 161–2, 176–7, 200–1, 218, 221, 265, 268, 275, 283, 398
Ronalds, Mary Frances 85 thereafter *passim*
Ronalds, Peter (Pierre) Lorillard 88, 438
Ronalds, Pierre jun. 89
Ronalds, 'Reg(g)ie' 89, 128, 200, 221, 275, 277, 283, 295
Röntgen, Engelbert 21
Roose, Dr Robson 336
Roosevelt, Blanche Tucker 132, 136, 137, 353, 441
Rorke, Kate 293
Rosa (Rose), Carl 23, 25, 36, 91, 93
Rosebery, Lord (and Lady) 81, 386, 437
Rosenfield, Sydney 226
Ross (?) 254–5
Rossetti, Christina 58
Rossetti, Dante Gabriel 32, 81
Rossini, Gioachino 35–6
Rothmühl, Nikolaus 258
Rothschild, Alfred 81, 162, 186, 215–16, 286, 303, 305, 364, 447
Rothschild, Alphonse 447
Rothschild, Ferdinand 186, 204
Rothschild, Hannah (daughter of Meyer) 81, 438
Rothschild, Hannah (daughter of Nathan) 438
Rothschild, Leopold (and Mrs) 81, 186, 272, 374, 403, 447
Rothschild, Lionel 81, 437
Rothschild, Meyer 81, 437
Rothschild, Nathan Mayer 438
Routley, Erik 426
Rouzeaud, Auguste (for wife *see* Nilsson, Christine) 82–3
Rowell, George 97
Rubinstein, Anton 155, 440
Rummel, Franz 214–15
Ruskin, John 85, 157
Russell, Alice Scott 55
Russell, Sir Charles (and Lady) 154–5, 251, 350, 399
Russell, Ella 261, 272
Russell, John Scott 44, 53–5, 126, 435
Russell, Lillian 191–2, 443–4

Russell, Louise Scott 56, 161
Russell, Rachel Scott 54–7, 163, 167, 359
Ruth (servant) 338
Ryley, J.H. 181

St John, Florence 358, 448
Saint-Saëns, Camille 237, 239, 261, 411
Sainton-Dolby, Charlotte 37
Sala, *See* Della Sala
Salaman, Charles K. 432–3
Salisbury, Lord and Lady 286, 377–8
Salmond, Norman 343
Salvioni (ballerina) 39
Sam (train attendant) 221
Sanderson, Sybil 227
Santley, Sir Charles 31, 34, 42, 61, 78,
    110–11, 148, 215, 261
Santurca, Mme 202
Sarah (servant) 252
Sarasate, Pablo de 216, 301, 428
Saremba, Meinhard 427
Sartoris, E.J. 209
Sassoon, Arthur 447
Sassoon, Reuben 162, 272, 286, 289,
    305, 446–7
Saxon, Avon 330
Schallehn, Henry 17
Schiff, Sydney 376
Schneider, Eduard 46
Schnitzer, Ignaz 357
Schoenberger, Bruno 260
Schubert, Franz 45–7
Schumann, Clara 46, 208
Schumann, Robert 20
Scott, Clement 359
Scott, Gilbert 58
Scott, Mrs 201
Scott Russell (family), *See* Russell
Seckendorff, Count 285–6
Seeger, Dr. 187
Seidl, Anton 382–3
Seligman, David and Sybil 372, 376
Serrés, Mme de 291
Sewell (veterinary surgeon) 328
Shakespeare, William (singer) 101
Sharpe, Mrs Parkinson 374
Shaw, Mrs Alice 272, 286
Shaw, Capt Eyre Massey 179
Shaw, George Bernard 16, 41, 209, 332,
    335, 347, 355–6, 359, 383,
    411–12
Shaw, Norman 351

Shepherd (orchestral manager) 99, 101,
    121, 440
Sherson, Erroll 103
Shrewsbury, Earl and Countess of 80,
    201
Silas, Edouard 85
Silva (servant) 99–101, 120
Silvestre, Armand 309–11
Silvestre, Victor 309–11
Smart, Sir George (and Lady) 8, 12,
    18–22, 34–5, 430
Smart, Henry Thomas 74
Smith, W.H. 119
Smyth, Dame Ethel 248, 325, 337,
    382–3, 390
Smyth, Maj.-Gen. J.H. 325
Smythe, Walter 147, 162, 164–7, 170,
    173, 180–2, 187–8, 191, 205,
    217–18, 221–2, 224, 232–3, 239,
    243, 245, 252, 255–6, 269, 286,
    291, 309–10, 336, 343, 362–3,
    445
Solomon, Edward 191
Solomon, John 387
Sontag, Henriette 223
Sophie, Princess (Princess Louis of Hess)
    376
Sothern, Edward 137
Spark, F.R. 173, 233, 236, 242–3, 269,
    302, 313, 344, 348, 394–5
Spark, William 242
Spina, Carl Anton 46
Spohr, Louis 25, 42
Spurgeon, C.H. 30
Stafford, Lord and Lady 80
Stainer, Sir John 243, 262, 437
Stanford, Sir Charles Villiers 199, 247,
    262, 273, 300, 367, 382, 386,
    389–90, 405
Stanhope, Mrs Spencer 176
Stanley, Dean Arthur 58, 146
Stedman, Jane W. 436
Stephenson, B.C. 95, 293
Sterling, Antionette 111, 216, 239
Sterling, Mr 201
Stetson, John 219–20, 225
Stevens (driver) 225
Stockman (servant) 69
Stoker, Bram 282–3
Stoppard, Tom 409
Strafford, Lord, *See* Byng
Straus, Ludwig 45, 48

Strauss, Eduard 364
Strauss, Johann, jun. 45, 364, 409
Stravinsky, Igor 376, 409
Stuart, Leslie 387
Sturgis, Julian Russell 288, 294, 298,
    313, 324, 326–8, 329, 332
Sturt, Lady Feodora 246
Sullivan, Amy 99, 109, 127, 154, 212–13,
    224, 338, 404
Sullivan, Arthur [Seymour]
  addresses (home) 5, 7, 8, 13, 14, 17,
    26, 34, 38, 44, 68, 108, 109,
    165, 176
  appointments
    academic 77, 103–5, 111, 121, 155
    church organist 26, 45, 58, 79–80
    conductor
      Leeds Musical Festival 144–5,
        146–51, 189, 234, 236, 245–8,
        268–9, 296–303, 342–4, 348–50,
        362, 367–9, 388–91, 411, 442
      other 45, 75, 99, 101–2, 108
      Philharmonic Society 145, 204–5,
        207–8, 214–15, 234–5, 237–9,
        260–2, 264–5, 411
    theatre organist 38
  birth and early upbringing 1, 5–9,
    452–3, 454–5
  contracts and remuneration 36–7, 54,
    58, 61–2, 85–6, 86, 104–5, 113,
    131, 134, 142, 144–5, 151, 157,
    159–60, 204–5, 212, 241, 270,
    282, 296, 314–15, 324, 341–2,
    357, 380, 387, 392–3, 404
  death 402–3
  diaries 130–1, 154–6 (and quotations
    passim)
  education 10–25
  Freemasonry 40
  funeral and will 403–4, 408
  honours and honorary degrees 82, 83,
    125, 150, 185–6, 381
  legal actions 131, 154, 252, 324
  love-affairs 38, 54–7, 161–6, 166–7,
    176, 203, 295, 312, 325, 334,
    337, 373, 376, 411
  medical history 112, 120–1, 128, 147,
    155, 166, 173, 175, 179, 212,
    265, 267–8, 272, 325–6, 336–7,
    341, 348–9, 386, 399, 401–2
  method of composition 179

  personal descriptions of 12, 22, 133,
    219, 228, 249, 409–10
  political and ethical views 58, 168,
    171–2, 202, 281–2, 411
  portraiture 271–2, 446
  travel abroad
    Algeria 271
    Egypt 168–71
    Europe 21–5, 45–8, 63–4, 68–9,
      81–4, 97–9, 106, 118–24, 147–8,
      154, 160–1, 163–7, 185, 193,
      202, 256–60, 262–3, 269–71,
      286–93, 312, 336–8, 341, 350,
      358, 372, 374–80, 382–3, 386–7,
      391, 398–401
    USA and Canada 127–8, 130–8,
      217–30
  works
    arrangements and editions of others'
      music 12, 63, 411–12
    ballets
      'L'Ile enchantée' 39, 79, 377–9,
        418
      'Victoria and Merrie England'
        377–81, 384, 392, 418
    choral works with orchestra
      'Festival Te Deum' 77–8, 80, 146,
        243, 405
      'Golden Legend, The' 111, 149,
        232–3, 239, 241–8, 250, 252–3,
        254–9, 264, 266, 268, 272–6,
        313–14, 346, 349, 350, 368–9,
        377, 385, 388, 395, 405, 409,
        416–17, 447
      'Kenilworth' 39, 42, 313
      'Light of the World, The' 77–8,
        83, 86, 91–2, 108, 124, 237,
        295, 369
      'Martyr of Antioch, The' 144,
        146–50, 167, 181, 236, 295, 326,
        350, 385, 405, 409, 416, 441
      Odes 238, 262, 351
      'On Shore and Sea' 67–8, 92, 93,
        131
      'Prodigal Son, The' 56, 60–1, 111,
        132, 134, 441
      'Te Deum' (1900) 399, 405
    hymns and other church music
      'Onward Christian Soldiers' 74–5,
        227, 398, 407, 412, 426
      other 8, 11, 62, 76, 77, 137, 143,
        188, 376–7, 381

incidental music and individual
 songs for theatre
 'Foresters, The' 340, 447
 'Henry VIII' 112–13, 116, 120,
  243, 369, 407
 'King Arthur' 359
 'Macbeth' 282–4, 362, 405, 407,
  417
 'Merchant of Venice, The' 70,
  101, 107, 120, 126, 141, 405,
  418
 'Merry Wives of Windsor, The'
  78–80, 252, 418
 'Old Jew, An' 357
 'Olivia' 121
 'Profligate, The' 293–4
 'Tempest, The' 25, 28–9, 31, 33,
  35, 40, 70, 79, 108, 141, 168,
  350, 360, 362, 405, 407, 417,
  420, 433
operas and operettas
 'Beauty Stone, The' 384–5
 'Chieftain, The' 53, 357–9, 369
 'Contrabandista, The' 53–4, 64,
  66, 86, 357–8
 'Cox and Box' 48, 51–5, 64, 86,
  92, 119, 158, 233, 412
 'Emerald Isle, The' 397, 400–2,
  405
 'Gondoliers, The' 73, 76, 294,
  297–9, 303–10, 312–13, 316–18,
  321, 324, 326, 329, 334–5, 356,
  384, 412, 414–15
 'Grand Duke, The' 65, 71, 140,
  294, 363, 365–9, 371–2, 384,
  408, 414
 'Haddon Hall' 341–2, 345–8, 351
 'HMS Pinafore' 85, 108, 117–19,
  122–3, 125–9, 134, 136–7,
  139–40, 145, 149–50, 152, 155,
  164–5, 220, 222–4, 226, 231,
  253, 266–8, 284, 308, 406, 412
 'Iolanthe' 173, 179–86, 231, 329,
  347, 409, 414, 420, 425, 443
 'Ivanhoe' 25, 149, 312–15, 317,
  322–3, 329–35, 350, 361,
  368–70, 416, 448
 'Mikado, The' 67, 75, 118, 199,
  202–5, 207–13, 215, 219–20,
  231–2, 240–1, 249–50, 253–5,
  259–60, 270, 277, 284, 291,
  294, 308–11, 314, 326, 356,
  359, 365, 370, 393, 399–402,
  406, 409, 413–15, 419, 422,
  424, 426, 448
 'Patience' 67, 90, 91, 111, 140,
  153–8, 160–1, 167–9, 177, 204,
  224, 231, 259, 294, 356, 409,
  442
 'Pirates of Penzance, The' 35, 53,
  73, 94, 134–44, 152, 285,
  291–2, 408–9, 442, 450
 'Princess Ida' 118, 186–94, 371
 'Rose of Persia, The' 392, 396–7,
  449
 'Ruddigore' ('Ruddygore') 140,
  228, 235–6, 251–5, 266, 371,
  408–9
 'Sapphire Necklace, The' ('The
  False Heiress') 35, 42, 44, 49,
  51, 108, 252, 378, 417, 432
 'Sorcerer, The' 5, 108, 113–17,
  119, 121–23, 192, 195–6, 200,
  371, 391
 'Thespis' 72–3, 75, 77, 136,
  417–18
 'Trial by Jury' 65, 92–7, 102, 105,
  150, 181, 200, 227, 250, 412
 'Utopia (Limited)' 32, 352–6, 364,
  371, 384, 408
 'Yeomen of the Guard, The' 268,
  274–81, 284–5, 287–8, 291,
  307–9, 314, 323, 356, 380–1,
  384, 405, 409
 'Zoo, The' 95–6
orchestral works
 Cello concerto 43, 411
 'Imperial March' 62, 351, 369,
  382
 'In Memoriam' 44, 47, 49, 63,
  101, 110, 125, 162, 349, 369,
  405, 417, 447
 juvenile works 18, 24
 'Marmion' 40, 44, 47, 91, 313,
  359, 438
 'Overtura di Ballo' 62, 101, 120,
  124–6, 131, 141, 158, 233, 262,
  269, 369, 417, 419
 'Procession March' ('Royal
  Wedding March') 36, 102
 symphony 37, 42, 46, 49, 106,
  144, 239, 359–60, 411, 435, 445
part-songs 62, 101, 136

solo instrumental and chamber
music 25, 36, 43, 433
songs (other than for plays)
'Absent-Minded Beggar, The'
395–6, 399–400, 406–7
'Lost Chord, The, 110–11, 129,
167, 222, 238, 285, 336, 404,
406–7, 412
Shakespeare settings 37, 40, 42,
85, 407
'Window, The' (Tennyson cycle)
59–60, 340
other 36, 85, 120, 212, 407, 412,
435
Sullivan, Charlotte, *See* Lacy, Charlotte
Louisa
Sullivan, Edith Mary 109
Sullivan, Elena M., *See* Bashford, Elena
M.
Sullivan, Elizabeth Agatha ('Lizzie'), *See*
Findon
Sullivan, Florence 109, 127, 212–13, 224,
226, 230, 338
Sullivan, Frederic 5, 12, 16, 18, 22,
22–3, 26, 44–5, 72, 84, 86, 93,
109–10, 404
Sullivan, Frederic Richard ('Dickie') 109,
154, 162, 224
Sullivan, George Arthur 109, 224, 338,
404
Sullivan, Herbert Thomas ('Bertie') (for
wife see Bashford, Elena M.) 6,
89, 109, 127, 188, 202, 217,
229, 251, 273, 283, 293, 295–6,
325–6, 334, 341, 351–2, 362,
369–70, 374, 377–8, 383, 389,
398–400, 403–4, 408
Sullivan, Jane 251, 272, 403
Sullivan, John 188, 233, 251–2, 267, 272,
299, 363, 403
Sullivan, Mary Clementina 5, 15, 19, 69,
79, 109–10, 126, 141, 178, 411
Sullivan, Maude ('Cissie') 109, 224, 338,
404
Sullivan, Rosa/Rose 272
Sullivan, Thomas (Arthur's father) 6, 13,
16–17, 24, 31, 44, 429
Sullivan, Thomas (Arthur's grandfather)
6
Sullivan, William Lacy 109, 224, 338,
404
Sutro, Otto 141

Swinburne, Algernon Charles 32, 79, 437
Sykes, Lady 201
Sylvain, *See* Silva
Sylvan, Sanford 417

Taylor, J. Franklin (and Mrs) 235
Taylor, Sedley 302
Taylor, Tom 67–8
Tchaikovsky, Pyotr Ilyich 165
Teck, Duke of (Prince Teck) and
Duchess 156, 374, 448
Temperley, Nicholas 11, 111
Tempest, Dame Marie 257
Temple, Richard 119, 157, 209, 274,
276–8, 289, 358
Tennent, Annie 38
Tennent, Robert 433
Tennyson, Alfred Lord 32, 58–60, 187,
238, 262, 340, 349, 410, 431
Terry, Dame Ellen 51, 282, 284, 308,
446
Terry, Kate 51
Theresa (servant) 200
Thiers, Adolphe 68
Thomas, Ambroise 64, 125, 263
Thomas, Arthur Goring 322, 343
Thomas, Brandon 201
Thomas, John 215
Thomas, Theodore 131
Thompson, Sir Henry 162–3, 178, 201
Thornton, Frank 157
Thornton, William 369
Thring, Sir Henry 168, 235
Thudicum, Charlotte 330
Tietjens, Therese 31, 61, 78
Tigrane Bey (and Mme) 169, 201
Tillett, Selwyn 377, 418
Tippett, Sir Michael 409
Titiens, *See* Tietjens
Tomlins, William 264
Toole, J.L. 71–2
'Tootsie' or 'Tootie' 176, 178–9
Tosti, Sir Paolo 110, 201, 246, 403
Tours, Berthold 240, 243
Tovey, Bramwell 414
Tovey, Sir Donald 439
Townsend, Mr. 14
Toye, Geoffrey 408
Tracey, George Lowell 219
Trebelli, Antoinette 234
Trebelli, Zelia 78
Tree, Sir Herbert Beerbohm 284, 357,
440

Trollope, Anthony 81, 162
Tufnail, Musgrove 236, 445
Twiss, Quintin 52

Ulmar, Geraldine ('Dolly') 220, 226, 233, 266, 274, 277, 289, 299–300, 307, 322, 334, 448
Ulrick (servant) 252

Van Dyck, Ernest 291, 382–3, 446
Vanderbilt (family) 219, 241
Van Rooy, Anton 382
Van Zandt, Marie 201–2, 215–16
Vanzini, Mlle 61
Vaughan, Rev. 15
Vaughan Williams, Ralph 41
Verdi, Giuseppe 4
Vert, Nathaniel 378–9
Viardot-Garcia, Pauline 25, 35, 46, 431, 446
Victoria, Lady (unidentified) 56
Victoria, Princess (daughter of Queen Victoria, later Empress Frederick of Germany) 105, 217, 257, 263, 270, 285–6, 330, 376
Victoria, Princess (grand-daughter of Queen Victoria, later Princess Adolf of Schaumburg-Lippe) 257, 263, 270, 376
Victoria, Queen 1, 12, 37, 67, 75, 77, 82, 89, 91, 105, 186, 238, 262, 272, 330, 334, 341, 376, 378, 383, 405, 437
Vieuxtemps, Ernest 31
Vincent (unidentified) 398
Vincent, Ruth 385
Visetti, Alberto 98, 110, 113, 400

Waddington, W.H. 216
Wade, Wyn and Barbara 449
Wagg, Arthur 363, 382
Wagner, Cosima 383
Wagner, Johanna 22
Wagner, Richard 4, 243
Wagner, Siegfried 382–3
Wales, Prince of (later Edward VII) and Princess 36, 67, 77, 81, 90, 104, 110, 124, 154–6, 166, 186, 201–2, 204, 215–17, 235, 238–9, 251, 257, 260, 272, 285–6, 295–6, 312–13, 316, 324, 329–30, 334, 336, 357, 368, 378–82, 407

Walker, Ernest 407
Walker, Russell D. 250–1, 254, 273, 304, 317, 326, 328, 363
Waller, Lewis 293
Walton, Sir William 41
Walzel, Camillo 219, 255, 285, 292, 309, 326
Ward, John 297
Warnots, Elly 207
Warwick, Giulia 115
Washburn (hotel-keeper) 225
Waterfield (tutor) 100
Weaver, Leslie 429
Weckerlin, Jean-Baptiste 286
Weissmann, Adolf 401
Welch, Maj. 164
Weldon, Georgina 111
Wells, H.G. 391
Wessely, Hans 272
West, William Cornwallis (and Mrs) 170
Westminster, Duke and Duchess of 110, 433
Wharncliffe, Lord and Lady 201
Wheat, Leonidas Polk 142
Whistler, James McNeill 157, 207, 263
Whiting, Miss 201
Wieniawski, Henryk 107, 439
Wilbraham, Lady Bertha 246
Wilcox (undertaker) 178
Wilde, Oscar 153, 157, 361
Wilhelmj, August 205
Wilkinson 392
Willeby, Charles 433
William (houseboy) 200
William I, Emperor of Prussia (later of Germany) 257, 270
William, Prince of Prussia, later Emperor William II 165, 240, 257, 270, 285, 370, 399
Williams, Hwfa (and Mrs) 297
Wilson, Leslie J. 434
Wilton, Isabella Countess of 201
Wingham, Thomas 214
Wittgenstein, Princess 238
Wolfson, John 357, 359, 371
Wolseley, Lord (Sir Garnet) and Lady 91, 172, 201
Wood, Ellen (Mrs Henry) 438
Wood, Sir Henry J. 274, 368, 390–1, 405, 407, 416

Woodhouse, Dr Thomas 116, 178
Woods, Francis Cunningham 336
Woolsey, Mr and Mrs 137
Worthy, Charles (and Mrs) 382
Wren (servant) 112
Wright (fiddler) 225
Wyatt, Frank 308
Wylde, Henry C. 30
Wyndham, Charles (and Mrs) 272,
    374–5
Wynne, Edith 42, 44, 102

Yates, Edmund 192
Yaw, Ellen Beach 397, 449
York, Duke and Duchess of 374
Young, Bicknell 222, 444
Young, Percy M. 26, 409, 454
Yznaga, Consuelo 89, 263, 447
Yznaga, Emily 263, 382
Yznaga, Mrs. 241

Zell, *See* Walzel
Ziegler, Mrs. 101